THE ITALIAN PARLIAMENT IN THE EUROPEAN UNION

This important new collection explores the role of the Italian Parliament in the Euro-national parliamentary system as an example of an increased role for national parliaments within the composite European constitutional order. It illustrates how parliamentary interactions within the European Union are highly systematic, with integrated procedures and mutual interdependence between the various institutions and stakeholders. The book argues that this dynamic is vital for both the functioning and the future equilibrium of democracy in the EU. This is significant, particularly given the challenges posed to democracy within the EU institutions and the Member States.

Notwithstanding its peculiarities (a symmetrical bicameral system in which both Houses are directly elected, hold the same powers and are linked through a confidence relationship with the government), the Italian Parliament deserves specific attention as a lively active player of the European polity. The grid for its analysis proposed by this collection may also be applied to other national parliaments, so contributing to the development of comparative research in this field.

Volume 2 in the series Parliamentary Democracy in Europe

Parliamentary Democracy in Europe

The European Union is founded on the idea of 'representative democracy'. Its citizens are directly represented in the European Parliament, but Union democracy is equally based on indirect forms of representation especially through the European Council and the Council—two Union institutions whose members will be democratically accountable to their national parliaments. The good functioning of the Union democracy assumes, therefore, the good functioning of the democratic institutions of each Member State.

What is the role and relationship between the European and the national parliaments in the democratic functioning of the Union? Do they exercise distinct or complementary functions? Has the European Parliament adopted a structure similar to national parliaments; and how do national parliaments assume their 'European' functions? These questions have gained particular relevance in recent years. Not only has the Lisbon Treaty conferred new functions upon national parliaments, especially concerning the scrutiny on the compliance with the subsidiarity principle (the so called 'Early Warning System'), the coordination of fiscal and economic policies at the European level has led to significant restrictions of national parliamentary powers.

The new Hart Series on 'Parliamentary Democracy in Europe', encompassing both monographs and edited collections, aims to answer some of these questions. The series offers new insights into rules and conventions shaping parliaments and parliamentary democracy in Europe. Its aim is to provide a better understanding of the role parliaments are playing in European constitutional law and its idea of 'representative democracy'.

Series Editors

Nicola Lupo
Robert Schütze

Interparliamentary Cooperation in the Composite European Constitution
Edited by Nicola Lupo and Cristina Fasone

The Italian Parliament in the European Union

Edited by
Nicola Lupo and Giovanni Piccirilli

• HART •
OXFORD • LONDON • NEW YORK • NEW DELHI • SYDNEY

HART PUBLISHING
Bloomsbury Publishing Plc
Kemp House, Chawley Park, Cumnor Hill, Oxford, OX2 9PH, UK

HART PUBLISHING, the Hart/Stag logo, BLOOMSBURY and the Diana logo are trademarks of Bloomsbury Publishing Plc
First published in Great Britain 2017

First published in hardback, 2017
Paperback edition, 2020

A catalogue record for this book is available from the British Library.

Library of Congress Cataloging-in-Publication Data

Names: Lupo, Nicola, editor. | Piccirilli, Giovanni, editor.

Title: The Italian parliament in the European Union / Edited by Nicola Lupo and Giovanni Piccirilli.

Description: Portland, OR : Hart Publishing, 2017. | Series: Parliamentary democracy in europe ; volume 2 | Includes bibliographical references and index.

Identifiers: LCCN 2017022889 (print) | LCCN 2017023221 (ebook) | ISBN 9781782258742 (epub) | ISBN 9781782258735 (hardback)

Subjects: LCSH: Legislative bodies—Italy. | Legislative bodies—European Union countries. | European Union—Italy. | Italy. Parlamento.

Classification: LCC KKH2514 (ebook) | LCC KKH2514 .I83 2017 (print) | DDC 328.45—dc23

LC record available at https://lccn.loc.gov/2017022889

ISBN: HB: 978-1-78225-873-5
PB: 978-1-50993-667-0
ePDF: 978-1-78225-872-8
ePub: 978-1-78225-874-2

Typeset by Compuscript Ltd, Shannon

To find out more about our authors and books visit www.hartpublishing.co.uk. Here you will find extracts, author information, details of forthcoming events and the option to sign up for our newsletters.

CONTENTS

NOTES ON CONTRIBUTORS

Davide Alberto Capuano is Counsellor of the Italian Senate and Head of the Secretariat of the Committee on EU Policies. He worked also for the International Affairs Department of the Senate (2003–13) and headed the Interparliamentary Relations Office (2009–13). Other experiences saw him as an official of the Italian Authority of the Stock Exchange (2000–03) and as a practising lawyer (1997–99). He wrote book chapters on 'The Role of National Parliaments in the Legislative Process of the EU. A View from the Italian Parliament' in M Cartabia, N Lupo, A Simoncini (eds), *Democracy and Subsidiarity in the EU* (Il Mulino, 2013) and on 'La nuova governance economica europea. I risvolti sulle procedure parlamentari italiane' (with E Griglio) in N Lupo and A Manzella (eds), *Il sistema parlamentare euro-nazionale* (Giappichelli, 2014).

Alessandro Chiaramonte is Full Professor of Political Science at the University of Florence, where he received his doctorate and now teaches 'Italian Politics' and 'Elections and Electoral Systems'. He is co-founder of CISE, the 'Italian Center for Electoral Studies' at the University of Florence and LUISS Guido Carli University in Rome, and member of the executive boards of the 'Italian Political Science Society' (SISP) and the 'Italian Electoral Studies Society' (SISE). He has published various books and articles on elections, electoral systems and party system change in Italy and in comparative perspective.

Lorenzo De Sio is Associate Professor of Political Science at the LUISS Guido Carli University, Rome, where he teaches several courses at all levels. Formerly Visiting Research Fellow at UC Irvine, Jean Monnet Fellow at the Robert Schuman Centre of the European University Institute, Campbell National Fellow at Stanford University, he is the coordinator of the CISE (Italian Center for Electoral Studies) and a member of the Scientific Council of the ITANES (Italian National Election Studies). A member of the Methods Working Group of the 'True European Voter' international research project (ESF-COST Action IS0806), he participates to the EUDO Observatory on Public Opinion, Political Elites and the Media. His research interests are broadly into elections, voting behaviour and party competition in comparative perspective. Among his publications, beyond several books and edited books in Italian and English, are articles appearing in the *American Political Science Review*, *Comparative Political Studies*, *Electoral Studies*, *Party Politics*, *West European Politics*, *South European Society and Politics*, and all major Italian political science journals.

Vincenzo Emanuele is Post-doctoral Research Fellow in Political Science and Adjunct Professor of Italian Political System at LUISS Guido Carli University in Rome. He is member of CISE (Italian Center for Electoral Studies) and of ITANES (Italian National Election Studies). His field of research is comparative politics with a particular emphasis on elections and party systems. He has also worked on voting behaviour, electoral systems, issues and party competition, party leader selection rules, personal vote and territorial politics.

His research has appeared on *Party Politics, Regional and Federal Studies, Journal of Contemporary European Research, Italian Political Science Review, Contemporary Italian Politics.* He has co-edited five e-books on Italian local and national elections and on the European Parliament elections published by CISE and he is author of several book chapters focusing on party systems, voting behaviour, Italian and European politics.

Antonio Esposito is Counsellor of the Italian Chamber of Deputies. After working for more than a decade at the EU Affairs Department, he is currently Head of Secretariat of the Speaker. He has published articles and essays on EU affairs, especially on the role of the National Parliaments in the European constitutional framework and on comitology. Among his most recent publications: 'La cooperazione interparlamentare: principi, strumenti e prospettive' in A Manzella, N Lupo (eds), *Il sistema parlamentare euro-nazionale. Lezioni* (Giappichelli, 2014) and 'The Role of COSAC in EU Interparliamentary Cooperation: An (Endless) Quest for an Identity' in N Lupo and C Fasone (eds), *Interparliamentary Cooperation in the Composite European Constitution* (Hart Publishing, 2016).

Pietro Falletta is Assistant Professor of Administrative Law, Department of Humanities and Education, University of Molise, Campobasso. He is also Coordinator of @LawLab-Laboratorio di diritto del digitale at LUISS Guido Carli University, Rome, where he teaches Information and Communication Law and New Media Law. In the same University he had a Research Grant in Public Law (2008–12). He is Invited Professor at the University of Sorbonne-Pantheon I, Paris. He was legal advisor to the Antidiscrimination Unit at Italian Prime Minister's Office and to the Ministry of Environment. His research focuses on the public law, electronic communications, environmental information and the freedom of expression. Among his publications, *Le funzioni amministrative locali tra attuazione e inattuazione del Titolo V* (Aracne, 2012) and a co-authored handbook on Internet Law, *Il diritto del web. Casi e materiali* (together with M Mensi, CEDAM 2015).

Cristina Fasone is Assistant Professor of Comparative Public Law, Department of Political Science, LUISS Guido Carli University, Rome. She is holder of a Jean Monnet Module on Parliamentary accountability and technical expertise: budgetary powers, information and communication technologies and elections (PATEU) (2017–19) within the Summer School on 'Parliamentary democracy in Europe' at LUISS School of Government, and is one of the Academic Coordinators of the EU Joint Master on 'Parliamentary procedures and legislative drafting (EUPADRA)'. She holds a PhD in Comparative Public Law from the University of Siena and she has been Max Weber Postdoctoral Fellow (2013–15), Law Department, European University Institute. She has been Visiting Researcher at the Georgetown University Law Center, Washington DC (USA) (2011), Erasmus Mundus Visiting Scholar at the Victoria University of Wellington (NZ) (2013), Visiting Fellow at the Law Department, European University Institute, Florence (2015), where she has also been part of the EUI Law Research Team of the Horizon 2020 project on 'A Dynamic Economic and Monetary Union' (ADEMU). In 2016 she has held an International Chair at Uppsala University, Faculty of Law. Her research focuses on Parliaments and Constitutional Courts in the EU and in the Eurozone crisis, parliamentary committee systems and forms of government (*Sistemi di commissioni parlamentari e forme di governo* is the title of her monograph, CEDAM 2012), and national and EU budgets and budgetary powers. She has authored several essays on these topics, published on national and international journals like the *European Law Journal*, *The Journal of Legislative Studies* and *German Law Journal* and has co-edited a book with Nicola Lupo, *Interparliamentary Cooperation in the Composite European Constitution* (Hart Publishing, 2016).

Luigi Gianniti is Counsellor of the Italian Senate, where he directs the Research Service. He holds a PhD in Public Law from the University of Bologna. He has been Head of Cabinet of the Minister of European Affairs. In addition to his professional activity, he has held courses and conducted research activities in constitutional law. Since 1998, he has held seminars on public law and legal theory at 'Sapienza' University and the University of Firenze. Currently he is Professor of Parliamentary Law at the Department of political science, 'Roma Tre' University and at the LUISS School of Government. He is a frequent speaker at conferences on Constitutional Law and European Law organised by other Italian universities. He is the author of several essays, among which in *Giurisprudenza costituzionale*, *Quaderni costituzionali* and *Astrid on line*. His recent publications include *Corso di diritto parlamentare* (co-authored with N Lupo, Il Mulino, 2nd edn, 2013).

Elena Griglio is Counsellor of the Italian Senate with the responsibility of Acting Head of the Office for Parliamentary Delegations. She teaches Legal Drafting at the ad hoc Laboratory of the Department of Political Sciences of the LUISS University of Rome. She holds a Course in 'Drafting and follow-up of non-legislative acts' within the Master on Parliament and Public Policies of the LUISS School of Government and a Course in 'Sub-national parliaments' within the Joint Master in Parliamentary Procedures and Legislative Drafting EUPADRA, under the Erasmus+ programme. She holds a PhD in Public Law from the University of Turin (2007), she has been post-doc Fellow in Public Comparative Law at the Luiss Guido Carli University of Rome (January 2010–February 2012) and adjunct professor in Administrative Law at the University 'Cattolica del Sacro Cuore' in Rome. Her research focuses on parliamentary procedures, parliamentary democracy in the EU, social rights and federalism/regionalism (*Principio unitario e neo-policentrismo. Le esperienze italiana e spagnola a confronto*, CEDAM 2008, I–XXII, 1–482). She has authored several essays on these topics. Among the most recent ones, 'Parliamentary oversight in the European economic governance: the Conference on Stability, Economic Coordination and Governance', co-written with Nicola Lupo, in *Journal of European Integration* (forthcoming, 2017).

Barbara Guastaferro is Tenured Assistant Professor of Constitutional Law, Department of Political Science, University of Naples "Federico II" and Research Fellow in Law at Durham University within the framework of the 'Neo-Federalism' Project, funded by the European Research Council. She is qualified as an Associate Professor in both Comparative and Constitutional Law in Italy. She currently serves as the national constitutional expert for Italy in an ERC research project on 'The Role and Future of National Constitutions in European and Global Governance' run by the Kent Law School and in a research project on 'Member States' Constitutions and EU Integration' run by the University of Salzburg. In 2011 she was awarded the Hauser Global Law Scholarship to financially support her post-doctoral studies at New York University School of Law, where she was Emile Noël Fellow 2011–12 at the Jean Monnet Center for Regional and International Economic Law and Justice. She is author of several publications in the field of EU Law, Comparative and Constitutional Law, and Constitutional and Democratic Theory, among which 'Beyond the Exceptionalism of Constitutional Conflicts. The Ordinary Functions of the Identity Clause', in *Yearbook of*

European Law 2012 and the book *Legalità costituzionale e legalità sovranazionale. Tensioni constitutive e giunture ordinamentali* (Giappichelli, 2013).

Renato Ibrido is Post-doctoral Research Fellow in Public Law at LUISS Guido Carli University, Department of Political Science. He holds a PhD in Comparative Public Law from the University of Siena. He is instructor and Academic Coordinator of the Master in 'Parliament and Public Policies' organised by LUISS-School of Government as well as of the Joint Master Erasmus+ in 'Parliamentary procedures and legislative drafting' (EUPADRA). He has been Visiting professor at the Complutense University of Madrid. Its monograph on *L'interpretazione del diritto parlamentare* (Franco Angeli, 2015) won the annual Prize of the Italian Constitutional Law Scholars' Association for young scholars and the Franco Angeli—Collana 'Studi di diritto pubblico' annual Prize for the best book proposal in the field of Public Law. He is author of a second monograph on *L'Unione bancaria europea. Profili costituzionali* (Giappichelli, 2017).

Amie Kreppel holds a Jean Monnet Chair (*ad personam*) at the University of Florida where she is also Director of the Center for European Studies. She was the 2016 Fulbright-Schuman Chair at the College of Europe and a past Fernand Braudel Senior Fellow at the European University Institute (EUI). In addition, she has served as international visiting faculty at the Université Louis Pasteur (ULP), Strasbourg, France, Institut für Höhere Studien (Institute for Advanced Studies) Vienna, Austria, and the l'Institut d'Etudes Européennes, Université Libre Bruxelles (ULB), Brussels Belgium and at the LUISS Guido Carli University in Rome. She has written extensively on the political institutions of Europe in general and the European Union and Italy more specifically. Her publications include a book on the *Development of the European Parliament and Supranational Party System*, published by Cambridge University Press (2002) as well as articles in a wide variety of journals including *Comparative Political Studies*, the *British Journal of Political Research*, *European Union Politics*, the *European Journal of Political Research*, *Political Research Quarterly*, the *Journal of European Public Policy* and the *Journal of Common Market Studies*. She is currently Co-Editor of the *Italian Political Science Review*. From April 2011–April 2013 she served as the President of the European Union Studies Association (EUSA). She is also a past president of the Conference Group on Italian Politics and sits on the steering committee of the European Consortia for Political Research Standing Group on the European Union (ECPR-SGEU) and the ECPR Standing Group on Parliaments.

Peter L Lindseth is Olimpiad S Ioffe Professor of International and Comparative Law at the University of Connecticut School of Law, where he is also Director of International Programs and Co-Director in the Professional Certificate Program in Corporate and Regulatory Compliance. He is also a regular Visiting Professor in the School of Law at Queen Mary University of London as well as a Research Associate at the Centre for International Studies at the University of Oxford. He has held fellowships at the American Academy in Berlin, the European University Institute, the French Conseil d'Etat, the Max Planck Institute for European Legal History, Princeton University (Law and Public Affairs), and New York University School of Law. His research and teaching focuses on administrative law, compliance, European integration, and legal history and theory. His books include *Power and Legitimacy: Reconciling Europe and the Nation-State* (Oxford University Press, 2010), *Transatlantic Regulatory Cooperation: Legal Problems and Political Prospects* (co-editor,

Oxford University Press, 2000), and *Digital Democracy in a Globalized World* (co-editor, Edward Elgar forthcoming). His articles have appeared in the *Columbia Law Review*, *Contemporary European History*, the *European Law Journal*, and the *Yale Law Journal*, among other publications. He holds a BA and JD from Cornell and a PhD in European history from Columbia.

Nicola Lupo is Full Professor of Public Law and Director of the Center for Parliamentary Studies at LUISS Guido Carli University in Rome. At LUISS School of Government he is Director of the Master programme 'Parliament and Public Policies', of the Summer School on 'Parliamentary Democracy in Europe' and of the Erasmus+ Joint Master Degree in 'Parliamentary Procedures and Legislative Drafting' (EUPADRA). He was counsellor at the Italian Chamber of Deputies (1997–2005), member of the Prime Minister's Simplification Unit (2006–2008) and of the Drafting Committee of the Commission for Constitutional Reform (2013). He has been a visiting scholar at George Washington University Law School (US), at the Institute of Advanced Legal Studies in London, at the Institut d'Etudes Europeénnes at the Université Libre de Bruxelles, at the Australian National University in Canberra, at the Department of Politics of the University of Sheffield, at the Law School of Copenhagen University and at Science-Po, Paris. His publications concern sources of law, parliamentary rules of procedures, legal drafting, budgetary procedures, regional councils, parliaments in the EU. Co-author of a textbook on Italian Parliamentary Law—L Gianniti, N Lupo, *Corso di diritto parlamentare* (2nd edn, Il Mulino, 2013)—he has co-edited *Democracy and Subsidiarity in the EU* (Il Mulino, 2013) (with M Cartabia and A Simoncini), *Comparative Law in Legislative Drafting* (Eleven International Publishing, 2014) (with L Scaffardi) and *Interparliamentary Cooperation in the Composite European Constitution* (Hart Publishing, 2016) (with C Fasone).

Andrea Manzella is President of the Centre for Parliamentary Studies, LUISS Guido Carli University, Rome, where he was Full Professor of Parliamentary Law and later held a Jean Monnet *ad personam* Chair on the democratic principles in the European Union. He gave courses in the Universities of Trento, Genova, Padova and Roma. Among his publications the volumes *Sui principi democratici dell'Unione Europea* (ES, 2013) and *Il sistema parlamentare euro-nazionale. Lezioni* (co-edited with N. Lupo, Giappichelli, 2014) are linked to the Jean Monnet *ad personam* Chair. He is author of *Il parlamento* (3rd edn, Il mulino, 2003). Among his most recent works, 'The European Parliament and the National Parliaments as a system' in *The Consequences of the Crisis on the European Integration and on the Member States* (Springer, 2017). He served as Member of the European Parliament and as Italian senator, also as Chairman of the Committee on EU affairs of the Italian Senate of the Republic. He was also member of the Parliamentary Assembly of the Council of Europe and member of the Convention that drafted the Charter of fundamental rights of the European Union.

Massimo Nardini holds a PhD in Public Law from LUISS Guido Carli University in Rome and is a Carabinieri Officer. He is now deputy Head of the Legislative Office at the Environment Ministry and responsible for the Parliamentary/Legislation Sector. His research focuses on constitutional law, public budgeting and parliamentary procedures. He has published articles and essays on electoral systems, budgetary legal framework, Italian constitutional history. Among his most recent publications: 'Il d.lgs. 126/2014: l'"armonizzazione" dei bilanci regionali nel quadro del nuovo principio di "equilibrio" ed i riflessi sull'autonomia del Consiglio' (2014) 5/6 *Le Regioni*, 'Il ruolo "notarile" di Einaudi nella formazione del VII governo De Gasperi e le dinamiche sul "modello Westminster" della prima legislatura repubblicana: realtà o illusioni?' (2015) 12 *Federalismi.it*, and with S Pajno 'Il potere sostitutivo dello Stato (art 120, comma 2, Cost)' in *Commentario alla riforma costituzionale del 2016* (ESI, 2016).

Giovanni Piccirilli is Assistant Professor of Constitutional Law, Department of Law, LUISS Guido Carli University in Rome, where he is also Coordinator of the Centre for Parliamentary Studies and of the Erasmus+ Joint Master Degree on 'Parliamentary procedures and legislative drafting' (EUPADRA). He holds a PhD in Law, Methods and techniques of Lawmaking and Assessment from the University of Genova and was previously Emile Noel Fellow at the NYU School of Law, Jean Monnet Center for International and Regional Economic Law and Justice (Fall 2013). He has been Jean Monnet Centre of Excellence Visiting Professor 2012 at the University of Florida, Centre for European Studies and Erasmus Mundus Visiting Scholar at the Monash University of Melbourne. He was advisor to the Chairman of the Committee on Legislation, Italian Chamber of Deputies (2009–10) and Legal expert in the staff of the Minister of Economic Development (2014–15). His research focuses on sources of law, parliaments and lawmaking processes. His monograph *L'emendamento nel processo di decisione parlamentare* (CEDAM 2008) was awarded with the annual Prize of the Italian Constitutional Law Scholars' Association. He is coordinator and module leader of the Jean Monnet Module on 'Legislative drafting in implementing EU law in Italy', funded by the EACEA in 2017–19.

Giovanni Rizzoni is Counsellor of the Italian Chamber of Deputies and Head of the International Relations Department of the Italian Chamber of deputies. He is Professor of Comparative Public Law at LUISS Guido Carli University in Rome. Since 2002 he has served as international expert in several missions to assists partner countries in strengthening policy-making and strategic capacities and in setting up co-ordination mechanisms at the centre of government. He is author of several publications in the field of comparative constitutional law and parliamentary law, among which the book *Opposizione parlamentare e democrazia deliberativa* (il Mulino, 2012).

Maria Romaniello holds a PhD in Political Systems and institutional change from the IMT Lucca Institute for advanced Studies. She discussed a thesis dealing with the involvement of National Parliaments in the EU decision-making process, with a specific focus on Upper Houses. She was visiting research scholar at UM Maastricht University, in the Department of Public law and she attended the Master of Arts in European Political and Administrative Studies at the College of Europe. She is lecturer within the Master in European Studies of the LUISS School of Government and academic coordinator of the Erasmus+ Joint Master in 'Parliamentary Procedures and Legislative Drafting' (EUPADRA). She conducts researches mainly in the field of comparative constitutional law, dealing with federal issues, parliamentary institutions and European Union law and policies.

Giuliano Vosa is Post-doctoral Research Fellow in Constitutional Law at LUISS Guido Carli University in Rome, Department of Law, where he is also Teaching Assistant in Constitutional Law. He has spent various research periods at the Central European University, Budapest, at the Erik Castren Institute for International Studies, Helsinki, at the European University Institute, Florence and at the Kozminski University, Department of Law, Warsaw, as well as at the European Parliament, where he has worked for almost two years. His main interests lie in European and Comparative Constitutional Law, with a special focus for law-making process in a post-State scenario. Among its numerous publications, in English and Italian, a few articles appearing in major Public Law reviews dwell on or refer to the role of Parliaments in the European context.

Werner Vandenbruwaene is a research fellow of the Research Foundation Flanders (FWO) affiliated with the research group Government & Law at the University of Antwerp. As a visiting professor, he teaches introduction to political science (BA course) and taught comparative constitutional law (MA course). He defended his doctoral thesis on the judicial enforcement of the principle of subsidiarity in the fall of 2014. He was a visiting researcher at the UCLA School of Law during the Spring term 2014, and a Visiting Scholar at NYU Law School in 2017. His main research interests are federalism, comparative constitutional law, fiscal and budgetary law, legislative studies and constitutional law & economics.

FOREWORD: A MORE EFFECTIVE, CONNECTED AND DEMOCRATIC EU

ANDREA MANZELLA

I. Introduction. The Italian Parliament, Today

To what extent is the Parliament of a Member State of the European Union still sovereign? In what terms can one still speak of 'national' parliamentary sovereignty? Can there be a parliamentary sovereignty shared among the 28 national assemblies and the European Parliament?

These are questions that all the parliamentary democracies of the Member States of the Union are asking themselves. The answers to these questions will be given here below, starting from the condition of the Italian Parliament, which is a particular one since it is the Parliament of one of the 'founding' States: the promoters of the European integration process (Rome, 1957). A state which, according to the 1948 Constitution (article 11), has had since its very origins the obligation to agree, 'on conditions of equality with other States, to the limitations of sovereignty that may be necessary to a world order ensuring peace and justice among the Nations'.

More recently (2001, 2012), its legislative sovereignty was conditioned by the 'respect for the constraints deriving from EU legislation' (article 117.1) and its financial autonomy has been carefully regulated by the norms of the Fiscal compact (2013) which brought about the modification of article 81 of the Constitution on state budget and the approval of the correlated constitutional law (20 April 2012, No 1). As it belongs to the common monetary zone, the Italian Parliament is therefore conditioned as well as by the general constraints of the EU legal order, also by those that are specific to the 'enhanced cooperation' which is the Eurozone: a true 'union in the Union' (article 3.4 Treaty on European Union (TEU)).

In other words, to all effects and purposes the Italian Parliament has become the political assembly of a state with self-limited sovereignty: the 'community State'.[1] In fact, with its adhesion to the European Union, the Italian state, like the other Member States, has limited its sovereignty in a collective contractual way. The 'contract of sovereignty', stipulated with the concurrence of all the other states in a condition of reciprocal equality, gave rise to a legal order whose norms have, formally and materially, a superior force to those laid down by the original state legal systems. With respect to these systems the European Union poses itself as a legal order with objective autonomy, even though recognising in them the character of constituting prerequisites and remaining linked to them for a number of relations of 'juridical relevance'.

[1] A Manzella, Lo Stato 'comunitario',(2003) *Quaderni costituzionali* 273 ff.

The essential aim of the Union is to carry out policies and achieve objectives that constitute a common good for the Member States, but which the democratic self-conscience of the single states shows as being no longer achievable with its own powers alone. For this mission that cannot be limited to within national boundaries, the legal system born from the conferral of sovereign state powers has taken on, through the very effect of their reciprocal integration, an autonomy of exercise and development that is not ascribable to the sum of the original state powers. The autonomous supranational power arising from this asserts itself on both the states that founded the new legal order and, directly or indirectly, on their citizens. They are thus subjects in two legal orders: the state one and the supranational one.

II. Dual Citizenship, Dual Representation

This 'duality' of interconnected citizen status (see article 9 TEU: 'Citizenship of the Union shall be additional to and not replace national citizenship') is at the basis of a duality and interconnection also in the order of political representation. Citizenship is not only a centre of application of rights and duties but it is above all the *status activae civitatis*: that is, the way for each single individual to take part in the political life of the community of reference. This means that for the whole exercise of citizenship, the national Parliament cannot be considered the only organ of political representation: to this must be added the European Parliament, without prejudice to the limit of obligations of each assembly. If this interconnection is missing, in terms of interparliamentary cooperation, phenomena of democratic deficit arise which are a source of risks, not only for the very stability and legitimation of the Union's legislation, but also, by a sort of 'contagion', for the national representative bodies themselves.

If therefore the functions of the Italian Parliament are in recession insofar as they are conditioned by the 'constraints deriving from EU legislation' (article 117 Constitution), such functions are nonetheless in expansion in as much as active in the EU legislation, that is, in a sphere going beyond state borders. This expansion goes in three directions: a) in the upholding of the government's responsibility for its management of European affairs; b) in the control of European legislation: from normative initiative to its execution and implementation; c) in the expression of opinions during parliamentary procedures relative to the banking Union, particularly in the one regulating the single resolution mechanism;[2] d) in the direct participation in the form of 'political' and 'economic' dialogue with the European Commission and the 'pertinent' economic committee of the European Parliament in the 'European semester' procedures and, above all, in the form of organic union with the European Parliament and the other national Parliaments in the interparliamentary conferences (COSAC, Conference for economic governance, Conference for common foreign and defence policy).[3]

[2] See R Ibrido, *The Banking Union and the 'Euro-national Parliamentary System'. Constitutional Implications*, paper presented at the 2nd Annual Conference of the Erasmus Academic Network on Parliamentary Democracy in Europe—PADEMIA, Brussels, 2–3 July 2015; R Ibrido, *L'Unione bancaria europea. Profili costituzionali* (Turin, Giappichelli, 2017) 248 ff.

[3] See the volume, edited by N Lupo and C Fasone, *Interparliamentary Cooperation in the Composite European Constitution* (Oxford, Hart Publishing, 2016).

By reason also of the existence of a national Parliament, fully participant in the legal potentialities contained in the Union's legislation, the European state with self-limited sovereignty is therefore in the end like an 'enhanced' state: because it manages to carry out functions reaching beyond its legal and economic forces; because it is in a wider legitimation process than the domestic one; because by means of the subsidiarity principle it always keeps the tasks that in size and efficacy it can adequately fulfil; because it is more 'defended'—on the basis of the establishment of shared powers in the supranational system—against the drive towards fragmentation as a result of claims of territorial independentism coming from inside.

From the self-limitations of sovereignty thus emerges a parliamentary state that is different but not at all weakened, but rather 'enhanced', with respect to the fully sovereign state, which is now something of the past owing to its obvious lack of power in the global world.[4]

The thus 'enhanced' state must nevertheless be radically rethought in all its aspects, in the light of the constitutional process transforming it: the integration process. Rudolf Smend would have said that now all the elements of the political order must be reconsidered in the new system: 'like the elements of a magnetic field that has been received a new pole in a different position'.[5] In the transformation of the state and its sovereignty the role of the Parliament, owing to its very flexibility and resilience, is essential for the stability of democratic values in the change. Despite the falls in political tension caused by a sort of creeping parliamentary revisionism, this is a tension that the Italian Parliament is certainly not immune to.

III. A Devil's Alternative for Parliaments in the EU

In which context can one however still speak of 'national' parliamentary sovereignty? In order to establish this, it is necessary to refer to two precise provisions of the same Union legislation.

The first one is article 4.2 TEU. In this norm the problem of the respect for the national 'identity' of the Member States by the Union is posed in new terms with respect to the past. In fact, national 'identity' is specified both in the 'fundamental, political and constitutional structure' and in the 'essential functions' of the state. There is therefore a structural and functional aspect characterising national identity. It is not at all absorbed by belonging to the EU. The state sphere can undergo, and does actually undergo, 'limitations' from the very moment of adhesion to the EU, in the fulfilment of the 'admissibility conditions' (see 'Copenhagen criteria' and article 9 TEU). However, this 'sovereign' sphere cannot be annulled in its fundamental nucleus: if this were the case, the very constitutional identity of the EU would be violated, whose motto 'unity in diversity' (see Declaration No 52) does not only express the essence of a cultural pluralism in the EU structure but also a precise juridical element: the concept of national sovereignty—with its limitations and perseverance—has always been at the basis of the decision-making process of the European Union and, definitively, of its legitimation.

[4] AS Milward, *The European Rescue of the Nation-State* 2nd edn (London, Routledge, 2000).

[5] R Smend, *Verfassung und Verfassungsrecht* (München, Duncker & Humblot, 1928).

The second defining provision of the area of national parliamentary sovereignty is article 53 of the Charter of Fundamental Rights of the European Union. Here it states that 'Nothing in this Charter shall be interpreted as restricting or adversely affecting human rights and fundamental freedoms as recognised, ... by the Member States' constitutions'.

In this far-reaching formulation, there nonetheless lurks, also for the Italian Parliament (and for the Constitutional Court), the difficult issue of social rights, that is, of that particular aspect of sovereignty—essential in the state of the 1900s—that can be called 'social sovereignty'.

In fact there is a widespread problem of the constitutional legitimacy of a possible deterioration of national social rights possibly caused by the application of Union provisions, indirectly restrictive of the social policy of the governments of the Member States. Here a real devil's alternative can be seen for each national Parliament. Either to keep (and perhaps improve) the existing conditions of the *welfare state*, breaching the EU financial parameters and the same new national budget constraints, or to respect those parameters and constraints at the cost of creating a new—and more dangerous—democratic deficit, with the distancing and repulsion of citizens with respect to the national representative institution and with the danger of running into the sanction of their own Constitutional Court.

With regard to this last point, it must in fact be noted that the Italian Constitutional Court, even though accepting the essential principles of EU law (direct applicability and primacy), has reserved its right to the conservation of legislative dualism (national and European) as an extreme counter-limitation. Thus, the power to judge the compatibility of 'European legislation' has been maintained with the 'supreme principles of the legal system of the Republic'. Even though as *extrema ratio*, this is a rather elastic assessment of last resort.

However, apart from this exceptional remedy, in order to get out of the impasse of the question of social rights, a 'Europeanisation' of social policy would be decisive (at least in its less 'identity' oriented connotations), with the fixing of standards and sharing mechanisms of the relative 'sovereignty'. An application of 'social responsibility' also on the European institutions should result from this. This would however only be possible if the Eurozone achieved a real 'budget union', a fiscal capacity, parallel with the budget powers that are up to the EU in its entirety.

The national Parliament and the European Parliament would thus find themselves before a real economic and social policy implemented by an institutional platform with a corresponding political responsibility: to a 'government', in short, that would rectify the present isolation of the monetary power of the European Central Bank. In this way, there would be democratic decisions—and not jurisdictional ones—that would guarantee (with the same co-decision structure congenial to it) the social imbalances in the Union's citizenship.

IV. The Active Contribution of National Parliaments to the Good Functioning of EU Democracy

In the present state of the Union, the Italian Parliament is also affected by the 'protagonism' which for national Parliaments was framed in the Treaty of Lisbon. In particular, in the formula of article 12(1) TEU ('National Parliaments contribute actively to the good functioning of the Union') are two expressions rich in meaning.

The first is the adverb '*actively*', referring to the concept of a dynamic subjectivity in the life of the Union. Its scope is to underline that the position of the national Parliament in the EU is the opposite of the mere passive right to be informed that characterised their position for a certain period of time.

The second expression is the word '*functioning*': a word that in the Treaties (see article 1(1) Treaty on the Functioning of the European Union (TFEU)) is used to indicate the overall activity of the Union's institutions, as stated in the preamble (seventh paragraph) of the Treaty of the Union and even by the very name of the 'second' Treaty which lays down the basis 'on the *functioning* of the Union'. In this second preamble the emphasis is on a 'concerted action' for the 'removal of existing obstacles' for the achievement of the Union's objectives (fourth paragraph). In this case too, a role of active participation is delineated. For the purposes of the functioning of the Union which must be 'good' in the multi-faceted sense of 'democratic', 'efficient', interconnected 'within a single institutional framework' (these are the three specifications of the adjective 'good' that can be drawn from the seventh paragraph of the TEU preamble). Is there therefore a 'responsibility for integration' thus defined that weighs on the Italian Parliament as it does on the other national Parliaments?[6]

From the formula of the Treaties it also follows that the 'participation of the national parliaments in the activity of the Union' (paragraph 2 of the preamble to Protocol No 1), albeit respectful of the fundamental principle of attribution (article 5(2) TEU), is not a sectoral participation. Instead, there is a general condition of interference of national parliamentarism, which, also within the normative limits and constraints of the Treaties, tends to characterise the entire functional physiognomy of the Union. This is a natural consequence: as a juridical phenomenon of political intermediation between institutions and citizenship, parliamentarism characterises virtually the whole legal system to which it refers, other than the specific normative nucleus limiting its functions.

When, therefore, article 10(1) TEU states that 'the functioning [yet again recourse is made to this key expression] of the Union shall be founded on representative democracy', it uses an important phrase: in fact, referring inclusively to both European parliamentarism and national parliamentarism, it attests the necessary interconnection. On both must the good functioning of the Union be 'founded'.

The formal definitions aside, the awareness is thus becoming more diffused—in the Italian Parliament and public opinion—of a basic fact that associates national Parliaments and the European Parliament. This is the electoral factor, an expression of the same 'right to parliament'[7] set down extensively in article 39 of the EU Charter of Fundamental Rights. Leading to this conclusion is the concrete fact of a same electorate, which is apparently divided—incoming—by national geographic seats but then unified—outgoing—in the

[6] The expression was notoriously coined in the jurisprudence of the *Bundesverfassungsgericht* on the occasion of the judgment on the Treaty of Lisbon of 30 June 2009.

[7] ... following the formulation given by the European Court of Human Rights in the famous judgment of 18 February 1999 *Matthews v United Kingdom* (Application No 24833/94).

shape of a collegial body, the European Parliament, which votes by merging (that is, with no national distinction among the voting Members of European Parliament (MEPs)).

The electoral factor is turning out to be—even in the chaos of the economic crisis—the most powerful and incisive factor for the formation of a 'European' public space: that is, a space that is no longer dominated by domestic questions but by common issues, a ground for political convergences and divergences going beyond the boundaries of the Member States. At the basis of this new energy of the electoral factor lie three causes.

The first can be found in the parliamentary choice of the president of the European Commission, after the 2014 elections. The big European political 'families' managed to express a unifying candidature, despite the variety of parties and peoples, languages and spirits within each of these. Furthermore, by asking the electors to vote for a 'foreign' leader, there was a radical refusal of any kind of national discrimination, right at the moment of greatest importance in the life of the Union. Lastly, by establishing a connection between elections for representation and elections for the European 'government', it was demonstrated that with the force of the electoral factor it is possible to break the curse of the democratic *deficit*. During the last European electoral campaign, the *Spitzenkandidaten* turned out to be elements of orientation, if not political cohesion, before the obsolescence of old style party memberships.

The almost confidence vote of the president of the Commission—an institutional consistent follow-up of the *Spitzenkandidaten* in the European Parliament—has thus led to the mapping out of a political geography of the supranational Assembly distinguished by a profound cleavage between the staunch pro-European majority and the Euro-hostile groups. This same geography is beginning to spread to the national political geography of party and parliamentary alliances. The separateness between the two spaces—the domestic and European ones—has thus been substituted by a process of communication of political matters from the European Parliament to the national Parliaments.

The second cause marking the formation process of a European public space is the polarisation of a political debate involving the whole Union on its position with regard to the problems of globalisation. There is a fault line transversally dividing nationalities, as the dramatic events in Greece in summer 2015 have demonstrated.

On the one hand, there are political debates and movements that perceive the Union as a vehicle for the transmission and enhancement of the 'subjections' generated by globalisation. On the other hand, are opinions and camps which, on the contrary, see the Union as the 'first level' of institutional resistance to anonymous market laws. Such a radical contrast should not allow, as can easily be seen, differentiated behaviour at European and national level. Also from this point of view, there is a transposition from one level to another and a reciprocal influence in a field that has become common.

Closely connected is the third cause that contributes to the opening of a common public space. This is the holding of a debate—a perfect example of which is to be found in the United Kingdom—on the attributions of the Union. On the one hand, the idea of a 'repatriation' of a number of competences (moreover never actually defined), which means a return to an '*un-closer Union*', in all likelihood downgraded to being a simple space of the single market. On the other hand, the idea of a forward thrust, perhaps with the method of enhanced cooperation (article 20 TEU; article 10 Fiscal compact) towards a political Union marked by a *fiscal capacity*: that is, the thrust towards an institutionalised differentiation.

These three causes, with their divisive effects, are all to be found in the Italian Parliament: after the clamorous alliances established in the European Parliament by important national parties with Euro-hostile movements (the Northern League party merged into the group 'Europe of Nations and Freedom' group with Marine Le Pen's National Front, and the 5 Star Movement merged into the 'Europe of Freedom and Direct Democracy' group with Nigel Farage's UKIP).

Nevertheless, only the next Italian general election (the expiration date of which is 2018, unless there is an anticipated dissolution) will show whether the boundary lines, now well marked in the European public space, will be maintained at home, or whether the long-standing Italian pro-European tradition and the positive developments of the European crisis will manage to prevail, lessening the present divergences.

V. The Need for a Pact Among Parliaments, within the New Institutional Framework

Dual citizenship and the electoral factor are the roots connecting the European Parliament with the national Parliaments, and justify the legal basis of their 'active contribution' to the 'good functioning' of the Union (article 12 TEU). The question however remains whether this 'contribution' can achieve the configuration of the exercise of a 'shared' parliamentary sovereignty, without prejudice to the respect for the—non 'sharable'—identity nucleus of which each Parliament is an active holder and by which it is at the same time conditioned.

It is a question that involves the Italian Parliament, just as it does the other national Parliaments, since it is a crucial issue for the democratic quality of the entire institutional apparatus of the Union and, in particular, of the Eurozone. In principle, there is the assuming of government responsibility at the top by the European institutions (above all the European Council and the European Central Bank, and even the 'European Troika' despite the cumbersome presence of the International Monetary Fund).

The 'lift' of the principle of subsidiarity has above all worked upwards in closely pursuing the economic crisis. And this has given rise to big problems of democratic accountability. The powers of the European Parliament are devoid of real sanctioning mechanisms and those of the national Parliaments are split and segmented in the mere confrontation with the 'respective governments' (article 10(2) TEU): a whole grey area has opened up in which the European institutional powers are not balanced by actual instruments able to enforce political responsibility.

This is a grey but also indivisible area that cannot be overseen, at least in the present stage of EU law, by the European Parliament alone. At the same time in its intergovernmental unity it is outside the range of action of national Parliaments.

It is this situation of disconnection in the democratic functioning of the Union that in various Treaties 'calls for' an ever more juridicially intense application of Protocol No 1 of the Treaty of Lisbon in the part dedicated to 'interparliamentary cooperation' (article 9 TEU). It is in this cooperation that the exercise of shared sovereignty can be fulfilled by the Parliaments of the Union and a Euro-national parliamentary system can take shape.[8]

[8] See the volume edited by A Manzella and N Lupo, *Il sistema parlamentare euro-nazionale. Lezioni* (Giappichelli, Turin, 2014); N Lupo, 'Parlamento europeo e Parlamenti Nazionali nella costituzione 'composita'

Of course this need for interparliamentary cooperation, involving the whole Union (as the recent setting up of the interparliamentary Conference for foreign policy and defence shows), is particularly felt in the Eurozone.

In this 'union of the Union' (article 3(4) TEU) the so-called Fiscal Compact contract realised, albeit with the terminological caution of 'informality', a parallel recomposition of the 'head of government' of the Union. From this point of view, the Fiscal Compact basically acted as a real 'institutional treaty' of the Eurozone, with specific variations with respect to the Lisbon Treaty.

The European Council became the Euro Summit (article 12 Fiscal Compact). The ECOFIN Council became the Eurogroup (article 137 TFEU) with different functioning modalities with regard to sensitive points from the ECOFIN rules (Protocol No 14 on the Eurogroup; article 136(2) TFEU). The same Commission has its own diversity in the Eurozone because it has taken on tasks and power (with the *reverse majority*) not foreseen by the Treaty (articles 5, 6 and 7 Fiscal Compact). And moreover as far as concerns democratic scrutiny, the Fiscal Compact, at the same time a summary and an innovative text of the provisions on the economic governance of the Eurozone, introduced an interparliamentary Conference on economic and financial governance (article 13), that is a venue at which national and European Parliaments can agree on common actions by debate concerning the line of action of the Commission and Council.

These institutional bodies of the Eurozone could have an institutional cover—as again foreseen by the Fiscal Compact (article 10)—by means of the formal recognition of the 'union of the Union' as 'enhanced cooperation' (according to articles 20 TEU and 326–334 TFEU). After all, this is a finalisation that has already traversed the whole crisis legislation.

The same Fiscal Compact, as a 'summary', which foresees the possibility of such 'enhanced cooperation' in essential matters for the good functioning of the Eurozone, furthermore sets down the incorporation of its 'measures' within the legal framework of the Union with the aim of realising an 'enhanced' economic and monetary union (article 16). Before this the preamble on the institution of the Eurogroup already spoke of 'enhanced dialogue' 'pending the Euro becoming the currency of all Member States of the Union' (Protocol No 14). While as confirmation that the enhanced cooperation shall be 'open at any time to all Member States' (article 20(1) TEU) 'subject to compliance with any conditions of participation laid down by the authorising decision' (article 328 TFEU), there is Protocol No 15(9) which lays down that 'The United Kingdom may notify the Council at any time of its intention to adopt the euro'.

It should be highlighted that the recourse to flexible 'enhanced cooperation', in this phase of the integration process, is by far preferable to a review of the Treaties that would instead inevitably crystallise the present European monetary 'disunion' with potential irreversible effects.

The institutional link, with the formal instrument of 'enhanced cooperation', could bring about an actual government dynamic (and no longer of simple governance) of the Eurozone, with 'specific provisions' and simplified decision-making procedures

nell'UE: le diverse letture possibili' (2014) 3 *RivistaAIC*; A Manzella, 'Parlamento europeo e Parlamenti Nazionali come sistema' (2015) 1 *RivistaAIC*; A Manzella, 'The European Parliament and National Parliaments as a System', in S Mangiameli (ed), *The Consequences of the Crisis on European Integration and on the Member States* (Cham, Springer, 2017) 47–63.

(cf article 20(4) TEU and article 136 TFEU), above all with the possibility of establishing autonomy in expenditure (article 332 TFEU) to the point of defining a fiscal capacity of the zone, structured for funds and powered by its own resources.

The completion of the construction of the Eurozone is functional in obtaining a twofold effect. The first is that of transforming the present 'set of rules' into a real structured legal order in the natural connection between rules and institutions. The second is that of guaranteeing the stability of the Eurozone, accompanying the intervention powers, alone, of the European Central Bank, with the guarantee of a political system. Within this framework there exists a parliamentary question for the Eurozone, with two possible outcomes.

The first is that it develops the choice, already institutionalised in article 13 of the Fiscal Compact, of interparliamentary cooperation. The presently used instrument is that of the 'Conference' that unites the representatives of the 'pertinent' committee of the European Parliament and the national Parliaments in a collegial body. This is nevertheless an outcome against which, in its first real concrete expressions, attempts were quite obviously made to weaken by means of the insertion of the Conference in an ambiguous six-monthly 'European parliamentary week', almost making it appear more as an 'event' than as a body.[9]

This attempt to downsize was the result of institutional short-sightedness giving rise to two concerns. On the one hand, the concern of the European Parliament that it would lose powers in favour of national Parliaments in areas that are supranational by destination. On the other hand, the concern of various national Parliaments to not deepen the present gap between the countries in the Eurozone and the area of those that are outside it.

As far as they may be justified, these concerns cannot be above the absolute need to guarantee the democratic responsibility of a decision-making body characterised by the interweaving of supranational and national components. The instruments of interparliamentary cooperation, in which a symmetrical sharing of parliamentary sovereignties is implemented, are crucial for the necessary supply of guarantee.

The second possible outcome is that of the introduction into the European Parliament of a differentiated organisation among the deputies according to whether their country is outside or inside the Eurozone. This would be a question of achieving mechanisms that are analogous to those being studied in the British Parliament for the so-called 'West Lothian Question'. As well as affecting the fundamental principle of non-discrimination by nationality of European Parliaments, this solution would however also have the defect of not completely covering the area of government of the Eurozone, where the principle of subsidiarity would continue to exist with its delicate equilibriums of attributions among parliamentary assemblies too.

With regard to this, there is no doubt at all that the European Parliament, bearing in mind the juridical basis set down by article 13 of the Fiscal Compact, could give rise to a 'pertinent'—even under the profile of a differentiated personal composition—empowered committee for the participation in the interparliamentary Conference for economic and financial governance. Nonetheless, its plenum should instead always continue to guarantee the principle of equality among its members in order to carry out a function of guarantee

[9] I Cooper, *Parliamentary Oversight of the EU after the Crisis: on the Creation of the 'Article 13' Interparliamentary Conference*, LUISS SOG Working Papers No 21, August 2014; E Griglio and N Lupo, 'Parliamentary Democracy and the Eurozone Crisis' (2012) 1(2) *Law and Economics Yearly Review* 314 ff.

and balance between the two monetary areas, euro and non-euro. The harmonious development of the Union and all its other sectors depends on this function. The 'functioning' of the Union founded on 'representative democracy' (article 10(1) TEU) in fact establishes a primary responsibility on the European Parliament for integration in all the matters foreseen by the Treaties: from the internal market to the 'area of freedom, security and justice'; from the 'common commercial policy' to 'common foreign and security policy', and so on. In all these areas, owing to the pervasive integration process that has been going on for over half a century, it is now difficult to separate the powers of the European Parliament from those of the national Parliaments: even when forms of interparliamentary cooperation are not actually achieved.

Just as the national state in the Union is stronger than the isolated national state, in the same way national Parliaments, in cooperation with the European Parliament, are stronger than they are alone. Hence the need, by the sheer logic of things and beyond the current narrow-mindedness, not only for a 'dialogue' but for a real 'pact' among Parliaments, as the driving force of a Euro-national parliamentary system that confers an overall legitimation to the system of government of the Union. This perspective of 'parliamentary Union' is closer to the present condition and future of the Italian Parliament.

Introduction: The Italian Parliament and the New Role of National Parliaments in the European Union

NICOLA LUPO AND GIOVANNI PICCIRILLI

I. National Parliaments within the 'Euro-national Parliamentary System'

The role of national parliaments in the European Union has been one of the trending topics in EU legal and political studies over the last few years, especially after the entry into force of the Treaty of Lisbon. That is not by chance.

National parliaments have always been and still are the institutional symbols of national politics, too often dissociated from (mostly Europeanised) policies—a dissociation that causes, as is well-known,[1] negative effects both on European policies, almost devoid of any salient political debate especially before the economic crisis, as well as on national politics, which, once deprived of policies, risk becoming easy victims of populism and demagogy. A more active participation of national parliaments in the institutional life of the EU aims at strengthening the democratic legitimacy of the decisions taken at European level, so reducing the democratic disconnect that characterises European democracy and helping to strengthen the mechanisms of political responsibility and accountability on which the functioning of parliamentary democracy is founded.[2]

[1] V Schmidt, *Democracy in Europe: The EU and National Polities* (Oxford, Oxford University Press, 2006) 5 ff.

[2] PL Lindseth, *Power and Legitimacy. Reconciling Europe and the Nation-State* (Oxford, Oxford University Press, 2010) 225 ff. See also, on the reasons of the resurgence of interest around national parliaments, A Jonsson Cornell and M Goldoni, 'Introduction' in A Jonsson Cornell and M Goldoni (eds), *National and Regional Parliaments in the EU-Legislative Procedure Post-Lisbon. The Impact of the Early Warning Mechanism* (Oxford, Hart Publishing, 2017) 1.

The regulation of the European powers of national parliaments is contained partly in EU law, partly in national constitutional law. Regarding the former, a fundamental premise of the European role of national parliaments can be found in Article 10 Treaty on European Union (TEU), which clarifies that European representative democracy develops through a twofold channel—both through the European Parliament and through the national parliaments.[3] This acknowledgement that the EU legitimacy has its foundation in national representative democracy opens the way for the EU to directly recognise the contribution of the institutions that traditionally embody it. The enumeration of the national parliaments' attribution to the 'good functioning' of the EU is then completed in Article 12 TEU.[4]

However, the concrete exercise of those powers listed in Article 12 TEU also derives from the constitutional law of each Member State. Just like the way in which each government is democratically accountable to its own parliament (and to its citizens)—to use the wording of Article 10 TEU—is not specified by EU law and is instead entirely ruled by national constitutional provisions, similarly the ways in which Member States contribute to treaty revisions, check subsidiarity and alike must be specified at national level, in the light of the peculiarities of the individual legal system and institutional traditions.

That is why, in order to fully grasp the role of national parliaments in the EU, it is essential to study not only the legal provisions and the procedures provided by EU law, but also the legal provisions and the procedures existing in every Member State (and even in each individual House in the case of the 13 bicameral parliaments). Constitutional norms, parliamentary rules and parliamentary practices determine how each House is composed and organised. They also guide whether, how and when each House can exercise its own function of scrutiny and direction of the government's EU policies, and address other policy areas, so ensuring democratic accountability for its action at European level.

The object of this compound of EU and national law can be defined as a 'Euro-national parliamentary system',[5] which actually seems to have always been in the background of European integration. Even when national parliaments had no explicit acknowledgment in EU law, their functions of political direction and scrutiny of governmental activity already played a significant role (albeit indirectly) in shaping the functioning of European institutions and legitimising them within the dynamics of the national forms of government. Suffice it to say that all the six founding Member States of the European Communities were characterised by a parliamentary form of government and that a confidence relationship is still required with one of the Houses in 27 out of the 28 current Member States (the unique exception being the presidential government of Cyprus).

[3] R Bellamy and S Kröger, 'Domesticating the Democratic Deficit? The Role of National Parliaments and Parties in the EU's System of Governance' (2012) 4 *Parliamentary Affairs* 775.

[4] A Manzella, *Sui principi democratici dell'Unione europea (Lezioni Jean Monnet 2010–2012)* (Napoli, Editoriale Scientifica, 2012); E Griglio and N Lupo, 'Parliamentary Democracy and the Eurozone Crisis' (2012) 1 *Law and Economics Yearly Review* 314 ff; C Pinelli, 'Le disposizioni relative ai principi democratici' in F Bassanini and G Tiberi (eds), *Le nuove istituzioni europee. Commento al trattato di Lisbona* (Bologna, Il Mulino, 2010) 135 ff.

[5] The definition has been forged in Italian in what has to be considered the necessary premise for the present book: *Il sistema parlamentare euro-nazionale. Lezioni*, edited by A Manzella and N Lupo (Turin, Giappichelli, 2014). See also A Manzella, 'Parlamento europeo e parlamenti nazionali come sistema' (2015) 1 *Rivista AIC* 1–16; N Lupo 'Parlamento europeo e Parlamenti nazionali nella Costituzione "composita" nell'Unione europea: le diverse letture possibili' (2014) 3 *Rivista AIC* 1–27; C Fasone and N Lupo, 'Conclusion. Interparliamentary Cooperation in the Framework of a Euro-national Parliamentary System' in N Lupo and C Fasone (eds), *Interparliamentary Cooperation in the Composite European Constitution* (Oxford, Hart Publishing, 2016) 345–60.

Now more clearly, since they are in some circumstances explicitly involved in and directly called to contribute to EU policies, national parliaments' activity includes participation in a broad set of interinstitutional relationships and procedures with national as well as EU institutions. Also at EU level, the innovations brought by the Spitzenkandidaten practice seem to move towards some parliamentarisation of the relationship between the European Parliament (EP) and the Commission, making it not too far from the dynamics of a parliamentary form of government.[6] If taken seriously, the Spitzenkandidaten practice could even become the first step of a 'constitutional convention' reconceiving and shaping the relationship between EU institutions, that is the EU 'form of government'.

Therefore, in our view, national parliaments (but also sub-national parliaments)[7] in the EU do not form a mere (multilevel) parliamentary 'field', as argued by some scholarship.[8] Parliaments are not playing on a field in which there are only other parliaments, but instead are part of the same institutional and procedural system that includes the executives, at the EU as well as at the national levels (and the main systematic linkage, for many of them, is still the confidence relationship with their own government).[9]

The result appears to be an accomplished (although ever-refining) Euro-national parliamentary 'system', consisting of parliamentary and interinstitutional procedures that can be bilateral or multilateral, innovating the traditional parliamentary institutional mission but always pursuing the participative and legitimising function of representative bodies in complex constitutional orders.[10]

II. The European Powers of National Parliaments

The same conclusion, on the need to analyse individually the rules and procedures of each national parliament, results, upon a closer look, also when considering only those European powers enumerated by Article 12 TEU and other Treaty provisions. In order to clarify this, it can be useful to recall the main possible classifications of these powers.

[6] On the origins of the Spitzenkandidaten practice see J Priestley et al, *The Making of a European President* (Basingstoke, Palgrave MacMillan, 2015). On its first effects, with different approaches, SB Hobolt, 'A Vote for the President? The Role of Spitzenkandidaten in the 2014 European Parliament Elections' (2014) *Journal of European Public Policy* 10, 1528–40; S Fabbrini, 'The European Union and the Puzzle of Parliamentary Government' (2015) 5 *Journal of European Integration* 571–86; M Goldoni, 'Politicising EU Lawmaking? The Spitzenkandidaten Experiment as a Cautionary Tale' (2016) 2 *European Law Journal* 279–95.

[7] In this case, including sub-national parliaments with legislative powers, the number of parliaments of the EU is 74. See G Abels, 'Subnational Parliaments as 'Latecomers' in the EU Multi-Level Parliamentary System. Introduction', in G Abels (ed), *Subnational Parliaments in the EU Multi-Level Parliamentary System: Taking Stock of the Post-Lisbon Era* (Innsbruck, StudienVerlag, 2016) and Jonsson Cornell and Goldoni (eds), above n 2.

[8] On the EU fragmented executive see P Magnette, 'Appointing and Censuring the European Commission: The Adaptation of Parliamentary Institutions to the Community Context' (2001) 3 *European Law Journal* 292 ff, and D Curtin, 'Challenging Executive Dominance in European Democracy' (2014) 77 *Modern Law Review* 1, 1–32.

[9] The reference goes to the foundational study by B Crum and JE Fossum 'The Multilevel Parliamentary Field: a Framework for Theorizing Representative Democracy in the EU' (2009) 2 *European Political Science Review* 249 ff. Further applications of the same model include A Herranz Surrales, 'The EU's Multilevel Parliamentary (Battle) Field: Explaining Inter-parliamentary Cooperation and Conflict in the Area of Foreign and Security Policy' (2014) 27 *West European Politics* 957.

[10] On the representative function and its transformation in the EU see C Lord and J Pollak, 'The EU's many Representative Models: Colliding? Cohering?' (2010) 1 *Journal of European Public Policy* 117–36 and S Kroger (ed), *Political Representation in the European Union: Still Democratic in Times of Crisis?* (London, Routledge, 2014).

A first classification is based upon the nature of the power conferred upon national parliaments on each occasion.[11] Thus, one can distinguish between 'rights' that are more passive (as, for instance, the right to be informed) and more active 'functions', in which national parliaments are called upon to give their own views. In turn, the active role can include functions of a 'positive' type (the participation of representatives from the national parliaments at the conventions for the revision of treaties; interparliamentary cooperation, be it generic or specific; and the so-called 'political dialogue' all come to the fore here) or functions of a 'negative' type (such as the veto on the 'passerelle' clauses or the mechanism to ascertain that the principle of subsidiarity is being respected).

A second classification considers the aims and the scopes of the individual powers granted to national parliaments.[12] In this sense, once the information and cooperation powers have been isolated (both of which can be used to different ends), a distinction is made between the powers aimed at protecting national prerogatives on the one hand and those that correspond to 'classic' parliamentary scrutiny on the other. In the former category, it is possible to place not only the check on the respect of the principle of subsidiarity, but also the veto powers and the participation in treaty revisions. In the latter category are located the scrutiny powers relating to areas of freedom, security and justice (AFSJ) and common foreign and security policy (CFSP), as well as those that concern economic governance.

Finally, a third classification can apply concerning the subject to which the power is attributed, thereby emphasising the 'formation' whereby the power in question is—in an exclusive or preferential way—exercised. Based upon this criterion, one can deduce that some powers are individually attributed to each House (the right to be informed; the power of expressing motivated opinions and contributions to the Commission, in the sphere of 'political dialogue'; those which enable an act to be brought before the Court of Justice); others (such as the veto powers in the 'passerelle' clauses, as well as in the case of measures concerning family law with cross-border implications entailed in article 81(3) Treaty on the Functioning of the European Union (TFEU)) are given to each national parliament, thus requiring a double approval or at least a mandatory coordination of bicameral parliaments; others require approval in 'groups of chambers', which are variously composed, on condition that they reach a certain threshold (this is the case of the 'yellow' and 'orange' cards, issued when an alleged violation of the principle of subsidiarity is seen and asserted by a certain number of national parliaments);[13] and still others, finally, for reasons of necessity are approved in collective form, usually with the involvement of the European Parliament (as, for example, with the 'convention method'[14] and the many multiple forms that interparliamentary cooperation can assume).[15]

[11] P Kiiver, *The Early Warning System for the Principle of Subsidiarity. Constitutional Theory and Empirical Reality* (Oxford-New York, Routledge, 2012).

[12] M Olivetti, 'Commentary to Article 12 TEU' in H-J Blanke and S Mangiameli (eds), *Commentary on the Treaty of European Union* (Berlin-New York, Springer, 2013).

[13] P Popelier and W Vandenbruwaene 'The Subsidiarity Mechanism as a Tool for Inter-level Dialogue in Belgium: On "Regional Blindness" and Cooperative Flaws' (2011) 7 *European Constitutional Law Review* 204 ff.

[14] See C Pinelli, 'The Convention Method' in Lupo and Fasone (eds), above n 5.

[15] This has been interpreted also as establishing a new body, albeit virtual, among the European institutions: I Cooper 'A "Virtual Third Chamber" for the European Union? National Parliaments after the Treaty of Lisbon' (2012) 3 *West European Politics* 441 ff.

The third classification is obviously the most consistent with the approach adopted in this volume, in which these European parliamentary powers are analysed through a single national parliament and considered together with those powers attributed directly by national constitutional law. The other two classifications, however, also may be useful, depending on the specific power discussed.

This variety of typologies into which European parliamentary powers can be classified emphasises the richness and the multi-faceted nature of national parliaments' involvement in the functioning of the European Union. As it has been recently remarked, this unmediated role of national Parliaments (NPs) within the EU's constitutional and legislative process transforms the NPs into 'multi-arena players'.[16] The analysis of their European powers represents only a partial view of the concrete practice of the procedures followed in each national parliament. The study of individual powers needs to be completed with the national implementation given to them[17]—also in consideration of the wide margin left to national adjustment—and the subsequent parliamentary practice, when already developed.

III. The Ambiguities of the Role of National Parliaments in the EU and the Debate on their Perspectives

The role of national parliaments in the EU was subject to at least a twofold interpretation. The progressive loss of the centrality in their respective domestic arenas led to a general qualification of them as the main 'losers' in the overall process of European integration. On the other hand, the recognition of their significance in boosting the democratic legitimacy of the EU, first in the Treaty of Amsterdam and then, even more clearly, with the constitutional treaty and the Treaty of Lisbon, has led some to reconsider them as being mere 'latecomers'.[18]

The narrative according to which national parliaments made their appearance on the European scene only after the Treaty of Lisbon—sometimes rhetorically referred to as the 'Treaty of Parliaments', as it also significantly strengthened the powers of the EP[19]—or

[16] *cf* K Auel and C Neuhold, 'Multi-arena Players in the Making? Conceptualizing the Role of National Parliaments since the Lisbon Treaty' (2017), 24 *Journal of Public Policy*, 1547–1561. According to these authors, 'the unmediated role of NPs within the EU's constitutional and legislative process, as well as their direct relation to the EU institutions, clearly eliminates the demarcation of levels within the multilevel system'. In our view, this approach exaggerates a bit the significance of the European powers of NPs, as they are not fully independent actors, being linked with their governments, and as they still have their core function in the scrutiny of their own government.

[17] With regard to the provisions that may enlarge EU competences, a comprehensive in depth study was commissioned by the European Parliament (PE 493.046) and conducted by L Besselink et al, *National Constitutional Avenues for Further EU Integration* (Brussels, European Parliament, 2014), available also at www.europarl.europa.eu/RegData/etudes/etudes/join/2014/493046/IPOL-JURI_ET(2014)493046_EN.pdf.

[18] A Maurer and W Wessels (eds), *National Parliaments on their way to Europe: Losers or Latecomers?* (Baden-Baden, Nomos, 2001).

[19] The qualification of the Lisbon Treaty as the 'Treaty of Parliaments' started to be used during the process of ratification of the latter, both at the European level and at national one. As for official documents, the first appearance seems to be in the EP draft report 2008/2120(INI) that later led to the approval of the resolution of 7 May 2009 on the development of the relations between the European Parliament and national parliaments under the Treaty of Lisbon. See also E Brok and M Selmayr, "Der Vertrag Der Parlamente' Als Gefahr für Die Demokratie?,

immediately before, thanks to the 'political dialogue',[20] is substantially incorrect: they have always been part of the EU polity, although normally hidden behind their governments and called upon to play a major direct role only in limited and extraordinary occasions like the ratification of Treaty reforms.

As under these conditions it was revealed—apart from some exceptions[21]—to be almost impossible for national parliaments to effectively scrutinise and direct the EU policies pursued by their governments, new and more direct channels with EU institutions had to be built. This explains why national parliaments acquired the right to receive direct information from the EU institutions and also, in some limited cases, to speak autonomously—ie independently from its own government—to the EU institutions to signal a potential violation of the principle of subsidiarity or just, according to a more collaborative approach, to add some more elements to a draft act as proposed by the Commission.

Along the same lines, the enrichment of the bodies and procedures of interparliamentary cooperation in the EU may be better understood. Constant exchanges of information and best practices also with the EP and with other EU institutions—which is the minimum outcome of interparliamentary cooperation[22]—aim at helping national parliaments to get a more complete picture of EU policies and their complex negotiations. Therefore, interparliamentary cooperation allows national parliaments to make a more incisive use of their powers of scrutiny and political direction towards the government, sometimes even to decide to move in conflict with it, or just threaten to do so, if they so desire.

Indeed, national parliaments were, generally speaking, the last national institutions to undertake a Europeanisation process, after the executive and the judiciary, which drove this evolution,[23] although in different orders and speeds in each Member State.[24] The collegial structure of national parliaments and their native reference to Nation-States slowed the process of their adaptation to the European integration process, which in many cases consisted only in the setting up of specialised committees for EU affairs.[25] This provided a way of adapting to the European integration process, but often also—especially in the

Zu Den Offensichtlich unbegründeten Verfassungsklagen Gegen Den Vertrag Von Lissabon' (2008) 3 *Integration* 217–34. Moreover, see Bernard Accoyer, Speaker of the French Assemblée Nationale, Report on *The implementation of the provisions of the Treaty of Lisbon by national parliaments*, 28 February 2009, 3 (available www.assemblee-nationale.fr/europe/conf_presidents/rapport/report_accoyer_en.pdf). See also the Dutch Tweede Kamer, 'Ahead in Europe. On the Role of the Dutch House of Representatives and National Parliaments in the European Union' (2014) *Final Report on Democratic Legitimacy*, 9 May 2014, 8.

[20] See chapters by DA Capuano, A Esposito and N Lupo in this volume.

[21] On the Danish case see M Buskjœr Christensen, 'The Danish Folketing and EU Affairs: Is the Danish Model of Parliamentary Scrutiny Still Best Practice?' in C Hefftler et al (eds), *The Palgrave Handbook of National Parliaments and the European Union* (Basingstoke, Palgrave MacMillan, 2015) 275 ff.

[22] Lupo and Fasone (eds), above n 5.

[23] A Stone Sweet, *The Judicial Construction of Europe* (Oxford, Oxford University Press, 2004).

[24] For a compared picture see S Bulmer-C Lequesne (eds), *The Member States of the European Union* 1st edn (Oxford, Oxford University Press, 2005). The second edition (Oxford, Oxford University Press, 2012) offers an updated, although less complete view, as it deliberately does not consider all the Member States, given the enlargement that took place in 2004, but just eight among them, restricting the analysis only to one or two examples for each 'wave' (UK for the first enlargement, Spain for the post dictatorial countries entered in the 1980s, Sweden for the post-Maastricht adhesions, Poland and Estonia for the 2004 enlargement, and finally Romania).

[25] D Fromage, *Les Parlements dans l'Union Européenne après le Traité de Lisbonne. La Participation des Parlements allemands, britanniques, espagnols, français et italiens* (Paris, Harmattan, 2015) 39 ff.

first years—of delegating and relegating all the EU issues to a specific body, and to a limited number of MPs.

The European powers directly provided by the Treaty of Lisbon accelerated the Europeanisation process of all national parliaments, at different speeds and following articulated paths. In fact, a larger number of national MPs gradually realised that they were called to play a major role also in the European scene, first by scrutinising their executive's activity in the EU and then taking an active role in EU decision-making, addressing their positions directly to the EU institutions (in this case, skipping the possible filtering function of their own government).

After the Treaty of Lisbon, the debate on the role of national parliaments has developed further and increased in its dimension. The financial crisis and the measures taken, at European level, to face it showed even more dramatically the need of a clearer democratic legitimacy for the EU institutions and called for more effective forms of political accountability of intergovernmental decision-making.[26]

This caused an apparent paradox. There is, in fact, a very wide consensus, especially among political actors, on the opportunity to increase the involvement of national parliaments in EU decision-making. Both supporters of national sovereignties and promoters of a deeper European integration agreed, at least in general terms, on the need for a larger place for national parliaments in the EU. An example may suffice. During the negotiations that preceded the referendum on Brexit, the 'basket' in which the UK government asked for 'more powers to national parliaments' has been probably the easiest to be agreed on, through the concession of a so-called 'red card', which would have allowed a two-third majority of national parliaments to compel the Commission to withdraw its proposal.[27]

Of course, disagreements persist, both on the efficacy of the instruments and procedures currently provided and on the perspectives of how to achieve these goals. Regarding the former, some have argued that 'the EWS [Early Warning System] is a loss of time both for MPs and for scholars',[28] while others have seen in this procedure a chance for increasing the democratic legitimacy of the EU.[29] Regarding the latter, some argue in favour of setting up

[26] Within a wide debate see J Habermas, 'The Crisis of the European Union in the Light of a Constitutionalization of International Law' (2012) 23(2) *The European Journal of International Law* 335–48; A Hinarejos, *The Euro Area Crisis in Constitutional Perspective* (Oxford, Oxford University Press, 2015) 159 ff; M Dawson, 'Opening Pandora's Box? The Crisis and the EU Institutions' in M Dawson, H Enderlein and C Joerges (eds), *Beyond the Crisis. The Governance of Europe's Economic, Political and Legal Transformations* (Oxford, Oxford University Press, 2015) 85–93; S Hix, 'Democratizing a Macroeconomic Union in Europe' in O Cramme and SB Hobolt (eds), *Democratic Politics in a European Union under Stress* (Oxford, Oxford University Press, 2015) 180–98.

[27] K Granat 'The Draft Renegotiation Deal: A Genuine Red Card? Tusk's Proposal and National Parliaments' (2016) in http://eulawanalysis.blogspot.it/2016/02/the-draft-renegotiation-deal-genuine.html.

[28] See P De Wilde, 'Why the Early Warning Mechanism does not alleviate the Democratic Deficit', OPAL Online Paper 6, 2012, and T Raunio, 'National Legislatures in the EU Constitutional Treaty' in JO'Brennan and T Raunio (eds), *National Parliaments within the Enlarged European Union. From 'Victims' of Integration to Competitive Actors?* (Routledge, Abingdon, 2007) 79–92. Less critical is now the assessment expressed by T Raunio, 'The Role of National Legislatures in EU Politics', in Cramme and Hobolt (eds), n 26 above, 103 ff.

[29] See U Villani, *Valori comuni e rilevanza delle identità nazionali e locali nel processo d'integrazione europea* (Napoli, Editoriale scientifica, 2011) 86 ff; N Lupo, 'National Parliaments in the European Integration Process: Re-aligning Politics and Policies' in M Cartabia, N Lupo, A Simoncini (eds), *Democracy and Subsidiarity the EU. National Parliaments, Regions and Civil Society in the Decision-Making Process* (Bologna, Il mulino, 2013) 107–32; J Nyer, 'Justified Multi-level Parliamentarism: Situating National Parliaments in the European Polity' (2014) 20(1) *Journal of Legislative Studies* 125–38; D Fromage, n 25 above, at 415 ff.

a new parliamentary body, composed of representatives of national parliaments in the EU (or in the Eurozone, according to other proposals),[30] while others prefer a further increase of the powers conferred to national parliaments, eventually through the introduction of some sort of veto power to a certain quota of them, easily presented as a 'red card'.[31]

Indeed, neither of the two perspectives looks fully convincing. The first is far from being new, as it has been put forward since the first direct election of the European Parliament, and it regularly encounters the firm opposition of the European Parliament, which obviously would see its role dramatically reduced by the setting up of another European parliamentary assembly. The second is unsatisfactory because increasing the veto powers conferred to national parliaments determines, especially if the relative weight criteria provided by Protocol No 2 confirm their validity, a strong advantage for the parliaments of the small Member States, normally unicameral. Just to cite an example, in these procedures the weight of the Maltese House of Representatives is double that of the German Bundestag. It is clear that following this criterion would make it almost impossible to reach the aim of strengthening the European democracy.

Also, the hurdles set up in October 2016 by one of the seven Belgian Parliaments,[32] the Parliament of Wallonia, to the ratification of an important EU-Canada trade deal (Comprehensive Economic and Trade Agreement—CETA), showed once more that the involvement of parliaments is a very delicate matter, especially in a complex legal order like the EU. Most of all, it clarified that it does not necessarily create more democracy, at least if democracy is interpreted as the possibility for the majority to prevail (respecting, of course, the minorities). Once the trade deal was qualified, in conformity with COSAC requests, as a 'mixed agreement'—meaning that it includes areas where Member States as well as the EU exercise competence and thus requires the ratification by not only the EU but all the Member States—a single regional parliament, representing 3.5 million citizens, was in this case able nearly to veto a treaty whose contents was substantially shared by the EP and other 37 parliaments (including some regional parliaments).[33]

[30] Among others, CE de Vries, 'Rethinking Electoral Democracy in Europe', in Cramme and Hobolt (eds), n 26 above, 217–35. For an updated synthesis, see V Kreilinger and M Larhant, 'Does the Eurozone need a Parliament', Policy Paper No 176, Jacques Delors Institut, 14 November 2016 (at institutdelors.eu). According to other scholars, a new EU Senate, composed of representatives of national governments, should derive from the transformation of the European Council: see, F Fabbrini, 'The Relation Between the European Council and the Council: Institutional Arguments in Favour of an EU Senate' (2016) 3 *European Public Law* 485–500. Recently see S Hennette et al, *Pour un traité dé democratisation de l'Europe* (Paris, Seuil, 2017).

[31] On the red card, see D Chalmers, 'Democratic Self-Government in Europe. Domestic Solutions to the EU Legitimacy Crisis' (2013) *Policy network papers*; D Jancic, 'The Game of Cards: National Parliaments in the EU and the Future of the Early Warning Mechanism and the Political Dialogue' (2015) 4 *Common Market Law Review* 939–76 and I Cooper, 'How the "Red Card" System could Increase the Power of National Parliaments within the EU' in http://blogs.lse.ac.uk/europpblog/2016/06/13/how-the-red-card-system-could-increase-the-power-of-national-parliaments-within-the-eu/, 13 June 2016.

[32] On the specificities of the Belgian 'national parliament', recognised by declaration no 51 annexed to the Treaty of Lisbon, see M Romaniello, 'Upper Chambers in EU Affairs. Scrutinising German and Belgian federalism' (2015) 16 *Federalismi.it* 28 ff, P Popelier and K Lemmens, *The Constitution of Belgium. A Contextual Analysis* (Oxford, Hart Publishing, 2015) 100 ff, and W Vandenbruwaene and P Popelier, 'Belgian Parliaments and the Early Warning System', in Jonsson Cornell and Goldoni (eds), above n 2.

[33] See the interview of Paul Magnette, president of Wallonian region, in *Corriere della Sera*, 22 October 2016 (remarking that in the EU there are national parliaments representing fewer European citizens than the Wallonian Parliament).

IV. The Need to Analyse each National Parliament Placed within the Euro-national Parliamentary System

What clearly emerges, in any case, is a high degree of simplification required when national parliaments are considered, as necessarily happens when adopting an EU perspective as a whole. The variety of the institutional histories and constitutional identities of Member States—often represented by some pictures of their parliaments—strongly recommend analysing Member States individually, with their many particularities and, of course, some common elements. The objective is to understand how and why they are changing and, more specifically, to identify which, among the many and deep transformations they are facing, directly or indirectly derives from their being the parliaments of EU Member States.

Some comparative analysis has already been conducted, but it still looks exclusively at the European powers of national parliaments[34] or is aimed mostly at spotting some common transformative trends from a political science perspective.[35] The transformation is indeed deeper and involves the main structural and functional features of every parliament of the EU Member States (and up to a certain extent even of those States that have asked to join the EU, which have to adapt almost at once to the 'acquis communautaire').[36]

The EU's existence changes and challenges in a deep way the legal and institutional framework in which each national parliament is called upon to act. This is not only because of a number of functions which are attributed to them directly by EU law, especially after the Treaty of Lisbon, whose Article 12 TEU ideally adds up to the enumeration of its functions conferred by each national Constitution. But, more generally, it is also because their natural interlocutor, ie their executive, has acquired a new and very relevant dimension of activity within the European Union.

As Federica Mogherini, at the time just appointed as Minister for Foreign Affairs of the Italian Government, stated: 'Italy has two capitals: Rome and Brussels'.[37] The same idea can be repeated by any Member State, as the institutions that define the 'general political direction' of an EU Member State, intended as something different from a Nation-State,[38] are located not only in its capital but also in Brussels. A high number of policies are indeed defined in Brussels, with the important and often decisive contribution of Member States' executives.

The fact that the politicians who compose national executives often tend to deny responsibility for the decisions collectively taken in Brussels, blaming EU bureaucrats or other

[34] This is the case of Fromage, above n 25.

[35] See *The Palgrave Handbook of National Parliaments and the European Union*, above n 21.

[36] For this remark, as well for an interesting example, see E Albanesi, 'Il 'ritiro' della domanda di adesione dell'Islanda all'Unione europea. Profili di diritto costituzionale' (2016) 2 *Diritto pubblico comparato ed europeo* 21.

[37] Statement made at the National board of the Democratic party, 27 February 2014, two days after the vote of confidence of the Renzi Government: www.askanews.it/politica/pd-mogherini-italia-ha-due-capitali-roma-e-bruxelles_711389912.htm.

[38] See CJ Bickerton, *European Integration: From Nation-States to Member States* (Oxford, Oxford University Press, 2012). A similar concept had been proposed by A Manzella, '*Lo Stato comunitario*' (2003) 2 *Quaderni costituzionali* 273.

(big) Member States for them,[39] should not impede a clear understanding of the strict connection and the overlapping—in the Council and the European Council, but also in most of the committees that assist the work of the European Commission[40]—between EU and national institutions. This means that the forms of government of EU Member States—each one with its own evolution and specificities—have been deeply influenced and often transformed by the European integration process. Researchers, generally speaking, tend to agree that the EU has empowered the executives,[41] and this is true. However, the empowerment of the national governments is only an element of a deeper and wider process of transformation that determines an overall effect of altering almost every dynamic institutional relation structuring the national forms of government.

Reciprocally, the dynamics of the EU form of government also cannot be correctly understood without inserting into the picture the institutions of its Member States. It is for this reason that the problem of the EU is not definable as a 'democratic deficit,' but rather, as it has been already called, as a 'democratic disconnect'—and the steady empowerment of the European Parliament was indeed insufficient to solve the problems of EU democracy.

Not only do the compositions of the European Council and Council structurally depend, as is well-known, on constitutional choices made by each Member State,[42] but also the timing and often the contents of the decisions taken by these bodies derive from national circumstances. In fact, an approaching election (at national or even at sub-national level), a referendum, or even a judicial decision could influence the rhythm of EU democracy, often in intended or unintended conflict with the traditional rhythm of representative democracy.[43]

The fulfilment of this aim calls for the development of both bilateral and multi-lateral parliamentary and inter-institutional procedures, which are able to structure a real and effective 'system' not only among parliaments (including the European Parliament), but also, first and foremost, between each parliament and its own government. No executive—including the fragmented executive of the EU—can legitimately exist or act in the composite EU Constitution without an 'intermediate' institution, namely a parliament, with

[39] SB Hobolt and J Tilley (eds) Blaming Europe? Responsibility Without Accountability in the European Union (Oxford, Oxford University Press, 2014).

[40] Among many, see C Joerges and E Vos (eds), *EU Committees: Social Regulation Law and Politics* (Oxford, Hart Publishing, 1999); A Esposito, *La delega di poteri dal Consiglio alla Commisione. Profili giuridici della comitologia* (Roma, Philos 2004); CF Bergstrom, *Comitology: Delegation of Powers in the European Union and the Committee System* (Oxford, Oxford University Press, 2006); J Blom-Hansen, *The EU Comitology System in Theory and Practice: Keeping an Eye on the Commission?* (Basingstoke, Palgrave, 2011).

[41] P Caretti, already in 'I riflessi dell'ordinamento comunitario nella forma di governo italiana' (1981) 2 *Quaderni costituzionali* 311 ff and then in 'Il ruolo dei Parlamenti nazionali prima e dopo il trattato di Lisbona' in *Studi in onore di Franco Modugno* (Napoli, Editoriale scientifica, 2011) 535 ff, and, taking into account more recent developments, D Curtin, 'Democratic Accountability of EU Executive Power: A Reform Agenda for Parliaments' in F Fabbrini (ed), *What Form of Government for the European Union and the Eurozone?* (Oxford, Hart Publishing, 2015).

[42] See T Raunio, 'Semi-presidentialism and European Integration: Lesson from Finland for Constitutional Design' (2012) 19(4) *Journal of European Public Policy* 567–84 (observing that 11 of the then 27 EU Member States had semi-presidential forms of government, at least in a wide meaning).

[43] J White, 'Politicizing Eur this is the Case of Executive Discretion' in Cramme and Hobolt (eds), n 26 above, 87–102 (arguing that in the EU there is 'politics without rhythm', given the plurality of political systems that compose the EU). See also KH Goetz, 'How does the EU Tick? Five Propositions on Political Time' (2009) 16 *Journal of European Public Policy* 202–20.

the function of making it accountable to citizens. Thus, in order to grasp the reality of the 'Euro-national parliamentary system', it is essential to look dynamically not only at the horizontal relationship between national parliaments, but also at their involvement in a specific form of government (and consequently with their executive branch), and their relationship with the European Parliament and other EU institutions.

Procedures such as the 'European semester' in the elaboration of national budgets cannot simply be labelled as either national or supranational.[44] They entail elements of both levels of government and assume the interaction of the two in order to fully accomplish their tasks. The same can be said about the 'Early Warning System'—the already recalled procedure for the subsidiarity check of the draft legislative proposals in the EU law-making process—or even for the amendment of the European Treaties.

In the framework of this Euro-national parliamentary system, the focus on the features of the Italian institutions and especially of the Italian Parliament is exactly the aim of this edited volume. This book seeks to investigate the parliamentary role in these procedures as interpreted in the Italian legal order underlining how they contributed to a deep transformation of the parliament—namely the most 'national' among Italian constitutional bodies, because of its nature of embodying 'national' political representation (Article 67 Constitution)—that has been attaining a level of Europeanisation unknown in the past.

V. The Italian Parliament

The topic is addressed—through an outline that may be replicated, with adaptations, for national parliaments of other Member States—from the point of view of the Italian Parliament, as an example of one of the founding Member States of the European Communities, structured in two Houses with symmetrical powers and functions towards the executive. Hence, Italy is a paradigmatic case of a progressive adaptation to the EU's institutional innovations, as it is among the first Member States to have set up a dedicated collegial body on European affairs (back in the late 1960s, within the Senate) and among the last to fully implement the parliamentary powers introduced by the Treaty of Lisbon (only in December 2012, through Law No 234/2012).

The aim is also to start from the Italian case to create an analysis model and methodology that can be further applied to the parliaments of other Member States, in order to realise a more comprehensive understanding of the role of parliamentary bodies in the new constitutional framework of the EU. The example of Italy is paradigmatic, for at least a couple of reasons: one is more generally related to the evolution of the Italian Parliament's position in its institutional system; the other one is more specifically connected to its relationship with the European integration process, including its most recent developments.

In the comparative analysis, the Italian Parliament has for a long time—roughly, from 1948 to 1992—been seen as an example of a rather powerful and transformative legislature, especially if compared with other parliaments of European countries, inserted

[44] Generally on the European semester K Armstrong, 'The New Governance of EU Fiscal Discipline' (2013) 5 *European Law Review* 601 ff; specifically on the Italian parliament DA Capuano-E Griglio, 'La nuova governance economica europea: i risvolti sulle procedure parlamentari italiane' in Manzella and Lupo (eds), above n 5.

in a framework of a parliamentary form of government. Not by chance, its point of reference—both for scholars[45] and for the same parliamentary administrations[46]—has often been found more in the US Congress than in any other parliament of EU Member States. However, its prominence started to decline during the 1980s and has been significantly reduced in the following decades, partially as a consequence of the rather complete change of the party system and the passage of a majoritarian electoral law.[47]

Regarding its relationship with European law, the Italian legal order has a longstanding tradition of a dualist but very open approach to the legal integration between national and Community law and then EU law, affirmed by the case law of the Constitutional Court since the early 1960s and consistent with legislation and the prevalent institutional practice. After the latest innovations introduced by the Treaty of Lisbon and the subsequent evolution of the new economic governance, the domestic legal framework has been significantly amended, both at the constitutional and statutory levels.

The year 2012 was particularly important because in the space of a few months the Italian Constitution was amended with the introduction of the balanced budget clause (in the new Article 81), after the Euro-Plus Pact and the Fiscal Compact, and new legal provisions were reshaped in order to insert (further) 'European' elements within the domestic part of the European composite constitution. Moreover, by the end of the year, Law No 234/2012 finally regulated the new parliamentary powers and the further innovations introduced by the Treaty of Lisbon on Italian participation in the EU. The result of this process was a completely new relationship framework between domestic and European procedures that is more integrated, with the two Houses becoming a crucial vehicle for ensuring the connection between the democratic principles and the new European institutional architecture.

In sum, the Italian case deserves to be investigated, and assuming its parliament as point of observation might offer interesting and innovative findings for the research on the functioning of the EU. It is true that broader analyses on the role of Italy in the European Union have been already conducted in past scholarship, but mostly from the political science perspective.[48] The legal (constitutional) studies seem to have embraced either a broad-spectrum approach with the aim of investigating the mutual interactions between the two legal orders[49] or a very sectoral lens, focusing on an individual topic.[50] No specific studies

[45] For instance, with reference to the strength of parliamentary standing committees, see M Shaw and J Lees (eds), *Committees in Legislatures. A Comparative Analysis* (Durham, Duke University Press, 1979) 384 ff (where the Italian Parliament's committee system is ranked second for relative importance, second only to the US Congress). An updated analysis is conducted by C Fasone, *Sistemi di commissioni parlamentari e forme di governo* (Padova, CEDAM, 2012) 330 ff (highlighting how the committee system of the Italian Parliament could be qualified as 'predominant' till the end of the 1980s, but not later on).

[46] For two examples see L Elia, *Forma di governo e procedimento legislativo negli USA* (Milano, Giuffrè, 1961), and M Meschino, *Le procedure del bilancio federale negli Stati Uniti* (Rome, Camera dei deputati, 1981).

[47] See, inter alia, S Vassallo, 'Parliament' in E Jones and G Pasquino (eds), *The Oxford Handbook of Italian Politics* (Oxford-New York, Oxford University Press, 2015), 108. And the chapter by A Kreppel, in this volume.

[48] See S Fabbrini and S Piattoni (eds), *Italy in the European Union. Redefining National Interest in a Compound Polity* (Plymouth, Rowman & Littlefield, 2008) and F Bindi, *Italy and the European Union* (Rome-Washington, SSPA-Brookings, 2011).

[49] See the seminal book by M Cartabia and JHH Weiler, *L'Italia in Europa. Profili istituzionali e costituzionali* (Bologna, Il Mulino, 2000). See also S Mangiameli, *Integrazione europea e Diritto costituzionale* (Milan, Giuffrè, 2001).

[50] This is the case of G Di Cosimo (ed), *Implementing EU Environmental Law in Italy* (The Hague, Eleven International Publishing, 2013) or S Mangiameli (ed) *The Consequences of the Crisis on European Integration and on the Member States: The European Governance Between Lisbon and the Fiscal Compact* (Berlin, Springer, 2017).

have been undertaken, so far, on the evolution of a specific institution (in our case, the parliament) and its transformations based on or however related to the process of European integration.

Taking stock of the Italian Parliament at this point of its evolution is all the more interesting as important transformations took place while this book was being conceived and written. It seems useful to recall them here to better understand the references made in some of the chapters.

With the decision no 1/2014 the Constitutional Court annulled significant parts of the electoral law in force since 2005, according to which three general elections had been held (in 2006, 2008 and 2013).[51] This historical decision has shaken the political system and pushed for an electoral reform that had been long-awaited in the previous decade. The electoral reform was soon approved in 2015 under the initiative of the Renzi Government,[52] that ideally linked it to the draft constitutional amendment being debated in the same period, aiming to completely subvert the symmetrical bicameral system.[53]

This attempt at institutional renovation had two setbacks. First, a popular referendum held on 4 December 2016 rejected the constitutional amendment,[54] causing a political crisis (with Renzi resigning shortly after the referendum results). Second, also the new electoral law for the Chamber of deputies was partially declared as unconstitutional by the Constitutional Court[55] on the basis of the precedent constituted by decision no 1/2014 and before any application.

The symmetrical bicameralism was therefore confirmed, with equal powers for the two Houses, including, in particular, the need for the government to obtain and maintain the confidence of both Houses. Thus, this evolution results in a strong call for homogeneity in the political composition of the two branches of the Parliament. Not an easy target in a context in which the fragmentation and the instability the party system are increasingly and in which the electorate for the two Houses is very significantly differentiated.[56]

VI. The Structure of the Book

The volume aims to foster and disseminate to a wider audience the findings of long lasting research undertaken in the framework of the LUISS CESP-Center for Parliamentary

[51] On the decision no 1/2014 see A Pin and E Longo, 'Don't Waste Your Vote (Again!). The Italian Constitutional Court's Decision on Election Laws: An Episode of Strict Comparative Scrutiny' (May 7, 2015). ICON·S Working Paper—Conference Proceedings Series 1, no 10/2015. Available at SSRN: http://ssrn.com/abstract=2670634.

[52] Law No 52/2015, on which R D'Alimonte, 'The New Italian Electoral System: Majority-assuring but Minority-friendly' (2015) 7(3) in *Contemporary Italian Politics* 286–92.

[53] The connection (both procedural and substantial) between the electoral and constitutional reforms is developed in N Lupo and G Piccirilli (eds), *Legge elettorale e riforma costituzionale: procedure parlamentari 'sotto stress'* (Bologna, Il Mulino, 2016).

[54] The referendum registered a significantly high turnout (64.47%) and a victory of the 'Nos' with a clear margin (59.12%).

[55] Decision No 35/2017.

[56] The voting age is significantly different between the two Houses: 18 for the Chamber and the 25 for the Senate: in order to be elected, 25 for the Chamber and 40 for the Senate.

Studies,[57] in which a permanent bridge has been built between scholars (of different origins and background) and practitioners focused on parliamentary studies in both national and European contexts.

It relies largely on a series of courses, seminars and summer schools organised mainly within the two main educational initiatives of the Center: the Master of Arts (Master universitario di secondo livello) in 'Parliament and Public Policies' and the Summer School on 'Parliamentary Democracy in Europe', both based at the LUISS School of Government in Rome. More recently, it relies also on the first year of teaching within the new Erasmus+ Joint Master Degree in Parliamentary Procedures and Legislative Drafting (EUPADRA), co-organised by LUISS, Universidad Complutense-Instituto de Derecho Parlamentario of Madrid and University of London-Institute of Advanced Legal Studies.

The book constitutes an attempt to transpose the structure and methodology developed in the LUISS CESP by mixing scholars (mainly of constitutional law, but with the addition of some qualified scholars of political science) and practitioners with an academic background and proposing an approach to parliamentary law and practice as an integral and essential part of constitutional law. Thus, if constitutional law at the EU level underwent a process of deep transformations to reach a 'composite' dimension (that is to say, to be now constituted both by the EU Treaties and by the Constitutions of the Member States),[58] the same can be affirmed with regard to parliamentary law, which became 'composite' too.

No longer being merely 'national' institutions, parliaments of EU Member States need to be evaluated by both scholars and citizens on their performance in the European system. Operating in a system—a 'Euro-national parliamentary system'—in which by definition every change in one of its parts influences all the others, any process of reform or the rebalancing of powers within the national institutional framework must take into account this situation: the powers directly conferred to national parliaments by European Treaties set a series of constraints and opportunities on domestic institutions and even on the power to pass constitutional amendment.

The format of the book follows the procedures and the relationships that, seen from the perspective of the Italian Parliament, structure the Euro-national parliamentary system.

The Foreword by Andrea Manzella has already opened the discussion on the role of the national parliaments in the European Union, connecting the dots among the provisions of the Treaties and fostering a closer interaction among parliaments to the benefit of both the European Union and the Member States.

The first part of the volume is composed of four chapters examining the specificities of the Europeanisation process of the Italian Parliament and the Italian Members of the European Parliament (MEPs). Pietro Falletta offers an overview of the role of the Parliament in the constitutional system and its evolution, specifically giving account of the function of the political parties—before and after the crisis of 1993—and of the incomplete shift to a majoritarian democracy. Giuliano Vosa goes back to the original role of the Italian Parliament, which was limited to the approval of legislation authorising the ratification of

[57] http://scienzepolitiche.luiss.it/en/research/research-centers/cesp-centre-parliamentary-studies.

[58] A von Bogdandy-J Bast, 'The Constitutional Approach to EU Law. From Taming Intergovernmental Relationships to Framing Political Processes' in A von Bogdandy and J Bast (eds), *Principles of European Constitutional Law* (Oxford-München, Hart-Beck-Nomos, 2009). L Azoulai, 'The Force and Forms of European Legal Integration' (2011) 6 EUI working paper, available at http://ssrn.com/abstract=1899484.

European Treaties, and sets it in the broader understanding of parliamentary intervention in foreign affairs. Renato Ibrido deals with the dichotomy between the so-called 'ascending' and 'descending' phases (roughly corresponding to the formation of EU policies and their later implementation at the national level), which dominates the domestic scholarly debate on the role of the Italian parliament in European affairs. In doing this, he offers also a synopsis of the evolution of the general laws that, since 1989, disciplined the Italian participation in the EU. Finally, Alessandro Chiaramonte, Lorenzo De Sio and Vincenzo Emanuele, adopting a political science perspective, focus on the Italian legislation for the election of the European Parliament, as well as on the impact of the electoral system for choosing the Italian MEPs on the overall political system at the domestic level. Indeed, even the election of the European Parliament is the outcome of a Euro-national procedure, with its rules given by both EU law and national law.[59]

The second part, with chapters written mainly by parliamentary officials, then examines the instruments whereby the Italian elected assemblies influence the formation of the Italian position in the EU. Giovanni Rizzoni helps to set the parliamentary activities related to the EU within the general framework and procedures pursued in non-legislative activities, such as those of scrutiny and political direction, thus focusing specifically on the relations between the Parliament and the Government. Then, in two separate chapters, Antonio Esposito and Davide A Capuano focus on the specificities of each House (the Chamber of Deputies and the Senate, respectively), highlighting the different nuances in the individual Rules of Procedure, which diverged rather significantly on the design of the Euro-national procedures. Finally, Cristina Fasone broadens the perspective, adding a chapter on regional 'parliaments' and their (uneasy) coordination with the national one, highlighting the coordination role recently played by the Senate.

The third and most innovative part considers the Italian Parliament as one of the institutions comprising the Euro-national parliamentary system analysing the Italian parliamentary procedures in direct relationships with the individual institutions of the European Union. In six chapters, the bilateral or multilateral relationships of national parliaments in the EU are presented from the perspective of the Italian Parliament, highlighting the implementation that Italy has given to the Treaties' provisions and the practice that has emerged thus far. The idea in the background is that the European role of any individual national parliament can be fully understood not solely through the study and observation of the individual institution, but instead also through the study of its steady interaction with its 'partners' in the more comprehensive picture of continental integration. Hence, such a focus on the interaction between the Italian Parliament and its partner institutions helps to understand the dialogic and procedural nature of the European composite Constitution and the role that national parliaments play in it.[60] Moreover, the focus on procedures may allow an easier comparison with other national parliaments.

[59] On some of the issues so originated see G Piccirilli, 'Maintaining a 4% Electoral Threshold for European Elections, in Order to Clarify Access to Constitutional Justice in Electoral Matters' (2016) 1 *European Constitutional Law Review* 164–76.

[60] The procedural nature of constitutional law (and so, in the perspective adopted in this book, also of European constitutional law) has been underlined by A Manzella, 'Il parlamento federatore' (2002) 1 *Quaderni costituzionali*, 35–49, who emphasises also the peculiar role of parliaments as crossroads of this procedure (at 38) also on the basis of the idea of parliaments as 'structures of integration of the pluralism' elaborated by L Elia, 'Relazione generale' in *Il Parlamento-Annuario AIC 2000* (Padua, CEDAM, 2001) 15.

Going into detail about the chapters of the third part, Nicola Lupo deepens the discussion on the relationship with the European Commission, in particular from the point of view of the subsidiarity scrutiny and the political dialogue, which are seen as ways to 'reconnect' the different levels of EU democracy, and highlights the political interpretation of subsidiarity most frequently adopted, especially by the Senate. Giovanni Piccirilli deals with the compound procedures that involve the Italian Parliament as a counterpart of the Council or the European Council in the definition of a multilevel decision, emphasising the differences between those cases that make reference to the legislative procedure and those that opt for other solutions. Elena Griglio presents interparliamentary cooperation as a necessary component of the European role of the Italian Parliament in dialoguing both with other national parliaments and with the EP. Verner Wanderbuwaene looks at the newly established possibility of a direct dialogue between each national parliament and the Court of Justice in cases of an ex post subsidiarity scrutiny, also seen as a culmination of the activity started in the pre-legislative phase in the framework of the Early Warning Mechanism. Massimo Nardini focuses on the interaction of the Italian Parliament with the European institutions of the new economic governance, highlighting the growing complexity in this field especially after the economic crisis (and the countermeasures taken against it). Barbara Guastaferro completes this part by explicating the role exerted by the Italian Parliament in the treaty revision procedure (so putting it in dialogue with the Member States 'Masters of the Treaties'), both in the ordinary procedure (either in the case of the involvement of a Convention method or not) and the simplified procedure.

The last part of the book is devoted to placing the Italian Parliament in a broader perspective, both in comparative terms and in consideration of the most recent attempt for a reform. Amie Kreppel helps to look at the Italian Parliament in the comparative framework, something even more useful for a non-Italian reader. Maria Romaniello focuses specifically on the Italian uniqueness of a perfectly symmetrical bicameral system with its (limited and probably obsolete pros) and its many cons. Luigi Gianniti reflects on the contents of the constitutional reform rejected by popular referendum on 4 December 2016, trying to elaborate on its potential impact on the functionality of the Italian Parliament in the European Union.

Finally, following the conclusions that make an attempt to recap the constitutional features of the Italian Parliament and evaluate its contribution to the 'composite' Constitution of the EU, an afterword written by Peter L Lindseth reflects on the current trends of EU democracy, using as points of reference a number of speeches by Matteo Renzi,[61] the former Italian Prime Minister, at the beginning of its government, that is, during the semester of the Italian presidency of the EU Council (July to December 2014), and at the final stage of its experience (December 2016).

[61] The novelty in the approach followed by Renzi in guiding the Italian participation to the EU has been underlined also in the scholarly debate, so independently from the political evaluation. See M Brunazzo-V Della Sala, '"Things Are Now Changed": Matteo Renzi and the European Union' (2016) 1 *Rivista Italiana di Politiche Pubbliche* 115–34, and E Jones, 'Relations with Europe: Beyond the *Vincolo Esterno*', available at https://ces.fas.harvard.edu/events/2017/02/talk-on-italy-with-erik-jones-from-john-hopkins-university-boronia.

Part I

Italy Coping with the Process of European Integration

1

The Transformative Role of the Parliament in the Italian Experience

PIETRO FALLETTA

I. The First Long Phase of the Italian Parliamentary System

Any discussion on the role of the Italian Parliament in the republican constitutional system relies on the necessary acknowledgment of the invariance of the constitutional provisions on the organisation of powers since the entry into force of the Constitution in 1948. Therefore, it is essential to bear in mind that changes (or, sometimes, upheavals) in the law-making process, the participation in European decision-making processes, or even in the mechanisms to trigger political responsibility, occurred within an essentially unchanged constitutional framework. The rather obvious (but undeniable) conclusion follows that the causes and reasons for the evolution that has come about in the institutional system have to be found elsewhere.

The identification of this 'elsewhere' inevitably implies the historical context and the evolution of the political system in the second half of the twentieth century. As is widely known, between 1948 and the early 1990s the balance between Parliament and Government was characterised by an extreme fragmentation of the party system and the polarisation of parties at the extreme sides of the political spectrum,[1] both converging in determining an extremely low stability of governments (on average in charge for less than one year).[2]

[1] At least until the early 1990s, Italy represented the paradigmatic example of 'polarised pluralism', according to the renowned classification by G Sartori, *Parties and Party Systems. A Framework for Analysis* (Cambridge, Cambridge University Press, 1976), namely a system with a high number of relevant parties with huge differences in the respective platform and core values.

[2] Just to look at the figures: Italy had 52 governments (with 20 different Presidents of the Council of Ministers) between 1948 and 1994. The instability remained high also after 1994: 11 governments with eight different leaders.

Up to 1993, all the governments were supported by a parliamentary majority including Christian-democrats alternatively backed up by minor 'secular' parties (including Liberals, Republicans, Social-democrats or, since the mid-1960s, even Socialists). Those coalitions, that characterised both the 'centrism' (1948–60) and the 'center-left' (1964–76) periods were however deeply rooted in Republican values, acknowledging the crucial role of the state in the Resistance Movement and decisively adhering to the European and Atlantic option.

On the contrary, the opposition consisted of two very different kinds of political subjects, placed at both sides of the leading party: the post-fascist or monarchic right (excluded from any participation in the definition of policies, however present in a marginal part of the electorate) and, on the left, the strongest Communist party among Western European countries. The latter fully participated in the liberation war, as well as in the adoption of the Republican Constitution and even in the Government up to 1947.[3] However, when the evolution of the Cold War made it clear that the international position of the Communist Party was incompatible with assuming full Government responsibility, it fell into the so-called *conventio ad excludendum*: because of its 'anti-system' standing, it was practically impossible for the communists to have any direct participation in the government.[4]

This exclusion was however balanced—in order to avoid head-on clashes and to meet the needs of a composite (and wider) majority in society—in a sort of friend-enemy dialectic: the opposite of a *conventio ad includendum* (or *ad consociandum*) had been established in the main public and social policies. The Communist party was in fact involved in the legislation also by exploiting the possibility to approve laws directly at the committee stage in most subject matters,[5] with the twofold advantage of a higher degree of informality and a lower degree of publicity that would have limited the possibility to reach a compromise.[6] The laws passed according to this procedure had been the vast majority in the first 10 legislative terms (1948–87). Their percentage dropped after 1996 and became marginal after 2001.[7]

In the same time span, Germany had six Chancellors from 1948–98 and only two afterwards; the UK had 14 different Prime Ministers between 1958 and 2017 (considering that Harold Wilson served twice); even France, much more unstable than other major European countries, had 21 different Prime Ministers (and seven Presidents of the Republic).

[3] Palmiro Togliatti, Secretary of the Communist party, was Vice President of the Council of Ministers and then Ministry of Justice between 1944 and 1946.

[4] The iconic expression '*conventio ad excludendum*', widely circulated both in the political and scholarly debate, is due to the seminal masterpiece of L Elia, 'Governo (forme di)' in *Enciclopedia del diritto* XIX (Milan, Giuffrè, 1970), probably the most influential (and most quoted) piece of work on the organisation of the Republic after WWII.

[5] Art 72 Const allows committees to pass legislation with the exclusion of bills on constitutional and electoral matters, bills delegating legislation, bills authorising the ratification of international treaties and bills approving budgets and accounts. Significantly, the same provision sets a very high quorum to avoid the approval by the plenary: the Government, one-tenth of the members of the House or one-fifth of the Committee can refer the bill back to the ordinary procedure.

[6] See, in a comparative analysis, N Lupo and C Fasone, 'Transparency vs Informality in Legislative Committees: Comparing the US House of Representatives, the Italian Chamber of Deputies and the European Parliament' (2015) 3 *Journal of Legislative Studies* 342–59.

[7] Figures in V Di Porto, 'I numeri delle leggi. Un percorso tra le statistiche delle legislature repubblicane' in V Lippolis (ed), *Il Filangieri. Il Parlamento del bipolarismo: un decennio di riforme dei regolamenti delle Camere* (Neaples, Jovene, 2008) 179–200.

Notwithstanding this wide participation in the legislation (and even in the reforms of the rules of procedure),[8] the impossibility of any alternation to the government led to several consequences. First, it gave Italy a paradoxical stability with regard to parliamentary majority (and the ruling party) that somehow clashed with the need for a 'true dynamism in political decision-making'.[9] Second, this context led to the transfer of the 'ordinary' conflict between majority and opposition to a unique struggle within the governing coalition and even among the various inner currents of the Christian-democrats. Third, the inability of the Christian-democrats to achieve an absolute majority in Parliament forced them to accept a relevant influence even by modestly sized political parties, so enhancing the governmental instability through 'repeated swings between the often very long crises of government and the often very short governments in crisis'.[10] Fourth, the all so frequent renewals of Government leadership consisted in an oligarchic rotation in a relatively small number of party leaders of the Christian-democrats (only in the 1980s with Giovanni Spadolini was there a President of the Council of Ministers from a different party of the coalition). Last, this paradoxical stability in the political majority vis-à-vis the extreme fragility of the individual cabinets strengthened the perception of the Government as a mere (and temporary) executive committee of Parliament. Therefore it was no coincidence that, at least until the late 1960s and the need to rethink the relationship between the Parliament and society, there was no real planning of parliamentary work, nor did the Government play a significant part in this.[11]

The same internal organisational model of the Christian-democrats caused even further causes of instability. The affirmation of a necessary separation between the office of the President of the Council of Ministers and the Party Secretary constituted a further distinctive feature from other parliamentary forms of government in Europe where, either by custom or by law, leadership of the party and premiership had always gone hand in hand, so enabling a stronger consolidation and support of the parliamentary majority for the head of the executive and so ultimately for government stability and the effectiveness of its policies.

In this type of context, it is clear how the choice of the electoral system had to be fully instrumental in a necessarily locked system, both outside the majority (due to the *conventio ad excludendum*) and internally (due to the heterogeneous and complex nature of the government coalitions). A proportional system devoid of significant elements of rationalisation was therefore the only possible choice for the self-preservation of the model as at the same time it ensured the achievement of a twofold target: to perfectly mirror the complexity of society in the Parliament; and to weight minor parties in order to determine their coalition-power.

This perfect adherence of the proportional system to the needs of those years even led to considering its adoption as required in order to fully implement the constitutional

[8] The main reform of the rules of procedures of both Houses was conducted in 1969–70 (and finalised in 1971) and was fully participated in by the Communist party. A reconstruction of those works have been recently offered by A Manzella (ed), *I regolamenti parlamentari a quarant'anni dal 1971* (Bologna, il Mulino, 2013).

[9] See A Manzella, *Il Parlamento* 3rd edn (Bologna, il Mulino, 2003) 79, on this point referring to G Galli, *Il bipartitismo imperfetto. Comunisti e democristiani in Italia* (Bologna, il Mulino, 1966).

[10] N Bobbio, 'The Permanent Crisis' (1981) 18 *Pouvoirs* 3.

[11] See the detailed reconstruction of the reasons why the opposition was not institutionally recognised offered by S Ceccanti and S Curreri, 'L'opposizione politica in Italia' (2015) 22 *Federalismi.it*.

principles of democracy and popular sovereignty.[12] Moreover, any change to the majoritarian system was largely seen as incompatible with the intrinsic nature of the Italian parliamentary system, and even as an unacceptable distortion of the mechanisms of democratic participation that even before the advent of the Republic had been deeply rooted in the mediation conducted by political parties, to be considered the real founders of the constitutional order.[13]

However, the proportional electoral system and the subjection of the Parliament to the political parties played a big role in the long stagnation of the Italian political system right up the 1990s.[14] Furthermore, a democracy without alternation—ie a locked-in democracy, where parliamentary opposition cannot compete for leadership—is a democracy that risks being violently challenged from outside the parliamentary spectrum. Moreover, it should be noted that the apparent fragility and instability of political power nevertheless matched the permanence and continuity of real political power: beneath the official and visible government, a 'shadow' government, a sort of 'patronage', had been developed by public bodies and public interests that held most of the levers of economic life in the country. Governing parties negotiated amongst themselves over the division of management positions within these bodies according to a practice of 'allotment' and the executives they appointed gave a return to the parties in the form of illegal financing. This political-administrative system led to a series of increasingly serious and alarming economic and socio-cultural data that progressively fuelled factors of a permanent institutional crisis.

II. Reasons for and Context of the 1993 Crisis

In the first 40 years of the Republic, the main challenge for the Italian representative democracy was thus constituted by the anomaly of an opposition unfit to govern, potentially subversive of the democratic order that it had itself contributed to creating, and the role of the same opposition as a co-protagonist of a consensual legislative activity. Between the late 1980s and the early 1990s most (if not all) of the external factors that underpinned that blocked system suddenly lost their significance.

First of all, as evident as it may appear, the fall of the Berlin Wall made the anomaly evaporate. The model of a consensual democracy (even defined as 'consociationalism', in Italian '*consociativismo*')[15] lost its reasons to survive, considering the costs it implied in terms of instability and inefficiency of governments, but also considering its economic and

[12] C Lavagna, 'Il sistema elettorale nella Costituzione italiana' (1952) 2(3) *Rivista trimestrale di diritto pubblico*, 849.

[13] The relevance of the political parties at the core of the constitutional order, as well as of the public discussion even as a brake to a complete development of the democratic principles has been significantly underlined by P Scoppola, *La repubblica dei partiti. Evoluzione e crisi di un sistema politico* (Bologna, Il Mulino, 1997).

[14] G Pasquino, 'I sistemi elettorali' in G Amato and A Barbera (eds), *Manuale di diritto pubblico* 2nd edn (Bologna, il Mulino, 1997) 85.

[15] A Lijphart, 'Typologies of Democratic Systems' (1968) 1 *Comparative Political Studies* 3–44. Recently see also M Bogaards, 'The Italian First Republic: 'Degenerated Consociationalism' in a Polarised Party System' (2005) 3 *West European Politics* 503–20.

social consequences.[16] It does not seem by chance that, shortly before the collapse of the Soviet Union, a major reform of the parliamentary rules of procedure was approved in Italy, putting at risk any continuation of the consensual democracy model: by replacing the secret ballot rule with the opposite principle of the primacy of open ballot[17] the aim was to force the assumption of responsibility by individual Members of Parliament (MPs), in order to strengthen party discipline and avoid informal (and so 'silent') agreements with the opposition.

Second, another international factor contributed decisively to shaking the already fragile hold of the internal systemic equilibrium. The transformations induced by the process of European integration took on an increasingly important role in national politics. In the 1980s, the Italian party system found one of its rare points of convergence in a general agreement supporting European integration. The often-underestimated road to the referendum held in 1989 may offer useful references to recall the context of those years. On 10 February 1988, the Committee on Foreign and Community Affairs of the Chamber of Deputies approved a resolution submitted by MPs of the Radical party almost unanimously, containing some 260 signatures from many political groups. According to the text approved, Resolution No 7-00091, the government was invited to 'support the democratic policy and the economic and social cohesion of the European community, with consistency and continuity', as well as to support any effort in order to hold 'a referendum on the political union of the Europe and a constituent mandate to the European Parliament at the time of its re-election'. The ultimate aim of the resolution was to stress the focus on institutional and political integration (meaning political democratic scrutiny of European institutions) in order to reaffirm the European outlook of their respective political parties and the country in general. The aim was also to strengthen the political responsiveness to the situation of progressive Europeanisation of decision-making powers, fostering also a popular involvement and so limiting the economic-financial aspects in the integration process. Later, in May 1988, the European Parliament (EP) approved a declaration to support the intents of the Italian resolution, also in the perspective of the election to be held in 1989.

The outcome of this phase was first of all a consultative referendum in June 1989 (held on the same day as the elections of the EP), in which the Italians were asked to express their opinion on the possibility to confer a 'constituent power' to the European Parliament in order to create a European government responsible before the European Parliament.[18] The turnout of the referendum was very high—80.68 per cent, in line with the trends of that time—and the overwhelming majority (88.03 per cent) supported the pro-integration spirit of the referendum.

[16] On this point S Fabbrini, 'La riforma del Governo: tra dogmatismo costituzionale e costituzionalismo unilaterale' (2004) *Forumcostituzionale.it*, who consider the Italian Constitution as traditionally marked by the need for consent rather than by competition or alternation. For this reason, he advocated for changing or adapting it to the evolved political system.

[17] C De Caro Bonella, 'Ostruzionismo, addio' (1991) 11(2) *Quaderni costituzionali* 308, describes it as a 'parliamentary mini-revolution'; S Curreri, 'Il voto segreto: uso, abuso, eccezione' in L Violante (ed), *Storia d'Italia: Il Parlamento* (Turin, Einaudi, 2001) 537, sees the modification of the rules of procedure on the open/secret ballot as a moment of fundamental change in the relationship between majority and minorities.

[18] The referendum question also indicated that the draft Constitution elaborated by the European Parliament would have to be submitted directly to Member States for ratification (ie without passing through an intergovernmental conference).

The 1989 referendum perhaps represented the climax of the traditional Italian pro-European position of the first decades after the Treaties of Rome,[19] just before the less appealing constraints of the economic integration were about to lead to a sudden shift in the 'European rhetoric'. The perception of the European integration as an 'external constraint'[20] started to arise together with the awareness of the country's serious and blameworthy delays.

A third factor that contributed to dismantling the previous equilibrium in Italian politics was undeniably the disastrous financial-economic situation of the country, that was even about to exclude Italy from the road to European integration, considering also the priority given in the Treaty to the economic and monetary union and the strict monetarist line demanded by then re-unified Germany.[21] The incompatibility of keeping up with redistributive policies and complying with the financial constraints requested by the European partners started a slow but decisive turn in the perception of the economic (and political) advantage of participating in the European Communities.

Eventually, the maybe decisive pushes toward an eventual shift of the political system were determined by two factors, both coming not from outside the country but outside the party system. Corruption scandals and the obscure interconnections between politics, finance and party financing received an extremely raw and huge media exposure leading to the failure of the parties in government up to that point and the deep financial and economic stagnation in the country.[22] Falling into the spiral of political and social turmoil starting in February 1992 with the judicial inquiries, climaxing with the Mafia bomb attacks, the Treaty of the European Union tore the veil off pro-European rhetoric, speeding up the necessary and radical changes taking place in the Italian political system scenario.[23]

The final blow to the political system arrived shortly after that in 1993, via the popular referendum against the perfect proportional representation system, which tailored for the post-war context of extreme social and ideological homogeneity and characterised by the presence of anti-system parties excluded from Government teams.[24] The consequent amendment of the electoral law in 1993 introduced a strongly majoritarian logic in the allocation of seats[25] and thus pushed political parties to come together in coalitions presenting

[19] Diffusely on the ideas of (and within) Italian political parties about the European integration see L Castellina, *Cinquant'anni d'Europa. Una lettura antiretorica* (Turin, UTET, 2007).

[20] G Carli, *Cinquant'anni di vita italiana* (Rome-Bari, Laterza, 1996) 8 and 435; L Caracciolo, *Euro no Non morire per Maastricht*, (Rome-Bari, Laterza, 1997) 57.

[21] M Piermattei, 'Le culture politiche italiane e il Trattato di Maastricht (1992–1994)' (2011) *Officinadellastoria.info*.

[22] For more information on the history of the Italian parties and an analysis of a number of cases of corruption, see S Fabbrini and V Della Sala (eds), *Italian Politics: Italy Between Europeanization and Domestic Politics* (Oxford-New York, Berghahn Books, 2004) 196, and S Fabbrini, 'The Transformation of Italian Democracy'(2009) 1(1) *Bulletin of Italian Politics* 31.

[23] Connecting the overturning of the form of Italian government towards emphasising the role of Government in the European integration process, P Caretti, 'Le svolte della politica italiana nella riforma dei regolamenti parlamentari' in Violante, n 17 above 600 ff.

[24] To be complete, a premise to the electoral referendum in 1993 there had already been in 1991, when a further (prior) popular vote reduced the multi-preferential vote in general elections to a single-preferential vote, so dismantling the chains of candidates that constituted one of the most practical evidences of the powers of the currents within the individual parties.

[25] The new electoral system, in force from 1993 to 2005 and used in three elections (1994, 1996, 2001), provided a three-quarter *plurality* formula in single-member constituencies and a quarter proportional for party lists, with

shared platforms to the electorate. The reform of the electoral law cannot be considered as detached either from the huge renewal in the party system (in its turn, also linked to the novelties on the international scenario) or from the aforementioned judicial scandals on illegal party financing. These two factors brought to the transformation (if not the disappearance) of all the political forces that formed the parliamentary majority in the previous 50 years, including the Christian-democrats, reconverted into a new 'Popular Party' and in various other centrist smaller parties. This new majoritarian logic determined quite a paradoxical increase in the number of the political parties forced to join to catch-all coalitions and decisively influenced by Silvio Berlusconi's entry into politics, whose divisive personality was to polarise the following 20 years of Italian politics.[26]

In the early 1990s (with a climax in 1993)[27] there was, in short, a convergence of events that disrupted the foundations of the political and institutional balance of the previous 50 years. The profound changes in the international scenario deprived the Italian system of government of any excuse for self-preservation and revealed the institutional inertia and operational inefficiencies that were no longer admissible in an increasingly globalised context.

III. The Incomplete Shift to a Majoritarian Democracy

The novelties in the international and national contexts had an immediate impact on the party-based form of government, fostering a fresh start and a brand new season in the life of the Republic.

The most urgent changes concerned the simplification of the political framework, also in the light of the revolution that was taking place in the party system, which was widely delegitimised by the judicial inquiries. The main objective was to accompany the innovations in the actors with parallel ones in the institutional framework, in order to strengthen the stability and cohesion of the parliamentary majorities, so as to sustain the role of the executive in the constitutional system. These innovations concerned first and foremost the constitutional rules of the form of government and also the internal rules of procedure of the two Houses.

A. Attempts at (Comprehensive) Constitutional Reforms

The most natural and consistent way to achieve these objectives would have consisted in a total rewriting of the rules of the game, a new constitutional design aiming at renewing

an electoral threshold at four per cent on a national scale to participate to the distribution of seats. See S Bartolini and R D'Alimonte (eds), *Maggioritario ma non troppo. Le elezioni politiche del 1994* (Bologna, Il Mulino, 1995).

[26] G Orsina, *Il berlusconismo nella storia d'Italia* (Padua, Marsilio, 2013).

[27] Manzella, at n 9, 7, to some extent compares the events in 1993 to those of 1793, underlining their revolutionary nature vis-à-vis the pre-existing situation. Actually, together with the Treaty of Maastricht and the quoted referendum on the electoral law, Manzella mentions also the modification of the electoral law for the municipalities—Law No 81/1993, which introduced the direct elections for majors—as a further factor of disruptive innovation.

the part of the Constitution concerning the organisation of the powers, so fully opening a 'second' Republic.[28] Indeed, the Constitution in force was (and still is) pervaded by the (quite outdated) need to preserve the logic of consensualism, rather than that of alternation, precisely in order to reduce the fracture represented by extremist parties and now healed within an institutional fabric. A reform would have had to rewrite most of the rules of the parliamentary system, and to push resolutely, on the one hand in the direction of the model of fierce competition among political players and, on the other, in the direction of solutions of stability and government effectiveness. This reform remained largely incomplete and the transition that began with the 1993 crisis does not seem to have reached an end yet.

In fact, apart from an amendment to Article 68 of the Constitution related to parliamentary immunities that tended to give some 'ethical recovery'[29] after the corruption scandals in the early 1990s, the constitutional provisions governing the traditional political cleavages remained entirely unchanged.

At least two major attempts to reach a comprehensive reform of the Constitution deserve to be mentioned here, both because of the methods that were followed in the individual cases, and because of the substantial options that they entailed.[30] The first attempt was that of the Joint Commission for constitutional reforms, the so-called 'Bicamerale', set up in 1997 in the framework of an ad hoc procedure that was opened by Constitutional Law No 1/1997. According to this procedure, the Joint Commission (consisting of 70 MPs, half deputies and half senators) was in charge of drawing up a text for a comprehensive revision of the second part of the Constitution, to be then submitted to the Houses and finally to a popular referendum before its entry into force. The option elaborated therein was aiming to introduce a semi-presidential form of government, with a President of the Republic elected by universal and direct suffrage and a Prime Minister depending on the confidence of the (sole) Chamber of Deputies. Major innovations were also proposed with regard to the bicameral system (that was meant to be no longer symmetrical) and with regard to the 'federal' nature of the country, in a deep revision of the relationship with the regions and local communities.[31] The Bicamerale failed politically, with the coalition led by Berlusconi withdrawing its support of the text. However, the options elaborated in that context have been more or less directly at the basis of partial constitutional revisions, especially related to the regions and their powers.[32]

[28] The expression 'second' republic is extremely controversial in the scholarly debate. If it has been widely used by both historians (see Scoppola, above n 13; S Colarizi and M Gervasoni, *La tela di Penelope: storia della seconda repubblica, 1989–2011* (Rome-Bari, Laterza, 2012)) and political scientists (M Cotta and L Verzichelli, Il *sistema politico italiano* 2nd edn (Bologna, Il Mulino, 2011)), only few constitutional legal scholars accepted it (see V Lippolis and G Pitruzzella, *Il bipolarismo conflittuale: il regime politico della seconda repubblica* (Soveria Mannelli, Rubbettino, 2007)), whereas the majority relied on the stability of the constitutional framework in order to stress the continuity.

[29] Manzella, quoted at n 9 above, 8.

[30] To be complete, further attempts at constitutional reforms had been conducted even before, in 1983 (by a Bicameral commission chaired by Aldo Bozzi) and in 1992 (by a further Bicameral commission chaired initially by Ciriaco De Mita and later by Nilde Iotti). However, the activity of these bodies, although important for the development of options and for engaging the public debate, did not attain concrete results.

[31] Records and results of the Bicamerale are collected in P Costanzo et al, *La Commissione bicamerale per le riforme costituzionali. I progetti, i lavori, i testi approvati* (Padova, CEDAM, 1998).

[32] The proposals made by the Bicameral Commission concerning the form of the state translated into adoption of two constitutional laws: the first (Const Law 22 November 1999, no 1) on the reform of the electoral system in

The second attempt at a comprehensive reform of the system went further and was also approved by Parliament in 2005 by the then centre-right leading coalition. As for the procedure, it followed the (ordinary) constitutional amendment procedure, foreseen in Article 138 of the Constitution. This procedure asks either to reach a two thirds majority in parliament in the second reading or allows the people (and the parliamentary minorities) to call for a popular referendum. In that case, the reform did not reach the supermajority in Parliament and was then eventually rejected by a referendum held on 25–26 June 2006. As for its contents, it was quite ambitious and innovative. It entailed an extremely strong role of the Prime Minister, who was meant to be directly elected by the people. The confidence relationship with the Chamber of Deputies was emptied by the fact that the same Prime Minister was able to call for the dissolution of that House. Moreover, that project contained the transformation of the Upper House into a '*Federal* Senate of the Republic', together with further innovation in the relationship between the state and the regions.

Besides an evaluation on the actual desirability of the text rejected by the electorate, there are at least two possible considerations that can be drawn from them. The same considerations—to some extent—can be applied also to the further attempt at constitutional reform stopped by the referendum on 4 December 2016. First, such large majorities rejecting the modification of the form of government might let one presuppose some identification of the electorate with the parliamentary form of government, so that it could even be considered as part of national identity.[33] If this is so, it should not be the original Constitution that is seen as being responsible for the crisis in the early 1990s. Second, the failure in the referendum of such comprehensive modification of the fundamental Charter could encourage a different approach to constitutional reforms, trying to pursue more limited corrections to specific mechanisms of the form of government to be approved with the required majority in parliament.

B. Parallel and Alternative Ways to Strengthen the Majoritarian Breakthrough

i. *Incomplete Modifications of Parliamentary Rules of Procedure*

The failure of projects of comprehensive constitutional reforms shifts the attention to further instruments that have been pursued to reach the redefinition of the form of government in line with the evolution of the party system in the early 1990s. Here the focus has to be placed both on the (attained or failed) modification of the parliamentary rules of procedure and on the further electoral reforms.

respect of the Presidents of regional councils and statutory autonomy of the regions, was quickly approved with the consent both of the majority and the opposition; the second (Const Law 18 October 2001, no 3) on comprehensive reform and strengthening of the system of autonomies was voted by the centre-left majority alone—and then confirmed at a constitutional referendum—due to the very effects of the clash that had taken place in the Bicameral Commission over the reform of the new system of government.

[33] See, with reference to the constitutional referendum in 2006, F Bassanini, 'Portata e conoscenze del referendum' (2006) 40(4) *Il Mulino*, who considers that vote a 'turning point', destined to mark our constitutional history; similarly L Elia, 'Cinquantanove anni dopo' (2006) *Astridonline.it*, describes it as an 'historical event'.

The adoption of the (mostly) majoritarian electoral law in 1993 required the Parliament to rethink its rules of functioning. The twofold aim of this new phase was to both ensure the right of the majority to reach the decision and the right of the minority to a fair opposition, now intended as a potential 'alternative' for the government. This adversarial perspective implied a rejection of the consociational inspiration that characterised the rules of procedure adopted in 1971,[34] that were functional in the previous system and its logics. It was in particular the Chamber of Deputies that opened the debate on revising its procedures, because the rules of procedure of the Senate had already been subjected to an extensive review some years before in 1988, on the occasion of the secret/open ballot reform, that included also significant modifications to the organisation of parliamentary work.

A crucial role was played by the President of the Chamber, Honourable Luciano Violante, who repeatedly underlined the need to shift to a 'deciding democracy' (where the stress was more on the adjective rather than on the noun). The reform process started under his guidance with a debate held in 1996 in the Committee on the rules of procedure of the Chamber of Deputies and was approved in 1997, at the same time as the establishment of the aforementioned Joint Commission for Constitutional Reforms, sharing the same inspiration and the same aim of facilitating the development of the new bipolar declination of the form of government. In this regard, on the one hand the intention was to immediately create the conditions for a rational functioning of the House; on the other, in an unchanged constitutional framework, it anticipated part of the evolution of the form of government that had already emerged after the transition to the majority and that would have been debated within the Bicameral Commission.

The main innovations were related to the allocations of time to parliamentary groups on the basis of their size, capping the total amount of time available for each group. Further innovations concerned new procedures for parliamentary oversight, among which was the (very) unsuccessful introduction of question time.[35] However, albeit relevant, the reform did not touch some other aspects that might have resulted as crucial in strengthening a new majoritarian rationale of functioning of the Parliament. Just to make some examples with regard to the legislative procedure, no significant priority procedures were introduced, nor actual limitations to the submission of amendments. The individual MP was still entitled to submit as many amendments as he or she wished, both at Committee stage and in the plenary. Anti-filibustering mechanisms were rather oriented at dissociating the right to

[34] On this point, V Cozzoli and F Castaldi, 'I gruppi parlamentari alla Camera dei Deputati tra rappresentanza democratica e funzionalità politico-parlamentare' in Lippolis above n 7, 339–67, according to whom the objectives of the reform were to strengthen both the government and the groups, without ignoring the existence of the smaller formations (ie the so called 'political components' of Mixed Group); recovery of collective time of parliamentary action, providing a minimum quorum of deputies to activate a number of important procedural institutions. On the instrumental nature of the regulatory procedures to renewed political system, in the absence of a constitutional revision, N Lupo, 'I regolamenti parlamentari nelle "retrovie" del diritto costituzionale' in E Rossi (ed), *Studi pisani del Parlamento* (Pisa, PLUS, 2007) 7; V Lippolis, 'La riforma del regolamento della Camera dei deputati del 1997 e il Parlamento del bipolarismo' in Lippolis above n 7, 5, highlighted that, as before in the Italian constitutional history, parliamentary rules of procedure were means to the evolution of the form of government.

[35] N Lupo, 'Alcuni dati e qualche considerazione sulle procedure (tradizionali e nuove) di controllo parlamentare' in E Rossi (ed), *Maggioranza e opposizioni nelle procedure parlamentari* (Padova, CEDAM, 2004) 109 ff, and G Rivosecchi, 'I poteri ispettivi e il controllo parlamentare a dieci anni dalla riforma del regolamento della Camera dei deputati' in *Il Filangieri* quoted at n 7 above, 201 ff.

introduce amendments from that of voting on them, also granting political groups some limited powers to select them for the plenary debate.

In short, the reforms of the parliamentary rules of procedure did not produce the expected results, also considering the partial approach of introducing few corrections to the general framework that remained based on the proportional and group-focused set of 1971.[36]

In particular, the rules for the creation of political groups confirmed the same minimum number set back in 1920 and were not adapted to the various electoral reforms; at the same time, on the side of the dynamics of the legislative procedure, the intertwining between 'maxi-amendments' with votes of confidence has gradually dismissed the examination of the relevant legislative measures at committee level.

ii. The 'Escalation' of Majoritarian Electoral Reforms

The other pillar of institutional reforms other than constitutional amendments has been represented by the electoral legislation, subject to subsequent amendments after the system shift in 1993.[37] After only three Parliaments elected according to the law resulting from the 1993 referendum, a new electoral law was approved in 2005, introducing a proportionally structured system, with a majority ensuring outcome—certain in the Chamber, probable in the Senate—that imposed the creation of coalitions before the election, guaranteed the formation of a majority of seats in the Chamber and prevented the fragmentation by introducing a very high electoral threshold for lists external to coalitions.[38]

Despite this large number of elements oriented at strengthening the majoritarian logic, the result of this electoral formula was to enhance the creation of (too) large and heterogeneous coalitions, built to win the elections and later destined to be dissolved or, anyway, to deteriorate during the legislative term. Notwithstanding the majority prize, leading coalitions have always suffered from a significant erosion of their parliamentary basis after the first two years following the elections.[39] The absence of significant anti-fragmentation norms (such as to prevent the creation of new parliamentary groups without any link to the lists present on the electoral ballot) led to an increasing personalisation of the minor parties, stimulating in their leaders the ambitions either to enter the government team or to increase their coalition power. However, similar disruption also concerned the majority coalitions, in both the centre-right and the centre-left. Thus, pre-electoral coalitions

[36] In this sense, see P Gambale, 'L'organizzazione interna e le prerogative parlamentari nelle proposte di riforma dei regolamenti delle Camere nella XVI legislatura' (2009) 1 *Osservatoriosullefonti.it* 19 ff; also N Lupo, 'La persistente ispirazione proporzionalistica dei regolamenti parlamentari dal 1920 ad oggi' (2009) *Ventunesimo Secolo* 77–94, underlines how the parliamentary rules of procedure were inspired by proportional system, even after the reform of the 1990s.

[37] A summary of the evolution in the Italian electoral legislation is offered by C Fusaro, 'Party System Developments and Electoral Legislation in Italy (1948–2009)' (2009) 1 *Bulletin of Italian Politics* 49–68.

[38] Law No 270/2005 on which see A Chiaramonte and R D'Alimonte (eds), *Proporzionale ma non solo. Le elezioni politiche del 2006* (Bologna, Il Mulino, 2007) introduced an electoral threshold at four per cent at national level for the Chamber and eight per cent at regional level for the Senate, both related to lists independent from coalitions.

[39] For a detailed analysis of ineffectiveness of electoral law in terms of parliamentary coalition stability, also in connection with the unchanged norms on the formation of parliamentary groups see N Lupo, 'I gruppi parlamentari nel parlamentarismo maggioritario' (2009) 46(3–4) *Democrazia e diritto* 97 ff.

became equally precarious because of the tendency to aggregate more electoral cartels rather than programmatic coalitions, so ready to fall apart for the same reasons of visibility.

Ultimately, the strange mix of a 'super-majoritarian' electoral law with the persistence of parliamentary regulations still based on a proportional and group-centric type of setting has inevitably brought about strong contradictions in the functioning of the system.

First of all, it excluded what should be natural in a majoritarian and bipolar system, ie a general agreement on the rules of parliamentary law (equally supported and enforced by the two major coalitions) as well as the rigidity of the latter (intended as their binding nature). In other words, there was the failure to identify an adequate balance between the guarantees for the 'decision' and those for the 'participation' within the new political formula which determined a gradual but decisive estrangement from constitutional and regulatory principles[40] inside and outside the Houses.

The most obvious consequence of these contradictions was the political-institutional climate permanently consecrated to the conflict, and the related inability of any majority to approve comprehensive and long-lasting reforms. This is unequivocally demonstrated by the approval of the three aforementioned global reforms of the constitutional structure, all passed by a narrow margin beyond the minimum requirement of the absolute majority of the votes cast in Parliament. Only the first of these three reforms was confirmed by the referendum in 2001, whereas those in 2006 and 2016 were rejected by popular referendum.

Thus, the most advantageous corollary of a majoritarian system, that is the guarantee of governability, was ultimately neutralised by a climate of permanent election campaigns and the debasement of the institutions and democratic mechanisms to mere instruments for the search for consensus.

The current tripolar configuration of the party system—significantly innovated by the rise of the 5 Star Movement in the general elections held in 2013—seems to confirm this conflictual attitude. Hopes for the enhancement of stability and governability have been undermined since the genetic moment of legislature, and abandoned through post-electoral coalitions typical of a proportional representation system.

It can be said that the attempt to achieve a transition from a proportional democracy to a majoritarian one had not produced that impulse towards the great reforms and the governability of the system that the change set out to create. It thus seems possible to affirm a full continuity between the pre-1993 and post-1993 phases, with the partial (and maybe marginal) exception of the starting moments of the legislative terms, when often (but not always: see 2013) the first government appointed after the election was supported by the entire coalitions that won the elections without further enlargements to its competitors.[41] Anyway, the paradox seems to be self-evident: in the proportional 50-year period, the exclusion of anti-systemic forces from government and the self-preservation of the party system determined immobility, while ensuring a basic stability; with the majority breakthrough, the continuous shuffling of the political-institutional framework did not ensure

[40] N Lupo, 'Emendamenti, maxi-emendamenti e questione di fiducia nelle legislature del maggioritario' in E Gianfrancesco and N Lupo (eds), *Le regole del diritto parlamentare nella dialettica tra maggioranza e opposizione* (Roma, LUISS Univerisy Press, 2007) 41 ff.

[41] N Lupo and G Piccirilli, 'Le recenti evoluzioni della forma di governo italiana: una conferma della sua natura parlamentare' (2012) 1 *Democrazia e diritto* 85–110.

the Parliament a centre-stage position, but actually confirmed a 'perpetual motion' tending more to an antithesis rather than to a synthesis.

IV. Current Issues in the Political Representation System

We live in an era where the prefix 'post' is increasingly used for all kinds of human activities, as if everything was an epochal surmounting or, better stated, an overturning of a previous reality.

Against a more general backdrop of post-modernity, which marks an overcoming of the cognitive processes of the modern age, the dynamics regarding forms of political representation are also seen through the prism of analogy. It seems to function earlier in the process in terms of the relationship between public authorities and civil society, and later on in a definition and implementation of political guidance and therefore, the relationship applying to the legislative and executive branches.

In the first sense, we speak of post-democracy to censure a global rhetoric of elective/representative systems from a critique of the liberal-elitist conception of democracy; in these terms, the focus of political representation, namely an election, is reduced to a tightly controlled spectacle and led by rival groups of professionals who are experts in techniques of persuasion, and which covers a limited number of issues selected by these groups.[42] The result is inevitably that the political decision is entrusted almost entirely to the integration between elected governments and elites, who represent almost exclusively economic interests.

A conditioned reflex to the post-democratic reality is a profound transformation of the respective roles of parliament and the government as compared to the original structure of representative democracies. The centrality of the government is increasingly undisputed, also considering the new configuration of the public power in a globalised world. Conversely, the parliament suffers from a transformation from the role of decision-maker and representative of social interests to that of controlling decisions already taken (in the more reductive sense of giving legitimacy to them).

The underlying reasons for this transformation of the political representation model first of all lie in the size of those represented, meaning the political extension of a contemporary party. Again, the more general context of the post-modern dissolution of the party into a 'single dimensional man'[43] may be a key to the reading of the situation most appropriate to understanding the meaning of the fragmentation of interests and the exaltation of their individual dimension.[44] A collective loss of identity and a slow expiration of the

[42] C Crouch, *Post-Democracy* (Cambridge, Polity Press, 2003) 6.

[43] H Marcuse, *One-Dimensional Man* (Boston, Beacon, 1964).

[44] According to A Manzella, 'La riforma del bicameralismo' (2013) *Rivista AIC* 4, there is a shift from 'vertical' sovereignty to 'circular' sovereignty which evokes a 'series of pluralisms'. For more information on this point, in particular, the relationship between the individual and technology, see D De Kerckhove, *The Skin of Culture: Investigating the new Electronic Reality* (London, Kogan Page, 1998) 210.

dominant ideologies may indeed be behind the opening of an unravelling process of the socio-political fabric.[45]

Italy and the Italian Parliament are part of this process and seem to fit into the global trends of transformations of parliamentary representation. The effects of the aforementioned fragmentation are decisive in the creation and development of phenomena such as the mediatisation and leaderisation (or, alternatively, 'presidentialisation')[46] of politics, resulting in centralising the decision making power in the government and its guide.

Moreover, the long-lasting economic crisis contributed to exacerbating the loss of the sense of belonging to a homogeneous social group that is able to identify with a particular representative filter. The same idea of the output-legitimacy of the European integration has been completely reversed by austerity policies, making it increasingly difficult for pro-European parties to be appealing to voters.[47] In this sense, the role of political parties can no longer be the traditional one of mediation between a social group and political decision-makers. Now a party must offer, almost in the same way as any other media product, guarantees of adaptability to the most varied uses, and thus an ideological fluidity if not impermeability. Citizens, also in the light of the 'digital revolution', are being used to directly interact with the rest of the society, increasing processes of disintermediation. Moreover, the experience of the 5 Star Movement confirms that the same logic can be extended to political representation. It is not surprising that citizens increasingly demand to have answers that are simple and immediate from leaders that are charismatic and decisive.[48]

The consequences of these processes on the role of Parliament are, as mentioned, disruptive. The disjunction between the perspective of the represented and that of the representative puts the Houses' function of decision-making into a bind. The search for a convergence of interests becomes a sterile self-referential comparison that is often unable to achieve any solution at all. By way of example, the last few years offered the case of the bill concerning 'civil unions',[49] which highlighted the inability to reach an agreement among the political parties until the intervention of the government that broke the negotiation by imposing a vote of confidence.[50]

These deep transformation processes highlight the progressive marginalisation of the role of the Italian Parliament, not only in its decision-making function (which is all the more attracted by the government[51]), but also in its general representative capacity, along the

[45] N Lupo, 'La (ancora) incerta natura del nuovo Senato: prevarrà il cleavage politico, territoriale o istituzionale?' (2016) 4 *Federalismi.it* 8, highlights the *cleavages* influencing the functioning of each elected assembly: different permanent fracture lines that can divide the plenum and that each MP must somehow try to reconcile in the manner deemed most appropriate while exercising his/her functions.

[46] T Poguntke and P Webb (eds), *The Presidentialization of Politics. A Comparative Study of Modern Democracies* (Oxford, Oxford University Press, 2005).

[47] VA Schmidt, 'Democracy and Legitimacy in the European Union Revisited: Input, Output and "Throughput"' (2013) 61 *Political Studies* 2–22.

[48] N Lupo, 'Il controllo parlamentare sui Governi degli Stati membri dell'Unione europea, tra trasparenza e privacy' in (2015) 3 *Federalismi.it.*

[49] Approved as Law No 76/2016.

[50] See A Schillaci, 'Le unioni civili in Senato: diritto parlamentare e lotta per il riconoscimento' (2016) 2 *GenIUS. Rivista di studi giuridici sull'orientamento sessuale e l'identità di genere* 18–45.

[51] For a critical analysis on the progressive marginalisation of the role of Parliament, looking specifically at legislative production, see R Zaccaria, 'Introduzione' in R Zaccaria (ed), *Fuga dalla legge?* (Brescia, Grafo, 2011) 16. In particular, the author says that traditional parliamentary law (ie rules of procedure) has been replaced by a series of other regulatory sources of uncertain rank, in some cases of disputable constitutional compatibility. See also N Lupo (ed), *Il precedente parlamentare tra diritto e politica* (Bologna, Il Mulino, 2013).

global trend of the crisis of parliamentary democracy. The Italian specificity in this global trend might be classified as a 'disruptive inaction', meaning an overt inability of the Italian Parliament to renew its structure and internal organisation, as well as the rules for conducting parliamentary business. Many factors seem to confirm this statement: the impassable permanence of the symmetrical bicameralism,[52] recently confirmed by the result of the referendum held on 4 December 2016;[53] the failure of any major reform of parliamentary rules of procedure;[54] then, in a more substantive sense, the inadequate mechanisms for selecting the parliamentary class[55] and the opacity of parliamentary logics.[56] These are all factors enhancing the disconnection between the Parliament and civil society, opening wide gaps through which the aforementioned phenomena of presidentialisation and mediatisation of politics may break in.

A further more recent specificity is the emergence of a relevant political movement (which amounts around one fourth of the electorate)[57] that, at the same time, radically contests the classical mechanisms of political representation, fosters the idea of a direct participation through citizens' electronic vote (so entirely overcoming parliamentary institutions) and campaigns for exiting from the European Union (and/or from the single currency). Eurosceptical parties are nowadays present in all Member States[58] but the specific challenge brought into Italian politics by the 5 Star Movement deserves specific attention, not only because of its critical position on representative democracy but especially because of its significant support and, ultimately, the possibility of it succeeding in ruling the country.

As has been authoritatively stated within the historical analysis, rejecting an unacceptable situation is not necessarily the same as formulating a solution to one's problems.[59] In this sense, a wise approach to this state of things might be to discern what is reversible from what is not, looking for a more sustainable model of political representation as compared with democratic theories of popular sovereignty.

In this respect, the aforementioned phenomena of a technological conversion of social relations and precarious economic and labour realities appear difficult to stop, especially due to their relevance and transnational consistency. Diversely, what seems to be possible to reverse is an adaptation of the organisation and operation of the Chambers to the new scenario, applying it in particular to the changed conditions and needs of those represented.

[52] On the need of a reform of the bicameral system, N Lupo, 'La riforma del bicameralismo: un nodo non più eludibile' (2009) 4 *Italianieuropei* 2. Also see A Manzella, 'La riforma del bicameralismo', quoted at n 44 above, 2.

[53] See the chapter by L Gianniti, in this book.

[54] On the need of reforming the parliamentary rules of procedure, considering also the disappointing results of the reforms in the 1990s, see N Lupo, '"Codificazione" dei precedenti o valorizzazione del Parlamento? I presupposti dell'ipotesi di riforma del regolamento della Camera e alcune possibili integrazioni' (2014) 1 *Osservatoriosullefonti* 1.

[55] On the method of parliamentary selection, see I Nicotra, 'Governo Renzi direzione Italicum?' (2014) 5 *Federalismi.it* 18.

[56] Lupo at n 34 above, 25.

[57] The 5 Star Movement got 25.55 per cent at the Chamber of deputies and 23.79 per cent at the Senate of the Republic.

[58] See the special issue of (2015) 3 *International Political Science Review*, edited by N Brack and N Startin, 'Euroscepticism, from the Margins to the Mainstream'.

[59] EJ Hobsbawm, *The Age of Extremes. 1914–1991* (London, Penguin, 1994).

In other words, what is needed is a structural and functional upgrading of Parliament, in order to better meet the transformations in the shape and instruments of civil society.[60]

In conclusion, it could be helpful to elaborate on three different contexts in which we need to redefine parliamentary action, in order to find a better suited placing within the circuits of representative democracy.

The first concerns the complex institutional relations with the process of European integration; more specifically, it is necessary to implement the most effective remedies to ensure that parliamentary procedures of political direction and oversight are not marginal within EU decision-making processes, but rather impact upon European decision-making.

The second one looks more closely at the mechanisms of political representation and concerns forms of a more effective bond being created between parliamentary assemblies and civil society, especially in view of the new demands and the manner of participation emerging through technological innovation.

The last scenario pertains to the dynamics of the form of government, and so the relationship with the Executives in defining policy and law-making processes. It is in this context that the Parliament can play a role, counterbalancing the ever-expanding power of the government. However, the capacity of a self-reform, starting from the internal rules of procedure, seems to constitute a pre-condition even with regard to more decisive (albeit far less likely) revisions of the same form of government.

[60] For a reconstruction of the relationship that exists between the needs of civil society and the role of mediation of Parliament see G Amato (ed), 'Parlamento, partiti e società civile. Un'intervista con Pietro Ingrao' (1978) 31(1) *Mondo Operaio*. In this interview a reflection already comes to light concerning the upheavals taking place in the great apparatuses of hegemony and the reproduction of society and the moment of general political mediation, ie the moment when society girds itself for a 'distant goal', using Gramsci's words.

2

The Role of the Italian Parliament in the Stipulation of International Treaties: Rise and Decline of the 'Authorisation Model'

GIULIANO VOSA

I. Introduction. Parliamentary Authorisation: A Model for a State-based Law-making

Under the 1948 Italian Constitution, the ratification of international treaties in certain subject-matters listed in Article 80 requires parliamentary authorisation in legislative form, named '*Legge di autorizzazione alla ratifica*'. A general clause features in the list, too, pursuant to which the Parliament shall proceed to such *Legge di autorizzazione alla ratifica* whenever the treaty is of a 'political nature'. Pursuant to the ratification, the legislative *ordre d'execution* of the treaty concerned allows the international norms contained therein to enter the domestic order.

Nonetheless, in the Italian system, the idea of a genuine co-determination of international affairs between Parliament and the Government has needed to adjust to contingent needs. Contrary to the direct relationship enshrined in Article 80, the relationship between 'political sensitivity' and parliamentary involvement has come to be read in light of the Government's interest: the more politically sensitive a certain matter is, the higher the degree of secrecy and the greater reluctance there is to expose the motives, goals and terms of the bargaining in a public debate, unless the Executive deems it opportune.

This chapter deals with the development of the 'authorisation model' as a tool for the interplay among legal orders. This model works as follows: on the national level, Parliament and Government are entitled to co-decide on the stipulation of an international treaty according to their respective autonomous evaluations of its political sensitivity. This chapter will provide evidence that this model reflects the allocation of sovereign powers at the national level: it is the model for a state-based law-making, as it is based upon the national-international dimensions of sovereignty. A brief comparative analysis of the English and the French systems, both concerned with parliamentary sovereignty but in a quite diverging manner, will be carried out; pursuant to that, the chapter will focus on the evolution of Italian parliamentary practices for the stipulation of international treaties. In this vein, a few cases will be detailed to show how this model has been put into practice and how it is developing in the manifold post-State public sphere.[1]

Authorisation to ratify is a tie between two law-making processes—national and international[2]—and the key to elucidate each order's mutual sphere is the concept of sovereignty as elaborated in the early-twentieth-century debate.[3] In that respect, sovereignty comes at stake as a twofold concept. From a domestic standpoint, it defines national law-making, including the national bodies responsible for international affairs. From an international standpoint, it serves as a shield to protect national autonomy while accessing an international sphere in which every state, though ultimately free, was recognised as an interlocutor. Therefore, sovereignty policed the borders of these national-international spheres' reciprocal interaction, where the liberty of one state was guaranteed in the light of the other states' liberty.[4]

Two consequences need to be highlighted at this point. First, the king was historically entitled to carry out the related activity at the international level on behalf of the whole state; understandably so, as absolute monarchy was the most common *régime* of any nation at the dawn of the states' age. Second, sovereignty has come to shape the formation of meta-norms for the production of international and domestic law; that is, it concretely determines the operative modalities of the 'authorisation model' as a tie between the two legal orders.

Internationally, meta-norms stem from free interaction of sovereign entities and acquire legal value according to the mutual acknowledgement of this fluid practice. On the domestic side, meta-norms are shaped like a pyramid, as domestically sovereignty is to be concentrated at the top of the state: the state as one is entitled to bargain in the international arena. Transposing a legal international norm into domestic law is thus a matter of hierarchy as long as the hierarchical model remains unchallenged in the national legal order. A formal

[1] 'Public sphere' is to be understood as the conceptual place in which a decision is debated in light of its adoption. It comprises all those who influence its outcome, that is, a number of institutional actors endowed with autonomous legitimation and other non-institutional entities participating in public debates. The term is a translation from the German *Öffentlichkeit* and has entered the scholarly debate thanks to works such as J Habermas, *The Structural Transformation of the Public Sphere: An Inquiry into a Category of Bourgeois Society* (Cambridge, MIT Press, 1989) 6 ff.

[2] B Mirkine-Guetzevich, *Droit constitutionnel international* (Paris, Sirey, 1933) 97.

[3] H Kelsen, *Das Problem der Souveränität und die Theorie des Völkerrechts. Beitrag zu einer reinen Rechstlehre* (Tübingen, Mohr, 1920) 370 ff; M Cartabia, 'The Legacy of Sovereignty in Italian Constitutional Debate' in N Walker (ed), 'Sovereignty in Transition' (Oxford, Hart Publishing, 2003) 305 ff.

[4] Sovereignty was 'a gift for civilization' according to M Koskenniemi, *The Gentle Civilizer of the Nations: the Rise and Fall of International Law* (Cambridge, Cambridge University Press, 2002) 68 ff; see also I Brownlie, *Principles of International Law* 8th edn (Oxford, Oxford University Press, 2012) 203 ff; J Von Bernstorff, *The Public International Law's Theory of Hans Kelsen: Believing in Universal Law* (Cambridge, Cambridge University Press, 2010) 61 ff.

process governs the acquisition of an international rule into the domestic legal system: the goal is to *internalise* such rule according to the national meta-norms.

This passage displays the main characteristics of the authorisation model. First, it explains why the Executive is said to enjoy a strong legitimation in international activity, one that is attached to the prime nucleus of its sovereign prerogatives as grown in a state-based international public sphere. This structural feature makes it harder for Parliament to effectively counter the Executive's primacy in carrying out international affairs. The Government's position allows it to construe a political strategy encompassing both national and international levels; and to function on both levels as a mediator—thus hampering Parliament's acquisition of first-hand knowledge—whenever it deems necessary or whenever it manages to do so. Second, it accounts for the authorisation model as a tool for sharing law-making competences in light of the national separation of powers.

Pursuant to that, it is clear that the parliamentary role in the international affairs of a state ultimately depends on the way sovereignty is understood at the national level: it is tied to parliamentary role in national law-making, and it must face the strong legitimation that the Executive has come to possess—for the aforementioned reasons—in the specific field of international affairs.[5]

II. The Functioning of the 'Authorisation Model' in a Comparative Perspective

A quick overview of what happens in some Western countries casts light on a twofold assumption: on the political-institutional level, parliamentary involvement in international affairs is consistent with the role of the Parliament in national law-making and follows the course of the relation with the Executive; from a legal perspective, the architecture of the authorisation model varies according to the domestic concept of sovereignty—in particular, whether the holder of sovereign powers is a single monolith or a composite entity.

A treaty is thus subjected to parliamentary intervention according to its *political sensitivity*, and how to define this sensitivity and who defines it comes as a result of a Parliament-Government interplay. Specifically, a legal framework is more likely to arise in systems which are not grounded in a monolithic concept of sovereignty, due to the mutual recognition of diversity among the institutions endowed with sovereign powers. Conversely, when the Parliament-Government relationship is a mere question of political trust, the binding value of the legal rules concerned is weakened.

The United Kingdom is a very illustrative case. Since the *Glorious* Revolution, it was clear that any power related to foreign affairs belonged to the Crown. Nonetheless, pursuant to the British concept of parliamentary sovereignty and the consequent shape of its separation of powers, this prerogative was conferred on the institutional pair 'King-in-Parliament' that evolved into a trilateral relationship including the Crown, the Cabinet and the Parliament. Their mutual relations were still a matter of political trust; but in the context of a fully

[5] E Palazzolo, *Ordinamento costituzionale e formazione dei trattati* (Milan, Giuffrè, 2003) 8 ff.

recognised institutional diversity. As a consequence of the general understanding of sovereignty at domestic level, many practices developed in the inter-institutional dialogue and sometimes were rationalised into specific rules. Accordingly, the Executive was responsible for international business, but Parliament was involved to a substantial extent, both prior to and after the conclusion of an international treaty.[6]

Some tools aiming at a rationalisation of the political relations in international affairs have emerged in the form of constitutional conventions and apply to the ratification and implementation of the to-be-concluded treaty. A constitutional convention called the *Ponsonby rule* has existed since 1924.[7] Accordingly, the Parliament is entitled to a 21-day 'period of reflection' before the UK stipulates to any treaty deemed of political importance.

There is also an ultimate criterion for parliamentary intervention, namely the possibility of conflict with domestic legislation.[8] The preparation of the legislative measure is requested often in a formal hearing by the Secretary of State, prior to the ratification of the treaty, in order to avoid problems in its implementation.

It is noteworthy that the Legislative-Executive interaction can be tracked on a scale of progressive rationalisation. In the first step, we find the political dimension of sovereignty, embedded in the trilateral Crown-Cabinet-Parliament relationship and dominated by the tools for parliamentary oversight and direction. In an intermediate step, specific conventional rules for international activity come to light under constitutional law. In the ultimate step, a fully-fledged legal rule exists, entailing legislative activity in case of possible contrast with national legislation. Parliamentary intervention is thus more intense where the interference with domestic sovereignty is the strongest, namely when it comes to formalising a domestic legal rule; it takes the form of legislation, and thus it possesses binding value erga omnes by definition. The evaluation of a treaty's political sensitivity comes as a result of the institutional interplay and ratification is the ultimate step in the rationalisation of the political relationships between law-making actors.

In a different perspective, France tried to set up the terms of a strong parliamentary involvement in international affairs ever since the Révolution had put an end to the Ancien Régime. Parliament's role became dominant in the light of the *confiance* relation with the Executive. In particular, the 1791 Constitution endowed the Parliament with remarkable powers of co-determination but left with the Executive the initiation and management of international relations; the 1793 Constitution provided that the Executive

[6] J Goldsworthy, *Parliamentary Sovereignty* (Cambridge, Cambridge University Press, 2010) 37 ff. The Secretary of State for Commonwealth and Foreign Affairs holds a de facto competence on the matter, under the direction of the Cabinet and the Prime Minister, the latter being ultimately responsible for any act of the Government.

[7] Select Committee on Constitution—15th *Report*, January 2001, at www.publications.parliament.uk. Although it is not certain whether it has achieved the level of customary law, the *Ponsonby rule* has been intensively applied and testifies to the growth of specific tools, vested with legal form, for Parliament-Government interaction in substantive co-determination of an international obligation. See A Aust, *Handbook of International Law* 2nd edn (Cambridge, Cambridge University Press, 2010) 76 ff, and L Lai, 'Il controllo parlamentare sul potere estero del Governo: l'autorizzazione a stipulare i Trattati in prospettiva comparata', in *Il Parlamento della Repubblica: organi, procedure, apparati* (Rome, Chamber of Deputies, 2013) 999 ff; see in particular at 1031 and 1036 ff.

[8] As highlighted by Lord Atkin in *Attorney General for Canada v Attorney General for Ontario*, 'Within the British Empire it is a well-established rule that the making of a treaty is an executive act, while the performance of its obligations, if they entail alteration of the existing domestic law, requires legislative action'. See the judgment in (1937) 2 *The American Journal of International Law* 348 ff.

Council—delegated by the Legislative—was in charge of the overall process, the Assemblée also being entitled to the last word on the stipulation.

However, in the post-Napoleon age the primacy of the Executive and the royal prerogative alike were generally restored, although tools for parliamentary involvement were provided for in the Constitution.[9] While in 1814 the Crown's power to direct foreign affairs was reaffirmed, a fine-tuned equilibrium was sought in the aftermath of the July Revolution and found a more stable balance under the III République. Such a balance formally consisted in a co-determination, but ended up substantially in a delegation of international activity to the Executive, often in the guise of a carte blanche.

The *rélation de confiance* resulted in a substantial compression of the spaces for institutional interaction, and was confined to a fully political dimension: the Parliament, being the sole holder of sovereign powers, could basically choose to do whatever it liked, including to delegate substantive law-making powers to the Executive. As far as a unitary concept such as the *volonté générale* was the sole source of legitimate power, no genuine institutional interaction could take place, for any other source of legitimation would be subordinate and could not counter it from an equal level.

Instruments for parliamentary participation found no grasp in this context of political homogeneity coupled with weak institutional awareness. The Parliament was in fact marginalised and the ratification relegated to a mere execution of decisions taken elsewhere. In most cases, eventually, the practice of simplified agreements entering the national order without prior ratification replaced any other formality. In spite of the 1875 Constitution itself, national sovereignty was thereby curtailed to a remarkable extent.

The allocation of powers in international affairs proved to be one tile in the state's overall law-making mosaic. A general trend toward the empowerment of the French Executive is clearly visible in the first half of the twentieth century, as confirmed by the emergence of delegated legislation and the establishment of a merely formal concept of legislation.[10]

In view of an enhancement of the President's position within the peculiar constitutional arrangement of the *V République*—echoing the royal prerogative and thus grounded on autonomous legitimation—the shift from Legislative to Executive powers in dealing with international affairs was completed under the 1958 Constitution. The set of instruments for parliamentary participation in international business may be shortly presented as such. At the first level, political relations are further complicated by the presidential figure, who entertains no formal *rélation de confiance* with the Parliament but enjoys a legitimation on its own by virtue of an election. At an intermediate level, there are international agreements not subjected to ratification but formally approved through parliamentary legislation (not to be confused with simplified agreements, where no formal parliamentary intervention is provided at all) and, at an allegedly superior level, those agreements requiring a law for ratification.

Yet the latter instruments remain confined to a purely hypothetical, formal dimension. According to Article 55 of the 1958 Constitution, a few types of treaties are explicitly subjected to 'ratification or approbation'. The list largely does not depart from the categories

[9] A Ésmein, *Élements de droit constitutionnel français et comparé* 8th edn (Paris, Sirey, 1896, this edn 1927) 564 ff.

[10] Ésmein, ibid 75f; R Carré de Malberg, *La loi, expression de la volonté générale. Étude sur la notion de loi dans la Constitution de 1875* (Paris, Sirey, 1931) 14–15.

elaborated in the UK system. Nevertheless, it possesses little binding value, for the Executive alone is entitled to say whether a treaty or an agreement falls within the categories laid down in the Constitution and is consequently submitted to the Parliament. Furthermore, even when Parliament has consented, the President is under no obligation to actually conclude the agreement; nor is he bound to proceed to publication. As meta-norms stemming from a single legitimate power, all these instruments hardly meet with effectiveness in the inter-institutional practice, unless so decided by the holder of sovereign powers, whose decision stays within the shadows of politics.

Ratification and approbation are in practice merely formal laws: they cannot even amend the content of the treaty, for such a limitation is expressly provided for in the Rules of Procedure of the Assemblée Nationale (Article 128). The impact of the international norms on the domestic level is the highest: pursuant to Article 55 of the 1958 Constitution, they have a higher rank than ordinary legislation, meaning that they can derogate the Parliament's sovereignty and create a law-making competence that is explicitly grounded on the President's prerogative.[11]

Under such conditions, political sensitivity is de facto a subjective category, one which is largely in the hands of the executive branch and depends on the political relations it entertains with the Parliament, being scarcely rationalised into legal norms.

III. Authorisation Model: The Italian Way

The Italian authorisation model has grown in a strongly conservative political environment, inspired by the French concept of legislation and infused with German legal doctrines. Under the Statuto Albertino, the King held the power to conclude international agreements, and only in cases of financial implications or territorial modification could the Parliament have a say on the stipulation (Article 5). The 1948 Constitution sought to introduce a rather different figure, entailing the co-participation of Parliament and Government, as the institutional duo held the function of general political direction.[12]

Discussions on this point started within the Ministero per la Costituente, where a Committee for the Reorganisation of the State was established. The Report on the 'State's International Relations'[13] focused on three main questions: 1) the opportunity of a general declaration of principle about Italy's prospective international policy; 2) the issue of the national organs competent to represent the state at the international level; and 3) the legal mechanism for the acquisition of international norms to the domestic order, that is, what Italian scholars call the 'adaptation mechanism'.[14] At the Assemblea Costituente, the Report on the 'State's International Relations' was discussed together with (and in light of) the

[11] See Lai, above n 7 at 1038 ff.

[12] See V Lippolis, *La Costituzione italiana e la formazione dei trattati internazionali* (Rimini, Maggioli, 1989) 62f.

[13] Two celebrated professors of international law (Roberto Ago, Gaetano Morelli) were appointed as rapporteurs. See A Cassese, 'Il contributo degli internazionalisti ai lavori del Ministero per la Costituente' (1977) *Rivista di Diritto Internazionale* 47 ff; in general, Palazzolo, above n 5 at 91 ff.

[14] On the theories related to the adaptation mechanisms adopted in the Constitution, see A La Pergola, *Costituzione e adattamento interno del diritto interno al diritto internazionale* (Milan, Giuffré, 1961) 73f.

Report on 'Legislative Power'.[15] From that distinguished debate, arguably the rapporteurs were fully aware of the tie between the national concept of sovereignty and its projection at the international level. The chosen constitutional formulas came as a result of a compromise between the advocates of a full involvement of the Parliament and those who preferred to leave the Government free to stipulate at least some kinds of agreements.[16] The overall constitutional architecture was designed for substantial Parliament-Government co-determination in elaborating the 'national will' when the treaty is negotiated at the international level, in order for the Parliament to have an influence on the content. Consistently, the adaptation mechanism is of a formal nature, requiring positive legislation—'*ordre d'execution*'—for an international rule to acquire binding force under domestic law.

The 'political sensitivity' as an indicator of the degree of the parliamentary involvement follows a tripartite structure. According to Article 78 and Article 87 paragraph 9 of the Constitution, Parliament's deliberation on the state of war takes the form of a legislative act conferring on the Government all the powers concerned; the official declaration is signed by the President, who is the Head of the State and the gateway between the national and international levels. Then, there are those treaties which require a legislative act authorising the Government to stipulate to and the President to formally ratify them (Article 80). The list fixes some legal norms for a treaty to have in order fall within this category (including clauses of arbitration or other forms of judicial settlement involving the state, territorial modifications, financial burdens or legislative modifications). A general category is provided, too, requiring parliamentary authorisation of ratification whenever the treaty is 'of a political nature'; in the way highlighted above, this means that the determination of the political sensitivity in pre-rationalised cases depends on the Legislative-Executive relationship. Other treaties which do not make it to the threshold of political sensitivity would not be submitted to the Parliament and would be concluded by the Government alone: those treaties are concluded in a simplified form and do not fall within the scope of Article 80. Thus, as a general rule, the lesser the political sensitivity, the less intense the constraints to the Executive's activity are.

Conclusively, the Italian authorisation model can be drawn as follows. According to a treaty's 'political sensitivity' as determined by the Parliament-Government interaction, the stipulation of treaties features increasing parliamentary powers: such co-determination is formally recognised in the '*legge di autorizzazione alla ratifica*' by which the Parliament takes on the responsibility for the treaty to be concluded prior to its ratification and pursuant to a Government proposal. This piece of legislation follows the 'normal parliamentary procedure': it must be referred to the competent committee(s) for a fully-fledged scrutiny (Article 72, last paragraph, of the Italian Constitution) and is approved pursuant to a

[15] Edited by the celebrated constitutional law scholar Costantino Mortati. See Palazzolo, above n 5 at 96–97; A Cassese, 'Articles 10–11' in V Scialoja and G Branca (eds), *Commentario della Costituzione. Principi Fondamentali* (Bologna, Zanichelli, 1975) 461 ff.

[16] The competence of the Parliament and that of the President were expressly laid down in the Constitution, while the Government's function was left implicit, embedded in a historical-systematic argument. See Palazzolo, above n 5; W Leisner, 'La funzione governativa di politica estera e la separazione dei poteri' (1960) *Rivista Trimestrale di diritto pubblico* 342 ff; Lippolis, above n 12 at 16 ff; Cassese, n 15 above, 150 f; C Mortati, *Istituzioni di Diritto Pubblico* 9th edn (Padova, CEDAM, 1976) 681 ff.

discussion in plenary. Furthermore, the Parliament needs to produce an *ordre d'execution* for the international norms to be incorporated into domestic law.

Confronted with the allocation of sovereign powers in national law-making, the coherence of the internationally relevant powers is manifest. The centrality of the Parliament as the locus of the Nation's representatives (Article 67) in accordance with the people's sovereignty (Article 1, paragraph 2) results in a power of direction-control of the international activities carried out by the Executive; the Head of the State, representing the national unity (Article 87) is entitled to the last word on the national commitment to an international obligation vis-à-vis the community of states. Political sensitivity is understood from the perspective of the national interest being pursued through parliamentarisation: the more sensitive the issue, the higher the openness and inclusion of the process, which results in more extensive parliamentary debates with a higher level of formality and publicity.

Pursuant to the Italian Constitution, the involvement of the Parliament in politically sensitive treaties was initially substantial. The prototype of such treaties is the ratification of NATO and the overall debate leading to the enactment of *Legge* No 465 of 1 August 1949; another good example, in the view of prospective developments of the authorisation model, is the Treaty establishing the European Economic Community. Hence it is helpful to provide a short recall of what happened a few decades ago.

A. The NATO Treaty: A Major Political Discussion

The North Atlantic Treaty Organization (NATO) concluded in Washington originated from a failure to accommodate USSR and Western countries into a single framework in order to prevent geopolitical tensions. It arose out of two separate plans of integration among Western countries, in Europe and in North America, with UK Foreign Affairs Secretary Ernest Bevin acting as a mediator between the two levels. On 17 March 1948 the UK, the Netherlands, Luxembourg, France and Belgium signed the Brussels Treaty, providing for strong duties of mutual military defence. Five days later, US, Canadian and UK officials started intense secret talks to agree on a transatlantic pact for mutual defence and, at the same time, negotiations began with a few key members of the US Congress, in order to gain parliamentary support for the initiative before it was even officially presented.[17]

The secret negotiations went on to include all the Brussels Treaty powers, Canada and the United States, and in July those talks went public. France pushed for a North American strong military commitment in Europe and urged the US to associate with the Brussels Treaty. But France was not aware of the Pentagon's proposals at the beginning, nor did it know that the US (and UK) government(s) were becoming increasingly interested in a transatlantic defence arrangement. So the US government had a double situational advantage, which was of great help in dealing with the case at both the national and international levels.

At the national level, a certain US involvement in European affairs had the support of the majority of congressmen. The interlude between the two World Wars was characterised

[17] SR Sloan, 'Negotiating Art 5' (2006) *NATO Review*, available at www.nato.int/docu/review/2006/Invokation-Article-5/Negotiating_Article_5/EN/index.htm.

by isolationism, which afterwards was recognised as a mistake.[18] However, Congress would have never accepted that the United States could enter a war pursuant to a government's acknowledgement of an 'act of aggression' that occurred in another country: to deliberate on the state of war is one of Congress' major competences under US constitutional law. The US government was willing to commit to a Western alliance contemplating military intervention in Europe; but it was not excited to enter into the Brussels Treaty, preferring a form of military support that could be more easily and directly controlled from Washington. Yet, at the international level, the US government could sell to the international interlocutors that a US military commitment in Europe was only going to be accepted by Congress in a transatlantic perspective and thus obtained a 'politically sustainable' wording of the Treaty, *in primis* of what was going to be Article 5 on mutual defence duties. At the same time, it referred to Congress that some sort of military commitment was necessary for any agreement to be reached with European powers. Acting on separate tables by a coherent undisclosed strategy, the US government got the best out of the negotiations and the Washington Treaty was signed on 4 April 1949.[19]

Italy was admitted to the table in the last rounds of the negotiations as a country 'invited to adhere' to the pact. The Government submitted the issue to the Chamber of Deputies on 11 March 1949 but the Prime Minister declared 'not to be in the position' to present a complete draft treaty. A seven-day discussion took place; after a 51-hour plenary session on the last day, a motion (*ordine del giorno*) was approved in support of a prospective adhesion.[20]

From the short survey of the bargaining reported above, it is manifest that Italy was not really a big player at the negotiation table and had little voice in shaping the content of the Treaty, although its key position in the Mediterranean and the strong presence of socialist parties made it crucial for the United States to have it as a member of the North Atlantic Alliance. Therefore, whether to enter NATO was a yes-or-no question, although to be sure, one entailing a strategic choice of supreme political sensitivity, let alone the indirect but massive effect on domestic policies in general.[21]

A governmental legislative initiative presented at the Chamber of Deputies on 10 June 1949 (one year after the US Senate had approved the initiation of a treaty, and two months after the treaty itself had been signed) inaugurated the talks on the ratification of NATO.[22] Advocates of the ratification were the parties of the Democrazia Cristiana (Christian Democrats) as opposed to the Communist and Socialist Parties, and others, who endorsed a radically divergent approach to international affairs as well as to regulation of society in general. Within the Parliament, competent on the subject-matter was the Foreign Affairs Committee, whose Report gave also full account of the oppositions' theses.

Seven plenary sessions were devoted to the discussion. Speeches were given by the most relevant political leaders of all parties, and procedural instruments relating to parliamentary

[18] A Johnstone, 'Isolationism and Internationalism in US Foreign Relations' (2011) 1 *Journal of Transatlantic Studies* 7 ff.

[19] The Senate authorised to ratify this on 21 July by a vote of 82–13.

[20] The Communications by the Premier Alcide De Gasperi (Christian-Democrats) opened the floor to one of the most intense parliamentary debates. See www.storiadc.it/doc/1949_cnato_degasperi.html.

[21] See G Mammarella and P Cacace, *La politica estera dell'Italia: dallo Stato unitario ai giorni nostri* (Rome-Bari, Laterza, 2006) 180 ff.

[22] Gaspare Ambrosini (Chairman of the Committee, Christian Democrat) and Antigono Donati (Socialist) were appointed as rapporteurs. See the full account of the debates at www.legislature.camera.it and also from the website www.normattiva.it.

debates were fully exploited; the arguments were undoubtedly profound and well-crafted: nowadays they still should be read as a contribution to the ongoing debate on the Alliance. Ideological divergences added to the idea that the Alliance was in fact the pretext for future wars planned outside Italy and in which Italy had no interest; implications for domestic policies, too, were discussed in depth. Critics of the Government focused also on its 'zeal and hurry' in presenting the *Legge* to authorise the ratification of the NATO Treaty, rather than 'in preparing those laws which would implement the Constitution'; but, perhaps most incisively, in the first session MP Pajetta (Communist Party) raised the issue of the lack of autonomy in the negotiations. While recalling the plan agreed upon with the UK in late 1948 on the settlement of African territories belonging to Italy prior to World War II—eventually rejected by the UN and yet presented back to the Parliament as a prospective victory—Pajetta accused the Government of having forced Italy into a diplomatic bottleneck, and of having purposely done so to compel the Parliament to authorise NATO ratification, with the sole objective to put pressure on the USSR as well as on the domestic Communist-Socialist oppositions. The Parliament—he rightly emphasised—was called to say yes or no with no complete formal document being available prior to the discussion.[23]

A few motions put forward by political groups gained attention, especially those looking at NATO as a first step towards an enhanced supranational integration. It is interesting to recall that, in an order of business presented on 20 July 1949, fellow MPs Adonnino and Chiesa Tibaldi pointed to the difference between 'agreements among nations' and 'agreements among peoples', the latter being eventually what they wished to promote. In a world-based federalist view, NATO was only acceptable in the perspective of a deeper integration among peoples, which would constitute the sole real guarantee of peace, safety and security. Most notably, they recalled that 84 members of the US Congress had formulated a similar motion a few days prior.[24]

The authorisation passed on 21 July by a split vote (partially secret) and was referred to the Senate for debate on 26 July. A debate was held during four days, and an *ordine del giorno* was eventually approved, the final *Legge di autorizzazione alla ratifica* being promulgated on 1 August.

B. Beyond the Authorisation Model: European Treaties and the Emergence of a (Manifold) European Public Sphere

The Italian Parliament was again involved to a substantial extent in the ratification of the Treaties establishing the European Communities, in particular the Treaty establishing the European Economic Community (TEEC). Debates on an instrument for enhanced European economic integration had been on the table for a decade and, pursuant to the foundation of the European Coal and Steel Community (the ECSC, in 1951) a few conferences were held (the last one taking place in Messina in June 1955) among Prime Ministers and Foreign Affairs Ministers of Italy, France, Germany, Belgium, The Netherlands and

[23] Chamber of Deputies, II Legislatura, *Atti parlamentari, Seduta antimeridiana del 14 luglio 1949.*

[24] Fellow MPs raised a sort of *inter-parlamentarian* argument with a view to endorsing a mutual legitimation among directly representative bodies. See Chamber of Deputies, ibid, *Seduta pomeridiana del 14 luglio 1949.*

Luxembourg. An ad hoc committee chaired by Paul Henri Spaak—a Belgian Social-Democrat—led to the mandate to negotiate for the European Atomic Energy Community (EAEC) and EEC being issued by the ECSC Council of Ministers held in Venice in 1956. Negotiations lasted for a year and the structure of the EEC followed the 'Jean Monnet method' which had inspired the ECSC itself: functionalism in the achievement of a common market and a progressive harmonisation of national legislations in those fields, within the framework of an *élites*-driven integration.[25]

Italy was a big player in the negotiations and hosted the crucial meetings; debates were reported to the Parliament regularly; a draft of the legislative authorisation was presented to the Chamber of Deputies on March 1957, and its full text was discussed from 18 July onward. Three rapporteurs had been appointed and the report was delivered on 16 July, including a detailed minority report. The general enthusiasm from conservative parties was anyhow mitigated by 'a mixture of disapproval, scepticism and compassion' from most leftists, as reported by fellow MP Montagnana (Communist Party) in light of the 'past and current experiences' of common market pacts. The left parties declared themselves 'not contrary in principle' to the idea of a common market, and in favour of any initiative aiming at 'getting peoples closer to each other'. What they stigmatised was the lack of any such intention in the draft treaty, absent any provision of social integration and given the fact that 'not only Washington and Bonn wanted the EEC, but the most powerful monopolies of Europe and Italy alike'. In this vein, they looked at those Treaties as a further step towards the division of the world and a concession to the 'German *revanchisme*'.[26]

Nine full sessions were devoted to the debate (plus six at the Senate, from 1 October onwards); the *Legge* No 1203 of 1957 authorising the Government to ratify the Treaty passed on 14 October.[27] That was probably the last occasion in which the ratification mechanisms have been exploited to their fullest. This has never happened to a comparable extent in the aftermath, nor have the relevant subsequent debates reached the same quality and intensity.[28]

Italy since then has slightly but constantly turned to a 'blocked democracy,'[29] and the so-called *conventio ad excludendum* (from government offices) against Communists was perpetuated to marginalise radical dissent on key issues.[30] Against this background, political choices which were made a few decades prior, such as the adherence to NATO and the commitment to European integration, were in fact no longer openly contestable.

The decline of sovereignty as a legal and political concept worked against the authorisation model for parliamentarisation of international affairs, whereas the fading of general

[25] See Mammarella and Cacace at n 21, 202f.

[26] Chamber of Deputies, above n.

[27] It is noteworthy that Art 4 of the *Legge* contained a delegation to the Government to implement the Treaty in several points, according to Art 76 (delegated legislation having the same formal rank as parliamentary legislation) whereas the 'principles and directive criteria' required by the Constitution in order for delegated legislation to be effective were to be sought 'in the Treaties themselves'.

[28] Lai, above n 7 at 1043f. An overview of the parliamentary proceedings for ratification in R Dickmann, *Processo legislativo e limiti della legge* (Neaples, Jovene, 2006) 215 ff.

[29] B Caravita and M Luciani, 'Oltre la democrazia bloccata. Ipotesi sui meccanismi elettorali' (1992) 6 *Democrazia e diritto* 12f. On the history of Italian political *élites* G Maranini, *Storia del potere in Italia (1848–1967)* (Rome, Corbaccio, 1995) 20 ff.

[30] G Galli, *I partiti politici italiani (1943–2004)* (Milan, SuperBur, 2004) 78f, 101f; P Ginsborg *A History of Contemporary Italy. Society and Politics 1943–1989* (London, Palgrave McMillan, 2003) 258 ff, at 348 ff.

representation as the key to legitimise public power deprived the Parliament itself of its centrality and paved the way for alternative forms of legitimation co-existing in a multi-faceted public sphere. However, a crucial point needs consideration. By the emergence of a European arena, we should say that 'international business' splits in a twofold dimension: those which relate to the growing European spheres and those which do not.

The growth of the European Community as a framework for multiple spheres of public debate, though highly specialised and restricted to a certain extent, may be said to have effectively replaced ratification as a model of interplay between national and international legal orders. In this context, the role of a parliament has changed, and its contribution, if any, follows patterns that sensibly differ from those enshrined in the authorisation model.[31] In this respect, a twofold point must be raised. First, the 'European public sphere' is actually a manifold one, as it has been construed on the ground of a conferral; still today, differentiated integration brings strong asymmetry in the balance of powers that the bodies of the supranational order seek from case to case.[32] Second, it is doubtful whether the decline of the authorisation model has been replaced by any other form of legitimation under EU law; and this is all the more true when it comes to those areas falling outside the best-integrated European sphere, which may be (generously) said to coincide with the scope of the ordinary legislative procedure.

If one abruptly jumps to more recent cases of ratification of European Treaties, she must note that, whereas the ratification of the Amsterdam Treaty was perceived as a follow-up to the Treaty of Maastricht's implementation, the early 2000s have been characterised by a stronger awareness of the democratic legitimation issue in the European public sphere. The involvement of the European Parliament in EU law-making reached the point of extending the co-decision procedure to several of the EU's key policy areas and claiming a more incisive role in the implementation phase—numerically, the bulk of EU legislation. The Treaty of Nice came together with the Charter of Fundamental Rights, the first document of that sort agreed on at the EU level, pursuant to a Convention; likewise, the Convention on the Future of Europe (established according to the same Treaty) was seen as the dawn of a new era, in which a supranational parliamentary-like public sphere was effectively being set in motion.[33]

Parliamentarisation of those issues in Italy mostly occurred through the ordinary channels for political debate, the debates on the legislative authorisation to ratify being confined to a merely formal dimension. As an example, we might look at the plenary debate that occurred after the Communications of the President of the Council of Ministers to the

[31] N Lupo, 'Parlamento europeo e Parlamenti nazionali nella costituzione "composita" dell'UE: le diverse letture possibili' (2014) 3 *Rivista AIC* 1–27.

[32] B De Witte et al (eds), *The Many Faces of Differentiation in EU Law* (Antwerp, Intersentia, 2001) in particular, G De Burca, 'Legal Principles as an Instrument of Differentiation? The Principles of Proportionality and Subsidiarity' 131 ff; see also T Beukers, 'The Eurozone Crisis and the Legitimacy of Differentiated Integration' (EUI MWP 2013/36) 1–18, at 6 ff.

[33] The most important documents of that kind were the Communication from the Commission 'European governance. A White Paper', 25 July 2001 and the Laeken 'Declaration on the Future of Europe' released by the Intergovernmental Conference, 15 December 2001. See eg N Nugent, *The Government and Politics of the European Union* 6th edn (Durham NC, Duke University Press, 2006) 82f, 135f; IP Karolewski, *Citizenship and Collective Identity in Europe* (London, Routledge, 2010) 107f; A Maurer, 'Deliberation and Compromise in the Shadow of Bargaining' in S Puntcher-Riekmann and W Wessels (eds), *The Making of the EU Constitution. Dynamics and limits of the Convention experience* (Wiesbaden, VS Verlag, 2006) 120 ff, at 127.

Senate concerning the European Council occurred in Feira and the prospective institutional reforms of the EU (13 July 2000). The specialised parliamentary body for European affairs (Giunta per gli Affari delle Comunità Europee)[34] presented two documents (relating to the Commission 2000–2005 Working Programme and to the state of the Italian participation in the EU legislative cycle). A dozen motions were tabled and most of them accepted and answered by the Executive. Hence, a full, well-informed and vivid discussion took place;[35] yet, it did not follow the authorisation tools.

The authorisation model, grounded on the functioning of the concept of sovereignty, had not survived the European Union, and new instruments were being sought to enhance the Parliament-Government interplay in drafting European Treaties. In this vein, the Convention method was created to respond to the need for the democratic legitimation of the European institutions: it was an ingenious attempt to create a new model for legitimising the multifaceted European public sphere in the view of the institutional reforms that were being planned.[36] The ex post ratification by national parliaments was to be preceded and completed by a structured participation of parliamentary delegations in a collective effort to draft the new Constitutional Treaty.[37]

Whether this instrument has actually worked is questionable. Some might say that the failed attempt to adopt a Constitution for Europe may amount to the Convention method proving ineffective and that usual intergovernmental bargaining was the best option to ease the negotiations and avoid stalemate after the French-Dutch *no* to the Constitutional Treaty. Yet some others may argue that the failure of the Constitution was a consequence of the Convention method in the sense that the latter was *too effective*, as it contributed to uncovering a substantive lack of political legitimacy involving all the institutions of the European public sphere, at the national and international levels.

Be that as it may, the decision to subscribe to a 'de-constitutionalised'[38] Treaty may alternatively be seen either as the return to a sound way to conduct European affairs or as an awkward attempt to hide the current problems. However, the Italian Parliament participated in the ratification of the Treaty of Lisbon with a certain zeal.[39] Some criticisms focused on the 'ambiguity' of provisions regarding complex issues transcending the European dimension; others evoked the 'wound' caused by the Constitutional Treaty's demise and assumed, in spite of the recent failures, that Lisbon was a first step toward a political union

34 C De Cesare, 'Adeguamento delle procedure e delle strutture della Camera dei Deputati in rapporto al Parlamento europeo', in *Il Parlamento nella costituzione e nella realtà*, Roma 21–23 October 1978 (Milan, Giuffrè, 1979) 413 ff; more recently A Mannino, *Diritto Parlamentare* (Milan, Giuffrè, 2014) 369 ff; G Ciaurro and V Di Ciolo, *Il diritto parlamentare nella teoria e nella pratica* 5th edn (Milan, Giuffrè, 2013) 320 ff; an overview in G Piccirilli, 'Il Parlamento italiano: le procedure europee nella legge n. 234 del 2012' in A Manzella and N Lupo (eds), *Il sistema parlamentare euro-nazionale. Lezioni* (Turin, Giappichelli, 2014) 205 ff, in part at 224.

35 Senato della Repubblica, *Atti parlamentari, Resoconto della Seduta antimeridiana n 885 del 13 luglio 2000*, www.senato.it/leg/13/BGT/Schede/ProcANL/ProcANLscheda4384.htm.

36 A survey on the *pros* and *contras* in A Maurer, *Less Bargaining—More Deliberation: The Convention Method for Enhancing EU Democracy* (IPG 1/2003) 167 ff; F Oberhuber, 'The Convention Method: An Institutional Device for Consensus-building' in Puntcher-Riekmann and Wessels, above n 33, 90 ff.

37 M Mokre, 'The Ratification of the Constitution and the European Public Sphere' in M Everson, J Eisner (eds) *The Making of a European Constitution: Judges and Law Beyond Constitutive Power* (London, Routledge, 2007) *i* 249 ff.

38 M Fragola, 'Osservazioni sul Trattato di Lisbona tra Costituzione europea e processo *decostituzionale*' (2008) *Diritto Comunitario e degli scambi internazionali* 205 ff.

39 See *Atti del Senato—Legislatura 16a—5a Commissione—Resoconto n 12 del 02/07/2008*, in www.senato.it.

which could overcome the asymmetries and inconsistencies of the merely economic and monetary Union.

It is noteworthy that no neat difference among political parties emerged; most criticisms were raised personally, and not on behalf of the party. Consent was accorded, but with no apparent enthusiasm and without a clear perspective of what was going to happen in fact.[40] To put it roughly, it was looked at mainly as the lesser evil, having regard to the stalemate in which the European Union had been caught since the Constitutional Treaty's demise. There was no further argument on underpinning the improvement of 'democratic principles' which nevertheless became a concern.

C. Overlapping Multiple Public Spheres in an Ultra-EU Dimension

Whereas the European debate proves to be vivid, in spite of the difficulties in approaching the multiple public spheres that it encompasses and notwithstanding the decline of the authorisation model, a more complicated situation concerns those treaties which do not belong to the EU.[41] In particular, because of the consequences that they may entail for both national and European law-making, attention must be devoted to some treaties, such as the Fiscal Compact, which only partially refer to the EU legal order but bring about a relevant influence on the law applicable in the European public space.

Most notably, the debates on the ratification of the Fiscal Compact deserve special attention. It is renowned that the Treaty in question is hybrid in nature, for it does not entirely belong to the realm of EU legal acts but affects EU law and policies to a substantial extent.[42] Talks were entertained at multiple levels, both European and intergovernmental, the Italian debate being quite a marginal moment for clarification of what was going to be planned elsewhere.

However, the process of approbation and implementation of the Fiscal Compact at domestic level needs to be considered from a dual perspective. It is well-known that the obligations contained in that Treaty required implementation through (preferably) constitutional legislation. Accordingly, *Legge costituzionale* No 1/2012 'for the modification of Article 81 and others of the Constitution' was discussed according to the procedure laid down in Article 138 Constitution; it was first presented in October 2011 at the Chamber of Deputies, where it was referred to the Constitutional Affairs and the Budget committees for joint discussion. Several hearings involving economists and constitutional law professors took place; it is noteworthy that talks on how to respond to the sovereign debt crisis were ongoing since 2010 at the supranational level and even earlier in Germany and France, and the same Treaty was in fact signed on 2 March 2012. As the chronology of

[40] *Legge* No 130, 2 Aug 2008 was adopted by unanimity in both Chambers. See the Chamber of Deputies dossier at leg.16.cam.it.

[41] R Ferrari Zumbini, 'Overcoming Overlappings ... in Other Words, beyond this Europe' (SoG WP-16, 2014) 3 ff.

[42] A vast debate has flourished over the nature of those acts and the overall legitimacy of the system that those acts have created. See, eg P Craig, 'Economic Governance and Euro-Crisis: Constitutional Architecture and Constitutional Implications' in M Adams et al, *The Constitutionalization of European Budgetary Constraints* (Oxford, Hart Publishing, 2014) 19f; C Joerges, 'Europe's Economic Constitution in Crisis and the Emergence of a New Constitutional Constellation' (2014) 5 *German Law Journal* 985 ff; Beukers, above n 32.

the events reveals, the key debates were being held within big EU States and at European level; as for the Italian debate, it is evident that the discussions were mainly concerned with the task to ex post inform and explain why Italy was brought to agree upon such obligations. All major political parties declared themselves ready to vote in favour of the constitutional reform as early as the first sitting, and a restricted sub-legislative committee (Comitato ristretto) was appointed on 3 November with a view to speeding up the works. Fellow deputies Tassone (Centrist for the then called 'Terzo Polo') Volpi (Lega Nord) and Zaccaria (PD-Democrats) expressed their personal concerns; their criticisms zeroed in on matters of principle (whether Italy can be urged to change its fundamental law because of international pacts taken in conditions of supreme emergency such as the economic crisis) as well as on matters of a technical nature (whether state-region relations, and other points as well, needed to be touched upon in the reform). On behalf of the major parties, most spokespersons pointed out that the proposed constitutional reforms 'proceeded in the spirit of the Constitution's drafters' and 'nothing really new' was going to be introduced.[43] A new text was adopted by the sub-legislative committee and approved in first reading; the Senate, too, referred it to the Constitutional Affairs and Budget committees jointly and approved it in six days. The second reading smoothly led to approbation by a two thirds majority of the members of both Houses—the possibility of a referendum being ruled out pursuant to Article 138 Constitution[44]—and the *Legge costituzionale* passed on 20 April 2012.

The procedure of the Fiscal Compact's *Legge di autorizzazione alla ratifica* started in the Senate on 3 April 2012, and discussions began on 12 July. Debates were quite limited, too, on the assumption that the main topics relating to the content of the Treaty had already been discussed in the debate on the constitutional reform. Two motions were raised and approved in the Senate's Foreign Affairs Committee:[45] it was mentioned that, while international obligations related to the Treaty had been promptly fulfilled, meetings had been held a month prior with the fellow deputies of the *Bundestag*'s competent committees and a common position had emerged to consider the Treaty as a first step toward a more integrated political Union.

In the light of the above, if one looks at the Italian experience, it seems that the lack of a structured 'parliamentarised' debate at the European level for those measures not following the most visible EU legislative channels—to put it clearly, which do not belong to the domain of the ordinary legislative procedure—is not balanced by a substantial parliamentarisation through national laws allowing for ratification, whether those laws be of an ordinary rank or of a constitutional one. This assumption is confirmed if account is taken of another Treaty of an even more accentuated hybrid nature: the Treaty establishing a European Gendarmerie Force (Eurogendfor).

This Treaty was concluded through a Declaration of Intent signed in Noordwijk on 17 March 2004 by six EU Member States: France, Italy, The Netherlands, Portugal, Romania and Spain, plus Poland and Lithuania entering in 2007 and Turkey being granted the status

[43] Chamber of Deputies, *Bollettino delle Commissioni* I–V, 2 November 2011, 3 ff, at http://leg16.camera.it.

[44] See Chamber of Deputies, *Resoconto della seduta del 5 March 2012*, http://leg16.camera.it/126?leg=16&pdl=4205.

[45] Resoconto, 'Emendamenti di Commissione relativi al DDL n 3239', at www.senato.it. The orders wished that further interparliamentary contact be made and urged the Government to submit to the European Council a 'proposal to put the Treaty under question, along with the Treaty establishing ESM, in a clear roadmap toward the Political Union'.

of 'observer'. Eurogendfor was declared operative from 20 July 2006 but only formalised in the Velsen Treaty on 18 October 2007. It is featured as a 'pre-organised, robust and rapidly deployable' force, 'exclusively comprising elements of police forces with military status of the Parties, in order to perform all police tasks within the scope of crisis management operations' (Article 1).[46] It is interesting to note that Italy hosts the Permanent Headquarters and has actively participated in all operations, but the *Legge di autorizzazione alla ratifica* was presented at the Chamber of Deputies only on 28 December 2009 and referred to the Defence and Foreign Affairs committees for joint discussion on 11 February 2010. Debates have been outstandingly laconic—mainly emphasising the high desirability of an enhanced cooperation between EU countries, as well as with NATO, without much else to say on the point—and en passant explained some of the content of the Treaty (and of the annexed Declaration).[47] Only the rapporteurs of the committees involved (and the Government representative) took the floor and, after four sessions in joint committee meetings, an overwhelming majority voted in favour of the authorisation to ratify.[48] Senate was as quick as the Camera and the *Legge* was eventually promulgated on 14 May 2010.

It appears that, although the Treaty in question was highly politically sensitive from the perspective of the rights of the individuals, the parliamentary involvement has been inadequate. The reason is that the qualification of political sensitivity is no longer understood in the parliamentary viewpoint, but it is assumed in the light of the Government's appreciation in the first place and goes relatively unchallenged during the parliamentary passages.

This is the most evident sign of the malfunctioning of the ratification mechanisms: the treaty is dealt with according to the dynamics of the trust relationship, despite the legal devices provided for. If a treaty is perceived by the Government—in light of its own interest, assumed as the national one—as peculiarly sensitive, in parliamentary stages it is debated to the extent (and in the terms) that the Government prefers, let alone the (im)possibility for the Parliament to have a say on the content of the international obligations to which Italy is subscribing. Coupled with the assumed merely formal nature of the parliamentary ratification law, this leads to a paradoxical subversion of the rationale behind Article 80 of the Constitution: The more sensitive the Treaty, the less substantive the parliamentary involvement.

In the case of the Fiscal Compact, the political importance of the obligations provided was de facto emphasised by the constitutional legislation required by the Treaty itself; the set of procedures has been formally consistent with the duties laid down in the Constitution.[49] Yet the debates on the merits have been scarce, for the bulk of the Treaty has been determined elsewhere, long before the Parliament was even called on to ratify it.

[46] Eurogendfor counts on 800–900 members ready to deploy plus about 2000 additional reinforcements available in standby. It can be also deployed under non EU structures, acting under both civilian and military chain of command: it has taken part in 'crisis management operations' in Bosnia-Herzegovina (2007) in the framework of EUFOR operation 'Althea'; in Afghanistan (2009) under NATO; in Haiti (2010) under the direction of the UN; in Central Africa (2013–14) under a mixed direction from EU and UN; in Mali (2014–ongoing) under EU control.

[47] See Chamber of Deputies, *Bollettino delle Commissioni* III–IV, 11 February 2010, at 16f, leg16.camera.it.

[48] Present and voters: 442. *Yes*: 441; *Abs* 1; *No* 0. *Resoconto votazione finale*, 9 March 2010, documenti.camera.it.

[49] N Lupo, 'La revisione costituzionale della disciplina di bilancio e il sistema delle fonti' (2011) *Il Filangieri* 89f, where such multilateral nature is taken as evidence of the 'European (and Italian) composite constitution' (91 ff) while emphasising the peculiarity of the implementing legislation 'which is to be adopted by absolute majority' (106 ff) in the like of the Spanish *ley orgànica.*

In the case of Eurogendfor, the hiatus between the national dimension of political sensitivity and the way the matter is dealt with is manifest. Parliamentarisation of the concerned issues hardly meets even the standard of formality. According to the Velsen Treaty, Eurogendfor is governed by the CIMIN (Comité Inter-Ministériel d'Haut Niveau) where each state counts on three members: a high representative of the Minister of Foreign Affairs, the Minister of Defence or the Minister of Interior, plus the General Commander or Director-General of the respective force. There is in fact little parliamentary control over those activities (apart from the ordinary means provided for at the national level); yet the powers with which Eurogendfor is endowed are not of minor relevance, and the subject-matter is closely related to personal individual liberties.

IV. Conclusions: Which Future for the 'Authorisation Model'?

Which lesson can be taken from the examples just illustrated? The cases of NATO and EEC were a manifesto of the high potential enshrined in the authorisation model as depicted in the Constitution. The Constitution was interpreted in the sense that the authorisation to ratify must include the full text of the treaty to be ratified, or at least a draft project, insofar as its content is fully understandable. But this possibility has not been exploited in such a way as to foster a substantive co-determination between the Parliament and the Government.

The *Legge di autorizzazione alla ratifica* is of a merely formal nature: this has been assumed by the Italian institutions unanimously, despite the opposite position maintained by some scholars.[50] As a consequence, no amendment can be tabled or discussed, and in general the parliamentary influence on the content of international obligations undertaken by the state is rather limited, as the unbalances with the Government are remarkable.[51] Authorising the Executive to ratify becomes a take-it-or-leave-it question; one which typically relates to the mutual trust between the Parliament and the Government. In this context, one might say, the provision contained in Article 72, last paragraph of the Constitution—admitting the sole 'normal', more inclusive procedure for the relevant draft legislative act authorising the ratification—has been in part deprived of its original substantive meaning.

The Constitution contained tracks of a pluralistic concept of sovereignty and pursued a strong parliamentarisation of international activities. Nonetheless, after its entry into force, a monolithic idea of sovereignty has proved to be quite solid in the understanding of most politicians and commentators, the possible explanation being that it was well-rooted in the

[50] For a detailed overview of the different positions, Lippolis, above n 12, 68f; Palazzolo, above n 5, 248f; Lai, above n 7, 1015 ff. Nonetheless, the decline of the category of 'merely formal legislation' was already highlighted by L Paladin, 'Ciò che rimane del concetto di legge in senso formale' in *Studi in onore di M Udina* (Milan, Giuffrè, 1975) 1753. On the notion of 'dual proceedings' leading to co-determined acts, see A Manzella, *Il Parlamento* 3rd edn (Bologna, Il Mulino, 2003) 339 ff. However, the possibility for the Parliament to formally urge the Government to put a reserve to the treaty has been held by scholars: see L Gianniti, 'Considerazioni sul ruolo del Parlamento e del Capo dello Stato nella stipulazione dei trattati internazionali' (2001) 4 *Diritto e Società* 682.

[51] The exclusive initiative of the Government has been maintained on the basis that it is the sole body that knows the details of the treaty and can provide the full text (Palazzolo, above n 5, 221–22). Yet, in some cases the legislative authorisation to ratify an international treaty has been tabled under parliamentary initiative: see L Gianniti-N Lupo, *Corso di diritto parlamentare* 3rd edn (Bologna, Il Mulino, 2013) 241–43.

Italian legal culture. Therefore, in the long run, the national position as defined by the Government has been merely validated by the Parliament (and by the President alike). While impacting the international sphere, the need for national unity preempts more articulated parliamentary debates, in spite of the wording of the Constitution itself.

Politically, this entails an enhanced supremacy of the Executive in deciding on and carrying out international business. As domestic diversity has been sacrificed to national unity, Italy has chosen to keep a fairly restricted internal public sphere, while progressively narrower room is being provided for a broader debate of major international choices.

From the perspective of constitutional law scholars, the legal devices shaped to vitalise the institutional diversity between the Parliament and the Government and to construe a broader public sphere seem to have resulted in formality, being often used by the Government itself to strengthen its position, in the view of emphasising national unity rather than accommodating domestic diversity. Getting absorbed into the relation of mutual trust between the Parliament and Government, these mechanisms became entrapped in the political dimension, and largely lost their legally mandatory force. The best evidence of this is the incorporation of the *ordre d'execution* in the same document as the authorisation to ratify, a practice which has gone uncontested since the very beginning and is directed at enhancing the unity of the Italian position in the international sphere.[52]

Along with that came the inadmissibility of amendments relating to the *ordre d'execution*, as well, maintained by the President of the Chamber of Deputies in 1981.[53] The rationale behind that was clear: if Article 80 is to be interpreted as giving to the Parliament the mere task of validating the content of an international obligation which was going to bind Italy, it would be inconsistent that the Parliament would give its consent but at the same time alter the substance of the obligation itself.[54]

Eventually, the overlap of the international and the national levels in a multifaceted global sphere results in the latter level being often neglected to the advantage of a more cohesive position vis-à-vis the global community. 'Political sensitivity' has been therefore mainly interpreted in the light of the national interest as pursued by the Government; that is, in prevalent consideration of what the Executive needs to defend itself and its strategies on the various levels it was called upon to act. The efforts provided by the Parliament in construing direct relations with European and supranational bodies—particularly in the EU framework[55]—show limited political impact in the global world. Faced with the overlapping legal orders in the global scenario, Italy has in fact reacted by restoring sovereignty in its prime sense—indeed, quite an anachronistic one. As late as 1902, Santi Romano said that

[52] See R Quadri, *Diritto internazionale pubblico* (Napoli, Liguori, 1989) 63–68; cp A Cassese, *Diritto internazionale* (Bologna, Il Mulino, 2003) 272–73.

[53] See G Piccirilli, *L'emendamento nel processo di decisione parlamentare* (Padova, CEDAM, 2008) 209, fn 126. The issue came at stake for the authorisation to the ratification of the Constitutional Treaty: see D Piccione, 'L'inemendabilità della legge di autorizzazione alla ratifica della Costituzione europea e il falso mito del "principio di non regressione"' (2005) *Archivio Rivista AIC*, 24/3/2005.

[54] It should be held possible—according to most scholars—to amend those provisions, ancillary to the executive clause, in a way which does not alter in an incoherent and inconsistent manner the content of the treaty.

[55] See A Esposito, 'Il Trattato di Lisbona e il nuovo ruolo dei Parlamenti nazionali: le prospettive per il Parlamento italiano' (2009) 4 *Rassegna Parlamentare* 1119 ff; A Esposito, 'La Legge 24 dicembre 2012, n. 234, sulla partecipazione dell'Italia alla formazione ed attuazione della normativa e delle politiche dell'UE. Parte I. Prime riflessioni sul ruolo delle Camere' (2013) 2 *Federalismi.it* 1–74.

> The Parliament cannot enact laws which would be in contradiction with the obligations that the State has undertaken with other States … that would be an illegal situation not only for international law, but also for constitutional law, which stands as a guarantee to the former and ensures its respect.[56]

The sharp contradiction with what Lord Atkin pointed out on international laws requiring an act of the Parliament before entering domestic law (footnote 8 of this chapter) witnesses to a radically different approach.

Confronted with the roles that parliaments are called to perform in the global arena, this approach is jarring. Whether it is consistent with the challenges of an ever-growing need for the 'inclusion of the other'[57] in a global law-making, whose implications on national level are yet to be fully uncovered, is still a matter for discussion.

[56] S Romano, 'Osservazioni preliminari per una teoria sui limiti della funzione legislativa nel diritto italiano' (1902) in S Romano, *Lo Stato moderno e la sua crisi* (Giuffrè, Milano, 1969) 145. As for the repercussions on the doctrine of national sovereignty, see G Arangio Ruiz, *Istituzioni di diritto costituzionale italiano* (Roma, F.lli Bocca, 1913) 21 ff. See P Costa, *Lo Stato immaginario. Metafore e paradigmi nella cultura giuridica italiana fra Ottocento e Novecento* (Milan, Giuffrè, 1986) 238 ff.

[57] Due reference to J Habermas, *Die Einbeziehung des Anderen. Studien zur politischen Theorie* (Frankfurt, Suhrkamp Verlag, 1996).

3

Formulating and Implementing EU Law and Policies: 'Ascending' and 'Descending' Phases and Beyond

RENATO IBRIDO

I. An Introduction: The Specificities of Italian Literature within European Constitutional Studies

For many reasons, the Italian constitutional literature is virtually inaccessible in the European debate concerning the integration process. These difficulties go beyond the simple problem of the linguistic barrier. Indeed, while in Germany federalism is a core part of the legal studies and has been the object of prestigious and well-crafted contributions by constitutional scholars, the 'centralistic' constitutional categories elaborated by Italian public law scholars are less easily adaptable in the study of the European constitutional Law.

Obviously there are some exceptions to this general trend, one example being the Italian 'counter-limits' doctrine, which had a certain resonance in foreign literature and recently was expressly cited in a concurring opinion of the Spanish Constitutional Court in the 'sequel' to the *Melloni* case about a European arrest warrant.[1] Further, some of the

[1] According to the so-called 'counter-limits' doctrine, art 11 of the Italian Constitution does not allow limitations to the sovereignty of the state when the European regulations could breach the fundamental principles of the constitutional order, especially those concerning fundamental rights (Judgment No 183, 18th December

Italian literature had the foresight to build or forecast future European constitutional scenarios before the others. Paradigmatic in particular are the contributions of Santi Romano,[2] Guido Calogero[3] and Giuseppe Barile[4] in 'imagining' the future of the constitutional state in Europe.

Furthermore, as some scholars have acknowledged, the origins (or better, the roots) of the 'federalist paradigm'—that is, a federalist interpretation of the role of the democratic principle in the European Union—can be traced back to the Ventotene Manifesto of Altiero Spinelli and Ernesto Rossi.[5]

However, despite these relevant contributions, the Italian constitutional 'lexicon' contained some concepts which—although in some cases were known by the scholarship in other countries—did not have a real impact on the European debate about the integration process. Such is the case, for example, of the dichotomy of the 'ascending/descending phase', which is employed to distinguish the process of elaboration/representation of the Italian position in Europe and the domestic procedures used to guarantee Italy's compliance with EU norms.

In light of these assumptions, this chapter questions the suitability of the 'ascending/descending phase' dichotomy. Indeed, this distinction acts as a 'litmus test', because it shows and summarises, in a paradigmatic way, some of the most important cultural and methodological peculiarities of the Italian literature within European studies.

1973, *Frontini* case). The 'counter-limits doctrine' was cited by Judge Roca Trías at the STC 26/2014 (see R Ibrido, 'L'esperienza costituzionale italiana negli itinerari argomentativi del Tribunale costituzionale spagnolo' (2014) 3 *Rassegna Parlamentare* 721 ff and above all 736).

[2] It is possible to remember an essay where Santi Romano highlighted the possibility that in future the states, or even just some of them, can remain 'included or absorbed' in larger organisations devoid of the character of state. When Santi Romano wrote this essay—'Oltre lo Stato' ('Beyond the State')—the German army was still stuck in Verdun and World War I had still not come to an end (S Romano, *Oltre lo stato. Discorso inaugurale dell'anno accademico del R Istituto di Scienze sociali 'Cesare Alfieri' letto il 18 novembre 1917* (Florence, Tip Galileiana, 1918).

[3] In 1945, Guido Calogero, intervening in the debate about the historicity of legal concepts, stressed that the problem of 'political representations' would concern if and when this concept would have a legal means within a supranational order, for example as a principle enforceable in the courts or as condition for the admission of a state in a supranational organisation (Guido Calogero, 'La polemica sui concetti giuridici' (1945) XLIII(I) *Rivista di diritto commerciale* 112 ff).

[4] Emblematic is an essay by Giuseppe Barile, written 10 years before the *Nold* decision. According to Barile, the TEEC must be applied with a consistent interpretation with the 'common factors' to the (spontaneous) domestic law of Member States. It is evident here the similarity between the category of 'constitutional traditions common to the member states' and the Barile's standard of 'common factors' (G Barile, 'Sulla struttura delle Comunità europee' (1964) *Rivista di diritto internazionale*, 17 ff).

[5] As Di Martino observes, the Ventotene Manifesto is a necessary step for the comprehension of Europistic opening of the Constitution after World War II. The political and constitutional heritage of the Manifesto can be fully appreciated in the long term: from the 1990s onward, this document, in its main lines, imposed itself again as a reference model (A Di Martino, 'Ventotene. Un progetto politico per l'unità federale europea' in A Buratti and M Fioravanti (eds), *Costituenti ombra* (Rome, Carocci editore, 2010) 68 ff and notably 79). On the impact of the Ventotene Manifesto in the constitutional debate, see also P Ridola, 'Federalismo europeo e modelli federali. Spunti di riflessione sul Trattato di Lisbona. L'Unione europea verso una res publica federalista?' in P Ridola, *Diritto comparato e diritto costituzionale europeo* (Turin, Giappichelli, 2010) 418 ff. The English translation of the Ventotene Manifesto is available at www.altierospinelli.org/manifesto/en/manifestoen_en.html.

II. Some General Definitions and an Attempt at Periodisation

In Italian legal scholarship, the concept of the 'ascending phase' refers to a set of rules and procedures that govern the Italian participation in the formation of EU Law and policies. Additionally, some authors distinguish between two main parts of the ascending phase: a) a sub-phase involving the elaboration of the Italian position in Europe, which consists of policy-setting and fact-finding procedures; and b) a sub-phase concerning the representation of this position at the European level. This second sub-phase involves those rules related to the composition of the national delegation to Europe.[6]

When Italian scholars and legal practitioners use the notion of the 'descending phase', they refer to the rules through which the constitutional and administrative bodies ensure compliance with the constraints imposed by European Union law. In particular, the 'descending phase' includes three different regulatory actions: a) the transposition of non-self-executing European rules into Italian law; b) the implementation of EU legal acts; and c) the repeal of domestic rules incompatible with EU law.

Italian constitutional jurisprudence also has adopted the vocabulary of the 'ascending/descending phases'. Referring to EU law, the Italian Constitutional Court used the expression 'ascending phase' for the first time in Decision No 239/2004. In it, the Constitutional Court confirmed the exclusive competence of the state in setting ascending phase procedures. More recently, with Decision No 63/2012, the Constitutional Court addressed the topic of the 'descending phase'. Precisely, it rejected, with a consistent interpretation, the claim filed against the Statute of Molise Region, which identifies the Regional Government as the body that is competent to implement EU law.

The reform of Title V—approved in 2001 to reshape the relationship between the state and regions—gives an indirect legal basis for these concepts, although it is limited to the five special autonomies.[7] Indeed, according to the new Article 117.5, the regions shall participate in the decision-making processes that lead to the adoption of European Union acts in the areas falling with their responsibilities and shall provide for the implementation and execution of EU measures.[8]

In light of the transformations of the legal framework, we could identify three distinct periods in the evolution of the connections between 'ascending phase' and 'descending phase'. After the first period, which was characterised by the absence of specific tools to rationalise the relations between Italy and Europe—and therefore the lack of the concepts

[6] P Costanzo and A Ruggeri, 'Unione europea ed autonomie territoriali' in P Costanzo, L Mezzetti and Antonio Ruggeri (eds), *Lineamenti di diritto costituzionale dell'Unione europea* (Turin, Giappichelli, 2014) notably 472.

[7] The five regions with a special status of autonomy are Friuli-Venezia Giulia, Sardinia, Sicily, Trentino-Alto Adige/Südtirol and Valle d'Aosta/Vallée d'Aoste (art 116.1 of the Constitution).

[8] 'The Regions and the autonomous provinces of Trent and Bolzano take part in the preparatory decision-making process of EU legislative acts in the areas that fall within their responsibilities. They are also responsible for the implementation of international agreements and EU measures, subject to the procedural rules set out in State legislation regulating the exercise of subsidiary powers by the State in the case of non-performance by the Regions and autonomous provinces' (art 117.5 of the Italian Constitution). Moreover, art 119.1 establishes that 'Municipalities, provinces, metropolitan cities and regions contribute to ensuring compliance with the economic and financial constraints imposed under European Union law'.

of the 'ascending phase' and the 'descending phase'—the second period started with the adoption of Law No 86/1989 conceived by the Minister for Coordinating Community Policies, Antonio La Pergola. From 1989 until the 2012 reform, there was a strict separation between the two phases. Finally, in the third period, with the adoption of the recent Law No 234/2012—which, inter alia, 'splits' the Annual Community Law ('*legge comunitaria*')—the Italian legal order started to valorise a more integrated approach between the two phases.

It is probably too early to acknowledge the definitive removal of the rigid separation between the 'descending' and 'ascending' phase. Indeed, the structure of Law No 234/2012 continues to reflect the signs of this dichotomy. In any case, some of this Act's innovations, like for example the so-called 'table of correspondence', show at least a change of mind. After all, it is not a coincidence that the scholarship emphasises with increasing frequency the necessity to strengthen the 'descending phase' through a stronger connection with the 'ascending phase'.[9]

III. The First Period: The Absence of Specific Tools to Organise the Relationships with the European Legal Order

As described above, in the first step of our periodisation there were no connections between the 'ascending phase' and 'descending phase' for the simple reason that, before Law No 86/1989, the implementation of European legislation and the involvement of non-governmental bodies in the formation of Community law (now EU law) were not done in 'phases', but only through a 'case-by-case' patchwork of decisions.

The delays and serious deficiencies in the implementation of European directives (which it is testified by the dismal constancy of infringement procedures) were gradually aggravated proportionally to the growth of the European competences. Indeed, in absence of a rationalisation of a 'descending phase', the transposition of European directives followed the logic of urgency without a coherent design. The implementation of the Annual Community Law was characterised '*ab origine*' by an unsystematic transposition of directives.[10]

The legal act most utilised by the Italian legal order in the implementation of EU law was the delegation of legislative powers to the Government.[11] This practice has been criticised for three fundamental reasons. First of all, to prevent a delegation of power on undefined matters, article 76 of the Italian Constitution requires parliamentary law of delegation to guide the legislative decree through the indication of principles and criteria. Hence there was at least some doubt whether delegating legislative powers for the implementation of European directives satisfies the condition established by article 76.

[9] See, for example, N Lupo, 'L'adeguamento del sistema istituzionale italiano al Trattato di Lisbona. Osservazioni sui disegni di legge di riforma della legge n 11 del 2005' (2011) www.astrid.eu; N Lupo, 'I Parlamenti nazionali nell'Unione europea e il principio di sussidiarietà: qualche suggestione per la Camera dei deputati' (2014) *Amministrazione in Cammino* 13.

[10] See F Astone, *Il processo normativo dell'Unione europea e le procedure nazionali per l'esecuzione degli obblighi comunitari* (Turin, Giappichelli, 2007) 193.

[11] 'The exercise of the legislative function may not be delegated to the Government unless principles and criteria have been established and then only for a limited time and for specified purposes' (art 76 of the Italian Constitution).

Second, legislative delegation—giving to the Parliament a marginal role in the European affairs—did not resolve the problem of the EU's 'democratic deficit'. On the contrary, it further strengthened the pivotal role of the Government in those affairs. Finally, this delegation produced a pathological and systematic delay in the transposition of European directives, which caused the copious infringement procedures against Italy.

Further, the structure of the European decision-making process, with the central position of the Council, and the traditional 'executive dominance'[12] within the international relations, led to an unsurprising absence of organisation of the coordination between Parliament, regions and Government in the 'ascending phase'. Consequently, the Italian Parliament and the regions for a long time were cast out of the European law-making process. Indeed, while the regions were suffering from the old European 'federal blindness',[13] at the national level the Chambers maintained only a generic oversight of Government. Inter alia, this function was rarely exercised in the field of European relations before the Lisbon Treaty.[14]

IV. The Second Period: The Annual Community Law 'Era' (1989–2012)

The first attempt to reorganise the European procedures dates from Law No 183/1987, which streamlines the tools for the implementation of European directives. In particular, Law No 183/1987 encouraged the transposition of European directives through government regulations and other administrative sources while directly providing for the implementation of 100 directives. Simultaneously, it recognised for the Chambers a generic 'right' to make observations about the drafts of European regulations, directives and recommendations.[15] Moreover, it also established the Governmental Department of Community Affairs to create a coordinated consultation on European proposals among Ministers, Parliament, regions and officials.

Act No 183/1987 was the first step on the path to Law No 86/1989, which two years later introduced the tool of the Annual Community Law. According to Law No 86/1989, the Government would introduce a specific bill including measures to 'reset' the backlog of European obligations awaiting fulfillment by 31 January of each year. The Annual Community Law was divided into three parts. The first part contained the legal measures which directly modified the Italian norms that conflict with the European obligations. The second part provided for the delegation of legislative power to the Government for the

[12] About the 'executive dominance issue', see D Curtin, 'Challenging Executive Dominance in European Democracy' (2014) 1 *Modern Law Review* 1 ff.

[13] According to Ipsen's well-known metaphor, at the beginning, the European Communities suffered from a 'federal blindness'. In other words, EU law could not 'see' the sub-national entities which existed within the Member States (HP Ipsen, 'Als Bundesstaat in der Gemeinschaft' in E von Caemmerer, H-J Schlochauer and E Steindorff (eds), *Probleme des Europäischen Rechts* (Berlin, Duncker & Humblot, 1966).

[14] On the lack of activation by the Chambers of the oversight powers within European affairs, see M Cartabia and JHH Weiler, *L'Italia in Europa. Profili istituzionali e costituzionali* (Bolonia, il Mulino, 2000) 141.

[15] In 1993, an investigation of the Senate of Republic concerning the participation of Italian Parliament at the formation of EU law highlighted that the 'right' to make observations did not pay off.

transposition of European directives. The third part authorised the Government to implement EU law through government regulations and administrative sources.[16]

The scholarship identified this Annual Law as the paradigmatic case of the 'dual legislative procedure',[17] that is a procedure characterised by the concurrence of two centres of legislative autonomy: on the one hand the autonomy of the Chambers, which coordinate and direct the implementation of EU law; and on the other hand the autonomy of other institutional actors (Government, regions, European institutions).

With the Annual Community Law, Italy showed that it could more effectively cope with the challenging obligations of membership in the European Union. In the over 20 years of adoption of Community laws, however, different signs of inefficiency regarding the transposition of EU law have emerged, especially in the chronic delays in the adoption of the Annual Law.

The responsibility for these delays is not exclusively on the slowness of Parliament's procedures but also concerns the Government.[18] Indeed, the Government's delay in the adoption of legislative decrees and the presentation of the Community law bills had a negative impact on the efficiency of the 'descending phase'. The delays take on pathological characteristics from 2011–2013, when, inter alia, the Senate found itself in the situation of examining and approving both the 2011 and 2012 Community laws at the same time.

In this framework, the main weakness of the model can be traced in the lack of a constitutional basis of the 'self-constraints' contained in Law No 86/1989.[19] In any case, Law No 86/1989 was repealed by Law No 11/2005 (the so-called 'Stucchi-Buttiglione Law'). Although it confirmed the overall architecture of Law No 86/1989, the Stucchi-Buttiglione Law upgraded the legislation concerning the descending and ascending phases in light of the new provisions contained in the constitutional reform of the Title V (Constitutional Law No 3/2011).[20]

With regard to the 'ascending phase', the Stucchi-Buttiglione Law, for the first time, created an organic regulation concerning the participation of the Italian Parliament in the European law-making process. In particular, it tried to combine the 'document-based model' with some elements of a 'mandating/procedural system'.[21] Indeed, while article 3 strengthened the background information provided to the Chambers—especially mandating that

[16] Moreover, art 7 of Law No 86/1986 introduced a Yearly Report about the developments of the European integration process which was to be presented by the Government to the Parliament by 31 January of each year.

[17] About the dual legislative procedure, see A Manzella, *Il Parlamento* 3rd edn (Bolonia, il Mulino, 2003) 339.

[18] According to V Boncinelli, 'Il mancato recepimento e la violazione del diritto comunitario imputabili a comportamenti, omissioni e ritardi del Governo' in S Baroncelli (ed), *Il ruolo del Governo nella formazione e applicazione del diritto dell'Unione europea. Le peculiarità di un sistema costituzionale multilivello* (Turin, Giappichelli, 2008), above all 212. Parliament took an average of 322 days for the approval of the Annual Community Law.

[19] This element of weakness is highlighted by B De Maria, 'I rapporti tra Parlamento e Governo nell'attuazione delle norme comunitarie' in R Dickmann and Sandro Staiano (eds), *Funzioni parlamentari non legislative e forma di governo: l'esperienza dell'Italia* (Milan, Giuffrè, 2008) notably 563 ff.

[20] The reform of 2001 was the most important reform of the Italian Constitution in quantitative terms. In particular, Constitutional Law No 3 of 2001 rewrote the allocation of legislative powers between state and regions, accelerating the process of decentralisation within the Italian legal order.

[21] In the comparative law, two models of parliamentary involvement in European affairs have emerged. The so-called 'document-based model' focuses on examining legislative proposals and other documents emanating from the EU institutions. The prototype of this model is the House of Commons of the United Kingdom. Instead, 'mandating' or 'procedural systems', as for example in Denmark and Finland, include a parliamentary power to give a direct mandate to a government before a minister can endorse legislation in Council meetings.

the Government provide the Parliament qualified and timely information on European affairs—article 4 introduced a special reservation of scrutiny for Parliament. Precisely, according to article 4, once a Chamber has started the scrutiny process of a European legislative proposal, they can request that the Government not take an official position on an issue until the Parliament has completed their scrutiny. After 20 days, however, the Government can proceed without a parliamentary decision. Thus, the scholarship has emphasised the 'double soul' of the scrutiny reserve: on one hand, it identifies a parliamentary constraint for the national Government within the European decision-making process; on the other hand, the scrutiny reserve represents a tool for applying pressure by which the Government tries to condition the European partners.[22]

Under the Stucchi-Buttiglione Law, the Annual Community Law continues to be the main tool for the 'descending phase', although its role is inevitably reduced by the allocation to the regions of the legislative residual competence. Indeed, within their own matters, the regions can give immediate implementation to the European directives, regardless of the Annual Community Law. In any case, the Stucchi-Buttiglione Act regulated state subsidiary powers regarding the hypothesis of regions' non-performance of EU measures.

Finally, Law No 11/2005 established the Interministerial Committee on European Community Affairs (CIACE), the governmental office for coordinating the Italian position at the European Union regarding cross-sectoral issues that involve more administrations.

V. The Third Period: Towards a Tighter Connection between the Two Phases? Law No 234/2012

More than 20 years after the introduction of the Annual Community Law, in 2012, the Italian Parliament—after a wide investigation by the two Chambers' Committees on EU Policies—approved Law No 234/2012 ('General Norms on the Italian Participation in the Formation and Implementation of European Union Law and Policies'), which integrally replaced the previous Stucchi-Buttiglione Law.

At the basis of the reform there were two fundamental necessities. First, Italy needed to adapt its own legislation in light of the new Lisbon Treaty[23] Aiming to strengthen the democratic legitimacy of the European Union, the Lisbon Treaty increased the role and powers of national parliaments in the EU decision-making process, in particular involving these parliaments in the Early Warning Mechanism.[24] However, while other

[22] See M Cartabia, 'I rapporti tra le istituzioni europee e i parlamenti nazionali: che cosa resta e che cosa si perde in caso di mancata ratifica?' in AIC, *L'integrazione dei sistemi costituzionali europeo e nazionali* (Padua, Cedam, 2007) 103 ff; P Gambale, 'Le "garanzie parlamentari" nella fase ascendente del diritto comunitario: cenni di diritto comparato e novità dell'ordinamento italiano' (2006) 3 *Rassegna Parlamentare* 833 ff.

[23] Although the Italian scholarship emphasised especially this first factor, according to Antonio Esposito the primary *ratio* of the Law No 234 of 2012 is to solve deficiencies, gaps and problems which had already emerged before the Treaty of Lisbon. However, Lisbon undoubtedly increased the awareness of the importance of a reform of the Buttiglione Law. See A Esposito, 'La legge 24 dicembre 2012, n 234, sulla partecipazione dell'Italia alla formazione e all'attuazione della normative e delle politiche dell'Unione europea. Parte I—Prime riflessioni sul ruolo delle Camere' (2013) 2 *Federalismi.it* 2–3.

[24] According to art 12 of the Treaty on the European Union, 'National Parliaments contribute actively to the good functioning of the Union'. Art 12 TEU, Protocol No 1 (on the role of the National Parliaments in the

parliaments—to exploit the new European prerogatives—modified their Constitutions, their legislation or at least their Rules of Procedure,[25] until 2012 the Italian Chambers merely introduced some 'experimental' and provisional procedures[26] by a letter of the President of the Senate and two opinions from the Committee on the Rules in the House.[27]

Second, the reform aimed to make the system of transposition and implementation of EU law more efficient, overtaking the rigid separation between the 'ascending' and 'descending' phases and, therefore, strengthening the link between the Government, the Parliament and the regions.

The most important sign of the connection between the two phases is contained in article 6, according to which the Government is expected to accompany the European Union draft legislation, 'in cases of particular relevance', with an explanatory note of assessment. Moreover, each Chamber can ask the Government for the explanatory note of assessment for every other EU act as well. The explanatory note provides a technical report on the compliance of the EU draft legislation with the EU competences. Moreover, the note is accompanied by a 'table of correspondence' between the provisions of the draft and the

European Union) and Protocol No 2 (on the application of the principles of subsidiarity and proportionality) group together the main prerogatives of the National Parliaments. For the new 'European powers' of the National Parliaments, see N Lupo, 'National Parliaments in the European Integration Process: Re-aligning Politics and Policies' in M Cartabia, N Lupo and A Simoncini (eds), *Democracy and Subsidiarity in the EU. National Parliaments, Regional and Civil Society in the Decision-making Process* (Bolonia, il Mulino, 2013) 107 ff; M Olivetti, 'Parlamenti nazionali nell'Unione europea' in *Digesto delle Discipline Pubblicistiche. Aggiornamento* (Turin, UTET, 2012) 485 ff; C Morviducci, 'Parlamenti nazionali (ruolo nell'UE)' in *Enciclopedia del diritto, Annali VII* (Milan, Giuffrè, 2013) 593 ff.

[25] For example, the new powers assigned to national parliaments are regulated in Spain by Law No 24/2009, which strengthened in particular the position of the Joint Committee for the EU. Moreover, with regard to the subsidiarity scrutiny a joint resolution of the Bureaux (*Mesas*) of the two Houses amended in 2010 a previous resolution of 1995. In France, *Loi constitutionelle* no 2008-103 of 4 February 2008 introduced seven new articles focused on relations with the EU. On the basis of this constitutional revision, the National Assembly and the Senate emended the provisions of their Standing Orders (Resolution No 292 of 27th May 2009 adopted by the National Assembly; Resolution of the 2nd June 2009 and Resolution of the 20th December 2010, no 34 adopted by the Senate).

[26] At the Chamber of Deputies, the Committee on the Rules at Procedure, with the opinion of 6 October 2009, conferred at the Standing Committee on European Affairs the power to express the position of the Chamber on the compliance with the principles of subsidiarity and proportionality. Instead, the competence on the merit of the EU draft legislation stays at the Standing Committee competent for the subject matter. With a second opinion, on 14 July 2010, the Committee on the Rules at Procedure established the possibility of a vote in the plenary on reasoned opinions. As Fasone, Griglio and Piccirilli underlined, 'notwithstanding this lack of specific procedures, the Italian Chamber of Deputies is one of the most active, at least in the numbers, in passing opinions in the framework of the early warning mechanism' (C Fasone, E Griglio and G Piccirilli, 'The Implementation of the Lisbon Treaty in the Parliamentary Rules of Procedure. The Italian "Zero-option" in Comparative Perspective', paper, 19th Conference of Europeanists-CES, Columbia University, NY).

[27] Giovanni Piccirilli argued that the delay of the Italian Parliament to adapt the legislation to the entry into force of the Lisbon Treaty was conditioned by two different factors. First of all, the heterogeneity of the solutions offered by the comparative law shows that the choice of the source of law which to intervene with was not taken for granted. For this reason, the Chambers preferred to wait and experiment some provisional procedures. Second, the political crisis of the government coalition determined the isolation of the Minister for European Affairs, Andrea Ronchi, who led the PDL party after the scission with 'Future and Freedom' ('*Futuro e libertà*'). Moreover, after the resignation of Ronchi in November 2010, the head of the Department for European Affairs remained vacant for nine months. In this context, the Law No 234 of 2012, mostly, is the fruit of parliamentary initiative and the technical support of parliamentary bureaucracy. See G Piccirilli, 'Le procedure europee nella legge n. 234 del 2012' in A Manzella and N Lupo, *Il sistema parlamentare euro-nazionale. Lezioni* (Turin, Giappichelli, 2014) 207.

current domestic rules. The reason for this new tool is to allow a more careful analysis of the impact of EU legislation on the Italian legal order 'with obvious benefit both in the phases of negotiation and implementation and transposition of EU obligation'.[28]

According to article 6, paragraph 4 of Law No 234/2012, the report of the competent administration needed to contain three main elements: a) the analysis of the draft in light of the principles of conferral, subsidiarity and proportionality; b) an assessment of the draft taking into consideration its perspectives of the EU negotiations; and c) the financial and legal impact of the draft. Oddly, these reports, although 'used and often quoted in the reasoned opinions expressed within' the Early Warning System, 'are not always published in parliamentary proceedings'.[29]

The new provisions tried to empower the Chambers in the formation process of the Italian position by strengthening the Government's duties to inform the Chambers[30] and introduced a better specification of the conditions needed for Parliament to invoke its reservation of scrutiny.[31]

With specific regard to the 'descending phase', Law No 234/2012 divides the previous 'Annual Community Law' into two separate legislative instruments: the annual 'European Law' ('legge europea') and 'European Delegation Law' ('legge di delegazione europea').

The 'European Delegation Law'—which is introduced by the Government by 28 February each year—provides for a parliamentary law of delegation to the Government to implement European directives. If necessary, a further law of delegation may be introduced by 31 July of each year.[32]

Meanwhile, the Annual European Law contains the amendments to current domestic laws which are necessary in consideration of pending infringement proceedings, rulings of the Court of Justice and the necessity to implement other EU acts. Unlike the 'European Delegation Law', the Annual European Law does not have a predetermined timeline for submission and approval. Thus, the previous 'Annual Community Law' was not only 'doubled' but also 'lightened', making transposition and implementation more timely and effective.[33]

The evaluation of the new provisions is controversial: according to some authors, the experience of the first years of application shows the further strengthening of the Government's role in the 'descending phase'. Indeed, Law No 234/2012 would seem to focus all the efforts on the individuation of tools able to solve the problem of the chronic delay

[28] P Falletta and N Lupo, 'Mechanism for Implementing EU Law at State Level' in G Di Cosimo (ed), *Implementing EU Environmental Law in Italy* (The Hague, Eleven International Publishing, 2013) 23 ff.

[29] N Lupo, 'The Scrutiny of the Principle of Subsidiarity in the Procedures and Reasoned Opinions of the Italian Chamber and Senate' in A Jonsson Cornell and M Goldoni (eds), *National and Regional Parliaments in the EU-legislative Procedure post-Lisbon: The Impact of the Early Warning Mechanism* (Oxford, Hart Publishing, 2017).

[30] For example, art 4, para 2 of the Law No 234/2012 introduces the duty of the Government to inform promptly the Chambers about the initiatives related to the Common Security and Defense Policy submitted to the Council. Relevant are also the 'informative rights' established by art 17 with regard to the appointment of Italian member in the EU institutions.

[31] In particular, the term for the activation of the parliamentary scrutiny reservation has been increased to 30 days.

[32] In conjunction with 'European Delegation Law', the Government shall introduce before Parliament a Yearly Report on the development of the European integration process, Italy's participation in the European law-making process and the implementation of economic and social cohesion policies.

[33] See L Bartolucci, 'Legge di delegazione europea e Legge europea: obiettivi e risultati di una prima volta' (2014) *Amministrazione in Cammino* 3; M Rosini, Legge di delegazione europea e Legge europea (Napoli, ESI, 2017).

in the implementation of EU law.[34] Conversely, other scholarship emphasises the innovations introduced in 2012 especially regarding the 'ascending phase' and considers Law No 234/2012 to be one of the most important legislative reforms adopted in recent years.[35]

VI. The Perspectives of Reform

As seen, with the exception of Article 117.5 of the Constitution, the dynamics of the relationship between Parliament and Government within the 'ascending' and 'descending' phases continue to move within the context of a substantial absence of a constitutional basis. Therefore, in the current legal framework, Italian participation in the formation and implementation of EU law finds its points of reference only in the ordinary legislation.

This scenario did not change after the constitutional referendum of 2016. Adopting the model of 'asymmetrical bicameralism', the constitutional bill approved in the same year by Parliament tried, inter alia, to strengthen the 'Europeanisation' of the second Chamber,[36] in particular establishing that the Senate 'participate in the decisions directed at the formation and implementation of the legal acts and policies of the European Union'.[37] Moreover, in the framework of the new asymmetrical bicameralism, the constitutional bill tried to introduce a specific exception to the principle of the prevalence of the House within the legislative process. Indeed, under the reform, both Houses would collectively exercise the legislative function for the law containing the general norms, the procedures and the terms of Italian participation in the formation and implementation of EU law. The involvement of the Regional Assemblies in the election of senators aimed to connect the autonomies and the state through the Senate in both the 'ascending' and 'descending' phases. However, on December 4, 59 per cent of voters rejected the proposed constitutional bill.

Another 'frontline' of the processes of institutional reform is the revision of the parliamentary Rules of Procedure. The original proposal of amendments to the Chamber of Deputies Rules of Procedure[38] seems to look more 'backward' rather than 'forward'. It codifies the 'experimental' procedures introduced in 2009, but it fails to exploit all the new 'European powers' that the Treaty of Lisbon recognised for the national parliaments. This is the case, for example, with the power established by article 8 of Protocol No 2, which requests that the Government notify the infringement of the principle of subsidiarity on behalf of

[34] This is the position of F Scuto, 'L'evoluzione nel rapporto Parlamento-Governo nella formazione e nell'attuazione della normativa e delle politiche dell'Unione europea' (2015) 1 *Rivista AIC* 41.

[35] For this perspective, see Esposito, above n 23.

[36] P Guasti, 'The Europeanisation of Parliaments in Central and Eastern Europe' (2011) 11 *RECON online Working Paper*, available at www.reconproject.eu/projectweb/portalproject/RECONWorkingPapers.html; P Kiiver, *The Early Warning System for the Principle of Subsidiarity. Constitutional theory and empirical reality* (London and New York, Routledge, 2012); R de Ruiter, 'Houses of Abstention or Houses of Reflection? Upper Houses in EU Member States and the Ex ante Scrutiny of EU Legislation' (2015) 3 *Journal of European Integration* 37.

[37] Art 55, para 5 as modified in the constitutional draft rejected in the referendum of 4 December 2016.

[38] About the original proposal of amendments to the Chamber of Deputies Rules of Procedure, see the special edition of the *Osservatorio sulle fonti.it* (vol 3, 2014) with essays of Nicola Lupo, Luca Bartolucci-Cristina Fasone, Renato Ibrido, Elena Griglio, Giovanni Piccirilli, Piero Gambale, Giovanna Perniciaro and in particular the essay of L Bartolucci and C Fasone, 'Le procedure di raccordo con l'Unione europea: un bilancio in attivo, ma con qualche occasione persa', at http://www.osservatoriosullefonti.it/mobile-saggi/speciali/revisione-dei-regolamenti-parlamentari-1-2014/693-osf-1-2014-bartolucci-fasone-speciale.

the national Parliament.[39] But this is also the case of the national parliaments' veto power within the 'simplified revision procedures' established by Articles 42 Treaty on European Union (TEU), 48(7) TEU, 81(3) Treaty on the Functioning of the European Union (TFEU), and 311 TFEU.

The proposal of amendments introduces, moreover, a special parliamentary European session. The business of the House and the Committees during the 45 days of this session shall be planned in a way to allow consideration of the 'European Delegation Law' to be completed within the set time limit, within 10 days from the conclusion of the Committee's work acting in a reporting capacity.

This innovation, although aiming to guarantee a timely approval of the 'European Delegation Law', also seems to look 'backward', however. Indeed, this procedure, which follows and imitates the model of the budgetary session, again reflects the idea of a rigid separation between the 'descending' and 'ascending' phases. Instead, as already noted, if the link between Parliament and the European Union today should be continuous and uninterrupted—representing a routine dimension of the actions of national institutions—the session model is inadequate.[40]

VII. Towards a Conclusion

In the comparative law, Italy is the only country which knows the distinction between 'descending' and 'ascending' phases. Indeed, with the exception of some Spanish authors who have directly dialogued with the Italian scholarship,[41] these categories have not influenced the European debate about the integration process in a significant way.

From a descriptive point of view, the dichotomy of the 'ascending' and 'descending' phases may have some utility: it allows greater clarity for understanding the organisation of the processes of formation and implementation of EU law, which is particularly useful for teaching purposes. Second, the structure of Law No 234/2012 continues to reflect the idea of the existence of two different phases and therefore offers a formalistic argument in favour of the use of these concepts.

At the same time, this distinction risks muddling and 'misleading': the decision-making process—both national and European—tends to be continuous and uninterrupted, with a constant maintenance and correction of the rules just entered into force.[42]

[39] According to art 8 of Protocol No 2 'The Court of Justice of the European Union shall have jurisdiction in actions on grounds of infringement of the principle of subsidiarity by a legislative act, brought in accordance with the rules laid down in Article 263 of the Treaty on the Functioning of the European Union by Member States, or notified by them in accordance with their legal order on behalf of their national Parliament or a chamber thereof'.

[40] Lupo, 'I Parlamenti nazionali nell'Unione europea e il principio di sussidiarietà: qualche suggestione per la Camera dei deputati', above n 9, notably 13.

[41] For example see J Tuñón, '¿Cómo las regiones influyen en el proceso decisional comunitario? Mecanismos de activación ascendente de las entidades sub-estales europeas' (2008) 17 *UNISCI Discussion Papers* 151; JA González-Aurioles, 'El federalismo alemán ante la integración europea' (2006) 6 *Revista de Derecho constitutional europeo* 195 ff.

[42] Lupo, 'L'adeguamento del sistema istituzionale italiano al Trattato di Lisbona. Osservazioni sui disegni di legge di riforma della legge n 11 del 2005', above n 9, notably 2. Moreover, see V Lippolis, 'L'adeguamento dell'ordinamento italiano all'ordinamento comunitario' (2006) *Scienza e tecnica della legislazione. Lezioni* 303 ff; V Lippolis, 'Il Parlamento nazional-comunitario' (1991) *Quaderni costituzionali* 319 ff.

The difficulties in implementing EU Law through the old 'Community law' can be traced back to the insufficient participation of the Parliament in the 'ascending phase'. Indeed, an inadequate participation in the formation of EU law entails that very often the national bodies find themselves in the situation of scrutinising EU arrangements without the ability to value in advance the problems of compatibility with the domestic legal order.[43]

As already noticed, 'it is probably no coincidence that since 2005 parliamentary scrutiny of EU draft legislation has gradually increased and, at the same time, the number of infringement procedures against Italy has gradually reduced to almost half.'[44] Indeed, this empirical element confirms that the most effective way to guarantee a full implementation and a correct transposition of EU law is the strength of the coordination between the Chambers and the Government and thus the increasing participation of Parliament in the formation of the Italian position in Europe. In other words, the so-called 'descending phase' 'would appear "less dramatic"' if 'the main political issues and the administrative ties would already be spotted and debated' in Parliaments.[45]

In conclusion, the dichotomy between the 'ascending' and 'descending' phases, reflecting a certain rigidity in the research methodology employed by Italian constitutional law scholars, exemplifies many of the particularities of the Italian approach to European studies. After all, while in other Member States, especially in the most Euro-skeptical countries, EU law implementation has always been a relevant matter in the national political agenda, in the culture of the Italian Parliament the compliance with EU Law for a long time has been considered to be a technical topic and a bureaucratic question. Paradoxically, the higher degree of consensus of the European integration process in the Italian public opinion led to the downgrade of the political dimension of the European affairs.[46] It is probably in this cultural 'mood' that the Italian scholarship developed its studies on the implementation of EU law with a perspective more oriented to the 'efficiency' of domestic parliamentary procedures concerning the EU than to the analysis of the relationships between the 'limitation' and 'legitimacy' of power.[47] Summarising the schematic but oversimplified representation of the dynamics of the European decision-making process contained in the use of the 'ascending' and 'descending' phases we could probably borrow the title of Max Frish's famous work: 'nostalgia for geometry'.[48]

[43] A Celotto, 'L'esperienza applicativa della legge comunitaria' in A Vignudelli (ed), *Istituzioni e dinamiche del diritto. I confini mobili della separazione dei poteri* (Milan, Giuffrè, 2009) 77 ff and notably 82.

[44] Falletta and Lupo, above n 28, notably 33.

[45] Falletta and Lupo, ibid.

[46] For an overview of the positions of Italian political parties towards the European integration process, see F Bindi, *Italy and the European Union* (Washington, Brookings Institution Press, 2011) 65 ff.

[47] On the relationship between the 'limitation' and 'legitimacy' of power, see Ridola, above n 5, 3 ff.

[48] M Frisch, 'Don Juan or The Love of Geometry' in O Mandel (ed), *The Theatre of Don Juan: A Collection of Plays and Views, 1630–1963* (Lincoln, University of Nebraska Press, 1986).

4

The Evolution of Italian Representation in the European Parliament: Electoral Laws, Systemic Effects and MPs' Characteristics

ALESSANDRO CHIARAMONTE, LORENZO DE SIO AND VINCENZO EMANUELE[1]

I. Introduction

This chapter focuses on the Italian electoral legislation for the European Parliament (hereinafter, EP) elections and on its political consequences. As highlighted by a very rich literature, electoral laws are fundamental institutional variables that provide a set of incentives and constraints that influence voters' behaviour and the competitive strategies of political actors. This process leads, in turn, to important consequences occurring both at the systemic level (the features of the party system) and at the individual level (the characteristics of the members of Parliament).[2]

Since the first EP election in 1979, the Italian electoral law has experienced relatively limited modifications, which have not changed its basic structure. However, this chapter

[1] The authors wish to thank Luca Verzichelli and all at CIRCAP (Centre for the Study of Political Change—University of Siena) for kindly providing the data on Italian MEPs used in s 3.

[2] The literature on the effects of electoral systems is extremely rich and complex. See in general M Duverger, *Political Parties* (Wiley, New York, 1954); G Sartori, *Comparative Constitutional Engineering. An Inquiry into Structures, Incentives and Outcomes* (London, MacMillan, 1994); A Lijphart, *Electoral Systems and Party Systems: A Study of Twenty-seven Democracies, 1945–1990* (Oxford, Oxford University Press, 1994); GW Cox, *Making Votes Count. Strategic Coordination in the World's Electoral Systems* (Cambridge, Cambridge University Press, 1997); M Gallagher and P Mitchell (eds), *The Politics of Electoral Systems* (Oxford, Oxford University Press, 2008).

will show how, in interaction with the changing structure of the party system, even minor modifications have produced significant effects.

The chapter consists of three parts. The first part provides a historical overview of the Italian electoral legislation for the EP. It explores the evolution of the electoral rules since the introduction of a proportional formula at the time of the EP's first direct election in 1979 up to the most recent changes taking place in the last years (national electoral threshold, gender preferences, abolition of the 'double mandate' and so on). The second part puts Italy in a comparative perspective, offering a synthetic cross-section analysis of the 28 Member States' electoral systems for the EP. Finally, the third part focuses on the effects of the Italian electoral law on political representation, considered in terms of systemic properties (number and size of parties, effective thresholds, territorial representation) and of Members of European Parliament's (MEPs) individual characteristics (mainly in terms of gender). Conclusions follow.

II. The Electoral Law for the Election of the Italian Members of the European Parliament

The election of Italian representatives in the EP is based on the Law No 18 of 24 January 1979 and its subsequent modifications and integrations. Its main features, and how they have changed over time, are here analysed according to the following dimensions: the number of representatives to be elected in the EP; the number and design of districts; the rules for running lists and candidates; the incompatibilities with the office of Member of European Parliament (MEP); the voting requirements and the ballot structure; and, finally, the electoral formula, ie how votes are converted into seats.

A. Number of Representatives

The number of Italian representatives in the EP has varied following the changes that have occurred in the membership and in the apportionment method (see Table 1). It was 81 for the first three elections and 87 in 1994 and 1999, then it went down to 78 in 2004 and to 72 in 2009. When the Lisbon Treaty apportionment rules have been applied transitionally in 2011 and for the first election in 2014, the number of Italian representatives to be elected to the EP has increased from 72 to 73.[3]

[3] The Lisbon Treaty states that the European Parliament is composed of 750 members, plus the President, bringing the total from 736 up to 751, and that the allocation of seats follows the principle of degressive proportionality, with a minimum threshold of six members and a maximum threshold of 96 members per Member State. Under the Decision No 2062 of 25 November 2009, the European Parliament has amended the protocol (no 36) on the transitional provisions and provided for the assignment of additional seats among the Member States. The new procedure, allowing one additional seat to be given to Italy, was ratified by the Italian Parliament with the Law No 2 of 2011. On the details of these aspects, see F Fabbrini, 'La composizione del Parlamento Europeo dopo il Trattato di Lisbona' (2011) 3 *Rivista Trimestrale di Diritto Pubblico* 859–74.

Table 1: The number of Italian representatives elected to the European Parliament (1979–2014)

	Election							
	1979	1984	1989	1994	1999	2004	2009[a]	2014
Number of Italian representatives	81	81	81	87	87	78	72	73

Notes:

[a] One additional seat was given to Italy following an amendment to the Lisbon Treaty and was assigned on the basis of the Law No 2 of 14 January 2011.

B. Districts

For the purpose of the presentation of party lists and the election of candidates, the national territory is divided up into five districts: North-West (consisting of the following regions: Aosta Valley, Piedmont, Lombardy, Liguria), North-East (Trentino-South Tirol, Friuli-Venezia Giulia, Veneto, Emilia Romagna), Centre (Tuscany, Umbria, Marche, Lazio), South (Abruzzo, Molise, Campania, Basilicata, Apulia, Calabria), Islands (Sardinia, Sicily).

C. Party Lists and Candidates

Lists of candidates have to be supported in each district by the signatures of no fewer than 30,000 and no more than 35,000 voters, provided that the signatures gathered in each region of the same district account for at least 10 per cent of the total number. No support is required for party lists: 1) that correspond to an existing group in the Italian Parliament; 2) that have won at least one seat in the latest election of either the two Chambers or of the EP running with their own symbol; 3) whose symbol contains the one of a party exempted.

The lists of candidates representing the French minority in the Aosta Valley, the German minority in the province of Bozen, and the Slovenian minority of the Friuli-Venezia Giulia may link to one national list in their respective districts for the purpose of seats allocation.

Candidates must be at least 25 years old[4] and accept to present themselves by a written declaration.

Since 2004, the lists of candidates have to comply with the rules on equal opportunities. Under the Law No 90 of 8 April 2004, each district list has to include at least one third of candidates belonging to the least represented gender, otherwise the due financial contribution is reduced of an extent proportional to the gender underrepresentation. New and more effective rules for the purpose of gender equality have been introduced by the Law No 65 of 22 April 2014, which, starting with the 2019 election, provides for the exclusion of lists not containing an equal number of candidates of both gender and whose top two rank ordered candidates are not of different gender.

[4] Note that the same age limit applies to the election of the Chamber of Deputies as set by the Constitution (art 56).

D. Incompatibilities

According to articles 5 and 6 of the Law No 18 of 24 January 1979, as amended by the Law No 9 of 18 January 1989, and by the Law No 78 of 27 March 2004—this latter implementing Council decision 2002/772/EC that prohibited the 'dual mandate'—and by the Law No 90 of 8 April 2004, the office of MEP is not compatible with a number of posts, among which are those of Deputy or Senator, member of the national Government, President of region, member of the Regional Government, member of regional Council, President of Province, or Mayor of a municipality with more than 15,000 inhabitants. Notwithstanding the incompatibilities, the persons in these posts may stand as a candidate for EP, and inasmuch as they are elected they have up to 30 days to choose which office to retain.

E. Voters and Votes

All Italian citizens who are at least 18 years old are entitled to vote. Citizens from other EU Member States can also vote, if registered in the electoral roll of their place of residence in Italy at least 90 days before the polling day. Furthermore, the electoral law as amended by the Decree-Law No 408 of 24 June 1994 allows: 1) Italian citizens residing in an EU Member State and enrolled in the AIRE (the Registry of Italians residing abroad), and, upon request, 2) Italian citizens and their relatives living together, who are temporarily in an EU Member State for study or business purposes, to vote abroad for the Italian MEPs.

In each district, voters can express their list vote for one of the competing party lists, each of them being characterised by a distinctive symbol on the ballot paper. They may also cast preferential votes for candidates belonging to the party list that they have chosen. Until the election of 1999, the maximum number of preference votes was dependent on the size of the district: it was three for North-West, two for North-East, Centre and South, and one for Islands.[5] The maximum number of preference votes that voters can express has been modified by the Law No 90 of 8 April 2004 and has since then become three for every district. Under the Law No 65 of 22 April 2014, starting with the election of 2014 voters who cast more than one preference vote are obliged to choose candidates of both gender, otherwise the second and third preference votes are declared as void.

F. From Votes to Seats

As for the procedure through which votes are translated into seats, the electoral law for the Italian MEPs provides for the application of a proportional representation system. Seats are distributed among the parties[6] in proportion to the total number of votes polled by them at the national level (upper distribution). However, since the introduction of the

[5] Until the 1999 election voters could express only one preference vote also when voting for party lists representing linguistic minorities linked to national parties.

[6] If there are party lists representing linguistic minorities linked to national parties, in the first instance these groups of parties take part as a whole in the distribution of seats. Then, seats assigned to groups of parties are proportionally allotted among their component party lists at the district level.

Law No 10 of 20 February 2009, only those parties that have succeeded in surmounting the four per cent threshold in the entire country are considered.

The mathematical formula for allocating seats is the largest remainders-Hare quota system. First, the total number of votes cast for parties surmounting the threshold is divided by the total number of seats to be assigned. The result of this calculation represents the (Hare) quota. Second, the total number of votes obtained by each party is divided by the quota and each party receives one seat for each whole number resulting from this calculation. Third, the remaining seats are assigned to the parties in the descending sequence of the largest reminders until all seats are allocated.

After the number of seats due to each party has been established, seats are distributed, separately for each party, among the five multi-member districts (lower distribution). A second calculation is therefore made, again according to the largest remainders-Hare quota system, to determine the total number of seats for each party at national level to be distributed among their district lists. Thus, for each party the numbers of votes of its district lists are divided by the quota, ie the total number of votes cast for the party divided by the number of seats assigned to it in the upper distribution. Each district list is then attributed a number of seats equal to whole number resulting from this calculation and possibly one additional seat through the largest reminders method.

For each district list there is thus elected a number of candidates equivalent to the number of seats assigned to it. Candidates are elected according to the order of their individual preference votes.

The way the lower distribution of seats works has changed in recent times following the ruling of 13 May 2011 (so called 'Gargani ruling')[7] by the Consiglio di Stato, the highest jurisdictional body on administrative matters. According to this ruling, the procedure for allocating seats under the Law No 18 of 24 January 1979 as amended by the Law No 10 of 20 February 2009 has since then changed and now it does not allow districts to return a number of elected representatives larger or smaller than the number of seats due to them on the basis of their population.

This phenomenon is known as *slittamento* (seats 'slipping') and has occurred in all Italian elections for the EP up to 2009, though to a different extent. As can be seen in Table 2, the number of 'slipped' seats goes from a minimum of two in 1984 to a maximum of seven in 1994. Moreover, the districts of South and Islands have always been penalised, obtaining fewer seats than expected on the basis of their population, while the opposite has happened for the remaining districts, who have often obtained more seats. This is due to the difference in turnout among the districts: the comparatively higher the turnout is—usually in the Centre and in the North of Italy—the more likely it is for a district to gain extra seats, 'stealing' them from the districts in Southern Italy with a lower turnout.

In 2011, the Consiglio di Stato not only ruled out the possibility of seat slipping, but also replaced de facto the norms on the lower distribution of seats with those of the electoral law for the Chamber of deputies then in force (DPR No 361 of 30 March 1957 as amended in 2005 by the Law No 270), on the consideration that the latter are built so as to ensure that every district in the end receives the number of seats due to it on the basis of its population. The new method has been utilised for the first time to retrospectively

[7] On the basis of this ruling the previously elected MEP Collino was replaced by Gargani.

correct the distribution of seats at the district level of the 2009 election and then in the 2014 election.

Table 2: The 'slipping' of seats across districts in the Italian elections for the European Parliament

Districts	Election							
	1979[a]	1984	1989	1994	1999	2004	2009	2014
Number of seats due based on population								
I—North-West	–	22	22	23	23	20	19	20
II—North-East	–	15	15	16	16	15	13	14
III—Center	–	16	16	17	17	15	14	14
IV—South	–	19	19	21	21	19	18	17
V—Islands	–	9	9	10	10	9	8	8
Number of seats allocated								
I—North-West	25	23	25	25	26	23	21	20
II—North-East	17	15	17	18	16	15	15	14
III—Center	17	17	16	20	18	16	15	14
IV—South	15	18	16	16	21	17	15	17
V—Islands	7	8	7	8	6	7	6	8
Number of 'slipped' seats								
I—North-West	–	+1	+3	+2	+3	+3	+2	0
II—North-East	–	0	+2	+2	0	0	+2	0
III—Center	–	+1	0	+3	+1	+1	+1	0
IV—South	–	−1	−3	−5	0	−2	−3	0
V—Islands	–	−1	−2	−2	−4	−2	−2	0
Total number of 'slipped' seats	–	2	5	7	4	4	5	0

Notes:

[a] In the 1979 election there are no (pre-) allocated seats to each district on the basis of their population. Therefore, there is not a formal 'slipping' of seats for this election.

III. How (Dis)proportional? The Italian Electoral Law in a Comparative Perspective

Having analysed the features of the Italian electoral legislation for the EP and its most relevant changes since 1979, it is worth enlarging the scope of the current analysis by putting Italy in a comparative perspective. How do the characteristics of the Italian electoral law for the EP discussed above stand in comparison with those of the other 27 European Union (EU) countries? Moreover, by considering features like the average district magnitude and the legal thresholds for representation, how disproportional—namely, how deviating from perfect proportionality in terms of transformation of votes into seats—is the Italian electoral law in a comparative perspective? The purpose of this paragraph is to offer a synthetic cross-section analysis of the 28 Member States' electoral systems for the EP.

With a decision of the Council (772/2002) approved by the EP in May 2002—amending the Act concerning the election of the representatives of the European Parliament by direct universal suffrage, annexed to the Council Decision 787/1976[8]—the EU has introduced some common principles to harmonise the elections for the EP, previously regulated under the jurisdiction of the Member States. Undertaking this decision the EU has established that the MEPs have to be elected with a system of proportional representation, using either the party list vote or the single transferable vote system. Member States may decide the adoption of an electoral threshold, albeit inferior to five per cent on a national basis. Member States can also decide if and how to split the national territory into different electoral districts for the allocation of seats, although this cannot generally affect the proportional nature of the voting system. Based on these general principles, the electoral systems in the 28 Member States have become more homogenous than in the past, albeit such principles have left a margin of manoeuvre for discretionary measures of the Member States. Apart from the number of electoral districts and the adoption of an election threshold, Member States are allowed to decide on the age of eligible voters and candidates, on the electoral formula (namely, the mechanism transforming votes into seats), on the election method of single deputies and on the presence of sanctions for eligible voters who decide to abstain. Table 3 offers a comprehensive overview of the main features of the electoral system for the EP in the 28 Member States. The overall picture is that of a proportional system with 28 national variants. This produces a range of formulas and election thresholds that in turn offer different incentives and constraints in the various national contexts.

Starting from the electoral rules that precede the features of the electoral system properly speaking, as we can see from Table 3, the minimum age to become an eligible voter is 18 in all countries with the exception of Austria, where voting age is 16. Greater variability can be observed for the minimum age of candidates: Italy, together with Cyprus and Greece, emerges as the country with the most restrictive rule (25 years). All the other countries have set a lower age of candidacy, granting eligibility for candidates at the age of 23 (Romania), 21 (Belgium, Ireland and the majority of Central and Eastern European countries), or even 18 (15 countries, among which are France, Germany, the Netherlands, Spain and Sweden). Moreover, in four countries (Belgium, Cyprus, Greece and Luxembourg) voting is compulsory, although any formal sanction is not applied, with the exception of Luxembourg. Here, abstainers receive a fine between 100€ and 250€ in case of first offence, while for repeat offenders the fine is increased up to 500€–1000€.

[8] This Act introduced the direct universal suffrage for the election of the Members of the European Parliament (now incorporated in the EC Treaty, art 190, para 1), following a provision included in the founding Treaties. In 1992, the Maastricht Treaty inserted a provision into the EC Treaty (art 190 para 4) stating that elections must be held in accordance with a uniform procedure in all Member States and Parliament should draw up a proposal to this effect, for unanimous adoption by the Council. However, the Council was unable to agree on a uniform procedure, in spite of the various proposals presented by Parliament. To resolve this deadlock, the Treaty of Amsterdam introduced into the EC Treaty the possibility, failing a uniform procedure, of 'common principles' with a view to enhancing the democratic legitimacy of the EP and the feeling of being a citizen of the European Union. On this basis it was possible to modify the 1976 Act by Council Decision 772/2002.

Table 3: Electoral system's features for the election of the EP in the 28 EU Member States

Country	Eligible voters	Eligible candidates	Compulsory vote	N seats	N electoral districts	Average M	Electoral formula	Election threshold	Election of single deputies
Austria	16	18	NO	18	1	18	D'Hondt	4%	Preferential voting
Belgium	18	21	YES	21	3	7	D'Hondt	NO	Preferential voting
Bulgaria	18	21	NO	17	1	17	Hare	NO	Preferential voting
Cyprus	18	25	YES	6	1	6	Hare	1.8%	Preferential voting
Croatia	18	18	NO	11	1	11	D'Hondt	5%	Preferential voting
Czech Republic	18	21	NO	21	1	21	D'Hondt	5%	Preferential voting
Denmark	18	18	NO	13	1	13	D'Hondt	NO	Preferential voting
Estonia	18	21	NO	6	1	6	D'Hondt	NO	Preferential voting
Finland	18	18	NO	13	1	13	D'Hondt	NO	Preferential voting
France	18	18	NO	74	8	9.25	D'Hondt	5%	Closed list
Germany	18	18	NO	96	1	96	Sainte-Laguë/Schepers	NO	Closed list
Greece	18	25	YES	21	1	21	Droop	3%	Closed list
Hungary	18	18	NO	21	1	21	D'Hondt	5%	Closed list
Ireland	18	21	NO	11	4	2.75	STV	NO	STV
Italy	**18**	**25**	NO	**73**	**5**	**73***	**Hare**	**4%**	**Preferential voting**
Latvia	18	21	NO	8	1	8	Sainte-Laguë	5%	Preferential voting
Lithuania	18	21	NO	11	1	11	Hagenbach-Bischoff	5%	Preferential voting
Luxembourg	18	18	YES	6	1	6	D'Hondt	NO	Preferential voting

(continued)

Table 3: ***(Continued)***

Country	Eligible voters	Eligible candidates	Compulsory vote	N seats	N electoral districts	Average M	Electoral formula	Election threshold	Election of single deputies
Malta	18	18	NO	6	1	6	STV	NO	STV
Netherlands	18	18	NO	26	1	26	D'Hondt	NO	Preferential voting
Poland	18	21	NO	51	13	3.92	D'Hondt	5%	Preferential voting
Portugal	18	18	NO	21	1	21	D'Hondt	NO	Closed list
Romania	18	23	NO	32	1	32	D'Hondt	5%	Closed list
Slovakia	18	21	NO	13	1	13	Hagenbach-Bischoff	5%	Preferential voting
Slovenia	18	18	NO	8	1	8	D'Hondt	NO	Preferential voting
Spain	18	18	NO	54	1	54	D'Hondt	NO	Closed list
Sweden	18	18	NO	20	1	20	Sainte-Laguë	4%	Preferential voting
UK	18	18	NO	73	12	6.08	D'Hondt**	NO	Closed list

* In Italy seats are allocated at the national level.
** The system adopted in the electoral district of Northern Ireland is the single transferable vote (STV).

Besides the different eligibility criteria for voters and candidates and the rules on compulsory voting, the most interesting differences of voting systems refer to the features of the electoral system, namely, the number of available seats, the number of electoral districts, the electoral formula and the election threshold. These elements have an influence on the competitive strategies of political actors as well as on voters' behaviour (these are the so-called 'psychological effects'), further than clearly affecting the transformation of the votes cast by the electorate into seats (the so-called 'mechanical effects').[9] In the vast majority of EU Member States representatives are elected within a unique national electoral district. Exceptions are represented by some large countries such as the United Kingdom, France and Poland, and by two small but culturally heterogeneous countries such as Belgium and Ireland, where seats are allocated through various electoral districts to protect local representativeness. As we have stated in the previous section, Italy has five districts, but they are only used to select the MEPs, while the allocation of seats is computed at the national level. Table 3 further reports the average district magnitude (M) in each country. This value is the ratio between the total available seats and the number of electoral districts (here to be meant as the territorial units where the allocation of seats takes place). There is a rather high degree of variability in the average value of M, as it ranges between 2.75, registered in Ireland, where 11 seats are allocated in four electoral districts, and 96, computed in Germany. With 73 deputies elected in a unique national district, Italy appears as the country with the second highest average district magnitude in Europe.

An additional difference can be detected in the electoral formulas. The most diffused mechanism of transformation of votes into seats is the highest averages method, and specifically the D'Hondt method, used in 17 countries, while the more proportional variant of the Sainte-Laguë method is adopted in three countries (Germany, Latvia and Sweden).[10] Italy belongs to the small group of countries adopting a largest remainder method: besides Italy, the classic Hare quota method is adopted in Bulgaria and Cyprus, while the more distortive variants of Hagenbach-Bischoff and Droop are adopted in Lithuania, Slovakia and Greece; finally, Ireland and Malta adopt the Single Transferable Vote (STV), a method used in their general elections as well. Only half of the countries have introduced a legal election threshold, generally set at five per cent (nine cases)[11] or in fewer cases four per cent (Austria, Italy and Sweden), three per cent (Greece), or 1.8 per cent (Cyprus). As regards the selection of candidates, about two thirds (18 out of 28) of the countries introduced a preference vote in their system, although following different specific procedures (for instance, open list in Italy, flexible list in Austria, or even *panachage* in Luxembourg), while eight countries vote with closed-list (in which the order of elected candidates is decided by party officials).

Given the abovementioned features, it is possible to categorise the 28 electoral systems in terms of expected disproportionality[12] regarding the transformation of votes into seats, so as to understand how Italy stands in comparative perspective. The electoral system represents a crucial variable influencing the party systems and its competitive dynamics.

[9] On the difference between psychological and mechanical effects, see Duverger, above n 2 and Cox, above n 2.

[10] On the functioning of the different electoral formulas, see Lijphart, above n 2.

[11] In France the election threshold of five per cent is applied at the district level. The other eight countries are Central and Eastern European Member States, where the five per cent threshold has the purpose to limit the excessive party system fragmentation detectable in the post-communist party systems.

[12] See M Gallagher, 'Proportionality, Disproportionality and Electoral Systems' (1991) 10 *Electoral Studies* 33–51.

A relatively disproportional system will tend to over-represent larger parties and under-represent smaller ones. As a consequence, these incentives will promote strategic behaviours both on the supply side (creation of electoral cartels and mergers among small parties) and on the demand side (voters will tend not to support small parties and prefer suboptimal political options with concrete possibilities of winning seats). In order to do so, we need to rely on a quantitative criterion that allows for cross-national comparisons. Therefore, our starting point can be represented by the concept (and the related formula) of *effective threshold*, formulated for the first time by Lijphart[13] and later refined by Taagepera.[14] The concept of effective threshold derives from the need to put in comparison countries where a legal threshold is imposed to parties in order to gain representation, with countries where there are no explicit thresholds but nonetheless where their electoral system imposes an implicit threshold, based mainly on district magnitude (ie the lower the district magnitude the higher the implicit threshold). The formula is the following: *effective threshold = 75%/ M+1*, where M is district magnitude.[15] The rationale is that the formula is approximately midway between the threshold of representation (the lowest level of support with which a party could win a seat under the most favourable conditions) and the threshold of exclusion (the highest level of support with which a party could fail to win a seat under the most unfavourable conditions). Obviously, our comparison also needs to take into account the effect of the legal threshold, if any: as a consequence, when the implicit threshold granted by district magnitude is higher than the legal threshold, this latter has no consequence, and the effective threshold is given exclusively by the abovementioned formula; on the contrary, when the legal threshold is higher than the implicit one, the effective threshold equals the legal one.

Based on these considerations, we have built a 5-point scale classification of the 28 electoral systems for the EP, according to their expected level of disproportionality granted by the respective effective threshold of representation.

Table 4: A classification of the 28 electoral systems for the EP based on their expected level of disproportionality

Expected disproportionality (Effective threshold)				
Very high (>15)	**High (10.1–15)**	**Average (5.1–10)**	**Low (2.5–5)**	**Very Low (<2.5)**
Ireland (20)	Cyprus (10.7)	Belgium (9.4)	Czech Republic (5)	Spain (1.4)
Poland (15.2)	Estonia (10.7)	Latvia (8.3)	Hungary (5)	Germany (0.8)
	Luxembourg (10.7)	Slovenia (8.3)	Romania (5)	
	Malta (10.7)	France (7.3)	Bulgaria (4.2)	
	UK (10.6)	Croatia (6.3)	Austria (4)	

(continued)

[13] Lijphart, above n 2.

[14] R Taagepera, 'Effective Magnitude and Effective Threshold' (1998) 17 *Electoral Studies* 393–404.

[15] Gallagher and Mitchell propose a different formula: M * (1 + log(E)), where M is average district magnitude and E is the number of districts (Gallagher and Mitchell, above n 2). Taagepera further refines its previous formula: $75\%/[(M+1)(S/M)^{0.5}]$, where M is average district magnitude and S is the number of seats to be allocated nationwide (R Taagepera, 'Nationwide Threshold of Representation' (2002) 21 *Electoral Studies* 383–401. We have decided not to use these more complicated formulas but only the original one, which is certainly more intuitive.

Table 4: ***(Continued)***

Expected disproportionality (Effective threshold)				
Very high (>15)	**High (10.1–15)**	**Average (5.1–10)**	**Low (2.5–5)**	**Very Low (<2.5)**
		Lithuania (6.3)	**Italy (4)**	
		Denmark (5.4)	Sweden (4)	
		Finland (5.4)	Greece (3.4)	
		Slovakia (5.4)	Portugal (3.4)	
			Netherlands (2.8)	

Source: authors' elaboration based on the method of calculation developed by Lijphart[16] and Taagepera.[17]

As one can see by looking at Table 4, there is a wide variability among the 28 EU Member States as regards their effective threshold of representation. The variable ranges from the extremely low level of Germany (0.8)—an almost purely proportional system where 96 deputies are elected in a unique electoral district without a legal threshold[18]—to the dramatic disproportionality of Ireland (20) where, given the very small district magnitude (2.75), a party needs to receive about 20 per cent of the national share to secure a representation in the EP. Overall, the average effective threshold in the sample is 6.9 per cent, which means that, on average, a party gains seats in the EP if it casts about seven per cent of the votes in its country. This means that the average effective threshold is higher than the maximum legal threshold of five per cent provided by the Council decision (772/2002): as many as 16 out of 28 countries show an effective threshold higher than five per cent. For many small countries this is an unavoidable consequence of the small number of representatives they elect to the European Parliament, while for some larger countries (Poland, UK, France) this is due to the legislator's choice as regards the number of electoral districts where seats are allocated (see again Table 3). Note that Western European countries (EU-15) display a lower expected disproportionality compared to their Central and Eastern European counterparts (6.2 versus 7.8), where no party with four per cent of the votes or less can have access to the EP (the lower threshold can be found in Bulgaria with 4.2 per cent). As regards the interaction between legal and implicit thresholds, in 22 out of 28 cases the effective threshold is determined by district magnitude, which means that the absolute majority of legal thresholds (eight cases out of 14) have actually no effect. The exceptions are represented by the Czech Republic, Hungary, Romania, Austria, Italy and Sweden, where the legal threshold (four or five per cent) is higher than the implicit one. In particular, before the introduction of the four per cent threshold in 2009, Italy had an even less distortive system, with an effective threshold of about 0.9 per cent, thus approaching Germany as the most purely proportional system of the EU. Today, notwithstanding the legislative change that occurred in 2009, the comparison with the other 27 EU countries reveals that Italy still belongs to the subgroup of countries with a low expected disproportionality.

[16] Lijphart, above n 2.

[17] Taagepera, above n 15.

[18] It is worth recalling the two rulings of the German Constitutional Court against the provision of a legal threshold for the election of the German representatives to the European Parliament (BWerfGE 2 BwC 4/10 et al of 9 November 2010; BWerfGE 2 BwE 2/13 et al of 26 February 2014).

IV. Effects on Political Representation

We have seen so far how the electoral legislation for the election of Italy's representatives at the EP has changed through time and how the Italian electoral system for the EP stands in comparative perspective. This section is now dedicated to an assessment and a discussion of the *effects* of such changes. We will focus on two key aspects: first, the effects on the *systemic properties* of the party system (number, size and relative importance of relevant actors, and potential consequences on voter-party interaction); secondly, the effects on the *political class*, ie the individual characteristics of the elected MEPs.

In order to test the presence and strength of any impact of legislative changes on the party system and the political class, we will pursue a simple design involving cross-time comparisons. To what extent do outcomes of interest *vary* in correspondence to specific events (namely, legislative changes)? In order to correctly state in advance our research hypotheses, it is then necessary to briefly recapitulate what are the critical events (and their location in time) which we expect to have an impact on our studied outcomes. In particular, it is relatively easy to identify a relatively long period of normative stability since the first election in 1979. Such stability was only interrupted in 2009 by the introduction of a minimum legal threshold of four per cent, and then, in 2014, by the adoption of minimum gender requirements for the expression of preference voting. As a result of such two events, then:

1. We expect most indicators of party system structure (number of parties, counted in different ways, and overall disproportionality of the electoral result) to remain relatively stable until the 2009 election, and to show a shrinkage of the number of relevant parties (along with an increased disproportionality) after that election;
2. we expect gender balance among Italian MEPs to change significantly in 2014, towards a more numerous representation of women.

Before assessing the hypotheses here presented in empirical terms, a last caveat is still necessary. During the observed period (from 1979 to 2014), there are significant changes that have affected the Italian party system: most importantly, the significant electoral reform of 1993, concerning the election of the national Parliament (followed by a second reform in 2005). Such reform, leading from a proportional representation (PR) system to a mixed system with a prevailing (75 per cent) plurality component, effectively fostered the emergence of a two-bloc, multi-party system (not far from what is emerging in France during the Fifth Republic). What is relevant to our research question is that, as several commentators observed, the new system actually led to an *increase* of the number of parties, in a context of what has been labelled as *fragmented bipolarism*.[19] We have to take into account that such a dynamic might exert a spillover effect even on election for the EP: thus, this might act as a confounding factor when assessing our core hypotheses. This said, we are now able to proceed to the empirical assessment of our two hypotheses.

[19] A Chiaramonte, 'Il nuovo sistema politico italiano tra bipolarismo e frammentazione' in R D'Alimonte and A Chiaramonte (eds), *Proporzionale ma non solo. Le elezioni politiche del 2006* (Bologna, il Mulino, 2007).

A. Systemic Effects

Concerning the first hypothesis, a cross-time trend of four key properties of the party system structure is quickly presented in Figure 1. The four indicators are the *Number of party lists with seats*, thus obtaining at least one MEP; the *effective number of electoral parties* (below: ENEP). Such measure derives from the application of the well-known formula introduced by Laakso and Taagepera[20] to *party vote shares*: it is calculated on *votes* (rather than seats), and as such it is an indicator of *electoral fragmentation*. This indicator counts the parties weighting for their relative electoral strength, so that larger parties count more than smaller ones in the computation of party system fragmentation. In the theoretical case of a system made up by two parties with 50 per cent of the vote each, the score of the indicator is two. ENEP captures to what extent *voters* distribute their vote choices across a large number of parties (ie without taking into account the party selection operated by the electoral system); the *effective number of parliamentary parties* (below: ENPP). This measure is the same as the previous one, except that it is calculated on party *seat* shares. As a result, it measures party system fragmentation at the *parliamentary* level, *after* the selection operated by the electoral system; the *Gallagher index*. This measure is calculated according to the well-known formula introduced by Gallagher,[21] which—by comparing vote shares with seat shares across all parties—effectively expresses the *disproportional effect* introduced by the electoral system, namely the deviations, from perfect proportionality, when votes are translated into seats. Therefore, the higher the Gallagher index, the higher the degree of distortion operated by the electoral system (ie larger parties will be overrepresented while smaller parties will be underrepresented in terms of seats they receive compared to the votes they get).

A quick summary inspection already reveals that our theoretical expectations are essentially confirmed, although in a nuanced fashion. First and foremost, the raw number of party lists obtaining at least a seat, quite predictably, shows a sharp decrease after the introduction of the four per cent legal threshold in the 2009 election. While hovering between 10 (in 1984) and even 19 (in 1999), the index then drops to six in 2009 and seven in 2014. This goes fully in line with the expectations, clearly showing the effectiveness of the legal threshold in limiting the number of parties obtaining at least one MEP.

However, the trend for the effective number of (both electoral and parliamentary) parties shows how the very high fragmentation suggested by the sheer number of represented parties might be partially misleading. Even in the 1999 election, which marked a record high with 19 parties represented, the effective number of parties was not larger than eight. The difference between the figures (the effective number of parties counts very small parties as less—or even much less—than one party) clearly shows how most of the 19 parties represented were actually very small (see Table 5). This has two implications: 1) that, as observed, the sheer number of parties might be partially exaggerating the actual fragmentation; 2) that the threshold might be effective in excluding *very small* parties (below four per cent), but might not be as effective in limiting the overall high fragmentation of the system, testified by an effective number of parties of about eight. Actually, in the highly

[20] M Laakso and R Taagepera, '"Effective" Number of Parties: A Measure with Application to West Europe' (1979) 12 *Comparative Political Studies* 3–27.

[21] Gallagher, above n 12.

fragmented 1999 election, eight parties were above four per cent, so as to potentially not be affected by the four per cent threshold introduced 10 years later.

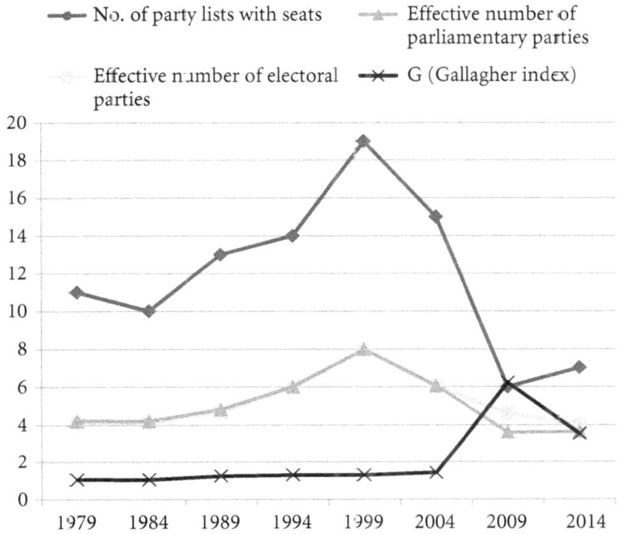

Figure 1: Evolution of several indicators of party system structure across the eight EP legislative terms

Both these implications are testified by the post-2009 trends for both versions of the effective number of parties. First, it is very clear that the reduction in *actual* fragmentation is in fact less pronounced. After the very fragmented election of 1999, both the effective number of electoral parties (ENEP) and the effective number of parliamentary parties (ENPP) had already decreased in 2004 to respectively 6.01 and 6.06. The enforcement of the legal threshold in 2009 in fact acted as a limitation to extreme fragmentation, leading to a further decrease of both indices, which became as low as in the first EP elections. It is however interesting to note how a typical Duvergerian mechanism of *mechanical* versus *psychological effects* is definitely taking place between the 2009 and 2014 elections. The 2009 election sees a sharp gap between ENEP (4.61) and ENPP (3.61). This clearly shows that voters were not fully aware of the four per cent threshold (or could not reliably predict which of the parties would pass it): as a result, a significant share of votes (13.89 per cent) went to parties that would not pass the legal threshold. This gap is much smaller in 2014 (ENEP=4.02, with ENPP=3.64): after realising in 2009 how many votes to small parties were actually wasted, many voters preferred to reward larger parties.[22] As a result, the share of votes going to parties below the threshold shrank by more than half, dropping to 6.65 per cent.[23]

[22] Besides this psychological effect taking place at voter level, we have to consider also the effect played by the changes in the supply side. In other words, the restructuring of the political offer (with, for example, the birth of a new large party as the 5 Star Movement, contesting the European elections for the first time in 2014) may have contributed to some extent to reduce the gap between ENEP and ENPP in 2014.

[23] Note that, of this 6.65 per cent, 3.67 per cent went to a single party, which thus—so close to four per cent—was expected before elections to have significant chances to pass the legal threshold.

This explains why, in 2014, the configuration of fragmentation in terms of both votes and seats appears much more similar. Of course, the emersion of a *psychological effect*—leading voters to avoid small parties, anticipating the potential effects of the electoral system—makes the legal regulation, in the long run, potentially only act as a deterrent, without heavily distorting the vote results. This is clearly visible in the trend of the last indicator, the Gallagher index of disproportionality. After the very low values recorded until 2009, it jumps to six in 2009, but then drops to less than four in 2014, showing how the electoral system places much less distortion on the vote results, when voters already take into account the risks of voting for small parties.

Table 5: Electoral results in the 1999 EP Election

Party list	Votes	Votes (%)	Seats
Forza Italia	7,813,948	25.16	22
Democratici Sinistra	5,387,729	17.34	15
An—Patto Segni	3,194,661	10.28	9
Lista Emma Bonino	2,625,881	8.45	7
I Democratici	2,402,435	7.73	6
Lega Nord	1,391,595	4.48	4
Rifondazione Comunista	1,327,327	4.27	4
Ppi	1,316,830	4.24	4
Ccd	805,320	2.59	2
Sdi	670,957	2.16	2
Cdu	669,919	2.16	2
Comunisti Italiani	622,261	2	2
Verdi	548,987	1.77	2
Udeur	498,742	1.61	1
Ms—Fiamma Tricolore	496,030	1.6	1
Dini-Rinnovamento Italiano	353,890	1.14	1
Partito Pensionati	233,874	0.75	1
Pri-Liberali	168,620	0.54	1
Svp	156,005	0.5	1
Liga Repubblica Veneta (and other allied local lists)	117,979	0.38	0
Lista Cito—Lega Azione Meridionale	94,181	0.3	0
Consumatori—Padroni in casa nostra	61,185	0.2	0
Partito Socialista	42,500	0.14	0
Union Valdotaine	40,970	0.13	0
Partito Umanista	16,168	0.05	0
Cobas per l'autorganizzazione	4,432	0.01	0
Total	31,062,426		87

B. Effects on the Political Class

Concerning the second hypothesis, we present in Table 6 the time trend of the number (and percentages) of women among Italian MEPs since the first legislative term of the EP. The first three columns respectively report the legislative term, the number of MEPs assigned to Italy, and the total number of political personnel involved as MEPs during the legislative term. The difference between these last two columns is due to the presence of a significant number of MEPs resigning before the end of the legislative term, so that replacement members increase the overall count. The fourth column counts the number of women, followed by a percentage, calculated over the total number of MEPs involved (including replacements).

Table 6: Gender balance among Italian MEPs across the eight EP legislative terms

EP Legislative term	N representatives	Total MEPs in office across the legislative term (T)	Total women in office across the legislative term (W)	Female representation ratio (W/T)
I (1979–1984)	81	90	12	13%
II (1984–1989)	81	97	11	11%
III (1989–1994)	81	93	14	15%
IV (1994–1999)	87	93	12	13%
V (1999–2004)	87	98	11	11%
VI (2004–2009)	78	82	14	17%
VII (2009–2014)	72	80	18	23%
VIII (2014–)	73	75	29	39%

The trend for this last indicator clearly testifies the effectiveness of the gender equality measures enforced since 2004. The percentage of women among MEPs had stayed consistently low (and with no apparent increase trend) until the 1999 election. The VI and VII legislative terms (2004 and 2009 election) saw an increase, which is related to the new rules on equal opportunities for party lists' candidates.[24] However, following the introduction of the gender preference vote, the 2014 election marks a record high level of 39 per cent, with a 16-point increase over the previous election.

V. Conclusions

As shown through the different sections of this chapter, the law for the election of the Italian representatives in the EP has seen only minor changes since its introduction in 1979, and its

[24] On the basis of the Law No 90 of 8 April 2004, no gender can be represented within the party list with more than two thirds of candidates.

basic structure still places it among the least disproportional electoral laws across EU countries. However, what clearly emerges from the examination of the *effects* of such relatively minor changes is that they have affected the party system—and representation in general—to a significant extent. Such impact goes essentially in two directions. The first one is related to the reduction of party system fragmentation. According to typical Duvergerian dynamics, such effect—due to the introduction of a legal threshold—has developed through two elections, with a clear *mechanical* impact in the election of 2009, and a clear *psychological* impact in the election of 2014. The second clearly present impact is instead observed in terms of gender balance. In this regard, the new regulations introduced in 2014 appear to have strengthened substantially a process of gender rebalancing, which had started in 2004, when a much weaker norm attempting at promoting equal opportunities was introduced.

As a result, what appears clear from our analysis is the neatly measurable effect of modifications in the EP electoral law. This is strongly consistent with the literature on the effects of electoral systems, which highlights their importance in shaping the competition context of political parties. It is of course still too early to draw conclusions about the future evolution of the Italian representation in the EP; however, we are confident that it will be very unlikely to reach the previous levels of fragmentation, and it will continue to provide a more accurate representation of both genders. We believe that both these aspects are going to improve the overall quality of Italian representation.

Part II

The Formation of the National Position in the EU

5

The Function of Scrutiny and Political Direction of the Government, Between Foreign Affairs and European Affairs

GIOVANNI RIZZONI

I. Parliamentary Instruments for Setting and Controlling the Government in the Domain of Foreign Affairs and European Affairs

As early as the 1990s, EU Member States began to find that, when framing public policies, it was increasingly hard to distinguish between European and purely domestic affairs as EU legislation extended its reach into new areas.

The need to tackle the economic and financial crisis that erupted in 2008 accentuated the overlap still further. As a result of new intergovernmental treaties and regulatory instruments (the 'Six Pack' and the 'Two Pack') the coordination of the economic policies of Eurozone Member States became much more tightly knit. New forms of direct oversight by the European authorities were established to enforce compliance with the strictures of the Stability and Growth Pact. With the introduction of the so-called 'European Semester', the oversight was extended to include the framing and approval of the national budget, which went to the core of one of the hitherto most jealously guarded prerogatives of national Parliaments, the national budgetary policy control.[1]

[1] K Lenaerts, 'EMU and the European's Union Constitutional Framework' (2014) 6 *European Law Review* 769.

At first, these developments seemed to confirm the opinion according to which national Parliaments were to be considered the 'losers' in the new drive towards European integration.[2] Such an interpretation was rejected by others maintaining that national Parliaments had successfully adapted to the new structures of the European governance.[3]

In reality, the learning process of national Parliaments in the new European decision-making environment is not yet complete and continues to evolve, with Parliaments proving themselves remarkably adept and resilient both at maintaining their internal coherence and at managing their relations with European institutions over the years. Many national Parliaments developed new techniques to deal with the changes in their deliberative procedures foisted upon them by the economic and financial crisis and its aftermath.

With respect to relations with European institutions, the new subsidiarity checks introduced in the Lisbon Treaty naturally acquired greater importance, as did the 'political dialogue' which serves as a direct channel through which national Parliaments can communicate with the European Commission. Major changes also took place in the nature of relations between Parliaments and their Governments. All the evidence suggests that, since the outbreak of the crisis, the national Parliaments of the EU have become increasingly intent on holding their Governments to account for their actions in the institutions of the EU.[4] This parliamentary oversight has been exercised both through prior (ex ante) activities and through the subsequent (ex post) verification and appraisal of Government action. The purpose of ex ante activities is to determine in advance the political stance of the national Government at the European Council and of national Government ministers at the EU Council. Ex post controls include parliamentary debates that hold the Government to account and assess whether it has successfully defended the national position at the EU level. Another approach being tested by national Parliaments—one that would seem to hold out more promise for the future of the European Union—regards the abovementioned 'European Semester'. The basic idea underpinning the 'parliamentarisation' of the European Semester is that oversight and scrutiny functions should be assigned to national Parliaments as part of the complex procedure by which national Governments design the policies that they submit to European bodies and to which they agree to be bound. With the introduction of the European Semester, national Parliaments were presented with a new challenge, with which they are still learning to cope.[5]

This chapter examines how over recent years the Italian Parliament has developed its own instruments for setting and controlling the policies that inform the Italian Government's position in European-level negotiations. To begin, the focus will be devoted to the traditional instruments used by the Italian Parliament in order to carry out the scrutiny and direction activity exercised over the Government in the domain of foreign and European affairs policies. The different parliamentary tools are analysed: from those implying a scrutiny function in the proper sense of the concept (as with questions and interpellations)

[2] See A Maurer and W Wessels (eds), *National Parliaments on their Ways to Europe: Losers or Latecomers?* (Nomos, Baden-Baden, 2001).

[3] T Raunio and S Hix, 'Backbenchers Learn to Fight Back: European Integration and Parliamentary Government' (2000) 23(4) *West European Politics* 142–68.

[4] C Hefftler and W Wessels, 'The Democratic Legitimacy of the EU's Economic Governance and National Parliaments' (2013) *IAI Working Papers* 1313.

[5] G Rizzoni, 'Il "Semestre europeo" fra sovranità di bilancio e auto vincoli costituzionali: Germania, Francia e Italia a confronto' (2011) 4 *Rivista AIC*.

to those oriented towards a more substantive direction of Government conduct (resolutions, motions). Mention will be made also of the formal political declarations made by the executive in front of the Assemblies (spontaneously or under the request of political groups), especially on the occasions of important meetings at the European level or of serious international crises. The most important innovations that have taken place in legislative and parliamentary practice in this area after the Lisbon Treaty will then be discussed. The chapter will proceed with an examination of how these new instruments have been brought to bear on a specific issue, namely, the attempts of the Italian Parliament to be part of the European deliberations on the migration emergency of the past two years.

In the complex game that is currently being played out between the EU and its Member States over the highly controversial subject of migration, national Parliaments have a great deal at stake. As the emergency measures adopted to deal with the financial crisis clearly showed, exceptional events such as forced migrations have the potential to bring about permanent changes in the European balance of power and can transform the scope of responsibilities of the European institutions that are called upon to respond to them. It is therefore worth looking in more detail at how the Italian Parliament has reacted to the rapidly changing decision-making environment and how it has sought to influence the position of the Italian Government in its dealings with European institutions (the EU Council and the European Council).

After reviewing the migration issue and the EU's response, some concluding remarks will be made on how national Parliaments have been adapting their procedures in order to keep pace with the rapid evolution of the European decision-making process.

II. The Traditional Parliamentary Tools

In the realm of foreign and European policy, the parliamentary scrutiny function over the Government is exercised through some traditional instruments, such as questions and interpellations. Questions are addressed by MPs to the executive concerning matters of fact. Typically, with questions the MPs ask the Government to confirm or deny allegations about a certain subject. Questions can be written or oral and can be debated in the plenary or in the relevant committees. Interpellations instead represent a more political tool because they concern the policy that the Government intends to pursue on a particular issue. After the debate, the questioner may table a resolution, an act intended to give a directive to the Government (see below in this section). Questions and interpellations are the typical instruments of parliamentary control, a function performed mainly on the initiative of the deputies of the opposition, although often the majority MPs (especially the backbenchers) also contribute to the presentation of these instruments. It must be added that normally a very limited percentage of questions and interpellations address the Ministry for Foreign Affairs (at the Chamber of Deputies these comprised only 2.8 per cent of the total from March 2013 to December 2016).

In the domain of foreign and European policy, however, the Parliament is not confined to merely discharging a control function, ie in scrutinising activities autonomously conducted by the executive. It may also issue directives regarding policies to be adopted by the Government. The tools used in this field are motions and resolutions.

Motions are standalone tools that can be presented by MPs in order to initiate a debate ending with a vote to which they plan to commit the government policy. During the debate, the Government expresses its opinion, indicating whether it is favourable or in opposition to accepting the commitment. Amendments can also be attached to the motion (which must be accepted by the presenters of the instrument). The vote adopted by Parliament has the value of being a political commitment for the Government but is not legally binding. Parliament may also vote for partially different motions on the same issue, even if it refrains from voting for documents that are contradictory to each other.

A recent interesting example in the field of foreign policy is represented by the motions passed by the Chamber of Deputies regarding the recognition of the Palestinian state. On 27 February 2015, the House passed two motions on this issue, submitted by MPs from different political groups of the ruling coalition. The motions suggested two different approaches to the issue. The motion tabled by the Democratic party (the leading party of the coalition) explicitly committed the Government to support the recognition of the Palestinian state. The second motion (tabled by the junior partner of the ruling coalition) did not engage directly the executive's recognition of the Palestinian state but called for continuing efforts to reach an agreement between the different political Palestinian factions as a condition for recognition of the Palestinian state. Despite the obvious difference between these two instruments, the Government accepted both the commitments. However, the non-binding nature of these instruments is confirmed by the fact that the Italian Government, despite the parliamentary vote, has not yet proceeded to formally recognise the Palestinian state (and neither does it seem willing to do so in the short term). The situation from this point of view has some analogies with what happened in France and the United Kingdom on the same subject: the lower Houses of the two countries recently passed motions in favour of recognising the Palestinian state, but those decisions did not lead the respective executives to implement the parliamentary vote.

Resolutions are documents that can be presented at the end of the debate on a certain issue with the aim of expressing a policy directive to the Government. Resolutions are usually voted on by the assemblies of both Houses when the Government makes communications to Parliament before important meetings of the European institutions, such as those of the European Council. This practice will be discussed in greater detail in section IV. Resolutions are also voted on at the end of the debate concerning the document of economics and finance (DEF), the document that the Government is required to present to the Parliament at the end of the first half of each year in order to set the parameters of its financial policy. The DEF defines the guidelines for the budget bill to be presented in the second half of the year. This process has taken on great importance for the involvement of Parliament in policy-setting regarding the European Semester. The DEF contains the National Reform Programme and the National Programme of Stability that the Government intends to present to the European institutions.

Resolutions are also voted on by the plenary bodies at the end of debate regarding the Government programme of activities at the EU level. According to the Italian legislation,[6] the Government is required to present annually a policy-setting document that lists the Italian priorities in the field of European policies. At the Chamber of Deputies and at the Senate the document is normally examined in plenary jointly with the European

[6] Art 13 Law No 234/2012.

Commission Work Programme on the basis of a report drafted by the European Affairs Committee. At the end of the debate, the plenary votes on a resolution that gives further guidance to the Government.

Finally, mention must be made of the parliamentary debates that take place when the Government makes communications in the House on a particular issue. It is a procedure widely used also for matters of foreign and European policy, especially to inform the Parliament about the latest political developments. Communications can be made by the Government on its own initiative or at the request of parliamentary groups. After the statements of the Government, a debate follows without vote, with the participation of all parliamentary groups. Government communications have become one of the preferred means to start debates on foreign and European policy in plenary and in the committees.[7]

III. Major Innovations after the Lisbon Treaty

In recent years, the Italian Parliament has completely overhauled its working methods as far as European affairs are concerned. The entry into force of the Lisbon Treaty accelerated this process. New procedures have been introduced in order to regulate parliamentary participation in the 'political dialogue' and the early warning mechanism, though the two Chambers of Parliament have each adopted their own solution. A new Act (Law No 234 of 2012) sets out rules on how Italy should participate in the formation of European Union legislation and policies and on how it should implement them. This chapter will not address the technicalities of this law.[8] Observations offered here will be limited to certain aspects of it that are particularly pertinent to the theme of this chapter, and further discussion left to the other contributors to this book.

The primary aim of the law was to enhance the system of relations between the various institutions of the Italian state (Government, Parliament, regional governments and local authorities) with a view to increasing the effectiveness with which Italy participates in the European decision-making process. The law is clearly configured to put an end to the practice of treating European Union business as part of the foreign affairs brief. It determines that the management of European policy is a matter for the upper echelons of Government—the Office of the Prime Minister and for the Minister for European Affairs (who acts on the instructions of the Prime Minister)—rather than for the Ministry of Foreign Affairs. In intent and content, the law reflects a clear awareness that an almost complete overlap now exists between European and national policies, the natural consequence of which is that the governance of these policies must necessarily be a central concern of the Head of Government to whom the Italian Constitution assigns responsibility for steering and coordinating the activities of all ministers.

[7] F Longo, *Parlamento e politica estera* (Bologna, il Mulino, 2011) 255.

[8] For a more comprehensive comment on the law, see A Esposito, 'La legge 24 Dicembre 2012, 234, sulla partecipazione dell'Italia alla formazione e all'attuazione della normativa e delle politiche dell'Unione Europea. Parte I—Prime riflessioni sul ruolo delle Camere' (2013) 2 *federalismi.it* and L Costato, LS Rossi and P Borghi (eds), *Commentario alla legge 24.12.2012, n 234* (Napoli, Editoriale Scientifica, 2015). On this subject see also the chapters by Esposito (ch 6) and Capuano (ch 7) in this volume.

The law is also intended to accord greater powers to Parliament to intervene in the determination of the Italian Government's position when dealing with European institutions. It regulates relations between Parliament and Government regarding the exercise of parliamentary control over the compliance with the principle of subsidiarity and the 'political dialogue'. It also sets out new rules on how Parliament may shape the political position to be adopted by the Government at the Council of the European Union. By means of this law, Italy at last has armed itself with a set of instruments that some other European countries have been using for some time already.[9]

The law reaffirms the power of the two Houses of Parliament to adopt policy-setting motions for the Government ahead of the approval of decisions in Europe and reaffirms that the Government is bound to respect these policies also when laying out the Italian position before the European Council or the EU Council. A debate and vote on the policy-setting motions can be begun either by a parliamentary committee or by the Floor of the House. Recently, it has become customary to hold the debate and vote on the Floor of the House in the run-up to a meeting of the European Council.[10] If the Government fails to adhere to the policies set by Parliament, it must then come before the debating chamber of Parliament and explain its motivations for adopting a different position.

The Italian law is flexible with regard to Parliament's right of scrutiny. Under the terms of the law, the Government is supposed to seek the suspension in the Council of a given proposal pending its scrutiny by Parliament. However, this right to scrutinise is not automatic and is granted only if there is an explicit request to this effect from one of the Houses of Parliament. In cases of particular political, economic and social importance, the Government itself may call for parliamentary scrutiny.

Thus, Italy now has detailed statutory provisions prescribing how Parliament may take part in the formation of European policies, which put it on par with its most advanced EU partners. Even so, while parliamentary activity in this field has significantly increased in recent years, it has not yet gathered sufficient critical mass.[11] Parliament's effective capacity to influence the Government's position in Europe remains weak. Even when Parliament intervenes to define policies for the Government, the parliamentary Houses show scant interest in following this up with ex post controls to ensure that the Government has actually complied with the instructions it was given.

IV. How the Italian Parliament Seeks to Influence the EU Policies: The Example of the Migrant Emergency

In this section, we shall consider how the instruments of parliamentary participation in the formation of European policies have been deployed in an effort to influence European

[9] On the ground-breaking role played on this field by the Danish Parliament see M Buskjaer Christensen, 'The Danish Folketing and EU Affairs: Is the Danish Model of Parliamentary Scrutiny Still Best Practice?' in C Hefftler, C Neuhold, O Rozenberg and J Smith (eds), *The Palgrave Handbook of National Parliaments and the European Union* (Basingstoke, Palgrave Macmillan, 2015) 275 ff.

[10] For some examples of this practice, see s 4 of this chapter.

[11] See ch 6 by Esposito in this volume.

measures to deal with the migrant emergency. The new European policies on migration have become a matter of enormous political relevance in Italy, and Parliament is therefore keen to have a direct line of contact with the Government so that it may have as great a say as possible in their formation.

Before considering the situation in Italy, we need to examine the sequence of the most recent actions taken by the European Union on migration. Since 2014, the European Union has been inundated by an exceptional influx of migrants, most of whom come from crisis-stricken regions of the Middle East and Africa. European law[12] states that the country into which an asylum-seeker first sets foot is responsible for processing the application for refugee status. The system, however, is being overwhelmed by the sheer size of the influx, and countries like Italy find themselves particularly exposed as they are often the first port of call for the arrivals. The immigration issue has come to dominate the political debate in many EU countries, and public and political opinion on the best way of dealing with the phenomenon is deeply divided. Not surprisingly, Italy is one of the EU Member States keenest to amend the current legislation on asylum and to introduce some sort of system that shares the burden by distributing the migrants among the different EU countries.

In recent times, European institutions have made repeated efforts to manage the migration emergency. On 23 April 2015, during a year replete with EU initiatives in this area, a special meeting of the European Council was called to consider the crisis after the sinking of an immigrant ship in the Mediterranean Sea with the loss of over 800 lives. The meeting came immediately after a joint Council session of foreign and home affairs ministers that was devoted to the migration question. Soon afterwards, on 13 May, the European Commission presented the European Agenda on Migration, which set out general policy guidelines. On 27 May, the Commission presented a first package of implementing measures to give practical effect to the Agenda. Amongst other things, the package provided for the relocation of a certain number of migrants (40,000) from Italy and Greece to other European countries over a period of two years. On 25 and 26 June, the European Council endorsed the Commission's proposals. On the following 20 July, however, the Justice and Home Affairs Council agreed to the relocation of a smaller number of migrants (32,256) than had been envisaged in the original provision, owing to the refusal of some Member States to accept the share of refugees allocated to them. The dramatic events of the summer, with new waves of arrivals coming through the Balkans corridor, prompted the Commission to present, on 9 September, a second package of implementing measures for the European Agenda on Migration. This second package contained a plan for the relocation of a further 120,000 asylum-seekers from Greece, Italy and Hungary to other Member States.

In addition to this emergency package, the European Commission also proposed two new regulations. One was for the creation of a permanent solidarity mechanism that the Commission may activate at any time to help a Member State that finds itself in a situation of crisis or is experiencing extreme pressure on its asylum system.[13] The other proposal was for the compilation of a list of safe countries of origin.[14] The purpose of the list is to

[12] The EU Law currently in force is Reg (EU) No 604/2013 of the European Parliament and of the Council of 26 June 2013 (so called Dublin III), establishing the criteria and mechanisms for determining the Member State responsible for examining an application for international protection lodged in one of the Member States by a third-country national or a stateless person (recast).

[13] See Com 2015 (450).

[14] See Com 2014 (452).

expedite the processing of asylum requests by excluding applicants who have come from countries that the EU deems to be safe for refugees. The chief aim of the first proposal for a regulation as described above was to establish a permanent derogation of the principle of the Dublin Regulation, according to which asylum requests must be considered only by the Member State into which the applicant first arrived. As a part of the permanent derogation of the Dublin principle, the Commission proposed that in cases of emergency a mandatory system of distribution, and hence a mandatory sharing of responsibilities, should be enacted.

The three proposals were predicated on different legal bases. The Proposal for a Council Decision was based on article 78(3) of the Treaty on the Functioning of the European Union (TFEU). Article 78(3) stipulates that in the event of one or more Member States being confronted by an emergency situation characterised by a sudden influx of nationals of third countries, the Council, on a proposal from the Commission and after consulting with the European Parliament, may adopt provisional measures for the benefit of the Member State(s) concerned. The other two regulations are based on article 78(2) TFEU, which allows the European Parliament and the Council to use ordinary legislative procedures to pass measures for a common European asylum system.

On 22 September 2015, having first secured the positive opinion of the European Parliament, an extraordinary session of the Justice and Home Affairs Council resolved in favour of the adoption of the relocation mechanism described above but excluded Hungary from its purview, since that country had dissented from the decision (which was therefore passed by a qualified majority rather than by unanimity). The two proposals for regulations are still being considered by the Council and the European Parliament (as of April 2017).[15]

On 23 September, an extraordinary informal meeting of the Heads of State and Government was held to discuss the refugee crisis, at the end of which a series of conclusions was approved to support Lebanon, Jordan and Turkey in dealing with the Syrian refugee crisis and to allocate one billion euros in funds to help the Office of the United Nations High Commissioner for Refugees (UNHCR), the World Food Programme and other agencies. On 8–9 October, the Justice and Home Affairs Council resolved, among other things, to provide additional funding by adjusting the EU budget so that more resources could be directed towards the refugee crisis. On the same occasion, the Council approved the conclusions on the future of the repatriation policy. On 15 and 16 October, the European Council reconvened once more with the immigration question at the top of its agenda.

How has the Italian Parliament tried to play a part in this rapidly evolving scenario? The current mechanisms were designed to facilitate Parliament's efforts, first to sway the actions of the Italian Government in its dealings with the European Union and second to affect the decision-making of the European institutions directly.

Under the terms of the aforementioned Act (ie Law No 234 of 2012), prior to a meeting of the European Council, the Government is obliged to appear before the Houses of Parliament to explain the course of action it intends to follow there. The Government's

[15] More recently, the European Commission has created a new proposal for a comprehensive revision of the Dublin regulation (see COM/2016/0270, Proposal for a regulation of the European Parliament and the Council establishing the criteria and mechanisms for determining the Member State responsible for examining an application for international protection lodged in one of the Member States by a third-country national or a stateless person—recast). This new proposal substantially substitutes the Com 2015 (452).

presentation of its case is followed by a debate in which all parliamentary groups take part, and may end with a vote on a policy-setting motion. In the first 10 months of 2015, four European Council meetings were held to discuss migration (23 April, 25–26 June, 23 September and 15–16 October). Ahead of three of the four meetings (those in April, June and October), the Government reported to the plenary assembly of the Chamber of Deputies and the Senate. In all three cases, both Houses passed a resolution at the conclusion of the debate containing directives to the Government on how to deal with the immigration issue at the European Council. The resolutions outlining the policies to which the Government was bound to adhere were notable for their depth of detail.

As for the specific proposals made by the European Commission to address the issue of migration (the two Proposals for a Regulation and the Proposal for a Council Decision on the provisional measures for the resettlement of migrants), Parliament's control activity consisted mainly in the work of the Chamber of Deputies and Senate Committees on Constitutional Affairs (two Standing Committees, one for each House of Parliament, whose remit extends to immigration issues), which examined the European proposals. On 14 and 20 October 2015, the Committees approved two documents setting out in considerable detail their position regarding the three proposals made by the European Commission.[16] The opinions were favourable to the proposed measures, but they also recommended some revisions that were by no means negligible in scope, including, for example, a call for the Dublin system of the processing of asylum claims to be abandoned altogether. As for the provisional measures for the relocation of migrants, while it is true that the parliamentary Committees reviewed the text only after it had already been definitively adopted by the European Council, the effort they expended in drafting a motivated opinion on the measures was noteworthy. The activism of the Committees of the Italian Parliament also needs to be weighed in the light of the fact that to date only a minority of national Parliaments of the EU have expressed themselves on the migration issue, although it is a matter of great political importance. If we take the proposal to amend the Dublin Regulation (COM (2015) 450) for example, we find that as of 15 December 2016, the document had been examined by just 11 national Parliaments. Some of them (the Senate and the Lower Chamber of the Czech Republic, the National Assembly of Hungary, the Chamber of Deputies of Romania and the National Council of Slovakia) have issued a reasoned opinion in which they maintain that the draft regulation fails to comply with the principle of subsidiarity.

V. Optimising the Participation Capabilities of National Parliaments in a Rapidly Changing Decision-making Environment

The summary account we have just given prompts two observations, the first regarding the manner in which the European institutions make their decisions and the second regarding the efforts of the Italian Parliament to influence them.

[16] For the Chamber of deputies, see the document passed by the Constitutional Affairs Committee (Doc XVIII, no 26) on 14 October 2015; for the Senate, see the resolutions passed by the Constitutional Affairs Committee (Doc XVIII, no 100 e 101) on 20 and 23 October 2015.

Generally, the way in which the EU has responded to the migration emergency raises some fundamental questions about the interpretation of the EU Treaties. Articles 78 and 79 of the TFEU grant the Union power to develop 'common policies' on asylum and immigration. By its nature, this is a concurrent competence with that of Member States.[17] The question, then, is how far the Union can go in exercising it. Can the imposition on Member States of compulsory refugee quotas really be considered a competence of the Union? The different possible answers to this question are the source of fierce disagreement among Member States. In any case, one thing is already certain: whatever the formal provisions of the Treaties might mean, the last year has seen a pronounced 'Europeanisation' of the migration issue. A problem that until only a few months ago was viewed as primarily the responsibility of the home affairs ministries of Member States is now almost unanimously recognised as one that demands the intervention of the EU institutions. It seems quite clear that no European country on its own can deal with the enormous problem of forced migration.

It must also be emphasised that the deliberative procedure of the European Union on the immigration emergency was characterised by the repeated intervention of the European Council as the main determiner of EU policy. The result of this approach has been to alter the ordinary relationship between the different bodies of the EU. Rather than limiting itself in setting the general political directions and priorities of the Union,[18] the European Council acted as a real executive institution engaged to draft concrete measures to face the migration emergency.

The Italian Parliament has taken steps to adapt itself to this fast-changing and complex decision-making process. Adapting has not always been easy, however, because it proved difficult to keep pace with the accelerating rhythm of change in the European decision-making procedures, which are being reshaped by the rapid succession of emergency situations. In short, the migration issue has given new currency to the problem of the time constraints imposed on national Parliaments when dealing with European decisions, a problem that already came to the fore when new instruments were introduced to deal with the financial emergencies of 2010–2011.[19]

The Italian Parliament's response to these challenges has been to organise plenary debates on the Floors of the Houses to discuss the general position of the Government when the Government is reporting to Parliament prior to a European Council meeting. Meanwhile, the task of delving into the minute details of the measures that European institutions propose to enforce was left to parliamentary committees. As it happens in other European Parliaments, the Italian Parliament has therefore adopted procedures aimed at optimising the participation capabilities of the different parliamentary bodies in EU decision-making.[20]

Most of the time, the function of the policy-setting documents approved on the Floor of the House or by the parliamentary committees was to lend substantive support to the political line that the Government resolves to follow in Europe. Yet the practice of aligning

[17] European parliament, Directorate General for internal policies, *Division of competences between the European Union and its Member States concerning immigration*, Note, Brussels, 2011.

[18] Art 15 TEU.

[19] M Dawson and F de Witte, 'Constitutional Balance in the EU after the Euro-Crisis' (2013) 76 (5) *Modern Law Review* 834.

[20] S Mangiameli, *The Role of National Parliaments in the European Union*, evidence given by prof Stelio Mangiameli to the House of Lords, 2013, at www.issirfa.cnr.it.

the opinions expressed in the parliamentary documents to the Government's political position has led, especially during plenary debates on the Floor of the House, to the opening of a fault line between Government and opposition parties, with the latter submitting minority draft motions with policies that diverge considerably from those espoused by the majority parties. Unlike what happens in other countries, especially in Northern Europe, where the negotiation mandates given to Governments are the result of bipartisan collaboration between Government and opposition parties,[21] in Italy, the continuity between the majority parties and the Government prevails over the possibility that the national Parliament as a whole should enjoy independence of action and judgement when exercising its right to participate in the formation of European policies. The situation can be most plainly seen during plenary debates and voting, owing to the essentially political and public nature of this type of forum. We might consider this situation as simply another consequence of the almost complete 'domestication' of European policies and their inclusion in arena of national politics. In any case, there is no doubt that Italian MPs are primarily concerned with positively influencing European decisions rather than curbing EU powers through the use of the subsidiarity checks provided by Protocol No 2 annexed to the Lisbon Treaty.[22] The documents passed by the Standing Committees of the two Houses show exactly this attitude: normally, they give recommendations on how to improve the draft European regulations rather than questioning the right of the Commission to regulate on migration.

Even so, the activism of the Italian Parliament in the immigration debate might well serve as a template for national Parliaments anxious to prevent the expansion of EU powers in this particular area from turning into a more general 'de-parliamentarisation'.[23] In a Europe that is increasingly dominated by a decision-making process that is intergovernmental in scope, the best chance that the national Parliaments of Member States have of preserving their right to debate and having a say in European policies is for them show themselves capable of exercising their powers of control and guidance over their own national Governments. However, the prospect of securing improved accountability in the EU decision-making system is uncertain.[24] To be truly effective, these instruments must be constantly recalibrated to the constantly shifting and sometimes chaotic dynamics of European decision-making.

[21] L Gianniti and N Lupo, *Corso di diritto parlamentare* (Bologna, il Mulino, 2013) 286.

[22] S Cavatorto, 'Italy: Still Looking for a New Era in the making of EU Policy' in Hefftler, Neuhold, Rozenberg and Smith, above n 9, 209–31.

[23] J O'Brennen and T Raunio (eds), *National Parliaments and within the Enlarged European Union: From Victims of Integration to Competitive Actors?* (Abingdon, Routledge advances in European politics, 2007).

[24] A Cygan, *Accountability, Parliamentarism and Transparency in the EU: The Role of National Parliaments* (Cheltenham, Edward Elgar, 2007) 7.

6

European Affairs within the Chamber of Deputies

ANTONIO ESPOSITO

I. The Legal Framework

The Chamber of Deputies participates in framing EU legislation and policies through a combination of procedures established in the EU treaties, Italian legislation (notably Law No 234 of 2012)[1] and the Chamber's Rules of Procedure (hereinafter RoP).[2] Those

[1] On Law No 234/2012 see, among others, A Esposito, 'La legge 24 dicembre 2012, n 234, sulla partecipazione dell'Italia alla formazione e all'attuazione della normativa e delle politiche dell'UE. Parte 1, Prime riflessioni sul ruolo delle Camere' (2013) 9 (2) *Federalismi.it*; G Piccirilli, 'Il Parlamento italiano: le procedure europee nella legge n 234 del 2012' in A Manzella and N Lupo (eds), *Il sistema parlamentare euro-nazionale. Lezioni* (Turin, Giappichelli, 2014) 205–26; D Fromage, *Les parlements dans l'Union Européenne après le Traité de Lisbonne La participation des parlements allemands, britanniques, espagnols, français et italiens* (Paris, L'Harmattan, 2015) 157–62; R Adam, D Capuano et al, 'L'attuazione della legge n 234 del 24 dicembre 2012. Norme, prassi, risultati, dal livello statale a quello regionale' (2016) *Istituzioni del Federalismo*. On the EU-related provisions of the Italian Constitution see the chapter by D Capuano in this volume.

[2] The Chamber's RoP (enacted in 1971) contain specific procedures on EU affairs (Ch XXVIII 'Procedures for linkage with the activities of EU and international bodies'), which were significantly enhanced by amendments adopted in 1990, 1996 and 1999. The RoP have been complemented by three opinions (interpretative decisions) of the Rules Committee (Giunta per il regolamento), which is responsible for the consideration of amendments to the RoP and, together with the President, for their interpretation. An opinion issued on 9 February 2000 set out a procedure for the consideration of the European Commission Annual Work Programme and for any other political or legislative planning documents of the EU Institutions; two opinions, adopted on 6 October 2009 and on 14 July 2010, provided an experimental procedure for the subsidiarity check and clarified the application of some Rules or practices to make more effective the general scrutiny and the political dialogue. On the legal effects and value of the opinions of the Rules Committee, see the chapter by N Lupo in this volume.

provisions are complemented by a set of practices developed in the relations between the EU institutions and the national Parliaments (hereinafter NPs), by the cooperation among other Parliaments of the European Union, as well as by the relevant Chamber bodies.The legal framework in force gradually has been carved, especially in the last decade, to take into account the developments in the EU constitutional architecture as well as the increasing awareness of the importance of EU affairs in the Italian Parliament.[3] It enables the Chamber to contribute, directly or indirectly, to all the stages of EU policy-making and decision-making.

This chapter focuses on the four main channels through which the Chamber, like most NPs, can intervene in the EU affairs: the scrutiny (and direction) of the Italian Government's action; the political dialogue with the Commission and the European Parliament (hereinafter EP); the subsidiarity check under Protocol No 2 annexed to the Lisbon Treaty; and the EU interparliamentary cooperation.

II. The EU Scrutiny

The Chamber scrutinises the Government's action at EU level through specific procedures for each step or area of the EU policy-making and decision-making processes. In addition, the ordinary information, fact-finding or policy-setting procedures can be (and are actually) used.[4]

The general scope of the scrutiny is stated in Article 7 of Law No 234/2012, which makes it explicit and implements a principle enshrined in the Italian constitutional system that was for a long time neglected: the Government must take a position—within the Council or in the relations with other EU institutions or bodies—consistent with the policy guidelines issued by the two Houses. In the event that the Government is unable to follow the parliamentary guidelines, the President of the Council of Ministers or the relevant Minister shall report to the competent parliamentary bodies and explain the reasons why.

It is noteworthy that the Government's obligation of compliance may arise not only in the negotiations on legislative proposal within the Council but also in any other EU activity. Indeed the RoP and the legislation in force enable the Chamber to influence the broad priorities and the strategic framework of Italian EU policy, control and oversee the Government's action within the European Council as well as its negotiating position within the Council, participate in the elaboration of the Italian contribution to public

[3] Until a few years ago, in the Italian political culture a strong role of the Parliament in EU affairs or its direct interaction with the EU institutions was mostly considered detrimental to the Government's negotiating capacity. On the evolution of the parliamentary role in EU affairs, see A Esposito, 'Il Trattato di Lisbona e il nuovo ruolo costituzionale dei parlamenti nazionali: le prospettive per il parlamento italiano' (2009) *Rassegna parlamentare* 1156; R Matarazzo and J Leone, 'Sleeping Beauty Awakens: The Italian Parliament and the EU After the Lisbon Treaty' (2011) 46(3) *The International Spectator* 129–44; F Bindi, 'Italy and the European Union' (Washington, Brookings Institution Press, 2011) 65 ff; S Cavatorto, 'Italy: Still Looking for a New Era in the Making of EU Policy' in C Heffler et al (eds), *Palgrave Handbook of National Parliaments and the European Union* (Basingstoke, Palgrave McMillan, 2015) 209–31; Fromage, above n 1, 87–100; the chapters by R Ibrido, A Kreppel and M Romaniello in this volume.

[4] See also the chapter by G Rizzoni in this volume.

consultations launched by the Commission, and be informed and consulted during the negotiation of treaties or agreement on economic and financial issues.

It is very difficult to include the Chamber's system of scrutiny in the models identified by the most common classification.[5] On the one hand, it would be misleading to consider it as a 'document-based system', since the scrutiny of individual EU draft legislative acts or documents is a significant but not an overwhelming feature of the Chamber's EU activities. On the other hand, the Chamber does not follow a 'mandating system' as—according to the aforementioned Article 7—the Government is not obliged to seek the Houses' approval of its position before all the Council meetings. Only if the Chamber (and/or the Senate) adopts political guidelines does a 'comply or explain' rule apply, leaving to the Government a certain margin of flexibility to take into account the evolution of the negotiations at EU level.

The Chamber's model of scrutiny is therefore a '*tertium genus*' which aims at controlling and orienting the Government's action at the EU level through a pragmatic combination of tools and procedures. Such an approach takes into account that some trends of the EU constitutional system have severely affected the traditional mechanisms of parliamentary scrutiny. In particular, the leading role of the European Council in policy-making and the increase in early agreements during the EU legislative process reduce the effectiveness of both the mandate arrangements and the scrutiny of individual EU documents.[6] It has therefore become essential for the Chamber (and for all the national Parliaments) to be effectively involved in the definition of the national position within the European Council, generally in the pre-legislative stage, in order to influence the framing of EU policies and legislation.

A. The Government's Duty to Transmit Documents and to Provide Information

Law No 234/2012 obliges the Government to send to the Parliament various categories of EU documents and to provide information and assessments, in line with the most advanced NPs.[7] Such duties—which are mostly fulfilled electronically—follow a precise logical and chronological sequence with a twofold objective:

— To support the Houses in selecting the EU documents to be scrutinised (or checked under the Early Warning System, hereinafter EWS) and in assessing all the legal and substantial issues at stake; and

— to promote, as far as possible, a consistency between the Parliament and the Government's positions for the purposes of the EWS and the political dialogue.

[5] The most common classification of the different systems of EU parliamentary scrutiny is based on a distinction between the 'document-based', 'mandating' and 'mixed' models (see the COSAC website: www.cosac.eu/eu-scrutiny-models). The Italian Parliament is generally included among the 'document-based' systems. Cavatorto above n 3, 212, argues that Law 234/2012 has reshaped the Italian document-based model reinforcing it with some instruments more typical of a mandating system.

[6] See MD Jensen and D Martinsen, 'Out of Time? National Parliaments and Early Decision-Making in the European Union' (2015) 50 *Government and Opposition* 240–70.

[7] See, for instance, S 6 of the Act on Cooperation between the Federal Government and the German Bundestag in matters concerning the EU (www.bundestag.de/htdocs_e/bundestag/Committees/a21/legalbasis/euzbbg/248870). A survey and an assessment of the EU scrutiny in the national Parliaments is contained in Heffler et al, above n 3; Fromage, above n 1.

The first step of this sequence, according to Article 6.1 of Law No 234/2012, is the transmission of all the draft legislative acts, their preparatory documents as well as the consultation and policy-setting acts adopted by EU institutions. It allows the formal referral of the EU documents to parliamentary committees (unless they have been already sent directly to the NPs by the Commission or other EU institutions under Protocols No 1 and 2 annexed to the Lisbon Treaty).[8]

If the Government considers a draft legislative act of particular importance, it must transmit along with it an information note containing an evaluation, an assessment of its urgency and a recommendation of the level of priority to be accorded to it. In practice, the Government fulfils this duty just annexing to each transmission sheet (generally twice a week) a list and a short summary of the documents it deems particularly important (without justifying the selection).[9]

The second step (Article 6.4) is the duty of the competent Ministry to submit to the Houses a report on each draft legislative act (within 20 days from its transmission) assessing:

a) The compliance with the principles of conferral (choice of the legal basis), subsidiarity and proportionality;
b) the coherence with the national interest and the need or opportunity to amend it during the negotiations;
c) the perspectives of the negotiations at EU level; and
d) the impact on EU and national budgets on the domestic legal system (including the regional and local competences), on the public administration and on business and citizens.

Along with the report, the Government must provide a table of correspondence between the provisions of the draft legislative act and the relevant domestic legislation.[10] The reports are transmitted to the relevant committees which circulate them among their respective members. However, the reports are not made publicly accessible (in particular, they are not published in the Chamber website).

The Government regularly fulfils such information duties albeit with some delays. However, the reports' content and quality vary widely depending on the Ministries which draft them: despite an ongoing improvement, some reports just summarise the content of the EU documents without an in-depth assessment of all relevant elements.[11]

B. Participation in Consultations

According to Article 6.2 of Law No 234/2012, the Government must forward to the Parliament all the contributions it sends to the EU institutions within the framework of a (formal or informal) consultation. The objective is to make the Parliament fully aware of the

[8] A notice of all the EU documents referred to the standing committees is annexed to the full transcript of the Plenary sittings.

[9] The list is included in the notice annexed to the full transcript of the Plenary.

[10] The table must be drafted following the procedures set out in a specific Decree of the President of the Council of Ministers (DPCM) of 17 March 2015.

[11] Until December 2016 the Government has transmitted such reports on 215 draft legal acts or other EU documents.

position expressed by the Government in the pre-legislative stage in view of the consideration of a Commission consultation document by the relevant committees of each House.

To date, such obligation has been fulfilled only in some cases; in other cases the Parliament was informed of the Government's contributions only after they had been made public by the Government itself or on the Commission's website.[12]

C. Participation in the European Council and the Council

According to Article 4.1 of Law No 234/2012 (which reproduces a provision already contained in Law No 11/2005), the Government must:

— Report to the Houses the position it intends to take at meetings of the European Council;
— report to the competent standing committees, at their request, before the Council meeting; and
— inform the competent standing committees about the outcome of the meetings of the European Council and the Council, within 15 days after they took place.

In practice, such provisions have been fully implemented with regard to the European Council while being rarely applied for the Council meetings. Since November 2011, the Italian President of the Council reports to the Plenary of each House before all the meetings of the European Council; each House debates and votes on resolutions setting out the parliamentary position on the items on the European Council's agenda.[13] The Minister (or Secretary of State) for EU Affairs reports to both Houses' joint Committees on Foreign Affairs and EU Policies on the outcome of the European Council and on the follow-up given to the parliamentary resolutions adopted before the meeting.

The Italian participation in the European Council therefore lies on a well-established coordination between Parliament and Government, which reflects the awareness among political parties and MPs of the increasing role played by the European Council in shaping the EU's political and legislative priorities.

Conversely, the Houses have rarely asked the Government to report (to the competent committees or to the Plenary) before and/or after Council's meetings.[14] The lack of a regular scrutiny of the Council workings—which is well-developed in other NPs—mostly stems from the approach of the standing committees. They usually prefer to hold a debate with the competent Minister or Secretary of State (mostly in the form of hearings) when scrutinising individual EU documents or issues rather than discussing the whole agenda of a Council session. This approach prevents the Chamber from influencing the overall action

[12] Through December 2016, the Government has forwarded eight contributions to Commission's consultations.

[13] From April 2005 to November 2011, the Minister for Foreign Affairs used to report to the joint Committees on Foreign Affairs and EU policies of both the Houses before the meetings of the European Council. No resolutions were approved after the debate. The choice to report regularly to the plenary was taken by the President of the Council, Mario Monti, who was appointed in November 2011 after the former President Berlusconi resigned.

[14] Consequently, the committees have rarely applied Rule 126-bis which enables them to call 'a debate with the participation of the Minister, on proposals by the European Commission, where such proposals or specific subjects are to be included in the agenda of the Council or on matters concerning agreements pertaining to the EU or their activities or those of their bodies'.

of the Government within each Council composition and from getting a regular feedback on how the Government has taken into account the parliamentary positions.

D. Duties of Information and Consultation in the Field of Economic and Financial Affairs

Law No 234/2012 contains specific and partly overlapping provisions on the Parliament's involvement in EU decision-making in economic and financial affairs.[15] Indeed the general scrutiny tools are deemed ineffective towards, on the one hand, the international agreements stipulated among some Member States outside the EU institutional framework (such as the 'Fiscal Compact') or implemented through new bodies and procedures (such as the treaty establishing the European Stability Mechanism), and, on the other hand, the timeline of the European Semester for the coordination of economic policies.

Article 4.4 binds—with a very broad and generic wording—the Government to inform and consult the Houses regularly on the coordination of economic and budgetary policies as well as on the functioning of the financial stabilisation mechanisms 'established by act, draft acts or other EU documents, enhanced cooperation among Member States or agreements or draft agreements among EU Member States'. Article 5 obliges the Government to timely inform the Parliament about any initiative envisaging the conclusion of agreements among EU Member States which introduce or enhance financial or monetary rules or may have a significant impact on public finances. In addition, the Government must ensure that the Italian position in the negotiation of the agreements takes into account the parliamentary guidelines. If the Government does not follow such guidelines, it must report to the competent parliamentary bodies and explain its reasons.

Article 4.4 has been partially implemented so far. The Minister for Economic and Financial Affairs referred to the Plenary either before or after the adoption of some of the European Stability Mechanism governing bodies' decisions that had significant financial impact; in other cases, the Houses were neither provided with information nor consulted. Article 5 has never been applied despite a new intergovernmental agreement concerning the Banking Union that was negotiated after Law No 234/2012 entered into force.[16]

E. Information on CFSP/CSDP

According to Article 4.2 of Law No 234/2012 the Government is obliged to timely inform the competent parliamentary bodies on 'initiatives or issues' concerning the Common Foreign and Security Policy (CFSP) and the Common Security and Defence Policy (CSDP) which have been submitted to the Council or are under consideration within the Council itself. That provision takes into account that the particular decision-making

[15] More generally on the role of the Italian Parliament in the procedures of the EU economic governance, see the chapter by M Nardini in this book.

[16] See the Agreement on the transfer and mutualisation of contributions to the single resolution fund, signed on 21 May 2015 by 26 Member States and ratified by the Italian Parliament with Law No 188/2015.

mechanisms in the field of CFSP—as set out in Title V of the Treaty on European Union (TEU)—cannot be effectively scrutinised according to the ordinary procedures and require, in most Member States, additional information flows from the Governments to the NPs.[17]

Article 4.2 is substantially implemented through hearings of the Ministers for Foreign Affairs and/or Defence before the competent committees of the two Houses. The hearings are mostly held jointly by the Committees for Foreign Affairs and/or Defence of both the Houses. In addition, the Chamber's Committee for Foreign Affairs has established a subcommittee for European Foreign and Security policies.

F. Information Flows and Cooperation with the Permanent Representation

Law No 234/2012 contains specific provisions aimed at ensuring the cooperation between the Italian Permanent Representation to the EU and the Parliament. Such direct liaison is crucial for the effectiveness of the parliamentary scrutiny as it provides timely information on the developments of EU decision-making. In addition, it enables the Parliament to assess if the Government's action is coherent with the parliamentary guidelines.

Article 4.3 obliges the President of the Council of Ministers (or the Minister for EU Affairs) to forward to the Parliament reports and briefs prepared by the Permanent Representation concerning:[18]

a) Meetings of Council, Committee of Permanent Representatives in the EU (COREPER), Council working groups and committees as well as informal meetings at the ministerial level;
b) meetings of trilogues held in the EU legislative procedures;
c) acts or draft acts adopted by EU institutions;
d) other initiatives or issues concerning EU Institutions or policies; and
e) infringements and Case Law concerning Italy.

To fulfil these duties, the Government forwards to the Houses (some of) the briefs that the Permanent Representation sends on a regular basis to the Ministry for Foreign Affairs and the Department for EU Affairs, as well as the diplomatic advisers and other relevant parts of the competent Ministries.[19] The briefs are mainly used by the Chamber staff to prepare the documentation for the EU-related activities of the parliamentary bodies.

Under Article 3.3, the Government is also required to ensure, 'in the manner agreed by the President of the Council of Ministers and the Presidents of the two Houses', the assistance of the Permanent Representation by providing documentation and information

[17] See the XIV Biannual Report (2010) prepared by the COSAC Secretariat: www.cosac.eu.

[18] A similar provision is contained in s II (c) of the Agreement between the German Bundestag and the Federal Government on cooperation in matters concerning the EU in implementation of s 6 of the above mentioned Act on Cooperation.

[19] The Government usually recommends that the Houses treat the briefs confidentially; according to the Chamber's practice, the MPs can access the briefs on the premises of the Secretariat of the EU Affairs Committee or of the other relevant committees but cannot request a copy of them.

to the offices of the Chamber and the Senate for the liaison with the EU in Brussels.[20] Although these parties have not stipulated a formal agreement, their cooperation is performed according to well-established administrative practices.

G. Scrutiny Procedures

Rule 127 establishes a specific procedure for the consideration of EU acts, draft legislative acts, their 'preparatory documents' and any other EU document. Such documents are referred to the relevant sectoral committee, which is responsible for scrutiny, and to the EU Policies Committee, which issues an opinion.

EU documents concerning institutional issues[21] are referred to the EU Policies Committee, which under Rule 126 has 'an overall responsibility for the general legal aspects of the activity and measures' of the EU. Documents having a horizontal dimension (such as the Multiannual Financial Framework) as well as those concerning specific policy areas but having a significant institutional impact (such as the economic governance) can be referred to the EU Policies Committee jointly with the relevant sectoral committee.

According to Rule 125, the resolutions transmitted to the Chamber from the European Parliament are also referred to the relevant committee—which in turn can issue a resolution—and to the Committees for Foreign Affairs and on the EU Policies for their opinion. That procedure—which has been rarely activated[22]—allows the Chamber to express its position on issues which are not dealt with in specific Commission documents, also for the purpose of the political dialogue with the European Parliament.

The standing committees and the Plenary scrutinise only the EU documents that they consider significant for their scope, object or potential impact on national interests. In the current XVII legislative term (which started in March 2013 up to December 2016), 111 EU documents (out of about 3000 referred to the committees) have been scrutinised and 61 final documents have been issued; in the corresponding period of the XVI legislative term (April 2008–January 2012) the Chamber scrutinised more EU documents (126) but issued less final documents (50, excluding the subsidiarity checks).

The standing committees and the Plenary issue political guidelines for the Government's action on specific EU documents or matters also by using the ordinary policy-setting and fact-finding procedures provided in the RoP. It is noteworthy that in the current legislative term (until 31 December 2016) 139 resolutions on EU-related matters have already been adopted (31 by the Plenary before the meetings of the European Council) while in the corresponding period of the XVI legislative session only 54 resolutions had been issued.

Such figures confirm the peculiarity of the Chamber's system of scrutiny. While the most important draft legislative acts or pre-legislative documents are specifically scrutinised, the Chamber's position in EU affairs is mainly expressed through resolutions aimed at

[20] Also, this provision largely reproduces s VII of the aforementioned agreement between the German Bundestag and the Federal Government.

[21] See, for instance, the proposal for a Regulation on the Citizens' Initiative and the Package on the Better Regulation.

[22] In the XVI legislative term (2008–2013), the Chamber committees considered five EP resolutions and issued three resolutions. In the XVII legislative term (up to 31 December 2016), no EP resolution has been considered.

influencing the EU policy-making on broader issues. As a consequence, the Plenary is playing an increasing role in the definition of the Italian position even if the standing committees remain the main actors in this field.[23]

i. Selection of the EU Documents to be Scrutinised

Under Rule 25.4, the order of business of each committee should be established (by its Bureau including the representatives of all the political groups) 'in such a way as to ensure prompt consideration of EU documents and legislative drafts'. In practice, each committee has broad discretion for this purpose.

The Bureau of the EU Policies Committee regularly (at least twice a month) considers a list including the draft legislative acts transmitted under Protocol No 2 and the EU documents which the Government has indicated are important or which have been object of a Government report. The list is prepared by the parliamentary staff (notably, the EU Affairs Department) of the Chamber and contains explanatory notes and comments.[24] Each member of the Bureau (or of the Committee) can propose to start the scrutiny of any other EU documents.

In the sectoral committees, the Bureau decides to start scrutiny case by case, mainly taking into account briefs and analysis prepared by the Chamber's staff (always the EU Affairs Department) as well as inputs from stakeholders and regional or local authorities.

In the current legislative term, the Bureau of the EU Policies Committee decided to start the scrutiny of the EU documents that it selects only if the relevant sectoral committees do the same. This self-restraint pragmatically reflects the fact that the opinion of the EU Affairs Committee has no effect if the competent committee takes no action: it cannot formally be sent to the Government or transmitted to the EU institutions for the purpose of the political dialogue. In some cases, the Chairman of the EU Policies Committee (on behalf of the Bureau) formally invited the Chairpersons of the sectoral committees to start the scrutiny of specific EU documents. In the previous legislative term, the EU Policies Committee issued several opinions although the sectoral committee did not start the scrutiny. Through this practice the EU Policies Committee aimed at putting pressure on the sectoral committees. However, only in a few cases was this approach successful.[25]

The conduct for EU scrutiny in the standing committees varies dramatically on a qualitative and quantitative level, partly because of structural factors (the different impact of EU legislation in various policy areas) and partly because of contingencies (the committee Members' approach to EU affairs in each legislative term).[26]

[23] In the current legislative term (up to 31 December 2016), the Plenary considered EU-related issues in 73 meetings and the committees did so in 593 (in the corresponding period of the XVI legislative term, respectively, 35 and 835).

[24] In the XVI legislative term, the EU Policies Committee established a subcommittee with the task of selecting the EU documents to be considered (for the general scrutiny and subsidiarity check) The subcommittee usually met twice a month and submitted a list of the relevant EU documents to the Bureau of the Committee.

[25] Instead, the RoP of the Senate (Rule 144.5) enable the EU Policies Committee to send its opinion to the Government and to the EU institutions in case of no action of the sectoral Committees: see the chapter by D Capuano in this volume.

[26] The Committees on Environment, on Agriculture and on Transport are usually very active due to the prominent role of EU legislation in their respective fields of competence, while the Committee on Justice shows little interest in the EU affairs since it is more concentrated on internal and very sensitive legislation. Concerning the

ii. Consideration of Specific EU Documents

The sectoral committees and the EU Policies Committee usually carry out an in-depth consideration of the EU documents under scrutiny by holding hearings and fact-finding inquiries (as provided in Rule 79.4, 79.5 and 79.6 for the consideration of legislative bills).[27] The hearings mostly involve Ministers or Secretaries of State, Government senior officials, Agencies, European Commissioners, MEPs, other relevant EU institutions or bodies, regional governments or assemblies, stakeholders and experts.[28]

According to Rule 127.2, the relevant committees should conclude the scrutiny of an EU document 'in no more than thirty days'. That deadline is seldom respected, as the fact-finding activities are time-consuming. The scrutiny procedures are carried out taking into account the need to issue the Chamber's position in time to influence the Government's conduct in the EU negotiations. Due to the heavy agenda of the committees, sometimes the final documents are adopted after the Government has already expressed the Italian position and even after the Council adopted a general approach on a draft legislative act.

The EU Policies Committee systematically issues its opinion to the relevant sectoral committees (provided that the latter also started the scrutiny), focusing on the respect for the principles of conferral, subsidiarity and proportionality, on institutional and legal issues (for instance, the delegation clauses), on the impact of the EU initiatives upon the Italian institutional and economic systems, and on substantive issues of general scope.

Under Rule 127, the committees conclude the scrutiny by 'expressing in a final document their own opinion on the appropriateness of any possible initiatives'. The wording of this provision and the name of the act adopted ('final document') reflect the approach still prevailing when the section of the RoP concerning EU affairs was amended in 1996 and 1999. It was considered inappropriate for the Parliament to issue politically binding guidelines to the Government in EU affairs. It was feared that a parliamentary mandate would undermine the Government's negotiation capacity within the Council.[29]

Such an approach has been overcome by the legislation in force and by the practice.[30] Indeed, the final documents, while not being structured and worded as a resolution, politically bind the Government according to Article 7 of Law No 234/2012: they express a (positive or negative) position on the EU documents setting some conditions or observations which address specific guidelines to the Government.

contingent factors, impressive is the case of the Committee on Finance, which was very active in the XVI term (2008–2013) but did not consider any EU document in the current term despite the important initiatives in this field in the past two years (while holding several hearings on EU-related issues). Conversely, the Committees on Constitutional and Internal Affairs and on Employment increased dramatically their scrutiny activities in the current legislative term.

[27] In the current legislative term (up to 31 December 2016), 11 inquiries have been held by the standing committees (7 in the corresponding period of the past term).

[28] In the current legislative term (up to 31 December 2016), 222 hearings have been held (244 in the corresponding period of the XVI legislative term) on EU documents or issues (56 of Ministers/Secretaries of State, 18 of officials of the Italian Government/Agencies, 19 of European Commissioners, nine of MEPs, and 120 of experts, regional and local authorities, NGOs and others). Most hearings are held by the sectoral committees which usually invite the members of the EU Policies Committee to attend. Some hearings are held jointly by the relevant sectoral committee and the EU Policies Committee.

[29] See Matarazzo and Leone, above n 3.

[30] The RoP of the Senate on EU affairs, which were amended on 2003, are therefore more advanced both in its wording and in its procedures: see the chapter by D Capuano in this book.

Since the beginning of 2016, the Government started giving almost regular feedback on how it has complied with the Chamber's (or Senate's) guidelines to implement the 'comply or explain' rule stated in Article 7.[31]

iii. The Parliamentary Scrutiny Reserve

According to Article 10 of Law No 234/2012 (that mostly reproduces Article 4 of Law on 11/2005), a parliamentary scrutiny reserve may be invoked by one of the Houses of Parliament or the Government on its own initiative. The Government must place the reserve (for the whole draft legislative act or for one or more of its parts) within the Council, whereupon it may not proceed 'with the activities of its own competence' aimed at the adoption of a draft legislative act until the parliamentary scrutiny has been concluded or, even if Parliament has not adopted a position, until 30 days have elapsed from the notification to the Houses that the reserve has been invoked.

The procedure to invoke the reserve at the Chamber is set out in the opinion of the Rules Committee of 6 October 2009: at the request of the relevant committee, the President of the Chamber notifies the Government when the examination of a draft legislative act begins. In practice, each committee can decide if and when it is appropriate to invoke the reserve. The opinion also binds the committees to take into account the deadline of the reserve so as to issue a final document before it elapses.

The scrutiny reserve has been rarely used since its introduction in 2005 (four times overall). In the current legislative term, neither has the Chamber addressed a request to invoke the reserve nor has the Government invoked any reserve on its own initiative. This trend partially reflects the difficulty in carrying out an in-depth consideration of the EU document within the tight deadline provided for the scrutiny reserve. Also, however, in a few cases (in the past legislative term) the Government did not invoke the reserve in the Council despite the requests formally transmitted from the Chamber.[32] This failure was provoked by a lack of coordination among the Ministers of EU Affairs and for the Relations with the Parliament, who received the notifications from both the Chamber, on the one hand, and the Government's representatives who attended the relevant Council meeting, on the other hand.

The combination of these factors has led the committees to consider the reserve substantially useless to influence the definition of the Italian position.

H. Hearings of Representatives of EU Institutions

Rule 127-ter envisages another tool for a direct liaison of the Chamber with EU institutions which is increasingly used for the purposes of the general scrutiny and the political dialogue. It enables the committees to hold hearings of MEPs (mainly the Rapporteurs or the Italian members of the competent EP committees), members of the European Commission, and

[31] Until 31 December 2016, the Government sent to the Chambers 14 reports about the follow-up given to final documents adopted by the Chamber.

[32] See, among others, the reserve invoked on 9 June 2010 by the Committee on Budget on a proposal of Regulation on the quality of statistical data in the context of the excessive deficit procedure (COM(2010) 53).

(as specified in the opinion of the Rules Committee of 6 October 2009) representatives of other EU institutions and bodies.[33] Most hearings are held jointly with the corresponding Senate committees and concern broad issues rather than specific draft legislative acts.

The usefulness of the hearings varies significantly depending especially on the subjects and committees involved. In its documents on the Annual Reports of the European Commission on the relations with the National Parliaments, the EU Policies Committee has often underlined that the European Commissioners during their hearings should be open to a more effective and outspoken exchange of views, also with reference to specific legislative proposals.

III. The Subsidiarity Check

A. The Chamber's Procedure

The procedure for the Chamber's participation to the EWS was established on a transitional basis by means of two opinions issued by the Rules Committee.[34] Article 8 of Law No 234/2012 also deals with the participation of the Houses in the EWS but has no normative content, as it just recalls the provisions of Protocol No 2 and refers to the procedures established by each Chamber.

According to the aforementioned opinions, the EU Policies Committee has the competence to perform the subsidiarity check. It issues a document containing a reasoned opinion or a positive assessment of the compliance of the draft legislative act with subsidiarity (hereinafter 'positive decision') within 40 days of the referral; this sub-deadline is intended to leave enough time for a request to submit the decision to the Plenary. The request can be presented—within five days of the Committee decision—by the Government, a fifth of the members of the Committee itself (at least nine as the Committee is composed of 44 members) or a tenth of the members of the Chamber (at least 63). The Plenary can also refer the decision back to the Committee as long as this does not compromise the compliance with the deadlines envisaged by Protocol No 2. In this case, the new decision may be resubmitted to the Plenary for consideration.

Where a positive decision of the EU Policies Committee is re-submitted to the Plenary, 20 deputies (or one or more chairpersons of political groups having at least the same number of MPs) must submit a specific motion setting out the reasons why the draft legislative act under examination breaches the principle of subsidiarity (ie a 'draft reasoned opinion'). If no motion is presented, the matter will not be considered in Plenary. The motion is voted upon only if the positive decision of the EU Policies Committee is rejected. In any event, the procedure must be completed within the eight-week period. The possibility to re-submit

[33] See the figures on the hearings mentioned above.

[34] For a critical assessment of the Italian Chambers' procedures to implement the EWS, see the chapter by N Lupo in this volume. A survey of the procedures for the participation of NPs to the EWS is contained in the XVI biannual report (2011) of the COSAC Secretariat on Developments in EU Procedures and Practices relevant to Parliamentary Scrutiny' (www.cosac.eu).

the decisions on subsidiarity to the Plenary has been provided taking into account both the impact of a reasoned opinion on the Italian position in the negotiations and the effects that the EWS can produce on the EU legislative process (if the thresholds provided in Protocol No 2 are triggered). Up to now, no request to resubmit to the Plenary has been issued.

The President of the Chamber transmits to the EP, the Commission and the Council the reasoned opinion issued by the EU Policies Committee or the Plenary. The EU Policies Committee may also request the transmission of its positive decision (and it has always done so).

The decision to introduce such a specific procedure for the EWS (while in the Senate the same procedure as for the general scrutiny is followed) reflects three goals. First, it aims at ensuring that a single body develops coherent and well-established criteria and methods to assess the compliance of a draft legislative act with the subsidiarity principle. Indeed, the sectoral committees could follow divergent criteria and instrumentally use the EWS to assert substantial arguments against a draft legislative act. Second, given the eight-week deadline, the EU Policies Committee can carry out the check in a more timely and effective manner than the sectoral committees, which usually have an overburdened agenda. Third, the sectoral committees—the procedure for the EWS being completely autonomous—can conduct the general scrutiny of a draft legislative act well beyond the eight weeks by carrying out an in-depth consideration in compliance with the Chamber's approach.[35]

B. The Subsidiarity Check in Practice

Over six years of application of the EWS, the EU Policies Committee has developed a set of coherent criteria and methods to carry out the subsidiarity check.

First, the Committee does not check systematically all the draft legislative acts transmitted under Protocol No 2 but only those which—on the basis of the Government's reports, alerts from other NPs or stakeholders as well as the Chamber's staff analysis—require a more in-depth assessment. In the past legislative term, the Committee checked 20 draft legislative acts and issued four reasoned opinions and 14 positive documents. In the current legislative term (up to 31 December 2016), three draft legislative acts were checked and three positive documents were adopted. This approach reveals that the EU Policies Committee, despite its primary competence in this field, does not deem the EWS a priority, instead attaching more importance to substance of EU draft legislative acts through the general scrutiny and the political dialogue.

Second, the EU Policies Committee also includes in the subsidiarity check the assessment of the correct legal basis of draft legislative acts. Out of the four reasoned opinions issued to date, three alleged an incorrect legal basis or the adoption of provisions beyond the scope and the object of the correct legal basis. Conversely, the Committee—after debating different options—decided that a breach of proportionality would not justify the adoption of a

[35] According to the opinions of the Committee on RoP, a liaison between the general scrutiny and the EWS on the same draft legislative acts should be ensured by appointing a Rapporteur of the relevant committee who takes part in the proceedings of the EU Policies Committee. However this provision—set out in the opinions of the Rules Committee—has never been applied in practice.

reasoned opinion,[36] as the wording of Article 6 Protocol No 2, establishing the EWS, concerns only questions of subsidiarity. In addition, the Committee considered that the tests of subsidiarity and proportionality—while based on several common elements—demand partially separate criteria and methodologies. Indeed, subsidiarity concerns the actual existence of conditions to exercise non-exclusive EU competences (including if the EU can act and, if so, on which aspects of the policy field at stake); instead, proportionality deals with the choice of the tools and implies an accurate assessment of the legal, economic and social impact of the EU action at the national level, which are strictly connected with the substantive aspects of a draft legislative act. Therefore, the Committee decided to express its position on proportionality within the framework of the general scrutiny (and of the political dialogue).

Third, the EU Policies Committee carefully takes into account the Government's assessment of subsidiarity contained in the reports transmitted on each draft legislative act; in addition, it invites representatives of the Government to attend its meetings when the subsidiarity check is debated. This practice aims at reducing the risk of adopting a reasoned opinion without evaluating its potential impact on the Italian negotiating position within the Council.[37]

Some scholars have criticised the EWS procedure set up in the Chamber by underlining that it would be ineffective, burdensome and complex.[38] Such criticism does not take into account that the overall objective of the procedures and practices followed by the Chamber is to avoid an abuse or a misuse of the EWS. This tool is seen as exceptional, given its potential effect of blocking or delaying the EU decision-making process. Therefore, the Chamber's procedure aims at allowing the issuance of a reasoned opinion only where the EU Policies Committee (or the Plenary) finds an evident breach of subsidiarity or legal basis and the relevant draft legislative act is considered against the national interest. The low number of reasoned opinions issued by the Chamber is a coherent consequence of this approach rather than a sign of the procedural framework's weakness. In addition, the separation between the procedures for the general scrutiny (political dialogue) and the EWS allows the sectoral committees to carry out an in-depth assessment of the EU draft legislative acts, which generally requires more than eight weeks.

The distrust in the EWS is also the main reason for the Chamber's opposition to any attempt to establish within the Conference of Parliamentary Committees for Union Affairs of Parliaments of the European Union (COSAC) a coordination among the NPs to facilitate the triggering of the thresholds for the yellow or orange cards.[39]

[36] See the final document issued by the EU Policies Committee on the Commission Annual Report 2013 on subsidiarity and proportionality (COM(2014) 506) (www.ipex.eu/IPEXL-WEB/scrutiny/COM20140506/itcam.do).

[37] An interesting case of explicit divergence between the Chamber and the Government's position is the reasoned opinion on the proposal for a general Regulation on structural and investment funds (COM(2011) 615) issued by the EU Policies Committee on 14 December 2011, despite the Minister for Cohesion had recommended not to adopt it during the Committee meeting (www.ipex.eu/IPEXL-WEB/scrutiny/COD20110276/itcam.do).

[38] See, among others, the chapters by N Lupo and M Romaniello in this book. Both authors consider more effective the procedure set up by the Senate.

[39] See A Esposito, 'The Role of COSAC in EU Interparliamentary Cooperation: An (Endless) Quest for an Identity' in N Lupo and C Fasone (eds), *Interparliamentary Cooperation in the Composite European Constitution* (Oxford, Hart Publishing, 2016). The Senate follows a different approach: see the chapter by E Griglio in this book.

IV. The Political Dialogue[40]

The procedure for the Chamber's participation in the political dialogue with the EU institutions has been developed by practice. Indeed, no specific provision has been introduced in the RoP, while Article 9 of Law No 234/2012—which deals with the political dialogue—has no normative content. It merely provides that each of the Houses may forward to the EU—at the same time as to the Italian Government—any document pertaining to the framing of European policies. In substance, it acknowledges that the modes to carry out the political dialogue, in coherence with its informal nature, fall entirely within the autonomy of each House.[41]

In the Chamber's practice, the political dialogue is carried out together with the general scrutiny through a single procedure. The Chairpersons of the relevant committees usually request[42] the President to transmit to the European Commission, the EP and the Council the final documents (as well as resolutions or other policy-setting acts) adopted for the general scrutiny. Also, the positive decisions of the EU Policies Committee on subsidiarity are usually forwarded to the same EU institutions.

Most statements contained in the final documents (or other policy-setting acts) are not addressed specifically to the Government or to the EU institutions. However, some of them may be directed to the Government (as they contain negotiating mandates or concern purely internal aspects), while in a few cases they are expressly addressed to the EU institutions.[43]

In substance, the Chamber considers the political dialogue as complementary and not as alternative to the general scrutiny. The aim is to ensure the coherence of the Italian participation in the EU decision-making by avoiding the contrast of the Parliament's views with the Government's position within the Council.

From the introduction of the political dialogue in September 2006 to December 2016, the Chamber sent to the European Commission and to the EP 137 opinions: 25 from 2006 to 2009 (before the Lisbon Treaty entered into force) and 112 from 2010 to 2016[44] (almost 14 per year on average). Such figures—which are less impressive than those of the Italian Senate or other Parliaments—reflect the selective approach of the Chamber to the general scrutiny rather than an ineffective procedural framework.

The EU Policies Committee carries out an assessment of the political dialogue every year when considering the reports of the European Commission on the relations with the National Parliaments. In particular, in the final documents approved on such reports the committee has reiterated two arguments: the Commission's replies to NPs' opinions should

[40] For a critical assessment of the Italian Chambers' procedures to implement the political dialogue, see the chapters by N Lupo and M Romaniello in this volume.

[41] Instead N Lupo, see the chapter in this volume, considers that Art 8 has some legal effects.

[42] The request is generally based on a specific clause contained in the document to be transmitted or is reported in the minutes of the committee meeting when the document is approved.

[43] Some final documents, due to the content and the scope of the EU documents under scrutiny, are addressed exclusively to the EU institutions (such is the case of the annual reports on subsidiarity and proportionality and on the relations with the NPs).

[44] In detail the Chamber sent 25 opinions in 2010, 28 in 2011, 15 in 2012, six in 2013, 15 in 2014, seven in 2015 and 16 in 2016.

be more timely and focused on the argument raised by the NP; and the Commission should give overall feedback and assessment of the impact of NPs' opinions on the decision-making process, possibly considering some significant cases.

V. Consideration of the Government's and EU Political Planning Documents

A specific procedure set out in two opinions of the Rules Committee (issued on 9 February 2000 and 16 July 2010) enables the Chamber to consider jointly the Annual Work Programme of the European Commission, the Programme of the Trio Presidency of the Council and the Annual Report on the Government on the Italian priorities at EU level.[45] The procedure envisages a sort of 'EU Session' which involves all the relevant parliamentary bodies through three steps:

- The scrutiny by the sectoral standing committees (each in relation to the matters falling within their respective areas of competence), in which each of them issues an opinion;
- a general scrutiny (including hearings of Government, Italian MEPs, Regional Assemblies, stakeholders, and experts) by the EU Policies Committee, which submits a report to the Plenary; and
- a debate in the Plenary which can adopt one or more resolutions addressed to the Government (usually forwarded to the EP, the Council and the Commission within the framework of the political dialogue).

The EU Session enables all the relevant parliamentary bodies to scrutinise the political and legislative priorities of the EU institutions and the Government and to debate the state and the perspectives of the EU integration. The resolutions adopted by the Plenary can thus contribute to defining—at an early stage—the general approach and the main objectives of the Italian action at EU level. The application of such procedures has been initially deceiving because of delays in the first years of its conduct (notably 2011–2014). This was due partly to the late presentation of most Annual Reports from the Government to the Chambers[46] and partly to slowdowns in the Chamber's workings. As a consequence, since 2011 the consideration of the Government's and EU Political Planning Documents has been started three times and concluded only twice (in September 2015 and March 2016).[47]

[45] The Report must be submitted to the Chambers by 31 December each year according to Art 13.1 of Law No 234/2012. It illustrates the position that the Government intends to take during the subsequent year with regard to developments in the process of European integration, institutional issues and sectoral policies.

[46] Concerning the current Legislative term the Report for 2013 was transmitted on 5 June 2013 (due to the general elections held in February); the Report for 2014 on 10 January 2014 (however the scrutiny was slowed down due a Government reshuffle in February); the Report for 2015 on 5 March 2015; the Report for 2016 on 23 December 2015 and the Report for 2017 on 19 January 2017.

[47] See Resolutions No 6-00155 adopted on 10 September 2015 (http://aic.camera.it/aic/scheda.html?numero=6-00155&ramo=C&leg=17) and no 6-0023 adopted on 30 March 2016 (http://aic.camera.it/aic/scheda.html?numero=6-00223&ramo=C&leg=17).

VI. Consultation of the Regional Assemblies

The Chamber has not introduced specific rules or practices for the consultation of the regional assemblies within the EWS and the general scrutiny that thus takes place through the ordinary procedures.[48] As the legal framework in force (Article 6 of Protocol No 1 and Law No 234/2012) does not bind Parliament to consult the regional legislatures, the Chamber has opted to carry out such cooperation—which was already well-established before the Lisbon Treaty and Law No 234 of 2012 entered into force—in a very flexible way. This approach does not reflect a lack of commitment but aims at avoiding rigid procedures which would make the consultation more complicated and burdensome.

Concerning the general scrutiny (and the political dialogue), each standing committee can hold hearings of the Conference of Presidents of the regional Assemblies[49] and/or consider the resolutions the latter sends to the Chamber.[50] The regional resolutions are usually mentioned in the final documents adopted by the competent Committee as well as in the opinions of the EU Policies Committee.[51] The EU Policies Committee also can follow the same procedures for the purposes of the EWS, taking into account the deadlines to issue a reasoned opinion.

VII. Interparliamentary Cooperation

The Chamber of Deputies actively participates in all the fora and tools of the EU interparliamentary cooperation.[52] Representatives of the Chamber regularly attend the meetings of the parliamentary conferences as well as the meetings of the competent sectoral committees organised by the EP and/or by the Parliament of the country holding the Presidency of the Council.[53] A great attention is devoted also to the cooperation among parliamentary

[48] On the relationship between the Italian Parliament and regional Councils, see the chapter by C Fasone in this volume. A specific framework for cooperation with the Regional Assemblies has been developed by the Senate: see the chapters by DA Capuano and C Fasone in this volume.

[49] A hearing of the Conference of Presidents of the regional Assemblies takes place systematically during the consideration of the Annual Work Programme of the European Commission and the Annual Report on the Government on the Italian priorities at EU level.

[50] In 2016 the Chamber received 27 resolutions from regional assemblies.

[51] See, among others, the opinion issued on 23 July 2014 by the EU Policies Committee on the Communication 'A European Strategy for more Growth and Jobs in Coastal and Maritime Tourism' (COM(2014) 86 final): http://documenti.camera.it/leg17/resoconti/commissioni/bollettini/html/2014/07/23/14/comunic.htm#.

[52] In 2015, the Chamber attended 54 interparliamentary meetings at political and administrative levels. On the interparliamentary cooperation in the EU, see, among others, Lupo and Fasone (eds), at n 39; A Esposito, 'La cooperazione interparlamentare: principi, strumenti e prospettive' in Manzella and Lupo, above n 1, 133–82. On the different approaches of the two Italian Chambers to the cooperation, see the chapter by E Griglio in this volume.

[53] The President of the Chamber decides which committee is competent to participate and determines the size of the delegation (taking into account the rules or indication for each conference). The composition of the Chamber's delegations is decided by the Chairman of the relevant committee case by case, ensuring in principle the participation of majority and opposition MPs. Under a well-established practice, the COSAC delegation is composed by the Chairman of the EU Policies Committee and its two Deputies. On the composition of the Italian delegation, see also the chapter by E Griglio in this book.

administrations, especially through the IPEX system,[54] the network of representatives of NPs in Brussels, the contacts among officials attending COSAC meetings and other standing conferences.

In the Chamber's view, the primary object of the cooperation is to make more effective—through the exchange of information, views and best practices—the performance of the functions of the EP and of each NP, according to the logic of complementarity and minimising competition among them.[55] Hence, the Chamber opposes any proposal to express 'collective' or coordinate positions of the NPs for the purposes of the EWS and of the political dialogue[56] or to carry out shared advisory, policy-setting or oversight functions towards the EU institutions.[57]

Such an approach is based on the consideration that the role of NPs in the EU constitutional architecture—as set out in the Treaties (notably Articles 10(2) and 12 TEU, Protocols No 1 and No 2)—is to scrutinise the EU action of their respective Governments. The powers of direct intervention of the NPs in EU decision-making introduced by the Lisbon Treaty as well as the political dialogue are therefore an additional and ancillary channel to ensure the EU's democratic legitimacy.

In practice, the interparliamentary cooperation supports the Chamber's action on several levels. First, the participation in conferences and meetings as well as the relevant background documents (such as the biannual reports prepared by the COSAC Secretariat) provide the MPs and the Chamber staff with a valuable and updated survey of the positions, the procedures and methodologies of other parliaments (and sometimes of the EU institutions).[58] Second, the cooperation increases the awareness among the MPs and Chamber's staff of the European dimension of national policies by overcoming purely national visions. Third, the exchange of information and best practices—especially within COSAC—has stimulated a hybridisation of the procedures and practices for the EU scrutiny in the NPs. In particular—as mentioned above—several provisions of Law No 234/2012 evince an emulation of the mechanisms adopted in other Member States. Fourth, the administrative cooperation has promoted—in addition to the exchange of information—a convergence of working methods of the Chamber's staff with the best practices in other NPs that completes the process of cross-fertilisation of the legal framework.

VIII. Conclusions

The overall legal framework for the Italian Parliament's participation in EU affairs is one of the most advanced among the EU Member States. It potentially enables the Chamber and

[54] On IPEX see Esposito, above n 39.

[55] See A Esposito, 'The Role of COSAC in EU Interparliamentary Cooperation: An (Endless) Quest for an Identity', in Lupo and Fasone, above n 27.

[56] Such as the 'green card' allowing groups of NPs to propose to the Commission new legislative action, or the review, amendment of repeal of existing legislation).

[57] A different approach is followed by the Italian Senate: see chapters by D Capuano and E Griglio in this volume.

[58] To this end, the leading member of the Chamber's delegation submits to the competent committee a report on the outcome of each interparliamentary meeting. The report is attached to the official records of the relevant committee's meeting.

the Senate to intervene, directly or indirectly, in each stage of the EU policy-making and decision-making processes (from the policy-shaping phase to implementation).[59]

Within this framework, the Chamber has developed its EU-related procedures and practices following a fourfold logic: first, the concentration of its intervention on the most important EU issues and acts; second, an in-depth (but time-consuming) engagement in the scrutiny; third, the search for a close link with the Government not only for the general scrutiny but even for the political dialogue and the EWS which allow a direct relationship with the EU institutions; fourth, the promotion of a proactive contribution to the enhancement of the European integration rather than a potential slowdown of the EU action.[60]

This approach could be considered conservative or minimalist and unable to fully exploit the (alleged) potential of new powers conferred to the NPs by the Lisbon Treaty. Instead, the Chamber's attitude has a very solid and coherent legal foundation and is very pragmatic.

Concerning the legal and political foundations, the Chamber considers that—in compliance with the wording of Article 10(2) TEU—the primary role of NPs in the EU constitutional system is to scrutinise their respective governments. The powers of direct intervention of the NPs in the EU decision-making—such as the EWS—are therefore an additional and ancillary channel to ensure the democratic legitimacy of the EU.

As regards to the pragmatism, the Chamber's priority is to ensure the coherence and effectiveness of the overall Italian position in EU decision-making.[61] Without adequate and updated flows of information and a regular interaction with the Government, the scrutiny (as well as the political dialogue and the EWS) would be merely formal and ineffective. In addition, there would be the risk that Parliament and Government take contrasting positions on the same issue.

Despite its coherence, the actual impact of the Chamber's action in framing EU legislation and policies is questionable. On a quantitative level, the Chamber's EU-related activities have significantly increased over the last years. The most relevant EU draft legislative acts and pre-legislative acts are scrutinised in depth by the competent committees; also, the Plenary devotes increasing attention to major EU issues. In substance, although there have been some improvements, the overall capacity of the Chamber (and of the Senate) to influence the EU decision-making remains weak. Despite significant improvements in 2016, it is still hard to assess the contribution of the policy guidelines issued by the Houses to the definition of the national position. In some cases, the Chamber's position is adopted when the negotiations are already in an advanced state. In addition, the parliamentary reserve has seldom been invoked. Also, the real impact of the political dialogue and of the EWS can hardly be measured, as no real feedback on the follow up to the NPs' contribution is given.

The reasons behind this weakness stem from shortcomings of the political and administrative culture rather than the procedures and practices followed by the Chamber. First of all, the awareness of the importance of the Parliament's role in EU affairs is still asymmetrical among most MPs and within the political parties. In setting the political and the

[59] For a critical assessment of the legal framework in force, see the chapter by N Lupo in this book, who underlines the need for 'a formalisation and a simplification of the parliamentary procedures' especially as regards to the political dialogue and the EWS; C Fasone and L Bartolucci, 'Le procedure di raccordo con l'Unione europea: un bilancio in attivo, ma con qualche occasione persa' (2014) 1 *Osservatorio sulle fonti* 1–28.

[60] See the conclusions of the chapter by G Piccirilli in this volume.

[61] For an analysis of this approach, see the chapter by G Rizzoni, in this volume.

parliamentary agenda great attention is drawn to the European Council and to debates on major current issues; conversely, the scrutiny of individual EU documents is seldom considered a priority. This approach undermines the capacity of the Chamber to influence the EU negotiations.

Second, despite the provision of Law No 234/2012, the Ministries and the agencies tend to underestimate the Parliament's role in the definition of the national position on the EU dossier. While the Government's duties of information and consultation towards the House are regularly performed on a formal level, the quality and timeliness of the information provided is sometimes poor. In addition, the parliamentary guidelines seem not to be taken in due consideration by the Government's representatives during the negotiations in the Council.

Third, despite a significant improvement in recent years, the elaboration of the Italian position and even the definition of the national interest, especially on horizontal dossiers (such as the Multiannual Financial Framework), is complicated and slowed down by a weak inter-ministerial and intra-ministerial coordination, as well as poor coordination between the Government and other relevant actors (especially regions and stakeholders). This prevents the Parliament from having an early and effective interaction with the Government in all the stages of EU decision-making.

Such critical factors cannot be overcome by changing the legal framework.[62] Instead, a breakthrough in the attitude of the institutional actors and stakeholders towards EU affairs is required.

[62] On 8 January 2014, the Rules Committee adopted a basic test of amendments to the Chamber of Deputies' RoP. In October 2014, the consideration of the basic text was suspended—on a requests from the opposition political Groups—because of the ongoing consideration (at the time) of the Bill for a Constitutional Reform (later adopted by the Parliament in April 2016 but rejected because of the negative outcome of the referendum held on 4 December 2016). Concerning the EU affairs, the basic text mainly codified the 'experimental' procedures introduced by the aforementioned opinions issued by the Rules Committee in 2009 and 2010. On the basic text see the special edition of the (2014) 3 '*Osservatorio sulle fonti.it*'.

7

European Affairs within the Senate of the Republic

DAVIDE A CAPUANO[1]

I. The Constitutional Framework

The role of the Italian Senate in defining its position on EU affairs is directly linked to its constitutional role as a House of a national Parliament in the European Union, which works—in coordination with all the other relevant bodies of the Italian institutional system—to define and formalise the Italian position on EU draft legislation.

There are some provisions in the Italian Constitution that relate explicitly or implicitly to the EU: a non-explicit reference has been found in Article 11,[2] according to which 'Italy agrees, on conditions of equality with other States, to the limitations of sovereignty that may be necessary to a world order ensuring peace and justice among the Nations'; a direct one exists in Article 117, modified by the constitutional revision in 2001, according

[1] The opinions of the author are personal.
[2] The Constitutional Court, starting from the sentence no 183 of 1973, stated that Art 11 has been conceived not only for the participation of Italy at the supranational organisations, as the United Nations, but also for a stricter relationship in a specific European order.

to which 'Legislative powers shall be vested in the State ... in compliance with ... the constraints deriving from EU legislation ...'; and direct reference is also found in Articles 97 and 119 (in their 2012 versions stemming from the Constitutional Law on the Balanced Budget Rule),[3] which oblige the Public Administrations, the Regions and the territorial entities to respect budget constraints 'in coherence with' (for Article 97) or 'deriving from' (for Article 119) the European legal order.

These Articles do not explicitly foresee the active participation of the Houses in the forming of EU legislation. Nonetheless, in conjunction with the necessity for the Government to have the confidence of both Houses (Article 94 Constitution), the rules of procedure applied the constitutional power of the Senate and the Chamber of Deputies to hold debates on European matters. At the end of these debates, it is possible to vote on motions or documents that give direction to the Government on the positions to be assumed in the competent European bodies.

The Treaty of Lisbon has complemented the powers granted to national Parliaments by their respective Constitutions. Consequently, for the first time in the European integration process, national Parliaments exert powers not envisaged directly by their national Constitutions, but by the common European constitutional framework, constituted by the Treaty on the EU and the Treaty on the Functioning of the EU with their annexed protocols.

Furthermore, apart from what has been granted by the treaties, powers for national Parliaments have been envisaged by new European measures adopted in the years following the entry into force of the Treaty of Lisbon to counterbalance the devolution of power to the supranational level[4]—as is the case for example as concerns Regulation No 473/2013, on common provisions for monitoring and assessing draft budgetary plans, and Regulation (EU) No 1024/2013, on the Single Supervisory Mechanism (SSM).

According to this Euro-National constitutional framework,[5] the activities of individual houses of European parliaments in the European Union's decisional mechanisms can be summarised as follows: a) the procedure for monitoring the respect of the subsidiarity principle (early warning system), according to Protocol No 2; b) the political dialogue with the EU institutions, according to Protocol No 1; c) the procedure of monitoring and controlling the Government's activities in the Council; d) the interparliamentary cooperation between national Parliaments and with the European Parliament, which could be considered as a part of the political dialogue but because of its increasing importance is better described autonomously;[6] and e) the participation in the 'European Semester' process and in the economic governance cycle.

A few words must be made on the revision of the constitutional legal order, approved by the Italian Parliament but rejected by a large majority of citizens in the referendum held on 4 December 2016.

[3] Constitutional Law No 1 of 2012, adopted on 20 April 2012.

[4] On the limits of 'Democratisation' at EU level, see the Afterword by PL Lindseth, in this book.

[5] For the need to analyse each national parliament as an institution placed within the Euro-national parliamentary system, see the Introduction by N Lupo and G Piccirilli, in this book.

[6] On this categorisation, see DA Capuano, 'The Role of National Parliaments in the Legislative Process of the EU. A View from the Italian Parliament' in M Cartabia, N Lupo and A Simoncini (eds), *Democracy and Subsidiarity in the EU. National Parliaments, Regions and Civil Society in the Decision-making Process* (Bologna, Il Mulino, 2013) 229 ff; see also the chapter by A Esposito, in this volume.

This constitutional revision would have directly interfered with the powers granted to the houses at the national level without immediately altering the institutional balance made at the supranational level by the Treaty of Lisbon. In other words, according to the categorisation indicated above, it was only the scrutiny of the Government's activities in the Council that in theory could have been affected by the Senate's loss of the vote of confidence (even if it is possible to argue that the notion of scrutiny does not imply the necessity of a vote of confidence for the Government, as is for example the House of Lords' experience). Besides, Article 55 of the Italian Constitution after the revision would have devoted to the Senate, which would have 'represented' territorial institutions, the function of liaison between the state, the entities constituting the Republic and the European Union. It is not easy to understand in which ways this task would have been managed in concrete parliamentary activities; nor is it clear whether this proposition would have prescribed a new function for the Senate or whether it was merely a repetition of a power already provided elsewhere. What seemed more effective was the assumption that the Senate would have taken part in the preparatory decision-making process for EU legislative acts and EU policy definition. Also more promising would have been the Senate's role in the process of implementing EU measures and evaluating public policies (the new Article 55), even regarding the impact of European policies on the territories.[7]

The constitutional reform will not enter into force. But even if it had, the role and function of the Italian Senate in defining its position on EU affairs would not have been affected in a substantial manner in light of the Treaty of Lisbon's direct grant of power. Consequently, the description that follows is valid for the current constitutional order, but it would have substantially been the same if the Italian Constitution had been revised.

II. The Powers of National Chambers in the EU Legislative Process: The Scrutiny of the Government's Activities in the Council

The role of national Parliaments increased after the entry into force of the Treaty of Lisbon, which made them part of the European institutional balance under Article 12 of Treaty on European Union (TEU) and even holders of a 'responsibility for integration'.[8] The Treaty of Lisbon accelerated the Europeanisation of national Parliaments, realigning national politics with EU-determined policies.[9]

[7] On the European functions of the Senate after the reform, see the chapter by L Gianniti in this book; see also E Albanesi, 'Il nuovo Senato ed i raccordi con l'Unione europea' in P Costanzo, A Giovannelli and L Trucco (eds), *Forum sul d.d.l costituzionale 'Renzi-Boschi'* (Turin, Giappichelli, 2015) 73 ff.

[8] As recalled in the Foreword of this Book by A Manzella, quoting the expression coined by the *Bundesverfassungsgericht* on the judgement on the Treaty of Lisbon of 30 June 2009.

[9] For the concept of 'Europeanisation', to be intended as the transformation of national institutions deriving from (or inducted by) the participation of the Member States in the European Union, see N Lupo, 'National Parliaments in the European Integration Process: Re-aligning Politics and Policies' in Cartabia, Lupo and Simoncini, n 6 above, 130 ff; see, also, for an analysis of the European powers of national Parliaments after the first years of their use, N Lupo, 'I poteri europei dei Parlamenti nazionali: questioni terminologiche, classificazioni e primi effetti' in A Manzella and N Lupo (eds), *Il sistema parlamentare euro-nazionale. Lezioni* (Turin, Giappichelli, 2014) 128 ff.

In this framework, Law No 234/2012[10] aligned the powers of the Italian Houses with the new provisions introduced by the Treaty of Lisbon and also made substantial changes regarding the transposition process.[11]

Article 3, paragraph 1, of Law No 234/2012 sets out the general principle that Parliament participates in the decisional process of the European Union. The following paragraph, in a more detailed statement, ensures that both Chambers, 'in coordination with the Government', intervene in the formation phases of European legislation and European policies in accordance with the Treaty on the European Union and the Treaty on the Functioning of the European Union (TFEU).

Consequently, there is a strong connection between the two treaties and Law No 234/2012, which codified three forms of intervention for the Senate and the Chamber of Deputies in the EU decision-making process: the scrutiny of the Italian Government's activities in the Council, the subsidiarity check, and the political dialogue (see Articles 7, 8 and 9).[12]

We begin, in this part, with the scrutiny of the Government's activities in the Council. This task has remained substantially unchanged with the entry into force of the Treaty of Lisbon, both regarding its legal basis and the tools that Parliament use to do so. These tools are questions and interpellations for the scrutiny function and parliamentary motions and resolutions for the political direction of the Government.[13]

The Treaty of Lisbon has not intervened formally to regulate the internal relations between the legislative assemblies and their respective governments. It has only made a reference to each Member State's autonomous competence. The first recital of the preamble of Protocol No 1 recalls 'that the way in which national parliaments scrutinise their Governments in relation to the activities of the Union is a matter for the particular constitutional organization and practice of each Member State'.[14]

Concerning the Italian system, Law No 234/2012 establishes that every EU measure and the related preparatory work, including white and green papers as well as communications, should be sent by the Government to Parliament for referral to a Committee. On examining such draft measures, the Committee responsible for the subject matter shall issue an opinion and provide recommendations to the Government.

Article 6 of this Law demands that the Government provide a report to the Parliament on all draft proposals under consideration. This report includes elements on their respect

[10] On Law No 234/2012, see A Esposito, 'La legge 24 dicembre 2012, n 234, sulla partecipazione dell'Italia alla formazione e all'attuazione della normativa e delle politiche dell'Unione europea. Parte I—Prime riflessioni sul ruolo delle Camere' (2013) 2 *Federalismi.it*; for an investigation of the 'European' procedures, as reshaped by Law No 234/2012, G Piccirilli, 'Il Parlamento italiano: le procedure europee nella legge n 234 del 2012' in Manzella and Lupo, n 9 above, 205 ff.

[11] On the transposition activity and the need to connect it with the participation at the EU legislative process, see the chapter by R Ibrido, in this volume.

[12] In our categorisation we include also the interparliamentary cooperation and the participation in the EU economic governance. For other specific 'European' attributions of national Parliaments see the chapters by G Piccirilli and B Guastaferro, in this volume.

[13] See the chapter by G Rizzoni, in this volume.

[14] In this sense, the Constitutional Court of Slovenia, in its decision of 18 October 2012 (U-I-17/11-7), stated that the TEU, the TFEU, and the Protocols are not relevant for 'the regulation of how Member States are to form and adopt, in their national legal orders, the positions that the representatives of their governments support in the institutions of the European Union'; they are relevant, on the contrary, for 'the regulation of direct relationships between the national parliaments (and their individual chambers) and the European Union and its institutions'.

of the principles of conferral, subsidiarity and proportionality; an overall assessment on the status and the perspective of negotiations, with specific evidence of the points relevant to the 'national interest'; and the impact of the measure on Italian legislation. It is particularly important because it ensures both that the Parliament is aware of the Government's evaluation of the proposal or the single document under consideration and that the coordination between Parliament and Government, as envisaged by Article 3 of Law No 234/2012, is effective. Furthermore, the Parliament has the concrete chance to verify ex ante the possible position that the Government will assume in its activities in the Council and, if desired, adopt a parliamentary position to modify it.

At the end of the parliamentary consideration, Article 7 of Law No 234/2012 does in fact state that on draft EU acts and EU preparatory documents the competent parliamentary bodies—which currently are the Standing Committees—may adopt 'acts of direction', according to the relevant rules of procedure of both Houses of Parliament.[15]

The Government ensures that the position to be represented in the Council or in any other relevant EU institution is coherent with those expressed by the Chambers. Whenever the Government has difficulties in respecting the opinions and recommendations of the Chambers, the President of the Council or the competent Minister has the obligation to explain the different position assumed (under the 'comply or explain' rule).

As the Italian system is one of symmetrical bicameralism, the law does not envisage the supremacy of one House over the other. Therefore, in principle, it is possible that the two Chambers could adopt resolutions that are potentially in conflict with one another. However, the situation, whilst theoretically plausible, is extremely rare in practice, due to the central role of the Government, supported by the same parliamentary groups, in the Italian parliamentary system.

Regarding the parliamentary reserve, Article 10 of Law No 234/2012 establishes that a Chamber of Parliament, when considering legislation proposed by the Union or documents sent by the Government, may request the Government to withhold its legislative action in the Council, to be resumed only after parliamentary consideration has been completed or after 30 days have passed without any opinion having been issued. After the entry into force of the Treaty of Lisbon, the Senate never has triggered this reservation, while the Chamber of Deputies has done so only once, on the Citizen's Initiative proposal,[16] and only four times overall since its introduction in 2005 with Article 4 of Law No 11/2005.[17]

In addition, it is worth mentioning that Article 4 of Law No 234/2012 mandates that, before meetings of the European Council, the Government shall brief the Parliament on what position it will assume in the European Council. The Government shall take into account any position of the Senate or the Chamber of Deputies on the topics on the agenda.[18] The Government shall then report to Parliament on the outcome within 15 days from the conclusion of the European Council. The same procedure applies, upon request

15 This provision should have overcome the 'formal' difference between Art 144 of the Senate's rules of procedure (which use the word 'resolution') and Art 127 of the Chamber's rules of procedure (which use the words 'final document'). They both refer to 'substantial' considerations or observations expressed by the two Chambers, to be taken into account by the Government; see also the chapter by A Esposito, in this volume.

16 See Esposito, n 10 above, 39

17 See the chapter by A Esposito, in this volume.

18 See the chapter by G Rizzoni, in this volume.

of the relevant sectoral Committee, to the Council meetings. This provision, and its continuous implementation, is crucial for the Senate's involvement in the EU policy-making process. The bodies of the Senate are fully informed on the activities of the European Council and the Council, so that their opinions and recommendations to the Government can evaluate the state of play of the ongoing negotiations.

III. The Role of the Parliamentary Bodies of the Senate

A key instrument in ensuring the effectiveness of the scrutiny process is the consideration of draft EU acts by the relevant sectoral Committees of the Senate. Since the entry into force of the Treaty of Lisbon and Law No 234/2012, there have been no formal changes to the Senate's rules of procedure even though some Articles of Law No 234/2012 made a reference to changes to ensure the implementation of its provisions.[19]

However, it should be highlighted that the Senate's rules of procedure were modified in 2003 to take into account the parliamentary dimension in EU affairs as slated to be modified by the European Convention's deliberations.[20] These modifications gave the Rules of the Senate great flexibility, permitting them to adapt to the consideration of draft legislative proposals and other EU documents.

The cornerstone of the Senate's provisions is the widespread power amongst the relevant Committees in dealing with EU affairs, provided by Article 144 of the rules of procedure, which makes each one of them responsible for considering matters falling within their remit. On this topic, it is also worth recalling Article 29, paragraph 2-bis, of the rules of procedure. This Article states that the programme and calendar of business of each Committee 'shall' be drafted to ensure that preparatory documents for European Union legislation 'may be scrutinised in a timely manner', so making it possible to establish a direct connection between parliamentary consideration and its usefulness for the Government in its activities in the Council.

In 2003, parliamentary consideration included only scrutiny of Government activities in the Council, but the flexibility of the Senate's rules of procedure permitted later on—as we will see—the simultaneous consideration of the draft EU acts also for the early warning system and the political dialogue, without formal changes.

According to Article 144, paragraph 6, the consideration ends with the approval of a resolution 'laying down principles and guidelines, which shall apply to Italian policy in respect of the preparatory work for the development of Community measures'.[21] The resolution, at the request of the Government or one-third of the members of the Committee competent for the subject matter, shall be submitted to the Senate (Article 50, paragraph 3, of the rules of procedure). It acts as a sort of positive confirmation, at the highest deliberative

[19] Arts 4, 7, 8 and 15 of Law No 234/2012 make a reference to the rules of procedure of the two Houses.

[20] The modifications concerned a sweeping revision of Senate Rules concerning the relations between the Senate and the European Union and were adopted on 6 February 2003.

[21] The rules of procedure, having been approved in 2003, still maintain a reference to the 'Community' measures.

level within the Senate, or, alternatively, as a sort of appellate decision; and a Government defeated in the Committee's activity or a minority group may seek to activate this provision in order to have a second chance.

However, this sort of Senate appellate decision has never occurred in practice. Once a document has been adopted in a Committee, there is no real interest in involving the plenary, even by opposition groups. The plenary has instead a relevant role ahead of the European Councils, in discussing the topics of the Agenda with the Prime Minister and adopting through specific motions the positions to be represented by the Government. On these occasions, all parliamentary groups concentrate their political pressure.

The resolutions approved are then forwarded to the Government, provided to the Speaker of the Chamber of Deputies and, after the introduction of the 'political dialogue', also transmitted to the EU institutions.

If the relevant sectoral Committee does not conclude its consideration of an EU document within a given period (15 days after the transmission of the opinions of the obligatorily consulted Committees, which are the Foreign Affairs Committee and the Committee on European Union Policies), the consulted Committees may vote a document in its stead (Article 144, paragraph 5) in the presence of the majority of the Committee components. This substitutive power has been exercised, in the Senate's practice, only by the Committee on European Union Policies,[22] which—through the double membership of its members—assures the presence of all the competences represented in the Senate.

It must be argued that, according to Article 144, paragraph 5, of the rules of procedure, there should be no 'right' of the consultative Committees to deliberate in substitution of the competent Committee. The general principle of loyal cooperation between internal bodies of the Senate should prevent a conflict in adopting a resolution binding the Government on European issues. Therefore, the provision states that the consultative Committees—in cases of inactivity of the competent Committee—may request that their observations and proposals 'be forwarded to the Government, through the President of the Senate'. The President of the Senate has, consequently, the final word on sending the 'substitute' deliberation of the consultative Committee instead of the 'missing' deliberation of the competent Committee. It is for this reason that the consultative Committee (that is, in current practice, only the Committee on European Union Policies) usually consults the Committee competent for the subject matter before adopting the 'substitute' deliberation. The same substitutive power is not envisaged by the Rules of the Chamber of Deputies, which has a different approach towards the distribution of EU competences amongst the Standing Committees.[23]

[22] The Committee on European Union Policies (14th Committee) plays a major role in dealing with EU affairs in the Senate. Under the Senate Rules, the Committee on European Union Policies has general jurisdiction over the constitutional aspects of the activity of the EU and its bodies. It is responsible for relations with the European Parliament and the COSAC (Conference of Parliamentary Committees for Union Affairs of Parliaments of the European Union, established by Art 10 of Protocol No 1). It also has jurisdiction over compliance with European law and considers and reports to the Senate on the EU Delegation Bill and the European Bill (following Law No 234/2012), which are introduced yearly by the Government in order to fulfil Italy's European obligations. The Committee has had, since 2006, a Sub-Committee on the forming of EU legislation and a Sub-Committee on the transposition of EU legislation and, since 2014, a Sub-Committee on Regions.

[23] On the different role of the Committees of the Italian Parliament in dealing with EU affairs, see the chapter by A Esposito, in this volume.

IV. The Political Dialogue

The principal tool by which the Italian Senate proactively involves itself in the EU policy-making process is the political dialogue. Built upon the commitment of the European Commission in 2006[24] and endorsed by the June 2006 European Council,[25] it rapidly granted national parliaments the opportunity to truly engage in EU affairs. It now has an implicit reference in the Preamble of Protocol No 1, in which the High Contracting Parties express their desire 'to encourage greater involvement of national Parliaments in the activities of the European Union and to enhance their ability to express their views', not only 'on draft legislative acts of the Union', but also 'on other matters which may be of particular interest to them'.

The political dialogue is a more comprehensive procedure in comparison with the early warning system because it concerns not only legislative proposals, but any act related to the functioning of the European Union, and can address the substance of the draft acts under consideration. The European Commission supported this participation, stating that the political dialogue 'will allow both sides to engage in a broader, more political exchange of views, not only limited to legislative proposals and going well beyond the issue of subsidiarity'.[26] For the European Commission, the subsidiarity control mechanism and the political dialogue are interdependent as two sides of the same coin, with the former being part of a wider political relationship between the Commission and national parliaments.

The Italian Senate immediately followed this perspective of the political dialogue. The consideration of draft legislative proposals and other relevant European acts, with the view of 'laying down principles and guidelines' for the Government's activities in the Council—according to Article 144 of the Rules of Procedure—has also been extended to the possible reaction to the European Commission and other EU institutions in order 'to improve the process of policy formulation'.

According to the procedure shaped by the Senate's internal practice, the consideration of draft legislative proposals and other relevant European acts involves not only the substance of the proposals (to guide the Government in the Council), but also the subsidiarity and proportionality principles (as requested by the European Council). The aim is to provide the European Commission and the EU legislature with the Senate's perspective on all aspects of the proposals, with regards to its bodies, through a constructive approach instead of a mere opposition one, guided by a limited consideration of the aspects related to subsidiarity.

Two aspects make the Senate's approach preferable. First, there are real difficulties in making a clear distinction between the notion of subsidiarity and the notions of legal basis, proportionality and substance. Second, as has been argued, politicians tend to transmit into the subsidiarity check their prejudices about the proposal from their negative judgement

[24] With the Communication of 10 May 2006 (COM(2006) 211), the European Commission decided 'to transmit directly all new proposals and consultation papers to national Parliaments, inviting them to react so as to improve the process of policy formulation'.

[25] Point 37 of the European Council Conclusions of June 2006.

[26] Communication on relations between national Parliaments and the European Commission of 2009 (Annual Report 2009).

of the substance. If they agree with the substance, they will positively assess the subsidiarity profiles, whereas if they disagree with the substance, the contrary occurs.[27]

Also with the entry into force of the Treaty of Lisbon, the political dialogue within the Senate continues to follow the same procedural rules as applied for the procedure for monitoring and controlling the activities of the Government in the Council. So, Article 144 of the rules of procedure applies, in the exact terms as seen before. There is consequently a perfect overlap of the two procedures (scrutiny of the Government and political dialogue); they only differ in the 'resolution's' final destination: the Government, on one side, the EU institutions, on the other.

In the framework of the 'political dialogue', a new tool could be developed if the initiative of the so-called 'green card' succeeds in receiving a consensus of national parliaments and of the EU institutions. The 'green card' provides a certain number of national parliaments or chambers, through their relevant internal bodies, the possibility to suggest to the European Commission a reflection on certain topics, aiming at the adoption of a consultation document, a Communication, or even a legislative proposal.[28]

Some concerns have been raised about the possibility that the new initiative will alter the inter-institutional balance in a way similar to that of the European citizens' initiative (Article 11 TEU and Article 24 TFEU) or the European Parliament's request for a legislative initiative (Article 225 TFEU). However, within the Conference of Parliamentary Committees for Union Affairs (COSAC) there is an ongoing joint reflection, with the formal qualification of the 'green card' as 'a non-binding form of enhanced and coordinated political dialogue'.[29]

Thus, the framework of the political dialogue seems to offer a clear umbrella for a constructive participation of national Parliaments in the EU activities.[30] On this basis, the first green card was issued on 22 July 2015, on the initiative of the House of Lords and with the participation of 16 Parliaments/Chambers (including the Italian Senate), on the topic of reducing food waste within the EU; in 2016, the second green card was issued on the initiative of the Assemblée Nationale and with the participation of nine parliaments/chambers (including the Italian Senate), on the topic of corporate social responsibility.

V. The Subsidiarity Check

According to Article 12(b) TEU, national Parliaments contribute actively to the good functioning of the Union by ensuring the compliance of draft legislative proposals with

[27] See N Lupo, 'The Scrutiny of the Principle of Subsidiarity in the Procedures and Reasoned Opinions of the Italian Chamber and Senate' in A Jonsson Cornell and M Goldoni (eds), *National and Regional Parliaments in the EU Legislative Procedure Post-Lisbon: The Impact of the Early Warning Mechanism* (Oxford, Hart Publishing, 2017) 225 ff.

[28] See C Fasone and D Fromage, 'From Veto Players to Agenda-Setters? National Parliaments and their 'Green Card' to the European Commission' (2016) 23(2) *Maastricht Journal of European and Comparative Law* 294 ff.

[29] Point No 5.1 of the Contribution of the LIV COSAC (Luxembourg, 29 November–1 December 2015); see also point No 2.4 of the Contribution of the LIII COSAC (Riga, 31 May–2 June 2015).

[30] On the growing importance for national Parliaments to exert a constructive influence in the EU decision-making process, see C Fasone and D Fromage, 'National Parliaments and the EU Commission's Agenda: Limits and Recent Developments of a Difficult Partnership' in C Fasone, D Fromage and Z Lefkofridi (eds), *Parliaments, Public Opinion and Parliamentary Elections in Europe* (2015) EUI Max Weber Working Paper Series, 31–43.

the principle of subsidiarity, in accordance with the procedures provided for in Protocol No 2. The subsidiarity check is the typical procedure for the involvement of national parliaments in the EU legislative process. It is carried out on the draft legislative acts which do not fall into the exclusive competence of the European Union and may lead to the issuing of a 'yellow card' or an 'orange card' if the votes expressed by national parliaments reach, respectively, the threshold of a third (or a quarter for matters involving judicial cooperation in criminal matters or police cooperation) or the majority of all the votes allocated to them.[31]

The complex procedure laid down in the protocol has not had much success in the early years of entry into force of the Treaty of Lisbon. The threshold for the 'yellow card' so far has been reached in only three circumstances. The first time was in May 2012 and was related to a proposal on the right to strike (the so-called Monti II-regulation);[32] on that occasion, the Commission withdrew the proposal without taking into account the reasoned opinions of national Parliaments but instead merely referenced the lack of political support in the Council. In November 2013, the 'yellow card' was given to the proposal establishing a European Public Prosecutor's Office;[33] in that case, the European Commission decided to maintain the proposal as it was. In May 2016, the 'yellow card' was raised on the proposal for a directive amending the Posted Workers Directive;[34] the Commission decided to maintain the proposal.[35]

In all of these circumstances, quite surprisingly indeed, the European Commission neglected the 'collective' position of national Parliaments as concerns the subsidiarity profiles. On the contrary, the Commission reiterated its commitment to pursue its political dialogue with all national Parliaments on arguments going beyond compliance with the subsidiarity principle and affirming its readiness to engage in discussions with the European Parliament and the Council on the concerns raised.[36]

In all these cases, the Italian Senate expressed a positive statement on the respect of the principle of subsidiarity and so transmitted an opinion in the framework of the political dialogue. As concerns the Monti II-regulation and the Posted Workers Directive, the opinion was released pending the eight-week period envisaged by the treaty.[37] As concerns the European Public Prosecutor's Office, the opinion was released after the eight-week period elapsed,[38] and so in the full knowledge that the yellow card had been raised and in the spirit of supporting the Commission's proposal.

As mentioned above, after the entry into force of the Treaty of Lisbon, the Senate did not formally change the rules of procedure. One reason can be found in the capacity of the

[31] On the subsidiarity check, see C Fasone, 'Competing Concepts of Subsidiarity in the Early Warning System' in Cartabia, Lupo and Simoncini, n 6 above, 157 ff; B Guastaferro, 'Reframing Subsidiarity Inquiry from an "EU Value-added" to an "EU Non-encroachment" Test?' in Cartabia, Lupo and Simoncini, n 6 above, 133 ff.

[32] COM (2012) 130. The proposal regulates the exercise of the right to take collective action within the context of the freedom of establishment and the freedom to provide services.

[33] COM (2013) 534 final.

[34] COM(2016) 128 final. The proposal aims at ensuring that the implementation of the freedom to provide services in the Union takes place under conditions that guarantee a level playing field for businesses and respect for the rights of workers.

[35] In COM(2016) 505, adopted on 20 July 2016, the Commission justified the maintenance of the proposal.

[36] COM(2016) 505.

[37] By the Labour Committee, on 7 May 2011 and on 4 May 2016.

[38] By the Justice Committee, on 19 November 2013.

modifications of 2003 to absorb the new powers. Another is in the clear political approach of the Senate's bodies of not considering the early warning system in terms of acting as opposition, but instead including it in the general consideration of the proposals. In this perspective, the control of the subsidiarity principle is only a part of the general scrutiny of the Act, as Protocol No 30 on subsidiarity annexed to the Treaty of Amsterdam affirmed.

The President of the Senate's letter to the Presidents of Standing Committees, initially published on 1 December 2009, clearly reflected this approach.[39] Thus, each Committee, being responsible for the general scrutiny of the draft legislative proposal under Article 144, has the chance to include in the final resolution its view on the respect of the subsidiarity principle. This resolution, to be considered also as a reasoned opinion under Protocol No 2, must respect the five admissibility requirements imposed by the treaty:[40] opinions must originate in a national parliament or chamber; they must concern a draft legislative act; they must be sent on time; they must provide reasons (ie a blank objection is inadmissible); and the opinion must concern a breach of the principle of subsidiarity.

The letter of 1 December 2009, in order to respect the eight-week limit for the subsidiarity check, provided for the immediate deferral of draft legislative acts to the Committee competent in the subject matter, permitting the period to be fully exploited. The act of deferral fixes a date for the expression of the opinion of the consultative Committees and a date for the expression of the position of the Committee competent in the subject matter. These internal time limits are well before the eight-week period foreseen in Article 6 of Protocol No 2, in order to allow for a possible referral to the Plenary of the Senate, according to Article 50, paragraph 3, of the rules of procedure, expressly recalled by Article 144, last paragraph.[41]

The letter of 1 December 2009 maintains the substitutive power of the obligatorily consulted Committees under Article 144, paragraph 5, in the case of the competent Committee's inactivity. This power has never been exercised with reference to the subsidiarity checks.

The Senate adopted reasoned opinions in 12 cases. In nine out of the 12 cases, there has been coherence between the opinion of the Committee on European Union Policies, which detected a breach of the subsidiarity principle, and the 'reasoned opinion' of the competent Committee.[42] Only in the first reasoned opinion adopted

[39] For more details on this letter, see D A Capuano, 'Il Senato e l'attuazione del trattato di Lisbona, tra controllo di sussidiarietà e dialogo politico' in www.amministrazioneincammino.luiss.it, 2011.

[40] See, P Kiiver, *The Early Warning System for the Principle of Subsidiarity: Constitutional Theory and Empirical Reality* (New York-London, Routledge, 2012) 67.

[41] It must be noted, however, that the internal limits for the subsidiarity checks are not mandatory for the Committees.

[42] These nine cases of reasoned opinions adopted by Committees of the Italian Senate with a similar opinion of the Committee on European Union policies relate to: the Justice Committee, on COM(2011)126 (matters of matrimonial property regimes) and on COM(2011)127 (property consequences of registered partnerships); the Health Committee, on COM(2011)353 (food for special medical purposes) and on COM(2012) 788 (manufacture, presentation and sale of tobacco and related products); the Public Works, Communication Committee, on COM (2013) 296 (framework on market access to port services and financial transparency of ports) and on COM(2015) 613 (common rules in the field of civil aviation and establishing a European Union Safety Agency); the Agricultural Committee, on COM(2014) 4 and COM(2014) 5 (zoo-technical package) and on COM(2016) 750 (labeling and protection of geographical indications for spirit drinks); the Constitutional Affairs Committee, on COM(2016) 270 (reform of the Dublin system).

by the Senate,[43] in the reasoned opinion on the access to genetic resources,[44] and in the last reasoned opinion adopted on the standards for the reception of applicants for international protection[45] were there divergences between the Committee on European Union Policies and the competent Committee, the former having not detected a breach of the subsidiarity principle.

The final document to be approved under the subsidiarity check procedure is a resolution and could constitute a reasoned opinion if the Senate detects a breach of the principle of subsidiarity or a (simple) opinion in other cases. If the Senate adopts a reasoned opinion, under the treaties' requirements, it is sent to the EU institutions under Protocol No 2 and also to the Government and the Chamber of Deputies. In the same way, if the Senate adopts an opinion, it is sent to the EU institutions under Protocol No 1 (in the framework of the political dialogue) and also to the Government and the Chamber of Deputies.

It has been questioned whether a reasoned opinion, under the treaty requirements, automatically binds the Government. The question should have a positive answer in principle, but the problem has been preempted, in practice, in two cases of reasoned opinions adopted by the Senate, both containing a sentence which states that the reasoned opinion must also be considered binding upon the Government under Article 7 of Law No 234/2012, which obliges the latter to assure that the position to be represented in the Council or in other relevant EU institutions is coherent with the positions expressed by the Chambers.[46]

The complex content of the resolutions adopted by the Senate makes it easier to adapt them to one procedure or the other. The fact is that resolutions always contain paragraphs on the legal basis, the subsidiarity principle, the proportionality principle and the substance of the proposal. And, as has been highlighted, the Italian Senate (as well as the Italian Chamber of Deputies) uses a broad notion of subsidiarity that can at times overlap with the content of the other points of the consideration. Thus, it may more easily cover the aspects related to the political significance of the proposals, as politicians tend to prefer doing so. This approach is consistent with the predominantly political nature of the early warning system in its practical application.[47]

VI. The Involvement of Regional Legislative Assemblies

The direct involvement of regional legislative Assemblies in the European activities of the two Houses of Parliament is an important tool to help develop new forms of

[43] It was the case of the reasoned opinion adopted by the Agricultural Committee on COM(2010)176 (rules for imports into the European Union from Greenland of fishery products).

[44] The Environment Committee adopted a reasoned opinion on COM (2012) 576 (access to genetic resources and the fair and equitable sharing of benefits arising from their utilisation in the Union).

[45] The Constitutional Affairs Committee adopted a reasoned opinion on COM (2016) 465 (standards for the reception of applicants for international protection (recast)).

[46] The two cases refer to the reasoned opinions on COM(2013) 296 and on COM(2014) 4 and COM(2014) 5. The formula adopted is 'This document is to be understood as guidance to the Government within the meaning of Art 7 of Law No 234/2012'.

[47] See Lupo, n 27 above; see also the chapter by N Lupo, in this volume.

parliamentary democracy.[48] Law No 234/2012 provided for the involvement of regional Assemblies not only in the early warning system as regards the subsidiarity principle (Article 8), but also in the more general framework of the political dialogue (Article 9).

In this perspective, the Italian legislation went well beyond the spirit and the letter of Article 6 of Protocol No 2 annexed to the treaties, which—in the early warning system procedure—referred to the power of each national Parliament or each chamber of a national Parliament to consult, where appropriate, regional Parliaments with legislative powers.

Article 8, paragraph 3, of Law No 234/2012 repeated this clause, permitting the two Chambers to consult, according to their respective rules of procedure, the regional legislative Assemblies. Article 9, instead, went beyond this and opened political dialogue to the regional legislative Assemblies and (also) to the regional Governments.

Concerning the participation of regional legislative Assemblies in the Senate's European legislative tasks, a well-consolidated practice started in the wake of the approval of the political dialogue in 2006 and took a major step forwards with the establishment, on 12 March 2014, of a special Sub-Committee on Regions within the Committee on European Union Policies.[49] This Sub-Committee has been entrusted with the task of examining, in a preliminary manner, questions related to the European Union that were submitted by regional votes, as envisaged by Article 138 of the rules of procedure. The possibility of adopting such an assertive deliberation was founded on the competence granted to the Committee on European Union Policies by Article 23, paragraph 3, of the rules of procedure.[50]

Furthermore, another decisive step was made with the Resolution of the Committee on European Union Policies of 24 September 2014 (Document XXIV, no 35), which established an Annual Session between the Committee and the Conference of the Presidents of Regional Assemblies on themes of common interest for the year to come, starting from a joint consideration of the Commission's Legislative and Work Programme.

The procedural treatment of the documents transmitted by the Regions falls under Article 138 of the rules of procedure, dedicated to the 'Examination of the votes of the regional Councils'. The votes submitted by regional Councils are announced in the Plenary sitting of the Senate and referred to the Committee responsible for the subject matter.

The rules of procedure do not contain an adaptation of this Article to the Treaty of Lisbon, nor did the letter of 1 December 2009 take a position on the issue. The current practice of the Senate, however, refers the regional votes related to European Acts—either falling under the early warning system or the political dialogue—to the competent Committees,

[48] On the participation of regions in EU affairs and the principle of subsidiarity, see K Borońska-Hryniewiecka, 'Regions and Subsidiarity after the Treaty of Lisbon: Overcoming the "Regional Blindness"?' in Cartabia, Lupo and Simoncini, n 6 above, 341 ff; D Fromage, 'Regional Parliaments and the Early Warning System: An Assessment Six Years after the Entry into Force of the Lisbon Treaty' (2016) *SOG Working Papers #33*. On the impact of EU post-Lisbon procedures on the relationship between the Italian Parliament and Regional Councils, see C Fasone, 'Italian Regional Councils and the Positive Externalities of the Early Warning Mechanism for National Constitutional Law' in Jonsson Cornell and Goldoni n 27 above, 155 ff; see also the chapter by C Fasone, in this volume.

[49] See C Fasone, 'In attesa della riforma costituzionale, alcune recenti evoluzioni nella 14ª Commissione del Senato sui raccordi tra Stato, Regioni e Unione europea' (2011) www.forumcostituzionale.it.

[50] According to this Art, the Committee shall express its opinion or submit comments (also) 'with regard to … participation of the Regions and the Autonomous Provinces in the framing and implementation of EU legislation, … and compliance with the principle of subsidiarity in relations between the European Union and central and regional Governments'.

including the Committee on European Union Policies. The referral is made with a specific reference to Article 138 of the rules of procedure. If there is a European Act already referred to the Committees for consideration, it seems possible to extend the interpretation of Article 138, paragraph 2, so as to permit the joint discussion of the regional vote with the European Act under consideration.[51]

VII. The Follow-up of the Senate's Resolutions

As concerns the follow-up of the Senate's resolutions, it must be observed that they relate, in most cases, to a legislative procedure that sees the European Parliament and the Council as co-legislators.[52]

Thus, the Senate's resolutions that are 'reasoned opinions' are part of the European procedure that the treaties permit if the required thresholds have been reached.[53] However, even if the thresholds have not been reached, European institutions shall take into account the reasoned opinions issued either by national Parliaments or by a chamber of a national Parliament.[54]

In line with this last point, the European Commission, according to the letter sent by President Barroso to national Parliaments on 1 December 2009,[55] replies in writing to each reasoned opinion, explaining the rationale for sharing or declining to share the arguments expressed by each national chamber. The European Commission also sends a written reply to the opinions of national Parliaments issued in the framework of the political dialogue. All these replies are received electronically by the Senate and are sent to the competent Committees for a possible follow-up.

Resolutions adopted by the Senate's Committees are also sent to the European Parliament.[56] If these resolutions constitute a reasoned opinion, they fall under Article 42 of the rules of procedure of the European Parliament, dedicated to the 'Examination of respect for the principle of subsidiarity'. This Article states that if a national Parliament sends the President a reasoned opinion, that document shall be referred to the competent Committees, making these (reasoned) opinions part of the documents related to the legislative procedure. However, if the resolutions are simply 'opinions', thus falling under the political dialogue, Article 142 of the rules of procedure prescribes that they shall be forwarded to the Committee responsible for the subject matter addressed in that document. The resolutions adopted by the European Parliament, whether at the end of a legislative

[51] This para states that if a vote is relevant to a bill already referred to a Committee, it shall be referred to this Committee to be discussed jointly with the bill.

[52] The ongoing negotiations about draft legislative acts may be followed through the European data banks 'Prelex' and 'Oeil', while the positions of national Parliaments are collected in the IPEX website (www.ipex.eu).

[53] See Art 7, para 2, of Protocol No 2.

[54] See Art 7, para 1, of Protocol No 2.

[55] The European Commission, on the same date of entry into force of the Treaty of Lisbon, sent a letter to national Parliaments detailing its commitment in the enforcement of the provisions of the Treaty and the technical modalities for the reciprocal transmission of documents.

[56] See L Bartolucci, 'The European Parliament and the "Opinions" of National Parliaments', SOG Working Papers #14, February 2014.

procedure or not, are sent to national Parliaments. Article 143 of the Senate's rules of procedure permits the Committees to take a position on the European Parliament resolutions.[57]

Concerning the follow-up of the resolutions addressed to the Government for its activities in the Council, it must be said that formal sessions in order to discuss the results of the negotiations are not very common, even on the basis of Article 7 of Law No 234/2012, which establishes the 'comply or explain' rule. Nonetheless, in some recent cases, the Government—under Article 7 of Law No 234/2012—gave information about the ongoing negotiations, so providing parliamentarians a better understanding of the complex dynamism of forming EU legislation.[58]

In general, after the adoption of parliamentary resolutions on a certain European draft act and the successive steps of the three European institutions on that same draft, the Senate's parliamentary bodies engage in no formal evaluation of the results of their activity. They prefer, if it is the case, to engage the same topic again when scrutinising the next European proposal on the same subject matter or participating in a hearing of the responsible Commissioner.

VIII. The Senate and Interparliamentary Cooperation

The Senate actively participates in the different fora of interparliamentary cooperation: the general one, given by COSAC; the specific Conference on the Common Foreign and Security Policy (CFSP) and Common Security and Defence Policy (CSDP); the economic cooperation of Article 13 of the Fiscal Compact treaty; and other interparliamentary meetings, including the Conference of the Speakers and the Associations of the Senates of Europe.[59]

The Senate, through its participation, brings its view to the attention of the EU institutions and other Parliaments in a proactive and constructive way. In this perspective, a stronger role for the national Parliaments in the EU would not endanger the position of the European Parliament by causing potentially conflicting relations between them. On the contrary, the European Parliament would surely benefit from a constructive dialogue with the national Parliaments, closer to it for composition and wills.

Hence, it is easy to understand why, in general, the Senate has always promoted an approach in favour of the adoption of political conclusions at the end of interparliamentary meetings. This action maximises the effectiveness of such meetings by increasing the political engagement of national parliaments in EU affairs and ensuring that Parliaments' positions are better taken into account by legislators at European and national levels.

[57] In the current post-Lisbon practice, however, this Art has never been applied.

[58] For example, with two letters of 25 November 2015, the Minister for Internal Affairs informed the Senate about the ongoing negotiations concerning COM(2015) 450, on the establishment of a crisis relocation mechanism, and COM(2015) 452, on the establishment of an EU common list of safe countries of origin.

[59] On interparliamentary cooperation in general, in a system that puts together the national Parliaments and the European Parliament, see N Lupo and C Fasone (eds), *Interparliamentary Cooperation in the Composite European Constitution* (Oxford, Hart, 2016); N Lupo, 'The Role of International Parliamentary Cooperation: Political Tourism or Added Value for Intergovernmental relations? in W Hofmeister and J Melissem (eds.), *Rethinking International institutions: Diplomacy and Impact on the Emerging World Order* (World Scientific Pub Co Inc, 2016) 53–66; see also the chapter by E Griglio, in this volume.

Consequently, a regular and 'effective' interparliamentary cooperation is promoted, as is requested by Article 9 of Protocol No 1.

As has been affirmed,[60] in the 'connected' parliamentary system in progressive formation, the democratic legitimacy expressed through the vote of the national citizens, and recognised in the national parliamentary system, complements the other legitimacy expressed through the vote of the European citizens, and recognised in the European Parliament.

In this way, through the method of the so-called 'Conferences', a new European parliamentary system is emerging, ensuring the 'good functioning' of European democracy and European constitutionalism.[61] This system does not operate with the ordinary methods of joint decision-making or consultation, but through a process that is less than the former and more than the latter: it falls under the legal category of 'influence',[62] which envisages a special role for the national Parliaments and the European Parliament, different from their traditional and formalised one.

This special role derives from the system of the Conferences, where both national and European parliamentarians discuss together issues of common relevance and jointly adopt political conclusions as the meetings' outcome. These 'conclusions' may be used by representatives of national Parliaments and the European Parliament in order to exercise a power of informal influence on acts formally conferred to their competences. This process thus mutually interconnects national Parliaments and the European Parliament, consequently reinforcing the democratic legitimacy of the European integration process.

IX. The Participation in the 'European Semester' Process and the Economic Governance Cycle

In addition to the tasks already examined in the previous paragraphs, the Italian Senate is also involved in defining the position of the Italian Republic as concerns the so-called 'European Semester' in the framework of the new economic governance cycle.[63]

Taking into account the different phases that are part of the European Semester, the Senate applies the general procedures already described as well as some specific provisions. In particular, the consideration of the Annual Growth Survey follows the general consideration of non-legislative documents of the European Union, making it possible for the Committees or the Assembly to adopt resolutions for the Government (Article 144 of the rules of procedure) and to transmit opinions to the EU institutions in the framework of the political dialogue.

The consideration of the National Reform Programme and Stability and Convergence Programme has been adapted into the scrutiny of the Document of Economy and Finance

[60] A Manzella, *Sui principi democratici dell'Unione europea* (Napoli, Editoriale Scientifica, 2013) 137.

[61] Lupo, n 59 above, 56.

[62] Manzella, n 60 above, 143.

[63] For the procedural solutions chosen by the Italian Parliament with regard to the mechanisms of the new European economic governance, see DA Capuano and E Griglio, 'La nuova governance economica europea. I risvolti sulle procedure parlamentari italiane' in Lupo and Manzella, n 9 above, 227 ff; see also the chapter by M Nardini, in this volume.

(Article 125-bis of the rules of procedure). The two Programmes are, in fact, parts of the Document of Economy and Finance,[64] to be submitted by Government to the Parliament before 10 April for the consequent parliamentary deliberations.[65]

Article 125-bis of the rules of procedure states that the Economic and Fiscal Plan (now the Document of Economy and Finance) shall be referred to the Budget Committee for consideration and to the other Standing Committees, including the Committee on European Union Policies, for their opinions. It shall also be referred to the Parliamentary Committee on Regional Affairs for comments. The consideration ends with a report of the Budget Committee to the Plenary of the Senate, which adopts a resolution relevant for the European procedures (Article 3, paragraph 4, of Regulation (EC) No 1466/97 requires information about the parliamentary approval of the Stability and Convergence Programme).

The consideration of the draft Country Specific Recommendation follows the general consideration of EU non-legislative documents, making it possible for the Committees or the Assembly to adopt resolutions for the Government (Article 144 of the rules of procedure) and opinions for the EU institutions. Furthermore, the evaluation of the Country Specific Recommendation, once it is formally adopted by the Ecofin Council, occurs within the parliamentary procedure prescribed for the approval of the update to the Document of Economy and Finance, to be submitted to the Chambers by the 27 of September, prior to the presentation of the Draft Budget bill for the following year (Article 125-bis of the rules of procedure). Finally, the consideration of the opinion of the European Commission on the Draft Budget (adopted under Article 7 of Regulation (EU) No 473/2013) is made during the parliamentary procedure required for its approval during the 'National Semester'.

Consequently, as we have seen, the Senate's rules of procedure have proved to be flexible enough to incorporate the substantial changes stemming from the new economic governance cycle of the European Union, including the 'European Semester' process.

X. Conclusions

In drawing some conclusions about the role of the Italian Senate in EU affairs, it can be said that the procedures adopted are founded on a pro-integration attitude. This is quite clear if we consider that the subsidiarity checks are only a part of the overall consideration of the proposals. Also of note, the subsidiarity checks do not fall within the exclusive competence of the Committee on European Union Policies. They are, on the contrary, in the primary competence of the sectoral Committees, thus permitting responsibility for the consideration of EU acts to be disseminated throughout the Senate and in the various Committees. This engagement also looks more effective and suitable for the kind of involvement of national parliaments that the European Commission encouraged through the 'political dialogue'.[66]

[64] Art 9, para 1, of Law No 196 of 2009 (Public Finance and Accounting Act).

[65] Art 7, para 2, (let a), of Law No 196 of 2009.

[66] See Lupo, n 27 above.

Besides, the Senate's strong pro-integration attitude has been expressed through its constant participation in the various domains of interparliamentary cooperation among national Parliaments and with the European Parliament, supporting not only the European Parliament in its pivotal role as co-legislator, but also the role of the COSAC in its role as an engine—within a European framework—of the coordination of national parliaments' positions.

Importantly, the procedures involving national parliaments in the new economic governance and in the 'European Semester' have the possibility of becoming a counterbalance to the shifting of budgetary powers to the supranational, intergovernmental level. The Senate has efficiently dealt with the growing interconnection between the European and national dimensions of budgetary problems using its current rules of procedure.

Last but not least, the Italian Senate's participation in the initiatives concerning the so-called 'green card' makes it possible, in the general framework of the political dialogue, to have a new useful tool for a constructive involvement of national parliaments in the EU integration process, with full respect of the institutional balance.

An even further enhancement of the European attitude of the Senate could have been envisaged with the constitutional reform, if it had not been rejected by the referendum of 4 December 2016. All the powers granted by the Treaty of Lisbon to the single Chambers would have been maintained, thus allowing the renewed Senate bodies to exert their European functions in a more efficient and timely manner, because of their minor involvement in the national legislation, and with a 'federative' perspective, given the coordinating role between the EU, the state and the sub-national level of government.[67]

Even without the approval of the constitutional reform, the procedures described in the previous pages and the positive attitude of the Senate towards them show how the creation of instruments and tools to permit a concrete and constructive participation of national Parliaments in the European integration process, together with the European Parliament and the European Commission—in a spirit of cooperation and dialogue—contribute, as the treaty clearly affirms, to the good functioning of the Union (Article 12 TEU).[68]

There are however some critical remarks to make. Apart from the necessity of an ex ante political coordination of the positions of the two Houses of Parliaments and of the Government on European Affairs[69]—which Law No 234/2012 has, at least partly, granted—it is very difficult to assess the impact and the effectiveness of the Senate's (and Chamber's) increased action in shaping European policies.

It is possible to argue the necessity of promoting a breakthrough in the attitude of all the Italian stakeholders towards EU affairs[70] because their major positive stance could produce a significant influence on EU legal acts.

That is certainly true, but it is also possible to argue that legislating at the EU level is a complex process that requires the agreement of several actors of the European institutions

[67] See the chapter by C Fasone, in this volume.

[68] On the active contribution of national parliaments to the good functioning of the Union, see the Foreword of this volume by A Manzella.

[69] On the need of coordination mechanisms between the two Houses of Parliament and between the Parliament and the Government, see the chapter by M Romaniello, in this volume.

[70] In this sense, see the chapter by A Esposito, in this volume.

and of the Member States,[71] amongst which national Parliaments are only a small part of a broader 'Euro-National parliamentary system'.[72]

Hence, it is potentially impossible to define clearly which is the 'cause' that produced a certain legal 'effect'. As such, it is quite difficult to assess whether the position expressed by the Italian Chambers has determined a certain legal effect at the European level. Thus, the important aspect to underline is that documents reflecting the Italian position 'must' be on the (European) table. Their influence on the final decisions will then depend on their content and on the ability of Italian actors (at all levels) to influence the others in the European decision-making process.

[71] See the chapter by A Kreppel, in this volume.

[72] See N Lupo and G Piccirilli, in the Introduction of this volume.

8

The Coordination with the Regional Councils

CRISTINA FASONE

I. An Unsatisfactory Status Quo: The Historical Lack of Coordination Between the Italian Parliament and Regional Councils

The liaison between the national Parliament and regional councils in Italy has always been quite weak.[1] Until recently a sort of apathy has characterised the attitude of the Italian Parliament towards the regional councils and the regions[2] in general, although there are provisions at the constitutional and legislative levels that could have prompted the fostering of an effective cooperation.

For example, Article 121 Constitution enables regional councils to introduce bills before the Parliament. However, regional initiatives of national bills show a low degree of success in

[1] A Manzella, *Il parlamento* 3rd edn (Bologna, il Mulino, 2003) 19–20.

[2] Italy has 20 regions (and 2 autonomous provinces): 5 of them enjoy a special status, ie more autonomy, and were acknowledged by the Constitution itself and established in the aftermath of the adoption of the new Constitution. By contrast, the 15 ordinary regions were established only in the 1970s.

spite of a certain regional activism.[3] Article 126 Constitution provides for the consultation of a parliamentary committee on regional affairs—a bicameral committee with advisory powers and the only committee whose setting up is made mandatory by the Constitution—whenever the President of the Republic orders the dissolution of a regional council or the removal of the President of a region because of acts in breach of the Constitution or serious violations of law. Moreover Article 132, on the merging of existing regions or the creation of new regions, and Article 133, on the change in provincial boundaries or the establishment of new provinces, require the prior consultation of the Parliaments and, respectively, of the regional councils and the region concerned. The scope and the effects of such consultation nevertheless have been minimised under the case law of the Constitutional Court.[4]

Perhaps so far the most significant example of 'enhanced cooperation' between Parliament and regions, at least potentially, consisted in the provisions of Constitutional Law 3/2001 that require complementing the composition of the parliamentary committee on regional affairs with representatives of regions (and of local self-government), to be chosen at the 'parliamentary level', either from the regional councils or appointed by them (Article 11).[5] Article 11, which also increases the powers of this committee since its opinions on certain issues would have become somewhat binding for the committee responsible for the subject matter, has never been enforced. Although this was a provisional solution, waiting for a more comprehensive constitutional reform, the rules of procedure of the two Houses have not been amended. Amendments would have been particularly crucial, given the difficulty of coordination between national and regional legislatures in the aftermath of the 2001 revision and the confusing situation arising from the new division of legislative competences. The Italian Parliament has refrained from taking any action for bridging the gap between national and regional legislatures, often keeping on legislating as if constitutional amendments had not been approved.[6]

Furthermore, the weakening of regional councils following the decision to directly elect the Presidents of the regions in 1999[7] has made the cooperation between state and regions a matter mainly for inter-governmental relations.[8] Thus this cooperation has been modelled on Conferences that bring together representatives of the state and the regional

[3] In the Seventeenth Italian parliamentary term (so far 2013–2017) until May 2017 64 regional initiatives of national bills have been presented, 39 in the Chamber and 25 in the Senate (including those for amending the Statutes of the Regions enjoying special status), but only two of them (both constitutional laws amending the Statute of Friuli-Venezia Giulia) have been eventually approved (source: websites of the Italian Chamber of Deputies, http://www.camera.it, and of the Senate, http://www.senato.it).

[4] See judgment no 246/2010.

[5] See R Bifulco, 'L'integrazione della Commissione parlamentare per le questioni regionali: in attesa della Camera delle Regioni' in A Manzella and F Bassanini (eds), *Quarantaquattro modeste proposte per riformare il Parlamento* (Bologna, il Mulino, 2007) 87 and N Lupo, 'Sulla necessità costituzionale di integrare la Commissione parlamentare per le questioni regionali' (2007) 2 *Rassegna parlamentare*, 357.

[6] F Rosa, 'Parlamento e nuovo Titolo V. Interrogativi e riflessioni sulle "prime" conseguenze della riforma per le due Camere' (2003) 1–2 *Nuove Autonomie* 47–71 and G Rizzoni, 'Il "seguito" parlamentare della giurisprudenza costituzionale sul riparto di competenze Stato-Regioni dopo il nuovo Titolo V: il punto prospettico delle Commissioni affari costituzionali' in R Bin et al (eds), *'Effettività' e 'seguito' delle tecniche decisorie della Corte costituzionale* (Napoli, ESI, 2006) 473–92.

[7] M Olivetti, *Nuovi Statuti e forma di governo delle Regioni. Verso le Costituzioni regionali?* (Bologna, Il Mulino, 2003) 308–10.

[8] See I Ruggiu, *Contro la Camera delle Regioni: istituzioni e prassi della rappresentanza territoriale* (Napoli, Jovene, 2006) and G Rivosecchi, 'Consigli regionali e raccordi intergovernativi' in E Gianfrancesco et al (eds), *Il Filangieri. Quaderno 2009* (Napoli, Jovene, 2010) 263–303.

Governments (as well as local self-government, depending on the issue at stake), although some tools of interparliamentary cooperation had been also provided in the renewed constitutional framework.

Before Law No 234/2012 was enacted, some spot legislative provisions, like those of Law 42/2009 on the bicameral committee on the enforcement of fiscal federalism,[9] could have concurred to create a liaison between Parliament and regional councils, but in practice they have not changed this relationship. By the same token, the Rules of Procedure of the two Houses were not updated to incorporate the constitutional reform of 2001, which abolished the ex ante control by the state, including that by the Parliament on the merits, on regional legislation, and significantly extended the legislative competences of the regions.[10] According to the Rules of Procedure, and only in the Senate (Article 138), there is just one official channel of collaboration between Parliament and regions that does not find a legal basis directly in the Constitution or in legislative provisions: the so-called regional 'votes', which have experienced a sort of 'revival' in the post-Lisbon era. Indeed, these 'votes' are petitions or contributions submitted by regions to the Senate on issues of their interest that are then examined by the competent standing committee, possibly jointly with a bill dealing with the same subject-matter, if it exists. Interestingly, the number of 'votes' have increased since the entry into force of the Treaty of Lisbon because—since the parliamentary rules of procedure lack any provision that could regulate the regional councils' participation in the so-called early warning system (EWS), ie the control of compliance of EU legislative proposals with the principle of subsidiarity (see further, section II)—regional legislatures have started to transmit their opinions and observations, at least to the Senate, by means of this pre-existing tool.

Also, informal instruments of cooperation, such as hearings of regional councillors before national parliamentary committees, have been increasingly used in the last few years, even though they take place in camera like the hearings of interest groups, without any explicit recognition of the constitutional status of regional councils, in particular with regard to their relationship with the Parliament.[11]

Finally, in order to balance the lack of a Senate of the regions, by means of an inter-institutional agreement of 28 June 2007 between the Presidents of the Houses of the Italian Parliament and the Coordinator of the Conference of the Presidents of regional councils, a Joint Committee (Commissione paritietica) composed of an equal number of deputies, senators and regional councillors, plus the President of the parliamentary committee on regional affairs, has been established, outside of the parliamentary framework. This Joint Committee, which is the result of an informal process of cooperation started in 2002 in a joint working group, was enlarged in its composition and functions in 2009. Yet, it has

[9] See N Lupo, 'Il procedimento di attuazione della delega sul federalismo fiscale e le nuove sedi della collaborazione tra i livelli territoriali: Commissione bicamerale, Commissione tecnica paritetica e Conferenza permanente' (2009) 7: 23 *Federalismi.it*.

[10] Nowadays regions can legislate in all matters not expressly listed in Art 117 Const (residual clause) and in those listed in s 3 of Art 117 Const, provided that the state fixes the fundamental principles of the subject matter. By contrast, the state, in principle (since the Constitutional Court has interpreted the catalogue of competences aiming at broadening the scope of the State action), can intervene strictly in the matters listed in s 2. See, *ex multis*, T Martines et al, *Lineamenti di diritto regionale* 8th edn (Milano, Giuffrè, 2008).

[11] See Rule 48.5 of the Senate on the fact-finding inquiries and the practice of informal hearings, especially before the Bureau of the committees, developed from Rule 47 of the Senate.

been summoned fewer than 10 times. Indeed, in order to organise a meeting—where Italian members of the European Parliament also can be invited—of this Joint Committee, the activities of several Assemblies have to be coordinated together, and the outcomes of these meetings enjoy an uncertain legal status and effectiveness.

Given the weakness of the existing cooperation between Parliament and regional councils, in terms of both legal and more informal instruments, the Treaty of Lisbon and in particular Protocol No 2 has renewed this exhausted relationship. In other words, by imposing a direct dialogue among the legislatures of the Member States, the EWS could be the starting point to counter the state 'regional blindness' and to reshape this relationship in a more cooperative fashion.

This chapter deals with the impact of EU post-Lisbon procedures, in particular the EWS and the political dialogue, on the relationship between the Italian Parliament and regional councils. In order to analyse such a relationship the chapter is structured as follows: Section II considers how the Treaty of Lisbon has affected the role of regional parliaments with legislative powers in EU affairs. Section III focuses on Law No 234/2012, the main legal instrument implementing the Treaty of Lisbon's provisions in Italy, on the procedures established for the coordination between the Italian Parliament and regional councils and on the institutional practice developed by the two Houses and the Senate in particular. To this end, a case study of coordination with regional councils is presented, that of the second legislative package on circular economy. By drawing on the consolidated institutional practice of cooperation between the Senate and regional councils, Section IV considers Article 6 of Protocol No 2 annexed to the Treaty of Lisbon, Law No 234/2012 and the way they have been applied by the Senate as important steps toward the ultimately failed attempt to transform the Italian Upper House into a Chamber of regions and municipalities, where the representation of the regions was expected to largely rely on regional councils according to the constitutional reform bill rejected at the referendum of 4 December 2016. Finally, section V draws some conclusions on the level of coordination reached between the Italian Parliament, in particular the Senate, and regional councils in the light of the EU post-Lisbon procedures and the constitutional reform rejected.

II. The Treaty of Lisbon's Upgrade of Regional Parliaments' Position

The Treaty of Lisbon has created a new scenario with regard to the participation of 'regional parliaments'—as Article 6, Protocol No 2 annexed to the Treaty called them—in the European legislative processes. Each national parliament or each chamber thereof *can consult*, where appropriate, regional parliaments with legislative powers in the framework of the scrutiny of EU legislative proposals on the ground of subsidiarity through the EWS. The effects, the frequency and the procedures for the consultation of regional parliaments are settled autonomously in each of the eight Member States that acknowledge legislative powers for all or to some of their regions (Austria, Belgium, Finland, Germany, Italy, Portugal, Spain and the United Kingdom).

Article 6 does not define what a 'regional parliament' is. Indeed, it could not provide a specific definition. The EU cannot rule over the constitutional structure of the Member

States as entrenched in their constitutional identity (Article 4(2) Treaty on European Union (EU)): this matter is for each state only. Even the choice of the name 'regional parliament' is contested[12] as, for example, the Italian Constitutional Court has expressly forbidden to use the term 'parliament' beyond the national bicameral legislature, this legislature being the only constitutional body ensuring political representation at the national level (Article 67 Italian Constitution).[13]

The only requirement fixed by Article 6 is that the regional Parliaments concerned are solely those provided with legislative powers, a requirement that substantially restricts the number of institutions involved. In Italy it is clear that the institutions to which Article 6 refers are regionalcouncils.

While Article 6 certainly mentions regional Parliaments with legislative powers, at the same time it does not acknowledge to them any direct involvement in the EWS. The participation of regional legislatures in this procedure is mediated and conditioned by the national parliament or one of its Houses.

Regional parliaments, ie regional councils in Italy, *can be consulted* and the consultation, as is well-known, can take place in different forms. It can derive from an input of the regional legislature concerned or by the national Parliament; it can be mandatory or optional; it can entail binding effects or just an advisory role. On these issues, again, each Member State is free to decide.[14]

Finally, national constitutional law and national Parliaments also enjoy great discretion in defining under which circumstances a regional Parliament is consulted. The reference to the 'appropriateness' of the consultation of regional legislatures is justified on the ground of a domestic choice. Usually, should a regional parliament be provided with legislative powers in the field of an EU draft legislative act, this institution is consulted or at least allowed to send an opinion to the national Parliament. Indeed, a principle embedded in the Constitutions of many Member States, Italy included,[15] as well in European Treaties, the principle of sincere or loyal cooperation (Article 4 TEU), would argue in favour of a duty for the national Parliament to consult regional legislatures on an EU draft legislative act whenever the legislative competence of the latter is affected. Yet, no strictly legal enforcement of this provision is feasible either at the EU or domestic level to sanction the inaction of a national Parliament that has not consulted a regional Parliament.

Thus, determining what is appropriate for the consultation of regional Parliaments still lies with the discretionary decision of the national Parliament. In this regard, one chamber can also activate the procedure: it depends on the nature of the bicameral system, on the

[12] See N Lupo, 'National and Regional Parliaments in the EU decision-making process, after the Treaty of Lisbon and the Euro-crisis' (2013) 5(2) *Perspectives on Federalism* 11–13 and M Olivetti, 'The Regions in the EU decision-making processes' in M Cartabia, N Lupo and A Simoncini (eds), *Democracy and Subsidiarity in the EU* (Bologna, Il Mulino, 2013) 427.

[13] See Italian Constitutional Court, judgments no 106 and 306/2002. The Court mainly relied on a textual interpretation of the Constitution, in particular by comparing Art 55 and Art 121 It Const; by contrast it avoided defining what is a Parliament and thus providing a substantive notion useful to distinguish a parliament from other legislative assemblies, in addition to the national representation. The Court also rejected the view of the national Government which saw the notion of Parliament as linked to that of people's sovereignty.

[14] Except for Belgium (see Declaration 51 to the Treaty of Lisbon), the protocol does not allow a direct interaction between regional legislatures and EU institutions, first of all the Commission.

[15] See Art 120 Const and the case law of the Italian Constitutional Court since judgment no 219/1984 and, after the constitutional reform of 2001 eg judgment no 88/2003.

composition of the national Houses, and on formal or informal procedures for entertaining the inter-institutional relationship between the two levels of government. Moreover, the relationship can be one-to-one, ie each regional Parliament independently with the national Parliament, or can have two components, regional Parliaments together as a sort of collective actor, on the one hand, and the national Parliament on the other.

III. Law No 234/2012 as a Tool of Coordination between the Italian Parliament and Regional Councils

Despite the entry into force of the Treaty of Lisbon on 1 December 2009, until 2012 the Italian Parliament and Government substantially ignored the regional dimension of this Treaty by delaying the reform of Law No 11/2005 on the participation of Italy in EU affairs. Indeed, this law did not mandate any direct relationship between regional councils, either individually or collectively in the framework of the Conference of their Presidents, and the Parliament. Article 5 of that Law provided for the transmission of regional observations, both from regional councils and governments, directly to the President of the Council of Ministers or the Minister for European Policies. In particular, for regional councils the transmission was expected to take place through the Conference of the Presidents of Regional Councils within 20 days—so within a much shorter deadline compared to eight weeks—since the date when they received the relevant documents from the Government.

This notwithstanding, regional councils have shown a great commitment to revise their Statutes, regional laws and councils' Rules of Procedure in order to cope with the EWS and to engage in a constructive dialogue with the Parliament on it. With a few exceptions,[16] most regional councils have adopted updated rules—both in terms of regional legislation and new rules of procedure—on the participation in EU affairs after the Treaty revision and a few of them did it even before the Treaty entered into force.

The Italian Parliament eventually approved Law No 234/2012, repealing Law No 11/2005 and implementing most Treaty of Lisbon's provisions, including those on regional councils, only in December 2012.[17] However, neither the Chamber of Deputies nor the Senate has accommodated its rules of procedure to the new legal reality. New 'experimental and provisional' procedures have been put in place in both Houses, for example on the EWS,[18] but until recently they did not take into account regional councils and their new role under Article 6 of Protocol 2.

Nevertheless, in spite of the absence of legal provisions at national level, the cooperation between regional councils and the two Houses, especially the Senate, in the EWS has started to develop intensively de facto since the sixteenth parliamentary term (2008–2013).[19]

[16] Like Campania (Law No 18/2008), Puglia (Law No 24/2001) and Toscana (Law No 26/2009).

[17] See L Costato, LS Rossi and P Borghi (eds), *Commentario alla Legge 24.12.2012 n. 234. 'Norme generali sulla partecipazione dell'Italia alla formazione all'attuazione della normativa e delle politiche dell'Unione europea'* (Napoli, Editoriale Scientifica, 2015).

[18] See the chapter by N Lupo in this volume.

[19] See M Olivetti, 'Parlamenti nazionali nell'Unione europea' in R Bifulco et al (eds), *Digesto delle Discipline Pubblicistiche*, Aggiornamento V (Torino, UTET, 2012) 551–52.

Some regional legislatures, especially those of Abruzzo, Emilia-Romagna and Marche,[20] have begun to transmit their observations to both Houses.

Furthermore, the Senate has revitalised the procedure on the 'votes' of regional councils (see above Section I) treating regional observations under the EWS as if they were votes. It also started to inform the regional legislatures, by means of the Conference of their Presidents, on the EU draft legislative acts and documents which are to be examined by the Senate, whatever the competence affected (whether national or regional), and on when the eight-week deadline expires.[21]

A. The Early Warning System: Lights and Shadows

The participation of regional councils in the EWS is now provided by Article 8, section 3, and Article 25 of Law No 234/2012. The former takes the perspective of the Italian Parliament, locating the consultation of the regional councils within the national parliamentary scrutiny on subsidiarity, while the latter considers it from the standpoint of the regions and thus constitutes the 'legal basis' for the submission of observations on the subsidiarity principle from the councils to the Parliament. This is reflected also in the location of Article 8 within Title II of the law, on the participation of the Parliament in the formation of Italian position on EU policies and EU decision-making, and of Article 25 within Title IV, on the participation of the regions and the local self-government in EU law-making.

The option to split the regulation of a unitary procedure, like the EWS as it is conceived by Article 6 of Protocol No 2, into two articles may either appear as a duplication or remain unclear at first sight. However, analysing the two articles more in depth, it seems that the ratio behind them is the guarantee of a real participation of regional councils in the process.

Article 8, section 3, which follows the provisions on the adoption of reasoned opinions by the Parliament, states that the two Houses *may* (*possono*), and not *shall* (or even *must*), consult regional councils. Hence the fulfillment of an effective consultation can result in a discretionary choice of each House. For example, in principle, the Senate could proceed to consult regional legislatures, whereas the Chamber does not. In fact, the Senate and the Chamber have seldom used this article to call for a consultation of regional councils.[22] This is why Article 8, section 3, has beén depicted in the literature as a 'programmatic rule' (*norma programmatica*).[23] Indeed it fails to place any duty on the Parliament with regard to the effects and the frequency of the consultation—ie when such a consultation must

[20] B Sardella, 'La "dimensione comunitaria" dei nuovi Statuti regionali' (2007) 3/4 *Le istituzioni del federalismo* 431–77 and A Voltan, 'Il controllo della sussidiarietà dalla prospettiva dell'assemblea regionale dell'Emilia-Romagna' in J Woelk and P Bußjäger (eds), *Il Trattato di Lisbona e le Regioni: il controllo di sussidiarietà* (Bozen, EURAC Research, 2010) 141.

[21] DA Capuano, 'Funzioni delle Camere italiane nel procedimento legislativo dell'Unione europea' (2011) 3 *Rassegna parlamentare* 519.

[22] However, as it is pointed out in s III.C, since 2014 the Senate regularly informs regional councils when starting the scrutiny of an EU legislative proposal under the EWS and both Houses have arranged hearings of regional councillors and of the Representative of the Conference of Regional Councils' Presidents in charge for EU affairs.

[23] A Esposito, 'La legge 24 dicembre 2012, n 234, sulla partecipazione dell'Italia alla formazione e all'attuazione della normativa e delle politiche dell'UE. Parte I—Prime riflessioni sul ruolo delle Camere' (2013) 2 *Federalismi.it* 48.

occur—while simply referring to the Rules of Procedure for a detailed regulation of the matter. While according to Article 6 of Protocol No 2, national Parliaments seem bound to consult their regional legislatures when the issue at stake affects regional competences, reasonably EU provisions have not fixed any further obligations on national parliamentary procedures. Indeed, this matter should be regulated either by means of constitutional law—as it was in 2001 with the participation of regions in the committee on regional affairs—since it concerns the relationship between parliamentary institutions enjoying a constitutional status located at different levels of government of the Italian Republic, or, as seems preferable, by means of ordinary legislation. In the end, it is not the first time that an ordinary law provides in great detail the effects of parliamentary procedures or the activity of parliamentary bodies (see eg, Law No 124/2007 on security services and Law No 42/2009 on fiscal federalism), nor can such legislation be deemed to impair the autonomy of the Parliament. Indeed, this legislation would not jeopardise the opportunity for each House to further regulate its procedures and organisation while ensuring that the liaison between the Parliament and other institutions, namely the regional councils, is effective.

By contrast, much less can be provided by the Houses' Rules of Procedures because the whole process regards a Euro-national procedure and there is a risk of undermining the prerogatives conferred by the Treaty of Lisbon upon regional legislatures. What parliamentary Rules of Procedure could rationally establish, instead, are certain procedural but equally fundamental aspects, like the introduction of the 'votes' of regional councils also in the Chamber, the regulation of formal and video-broadcast hearings of regional councillors during the EWS, and the clarification of what effects regional observations have within the parliamentary scrutiny on subsidiarity: in particular, the kind of follow up on those observations given by standing committees, the timing and the form it should take, eg by publishing them as annexes of parliamentary opinions.

By contrast, Article 25 has been widely used, confirming the institutional practice already followed by the Parliament and the regional councils before the new law was enacted. The fact that now this practice has been codified into ordinary legislation should not be underestimated. Therefore, it can barely be argued that the provisions of Law No 234/2012 on the EWS are devoid of an autonomous legal value. On the contrary, they provide for the first time a national legal basis for the effective implementation of this procedure that takes into account not only the Parliament, but also regional legislatures, as provided by Protocol No 2.

Regardless of the opening of a consultation, Article 25 entitles regional councils to submit directly to the Parliament their observations on the principle of subsidiarity 'in due time' for the conclusion of the parliamentary scrutiny within the eight-week deadline. In other words, a sort of 'double-flow' procedure is established: whenever the top-down consultation is not accomplished, a bottom-up flow of observations from the regional councils can reach the Parliament anyway. This contributes to creating a long-term cooperation among legislatures.

This procedure shows another advantage for regional legislatures, since the submission of their observations under the EWS is not constrained by a rigid division of competences between regions and state. If regional councils had been allowed to express their positions only upon the summoning of a consultation on the part of each House, then it would have been likely that such consultation was arranged only with regard to draft legislative acts falling within the regional remit. The wording of Article 25, instead, guarantees to regional councils the chance to transmit observations on the principle of subsidiarity within the national stage of the EWS also on EU proposals that affect primarily state competences like immigration (Article 117, section 2, letter b) Constitution).

However, like Article 8, Article 25 also remains deliberately silent on certain issues. For example, it is worth mentioning the lack of a further (domestic) deadline for the transmission of the regional councils' observations in addition to the European one. The only time limit set for regional legislatures is that the submission must be made 'in due time as for the conclusion of the parliamentary scrutiny' (thus within the eight-week period); hence, the provision remains too vague. Indeed, the practice reveals that whenever one or both Houses can send opinions or reasoned opinions in advance (sometimes they cannot, and thus this case falls into the category of the 'political dialogue', on which see section III.B), they do not wait until the expiration of deadline for the submission of regional observations, but rather as soon as the parliamentary opinion is supposed to be finalised, either the committee concerned or the House votes on it and immediately transmits it to the EU institutions and to the executive. Article 25 does not prevent such a procedure. In other words, what 'due time' means is likely to be decided by the Parliament every time (20, 30, 40 days), thus giving to the Parliament a great discretion and damaging the predictability of the whole procedure.

Moreover, according to the Rules of Procedure of the Chamber (RC) and of the Senate (RS) (Articles 125 RC and 144 RS) and the experimental procedures in force, the time limit differs from one House to another: eg 40 days is the deadline for the Chamber of Deputies' Committee on EU Policies to express a reasoned opinion; by contrast, 15 days is the time limit for a Senate's sectoral committee to issue a reasoned opinion before the Committee on EU Policies asks to transmit its own observations to EU institutions on behalf of the whole Senate. Not only would a fixed deadline give legal certainty to the procedure, stimulating a more prompt reaction on the part of regional councils, but it would also resolve a possible mismatch which could occur with regard to the 30-day deadline fixed in Article 24 concerning the submission of regional observations, either by legislatures or by executives, to the President of the Council of Ministers or to the Minister for European Affairs. The content of these latter observations is not clarified by the law, but in principle they should not deal with the principle of subsidiarity in order to avoid overlapping with Article 25.

Finally, a positive element deriving from the new provisions deals with a clarification of the relationship within the 'triangle' of the Parliament, the regional councils and the Conference of their Presidents. Here Article 25 opts for setting up individual relationships between each regional legislature and the Parliament within the EWS, a choice which mirrors that of the EU Treaties providing for an individual participation of every Parliament or House thereof but without excluding the exchange of views and the coordination amongst Parliaments.[24] The ratio is the following:[25] a different degree of commitment and engagement can emerge across the councils when participating in the EWS and the same EU draft legislative act can raise a harsh debate in a certain region while passing basically ignored in another. Thus, it is not convenient to force regional councils to agree on a common position

[24] JV Louis, 'National Parliaments and the Principle of Subsidiarity. Legal Options and Practical Limits' in I Pernice and E Tanchev (eds), *Ceci n'est pas une Constitution. Constitutionalism without a Constitution* (Baden-Baden, Nomos, 2009) 131.

[25] P Bilancia et al, 'European Fitness of Italian Regions' (2010) 2(2) *Perspectives on Federalism* 124.

within the Conference of their Presidents, blocking the submission of regional observations in cases of diverging views.

B. Political Dialogue 'Italian Style': A Revolutionary Provision

The most 'revolutionary' provisions of Law No 234/2012 dealing with the relationship between regional councils and Parliament in EU policy-making are those concerning the (domestic) 'political dialogue'.[26]

The decision of the Italian Parliament—unique in a comparative perspective—to also include regional councils in a sort of national 'political dialogue' is extremely important with regard to the cooperation between the national and the regional legislatures. Indeed, Italy is the only Member State to have adopted legal provisions which enable regional legislatures to participate in this EU mechanism.[27] However, it does not mean that regional councils are entitled to send their observations directly to the Commission within the EWS as the Italian Houses do (Article 9, section 1, Law No 234/2012). Rather the same mechanism which is in force between the national legislature and the Commission is now 'transplanted' within the Italian Republic with regard to the relationship between regional councils and the Parliament. The submission of regional observations takes place under the same conditions provided by Article 25 on the EWS, but the impact is more far-reaching, in a twofold sense.

First of all, since it has become evident that legislatures, as political bodies, possibly are not the best equipped institutions to accomplish a strict legal scrutiny of the principle of subsidiarity,[28] both national and regional parliaments are accustomed to adopting opinions or contributions that also deal with the choice of the legal basis, the compliance with the principle of proportionality and, most of all, the substance or the merits of the prospective measures, both for EU draft legislative acts falling within the exclusive competence of the Union and EU documents more simply, which sometimes are crucial (like the Commission Annual Work Programme). Article 9 has strengthened a chain between regional, national and European institutions. Indeed, regional councils can submit to the two Houses observations on any EU draft legislative act or document, on any ground, and in principle without a deadline other than the parliamentary schedule, thus intervening before the Parliament's opinions are transmitted to the Commission. An interesting example is that of the scrutiny of the Annual Commission Work Programme that, according to Article 13, section 1 of Law No 234/2012, shall be examined jointly with the Annual Programme of the Government on the future participation of Italy in EU affairs, both of which are transmitted to the regional

[26] On the implementation in Italy of the 'constitutional convention' named since 2006 'political dialogue' between the European Commission and national parliaments, see A Esposito, DA Capuano and N Lupo in this volume.

[27] See D Fromage, 'Regional Parliaments and the Early Warning System: An Assessment and Some Suggestions for Reform' in A Jonsson Cornell and M Goldoni (eds), *National and Regional Parliaments in the EU-Legislative Procedure Post-Lisbon. The Impact of the Early Warning Mechanism* (Oxford, Hart, 2016) 132.

[28] G Martinico, 'Dating Cinderella: On Subsidiarity as a Political Safeguard of Federalism in the European Union' (2011) 17 *European Public Law* 649; against this idea see P Kiiver, *The Early Warning System for the Principle of Subsidiarity: Constitutional Theory and Empirical Reality* (London-New York, Routledge, 2012).

councils through the Conference of their Presidents (Article 24 and Article 13, section 3).[29] By way of the (national) 'political dialogue', each regional council can now make its voice heard in the Parliament for both documents, by submitting observations on the Annual Programme of the Government in the light of the Commission Work Programme (or vice versa) or also identifying its own priorities on EU legislative proposals, which is particularly important during the planning stage. Therefore, regional councils can have a say both on the national planning stage, and indirectly on the EU planning stage, since Parliament takes into account their observations when it transmits its opinions on the Commission Work Programme within the (European) 'political dialogue'.

Second, the impact of 'political dialogue' upon regional councils is deeper compared to the EWS because, despite lacking legal sanctions in the case of lack of compliance, Article 9 expressly imposes that the Parliament take regional observations into consideration in its opinions. Regional legislatures have been entitled to orient parliamentary procedures and guide the content of parliamentary deliberations at least when a residual and a shared competence of the regions is concerned. Therefore, the Parliament is bound by regional observations, while again (see above, Section III.A) no specific limitations are imposed upon regional councils regarding the submission of observations to the Parliament, which can regard in theory any issue, no matter if it falls within the regional or the state's remit. Although Article 9 marks a breakthrough with regard to the cooperation between national and regional legislatures, since, in principle, the observations of the latter could not be disregarded, to some extent it is a paradox that such a result is achieved on a procedure which is not even provided in the Treaties, whereas the EWS, regarded in the EU as one of the main innovations of the Treaty of Lisbon,[30] according to Law No 234/2012, only limitedly strengthens the tie between the national and regional legislatures.

Nonetheless, Article 9 also contains an ambiguous and maybe erroneous reference to the 'Regions and autonomous provinces' besides the regional legislatures, as if the councils were not part of the regional institutional setting. The norm is actually meant to involve in the 'political dialogue' with the Parliament also regional executives, with the same binding effects as the observations submitted by the regional councils, and aiming at increasing the information flow from regional political bodies to the national legislature. However, this new provision appears to disregard how the regional procedures linked to the EWS and the scrutiny of EU legislative proposals are designed at the regional level and how complicated the relationship between each regional legislature and executive is on this issue. Indeed, nowadays most regional laws that regulate this matter try to foster the adoption of a unitary position between the regional council and the executive,[31] given that, in addition to the domestic political dialogue with the Parliament, both regional legislatures and

[29] Art 16 of Law No 234/2012 adds a new document to be transmitted by the Government to the regional councils through the Conference of their Presidents (as well as to the regional executives through their Conference): the Report on the trend of the financial flow between Italy and the EU, which was already transmitted to the Parliament, according to Law 11/2005, and that contains very significant information for regional councils, for example on the incoming cohesion funds.

[30] F Fabbrini and K Granat, '"Yellow Card, but Not Foul": The Role of the National Parliaments Under the Subsidiarity Protocol and the Commission Proposal for an EU Regulation on the Right to Strike' (2013) 50(1) *Common Market Law Review* 115.

[31] See C Fasone, 'L'"europeizzazione" dei Consigli regionali. Il caso dell'Emilia-Romagna' (2010) *Studi parlamentari e di politica costituzionale* 167–68.

governments can transmit their opinions also to the national executive on any issue arising from an EU proposal by 30 days after its delivery (Article 24, see above Section III.A).

C. The Leading Role of the Italian Senate in the Coordination with Regional Councils

The participation of regional parliaments with legislative powers in the EWS as outlined in Protocol No 2 has triggered different reactions in the two Italian Houses: while the Senate has 'exploited' at best the provisions of the Protocol to enhance the coordination with regional legislatures on EU affairs, the Chamber of Deputies has not really taken advantage of them.

The two approaches can be explained on several grounds. First of all, the two branches of the Italian Parliament can be seen, even in the current constitutional context, as having a slightly different raison d'être. Although the development of a close cooperation with regional councils has happened only for EU policies, the Senate's discovery of a sense of institutional ownership over the relationship with regional legislatures can be evaluated as consistent with Article 57 Constitution, which indeed, despite a disputable interpretation in practice, makes the Senate the Chamber most strongly linked to regions as it 'is elected on a regional basis' (Article 57 Constitution). Such a regional background is lacking when it comes to the Chamber of Deputies.

Moreover, because of a political choice to focus mainly on the interaction with the national Government rather than interacting directly with EU institutions, the Chamber of Deputies is much more selective than the Senate in picking the EU legislative proposals to scrutinise, so that fewer proposals in the end complete the scrutiny within the EWS and the political dialogue.[32] At least since 2014, the Chamber of Deputies has de facto not participated in the EWS, and no reasoned opinion has been issued. By contrast, according to the European Commission, in 2015 the Italian Senate was ranked third in terms of activity of parliamentary Houses in delivering opinions (25) in the framework of the political dialogue and the EWS.[33] Even if one takes into account that the Chamber of Deputies frequently scrutinises consultation documents rather than legislative proposals, the disproportion in the number of resolutions and opinions delivered per year on EU documents remains patent: in 2016, there were 24 at the Chamber of Deputies and 66 at the Senate. The gap can be further justified by the different procedures in place in the Chamber of Deputies and the Senate for the scrutiny of EU affairs. In the Chamber, the scrutiny of the compliance with the principle of subsidiarity is centralised at the Committee on EU Policies alone, so that in case of inactivity the Chamber becomes unable to take a position. In the Senate, instead, this scrutiny is decentralised and is carried out by the committee competent for the subject matter with the Committee on EU Policies playing an ancillary and advisory role, unless the competent committee does not adopt the relevant resolution within 15 days since the delivery of the Committee on EU

[32] See N Lupo, 'The Scrutiny of the Principle of Subsidiarity in the Procedures and Reasoned Opinions of the Italian Chamber and Senate' in Jonsson Cornell and Goldoni, above n 27, 225.

[33] See European Commission, Annual Report 2015 on the relationship with national parliaments, Bruxelles, 15.7.2016, COM(2016) 471 final, 3.

Policies' opinion. Under these circumstances, the Senate Committee on EU Policies is entitled to replace the competent committee and its opinion is then transmitted to the Government, the Chamber of Deputies and the EU institutions.[34]

This explains why the most active regional councils—of Emilia-Romagna, Abruzzo, Friuli-Venezia Giulia and Marche—have found it strategically more convenient to build up a strong coordination with the Senate on the scrutiny of EU affairs.[35] By the same token, the Senate regards the opinions of regional councils as more and more important.[36] Indeed, the Senate regional councils' opinions are announced as regional votes in the Plenary, sent to the committee competent for the subject matter and the Committee on EU Policies and are then made publicly available on the Senate's website.[37] Moreover, regional councils' opinions (votes) are often quoted within the main report or resolution dealing with subsidiarity. In practice, in matters of cohesion policy and of common agricultural policy, for instance, the opinions of regional councils have been cited and have contributed to form the opinion of the Senate's standing Committee on EU Policies. In one case, the document adopted by the corresponding committee of the Chamber of Deputies was based on the arguments put forward by the regional legislatures.[38]

In the Senate, both the committee competent for the subject matter and the Committee on EU Policies have started referring to individual regional councils' opinions in their resolutions and opinions, and, although they do not report regional opinions as attachments, the influence of the regional legislatures on the position of the national Parliament in the EWS can be easily detected.[39]

Clear signals toward strengthening the relationship between the Senate and regional councils at institutional level can also be seen in recent developments in the Senate. On 12 March 2014, the Senate Committee on EU Policies set up a subcommittee for the relationship with the regions in matters of EU affairs. This is the only permanent subcommittee established in this standing committee besides that in charge to draft opinions on EU legislative proposals on behalf of the whole body; its peculiarity is a signal of the significance assigned to the cooperation between the Senate and the regions when EU law is at stake.

A few months later, on 24 September 2014, the same Committee of the Senate endorsed the inter-institutional agreement signed between the Committee and the Conference of the

[34] On those procedures see the chapters by DA Capuano and A Esposito in this volume.

[35] Despite being the most active, the number of opinions issued by regional councils is by no means comparable to those of each Chamber of the Italian Parliament. For example, the regional assembly of Emilia-Romagna has passed more than 30 opinions on the whole since 2010: see M Ricciardelli, 'L'attuazione della legge n. 234 del 24 dicembre 2012. Norme, prassi, risultati, dal livello statale a quello regionale' (2015) 3 *Le istituzioni del federalism* 51. Such an assessment can be extended, however, also to regional parliaments in other EU Member States, in particular Spain and Belgium: see D Fromage, 'Regional Parliaments and the Early Warning System: an Assessment Six Years after the Entry into Force of the Lisbon Treaty' *LUISS SoG Working Paper Series*, SOG-WP33/2016, 17–30.

[36] This argument has been fully developed by the author here: C Fasone, 'Italian Regional Councils and the Positive Externalities of the Early Warning Mechanism for National Constitutional Law' in Jonsson Cornell and Goldoni, above n 27. See also Fromage, above n 27.

[37] See D Capuano, 'L'attuazione della legge n. 234 del 24 dicembre 2012. Norme, prassi, risultati, dal livello statale a quello regionale' (2015) 3 *Le istituzioni del federalismo* (s 2.4) 23.

[38] See in detail C Odone, 'La collaborazione in fase ascendente tra il Parlamento e le assemblee legislative regionali: cinque casi pratici ed alcune riflessioni' (2013) *Federalismi.it*, 3 April, 13.

[39] C Odone, ibid 16–17 and, on the case studies of the reforms of the Common Agricultural Policy and of the Cohesion Policy, see Fasone, above n 36.

Presidents of Regional Councils as to ensure a better coordination between the Senate and the regional councils in the EWS, the political dialogue and the scrutiny of the Commission Work Programme.[40] Concerning the EWS, in particular, the inter-institutional agreement improves the cooperation between regional councils and the Senate, as it provides for:

1. The joint and coordinated selection among legislatures of the dossiers of common interest in the framework of the subsidiarity scrutiny (and the political dialogue);[41]
2. hearings of the Conference of the Presidents of Regional Councils' representatives in the Senate Committee on EU Policies before decisions of common concern are taken at European level;
3. the agreement among legislatures on a standard procedure for the EWS whereby regional councils are promptly informed about the Senate Committee on EU Policies' agenda for the meetings in order to send their opinions beforehand; and
4. the commitment of the Senate Committee on EU Policies to include and highlight in its opinions and resolutions within the EWS (and the political dialogue) the opinions issued by regional councils, a commitment that since then has always been fulfilled.

The latest institutional initiative in terms of collaboration between the Senate and regional councils is the Protocol signed on 3 December 2015 by the Speaker of the Senate and the Coordinator of the Conference of the Presidents of Regional Councils. Although the Protocol is not just focused on EU-related activities, a more coordinated scrutiny and implementation of EU policies is one of the final objectives pursued. Indeed, this aim can be better achieved through the instruments detailed in the Protocol such as sharing expertise and procedures, as well as jointly carrying out research and training activities for the Senate and regional councils' officials.

IV. The Coordination in the Case of the EU Second Legislative Package on Circular Economy

The case of the EU second legislative package on circular economy appears particularly important when looking at the growing coordination between regional councils and the Senate. Among other things, the package sets new waste management targets to be reached by 2030; provides for standard definitions, calculation methods and reporting obligations

[40] See the resolution passed by the Senate Committee on EU Policies on 24 September 2014, Doc XXIV, no 35 and the comments by L Bartolucci, 'In attesa del "nuovo" Senato, un canale di collegamento più fluido con i Consigli regionali negli affari dell'Unione europea' (2014) 3 *Osservatorio sulle fonti online* 10.

[41] See, as examples of implementation of the inter-institutional agreement, the resolution adopted by the Senate Committee on EU Policies on 4 March 2015 at the end of the analysis of the European Commission's *Work Programme 2015—A New Start*, COM(2014) 910 final, where the choice of dossier to be examined in 2015 has been also based upon the preference expressed in the regional councils' opinions; and the resolution of the Senate Committee on EU Policies of 17 February 2016 (Doc XXIV, no 56) on the European Commission's Work Programme 2016, the 18 month Programme of the Council (1 January 2016–30 June 2017) and the Planning Report of the Government on the Italian participation in the EU in 2016, where the joint document drafted by the Conference of the Presidents of regional councils, the opinion of the regional council of Marche and the vote of Friuli-Venezia Giulia on those documents are expressly cited.

for these targets; introduces an early warning system for checking the compliance with targets; and extends producers' responsibility.[42]

By affecting waste, the package concerns the state exclusive legislative competence on the environment,[43] a peculiar subject-matter: it is a shared competence between the EU and the Member States (Article 4 Treaty on the Functioning of the European Union (TFEU)) and, according to the Italian Constitutional Court's case law, it has been defined as a cross-sectional matter (*materia trasversale*) that lacks a clearly identified object but has several aims to be pursued, some of which intertwined with regional shared and residual competences. Because of this, although the subject-matter affected formally falls within the remit of the state, the Senate has taken regional councils' opinions into account through its Committees on the Environment and on EU Policies.

Those opinions, however, have been considered in the framework of the national and European political dialogue, since neither the Senate nor the Chamber of Deputies have participated in the EWS on the legislative package. Indeed, the deadline for the EWS expired on 2 February 2016. The Committee on EU Policies of the Italian Chamber of Deputies issued its positive opinion on 19 October 2016, but without reference to regional opinions; in the Senate, the Committee on EU Policies issued its opinion with several remarks on 10 February 2016, citing the opinions of regional councils, while the Committee on the Environment adopted a resolution on 14 June 2016 (Document XVIII, number 134). This confirms once more the consideration that regional councils are given within the Senate compared to the focus of the scrutiny in the Chamber.

Interestingly, the opinion of the Senate Committee on EU Policies refers to the document elaborated by the Conference of the Presidents of Regional Councils on the Commission 2016 Work Programme[44]—in which it was affirmed that, despite the state exclusive competence, waste and its treatment directly affect regional and local authorities in charge of drafting and adopting the plans on waste management, so that the legislative package could increase the responsibility of regions and local self-government—as well as to the resolution of the regional Assembly of Marche.

Furthermore, on 1 February 2016, the Senate Committee on Environment launched a public consultation (*consultazione pubblica*)—an institutional device aimed to collect contributions from anyone, from individuals to public authorities, on a certain legal act or proposal in order to move the decision-making process closer to citizens—on this legislative package, based on a questionnaire. The consultation, which lasted until 1 April 2016, benefitted from, among others, the opinions of the legislative assembly of Emilia-Romagna and of the regional council of Friuli-Venezia Giulia.[45] Although the text of the resolution

[42] The legislative package, published by the Commission on 2 December 2015, comprises 4 directives—Waste Framework Directive (COM(2015) 595 final), Packaging Directive (COM(2015) 596 final), Landfill Directive (COM(2015) 594 final) and Directive on end-of-life vehicles, batteries and accumulators, and waste electrical and electronic equipment (COM(2015) 593 final)—amending 6 EU legislative acts and a Communication on 'Closing the loop—An EU Action Plan for the Circular Economy' (COM(2015) 614 final).

[43] R Bifulco, Tutela dell'ambiente, dell'ecosistema e dei beni culturali (Art. 117.2.S) e valorizzazione dei beni culturali e ambientali e promozione e organizzazione di attività culturali (Art. 117.3) in R Bifulco and A Celotto (eds), *Le materie dell'art 117 nella giurisprudenza costituzionale dopo il 2001* (Napoli, Editoriale scientifica, 2015) 245. See, lately, judgment no 244/2016.

[44] In fact, on 10 February 2016 this Committee organised an informal hearing of the Conference of the Presidents of Regional Councils on the EU priorities for 2016.

[45] See the resolution no 2173 passed by the Committee on Budget, general and institutional affairs of the legislative assembly of Emilia-Romagna on 16 February 2016 and the resolution no 2 adopted by the Committee on

by the Committee on the Environment does not expressly recall the observations of these two regional councils, it shares and highlights similar concerns with the regional councils' opinions, like the need for the European Commission to set minimum requirements of quality for food and to set a minimum standard procedure for food recovery.

V. The Participation of Regional Councils in the EWS and the Political Dialogue as a Step Forward for the Reform of the Senate? The Legacy of the *Failed* Constitutional Reform

The idea of establishing a *Senato delle autonomie* (Senate of local and regional self-government) has recurred several times throughout Italian Republican history,[46] in particular after the revision of Title V of the Constitution (Constitution Law No 3/2001), but until 2016 those attempts had not regarded the reform of the Senate as a chance to strengthen the relationship between Parliament and regional councils.

By contrast, the 2016 failed attempt to reform the Italian Constitution to some extent has followed and endorsed the path traced during these years of more intense collaboration between the Senate and regional councils in EU affairs, after the Treaty of Lisbon and even more so after Law No 234/2012. Such a claim is based both on the composition of the Senate envisaged by the 2016 Constitutional Reform Bill and on the functions it would have assigned to the new Upper House.[47]

As for the composition, regional councils would have been represented in the Senate, becoming the most significant component of the newly established House. Indeed, according to the bill, the new Italian Senate would have been formed by altogether 100 senators, including 74 regional councillors elected within regional councils among their members in proportion to the population, 21 mayors chosen in each region and autonomous province by the regional council, and five senators appointed by the President of the Republic for a seven-year term. Compared to the original bill presented by the Government (Act of the Senate No 1429)—which aimed to include all the Presidents of the regions and autonomous provinces; the mayors of regional capitals in every region, two members elected

institutional affairs of the regional council of Friuli-Venezia Giulia on 17 February 2016. Also Lombardia, through its executive (*Giunta*) took part in the public consultation. See Senate of the Italian Republic, Servizio Studi and Servizio delle Commissioni, *Dossier sulla consultazione pubblica della 13a Commissione (Territorio, ambiente, beni ambientali) sull'economia circolare*, Rome, May 2016.

[46] Perhaps the most notable attempt to create a 'federal' Senate or a Senate of local and regional self-government in Italy before the 2016 failed constitutional reform was that pursued by the Constitutional Law amending the Second Part of the Constitution, 'Modifiche alla Parte II della Costituzione', published on the Official Journal on 18 November 2005 (Gazzetta Ufficiale no 269). That reform, later rejected on the occasion of the constitutional referendum of 25 and 26 June 2006, would have established a Senate composed of 250 senators elected at the same time as regional councils and not, as the most recent attempt of reform tried to do, from within the regional councils.

[47] See Constitutional Bill C 2613-D, Disposizioni per il superamento del bicameralismo paritario, la riduzione del numero dei parlamentari, il contenimento dei costi di funzionamento delle istituzioni, la soppressione del CNEL e la revisione del Titolo V della parte II della Costituzione, which was approved by the two Houses in two subsequent votes, according to Art 138 Const, and eventually rejected at the referendum of 4 December 2016.

by each regional council and two mayors elected within a constituency composed of all the mayors of the region concerned; plus 21 senators appointed by the President of the Republic—during the first reading, in 2014, the Senate managed to make the component of the regional councils largely predominant in the prospective Upper House;[48] a sign of the strong relationship built up over the last few years between the Senate and regional councils on the scrutiny of EU procedures.

All in all, the composition foreseen for the Senate, if reformed, would have led to the reframing of, and potentially to the enhancement of the participation of, regional legislatures in the EWS and in the political dialogue, within and outside of the Senate. Depending on the circumstances of a more or less coherent position reached by regional councils on EU legislative proposals and documents, these legislatures could either decide to act as a collective player within the new Senate and to issue a joint opinion to the EU institutions, or participate in the EWS as individual and autonomous players from a purely regional standpoint by sending their own opinions to the national parliament and government that then can try to mediate and find a compromise position.

Regarding the Senate's functions, the efforts to create a solid reputation toward both the EU institutions and regions as a reliable interlocutor when dealing with EU-related activities would have been confirmed by the amendments to the Constitution that ultimately were rejected (Article 1 of the Bill). The reformed Senate was expected to represent territorial institutions and acts as a connector between the state and the other constitutive entities of the Republic (Article 114 Constitution). Most important—since the provision was added by the Senate itself at the time of the first reading in 2014—the new Senate would have also exercised the liaison function between the EU, the state and the other constitutive entities of the Republic, a role that the Upper House has already taken on since the EWS and the political dialogue have been put in place.[49]

Given the outcome of the referendum, could the Senate, as it stands, nevertheless perform a role between the EU and regional councils similar to that assigned by the 2016 Constitutional Reform Bill? Although the Senate lacks this recognition at a constitutional level and a symmetrical bicameralism remains in place, we can reasonably expect that the process started by the Treaty of Lisbon, further reinforced by the prospect of a constitutional reform and leading to a de facto transformation of the Senate as the main *fil rouge* between regional councils and the Italian Parliament in the scrutiny of EU affairs, will endure over time. The shift from simple coordination with regional councils to inclusion of the latter in the Upper House will not be achieved. Yet the setting up of brand new procedures, like those introduced by the Senate Committee on EU Policies in 2014, the creation of an ad hoc subcommittee for the relationship with regions on EU issues and the latest Protocol signed with the Conference of the Presidents of Regional Councils (besides the joint training

[48] A Manzella, 'Il "nuovo" Senato' in G Gambetta (ed), *Proposte di riforma per le istituzioni e la cultura* (Bologna, Il Mulino, 2015). The Constitutional reform bill did not exclude, however, the possibility that Presidents of the regions would have eventually sat in the Senate: see G Piccirilli, 'Prospettive di organizzazione del nuovo Senato' (2016) 3 *Rivista dell'Associazione italiana dei costituzionalisti* 7.

[49] See C Fasone, 'Il rapporto tra bicameralismo e Regioni ridefinito dal controllo di sussidiariet . Spunti dal diritto comparato e riflessioni sulla riforma costituzionale in itinere', *diritticomparati.it*, 19 February 2015, and LS Rossi, 'La "funzione di raccordo" con l'Unione europea nella riforma dell'Article 55 Cost', *Forum di Quaderni costituzionali*, 19 September 2015.

activities carried out between Senate's officials and those of regional councils) make it likely for the Senate to fulfil a process of Europeanisation in cooperation with regional legislatures also in the future. The confirmation of this role for the Senate can rely both on entirely new procedures, preferably entrenched in the Senate's Rules, and on existing but unexploited tools like the bicameral committee on regional affairs, which would have been abolished in the failed constitutional reform and that, instead, after more than 15 years could be finally integrated with representatives of regional and local self-government. Consistently, with the design and performance of Upper Houses in other EU Member States, the Italian Senate can continue to show its truly European and, at the same time, 'federative'[50] vocation thanks to the coordinating role it has purposely taken up between the EU, the state and regional councils in particular.

[50] Own translation of '*funzione federatrice*' as described by A Manzella, 'Il parlamento federatore' (2002) 1 *Quaderni costituzionali* 35.

Part III

The Italian Parliament in the 'Euro-national' Parliamentary System

9

Procedures vis-à-vis the Commission: The Subsidiarity Scrutiny as a Way to 'Reconnect' EU Democracy

NICOLA LUPO

I. Introduction: National Parliaments and the European Commission, at the Opposite Extremes of EU Democracy

The active involvement of national Parliaments in EU decision-making is an instrument aimed at closing the gap between (mainly national) politics and (mainly European) policies.[1] As already remarked in the Introduction, through their representative institutions, national public opinions could have a say in decisions taken 'in Brussels', so being able to in some way diminish the 'democratic disconnect' with which the EU institutions, as well as the national ones, are struggling.[2]

One of the instruments to achieve this very ambitious aim consists in putting side by side, through 'ad hoc' Euro-national parliamentary procedures,[3] the institutions that are

[1] V Schmidt, *Democracy in Europe. The EU and National Polities* (New York, Oxford University Press, 2006) 5 ff.

[2] P Lindseth, *Power and Legitimacy. Reconciling Europe and the Nation State* (New York, Oxford University Press, 2010) 12 ff.

[3] As euro-national parliamentary procedures we may define the procedures that have two concurring features: first, they are characterised by interventions of both EU and Member States' parliamentary institutions (together with other bodies); second, they are regulated partly by EU law and partly by national constitutional/

seen as at opposite extremes of European democratic polity: on the one end, the symbols of national politics, ie national Parliaments; on the other end, the EU institution that traditionally represents, more than any other, the supranational and the technical-bureaucratic nature of EU policies, ie the European Commission.

This juxtaposition as just presented is at the same time oversimplified and static. Indeed, within national Parliaments there are also technical and bureaucratic elements supporting members of Parliaments, although in general they tend not to play formally a decisive role. Their role is usually increased, however, when national Parliaments need to deal with EU affairs, given their high level of complexity and specialisation.[4]

Reciprocally, within the European Commission political features, since the beginning, have been more than non-existent. Moreover, they have significantly increased after the 2014 European Parliament (EP) elections, essentially because of the so-called *Spitzenkandidaten* experiment (a sort of 'constitutional convention') and its subsequent parliamentary and administrative practices.[5]

The main Euro-national parliamentary procedure that allows a direct relationship of national Parliaments with the European Commission on daily activities, provided by Protocol No 2 annexed to the Treaty of Lisbon, is the Early Warning System (hereinafter EWS), ie the scrutiny on the compliance of EU draft proposals with the principle of subsidiarity. It is well known that this principle looks by its very nature ambiguous and multipurpose, somewhat in between law and politics, legal analysis and political assessment.[6]

Modelled on this procedure, another procedure was created by the European Commission even before the entry into force of the Treaty of Lisbon, through a letter of its President Barroso, called 'political dialogue'.[7] Through what can be defined as a sort of 'constitutional convention' originally conceived within COSAC (Conférence des Organes Spécialisés dans

parliamentary law, to which EU law often refers with a formula like 'in accordance with its own constitutional requirements' (see, for instance, within the TEU: Art 42(2), on CSDP; Art 48(4 and 6), on Treaty amendments; Art 49, on new membership; Art 50(1) on withdrawal; Art 54, on ratification).

[4] On parliamentary administrations see the research conducted by T Christiansen, A Hogenauer and C Neuhold: especially, *Parliamentary Administrations in the European Union* (Basingstoke, Palgrave, 2016). From an Italian perspective, see N Lupo, 'Il ruolo delle burocrazie parlamentari alla luce dei mutamenti dell'assetto istituzionale, nazionale e sopranazionale' (2012) 54(1) *Rassegna parlamentare* 51–89.

[5] The literature on *Spitzenkandidaten* is already very rich. For an accurate reconstruction of its origins see N Peñalver García and J Priestley, *The Making of a European President* (Basingstoke, Palgrave, 2015) 38 ff. About its constitutional effects see M Goldoni, 'The Representativeness of EU Law-Making: Lessons from the Spitzenkandidaten Experiment' in C Fasone, D Fromage and Z Lefkofridi (eds), *Parliaments, Public Opinion, and Parliamentary Elections in Europe* (2015) EUI Max Weber Working Paper Series 7–19; M Goldoni, 'Politicising EU Lawmaking? The Spitzenkandidaten Experiment as a Cautionary Tale' (2016) 3 *European Law Journal* 279 ff; T Christiansen, 'After the Spitzenkandidaten: Fundamental Change in the EU's Political System?' (2016) 5 *West European Politics* 992 ff.

[6] In the sense that the principle of subsidiarity is 'politically complex and legally uncertain' see, G de Búrca, 'The Principle of Subsidiarity and the Court of Justice as an Institutional Actor' (1998) 36 *Journal of Common Market Studies* 217; M Evans and A Zimmermans, 'Editors' Conclusions: Future Directions for Subsidiarity' in M Evans and A Zimmermans (eds), *Global Perspectives on Subsidiarity* (Springer, Heidelberg, 2014) 221 ff., especially 223, talk of a principle that is 'somewhat of a chameleon'. See also, more recently, M Goldoni and A Jonsson Cornell, 'The Trajectory of the Early Warning System' in A Jonsson Cornell and M Goldoni (eds), *National and Regional Parliaments in the EU-Legislative Procedure Post-Lisbon* (Oxford, Hart, 2017) 335–55.

[7] The letter of President Barroso is from 17 July 2006 and the procedure was originally called the 'Barroso initiative'. On the origins of the political dialogue see D Jančic, 'The Barroso Initiative: Window Dressing or Democracy Boost?' (2012) 8 *Utrecht Law Review* 78–91 and D Jančic, 'The Game of Cards: National Parliaments in the EU and the Future of the Early Warning Mechanism and the Political Dialogue' (2015) 52 *Common Market Law Review*, 939–76. On its application by the Italian Parliament see the chapters by A Esposito and D Capuano in this volume.

les Affaires Communautaires), the European Commission committed itself to apply ahead of time the information obligations provided by Protocol No 1 annexed to the Treaty of Lisbon and to take into consideration and reply to the opinions or contributions sent by national Parliaments on its own draft proposals.

Neither of these two procedures is to be deemed the main channel through which national Parliaments could play their role in the EU. The most important channel was and still is their relationship with their own Government.[8] The EU representative democracy is founded on the functions of scrutiny and political direction that each national Parliament exercises—according to the design and the procedures provided by the rules of each national Constitution regarding its form of government—towards all the policies pursued by the Government, including those on EU affairs.

Consistently with this reading of the involvement of national Parliaments in the EU decision-making process, the chapter examines—obviously, with reference to the Italian Parliament—the different procedures adopted by the Chamber of Deputies and the Senate in order to approve reasoned opinions according to Protocol No 2. It argues that, to better fulfil the function of reconnecting EU democracy, it is preferable that the Early Warning System be interpreted, as is the case for the Italian Parliament and especially for the Senate, mainly as a political rather than a merely legal instrument. It would not make much sense, indeed, to involve political bodies like national Parliaments and call upon them to play a role as a mere legal advisor on the compliance of the principle of subsidiarity interpreted in a strict meaning, as some scholars have maintained, probably aiming at reducing their role and the effects of their direct involvement on the EU decision-making.[9]

Nonetheless, the recognition of the political nature of the Early Warning System implies that the reasoned opinions approved sensibly differ depending on the style and on the concept of subsidiarity adopted in each assessment. As we will see, nothing excludes the situation that sometimes the Chamber or the Senate—or, as has happened to date, their standing committees—may wish to act almost like legal advisors, interpreting in a strict sense their role as guardians of the principle of subsidiarity. This is a possibility that is entirely left to them: as political bodies, they are rather free to interpret the parameters of their own assessment and to determine the scope of their intervention. Nothing impedes these interpretations from differing between the two Houses of the same national Parliament, although in this way they will probably weaken the effectiveness, at a European level, of their positions.

Considering the picture so described, this chapter examines the ways in which the Chamber and the Senate deal with EU policies and, more specifically, how they implemented the EWS (also in relationship with the political dialogue). Neither of the two Houses amended its rules of procedure after the entry into force of the Treaty of Lisbon. Indeed, the procedures for the EWS and the political dialogue have been determined in a provisional and

[8] See C Fasone and N Lupo, 'Conclusion. Interparliamentary Cooperation in the Framework of a Euro-national Parliamentary System' in N Lupo and C Fasone (eds), *Interparliamentary Cooperation in the Composite European Constitution* (Oxford, Hart, 2016) 345 ff.

[9] See, although with different approaches, P Kiiver, *The Early Warning System for the Principle of Subsidiarity: Constitutional Theory and Empirical Reality* (London, Routledge, 2012) (referring to national Parliaments as a sort of 'Council of State'); and F Fabbrini and K Granat, '"Yellow Card, but no Foul": The Role of the National Parliaments under the Subsidiarity Protocol and the Commission Proposal for an EU Regulation on the Right to Strike' (2013) 50 *Common Market Law Review* 115 (criticising the broad interpretation of the principle of subsidiarity adopted by national Parliaments in the first yellow card).

experimental way. These procedures have not been changed in the subsequent years, apart from a (rather generic) referral to both of them inserted in the law concerning the formation and implementation of EU policies in Italy (Law No 234/2012, in Articles 8 and 9 respectively). No procedure at all is currently provided for the so-called 'green card' or 'reinforced political dialogue' with the European Commission, at the moment used only by the Senate a couple of times, while the Chamber seems to look more cautiously and even critically at this new Euro-national parliamentary procedure.

As is more analytically shown in other chapters of this volume,[10] the two Houses follow rather different procedural paths. One of the main differences between the two Houses concerns precisely how the Early Warning System relates to the political dialogue, as well as to the powers of scrutiny and direction of the Government in EU affairs, already provided since the 1980s by the parliamentary rules of procedure. Other differences more specifically address the procedures of the Early Warning System. These differences regard, namely, the way in which the procedure starts and the respective roles assigned to the parliamentary bodies involved in the procedure (sectoral committee; EU policies committee; plenary). It is argued that, if compared to that in force at the Chamber, the procedure designed and followed by the Senate is more efficient and more consistent with the predominantly political nature of the Early Warning System in its practical application, although at the price of some inefficiencies and inconsistencies. This procedural difference contributes to explain the much higher numbers of reasoned opinions approved by the Senate.

The final part of the chapter deals with the implementation of these procedures especially after the full activation of the information channels provided by Law No 234/2012. A couple of recent reasoned opinions approved by the Senate on October 2016 regarding two proposals on migration issues are examined, as they represent a clear example of a political usage of the Early Warning System, in which some of the limits of the Italian Senate's procedures emerge.

This explains why, finally, a suggestion is formulated, in the direction of a formalisation and a simplification of the parliamentary procedures for issuing reasoned opinions (and contributions) by ensuring a constant presence of the Government. This formalisation would help not only the Italian political actors to better internalise and get accustomed to these procedures, but also the EU institutions in not getting lost, as sometimes happened, in the Italian procedural 'byzantinism'. Only in this way would these instruments be able to fully comply with the functions for which they have been originally conceived and to allow the Italian Parliament to participate more actively in the EU decision-making process.

II. Early Warning System and Political Dialogue: Their Complementary and Ancillary Role in the Function of Scrutiny and Direction on EU Affairs

According to the Italian Parliament, both the political dialogue and the early warning system not only are rather far from being the main channels for involvement in EU affairs,

[10] See the chapters by DA Capuano and A Esposito in this volume.

but also should not be seen as fully autonomous or independent instruments. Conversely, they are called upon to play a complementary and ancillary role, enriching the ordinary functions of scrutiny and political direction that both Houses are entitled to exercise with regards to the Government's policies on EU affairs.

As it is well known, because of the symmetrical Italian bicameralism, both the Chamber and the Senate are linked to the Government through a confidence relationship. This means that both Houses are fully entitled to exercise these functions, scrutinising and directing the members of the Government on their activity, including the one taking place at the EU level.[11] At the same time, this also means that, at least normally, neither of the two Houses is willing to play a role completely detached and independent from the preferences and positions expressed, in the past or in the future, by the Government at the EU level. Indeed, from the viewpoint of the parliamentary majority supporting the Government, it is rather improper to send an opinion or a contribution to the European Commission that is inconsistent with the position the same Government, as bearer of national interests, is going to express in the Council. Of course, there are exceptions, and they are not sporadic, as traditionally in Italian politics there is a vibrant dynamic between the Government and its parliamentary majority.[12] However, even in case of diverging visions between the Government and the Parliament, the most natural option would be that of trying first to redirect the action of the Government in the EU decision-making process, eventually coupling this attempt with the issuing of an opinion or a contribution that goes, even more clearly, along the same lines.

This fundamental approach in favour of the complementary and ancillary role of these new instruments is mirrored at the procedural level by the choice to use, at least at the beginning, the already existing parliamentary procedures, without adopting any 'ad hoc' amendment to parliamentary rules of procedure in order to implement them.[13] EU procedures have mostly been seen as a unique entity by the two Houses, up to a certain extent independent from the institution to which they were addressed: the Government or the Commission.

This choice, indeed, was also made easier by a couple of contextual elements. First, the fact that in the last decade the parliamentary rules of procedure of both Houses, different from what happened in the previous two decades, have not been amended frequently, and among the last amendments approved were precisely those regarding EU procedures.[14] Second, and more specifically, the informal instrument through which the political dialogue was introduced, consisting uniquely, as already noticed, in a letter sent by then-President of the European Commission Barroso.

[11] See the chapter by Rizzoni in this volume.

[12] On the inexistence, in the Italian parliamentary experience, of the so-called 'continuum' between the Government and its parliamentary majority see, among many, A Manzella, *Il parlamento*3 (Bologna, Il Mulino, 2003) 423.

[13] On this continuity, see, critically, C Fasone, 'Il Parlamento italiano dopo il Trattato di Lisbona, in vista dell'approvazione di una nuova legge sui rapporti con l'Unione europea' (2010) 169 *Studi parlamentari e di politica costituzionale* 41–71.

[14] The Senate Rules of Procedures were amended in February 2003 also in order to transform the pre-existing 'Giunta' for European Affairs into a (still rather peculiar) 14th standing committee. At the Chamber, the most recent updates of the Rules of Procedures concerning EU affairs were approved in July 1999.

A. The 'Experimental' Procedures for the EWS

This choice not to amend the parliamentary rules of procedure has been substantially confirmed after the entry into force of the Treaty of Lisbon, although different approaches were followed in each House. While in the Chamber the implementation of the EWS took place through two opinions approved by the Rules Committee (Giunta per il regolamento) in 2009 and 2010, in the Senate the procedure was introduced only by a letter of the President of the Assembly.

In more detail, the Rules Committee of the Chamber approved two 'interpretative decisions' (*pareri*):[15] one at the wake of the entry into force of the Treaty of Lisbon, on 6 October 2009; and the other, after some months of practical experience with the procedures, on 14 July 2010, partly singling out and partly reviewing some provisions of the first one (especially on the involvement of the Plenary). On the contrary, in the Senate the procedure was determined by a letter signed by the then-Speaker, Schifani, sent to all the standing committees' chairpersons, on the very day of the entry in to force of the Treaty of Lisbon, 1 December 2009.[16]

In both Houses, the procedural solutions were adopted expressly 'on an experimental basis' (and in the Senate also 'on a provisional basis'). This feature, indeed, was not completely unknown in recent parliamentary practice, as similar expressions have also accompanied other interpretative decisions taken by the two Rules Committees.[17] Their experimental and provisional character does not impede the procedures so constructed from being able to stay in place for years, if not for decades. Since 2010, in fact, no change has been made regarding their content, and the rules of procedure on the European powers of the Italian Parliament have not been modified further.

The first interpretative decision approved by the Rules Committee of the Chamber (on 6 October 2009), which addressed the main procedures linking the Chamber with the EU institutions, contained, precisely with regard to the EWS, an 'evaluation clause'. According to this clause, 'once the Treaty enters into force, the experimental procedure here envisaged will be the object of an evaluation with the particular aim of verifying the possibility, where certain circumstances are met, to involve the Plenary on decisions regarding subsidiarity'.[18] This is exactly what happened with the subsequent interpretative decision approved by the same Rules Committee on 14 July 2010, which is almost completely dedicated to the EWS: it complements the previous interpretative decision, allowing the possibility of an involvement of the Plenary and providing for the relevant norms ruling the Plenary debate.

[15] On the importance of the interpretative decisions of the Rules Committee (Giunta per il regolamento), see, in general, Manzella, above n 12, 52 and P Gambale, 'Le Giunte per il regolamento nella formazione e nell'interpretazione del diritto parlamentare' in N Lupo (ed), *Il precedente parlamentare tra diritto e politica* (Bologna, Il Mulino, 2013) 163–79.

[16] See A Esposito, 'Il Trattato di Lisbona e il nuovo ruolo costituzionale dei Parlamenti nazionali: le prospettive del Parlamento italiano' (2009) 51 *Rassegna parlamentare* 1119–73 and DA Capuano, 'Funzioni delle Camere italiane nel procedimento legislativo dell'Unione europea' (2011) 53 *Rassegna parlamentare* 519–50.

[17] For some examples and for a critical assessment of this practice, see R Ibrido, *L'interpretazione del diritto parlamentare* (Milano, FrancoAngeli, 2015) 82 ff.

[18] Our translation.

B. The Overlap with the Political Dialogue (and with the Function of Scrutiny and Direction)

In the Chamber Rules Committee's interpretative decisions and in the letter of the Senate's Speaker there was no specific reference to the political dialogue.

Both Houses agree that there is a full overlap between the documents through which the Parliament expresses its position in the exercise of the functions of scrutiny and direction (towards the Government), on the one hand, and the contributions issued in the context of the political dialogue (towards the European Commission or other EU institutions), on the other hand.

The difference is, conversely, the way in which the procedure for the EWS overlaps with the political dialogue and with the scrutiny and direction powers that both Houses are entitled to exercise within their confidence relationship with the Government—obviously, where all three procedures can be used, that is, in the case of EU draft legislative proposals. The two Houses tackle rather differently this triple overlapping.

In the Chamber, the assessment on the proportionality principle and on the substance of the draft proposals is a task for the competent sectoral committee, which may receive an opinion on these elements from the Committee on EU Policies. Similarly, it is up to each sectoral committee to exercise the function of scrutiny and direction of the Government's EU activity: according to Article 127 of the Rules of Procedure, this function is normally accomplished through the approval of a document after consultation with the Committee on EU Policies. The EWS, instead, pivots around the Committee on EU Policies: the task of issuing an assessment on the compliance with the subsidiarity principle is attributed exclusively to this Committee. If negative, it can stand alone as a reasoned opinion; if positive, it is not qualified as such, but can be transmitted to the EU institutions anyway, in the context of the political dialogue, only if the sectoral committee approves a document.[19]

Contrastingly, in the Senate an almost complete overlap between the EWS and the other two procedures, which create relationships between the Senate and the Government and between the Senate and the EU institutions, is intentionally pursued both in the Committee on EU Policies and in the sectoral committees.[20] Normally, the Committee on EU Policies should express its opinion at an earlier stage; in case of inactivity of the sectoral Committee in the subsequent 15 days after the issuing of the opinion of the Committee on EU Policies, however, the Committee on EU Policies' opinion, embedded in a resolution and after a second vote by the same Committee, can be sent directly to the Government and to the EU institutions. This implies that at least the Senate seems to share the idea that the EWS is not a separate procedure, but it is strictly intertwined with the political dialogue and with its powers of scrutiny and political direction of the Government.[21]

Finally, a certain degree of overlap between the EWS and the political dialogue, on the one hand, and the parliamentary powers of scrutiny and political direction, on the other

[19] On the problem that this coordination can cause and on some possible procedural solutions see the chapter by A Esposito.

[20] See Capuano, above n 16, 520. See also the chapter by DA Capuano in this volume.

[21] Similarly, see S Cavatorto, 'Italy: "Still Looking for a New Era in the Making of EU Policy"' in *The Palgrave Handbook of National Parliaments and the European Union* (Basingstoke, Palgrave, 2015) 209–31, especially 222 ff, referring indeed to both Houses and especially to the relationships between EWS and political dialogue, seen as 'two sides of the same coin'.

hand, has been codified by Articles 8 (for the EWS) and 9 (for the political dialogue) of Law No 234/2012. According to these provisions, all reasoned opinions and all contributions issued within the EWS and the political dialogue, although formally addressed to EU institutions, are to be sent to the Government too. In this way, these provisions involve the Government also in the procedures in which a direct conversation between the Italian Parliament and EU institutions should take place according to the EU legal provisions.

They are embraceable provisions, aimed at avoiding any bypasses of the Government by either of the Houses, in their activity related to the EU. This fear, indeed, for the moment should be excluded, as the current parliamentary rules of procedure already contain provisions toward the same aim and the Government usually actively follows all the parliamentary sittings in Plenary as well as in Committees. Apart from some criticisms regarding the language they use or the fact that Article 9 codifies—probably for the first time in Europe—an otherwise informal Euro-national parliamentary procedure like the political dialogue,[22] the two provisions of the Law No 234/2012 seem to further emphasise the necessary connections among all the channels, national and European, that each House is able to use in order to represent its own position on a EU draft legislative act.

These provisions were promptly implemented in the more recent reasoned opinions issued under the EWS, in which a new final formula was inserted, clarifying that their content is also to be deemed as a guidance for the EU activity of the Italian Government.[23]

C. The Differences in Implementing the EWS between the Two Houses

As has already been remarked, the main differences between the procedures adopted in the two Houses refer to the EWS. With regards to the initiation of this procedure, ie the identification of the acts to concretely check concerning the compliance with the principle of subsidiarity, the two Houses opted for very different solutions.

In the Senate, all the draft legislative acts transmitted according to Protocol No 2, that is on which a subsidiarity scrutiny could be exercised, are automatically assigned to the sectoral Committee competent in the subject matter, as well as to the Committee on EU Policies. The exception to the general rule, which leaves the request for a deferral of an EU draft legislative act to the sectoral Committee's discretion (Article 144(1) of the Rules of Procedure), is the result of a wish to respect, whenever possible, the eight-week deadline.[24] That is why in the assignment decision the Speaker of the Senate automatically indicates a deadline for the expression of the opinion by the sectoral Committee, as well as for the other committees consulted (including the Committee on EU Policies, which, as already seen, can also substitute the sectoral committee, in case of inactivity).

On the contrary, in the Chamber the selection of the draft legislative acts on which to start the EWS procedure is entirely left to the Committee on EU Policies, to which all

[22] A Esposito, 'La legge 24 dicembre 2012, n 234, sulla partecipazione dell'Italia alla formazione e all'attuazione della normativa e delle politiche dell'UE'. Parte 1, Prime riflessioni sul ruolo delle Camere' (2013) 9(2) *Federalismi.it* 45.

[23] The closing formula runs as follows: 'This document is to be understood as guidance to the Government within the meaning of Article 7 of Law No 234 of 24 December 2012' (for instance, see the resolution on zootechnics: Atto Senato, XVII legislatura, doc XVIII, n 59).

[24] Capuano, above n 16, 544.

these acts are assigned. The Chamber, in fact, decided not to systematically scrutinise all the EU draft legislative acts transmitted according to Protocol No 2 and, instead, to select only the proposals in which the respect of the principle of subsidiarity could be problematic and may therefore be deemed worthwhile for the Committee on EU Policies to begin examining.[25] This selection is decided by the Committee on EU Policies' Bureau, integrated with the political group representatives (that is, the chairpersons of every parliamentary group inside that committee). This body, which normally meets—without any form of publicity—once a week, in order to define the agenda of its standing committee, is called upon to select the acts to be examined, on the basis of technical notes prepared by the staff of the Chamber (EU Affairs Department).

As we will see, this difference in the initiation of the procedures contributes to the explanation as to why, in large part, there is a higher number of reasoned opinions approved by the Senate. However, this data can also find further explanations in other divergences that exist between the procedures adopted in the two Houses. In any case, as anticipated, the most significant difference between the two Houses relates to the allotment of tasks for the EWS among the Committee on EU Policies and the other sectoral committees, as well as to the ways of involving the Plenary.

In the Chamber, the 'reasoned opinion', included in a 'document' (*documento*), on the compliance with the principle of subsidiarity, can be issued exclusively by the Committee on EU Policies, to be expressed, in principle, within 40 days of its transmission and in theory—as this provision has never been implemented—with the participation of the rapporteur from the sectoral committee, who is invited to attend. The sectoral committees, instead, are competent regarding the substance of the draft legislative acts, as well as for the respect of the principle of proportionality. To these profiles the Committee on EU Policies can also add something, if desired, by issuing an opinion addressed (only) to the sectoral Committee, which must decide whether to use this opinion in drafting its own document, to be sent to the Government and to the EU institutions.

In the Senate, conversely, the Committee on EU Policies is asked to deal in its opinion with any aspect of the draft legislative act. In principle, its opinion should be addressed to the sectoral committee, which is also called upon to scrutinise the draft legislative act in its entirety and to issue a 'resolution' (*risoluzione*) addressed to the Executive and to the EU institutions relating to all the aspects of the proposal. However, in the case of the sectoral Committee's inactivity, the resolution approved by the Committee on EU Policies can also be transferred to the Executive and the EU institutions. In this way, a sort of substitutive power is given to the Senate Committee on EU Policies. It is founded on a (very) extensive interpretation of Article 144(5) of the Rules of Procedure—which does not refer to the EWS, as it has not been amended since February 2003—and, as already mentioned, it requires a second vote, with a higher attendance quorum,[26] by the Committee on EU Policies on the same resolution (Document XVIII-bis).[27]

[25] Esposito, above n 22, 41.

[26] The attendance quorum for the second vote is higher (50 per cent +1 of the committee members, instead of one-third), as it is on a document which will be sent to another institution and thus does not qualify as an affair to which the committee must refer to the plenary (or to another committee), according to Art 30 of the rules of procedure.

[27] Normally, the resolutions approved by the Committee on EU Policies are published as Doc XVIII. When transmitted directly to the Executive and to the EU institutions, they are (re-)published as Doc XVIII-bis.

In synthesis, by applying the classification imagined for the different models of national parliaments' scrutiny of EU draft legislative acts to the EWS,[28] the Senate adopted a decentralised scrutiny system, while the Chamber opted for a centralised model. Or, if one wishes to rely on a more recent and sophisticated typology,[29] the one preferred by the Senate could be better qualified as a 'mixed model', with the dominance of the Committee on EU Policies.

The option preferred by the Chamber presupposes the possibility of a clear-cut distinction between the assessment of the substance of the draft legislative act, on the one hand, and the scrutiny of the compliance with the principle of subsidiarity, on the other. According to this option, both tasks should be accomplished by the same political institution, the Chamber, although by different internal bodies: the first, maybe because it is deemed to be more important, by the sectoral Committee (with the opinion of the Committee on EU Policies); the second exclusively by the Committee on EU Policies, in order to distance it clearly from the scrutiny on the substance, and possibly to develop gradually a set of well-established criteria in order to assess the compliance with the principle of subsidiarity.[30]

It seems to be a fascinating attempt, however highly unlikely to succeed in practice, unfortunately. Members of Parliament naturally tend to express a positive assessment, either regarding the principle of subsidiarity or independently from it, if they agree with the content and the substance of the draft legislative act. On the contrary, they would evaluate negatively, on any possible parameter, a provision whose content they do not deem acceptable from a political point of view.

In both Houses, according to the experimental rules currently in force, the involvement of the Plenary would be possible, but in practice in neither of the two Houses has the Plenary exercised any role within the EWS to date. However, the rules for requesting the involvement of the Plenary are rather differently conceived in each of the two Houses.

In the Chamber, the power to move the procedure from the committee to the Plenary is attributed to either the Executive, 1/5 of the committee members, or 1/10 of the deputies. This option, which repeats exactly the same subjects that are allowed by Article 72(3) of the Italian Constitution to move to the Plenary a bill examined by a standing committee in its legislative capacity (*in sede legislativa*), seems consistent with other choices followed by the Chamber. Namely, it is consistent with the applicability of some provisions of the rules of procedure regarding the legislative process in the committee phase in a reporting capacity (*in sede referente*) to the examination of EU draft legislative acts: namely, Article 79, paragraphs 4, 5 and 6, to which the interpretative decision of the Rules Committee of 6 November 2009 expressly refers.

The interpretative decision of 14 July 2010 clarifies that this possibility must be exercised in the five days following the approval of the document by the Committee on EU Policies (which, as already discussed, must be approved within the first 40 days). If the document

[28] See P Kiiver, *The National Parliaments in the European Union. A Critical View on EU Constitution-Building* (The Hague, Kluwer, 2006) 47 ff.

[29] *cf* K Granat, *National Parliaments and the Policing of the Subsidiarity Principle*, PhD Thesis submitted for assessment with a view to obtaining the degree of Doctor of Laws of the European University Institute, Florence, December 2014, 134 ff (who does not include the Italian parliament in her proposed typology). See also D Fromage, 'Standing Committees in Interparliamentary Cooperation in the Post-Lisbon Era: Towards the End of the European Affairs Committees' Predominance?' in Lupo and Fasone, above n 8, 113 ff.

[30] The chapter by A Esposito effectively underlines, instead, the advantages of the procedures as designed in the Chamber.

is itself a reasoned opinion, there is no other requirement. But if the document contains instead a positive evaluation of the draft legislative act, a further document, called '*ordine del giorno*', will be also required, to be proposed in the Plenary (by at least 20 deputies or by a president of a parliamentary group composed of at least 20 deputies). This further document aims at complying with the need to justify, with some motivations, the negative opinion that could possibly be approved by the Plenary, in case it reverses the positive decision previously issued by the Committee on EU Policies. Through this '*ordine del giorno*', the Chamber would preemptively add the justification required for a proper reasoned opinion.

On the contrary, the Senate, consistent with the choice to make use of the resolution as a multi-purpose instrument, opted for analogising to the procedure constructed for the exercise of political directions to the Executive through resolutions issued by standing committees: ie to Article 50(3), recalled by Article 144(6), of the Rules of Procedure. This means that the power to involve the Plenary in the EWS is attributed either to the Executive or to 1/3 of the Committee members: that is, exactly the same subjects that have the power to move the discussion of a resolution from any standing committee to the Plenary. The procedures used as a point of reference in the Senate are, in fact, those provided by the rules of procedure for the approval of acts of political direction to the Government.[31]

III. A Senate More Active in EU Affairs, and Especially in the EWS

A. The Effect of Procedural Differences

The examined procedural differences between the two Houses contribute to explain why the overall number of both documents on EU draft legislative acts and reasoned opinions approved are, in fact, much higher in the Senate than in the Chamber.[32]

Indeed, the procedure adopted by the Senate, which does not isolate the principle of subsidiarity from the substance of the proposal, seems more effective and more suitable for the kind of involvement of national Parliaments that has been encouraged, especially through the political dialogue, by the Commission. In overlapping the different powers on EU affairs exercised by the Senate, this procedure also looks more consistent with the approach concretely followed by the Italian Parliament, which decided however to rely on the Government as the main channel of influence in EU matters, reserving a complementary role for both the political dialogue and the EWS.

On the contrary, the procedure imagined by the Chamber, although with the aim of ensuring a high level of consistency in the subsidiarity scrutiny conferred exclusively to the Committee on EU Policies, seems at the same time too ponderous and too subtle to be fully

[31] See the chapter by G Rizzoni in this volume.

[32] At the end of 2016, reasoned opinions approved have been 11 by the Senate and four by the Chamber. Furthermore, since the entry into force of the Treaty of Lisbon, the Senate has approved more than 400 resolutions, while the Chamber has approved slightly more than 100 final documents.

understood and implemented by the political actors. MPs are inevitably inclined to (also) express a political assessment of each proposal, which tends to prevail over its legal assessment. The latter may of course coexist with and accompany the former, if deemed useful, but it normally plays a secondary role. This outcome, indeed, had been foreseen, as doubts were raised about the practicability of a subsidiarity scrutiny independent and autonomous from the scrutiny on the political substance of the draft act. More specifically, an analogy was proposed with the failed attempt, in the Italian legal order in the 1980s, to isolate from the merits the parliamentary scrutiny centered on the existence of the prerequisites of necessity and urgency which, according to Article 77 Constitution, should concur in order to allow the Government to enact a decree-law. Also in this case, the parliamentary scrutiny saw the political assessment prevail over any kind of legal or constitutional evaluation of these prerequisites.[33]

The institutional arrangement of the Senate, thus, has been fundamental to explaining its high level of activity in the EU landscape.[34] However, the procedure followed in the Senate has its own downsides. The main one consists in giving an overly significant role to the Committee on EU Policies, especially in the case of inactivity of sectoral committees. Furthermore, it allows the other standing committees to make an instrumental use of the principle of subsidiarity: this happened in some cases, mainly during the first years of implementation of the EWS,[35] and again more recently, as will be discussed below in section V.B. The procedure adopted by the Senate also enhances—especially if the Plenary continues to be excluded by the process—the risk of a mixture of contradictory positions among the different committees, which would be reflected in the text of the single document that is sent 'to Brussels', clearly written by many different hands and often with divergent aims.[36]

B. Two Alternative Explanations: A Preview of the Then-under-approval (and Later Failed) Constitutional Reform? Upper Houses more Active on EU Affairs?

Apart from procedural differences, other explanations might theoretically be found for the Senate's greater use of European 'direct' powers, in either features typical of the Italian constitutional system, or else those common to all the EU upper Houses.

[33] See M Cartabia, 'I parlamenti nazionali nell'architettura costituzionale europea: che cosa resta in caso di mancata ratifica?' in *L'integrazione dei sistemi costituzionali europeo e nazionali*. Atti del XX Convegno annuale dell'Associazione italiana dei costituzionalisti, Catania, 14–15 October 2005 (Padova, CEDAM, 2007) 142f.

[34] A Baraggia, 'Bicameralism and Interparliamentary Cooperation' in Lupo and Fasone, above n 8, 93f.

[35] The clearest example is the first reasoned opinion approved by the Senate, on a decision on fishery products, on which see C Fasone, 'Il Senato approva il primo parere contrario sul rispetto del principio di sussidiarietà', (2010) 4 *Quaderni costituzionali* 824–27 (available also at www.forumcostituzionale.it/wordpress/imagboves/stories/pdf/documenti_forum/temi_attualita/parlamento/0012_fasone.pdf).

[36] For an example, in which the Senate sent a document deriving form a juxtaposition of texts issued by three different Committees, one favourable and two rather more critical, on the directive on Tobacco products, see N Lupo, 'The Scrutiny of the Principle of Subsidiarity in the Procedures and Reasoned Opinions of the Italian Chamber and Senate' in Goldoni and Jonsson Cornell, above n 6.

The first kind of explanation, considering typical features of the Senate, does not seem particularly meaningful, as in Italy the two Houses are both directly elected by citizens and hold exactly the same powers, including the confidence to the Government. It could even be supposed that the more active role of the Senate represented, to a certain extent, sort of a preview or a forecast of the future possible role of the new Senate. In fact, according to the constitutional reform rejected by the referendum held on 4 December 2016, the new Senate would not have voted any more the confidence to the Government and therefore would not have had, in a proper sense, scrutiny and direction powers over the Government. Instead, it should have been called upon to exercise a 'liaison function' (*funzione di raccordo*) between the State and the territorial autonomies and also among the State, the other entities which constitute the Republic and the European Union, as well as to participate in the decisions aimed at forming and implementing EU normative acts and policies. In other words, the new Senate would have—partially—compensated for the loss of the confidence relationship and the reduction of its legislative powers with an increase and a development of its European powers.[37]

In a way, a similar phenomenon of the 'early implementation' of the failed constitutional reform of the Italian bicameralism seemed to be happening in recent years, specifically regarding the creation of parliamentary procedures aimed at ensuring some forms of direct and specific 'dialogue' on EU affairs among the Senate and the regional councils (by which the new Senate would have been elected).[38]

However, to our ends, this does not seem to explain much, as the activism of the Senate on EU affairs dates back to the first years of the application of the EWS and the political dialogue, at a time when the recalled constitutional reform of the Senate was rather far from being conceived (although some proposals for reforming the symmetrical bicameralism were already debated, starting in the 1980s).

The second kind of explanation, based on common features of European bicameralisms, finds its roots in the observation that the EWS could represent an opportunity for the 'rise of the Senates'. The observation, in simplified terms, goes as follows. As Senates are generally more independent from the Government than lower Houses, because they do not vote the confidence, and as they are less engaged in legislative activity, this could 'offer a greater prospect that their opinion will not merely be a repetition of what the government thinks already'. This would seem consistent with the fact that generally speaking 'under the EWS Senates enjoy a voice that is completely out of proportion with the voice that they have' regarding domestic legislative competences.[39] Therefore, the EWS and especially the political dialogue as a result became among the few instruments for the upper Houses to make their voices heard at the EU level.[40] As has been noted, most of the institutionally strong

[37] See the chapter by L Gianniti in this volume.

[38] See L Bartolucci, 'In attesa del "nuovo" Senato, un canale di collegamento più fluido con i Consigli regionali negli affari dell'Unione europea' (2014) 3 *Osservatoriosullefonti.it*, and C Fasone, 'In attesa della riforma costituzionale, alcune recenti evoluzioni nella 14ª Commissione del Senato sui raccordi tra Stato, Regioni e Unione europea' (2015) www.forumcostituzionale.it. See the chapters by DA Capuano and C Fasone in this volume.

[39] *cf* Kiiver, above n 9, 64 ff.

[40] See E Mastenbroek et al, *Engaging with Europe. Evaluating National Parliamentary Control of EU Decision Making after the Lisbon Treaty. Part I: Report of Findings*, Nijmegen Institute for Management Research, Radboud University, 2014, 31 ff.

Parliaments 'see no added value in engagement in a dialogue with the European Commission and instead focus on domestic influence on their government', while some 'upper chambers in bicameral system try to evade the dominance of the lower chamber by getting involved directly at EU level'.[41]

Although following very different patterns, data confirm that 'upper houses—in absolute terms—were much more active than lower houses', considering both the reasoned opinions and the contributions expressed through the political dialogue.[42] Namely, four main groups have been observed:

> First, there are very active upper chambers, participating both in the political dialogue and in the EWS (Germany, Austria and France). Second, there are upper chambers mostly on equal footing in terms of subsidiarity concerns with the lower ones, but strongly involved in the 'political dialogue' (Czech Republic; Italian Senate; House of Lords). Third, there are upper chambers participating on the same grounds with the lower ones (Spain; Ireland; Netherlands; Poland; Romania). Finally, there are upper chamber characterised by a low degree of involvement in EU affairs (Belgium; Slovenia).[43]

However, in the cases of Belgium and Slovenia this result needs to be explained on the basis of specific national regulations, which—through national rules that in the case of Slovenia do not find any specific provision at EU level and therefore seem in contrast with Protocol No 2—limit the weight of the upper House.[44]

In the case of the Italian bicameralism, given its symmetrical features, the explanation founded on the inverse relationship between the institutional strength of a House and its activity towards the EU institutions cannot clearly be used. However, in some way, the overall trend of a higher level of EU activity of the other European Senates—that benefit from some 'ad hoc' informal opportunities for interparliamentary cooperation[45]—might have exercised some influence in encouraging the Italian Senate to take the new instruments seriously and to design procedures that would allow it to keep pace with other upper Houses in the EU.

IV. The Interpretation of the EWS as a Mainly Political Instrument

It is rather difficult to notice some clear trends or regularities in the documents or reasoned opinions issued by the two Houses, or even to spot constant features or differences between

[41] In these terms, K Auel, O Rozenberg and A Tacea, 'Fighting Back? And, If So, How? Measuring Parliamentary Strength and Activity in EU Affairs' in *The Palgrave Handbook of National Parliaments and the European Union*, above n 21, 60–93, specifically 86 ff.

[42] *cf* the analysis developed by M Romaniello, *Upper Chambers in EU Parliamentary Democracies*, PhD Thesis discussed at IMT Institute for Advanced Studies, Program in Political Systems and Institutional Change, Lucca, 2014, at 86, 279 and 268.

[43] Romaniello, ibid. at 86.

[44] See, specifically on these two systems, M Romaniello, *Assessing Upper Chambers' Role in the EU Decision-Making Process* (2015) *SoG-WP #26*, 17 ff.

[45] On the Association of European Senates see Baraggia, above n 34, 100, who wishes for a future increase of forms of interparliamentary cooperation for the EU Upper Houses.

the methodology and the content of the reasoned opinions and contributions approved by the Chamber or by the Senate. However, the formal aspect of the reasoned opinions underwent a gradual and partial standardisation process in both Houses, and partially even between them, although it did not alter the original differentiation in the names of the parliamentary acts to be adopted.

Regarding the content of the reasoned opinions issued, the kind of subsidiarity test followed varies a lot from case to case, depending on the political aim the Chamber or the Senate—or, more likely, the single committee at stake—wanted to achieve through the approval of a reasoned opinion. In other words, the bicameral and polycentric nature of the Italian Parliament is also reflected in the content and style of the reasoned opinions and contributions issued, ready to be adapted to the finality pursued in each case by the standing committee involved.

Both Houses, in fact, clearly opted for a political reading of this procedure and thus allowed the different committees, especially in the Senate, to choose the meaning of the subsidiarity check they found most convenient for each draft proposal. A rather broad and political concept of subsidiarity seems largely dominant in the Italian experience and is also affirmed, whenever possible, by Italian MPs on the EU scene, especially in the bodies of interparliamentary cooperation.

In particular, the Chamber was very clear in qualifying the EWS as a primarily political instrument 'rather than legal-formal in nature'. It is even qualified as a 'complementary instrument to support the national interest'. Both the subsidiarity and the proportionality principles are seen 'in a dynamic sense':[46] ie, not as a way of merely avoiding the expansion of the EU's jurisdiction, which is normally desired or accepted by the Italian public opinion,[47] but to allow for an enlargement of its policy areas where circumstances require it.[48]

At the same time, both Houses agreed, after the initial years of implementation, to ask the European Commission for more accurate impact analyses and subsidiarity reviews with quantitative and qualitative indicators, as well as for more timely replies and more accurate reconstructions of the follow-up of the contributions and reasoned opinions issued by national Parliaments.[49] These requests, shared by other national Parliaments and within COSAC, produced some effects during the first months of the Juncker Commission. Therefore, in 2016 the Senate assessed very positively the innovations introduced by the Juncker Commission. Namely, it appreciated that the replies by the Commission are co-signed by the first Vice-President Timmermans, responsible for interinstitutional relations together with the commissioner responsible for the subject matter. Also, the new approach according to which replies are not only received in a more timely fashion, but also

[46] See the document by which the EU Policies Committee of the Chamber approved, on 16 December 2014, the two Reports of the European Commission issued in 2014: specifically, AC, XVII legislatura, doc XVIII, n 18, 2 ff

[47] On the traditional approach of Italian public opinion, generally in favour of European integration, see M Telò, 'Italy and the Idea of Europe' in J Lacroix and K Nicolaidis (eds), *European Stories* (Oxford, Oxford University Press, 2010) 122–45.

[48] Above n 46.

[49] See, for the Chamber, the document cited above and for the Senate the resolutions issued on 6 November 2014 by the EU Policies Committee: AS, XVII legislatura, Doc XVIII, n 79.

written with a higher degree of political awareness, seems to go in the direction desired by national Parliaments.[50]

Furthermore, the individualistic approach to both the EWS and the political dialogue seems absolutely dominant in both Houses.[51] In fact, interparliamentary cooperation mechanisms are often recalled, but no collective subsidiarity check is envisaged or promoted, and bilateral dialogue with EU institutions is encouraged above all other means. In fact, from the Italian Parliament's viewpoint, the higher number of contributions compared to the reasoned opinions and the fact that only a limited number of yellow cards have been issued until now do not represent, if one adopts an individualistic reading of the EWS, an inefficient use of the mechanism.[52] On the contrary, as the Senate stated, these data confirm that the individual Parliaments have heterogeneous political interests, follow different priorities in choosing the proposals to be examined in the EWS, and also apply distinct criteria in order to verify the compliance with the subsidiarity principle.[53]

Nevertheless, it must be remarked that in the last few years the two Houses also seemed to diverge slightly regarding this perspective. While the Chamber firmly maintained its position in supporting only an individualistic usage of the EWS, the Senate gradually favoured some collective actions on the part of national Parliaments, for instance regarding the so-called 'green card' or reinforced political dialogue.[54]

V. The Implementation of Law No 234/2012: A Stronger Link with the Government, but Still to be Improved and Fully Proceduralised

A. An Increased Information Flow

Indeed, some effects on the Italian Parliament's EU activity seem to derive from the entry into force and the actual implementation of the new legislation on the EU procedures, the already discussed Law No 234/2012.[55] The law caused a steady increase of the information

[50] See the resolution approved, on 16 October 2016, by the Committee on EU Affairs of the Senate on reports of the Commission on 2015: AS, XVII legislatura, Doc XVIII, n 164, 5. The replies by the Commission are now systematically published, together with the opinions of national parliaments: http://ec.europa.eu/dgs/secretariat_general/relations/relations_other/npo/index_en.htm.

[51] On the general trend towards individual use of the EWS see N Lupo, 'National Parliaments in the European Integration Process' in M Cartabia, N Lupo and A Simoncini, *Democracy and Subsidiarity in the EU. National Parliaments, Regions and Civil Society in the Decision-making Process* (Bologna, Il Mulino, 2013) 124 ff. In the opposite sense, I Cooper, 'A "Virtual Third Chamber" for the European Union? National Parliaments after the Treaty of Lisbon' (2012) 35(3) *West European Politics* 441–65.

[52] AC, XVII legislatura, doc XVIII, n 18, 3.

[53] AS, XVII legislatura, doc XVIII, n 79, 3.

[54] On the participation of the Italian Senate, differently from the Italian Chamber, in the first 'green card', in 2015, see the chapter by E Griglio in this volume.

[55] On the different innovations deriving from Law No 243/2012 see the chapters by R Ibrido, G Rizzoni, A Esposito, DA Capuano, G Piccirilli in this volume.

transmitted by the Government to the Parliament on EU affairs, and more specifically on EU draft legislative acts. This information flow helped the Parliament to obtain a clearer picture of the issues at stake, although it still needs to be fully included in the political relationship between Parliament and Government, especially at the highest level.

The transmission of the informative notes on the most relevant draft legislative acts required by Article 6(1), the subsequent reports (including an assessment of its compliance with legal basis, subsidiarity and proportionality; its negotiations, highlighting the national interest; and its impact, accompanied by a correspondence table between the provisions of the draft legislative act and the national legislation) provided by Article 6(2), and some ex post documents on the follow-up of the directions given by the Parliament according to Article 7(2) caused some improvements in the parliamentary practice. Parliamentary committees are now in the position: to know in advance which among the many draft legislative acts transmitted by the European Commission in accordance with Protocol No 1 were deemed more important from the Italian viewpoint; to understand the Government's position on them; and, finally, to get a picture of the main issues regarding subsidiarity, proportionality and legal basis.

B. Two Cases of Reasoned Opinions Issued by the (Constitutional Affairs Committee of the) Senate

The effects of these new legislative provisions were initially rather limited; but increased as long as they were implemented by the Government. It is also to them that a new wave of reasoned opinions and contributions approved by the Senate in the second half of 2016 could be attributed. In parallel with the Renzi Government action at the EU level to obtain some recognition of the Italian role in the migration crisis, securing EU external borders and fulfilling EU's humanitarian obligations,[56] the Senate—ie the Senate Committee on Constitutional Affairs, competent for migration policies—issued two reasoned opinions: one on an EU draft directive and the other on an EU draft regulation, both related to the migration issue and components of the same package envisaged by the Commission through a communication significantly titled 'Towards a reform of the Common European Asylum System and enhancing legal avenues to Europe'.[57]

The first case is particularly clear, on the draft regulation reforming, although only as a recast, the Dublin III regulation on asylum.[58] The Senate Committee on Constitutional Affairs issued a reasoned opinion. It relied on the one hand on a negative assessment by the

[56] See, in this term, the reply by the Italian Economy and Finance Minister, Padoan, to the European Commission, on 27 October 2016 (available at http://download.repubblica.it/pdf/2016/economia/lettera_risposta_padoan.pdf).

[57] COM(2016) 197 final. On this communication see, from a European perspective, the chapter by G Rizzoni.

[58] Proposal for a Regulation of the European Parliament and of the Council establishing the criteria and mechanisms for determining the Member State responsible for examining an application for international protection lodged in one of the Member States by a third-country national or a stateless person (recast) (COM(2016) 270 final).

Government in its report transmitted according to Article 6(4) Law No 234/2012, motivated essentially on the basis of the national interest, as the proposal increased the difficulty of border control in Member States of first entry. It also took advantage, on the other hand, of negative advice of the Senate Committee on EU Policies, which highlighted some critiques regarding subsidiarity and proportionality principles. The reasoned opinion recognised that

> the purposes of the proposal, that is to say, to ensure fair responsibility burden-sharing between the Member States, especially at times of crisis, and to curb the secondary movements of Third country nationals between the Member States, cannot be achieved sufficiently by the Member States acting individually.[59]

Nevertheless, it remarked that

> the measures and mechanisms for which provision is made here fail to meet the need to address the present unprecedented migration levels as a Europe acting as a whole, and the overall effects of the amendments proposed fail to achieve the two main stated objectives.[60]

The second case, only some days later, is slightly less straightforward and relates to another proposal included in the same package, ie the EU draft directive on standards for the reception of applicants for international protection.[61] The final outcome was the same, as also in this case the Senate Committee on Constitutional Affairs issued a reasoned opinion, prepared by the same rapporteur, lamenting a violation of the subsidiarity and proportionality principles. In this case, however, the Government, in its report adopted according to Article 6(4) Law No 234/2012, had issued a positive assessment of the draft directive, specifically claiming its compliance with the principle of subsidiarity (as well as with the principle of conferral and the national interest), although signalling some concerns about the compliance with the principle of proportionality (specifically regarding the reception of minors). Similarly, the Senate Committee for EU Policies had issued a positive advice, in which it expressly affirmed the compliance with the subsidiarity and proportionality principles, as well as with the legal basis.

It comes as no surprise, therefore, that the legal reasoning supporting this second reasoned opinion on subsidiarity grounds is even less stringent and more 'political' than in the previous case. The reasoned opinion recognised that the aim of a better harmonisation of reception of asylum seekers is not achievable by single Member States, but it underlined that regulating more strictly internal movements is not the right way to obtain it. Moreover, it stressed that all

> the combined provisions of directives, regulations, and recasts that have accumulated merely prove the Commission's absolute impotence in achieving compliance with the key principles of managing migratory flows, that is to say, solidarity-based reception, redistribution of asylum seekers, and repatriation.[62]

[59] ibid.

[60] See the resolution approved by the Committee on Constitutional Affairs on 5 October 2016: AS, XVII legislatura, doc XVIII, n 156 (in the English translation available on ipex.eu).

[61] Proposal for a Directive of the European Parliament and of the Council laying down standards for the reception of applicants for international protection (recast) (COM(2016) 465 final).

[62] See the resolution approved by the Committee on Constitutional Affairs on 19 October 2016: AS, XVII legislatura, doc XVIII, n 165 (in the English translation available on ipex.eu).

To understand this reasoned opinion, thus, it is probably necessary to refer to the influence of the previous one, issued just two weeks earlier by the same Senate Committee, as well as to the worsening of the relationships between the European Commission and the Italian Government regarding the draft budgetary plan, taking place during the same time period.[63] Also the dynamic between the Parliament and the Government could indeed have played a role: in the Plenary seating devoted to the Government's communication in front of the Senate in view of the next European Council,[64] held in between the votes on the two proposals by the Constitutional Affairs Committee, the representative of the Government refused to support a motion submitted by some senators of the (leftist) opposition in which it was asked that the Government express a position against the reform of the Dublin regulation.[65] This also caused a reaction by some opposition senators within the Constitutional Affairs Committee, who accused the Government of ignoring the first reasoned opinion approved by the Committee.[66]

Of course, from the viewpoint of the Italian Government, there is a significant difference between sharing some doubts on the compliance with the subsidiarity principle of some provisions included in a draft regulation, addressed mainly to the European Commission, and committing to a negative position on the proposal for the future steps within the Council. However, it is true that this crucial issue in the European debate would have deserved a more specific and timely discussion, hopefully in the Plenary, in order to define a position to be later on fully expressed and supported at European level. On the contrary, neither of the two Houses of the Italian Parliament had any discussion, in Plenary or in Committee, regarding the already recalled communication issued on 6 April 2016 by the European Commission, and obviously timely transmitted to all the national Parliaments.

C. The Need for a more Formalised Approach and Better Coordination among Italian Institutional Actors

Overall, the lack of the Plenary's involvement and the high level of informality due to the continued absence of provisions for the EWS and the political dialogue in the Houses' rules of procedure increase neither transparency nor clarity. Furthermore, this loose regulatory framework, especially considering the highly polycentric nature of the Italian Parliament and the Italian Government, does not help to achieve a sufficient degree of consistency in the behaviours of political actors and institutions.

Some positive, although partial, effects have been produced by the entry into force of Law No 234/2012, which grants a sufficient level of information in parliamentary committees. However, at least for the moment, this increase in circulation of information remains, without a shared procedural scheme, insufficient to ensure effective forms of coordination

[63] See, for instance, www.ansa.it/english/news/2016/10/18/were-in-line-with-budget-rules-says-padoan_6260119d-a2eb-4b21-b629-a3a90bfd2c98.html.

[64] On the diffusion of this kind of Plenary debate in the Senate, see the chapter by D Capuano.

[65] See the motion n (6-00203) n 6 submitted by sen De Petris et al, on which the undersecretary of State for EU policies, Gozi, asked for its reformulation on the reference of Dublin regulation: AS, XVII legislatura, Plenary Seating, 12 October 2016, am.

[66] See the intervention of the sen De Petris in the Constitutional Affairs Committee: AS, XVII legislatura, 18 October 2016.

between the Chamber and the Senate, and even within the Italian Government. Further steps, thus, need to be taken in order to make possible an active and consistent participation of the Italian Parliament to EU decision-making, especially regarding its relationship with the European Commission.

The good functioning of the channels of communication between two fully political institutions, like the two Houses of the Italian Parliament, on the one hand, and a mainly technical institution, the European Commission, on the other hand, requires hard work on both sides, normally with the mediation of the national Government, which is embedded in the EU institutions and linked through a confidence relationship with both Houses.

10

Procedures vis-à-vis the European Council and the Council: Approval, Delay and Veto Powers

GIOVANNI PICCIRILLI

I. The Parliamentary Powers Concerned

This chapter focuses on those powers that the Treaty of Lisbon attributes to national parliaments in order to complete a compound decision-making process started either in the European Council or in the Council.

As this chapter will show, because the Italian Constitution enshrines a perfectly symmetrical bicameral parliamentary system, such powers have been implemented as requiring a joint or coordinated action by the two Houses. The bicameral Parliament's unitary or coordinated action to implement decisions at the European level is quite different from any independent activity that each of the Houses may undertake separately and can be considered one of the particularities of Italian participation in the EU. Thus, more broadly, a focus on those powers may help to define for the foreign reader the role played by the Italian Parliament as a whole—and so Italian bicameralism and the equilibrium therein—in the European Union.[1]

[1] Further (and more specific) considerations on this point are offered in the chapter by M Romaniello in this book.

In order to better pinpoint which specific parliamentary powers this chapter considers, it is worth recalling how those powers have been classified in the scholarship commenting on the Treaty of Lisbon's innovations regarding the role of national parliaments in the EU. For this discussion, however, it is important to remember that only a few provisions of the Treaties directly provide for parliamentary bodies' involvement.[2] More often, Parliaments partake in a 'Euro-national' decision-making process when the Treaties provide that, after the completion of the European part of the same process (within the Council or the European Council), an approval by the Member States is needed 'in accordance with their respective constitutional requirements',[3] so providing Member States a certain amount of autonomy in choosing the domestic means of implementation. This chapter will not consider some specific attributes when other parts of this book address them.[4]

The Introduction to this book provides a short list of the main classifications that the EU scholarship applies to the European powers of national parliaments. Among them it is worth recalling those focusing on the position of national parliaments according to their *active* or *passive* role in a particular procedure.[5] Another classification concerns the 'form' in which the power in question is exercised, such as: by the individual Houses independently from each other, as occurs with the subsidiarity scrutiny;[6] by the Parliament as a whole, so requiring—in cases of bicameral parliaments—coordination between the two Houses; or by the aggregation of individual actions of a certain number of parliaments/Houses[7]

[2] Apart from the general references in Arts 10 and 12 TEU (and further mentions in cases of rights to be informed, as in art 49 TEU, 70 and 71 TFEU), see: Art 5(3), second subparagraph, TEU, 69 and 352(2) TFEU, with reference to the activity aiming at ensuring compliance with the principle of subsidiarity in accordance with the procedure set out in Protocol No 2; 48(2) (notification of an initiative for a Treaty revision), (4) (participation to the Convention for the ordinary treaty revision) and (7) (general *passerelle* clause) TEU; 81(3) TFEU, concerning the opposition to decision determining those aspects of family law with cross-border implications.

[3] This wording occurs in a number of Treaty provisions that have been analysed in depth in a study commissioned by the European Parliament (PE 493.046) and conducted by L Besselink et al, *National Constitutional Avenues for Further EU Integration* (Brussels, European Parliament, 2014) at 14. These authors underline the different roles of different groups of provisions in allowing the entry into force of the Treaty of Lisbon (54 TEU and 357 TFEU), the amendment of the Treaties (48(4) and (6) TEU), the accession of new Member States (49, second subparagraph, TEU) and the withdrawal of existing ones (50(1) TEU). Finally, the *approval* by Member States 'in accordance with their respective constitutional requirements' is the common end of arts 42(2) TEU; 25, second subparagraph; 218(8); 223(1); 262; 311, second subparagraph TFEU. For the sake of completeness, it might be worth mentioning that the same wording has been used in the Decision of the Heads of State or Government concerning a new settlement for the United Kingdom within the European Union, attached to the conclusions of the European Council meeting held on 18–19 February 2016 (EUCO 1/16), as the procedural way to give 'substance' to the commitments stated therein: see in particular Annex 1, s A (Economic Governance), para 7, and s C (Sovereignty), para 1.

[4] For instance, the participation to the revision of EU Treaties is more completely tackled by B Guastaferro, in this book.

[5] Some attributions require in fact an (active) expression of will by the National Parliaments (ie a vote, in order to state their position in the dialogue with EU institutions), whereas some others merely register their entitlement to a (passive) right to receive something from the outside (eg the renewed powers of information of NPs are fully 'passive' and so it seems they can be better considered as 'rights'). See P Kiiver, *The Early Warning System for the Principle of Subsidiarity. Constitutional Theory and Empirical Reality* (London-New York, Routledge, 2012) 7.

[6] P Popelier and W Vandenbruwaene, 'The Subsidiarity Mechanism as a Tool for Inter-level Dialogue in Belgium: On 'Regional Blindness' and Cooperative Flaws' (2011) 7 *European Constitutional Law Review* 204.

[7] See N Lupo, 'National Parliaments in the European Integration Process: Re-aligning Politics and Policies' in M Cartabia et al (eds), *Democracy and Subsidiarity in the EU. National Parliaments, Regions and Civil Society in the Decision-making Process* (Bologna, Il Mulino, 2013) 114.

to reach the thresholds laid out by Protocol No 2, Article 7(3),[8] which is occasionally recognised as constituting a 'virtual' new body.[9] Finally, further classifications distinguish the nature of the individual parliamentary power concerned according to its *positive or negative* aims—either (contributing to) approving or blocking the EU procedure.[10]

Under this framework, the parliamentary powers analysed in this chapter are *active* (in the sense that they activate a procedure and pursue deliberation, so excluding those mere passive attributes, such as the right to be informed); hence, in the Italian legal order they will concern the Parliament as a whole and require the contribution of *both* Houses in order to express the position of Italy's Parliament (separate actions by two Houses individually being insufficient, even though in some cases the result of the comprehensive process is no more than the juxtaposition of two separate procedures); finally, they will include both *positive* and *negative* powers, depending on how the relevant Treaty provisions established the specific parliamentary attribute.

II. The Belated Implementation in Italy of Parliamentary Powers Requiring a Coordination between the Two Houses

As other chapters of this book show,[11] each House has implemented some of its individual European powers (that is, those independent from the use of the same power by the other branch of Parliament) through interpretative and often divergent approaches, as a manifestation of its institutional autonomy and even, to some extent, its independent understanding of the European integration. For instance, powers attributed to individual Houses by Protocols Nos 1 and 2, such as the subsidiarity scrutiny on draft legislative acts, or those more informally promoted, as the political dialogue between national assemblies and European institutions,[12] were informally systematised early on, which caused differences between the Chamber of Deputies and the Senate in both their form and content.[13] Those still are regulated in those (allegedly 'provisional') manners.

Conversely, other European powers either given to the national parliament in a more comprehensive and 'collective' sense or specifically requiring coordination of the two

[8] … but also, possibly in the future, the 'red card' prefigured in mentioned agreement with the UK (quoted at n 3 above), whose effectiveness was conditioned to the 'Remain' result in the Brexit referendum. Similar to the mechanism foreseen in art 7(2) Protocol No 2, a certain number of individual national Houses (ie 55 per cent) will have the possibility of blocking the debate of a legislative proposal, unless the latter is amended so to accommodate the concerns expressed in the reasoned opinions (see, again, the s C (Sovereignty), para 3).

[9] In this sense see I Cooper, 'A "Virtual Third Chamber" for the European Union? National Parliaments after the Treaty of Lisbon' (2012) 3 *West European Politics* 441.

[10] This classification has been proposed by M Olivetti, 'Parlamenti nazionali nell'Unione europea' in R Bifulco et al (eds), *Digesto delle discipline pubblicistiche* (Turin, UTET, 2012) 509.

[11] See chapters by N Lupo, A Esposito and DA Capuano.

[12] As is well-known, the same power has been interpreted as requiring joint execution by the two Houses in Spain via a bicameral Committee.

[13] In particular, at the Chamber of deputies, see the two opinions released by Committee on RoP (on 6 October 2009 and 14 July 2010), at the Senate, see the letter by the President Schifani to the President of Standing Committees on 1 December 2009.

Houses required an adjustment of the existing provisions pursuant to Law No 11/2005[14] and a subsequent adaptation of the rules of procedure of both Houses.

In implementing these new powers, Parliament preliminarily needed to choose the source of procedure (and so, the level of decision-making and the relevant actors) that was competent to proceed.[15] The full operability of the EU Treaty provisions necessitated interventions by bodies within the legal orders of the Member States, in keeping with the interpretation of the European legal framework as a *composite Constitution*:[16] an institutional and procedural architecture composed of sources that are both European and national, involving various levels of both legal orders.[17] Moreover, as is often the case in relationships between the European legal order and that of Member States, Member States are provided a significant margin of discretion in choosing the methods for implementing Treaty provisions. This margin of discretion acknowledges the EU's 'respect' for the Member States' 'national identities', including their political and constitutional fundamental structures.

Italy's choice in implementing such powers, in the light of its—at least momentarily[18]—perfectly symmetrical bicameral system, was to confirm the pivotal role of parliamentary legislation by requiring that the two Houses of Parliament jointly and equally decide these issues. This decision created norms that affected both Houses and their reciprocal collaboration, but also provided room for further detail by internal rules and practice.[19]

The option in favour of parliamentary legislation as the means for the implementation of the European parliamentary powers is not obvious or completely uncontroversial. By confirming it, Italy has excluded both a stronger, constitutional-level intervention and a more flexible adaptation of the rules of procedure, possibly through close cooperation between the two Houses.

However, the approval of the law implementing those European parliamentary powers in the Italian legal order suffered a significant delay and was reached only at the end of 2012, more than three years after the Treaty of Lisbon's entry into force, even though some

[14] Law No 11/2005 and the previous domestic framework for the participation of Italy to the EU are the specific subject of the chapter by R Ibrido, in this book.

[15] The set of options debated before the decision for the implementation is summarised by C Fasone, 'Quale è la fonte più idonea a recepire le novità del trattato di Lisbona sui parlamenti nazionali?' (2010) 3 *Osservatorio sulle fonti* and R Bifulco, 'La Costituzione italiana dopo il Trattato di Lisbona' (2012) *Rivista italiano di diritto pubblico comunitario* 1.

[16] In this sense, see L Besselink, *A Composite European Constitution* (Groningen, Europa Law Publishing, 2007); A von Bogdandy and J Bast, 'The Constitutional Approach to EU Law. From Taming Intergovernmental Relationships to Framing Political Processes' in A von Bogdandy and J Bast (eds), *Principles of European Constitutional Law* (Oxford-München, Hart, 2009) 1; R Schütze, *An Introduction to European Law* (Cambridge, Cambridge University Press, 2012) 105. In the Italian literature, in the same direction, see the formulation directed towards a 'composite' Constitution proposed by N Lupo in 'La revisione costituzionale della disciplina di bilancio e il sistema delle fonti' in V Lippolis et al (eds), *Costituzione e pareggio di bilancio. Il Filangieri. Quaderno 2011* (Naples, Jovene, 2012) 89, and N Lupo, n 7 above, 107.

[17] L Besselink and JH Reestman, 'The Fiscal Compact and the European Constitutions: "Europe speaking German"' (2012) 1 *European Constitutional Law Review* 1, insist on the interdependence (in the sense of reciprocal necessity) of the contribution of the European sources and domestic sources (at least in relation to the approach adopted with the Fiscal compact, but with considerations that seem to be able to be extended to the subject of this chapter).

[18] About the prospects of the ongoing constitutional revision bill, see the chapter by L Gianniti, in this book.

[19] The equal role of the two Houses in the legislation is succinctly (but thoroughly) described by the adverb '*collettivamente*' (collectively) used by art 70 of the Constitution (in its 1948 version) with regard to the way of exercising the legislative function. At this regard, see N Lupo, 'Art 70' in R Bifulco et al (eds), *Commentario alla Costituzione* (Turin, UTET, 2006) 1338, who values the bearing of the adverb 'collectively', beyond mere repetition of the bicameral established by Art 55.

(partial) modification already had been introduced with the annual 'community laws' in the early 2010s.

As the European Union's application of the Treaty of Lisbon was overwhelmed by the incumbent economic and financial crises (that ultimately led to some reshaping of the EU's institutional equilibrium, for example enhancing the role of the European Council),[20] so too was the Italian implementation of the Treaty of Lisbon's European parliamentary powers significantly delayed by Italy's great political instability at that time. Italy faced a major crisis involving the ruling coalition and the vacancy of the ministry in charge of EU affairs.[21] Only in November 2011, with the advent of the Monti government, was a more stable guide given to the Government's Department for EU Policies.[22] Thus, the regulatory framework underpinning the 'Euro-national'[23] role of the Italian Parliament was missing a fundamental part needed for its completion until the approval of Law 24 December 2012, No 234 (hereafter Law No 234/2012), only a few days before the Monti Government resigned and Parliament was dissolved.

III. Powers to 'Approve' Decisions by the Council and the European Council: The National Part of the Euro-national Decision-making

Law No 234/2012's choice of parliamentary legislation as the means for setting the framework for implementation did not result in a similar preference for parliamentary legislation as the tool for its concrete exercise. In fact, Law No 234/2012 distinguished cases that necessarily require the approval of a law, according to the procedures and the guarantees of articles 70 and 72 of the Constitution, from others in which the Italian Parliament could approve EU actions through a non-legislative procedure.

Although this Law establishes the necessity of the Italian Parliament's approval of certain EU actions, it fails to explain how the wills of the individual Houses must be exercised. The 'natural' way of expressing parliamentary will would obviously be by legislation. Requiring the approval of a law, however, may have some significant disadvantages. For example, it may have longer procedures than other forms of approval, since—as is the case in Italy—it may be constitutionally required to pass through a committee stage. Or, it may need to

[20] See U Puetter, *The European Council and the Council. New Intergovernmentalism and Institutional Change* (Oxford, Oxford University Press, 2014); W Wessels, *The European Council* (New York, Palgrave McMillian, 2015).

[21] In July 2010 Minister Andrea Ronchi took part in the party split led by the President of the Chamber of Deputies Gianfranco Fini, and after his resignation in November 2010 there was no substitution for several months, during which the portfolio was assumed provisionally by the President of the Council of Ministers, Silvio Berlusconi. Only in July 2011 was Anna Maria Bernini appointed to the office but after few months (in November 2011) the whole Berlusconi Government resigned and was replaced by Monti's.

[22] Significantly, the one appointed as Minister for EU Affairs of the Monti Government was Prof Enzo Moavero Milanesi, at the time Judge at the EU General Court. He was also confirmed in the office by the Letta Government, the only to stay in the same position held in the previous cabinet, so giving stability to the EU department after some years of troubled instability.

[23] With regard to this formulation, see A Manzella, *Sui principi democratici dell'Unione europea (Lezioni Jean Monnet 2010–2012)* (Naples, ES, 2013), and A Manzella and N Lupo (eds), *Il sistema parlamentare euro-nazionale. Lezioni* (Turin, Giappichelli, 2014).

undergo further procedural requirements, such as the involvement of the President of the Republic at the promulgation stage (and the associated possibility of a request for a new deliberation described in article 74 of the Italian Constitution).

In locating a domestic constitutional principle that may provide guidance on how to implement these European powers and, in particular, when to follow the form of the legislative process, it may be helpful to consider article 80 of the Italian Constitution, which lists those cases in which international treaties require legislative authorisation.[24] Obviously the context is different: legislative authorisation to the ratification of international treaties has little to do with participation in the EU and the exercise of European powers more or less directly attributed to national Parliaments to contribute to the 'good functioning of the EU'.[25] This provision lists those treaties that involve a 'political nature', 'require arbitration or a legal settlement', 'entail change of borders', and involve 'spending or new legislation'. It may provide some hints for implementing European parliamentary powers consistently with the Constitution by distinguishing between those European powers of the Italian Parliament that should be exercised via legislation to substantially conform to the spirit of the Constitution and those that can be exercised in a more informal way.[26] Although article 80 completely excludes Parliament from all treaties not explicitly requiring a legislative authorisation, Parliament will participate in these European powers either way, whether via the legislative procedure or by other, less formalised means.

Finally, the choice whether to pursue the legislative process in implementing the European powers concerned here has a further, and important, consequence: only legislative implementations may be subject to the scrutiny of the Constitutional Court, the jurisdiction of which is normally limited to legislative acts. In cases of implementation via non-legislative means, the Constitutional Court may only become involved in the controversy through the residual provision regarding disputes among the branches of government (*conflitto di attribuzioni*). Thus, deciding whether to require legislative approval matters not only from a procedural point of view, but also in order to have access or not to specific checks and balances.

A. The (Few) Cases of Necessary Approval by Parliamentary Legislation

The approach suggested here has not been that adopted by Law No 234/2012, and the identification of those cases in which the approval by parliamentary legislation is deemed necessary is based on different assumptions. Actually, Law No 234/2012's selection of those cases appears to have been based on a somewhat 'conservative' application of the previous practice, without a consideration of the Treaty of Lisbon's innovations or new elements

[24] 'The Houses authorise by law the ratification of international treaties which are of a political nature, or which call for arbitration or legal settlements, or which entail changes to the national territory or financial burdens or changes to legislation'.

[25] See art 12 TEU and, in particular, the reading of this formula presented in the Foreword by A Manzella, in this book.

[26] For a deeper analysis of this point, refer to G Piccirilli, 'Il ricorso alla legge per l'esercizio dei poteri "europei" da parte del Parlamento italiano. Spunti per una lettura costituzionalmente orientata' (2013) 2 *Osservatorio sulle fonti*. Also L Gianniti, in his chapter in this book, makes reference to art 80 of Italian Constitution in order to find a key for interpreting the settlement of European parliamentary powers that the rejected constitutional amendment would have created.

concerning the role of national Parliaments in the European Union's decision-making procedures.

From a general point of view, article 11(3) of Law No 234/2012 concerns the domestic follow-up of those decisions by either the European Council or the Council subject to national parliamentary approval. It—in a very undefined way—mandates Parliament's involvement in an 'appropriate deliberation' (*opportuna deliberazione*), requiring a 'positive vote' by both Houses.

There is an express requirement to follow the legislative procedure in only three circumstances,[27] in relation to those procedures pursuant to:

- Article 42(2) Treaty on European Union (TEU), framing a common defence following a decision of the European Council, adopted by unanimity, that 'recommends' that Member States do so;[28]
- article 48(6) TEU, assenting to simplified revisions upon a unanimous decision by the European Council made with consultation of the European Parliament, the Commission, and, in cases of institutional changes in the monetary sector, the European Central Bank;[29] and
- article 311(3) Treaty on the Functioning of the European Union (TFEU), concerning the determination of the Union's resources, upon a unanimous decision by the Council made with consultation of the European Parliament.[30]

These three cases do not appear to be fully consistent with each other, apart from their following a unanimous decision taken by either the Council or the European Council. Apart from that, there is a clear difference between Article 42(2) TEU's reference to domestic tools and those made by the other two provisions. And it is not by chance that the former is located in article11(2) of Law No 234/2012, and so before—and, apparently, independently from—the general clause provided the subsequent paragraph, article 11(3): the wording of Article 42(2) TEU is unclear in indicating whether decisions at the national level are really required in order to achieve a positive development of the overall procedure. The provision is in fact directed towards a 'recommendation' by the European Council, once the adoption of a common defence has been unanimously resolved, to be submitted to the Member States in order for them to adopt a decision based on that recommendation, in compliance with the relevant constitutional requirements. Hence, and in a more general sense, the first case appears to relate to a *una tantum* decision at the time in which the European Union may decide to initiate the process of unifying defence policies. By contrast, the other two provisions set procedures that are abstractly 'repeatable' as the Union develops (ie whenever a simplified revision will be approved or whenever the European Union's resources must be determined).

[27] LS Rossi, 'Art 11. Procedure di modifica di norme dei Trattati' in L Costato et al (eds), *Commentario alla legge 24.12.2012 n 234* (Neaples, ES, 2015) 124, defines this referral to the legislation as a proper 'riserva di legge', but actually it seems preferable not to use the classical lexicon of the mechanisms of fundamental rights protection in this context.

[28] Law No 234/2012, art 11(2).

[29] Law No 234/2012, art 11(4).

[30] Law No 234/2012, art 11(6). In this case the reference to the previous practice seems to have 'weighed heavily': in the past, the decisions concerning resources had followed the legislative route. For example, Council Decision (CE, Euratom) no 2000/597 related to the system of the resources within the European Communities was followed up with art 77 of Law 28 December 2001, no 448.

One aspect deserves particular consideration with regard to the procedure for the simplified revision of the Treaties under article 48(6) TEU because it received an earlier implementation prior to the approval of Law No 234/2012: between 2011 and 2012, the modification to article 136 TFEU was adopted according to this procedure,[31] but at that time in Italy there was no legislative framework describing the legal instrument to be followed at the domestic level.

The European Council made the unanimous decision to modify article 136 TFEU on 25 March 2011 and the Italian legal order completed its corresponding procedure with the approval of Law 23 July 2012, no 115. The domestic tool used was parliamentary legislation (similar to what Law No 234/2012 provides), but, somewhat oddly, it was carried out in a manner entirely identical to the procedure usually followed for the authorisation of the ratification of international treaties and agreements, so that Law No 115/2012 even includes the order of execution into the domestic legal order.[32] The choice to apply to a simplified revision the 'ordinary' procedure for parliamentary authorisation to ratification of international treaties ultimately led to considerably paradoxical implications inherent in equating a simplified revision to any new international agreement: acknowledging this procedure as equal to that followed for the (entire) Treaty of Lisbon (which seemed to outline a more flexible procedure with article 48(6) TEU).[33] Moreover, this process resulted in the related bill being assigned—in both Houses of Parliament, during the referral stage—to the competent Committee for Foreign Affairs and not, as might have been more appropriate given the specific topics covered by article 136 TFEU, to the Committee on the Budget (or even the Committee on EU Policies),[34] ultimately weakening the very guarantees instituted to safeguard the legislative procedure.

B. The (Vague) Residual Referral to a 'Positive Deliberation by both Houses'

In addition to the aforementioned cases, article 11(3) of Law No 234/2012 introduces a general clause for any additional Treaty provisions in which the entry into force of a deci-

[31] See Ka Tuori and Kl Tuori, *The Europzone Crisis. A constitutional Analysis* (Cambridge, Cambridge University Press, 2015) 145 ff.

[32] See art 2 of AS 2914, XVI leg. A significant element is a passage from the technical-normative analysis attached to the legislation, according to which 'the national measure in question is framed in the context of law that authorised the ratification of the various that, over time, led to the current configuration of the European Union's institutions and duties, from the Treaty establishing the European Community, signed in Rome on 25 March 1957 (ratified by Law 14 October 1957, no 1203) to the Treaty of Lisbon of 13 December 2007 (ratified by Law 2 August 2008, no 130)'.

[33] However, the domestic processes of approval were openly defined as 'ratification' (instead of that of 'approval' used in the wording of art 48(6) TEU) by the AFCO Committee of the European Parliament in the monitoring of the national follow up. On the profiles of interparliamentary cooperation in the implementation of the European Council decision, see K Granat, 'Interparliamentary Cooperation and the Simplified Revision Procedures' in N Lupo and C Fasone (eds), *Interparliamentary Cooperation in the Composite European Constitution* (Oxford-Portland, Hart Publishing, 2016) 86.

[34] See the process that led to approval of Law No 115/2012. If allowed, perhaps the perspective of the parliamentary examination in Foreign Affairs Committees—which are traditionally more 'controllable' by the Government than others—could have perhaps guided the choice to follow the route of the bill authorising the ratification in the complex parliamentary contingency of that period. The presentation took place in September 2011, ie in the final, frantic months of the Berlusconi Government, after months of the Department for EU Policies being guided by the Prime Minister himself in a caretaker role and the appointment of the new Minister Anna Maria Bernini.

sion by the European Council or the Council is subject to prior approval by the Member States 'in compliance with their respective constitutional requirements'.[35] This clause merely states that 'the decision shall be considered as approved in the event of a positive deliberation by both Houses'.

First, it is unclear whether this 'positive deliberation' can be made non-collectively, in a separate manner by the two Houses (and therefore potentially through autonomous acts and in the absence of any *navette*), or whether it is possible (or even necessary) to follow a more unusual procedure in the form of a 'non-legislative bicameral act', a document that does not create legislation but is approved in a procedure that follows a collective, legislative-like process.[36]

This confusion arises from the fact that, as these parliamentary powers are of a 'bicameral' nature, the contribution of only one of the two Houses of Italian Parliament is insufficient to contribute to the Euro-national decision. Thus, a procedural design merely juxtaposing two separated unicameral practices may be inconsistent with the spirit of the Treaties. As mentioned above, the Treaties distinguish between those powers conferred to individual Houses and those conferred on the 'National Parliaments' in their unity. Consequently, legislative provisions like those of Law No 234/2012, if interpreted as allowing 'positive deliberation' through two separated unicameral deliberations, may not meet Treaty requirements: a mere summation of the two juxtaposed unicameral procedures may be interpreted as undermining the requirement for a joint action of the two Houses. The juxtaposition of two parallel acts also creates the possibility of substantial divergences between the texts that each House approves. The Treaties surely provide Member States some room for manoeuvre by relying on 'national constitutional requirements'. Since the Treaties address differently individual Houses and 'national parliaments' as a whole, however, this difference should inhere also at the national stage of implementation.

At least for Italy, it may be useful to refer again to the lexicon of the Constitution and suggest that such deliberations of the 'national parliament' should be carried out in a 'collective' manner, reconnecting this parliamentary power to the bicameral principle under article 70 of the Constitution at least in its form, if not also in its result (ie parliamentary legislation).[37] In any case, since this power specifically requires a mere 'approval' by the national parliament, it is plausible that the procedures for discussion at each Assembly would be about dryly 'binary' choices, minimising the possible ambiguities in the outcomes of the two branches of Parliament.

In any case, a more detailed analysis of the additional Treaty provisions that require such 'approval' by the Member States in accordance with their respective constitutional norms,

[35] The list of the relevant Treaty provisions is at n 3 above. See there also the reference to the extensive work on this clause by L Besselink et al n 3 above.

[36] On this peculiar form of parliamentary deliberation, see in the literature L Elia, 'Gli atti bicamerali non legislativi' in Comitato nazionale per la celebrazione del primo decennale della promulgazione della costituzione (eds), *Studi sulla Costituzione* (Milan, Giuffrè, 1958) II, 421, and, more recently, G Rivosecchi, 'Atti bicamerali non legislativi' in S Mangiameli (eds) *Dizionario sistematico di Diritto costituzionale* (Milan, Il Sole 24 ore, 2008) 123.

[37] See n 19 above. When bicameral parliamentary functions are distinguished from those carried out individually by each House, it seems appropriate to recall the specific wording of the constitutional text, in which it would have been possible to state the specificity of the 'collective' process by both Houses.

which fall under article 11(3) of the Law No 234/2012, show that they appear important and problematic at the same time. They concern:

— Article 25(1) TFEU, regarding the adoption of provisions intended to complete the rights to citizenship listed under article 20(2) TFEU;
— article 218(8) TFEU, providing for EU accession to the ECHR;
— article 223(2) TFEU, allowing the adoption of a uniform procedure for the election of the European Parliament; and
— article 262(1) TFEU, assigning the Court of Justice jurisdiction over disputes related to acts adopted based on the Treaties that create European intellectual property rights.

Since these topics are unlikely to involve recurring parliamentary legislation, they would seem to need implementation consistent with Article 80 of the Constitution, as they have some 'political nature', concern the provision of at minimum preparatory frameworks for the judicial resolution of disputes or, at least, provide for amendments to laws.

Generally speaking, there is no doubt that parliamentary legislation (or even acts with the same legislative rank) can also be applied in cases where it is not considered mandatory).[38] But then, there seems to be a twofold paradoxical consequence if the procedure to be followed in the end depends on an evaluation of the individual circumstance at issue. First, it would seem to render useless the distinction made by Law No 234/2012 in highlighting only three cases in which the rules of the legislative procedure necessarily must be followed. Second, the 'general clause' under article 11(3) Law No 234/2012 would be equally misleading, as it promotes the use of some kind of acts that, even if bicameral, lack a legislative nature, even when in reality the option for the legislative procedure may be preferred anyway.[39]

IV. Delay Powers: The 'Emergency Brake'

National Parliaments are not only imbued with 'positive' powers of approval to complete at the domestic level the Euro-national decision-making process started by the Council or the European Council. They are also endowed with the ability to delay the adoption of a decision at the European level by calling on 'their' government to follow specific procedures for this purpose.

Unlike in the aforementioned cases, in this case there is no specific provision in the European Treaty that establishes a parliamentary power. Nevertheless, the national legislature, in adopting Law No 234/2012, better defined the relationship between the Italian Parliament and 'its' government in EU affairs to allow the former to direct and

[38] There are actually some cases in which it is not possible for legislation to substitute other forms of approval. See, for example the DEF (*Documento di economia e finanza*, Document on Economy and Finance), where the approval with a parliamentary deliberations (different from legislation) is foreseen by arts 7 and 10 Law No 196/2009.

[39] As observed by A Esposito, 'La legge 24 dicembre 2012, n 234, sulla partecipazione dell'Italia alla formazione e all'attuazione della normativa e delle politiche dell'Unione europea. Parte I—Prime riflessioni sul ruolo delle Camere' (2013) *Federalismi* 55, the exception that can be initiated by law derives from the residual nature of the reference to the 'positive decision by both Houses' in relation to the timely prediction of the approval of the previously mentioned cases by law (with the addition of the procedure pursuant to art 40(2) ESCB Statute, in a shareable manner). However, if the necessity of proceeding by law in the cited cases excludes any alternative hypothesis of inferior 'rank', nothing seems to be able to prevent proceeding in the forms of legislative procedure outside of the instances expressly identified by art 11(2) to (4) Law No 234/2012.

determine the position of the latter, especially when important aspects of the national constitutional and legal identity are at stake.

There are three cases in which the TFEU provides that individual governments may delay decisions on the basis of reasons connected to the national legal identity, under:

- Article 48, second subparagraph, when 'important aspects' of an individual Member State's 'social security system' may be affected by the adoption of 'measures in the field of social security as are necessary to provide freedom of movement for workers';
- article 82(3), when 'fundamental aspects' of an individual Member State's 'criminal justice system' may be affected by the adoption of a directive concerning: the mutual admissibility of evidence between Member States, the rights of individuals in criminal proceedings, the rights of crime victims, or any further procedures necessary to facilitate the mutual recognition of judgments and judicial decisions or provide for police and judicial cooperation in criminal matters having a cross-border dimension;
- article 83(3), when 'fundamental aspects' of an individual Member State's 'criminal justice system' may be affected by the adoption of a directive establishing 'minimum rules concerning the definition of criminal offences and sanctions in the areas of particularly serious crime with a cross-border dimension' or directives setting 'minimum rules with regard to the definition of criminal offences and sanctions in the area concerned'.

In all these cases, the Government of a Member State may request that proposal at issue is referred to the European Council, the highest political body—comprised of the heads of states and governments—so that it can consider how the proposal affects 'important' or even 'fundamental' aspects of core state functions, such as welfare and criminal justice.

Similarly, with regard to foreign and security policy, under article 31(3) TEU, a single government may ask not to proceed to a vote in the Council that must be held by qualified majority vote (QMV) by opposing it on grounds of 'vital and stated reasons of national policy'. In those cases, after a mediation attempt by the high representative, the Council, deciding by QMV, might refer the dossier to the European Council, which will decide it by unanimity. All these mechanisms have been informally described as an 'emergency brake',[40] as they do not necessarily prevent a final decision, but they aim to slow down the process, getting higher political actors involved in it.

As already has been mentioned, although there is no specific reference to national Parliaments in the aforementioned Treaty provisions, Law No 234/2012—similar to laws implemented by other States[41]—provided that Parliament could intervene in this procedure, causing the government to follow its direction.

The parliamentary action being different, the procedure of its implementation differs. Instead of the aforementioned (and quite undefined) 'positive deliberation' foreseen under article 11(3), article 12 Law No 234/2012 lays out a more specific procedure, requiring the

[40] The expression, widely used in the literature (see E Cloots, *National Identity in EU Law* (Oxford, Oxford University Press, 2015), occurs also in some official documents, such as the EP resolution approved on 22 May 2012 on an EU approach to criminal law (2010/2310(INI)), see in particular Point C. More recently, the same expression has been used in a completely different context, with regard to one of the requests (related to the containment of immigration in the UK) issued by the British Prime Minister David Cameron to the European Council in order to avoid the Brexit.

[41] See s 9 of the German *Integrationsverantwortungsgesetz*.

Houses to express themselves with acts of political direction (ie resolutions),[42] in order to orient to the Government's position at the European level.

In both cases, the Government has the duty to inform Parliament about the submission of relevant proposals and the Houses have 30 days from that time to request that the Government accede to these mechanisms at the European level. The Government is obliged to follow the direction of the Parliament. If there is no resolution from both Houses after those 30 days, the Government may proceed to give a positive vote in the Council.

For the sake of completeness, since this parliamentary power is not intended to be collective, Law No 234/2012 creates the 'parliamentary reserve', by which each individual House can delay the expression in the Council of the Italian position on whether a legal act should be adopted for an equal period of 30 days so that they can complete parliamentary scrutiny on that act. If the 30 days expire without the delineation of any parliamentary position, the government can freely decide at the European level.[43] A similar mechanism was formerly provided by article 4 of the Law No 11/2005. That provision was stricter than the one currently in force and obliged the Government to wait for parliamentary advice whenever a Commission started the scrutiny of a draft EU legal act, without Parliament needing to request it.[44]

The logic of these procedures seems to be as follows: it seems that the legislator was primarily concerned with permitting parliamentary intervention that would be as free from formalism as possible so as to minimise the risk that inertia (or a simple slowing-down) on the part of the parliamentary activities would hinder the Government's actions within Europe. Article 10 of Law No 234/2012's reference to procedures based on the classical model of political acts has the benefit of setting the exercise of the European parliamentary powers concerned as part of a consolidated framework and so avoiding any interpretative doubt that may arise with regard to the different procedure set by article 11 using the cryptic phrasing of the 'positive decision'.

V. Veto Powers on *Passerelle* Clauses and Family Law

Concerning those parliamentary powers of the national parliament as a whole that are intended to permit it to 'oppose'[45] decisions proposed or taken at the European level, the

[42] See art 117 of the Rules of Procedure of the Chamber of Deputies and art 50 of the Rules of Procedure of the Senate. On the general use of resolutions and other instruments of political directions and political oversight with regard to the Italian participation to the European Union, see the chapter by G Rizzoni, in this book.

[43] See art 10, Law No 234/2012. A similar parliamentary scrutiny reserve has been practised since the 1970s at least in those Member States that pursue a 'document based scrutiny' (about this notion, see the chapter by A Esposito, in this book). Then it was inserted, without a binding nature, in the 'Copenhagen Parliamentary Guidelines', adopted at the XXVIII COSAC held in Brussels on 27 January 2003 (2003/C 154/01). However the preamble Protocol No 1 to the Treaty of Lisbon still affirms that 'the way in which national Parliaments scrutinise their governments in relation to the activities of the Union is a matter for the particular constitutional organisation and practice of each Member State'.

[44] On the differences between the scrutiny reserve under Law No 11/2005 and Law No 234/2012 see S Righi, 'Art 10. Riserva di esame parlamentare' in L Costato et al, n 27 above, 116. On a case about the application of the scrutiny reserve before the law currently in force, see D Girotto, 'Sulla "riserva parlamentare" nella legge di attuazione del mandato di arresto europeo' (2006) *Quaderni costituzionali* 119.

[45] To qualify these prerogatives in the sense of rights to 'oppose', consideration should be made of the text in art 48(7) TEU (allowing the procedure to be positively concluded 'in the absence of opposition'), as well as the well-known ruling by the German Federal Constitutional Court of 30 June 2009, which describes these obligations as 'Oppositionsrecht' (points 318 ff). See also Kiiver, n 5 above, 7.

matrix of the decision-making system based on Law No 234/2012 changes. Indeed, the Italian Parliament is involved in a unitary sense: to assert its position at the European level and to prevent the adoption of a decision by the Council or the European Council, the two Houses must express their vote unitarily, such that an opposition submitted by a single House is legally irrelevant.

The nature of the power concerned—a mere power to oppose—and the necessity of a decision shared by the two Houses may replicate some of the peculiarities previously expressed with regard to the 'positive deliberation' of the Houses about the lack of any stipulation for a necessary 'collective' decision by the two Chambers. Again, in this case, there is nothing indicating that the two Houses must express the position of the 'national parliament' as the result of a coordinated (and, therefore, 'collective') procedure. Thus, they are allowed to act independently of each other.[46]

The absence of a provision requiring legislation (or a non-legislative bicameral act) is certainly not enough to prohibit the use of such bicameral 'collective' procedures. Nevertheless, a further element lacking a cohesive nature and a coherent dialogue can be highlighted within Law No 234/2012.

The reason that the Treaties include the possibility of stopping the procedure if even just one national parliament expresses opposition appears to be based on different assumptions in the two situations addressed. In the case of article 81(3) TFEU (related to 'family law with cross-border implications') the involvement of the national assemblies depends evidently on the political relevance of this specific subject matter. Differently, in the case of the general *passerelle* clause, the possibility to stop the shift of certain matters from unanimity to QMV is due to the necessity of not stripping the national parliaments of the power to have a bearing on decisive matters through the scrutiny and oversight of their respective Governments. In other words, as long as a given matter requires unanimity among the national Governments, the corresponding parliaments continue to hold a potentially determining position on the point; should the same matter become available to only a majority—albeit a qualified majority—of Member States, the individual Member State (and, therefore, 'its' parliament) would lose this ability to decisively object to new policies on that matter. For this reason, the ability to pass such a *passerelle* must be overseen by at least an abstract veto power held by the same parliament, in order to prevent the possible and irreversible loss of powers.[47]

[46] For a comparison with the French case, interesting also in the prospect of the (possible) Italian constitutional reform, art 88-7 of the French Constitution assigns Parliament the right to oppose the activation of the *passerelle* clause by passing of an identical motion by both the National Assembly and the Senate. So, notwithstanding the different composition and constitutional role of the lower and the upper House, an equal position in the exercise of the veto powers related to the *passerelle* clause is assigned to them.

[47] Furthermore, if allowed, it appears somehow debatable whether the general *passerelle* clauses are systematically located in the article providing the procedure for revising the Treaties (and even in the participation thereof dedicated to the 'simplified revision procedures' (in the plural!)). As can be seen, use of the mechanisms pursuant to art 48(7) TEU (and the further mechanisms of the specific *passerelle* clauses even more so) do not seem to be at all equivalent to amendments to the Treaties, even when 'simplified': the transition of a determined topic from a special legislative procedure to an ordinary legislative procedure, or the passage from unanimous approval to a qualified majority, do not constitute a formal modification of the Treaties but simply result as the implementation of a mechanism provided for by them, with obligatory procedural solutions expressly pre-established for its deployment. For an opinion contrasting with that given above, see LJ Quesada, 'The Revision Procedures of the Treaty' in HJ Blanke and S Mangiameli (eds), *The European Union after Lisbon. Constitutional Basis, Economic Order and External Actions* (Berlin, Springer, 2012) 327, as well as B Guastaferro, 'La partecipazione dei Parlamenti nazionali e del Parlamento europeo al procedimento di revisione dei trattati' in Manzella and Lupo,

Article 11(5) of Law No 234/2012 makes reference exclusively to cases pursuant to the general *passerelle* clause in article 48(7) TEU, and the opposition concerning family law pursuant to article 81(3) TFEU (ie the cases in which the Treaties exclusively provide for national parliaments' involvement in blocking the decision to be adopted). The same veto power does not apply to additional *passerelle* clauses that other specific provisions of the Treaties provide (such as that included in article 31(3) TEU, as well as those in article 86(4), article 153(2), article 192(2), article 312 and article 333 TFEU). On this point, Law No 234/2012 is consistent in not providing for similar procedures opposing the application of particular *passerelle* clauses, in relation to which the role of the individual national parliament seems to be necessarily limited to discussing with its 'own' government the position to be adopted within the European Council or the Council (in relation to which the information duty pursuant to article 11(1) equally applies).

VI. Conclusions: The 'Mild' Italian Parliamentary Model of Participation in the EU

In trying to evaluate the solutions pursued by the Italian Parliament in implementing its own 'collective' powers and also considering the different procedural solutions adopted in the other EU Member States, it seems possible to define the Italian model as a *mild* parliamentary one. It is 'parliamentary' because it pursues traditional parliamentary functions like legislation and political direction to the Government, incorporating the exercise of the new European powers into its own consolidated procedural framework. Hence, its fully 'parliamentary' nature comes from the decision to manage these new powers within the Parliament, without directly involving the people through referenda (as the British European Union Act 2011 does).[48] Finally, the kind of role self-attributed to parliament in the concrete exercise of the same powers tends to be quite 'mild', as it does not grant a necessary and pre-emptive power of authorisation for the exercise of the Government's role in the European institutions (as the German *Integrationsverantwortungsgesetz* tends to acknowledge, even with regard to the veto powers).[49]

Generally speaking, when compared to the other national cases, the Italian Parliament seems to be subject to fewer and less rigid external constraints.[50] It has no rigid legal framework given by an external source that limits its organisational and procedural autonomy (as is the German case with the Federal Constitutional Court, but also in France where the

n 23 above, 183. Also the Chapter by the same B Guastaferro and that of L Gianniti, in this book, present a different reading of the passerelle clause from that proposed here. Consistently with these latter interpretations, also the title of art 11 of Law No 234/2012 (which deals, among other things, with simplified Treaties' revisions and *passerelle* clauses) talks of 'simplified treaties' revisions'.

[48] … see in particular the s 6, where all decisions requiring both the approval by an Act of Parliament and by referendum are listed.

[49] This is the case of the *passerelle* clauses, 'transformed' by s 4 of the German *Integrationsverantwortungsgesetz* from a possible veto by the National Parliament to the necessity of an explicit authorisation (even to be approved under the procedure laid down by art 23 of the Basic Law) by the same Parliament, missing which the Government has to 'reject the proposal for a decision'.

[50] The same concept will be further elaborated in the Conclusion to the book.

Constitution deals directly and pervasively with the structure and the functioning of the Assemblies). It also did not come to the decision of assuming a mediating role between the institutions of the European Union and the sovereign people (as in the case of the UK), which has shown to be disastrous in the Brexit referendum case.

From a certain point of view, Coherently with the 'silent adaptation' to the European integration followed by the Italian Constitutional order[51] the Italian solution seems even more consistent with the spirit of the Treaties, which gave the national Parliaments a role in the EU's functioning with the aim of contributing to strengthening its role, not stopping its evolution. On the contrary, the solutions entailed in the implementation given by Member States like Germany, or the elusive choice pursued in the UK to bypass Parliament with a referendum, seems to constitute an extreme kind of gold plating (exactly in the sense of going 'beyond what is strictly required by EU legislation when they implement it at national level')[52] of what the Treaty actually attributed to the national Parliament.

This Italian mild kind of option, derived from the belated and difficult implementation of the same powers, might actually bring a chance for a better Europeanisation of the Italian Parliament. Through time, individual MPs (and the parliamentary bureaucracy itself) will become accustomed to applying similar rules and similar procedures to what is followed in internal affairs to European documents, and so will enhance their incorporation into 'ordinary' parliamentary activity and even their perception as non-exceptional tools. Of course, the results of such a combination need time to be evaluated, but they seem to constitute an opportunity for positive results, too.

[51] See more in detail in the Conclusion to this book.

[52] See the Communication from the Commission to the European Parliament, the Council, the European Economic and Social Committee and the Committee of the Regions, *Better regulation for better results—An EU agenda*, COM(2015) 215 final, 8–9.

11

Procedures vis-à-vis the European Parliament and the Other National Parliaments: Interparliamentary Cooperation

ELENA GRIGLIO

I. The Italian Parliament Facing Interparliamentary Relations in the EU Framework: Ongoing Trends

The Italian Parliament offers a solid tradition of 'external' relations with other Parliaments in the European Union.[1] Only in the last few years, however, has the Italian legislature

[1] C De Cesare,'L'Unione interparlamentare e le relazioni fra i Parlamenti' in *Il Parlamento italiano 1861–1988* Vol 20 (Milano, Nuova CEI Informatica, 1988) 213 ff; V Guizzi, 'La diplomazia parlamentare e la cooperazione tra Parlamenti: la nuova dimensione internazionale del Parlamento italiano' in *Divenire sociale e adeguamento del diritto. Studi in onore di Francesco Capotorti* Vol 1 (Milano, Giuffrè, 1999) 229 ff; R Dickmann, 'La "diplomazia parlamentare": esperienze, limiti, prospettive' (2005) 1 *Rivista trimestrale di scienza dell'amministrazione* 5; G Baiocchi, 'Profili e missioni della diplomazia parlamentare' (2005) 288 *Rivista di studi politici internazionali* 675; C Decaro and N Lupo (eds), *Il dialogo tra Parlamenti: obiettivi e risultati* (Roma, LUP, 2009).

experienced new forms of engagement in this field. These result from the evolutionary trends affecting interparliamentary cooperation in the EU institutional framework;[2] and partially also stem from the adaptations to the innovations brought about by the Treaty of Lisbon promoted in both Houses.

At the EU level, after the constructive experience of national Parliaments' participation in the Convention on the future of Europe, which concluded its work in 2003, interparliamentary cooperation has found formal recognition as a multidimensional experience in the Treaty of Lisbon. Before the Treaty's entry into force, interparliamentary relations in the EU were carried out mostly through occasional meetings (Joint Parliamentary Meetings, Joint Committee Meetings and Interparliamentary Committee Meetings). These meetings used to be promoted on a regular basis either by the European Parliament (EP) alone or jointly by the EP and the Parliament of the Member State holding the Presidency of the Council; they involved representatives of the EP and national Parliaments.[3]

Moreover, interparliamentary cooperation also was developed through the participation in two permanent and structured conferences: COSAC, the Conference of Community and European Affairs Committees of Parliaments of the European Union, established on 16–17 November 1989 in Paris and then formally recognised by article 10 of the Protocol on the Role of National Parliaments in the European Union of the Treaty of Amsterdam; and the Conference of the Speakers, devoid of a Treaty status, first convened in 1963 and more regularly, at least on an annual basis, since the 1980s.

The Treaty of Lisbon offered interparliamentary cooperation a double legal basis (article 12, paragraph f Treaty on European Union (TEU) and articles 9 and 10 of Protocol No 1, on the Role of National Parliaments in the European Union, annexed to the Treaty), thus reinforcing its placement among the 'democratic' toolbox of the EU.[4] Moreover, it also set the conditions for the creation of new, structural and policy-oriented forums for interparliamentary dialogue.[5] Two standing conferences were hence established:[6] the Conference on Common Foreign and Security Policy-Common Security and Defence Policy (CFSP-CSDP), based on Articles 9 and 10 of Protocol No 1 annexed to the Treaty of Lisbon;

[2] See C Heffler and K Gattermann, 'Interparliamentary Cooperation in the European Union: Patterns, Problems and Potential', in C Heffler, C Neuhold, O Rozenberg, and J Smith (eds), *The Palgrave Handbook of National Parliaments and the European Union* (2015) 94 ff; D Fromage, 'Increasing Interparliamentary cooperation in the EU: Current Trends and Challenges' (2016) 22 *European Public Law* 749 ff; N Bolleyer, 'Executive-legislative relations and inter-parliamentary cooperation in federal systems—lessons for the European Union' (2017) 24 *Journal of European Public Policy* 520 ff; O Rozenberg, *The Role of National Parliaments in the EU after Lisbon: Potentialities and Challenges* (Brussels, European Parliament, 2017) (http://www.europarl.europa.eu/supporting-analyses).

[3] On the origins of this practice, see the COSAC Sixth Bi-annual Report 'Developments in European Union. Procedures and practices relevant to parliamentary scrutiny' (2006) www.cosac.eu 5, 30. On its successive developments, see the Twenty-first Bi-annual Report 'Developments in European Union procedures and practices relevant to parliamentary scrutiny' (2014) www.cosac.eu 23 ff.

[4] S Roland, 'Quand le performatif tient lieu d'argumentatif: la contribution des Parlements nationaux au bon fonctionnement de l'Union' (2012) 556 *Revue du marche commun et de l'Union Européenne* 178; A Esposito, 'La cooperazione interparlamentare: principi, strumenti e prospettive' in A Manzella and N Lupo (eds), *Il sistema parlamentare euro-nazionale. Lezioni* (Torino, Giappichelli, 2014) 138–39; R Corbett, 'The Evolving Roles of the European Parliament and the National Parliaments' in A Biondi, P Eeckhout and S Ripley (eds), *EU After Lisbon* (Oxford, Oxford University Press, 2012) 248 ff.

[5] On the atypical nature of the EP's external relations, to be included in the traditional studies on International Parliamentary Institutions (IPIs) or, by contrast, to be considered a '*sui generis*' phenomenon, see A Cofelice and S Stavridis, 'The European Parliament as an International Parliamentary Institution (IPI)' (2014) 2 *European Foreign Affairs Review* 145 ff.

[6] N Lupo and C Fasone (eds), *Interparliamentary Cooperation in the Composite European Constitution* (Oxford, Hart, 2016).

and the Conference on Stability, Economic Coordination and Governance in the European Union (SECG), based on Article 13 of the Treaty on Stability, Coordination and Governance (called the 'Fiscal Compact').

The creation of such conferences paved the way for the consolidation of a network of interparliamentary cooperation in the EU: the latter is composed by an assortment of organisational and procedural arrangements not exclusively based on traditional methods and practices of parliamentary diplomacy.[7] The outcome is an interparliamentary network typified by the 'structural' (rather than 'sporadic') nature of the interaction among Parliaments, mostly developed on a multilateral (rather than bilateral) basis, supported by an interparliamentary institutional framework (rather than subject to the spontaneous initiative of Parliaments), directed at pursuing well-defined goals (rather than merely confronting general issues) and featured by recurring meetings (rather than by the unsystematic nature of the 'dialogue').[8]

Aside from these changes affecting the 'European' dimension of interparliamentary cooperation, other 'national' factors have lately influenced the Italian Houses' participation in EU interparliamentary cooperation. The reference is, in particular, to those institutional and political factors that, in the last few years, have led to a reconsideration and revitalisation of European affairs in the daily parliamentary practice.

The entry into force of the Treaty of Lisbon launched new forms of institutional engagement for the Italian Parliament in the consideration of European issues and in the participation in EU decision-making.[9] From the legal point of view, the need to comply with the revised EU institutional framework has found satisfaction mainly through the approval of Law No 234/2012, 'General rules on Italy's participation in the formation and implementation of legislation and policies of the European Union'.[10] This acceleration in the Italian Parliament's Europeanisation process has favoured a reconsideration of interparliamentary activities as a structural component of the 'European' powers of the two Houses. This evolution has occurred mostly informally, as the Houses have implemented the innovations of the Treaty of Lisbon not through a formal revision of their Rules of Procedure, but through 'internal' acts.[11] However, in a comparative perspective, this process has affected

[7] See FW Weisglas and G de Boer, 'Parliamentary Diplomacy' (2007) 2 *The Hague Journal of Diplomacy* 93 ff. On parliamentary diplomacy as 'parlomacy', see D Fiott, 'On the Value of Parliamentary Diplomacy' (2011) 4 *Madariaga Paper*. Italian scholars have spoken of a 'parallel' (Guizzi, above n 1, 246) or 'liquid' diplomacy (L Ciaurro, 'L'attività estera delle Commissioni parlamentari' in Decaro and Lupo, above n 1, 257; C Decaro, 'Esiste la diplomazia parlamentare?' in Decaro and Lupo, above n 1, 315 ff). See also G Baiocchi, 'Profili e missione della diplomazia palamentare' (2005) 72 *Rivista di studi politici internazionali* 676 and R Dickmann, 'Note sulla "diplomazia parlamentare" italiana' (2006) 18 *Federalismi.it*.

[8] See A Manzella, 'La cooperazione interparlamentare nel 'Trattato internazionale' europeo' (2012) www.astrid-online.it; B Crum and E Fossum, 'Practices of Interparliamentary Coordination in International Politics: the European Union and Beyond' in B Crum and E Fossum (eds), *Practices of Interparliamentary Coordination in International Politics* (Colchester, ECPR Press, 2013) 6 ff.

[9] See the chapters by Capuano, Esposito and Lupo in this Volume.

[10] See, *ex multis*, N Lupo,'L'adeguamento del sistema istituzionale italiano al trattato di Lisbona. Osservazioni sui disegni di legge di riforma della legge n. 11 del 2005' (2011) *Astrid Rassegna*, www.astrid.eu; P Caretti, 'La legge n 234/2012 che disciplina la partecipazione dell'Italia alla formazione e all'attuazione della normativa e delle politiche dell'Unione europea: un traguardo o ancora una tappa intermedia?' (2012) 5–6 *Le Regioni* 837 and G Rivosecchi, 'La partecipazione dell'Italia alla formazione e attuazione della normativa europea: il ruolo del Parlamento' (2013) 5 *Giornale di diritto amministrativo* 463 ff.

[11] See the Opinions dated 6 October 2009 and 14 July 2010 of the Commission for the Rules of Procedures of the Chamber of Deputies and the Letter of the Speaker of the Senate of the Republic released on the 1 December 2009. In literature, see C Fasone, 'Qual è la fonte più idonea a recepire le novità del Trattato di Lisbona sui

the Italian Parliament probably more than other national Parliaments because the former has always lacked a tradition of the scrutiny of EU affairs comparable to Northern Europe's standards.[12]

Other 'national' factors are more directly related to trends affecting the transformation of the Italian form of government and the relationship linking the Parliament to the Government in the management of EU affairs. The Italian legislature has always proved to be extremely weak in its capacity to influence governmental decision-making at a national level when EU interests are at stake. This weakness has significantly threatened existing channels of parliamentary scrutiny and oversight that enable the Parliament to intervene respectively in the ex ante stage (that precedes the assumption of formal decisions at EU level) and in the ex post stage (that follows EU decisions' implementation at the national level).[13] In this framework, participation in the different forms of interparliamentary cooperation has offered the Italian Parliament (and MPs as well) the opportunity to 'get involved' proactively in the debate on EU major political issues, thus overcoming the marginalisation experienced at the national level.

The present chapter aims at analysing the most recent developments affecting the Italian participation in the EU interparliamentary cooperation. Such trends are still ongoing and their outcomes remain uncertain. In particular, Section II analyses the apparent paradox of a symmetrical bicameralism featuring divergent practices and institutional approaches by the two Houses to interparliamentary cooperation. Sections III and IV respectively examine the rules, procedures and practices structuring the Italian Parliament's participation in this dimension. Section V highlights recent cases of manifest divergences between the two Houses in what will be defined as the 'macro' approach to interparliamentary cooperation in the EU (affecting the vision of the 'macro' elements—the nature, scope, purpose and way of functioning—of such relations). Finally, challenges featuring the Italian bicameralism vis-à-vis the requirements of unitary representation in EU interparliamentary relations are addressed in Section VI.

II. A Symmetric Bicameralism with Divergent Approaches to Interparliamentary Cooperation in the EU

Two Houses sharing the same powers both in the legislative and in the non-legislative procedures, including the confidence relationship with the Government, compose the Italian Parliament. Their entitlements in the field of European affairs are exactly the same.

Parlamenti nazionali' (2010) 3 *Osservatoriosullefonti.it*; D Capuano, 'Il Senato e l'attuazione del trattato di Lisbona, tra controllo di sussidiarietà e dialogo politico con la Commissione europea' (2011) *Amministrazione in cammino*, www.amministrazioneincammino.luiss.it; A Esposito, 'La legge 24 dicembre 2012, n 234, sulla partecipazione dell'Italia alla formazione e all'attuazione della normativa e delle politiche dell'UE. Parte I—Prime riflessioni sul ruolo delle Camere' (2013) 2 *Federalismi.it*.

[12] K Auel, O Rozenberg and A Thomas, 'Lost in Transaction? Parliamentary Reserves in EU Bargains' (2012) 10 *OPAL Online Paper Series*; A Buzogány, 'Learning from the Best? Interparliamentary Networks and the Parliamentary Scrutiny of the EU Decision-making' in Crum and Fossum (eds), above n 7, 17 ff.

[13] *Ex multis*, see M Cartabia and L Chieffi, 'Art 11' in A Celotto, M Olivetti and R Bifulco (eds), *Commentario alla Costituzione* (Torino, UTET, 2006); P Bilancia, *The Dynamics of the EU Integration and the Impact on the National Constitutional Law* (Milano, Giuffrè, 2012) 86 ff.

Bicameral symmetry affecting the Italian Houses' participation in the EU reveals itself to be fully consistent with the position entrusted on national Parliaments in the EU legal order. From the formal point of view, in fact, the latter does not make any difference according to the internal arrangement of national legislatures: European powers launched alongside the entry into force of the Treaty of Lisbon are entrusted to each House, irrespective of its composition, role in the national architecture and place in a bicameral or unicameral system.[14]

However, the symmetrical entitlements featuring the position of the Italian Houses in the EU policy area are not supported by convergent implementing procedures and practices. Each House has carried out a distinctive approach to the fulfilment of its European powers.[15] Moreover, because of the lack of a formal revision of the Rules of Procedure, this task has been developed mostly informally, adapting pre-existing practices (see below Section III). Such differentiation has also affected the participation in the EU interparliamentary cooperation.

Manifest asymmetries have arisen over the decades in the participation of the Italian bicameralism in EU interparliamentary relations, resulting in a diversification of the rules and practices driving the attitude of each House. In the absence of a formal, extended, regulation, both the Chamber of Deputies and the Senate of the Republic have developed internal praxis and attitudes not always fully consistent among themselves.

Divergences among the two Houses in the way of handling interparliamentary relations have been undergirded by extremely heterogeneous visions of this dimension. These have lately come to light on occasion of the drafting of the Rules of Procedure of the new interparliamentary Conferences established after the Treaty of Lisbon's entry into force (see below Section V).

Moreover, bicameral asymmetries have manifested themselves also in the participation in the 'Green Card' procedure: this procedure, although formally external to the framework of interparliamentary cooperation, can be included among the relational mechanisms linking national parliaments to EU institutions (see below Section V).

Generally speaking, a tricky cohabitation seems to characterise the position of the Italian Houses in their system of relations with the EP and the other national Parliaments. This factor potentially hinders the unitary representation and participation of the Italian Parliament in the network of EU interparliamentary relations.

[14] P Kiiver, *The Early Warning System for the Principle of Subsidiarity. Constitutional Theory and Empirical Reality* (London, Routledge, 2012) 66 ff; A Cygan, '"Collective" Subsidiarity Monitoring by National Parliaments after Lisbon: the Operation of the Early Warning Mechanism' in M Trybus and L Rubini (eds), *The Treaty of Lisbon and the Future of European Law and Policy* (Cheltenham, Edward Elgar Publishing, 2012) 55 ff; D Jançic, 'The Barroso Initiative: Window Dressing or Democracy Boost?' (2012) 8 *Utrecht Law Review* 78; PG Casalena, N Lupo and C Fasone, 'Commentary on Protocol No 1 annexed to the Treaty of Lisbon' (On the role of National Parliaments)' in HJ Blanke and S Mangiameli (eds), *The Treaty on European Union* (Berlin, Springer, 2013) 1529 ff. Among Italian scholars, see L Gianniti, 'Il ruolo dei Parlamenti nazionali' in F Bassanini and G Tiberi (eds), *Le nuovi istituzioni europee. Commento al Trattato di Lisbona* 2nd edn (Bologna, Il Mulino, 2010) 183 ff; N Lupo, 'I poteri europei dei Parlamenti nazionali: questioni terminologiche, classificazioni e primi effetti' in N Lupo and A Manzella (eds), above n 4, 101 ff.

[15] See Capuano, above n 11 and Esposito, above n 11.

III. Interparliamentary Cooperation from the Italian Perspective: An Issue Mostly Disregarded by the Two Houses' Rules of Procedure

Consistent with the idea of the EU's 'composite' Constitution[16] and the arrangements of a 'euro-national' parliamentary system,[17] the participation of national Parliaments in interparliamentary cooperation represents a 'dual' phenomenon. It finds its legal discipline both at the European level, in the rules and practices regulating the organisation and functioning of interparliamentary bodies and activities, and at the national level, in the rules and practices that, specifically, state the criteria for the formation of parliamentary delegations and determine the internal follow-up of supranational decisions.

With regard to this second level of regulation, very few norms are provided by the two Houses' Rules of Procedure. Such norms, moreover, limit themselves to stating general guidelines, inspired by a vision of interparliamentary relations in the EU that is somewhat out-dated, at least if compared to the innovations introduced by the Treaty of Lisbon.

The main reference norms are represented by article 23 of the Senate's Rules of Procedure (hereinafter RoP Senate) and article 126 of the Chamber's Rules of Procedure (hereinafter RoP Chamber): these identify the Committee for EU Policies as the organ entitled with a general competence on the activity and decisions of the EU, including interparliamentary relations.

Priority recognition of the EU Policies Committee does not prevent the involvement in the dialogue and cooperation with EU institutions of other standing committees, competent on specific policy areas. Such a setup is explicitly mentioned by article 144-quater RoP Senate and article 127-ter RoP Chamber: these rules allow standing committees, according to their areas of competence and with the consent of the respective Chairs, to invite members of the European Parliament to provide information on the tasks and activities of EU institutions. The two norms derive from amendments to the Rules of Procedure approved in 1999 (article 127-ter RoP Chamber) and 2003 (article 144-quater RoP Senate) respectively. A similar procedure is provided (article 144-quater RoP Senate and 127-ter RoP Chamber, paragraph 2) for the hearings of the members of the European Commission, to be promoted by standing committees according to their competence.

The aforementioned provisions must be read in connection with article 143 RoP Senate and article 125 RoP Chamber, which state the procedures for preparing and debating the resolutions approved by the European Parliament and the decisions adopted by international assemblies in which Italian parliamentary delegations participated. These acts are addressed to the Speakers of the Senate and the Chamber; after being announced to the plenary, they are deferred to the relevant standing committees.

[16] L Besselink, *A Composite European Constitution* (Groningen, Europa Law Publishing, 2007).

[17] Lupo and Manzella (eds), above n 3; A Manzella, 'Parlamento europeo e parlamenti nazionali come sistema' (2015) 1 *Rivista AIC*; N Lupo, 'Parlamento europeo e Parlamenti nazionali nella Costituzione "composita" dell'Unione europea: le diverse letture possibili' in A Ciancio (ed), *Nuove strategie per lo sviluppo democratico e l'integrazione politica in Europa* (Roma, Aracne, 2014) 365 ff and also in (2014) 3 *Rivista AIC*.

The two Houses' Rules of Procedure differ in the role entrusted to sectoral committees and to the Committee for EU Policies. At the Chamber of Deputies, in fact, the act is always deferred to the relevant sectoral committee, whereas the Committee for EU Policies, jointly with the Committee for Foreign Affairs, is asked to formulate advice. At the Senate, by contrast, the involvement of sectoral standing committees according to the aforementioned procedure is combined with the involvement of the Committee for EU Policies for those acts affecting the general policy of the European Union: to start a debate on such issues, the Committee must acquire the advice of the Committee for Constitutional Affairs and the Committee for Foreign Affairs. The role entrusted to the EU Policies Committee by the RoP Senate is designed to safeguard the unitary representation of the Senate's position when dealing with acts addressing the EU general policy. A not too dissimilar institutional mechanism is provided for the participation in the Early Warning System and the political dialogue: at the Senate, in fact, the EU Policies Committee is entitled with a sort of substitutive power in case of the sectoral committees' inertia in the scrutiny of EU proposals. The substitutive mechanism can affect the assessment of the act's political content or the compliance with the subsidiarity principle. The procedure implemented by the Chamber of Deputies, by contrast, distinguishes the participation in the political dialogue, entrusted to sectoral committees, from the subsidiarity monitoring, deferred to the EU Policies Committee.[18]

These norms complete the legal framework of the 'dialogue' with the other Parliaments of the EU; they are inspired by a somewhat traditional conception of the 'parliamentary diplomacy', typical of international relations. This conception has proved not fully suited to cover and possibly harmonise the variety of interparliamentary relations in the EU. Moreover, it addresses interparliamentary cooperation as a sphere of action with no clear distinction between the different formats. The only format of interparliamentary cooperation explicitly mentioned is COSAC: indeed, article 23 of the RoP Senate appoints the standing Committee for EU Policies responsible for the management of the relationship with the European Parliament and with COSAC. A similar provision is not included in the RoP Chamber, which however follows the same criteria.

It is somewhat peculiar that COSAC is the only interparliamentary format legally recognised and, besides, by only one of the two parliamentary Rules of Procedure. In the current framework, in fact, COSAC is probably not even the most strategic among existing interparliamentary formats.[19] The Conference is the most 'traditional' of the permanent EU interparliamentary conferences, being conceived in terms of cooperation among committees with a general competence on EU affairs[20] and having acted over the decades as a

[18] N Lupo, 'I Parlamenti nazionali nell'Unione europea e il principio di sussidiarietà: qualche suggestione per la Camera dei deputati' (2014) *Amministrazione in cammino*.

[19] M Knudsen and Y Carl, 'COSAC—its Role to Date and its Potential in the Future' in G Barrett (ed), *National Parliaments and the European Union* (Dublin, Clarus Press, 2008) 455 ff; D Capuano and C Fasone, *La Conferenza degli organi specializzati negli affari europei (COSAC). Evoluzione e prospettive*, Senato della Repubblica—Quaderni europei e internazionali (www.senato.it/application/xmanager/projects/leg17/file/Quad_Europei_Intern_18.pdf, 2010). See also A Cygan, 'COSAC: Birth, Evolution, Failures and Perspectives' in Lupo and Fasone, above n 5, 207 ff.

[20] K Neunreither, 'The European Parliament and National Parliaments: Conflict or Cooperation?' (2005) 11 *Journal of Legislative Studies* 466, 486.

forum of dialogue primarily between EU national Parliaments.[21] Due to this structure, the COSAC model is now facing some difficult challenges.[22] Problems have arisen because of its composition (characterised by the presence of generalists from EU affairs committees) and the changes affecting its role (shifting from the original idea of a space for interparliamentary exchange and debate to the recent development as a forum where representatives of the European executive[23] try to influence national parliamentarians).[24]

By contrast, the two sectoral interparliamentary Conferences on CFSP-CSDP and SECG do not find any reference in the two Houses' Rules of Procedure: the RoPs, in fact, have not been revised after the entry into force of the Treaty of Lisbon. This situation has inhibited the formal transposition of the innovations brought about by the new formats of interparliamentary cooperation embodied by such Conferences into the Italian parliamentary procedures. Based on article 9 of Protocol No 1 annexed to the Lisbon Treaty, these Conferences have found legitimacy in the search for a new form of cooperation that involves national Parliaments and the European Parliament on an equal footing. The institutional aims of the Conferences overcome the objectives entrusted to pre-existing interparliamentary formats. The latter consisted in the exchange of information and best practices, the effective exercise of national parliamentary competences in EU affairs, and the promotion of partnerships with Parliaments of third countries.[25] Being entitled to evaluate EU policies' implementation in those areas where the influence of the executive branch is overwhelming and oversight from representative assemblies represents a major issue of discussion,[26] the new Conferences are expected to achieve another more ambitious aim: that is, to strengthen the capacity of Parliaments to fulfil the oversight function and consequently to improve the democratic legitimacy of the European Union.[27]

Such changes in the concept of interparliamentary cooperation itself would have required an adaptation of the Italian Parliament's rules and practices concerning the formation of national delegations, the coordination of the two Houses' position and the follow-up on interparliamentary decisions. Nonetheless, because of the lack of a formal adjustment of the Rules of Procedure, each House has coped with the upcoming spirit of interparliamentary cooperation in the EU mostly by working on their internal practice, thus fostering further asymmetries.

[21] See, in particular, the Co-ordinated tests of the Subsidiarity check promoted by COSAC since 2004; on this point, Casalena, Fasone and Lupo, above n 14, 1598–99.

[22] See House of Lords, 'European Union Committee—Ninth Report. The role of the National Parliaments in the European Union' (2014) www.publications.parliament.uk, 115 ff.

[23] D Curtin, 'Challenging Executive Dominance in European Democracy' (2014) 77 *MLR* 1 ff.

[24] European Parliament, Annual Report 2013/2014 on 'Interparliamentary relations between the European Parliament and national Parliaments under the Treaty of Lisbon. 2009–2014' (2014) www.europarl.europa.eu.

[25] See the 'Guidelines for Interparliamentary Co-operation in the European Union', adopted by the Speakers' Conference during the Lisbon meeting, 19–21 June 2009. Among scholars, A Esposito, 'La cooperazione interparlamentare: principi, strumenti e prospettive' in Lupo and Manzella (eds), above n 4, 155–57.

[26] J Wouters and K Raube, 'Europe's Common Security and Defence Policy: the Case for Inter-Parliamentary Scrutiny' (2012) 90 *Leuven Centre for Global Governance Studies Working Paper*.

[27] I Cooper, 'Parliamentary Oversight of the EU after the Crisis: on the Creation of the "Article 13" Interparliamentary Conference' (2014) 21 *Luiss School of Government Working paper Series*.

IV. Representing the Italian Parliament in the Interparliamentary Cooperation at EU Level

Notwithstanding their variety, the formats for interparliamentary cooperation in the EU all share a common feature: their being participated in by delegations of MPs representing each national Parliament.

A dual set of rules regulates the formation and composition of national delegations. Basic criteria are defined at the European level. In the cases of Joint Committee Meetings and Joint Parliamentary Meetings, there are no fixed rules regulating the format of national delegations, as the latter are decided from time to time by their promoters. By contrast, permanent conferences find in their Rules of Procedure a more extended regulation of the format of parliamentary delegations, which usually also includes their size.

These rules, agreed upon at the European level, are integrated through national norms and practices; all further organisational and functional details are, in fact, deferred to the domestic jurisdiction of each national House/Parliament. Exception needs to be made for the Speakers' Conference, the composition of which, as defined in article 2.3 of the 'Guidelines for the Conference of Speakers of EU Parliaments', does not leave national Parliaments relevant room to manoeuvre. The Conference features participation by the Speakers, who can be represented by a Deputy Speaker/Vice-President.[28]

A. General Criteria for the Formation of National Delegations

The experience gained by the Italian Parliament in the formation of national delegations offers an example of the complexity driving the approach of bicameral parliaments in this sphere of activity.

Generally speaking, in the Italian practice of international and EU relations, the term 'delegation' is used to define a variety of experiences: the members of a standing committee's visit abroad in response to an enquiry; the participation of a group of MPs representing a standing committee, as 'observers', to the meeting of one of the EP committees; the mission of a bilateral group of friendship, created either within or outside the Italian Group by the Interparliamentary Union; a group of MPs' monitoring visit to an 'emergent democracy', promoted in cooperation with an international organisation or bilaterally; or the Speaker's visit to a foreign country or his/her attendance at one of the conferences promoted by international organisations.[29]

Among such experiences, a distinguished role is played by those delegations permanently representing the Italian Parliament in international organisations: such delegations, although devoid of a formal regulation in the two Houses' Rules of Procedure, have settled themselves into the parliamentary practice. The term 'delegation' (*delegazione*) must not be

[28] Adopted by the EU Speakers' Conference in Stockholm, 15 May 2010, the Guidelines are available at www.ipex.eu/IPEXL-WEB/dossier/files/download/082dbcc54b222e18014b505220e5365f.do.

[29] See V Di Ciolo and L Ciaurro, *Il diritto parlamentare nella teoria e nella pratica* 5th edn (Milano, Giuffrè, 20013) 465 ff.

confused with the term 'deputation' (*deputazione*), formally regulated by article 164 RoP Senate (no rule is provided by the RoP Chamber) to indicate a body composed by senators appointed by the Speaker as to assure maximum representation to all parliamentary groups and headed by the Speaker himself or by a Deputy Speaker. In the praxis of the Senate, article 164 RoP has never found implementation.[30]

In the Italian Parliament's experience, the 'international delegations' act as permanent bodies, elected by each House in the plenary or appointed by the Speaker and entitled with a representative mandate for the electoral term: members of the delegation are durably empowered to fulfil, in representation of their country, a certain mandate by an international parliamentary assembly. Their composition follows the proportions among political groups. Until 1979, delegations representing the Italian Parliament in the European Parliament also were formed accordingly. In the current legislative term, five international parliamentary delegations have been established, representing the Italian Parliament by NATO, the Council of Europe, the Organisation for Economic Development and Co-operation (OECD), the Central Europe Initiative (CEI) and the Union for the Mediterranean.

The proportional criterion used in the composition of international parliamentary delegations could have represented a guideline also for the formation of EU parliamentary delegations. However, both political and functional factors have contributed to inhibit such a solution. O1n the political ground, the nature of the Italian party model—which is still today featured by the presence of a plurality of medium-small parties that are hardly adjustable to the classical bipolar scheme and remain permanently unstable[31]—make the proportional criterion not always easy to apply in the composition of non-permanent collective bodies. In these cases, criteria of 'bipartisan' representation could only be interpreted in a flexible manner, directed at giving voice to the majority supporting the government and to at least one of the minorities playing the role of opposition.

On the functional ground, constitutive differences between EU and international delegations—EU delegations are appointed from time to time by the Chairs of the sectoral Committees and consequently lack a representative mandate—have led the two Houses to structure EU delegations on the basis of the different criterion of non-partisan representation. This criterion has been perceived as more suited to the functional demands of EU interparliamentary cooperation.

The non-partisan criterion is not completely new to the Italian parliamentary tradition for the formation of collective bodies.[32] Reference is made, in particular, to the Parliamentary Committee for the Security of the Republic (ruled by Law No 124/2007) and the Joint Committee for Legislation, established by the Italian Chamber of Deputies in 1997 (article 16-bis RoP Chamber), both formed with an equal proportion among the majority

[30] G Baiocchi (ed), *Manuale delle Delegazioni parlamentari internazionali* (Roma, Senato della Repubblica, 2005) 14–15.

[31] See C Fusaro,'Party System Developments and Electoral Legislation in Italy (1948–2009)' (2009) 1 *Bulletin of Italian Politics* 49 ff; M Cotta and L Verzichelli, *Il sistema politico italiano* (Bologna, Il Mulino, 2011); J Agnew, '*Genius loci*: the geography of Italian politics' in A Mammone, E Giap Parini, GA Veltri (eds), *The Routledge Handbook of Contemporary Italy: History, Politics, Society* (New York, Routledge, 2014) 157 ff.

[32] On the criteria for the composition of parliamentary collective bodies, see C Fasone,'Le commissioni parlamentari come "categoria a sè stante" di comitati', in *Le autonomie in cammino Scritti dedicati a Gian Candido De Martin* (Padova, CEDAM, 2012), specifically 341 ff.

and the minorities. However, it is in the participation at the European Union that it has found more promising conditions of implementation. Generally speaking, one of the prerequisites for the proactive participation in EU affairs is the involvement of representatives of both the majority supporting the Government and the opposition.[33] European affairs, in fact, do not usually follow the major political cleavage between the majority and the opposition: many studies on the functioning of the Early Warning System have rather proved that a proactive engagement of representative bodies in EU affairs is favoured by high levels of party political contestation over EU integration and consequently by the presence of diverging political positions.[34] When this condition is satisfied, parliamentary assemblies prove themselves capable of developing that role of 'unitary scrutiniser' advocated by some scholars in the transition to a new form of parliamentary democracy in the EU.[35]

With regard to their format, EU parliamentary delegations are usually smaller than international delegations and are formed from time to time. The occasional nature of EU delegations and their derivation from different parliamentary bodies has posed some problems in daily practice: their composition, in fact, needs to be weighed at every interparliamentary meeting, on the basis of the availability of MPs, the issue addressed and the search of a balance among different political positions.

For instance, delegations participating in the Joint Committee Meetings and the Joint Parliamentary Meetings are usually defined at the committee level. If the delegation is composed of two members per Parliament, participation is limited to the Chairs of the two sectoral committees of the Chamber and the Senate; in case of larger delegations, the Chair is usually joined by one other MP of the 'opposite' coalition; if the issue addressed involves the competence of more standing committees, the delegation is formed on the basis of an agreement among committee Chairs so as to grant bipartisan representation. By praxis, such decisions are taken by each House independently; however, they are usually preceded by informal consultations among parliamentary bureaucracies. The only practice derived from international delegations is the one related to the drafting of a report by the leading member of the delegation as a follow-up to interparliamentary meetings: the report must be announced in the first available committee meeting and attached to the official records.

A different arrangement guides the Italian Parliament's participation in interparliamentary organisations involving countries from outside the EU: in such circumstances, the two Houses are not always required to create a unitary parliamentary delegation in order to grant joint representation to the bicameral Parliament as a whole. This requirement is provided in the five aforementioned cases (participation in the interparliamentary organisations by the NATO, the Council of Europe, the Organisation for Economic Development and Co-operation (OECD), the Central Europe Initiative (CEI) and the

[33] See C Sprungk, 'Ever More or Ever Better Scrutiny? Analysing the Conditions of Effective National Parliamentary Involvement in EU Affairs' (2010) 14 *European Integration online Papers*.

[34] K Gattermann and C Hefftler, 'Political Motivation and Institutional Capacity: Assessing National Parliaments' Incentives to Participate in the Early Warning Mechanism' (2013) 15 *OPAL Online Paper Series*; C Neuhold and A Streklov, 'New Opportunity Structures for the "Unusual Suspects"? Implications of the Early Warning System for the Role of National Parliaments within the EU System of Governance' (2012) 4 *OPAL online Paper Series* 13.

[35] C Sprungk, 'A New Type of Representative Democracy? Reconsidering the Role of National Parliaments in the European Union' (2013) 35 *Journal of European Integration* 547.

Union for the Mediterranean), assisted by a permanent unitary parliamentary delegation. By contrast, participation in the other international organisations is addressed by each House mostly on a unicameral basis: there may be cases enabling the participation of only one of the two Houses and cases allowing the representation of each House at two different levels (for example Speaker and Deputy Speaker or Chair of the Committee); when both Houses participate in the meeting, their delegations are usually decided and managed separately. International interparliamentary organisations vary not just in the regional area involved, but also in the nature and frequency of meetings, the targets addressed and their organisational and functional features. Apart from the aforementioned five organisations, the most renowned ones are established by the Inter-Parliamentary Union (IPU), the Euro-Mediterranean Parliamentary Assembly, the Asia-Europe Parliamentary Partnership (ASEP), the Adriatic and Ionian Parliamentary Dimension, the Baltic Sea Parliamentary Assembly, and the Black Sea Economic Cooperation. There are, moreover, interparliamentary organisations specifically shaped for lower or upper Houses, as the Association of the 'Senates of Europe'. In such forums, notwithstanding the variety of formats and purposes,[36] the two Houses are called to interact not just with extra-EU Parliaments but also with the other Parliaments of the EU and in many cases with the EP itself. Due to the lack of an even formal unitary representation for the Italian Parliament, asymmetries in the management of interparliamentary relations between the two Houses are indirectly favoured.

To conclude, an attempt to strengthen the capacity to guide and oversee these processes was pursued by the Chamber of Deputies in the XIV legislative term (2001–2006),[37] when a commission for parliamentary diplomacy was established through a Decision of the Bureau of the Chamber of Deputies dated 6 November 2001. The commission was charged with the task of coordinating the multitude of initiatives affecting the areas of international and European relations and strengthening the connection among the international activities developed by standing committees, parliamentary delegations by international organisations and bilateral groups of friendship.

B. The Participation of National Delegations in the Interparliamentary Conferences

The non-partisan criteria for the formation of EU parliamentary delegations have provided a reference model also for the participation of the Italian Parliament in the permanent interparliamentary Conferences of the European Union. Such Conferences share a dual legal basis, being regulated both at the European level, by the norms shaping the internal organisation and functioning of the body, and at the national level, by the internal rules and practices of the two Houses.

With regard to COSAC, the subject is partially disciplined by article 4.1 of the COSAC RoP, approved on 4 November 2004, entrusting each Parliament to determine the composition of its delegation with a maximum of six members, without mentioning any other

[36] H Posdorf, 'International parliamentary cooperation', Lecture held at the Cambodian National Assembly, at the Senate and at the International Relations Institute (IRIC), 11 February 2008, www.kas.de/kambodscha/en/publications/12975/.

[37] For further details, see http://legislature.camera.it/europ_rap_int/892/901/9597/documentotesto.asp.

criterion. From the establishment of COSAC on 17 November 1989, the Italian Parliament has autonomously determined its delegation according to the unwritten rule enabling each House to be represented by the Chair and the two Deputy Chairs of the EU Policies Committee.

This rule, shared by tacit agreement by both branches of the Italian Parliament, has been honoured throughout the legislative terms and, notwithstanding the transformation of political majorities, it has not undergone any relevant change. Only occasionally and exceptionally, in fact, when the Chairs or Deputy Chairs of the EU Policies Committees were unable to join the Conference meeting, have delegations been formed by other members of the same Committees, selected by the Chairs within the political formation of the replaced component. The aforementioned format does not formally grant a representation both to the majority and to the opposition; this is due both to the criteria applicable to the election of the Chair and Deputy Chairs of the standing committees and to the peculiar features of the Italian party system. In fact, Article 19 RoP Chamber and article 21 RoP Senate, in line with article 72.3 of the Italian Constitution, only require that standing committees are formed as to mirror the proportions among political groups. No specific political commitment is prescribed for the election of the Chair (article 20.2 RoP Chamber; 27.2 RoP Senate), which nonetheless usually represents the majority,[38] and of the Deputy Chairs (article 20.3 RoP Chamber and article 27.3 RoP Senate), which however usually see one of their members chosen from the opposition. Notwithstanding the lack of binding rules, in practice at least one of the three senior positions of Italian delegations to COSAC is reserved for the opposition.

Criteria embraced by the Italian Houses in the composition of COSAC delegations are formally designed to favour a unitary representation of the Parliament as a whole. The Italian Parliament has gained a solid experience on this ground due to its long-established tradition of bicameral committees, composed by representatives of both Houses. Article 26 RoP Senate (and the corresponding practice followed by the Chamber) provides that, in view of the formation of bicameral collegial bodies, the Speaker of the Senate fosters an agreement with the Speaker of the Chamber as to assure, with due respect of the proportional criterion, representation for the highest possible number of parliamentary groups settled in the two branches of Parliament.[39]

In the case of COSAC delegations, however, the dismissal of the proportional representation principle, which in its turn determines the incapability of having all political parties represented, has raised, over time, more than one criticism, especially when the application of the aforementioned criterion has determined the exclusion of significant political formations. In the XIV legislative term, in particular, a debate was started in the EU Policies Committee of the Senate due to the structural exclusion of the Democratic Party (which at that time embodied the largest of the minority groups) from the Senate delegation to COSAC. The exclusion happened because the Deputy Chair of the Committee representing the 'opposition' belonged to another minority party (namely, *Italia dei valori*). The Democratic Party group manifested its disagreement by structurally abandoning the

[38] Exceptions to this trend are highlighted in N Lupo,'A proposito delle presidenze delle commissioni permanenti e, ancor prima, delle loro competenze e delle loro funzioni' (2006) *Forum di Quaderni Costituzionali.*

[39] For further details, see GF Ciaurro, 'Le Commissioni bicamerali nell'esperienza parlamentare italiana' in *Scritti in onore di Egidio Tosato* (Milano, Giuffrè, 1984) 301 ff.

meetings of the EU Policies Committee. In response to this criticism, the Chair of the Committee recalled the origins and the legitimacy itself of the ongoing practice, highlighting that the representation of the Democratic Party was in any case granted by the presence, in the national delegation to COSAC, of one Deputy Chair of the EU Policies Committee of the Chamber of Deputies belonging to this political formation.[40]

The precedent witnesses what difficulties oppose the conception of the Italian delegation not as a joint body, formed by the juxtaposition of unicameral delegations, but rather as a unitary subject, representing the Parliament as a whole.

The experience learned in the participation in COSAC has laid the ground for the formation of parliamentary delegations participating in the Conference on CFSP-CSDP. Generally speaking, the format of the Conference is completely different from COSAC, as it marks a rather unequal balance between the European Parliament—represented by 16 members—and national delegations, composed of only six members. On the national side, moreover, the policy area covered by the Conference falls within the competence of two standing Committees, established in both Houses: the Foreign Affairs and the Defence Committees.

Notwithstanding these original differences, since the first meeting of the Conference, which took place in Pafos on 9–10 September 2012, Italian delegations have been formed on the basis of criteria not too dissimilar from those followed for COSAC.[41] Dismissing the strict proportional rule, representation has been granted alternatively to the Chairs of the Committees for Foreign Affairs and Defence of the two Houses (who can delegate a Deputy Chair); the other four members of the delegation (two for each House) have always been selected among the permanent members of the same committees, as to give voice both to the majority and to minorities. Each House is formally autonomous in the selection of the three members of its pertinence. However, the experience from the last few years confirms that, mainly because of informal contacts among parliamentary administrations, the two Houses have coordinated their choices in the formation of the delegation, rotating Committee Chairs and representatives from different political formations.

Finally, participation of the Italian Parliament in the SECG Conference is shaped by the same requirement of bipartisan representation (although with no strict dependence on the proportional rule) that characterises the formation of delegations involved in COSAC or in the CFSP-CSDP Conference. Just like the latter, the SECG Conference mainly covers in its policy area the competence of two standing committees settled in both Houses: the Budget and the Finance Committees. As a consequence, since the first meeting in Vilnius on 16–17 October 2013, the formation of Italian delegations has been balanced on three factors: political affiliation, House of pertinence, and Committee membership.

Unlike COSAC and the Conference on CFSP-CSDP, however, the SECG Conference does not have a fixed format for national delegations set in the Rules of Procedure. This feature contributes to explain the intense variation in the number and selection of Italian MPs joining the Conference, swinging from the standard composition of the six members attending

[40] Committee for EU policies of the Italian Senate of the Republic, 21 July 2009 and 23 September 2009.

[41] See, among others, Committee for defence of the Italian Senate of the Republic, 21 December 2012, Allegato 2 'Sulla missione svolta dal 9 all'11 settembre 2012 a Cipro per la partecipazione alla Conferenza per il controllo parlamentare sulla politica estera e di sicurezza comune'.

the first meeting in Vilnius in October 2013[42] to the expanded delegation of 31 MPs joining the Conference of Rome held in September 2014 during the Italian Semester.[43] Some atypical precedents have occurred, with two senators attending the Brussels Conference organised during the European Parliamentary Week in February 2015,[44] whereas at the meeting of the Conference held in Luxembourg on 9–10 November 2015 the Italian Parliament was represented by one single member of the Budget Committee of the Chamber of Deputies,[45] as the Senate was meanwhile involved in the national budget session. The meeting held in Bratislava on 16–18 October 2016 saw for the first time the involvement of MPs selected from relevant committees other than the Budget and Finance Committees (namely, the Public and Private Sector Employment Committee of the Chamber and the Employment and Social Affairs Committee of the Senate). This choice, followed also by other national Parliaments, was consistent with the topics addressed in the Conference (involving the 'social dimension of the EMU') and with the invited speakers (including the European Commissioner for Employment, Social Affairs, Skills and Labour Mobility, Marianne Thyssen).

V. Other Divergences in the Italian Houses' 'Macro' Approach to Interparliamentary Cooperation in the EU

Over the last few years, the Italian Houses have had rather diverging visions of interparliamentary relations' nature, scope, purpose and way of functioning.

Some differences in the 'macro' approach to interparliamentary cooperation have specifically come to light in the establishment of the SECG Conference. The creation of the Conference was preceded by the organisation, in Luxembourg, of an atypical preparatory meeting, promoted by the Luxembourgish Parliament and involving only the founding Member States of the European Communities. The Italian Senate, but not the Chamber, joined the event, represented by one of its Deputy Speakers. From the very beginning, the Senate has approached the Conference as an opportunity for strengthening democratic oversight in the European economic governance.[46] By contrast, the abstention of the Italian Chamber confirms its scepticism about the role of the Conference, perceived as a mere

[42] Chamber of deputies, 114 *Bollettino delle Giunte e delle Commissioni parlamentari*, 30 October 2013, 84—Report to the Budget Committee on the participation at the first interparliamentary Conference on the economic and financial governance held in Vilnius, 16–17 October 2013.

[43] The Conference was held on 29–30 September 2014 (see http://ue2014.parlamento.it/34?appuntamento=25). The Italian delegation covered a large part of the Budget and Finance Committees of the two Houses.

[44] See the meeting held in Brussels on 3–4 February 2015 www.epgencms.europarl.europa.eu/cmsdata/upload/f72a6db2-29fe-4363-9a90-52f68001ffd5/FINAL%20EPW%20meeting%20-%203%20and%204%20February%202015%20-%20List%20of%20participants.pdf.

[45] www.eu2015parl.lu/Uploads/Documents/Doc/121_2_liste%20des%20participants_provisoire_05.11.2015.pdf.

[46] See the Press Declaration by Vannino Chiti, Deputy Chair of the Senate, released on the 11 January 2013 after the participation at the Luxembourg meeting (www.senato.it/leg16/2991?comunicato_giorno_mese_anno=11-01-2013).

opportunity for dialogue, sharing of opinions and exchange of best practices, thus excluding the entrustment of reinforced oversight powers in the economic and financial fields.[47]

Such divergences follow the more general cleavage dividing the supporters of this form of interparliamentary cooperation (the French Parliament, in first instance, followed by a number of national Parliaments) and its opponents or sceptics (such as the European Parliament). This cleavage has dominated the drafting of the Conference's Rules of Procedure, notably those provisions related to the title and scope of the Conference, the *quorum* (unanimity versus majority) for the adoption of non-binding conclusions, and the definition of the agenda.

Bicameral divergences on these organisational aspects needed to be reconciled during the Italian semester of the rotating presidency of the Council, when the Italian Parliament was called to play the role of mediator in the evaluation of amendments to the draft Rules of Procedure and adoption of a final text. This work was continued until the Speakers' Conference held in Rome on 20–21 April 2015 discussed and agreed on principles regarding the Rules of Procedure of the Conference, leaving for the following Conference under the Luxembourgish Presidency the formal adoption of the act. The Draft Conclusions and the final Presidency Conclusions of the Rome Speakers' Conference[48] mirror the different positions of the two Houses with regard to the procedure for the approval of the Conference's RoP: whereas the Chamber was favourable to leaving it up to the Speakers' Conference, the Senate defended the regulatory autonomy of the SECG Conference.

More generally speaking, the Italian semester of presidency confirmed relevant differences in the two Houses' macro attitude towards interparliamentary cooperation. The comparison of the agenda of the Conferences alternatively organised by the Chamber and by the Senate confirms such asymmetries. On the one hand, the agenda of the SECG Conference, whose secretariat belonged to the Chamber, featured the dominant participation of academics and experts rather than institutional representatives; this option represented a deliberate choice of the Chamber of Deputies, to be interpreted as an opportunity for discussing issues addressed on more concrete and informed bases.[49] On the other hand, the Conference on CSFP-CSDP, organised under the Secretariat of the Senate, focused its agenda on 'questions and answers' with the newly elected EU High Representative for Foreign Affairs, Federica Mogherini, thus promoting a conception of interparliamentary cooperation for the exercise effective parliamentary oversight.

The different attitudes of the two Italian Houses are clearly highlighted by another sphere of action: namely, the initiative labelled as 'Green Card' promoted by the UK House of Lords' Chair of the Committee for European Affairs, Lord Boswell, through a letter addressed to the Chairs of the corresponding Committees of the national parliaments of the EU and conveyed in the COSAC meeting of Riga on 1–2 June 2015.[50] The purpose was

[47] See Chamber of deputies, *Bollettino delle Giunte e delle Commissioni parlamentari*, no 114 of the 30 October 2013, cit, 84.

[48] Section 'Discussion and approval of principles on the Rules of Procedure of the Conference under Article 13 of the Treaty on Stability, Coordination and Governance in the Economic and Monetary Union', point 2, available in www.ipex.eu/IPEXL-WEB/euspeakers/getspeakers.do?id=082dbcc54a393144014a4d75e8690dec.

[49] Chamber of deputies, *Cifre e fatti. L'attività della Camera dei deputati nei primi 21 mesi di Legislatura* (Roma, 2014) 110.

[50] See the Chapter on the 'Green Card procedure' in the 23rd Bi-Annual COSAC Report 'Development in the European Union. Procedures and practices relevant to parliamentary scrutiny', released on 6 May 2015 and presented at the RIGA meeting, available www.parleu2015.lv/files/cosac_plenary/en-23-bi-annual-report-final-2.pdf.

to introduce a new procedure to enable a certain number of national Parliaments to solicit the European Commission to submit a legislative bill or another type of act if needed, also with the purpose of modifying in-force legislation. The initiative by Lord Boswell concerned specifically food waste reduction as one of the measures of the Circular Economy package.[51]

The Italian Houses adopted two opposite reactions to the proposal. The Senate's EU Policies Committee discussed the issue in its meeting of 6 May 2015, unanimously approving the proposal of the Chair to adhere to the initiative.[52] Discussions in support of the decision highlighted the potential contribution of the green card to the democratisation of the EU: by fully respecting the EU institutional architecture, the new mechanism is expected to support a more proactive involvement of national Parliaments in the European decision-making.

By contrast, the Chamber of Deputies, in the meeting of the EU Policies Committee of 29 July 2015, agreed not to adhere to the initiative. Arguments in support of the decision, presented by the Chair of the Committee,[53] emphasised that the tool would entitle a minority of national Parliaments with a power of initiative not too dissimilar from the one entrusted to the EP; the procedure, moreover, was perceived as a factor of further complexity in the European architecture; finally, it was argued that the decision to sponsor the initiative should have been taken by the Speakers' Conference rather than by COSAC.

Subsequent developments of the initiative at the European level seem to have rejected the objections raised, among others, by the Italian Chamber. Sixteen additional Chairpersons of relevant committees belonging to different national Parliaments of the EU supported the proposal. The Commission itself, in its reply to the initiative dated 17 November 2015, manifested its appreciation for the participatory mechanism. After such improvements, the procedure was started a second time by the Chair of the Committee for European Affairs of the French Assemblée Nationale to urge the provision of an initiative on the corporate social responsibility. The Senate's EU Policies Committee confirmed its adherence to the initiative,[54] whereas the Chamber, consistent with its original criticism, did not even take the proposal into consideration.

Finally, other challenges to the symmetrical bicameral rationale of the Italian Parliament come from interparliamentary relations involving the Speakers of the two Houses. In September 2015, the Speaker of the Chamber of Deputies, Laura Boldrini, launched the Declaration 'Greater European Integration: The Way Forward' that, after being signed by the Speakers of the German Bundestag, the French Assemblée Nationale and the Luxembourgish Chamber of Deputies, was presented in December 2015 at the European Parliament and the European Commission. Before being formally presented at the Speakers' Conference held in Luxembourg in May 2016, the Declaration also collected upper Houses'

[51] N Lupo, 'L'iniziativa legislativa nella forma di governo dell'Unione europea ed il ruolo dei Parlamenti nazionali' in *Il Filangieri. Quaderno 2014—Unione europea e principi democratici* (Napoli, Jovene, 2015) 17 ff; C Fasone and D Fromage, 'From Veto Players to "Agenda-setters"? National Parliaments and the EU Commission's Agenda-setting' in C Fasone, D Fromage and Z Lefkofridi (eds), 'Parliaments and Parliamentary Elections in Europe' (2015) 18 *EUI RSCAS Working paper*.

[52] EU Policies Committee, 6 May 2015, 'Communication of the Chair on the "Green card" of national parliaments related to food waste'.

[53] Chamber of deputies, 492 *Bollettino delle Giunte e delle Commissioni parlamentari*, 29 July 2015, 'Sulla riunione dei Presidenti COSAC svolta a Lussemburgo il 12 e 13 luglio 2015', 201 ff.

[54] EU Policies Committee, 27 January 2016 and 10 February 2016.

subscriptions. In the context of the Luxembourg Conference, the Rome Declaration represented a divisive issue for national Parliaments, not just on the merits of the proposal but rather also on the possibility itself to have such an act debated in the Conference and attached to the Speakers' Conclusions. As a compromise, the Declaration was mentioned in the Conclusions but not formally enclosed with the document. In this framework, the formal exclusion of the Italian Senate from the initiative—originally justified by the cleavage between lower and upper Houses—has become a further sign of the two Houses' divergent attitudes on the management of EU interparliamentary relations.

VI. Conclusions. The 'Europeanisation' of the Italian Symmetrical Bicameralism as a Leading Challenge for the Participation in Interparliamentary Relations

The response of the Italian Parliament to latest trends of interparliamentary cooperation in the EU can be assessed in terms of involuntary and indirect adaptations, partially driven by the transformations of the EU legal and political framework and partially linked to the general reconsideration of EU affairs scrutiny promoted at national level by the entry into force of the Treaty of Lisbon.

In the last few years, the Italian Houses have not adopted a formal revision of the internal rules and procedures regulating their participation in EU affairs; nor have they promoted the consolidation of bicameral synergies in practice to support their involvement in interparliamentary relations.

The lack of a consistent legal discipline concerning all the 'national' aspects of this dimension (namely, the formation of national delegations, the determination of the House's position with regard to interparliamentary decisions, and the follow-up of such acts) contributes to explain why participation in interparliamentary cooperation is managed in daily practice mostly based on general guidelines and looking at precedents, which however are never considered as binding.

Existing gaps in the legal discipline have been filled in according to a case-by-case approach, which has worsened the two Houses' abilities to promote structural, coordinated responses and inhibited the full exploitation of this dimension's potential. The result is the spread of manifest asymmetries that tend to appear not just in the diversification of the guidelines and practices, but eventually also in the 'macro' vision shaping the participation of each House in interparliamentary relations.

In the daily practice, the Italian Parliament's involvement in EU interparliamentary relations has had only sporadic and unsystematic forms of coordination between the two Houses. In the formation of delegations, for instance, each House is formally autonomous in the choice of MPs, the selection being adopted through a political unicameral decision usually entitled to the Chairs of relevant committees. Attempts to promote a unitary vision of the delegation, as a body whose political composition should necessarily be framed in a bicameral joint perspective, are ordinarily carried out mostly by the initiative of the two parliamentary administrations in their preparatory activities. However, these efforts function entirely on a voluntary basis and have as such experienced divergences on more than one occasion. Persistent difficulties seem to inhibit the conception of Italian parliamentary delegations as unitary subjects, representing the Parliament as a whole, rather than as joint bodies, formed by the juxtaposition of unicameral delegations.

Aside from these 'micro' differences, it is in the concept itself of interparliamentary cooperation that 'macro' divergences among the two Houses have come to light. The Chamber of Deputies has come to support the idea that relations among national Parliaments are meant to favour the exchange of best practices and encourage a confrontation on issues of common interest, with however no interference with the activities and role of the European Parliament. By contrast, the Senate has sponsored a rather different approach focused on the potential of interparliamentary cooperation as a means for strengthening democratic oversight by national Parliaments of the EU.

Such diverging attitudes towards the aim, scope and mission of interparliamentary relations align with two competing visions of parliamentary scrutiny in the EU:[55] respectively, the centralised scrutiny (advocated by the EP in particular, but supported also by some national Parliaments, among which is the Italian Chamber), assuming that democratic accountability of the EU executive is assured by the European Parliament alone, and the joint scrutiny (the position of those national Parliaments/Houses—such as the Italian Senate—more openly concerned with the protection of their sovereignty), which encourages the intervention of Parliaments, at all territorial levels, in order to hold the fragmented executive of the EU accountable.[56]

Traces of such visions can be detected in the diverging positions of the two Houses with regard to the place, functioning and purpose of interparliamentary meetings. It is however in the conceptualisation and regulation of the newly established Conferences, and in particular of the SECG Conference, that these asymmetries have become increasingly clear.

A different approach to the management of interparliamentary cooperation would have probably been started in the two Houses if the referendum on the constitutional revision of the Italian symmetrical bicameralism had resulted in a positive outcome.[57] Paradoxically, an asymmetrical bicameralism—featuring a strong limitation of the powers of the Senate vis-à-vis the Chamber of Deputies—could have indirectly favoured the research into symmetrical approaches to the management of EU relations.

The failure of the constitutional revision does not however prevent the Italian Parliament from promoting reforms aiming at revising its implication in the EU interparliamentary relations, acting on the internal Rules of Procedures and praxis. The unequal responses of the Italian Houses to the management of EU interparliamentary relations seem to endanger the unitary representation of the Italian Parliament vis-a-vis the other Parliaments of the EU. A potential solution would consequently lie in a further Europeanisation of the Italian legislature: to 'Europeanise' themselves, the two Houses should learn how to interact with a complex institutional framework which requires timely, consistent and informed

[55] On the competing visions affecting the role of Parliaments in the EU, see N Lupo,'Parlamento europeo e parlamenti nazionali nella Costituzione "composita" nell'Ue: le diverse letture possibili' (2014) 3 *Rivista AIC*.

[56] See Cooper, above n 27.

[57] On the 2016 constitutional revision of the Italian symmetrical bicameralism providing a differentiation of the powers of the two Houses also in the participation in EU affairs, see the chapter by Gianniti, in this volume.

decisions.[58] This process ought to be implemented through the full adaptation of their internal rules and practices to the requirements deriving from the involvement in the EU decision-making and the management of EU affairs.

Existing divergences are rooted in diverging visions of the role of national assemblies in the EU framework. As a consequence, the advocated Europeanisation of the two Houses should be pursued at two levels: on the empirical level, by promoting a greater coordination of the political and administrative activities; (first and foremost) on the institutional 'macro' level, by reconsidering in a unitary institutional perspective those issues related to the scope and purposes of interparliamentary relations. What is required, in other terms, is a rethinking of the capacity of the two Houses to fully exploit their hard and soft powers in the management of EU affairs, thus encouraging a proactive role of the Italian Parliament in coping with the difficulties 'of the "nascent" European demos to hold governments to account by means of "classical" assembly controls'.[59]

[58] N Lupo,'I Parlamenti nazionali nell'Unione europea e il principio di sussidiarietà: qualche suggestione per la Camera dei deputati' (2014) *Amministrazione in cammino*.

[59] DN Chryssochoou and S Stavridis and MJ Tsinisizelis, 'European Democracy, Parliamentary Decline and the "Democratic Deficit" of the European Union' (1998) 4 *The Journal of Legislative Studies* 117.

12

Procedures vis-à-vis the Court of Justice of the European Union: Ex Post Subsidiarity Scrutiny

WERNER VANDENBRUWAENE

I. Introduction

Because of its intimate connection to democratic theories,[1] subsidiarity has been hailed as a panacea for solving the democratic tension within the heart of the EU.[2] By expressing a preference for Member State action, so the dominant narrative goes, subsidiarity as it was conceived in the Maastricht Treaty in 1992 would protect a maximum scope of national discretion, allowing Europe to evolve, built on the shielded premise of nation states and their democratic space. At the same time, subsidiarity would allow—indeed, call for—EU action where and when a substantial additional benefit could be demonstrated.

The first decade of the legal conception of the subsidiarity clause governing the exercise of shared powers at EU level proved rather unsatisfactory. The case law of the Court of Justice was simultaneously lacking in quantity, and in quality: a mere reference to the added value of EU action was deemed sufficient to ensure compliance.[3] The rise to prominence

[1] See eg P Craig, 'Subsidiarity: a Legal and Political Analysis' (2012) *Journal of Common Market Studies* 73; A Gamper, 'Subsidiarity und Kompetenztheorie' in A Gamper and P Bussjäger (eds), *Subsidiarität anwenden* (Fribourg, Institut fur foderalismus, 2006) 109; A Follesdal, 'The Principle of Subsidiarity as a Constitutional Principle in International Law' (2013) 2 *Global Constitutionalism* 37–38; I Feichtner, 'Subsidiarity' in the *Max Planck Encyclopedia of Public International Law* (Oxford, Oxford University Press, 2007) 1.

[2] N Emiliou, 'Subsidiarity: Panacea or Fig Leaf?' in D O'Keeffe and P Towney (eds), *Legal Issues of the Maastricht Treaty* (London, Chancery Law, 1994) 78.

[3] Case 233/94 *Germany v Parliament and Council* [ECLI:EU:1997:231], paras 26–28.

of the national Parliaments culminating in the Lisbon reforms proved a valuable opportunity to connect the debate on the double legitimacy of the EU under article 12 Treaty on European Union (TEU),[4] the disconnect between the EU elite and the national political fora, and the weak enforcement of a clause that in theory should convey significant benefits to the Member States in terms of shielding their autonomy.

This chapter will analyse the different enforcement mechanisms from the vantage point of the Italian Parliament, focusing in particular on the hypothetical mutual reinforcement between the Reasoned Opinions (RO), emanating from the national Parliaments in the course of the Early Warning System, and an ex post judicial scrutiny of subsidiarity before the Court of Justice.

II. Subsidiarity and Article 5(3) TEU

A. Scope and Significance

Article 5(3) TEU requires the EU legislator to demonstrate the added value of legislative action at EU level, and the inability of action at the level of the Member States to achieve the objective. The question of subsidiarity is thus addressed from two different angles.[5] As the embodiment of a particular rule or instance of the broader legal principle of subsidiarity, Article 5(3) TEU limits its application in two ways: first it limits the scope of applicability of subsidiarity to the shared competences, and second, it requires compliance with two determinants; ie the insufficiency of Member State action (negative criterion), and the added value of EU action (positive criterion).

In the case of shared competences, Article 5(3) puts forward two tests that have to be met in order to ensure compliance with the principle of subsidiarity. The Treaty of Lisbon removed any doubts as to the twofold character of the test by changing 'and can therefore' (Maastricht version) into 'but can rather'.[6] Nevertheless, both criteria are not easily separated. They can be read as a trade-off between the rationales of efficiency and democratic legitimacy (presupposed to be higher in the national Member States).[7] Article 5(3) TEU aims to augment the legitimacy of EU legislative action, specifically by focusing on three dimensions of legitimacy: input-, output-, and vertical legitimacy.[8]

[4] eg JC Piris, *The Lisbon Treaty* (Cambridge, Cambridge Univeristy Press, 2010) 122–30; N Lupo, 'National and Regional Parliaments in the EU decision-making process, after the Treaty of Lisbon and the Euro-crisis' (2013) 5(2) *Perspectives on Federalism* 1–28.

[5] Case 547/14, *Philip Morris Brands SARL* [ECLI:EU:2015:853], Opinion of AG Kokott, para 275.

[6] A Estella, *The EU Principle of Subsidiarity and its Critique* (Oxford, Oxford University Press, 2002) 94.

[7] 'All other things being equal, democracy at the local level, especially when coupled with citizen mobility, is more representative of citizens' interests, allows for a greater satisfaction of diverse preferences, and is therefore more legitimate than democracy at a more distant level of governance.' D Halberstam, 'Comparative Federalism and the Role of the Judiciary' in K Whittington, R Keleman and G Caldeira (eds), *The Oxford Handbook of Law and Politics* (Oxford, Oxford University Press, 2008) 152.

[8] On the notion of legitimacy in a context of multilevel governance, see see eg P Craig, 'Integration, Democracy, and Legitimacy' in P Craig and G de Burca (eds), *The Evolution of EU Law* 2nd edn (Oxford, Oxford University Press, 2011) 13–40; P Popelier, 'Governance and Better Regulation: Dealing with the Legitimacy Paradox' (2011)

Subsidiarity thus functions as a two-faced principle: it simultaneously constrains and legitimises EU action.[9]

B. Venues for Enforcement

In order to render Article 5(3) TEU operative, several steps were taken, mostly to strengthen the procedural, ex ante, enforcement of subsidiarity. This section will briefly summarise the three different venues for enforcement, discerning the ex ante legislative phase and the ex post judicial scrutiny. In the ex ante phase, two different procedures draw attention. First, subsidiarity is included as a criterion in the Better Regulation agenda, and also functions according to Protocol 2 in the Early Warning System involving national Parliaments.

i. *Ex ante legislative preparation*

The European Commission is charged with the preparation of a legislative act. Protocol No 2 ensures that subsidiarity is taken into account at this preparatory stage. This is done, in particular, through the obligation that the Commission should consult widely in the legislative procedure, including stakeholders concerned with subsidiarity, and including regional and local governments.[10] Influenced by these consultations, the Commission following its monopoly of legislative initiative can present a draft legislative act to the Parliament and the Council. The justification requirement forces the Commission to add 'a detailed statement making it possible to appraise compliance with the principles of subsidiarity and proportionality'.[11] Article 5 of the Protocol goes on to clarify the content of this detailed statement:

> This statement should contain some assessment of the proposal's financial impact and, in the case of a directive, of its implications for the rules to be put in place by Member States, including, where necessary, the regional legislation. The reasons for concluding that a Union objective can be better achieved at Union level shall be substantiated by qualitative and, wherever possible, quantitative indicators. Draft legislative acts shall take account of the need for any burden, whether financial or administrative, falling upon the Union, national governments, regional or local authorities, economic operators and citizens, to be minimized and commensurate with the objective to be achieved.

Empty or standard formulae merely asserting compliance cannot suffice. Advocate-General Kokott opined that mere 'boilerplate language' may run counter to the obligation under Article 291 Treaty on the Functioning of the European Union (TFEU) to state reasons. However, the legislative fact-finding attesting to the two tests under Article 5(3) TEU should be derived from the whole of the legislation, ie including recitals and preparatory documents.[12]

17 *European Public Law* 555–69; W Vandenbruwaene, 'Multilevel Governance through a Constitutional Prism' (2014) 2 *Maastricht Journal of European and Comparative Law* 229–42.

[9] On this 'positive' and 'negative' ethos of subsidiarity, see for instance V Constantinesco, 'Who's Afraid of Subsidiarity' (1991) 11 *Yearbook of European Law* 33–55.

[10] Art 2 Protocol No 2.

[11] Art 5 Protocol No 2.

[12] Case 547/14, *Philip Morris*, above n 5, Opinion of AG Kokott, paras 286–96.

When drafting a proposal, the Commission follows a specific policy development process. This process consists in planning, initiating, and preparing a proposal. Subsidiarity features in each of these phases, most prominently in the preparation and the drafting of the proposal. This is demonstrated by Table 1.[13]

Table 1

Preparation		
	Roadmaps	Perform an 'early warning' function and contain a preliminary subsidiarity assessment
	Stakeholder consultations	Ensure a dialogue
	External studies	Deliver Additional data and evidence
	Impact assessments	Ensure a profound evidence-based subsidiarity argumentation
Legislative proposal		
	Explanatory memorandum	Includes a subsidiarity statement
	Recitals of the proposal	Serves to recall reasoning on subsidiarity

In summary, there are four key elements of the effective control of subsidiarity: first, checks are applied from early stages of policy development. Second, compliance with subsidiarity is verified in terms of necessity and added value of EU action. Third, the analysis is proportionate in scope and depth, depending on the nature of the initiative. Fourth, at different stages, transparency and an enhanced dialogue are important principles.

The scrutiny for compliance with subsidiarity has to take place in the Impact Assessment (IA), according to the Guidelines.[14] Five questions, reiterating the determinants on subsidiarity issued by the Edinburgh Council, address subsidiarity in particular:

1. Does the issue being addressed have transnational aspects which cannot be dealt with satisfactorily by action by Member States? (eg reduction of carbon dioxide emissions in the atmosphere)
2. Would actions by Member States alone, or the lack of Community action, conflict with the requirements of the Treaty? (eg discriminatory treatment of a stakeholder group)
3. Would actions by Member States alone, or the lack of Community action, significantly damage the interests of Member States? (eg action restricting the free circulation of goods)
4. Would action at Community level produce clear benefits compared with action at the level of Member States by reason of its scale?
5. Would action at Community level produce clear benefits compared with action at the level of Member States by reason of its effectiveness?

[13] B Schima, 'Verifying compliance with the principle of subsidiarity in the European Commission' presentation at ERA seminar, Trier, May 2012.

[14] European Commission, *Impact Assessment Guidelines* SEC(2009)92 at 22; European Commission, *Better Regulation Guidelines*, COM(2015) 215 at 20–21.

ii. Parliamentary Involvement

The Treaty of Lisbon heralded a shift in gears towards the enforcement of subsidiarity as laid down in article 5(3) TEU and Protocol No 2. Whereas the Amsterdam version consolidated weak attempts at clarifying the operation of article 5(3) through guidelines and several procedural requirements, the Lisbon version strengthened the implementation and monitoring of the principle of subsidiarity. The primary innovation consists in the Early Warning System as an instrument of ex ante political monitoring. This system is essentially a dialogical process, where the national Parliaments (NP) are attributed the role of guardians of the principle of subsidiarity.[15] Protocol No 2 installs four main mechanisms, laying down several procedural requirements to strengthen the implementation of subsidiarity in the legislative phase. All the EU institutions are obligated to 'ensure constant respect for the principle of subsidiarity'. Articles 6 and 7 of the Protocol set up an Early Warning System (EWS) to enable NPs to monitor the compliance with subsidiarity, and signal an eventual breach through the yellow and orange card procedures of article 7.

The Protocol furthermore complements the role of the NP in this EWS with standing rights to bring an action before the Court of Justice in annulment of a legislative act for breach of article 5(3). Additionally, it grants standing as a privileged applicant to the Committee of the Regions (CoR).

iii. Judicial scrutiny

Determining the proper judicial interpretation of subsidiarity is a daunting task. In general, the Court of Justice of the European Union (CJEU) does not employ an historical approach to the interpretation of EU law, since the constitutional and legislative deliberations are (were) often complex and—at best—incompletely published. Moreover, one fails to derive a clear and unequivocal meaning of subsidiarity based on the intent of the Treatymaker in 1992, or based on the wording in the Maastricht Treaty.[16] The judicial pendant finds itself between Scylla and Charybdis, faring between substantive legislative action, and weak procedural review. Under the model of functional political questions,[17] the problem resides with the socio-economic complexity of the assessment of subsidiarity. As it surfaces from the case-law, the main objection limiting the intensity of the judicial scrutiny has to do with the underlying questions of efficiency, added value and democratic legitimacy. The Court necessarily limits its review of compliance with subsidiarity to 'what it can usefully scrutinize'.[18] Confronted with functional political questions, the CJEU conducts a

[15] P Kiiver, *The Early Warning System for the Principle of Subsidiarity* (London, Routledge, 2012); D Fromage, *Les Parlements dans l'Union Européenne après le Traité de Lisbonne - La Participation des Parlements allemands, britanniques, espagnols, français et italiens* (Paris, Harmattan, 2015); A Jonsson and M Goldin (eds), *National and Regional Parliaments in the EU-legislative Procedure post-Lisbon: The Impact of the Early Warning Mechanism* (Oxford, Hart, 2016).

[16] K Van Keersbergen and B Verbeek, 'The Never-ending Story: How the Adoption of the Subsidiarity Principle Contributed to Old and New Conflicts in the EU' in J Loisen and F Deville (eds), *Subsidiarity and Multilevel Governance* (Brussels, KVAB, 2012) 37–38 (discerning four channels that lead up to the inclusion at the political level of subsidiarity in 1992).

[17] I have developed this analysis of subsidiarity as a political question at length in 'Multitiered Political Questions: The CJEU's Mandate in Enforcing Subsidiarity' (2012) 5 *Legisprudence* 321–45.

[18] 'Die richterliche Subsidiaritätskontrolle hat sich also auf das zu konzentrieren, was der Gemeinschaftsrichter in diesem Rahmen sinnvoller Weise überprüfen kann' T von Danwitz, 'Subsidiaritätskontrolle in der Europäischen

procedural review, ie orients itself towards reviewing procedural requirements.[19] The scope of this review extends over the compliance with procedural rules, the accurate statement of facts, and determining if a manifest error of appraisal or a misuse of powers occurred. The appraisal of the facts has to be careful and impartial. Moreover, all the relevant facts of the individual case have to support the conclusions. These requisites offer a starting template for a subsidiarity review.

The judicial scrutiny of compliance with subsidiarity is rather formal, displaying a large discretion towards the findings of the legislator on the two limbs of article 5(3): added value of EU action and Member State insufficiency. It is clear from the case law that the Court is not eager, nor particularly well equipped to strike down legislation for an infringement of subsidiarity.[20] The final outcome is, however, only contingent upon the legal inquiry. The poignant question concerns the intensity and structure of the review. How does the Court deal with the scope of legislative discretion, and more importantly, what arguments are accepted hereto? If subsidiarity is by its nature a political principle, then judicial deference is justified by the nature of the principle, and the political question is thus grounded by a textual argument. If *a contrario*, subsidiarity is a legal norm, but composed of socio-economic indicators that are hard to assess, judicial deference then comes into play as a second-order observation, which may be remedied. Indeed, Fritzsche observes that with respect to the justification of the scope of discretion granted, 'the "nature" of the question to be decided seems to serve as self-explanatory justifications for limited judicial review without addressing why and how the essentialist observation is connected to the courts' ability or authorization by Treaty to exercise their review powers.'[21] There is no textual basis to defer judgment on subsidiarity to the legislator in its entirety, well on the contrary, article 8 of the Protocol, confirming the jurisdiction of the Court, is merely a declarative confirmation of article 263 TFEU.[22]

In a setting of legislative discretion, the reviewing court applies a margin of appreciation. This deference to the legislature can be justified under different aspects of the political question doctrine. A political question in the context of judicial review is a question excluded from judicial determination, by express or implied constitutional principle, and therefore better left to be resolved by other—political—organs of government.[23] Generally, three possible approaches to this doctrine are employed: the classical, functional and prudential models. Concisely summarised, the first upholds political questions by express textual assignment to the political branch, while the functional model is based on considerations of judicial methodology, and the third on the deference due to branches of government for reasons of judicial self-restraint.

Union' in KP Dolde et al (eds), *Verfassung—Umwelt—Wirtschaft, Festschrift Dieter Sellner* (Munich, CH Beck, 2010) 39.

[19] See below, s III.

[20] W Vandenbruwaene, 'What Scope for Subnational Autonomy: the Issue of the Legal Enforcement of the Principle of Subsidiarity' (2014) 2 *Perspectives on Federalism* 55–58.

[21] A Fritzsche, 'Discretion, Scope of Judicial Review and Institutional Balance in European Law' (2010) 47(2) *Common Market Law Review* 380.

[22] The innovation of Art 8 Protocol No 2 is to confer standing upon national Parliaments and the Committee of the Regions.

[23] Vandenbruwaene, above n 17, 321–45.

Thus the functional argument of the difficulty of legally capturing elements of socio-economic complexity is the starting point.[24] This, however, needs to be nuanced, since 'the Court is exclusively a legal forum'.[25] A lack of legal basis for the consideration of norms or effects produces the logical result of an operatively closed system: '[T]he appraisal of any disadvantages of a possible, but not inevitable, increase in the rate of levy is a political and not a legal matter.'[26]

The question on the review of the socio-economic determinants underlying Article 5(3) TEU needs a reformulation: how can the judiciary be handed instruments that can guide the Court's interpretation of these questions? A margin of legislative discretion implies a demarcation, and traditionally this is heralded by the phrase 'manifest error'. In other words, the CJEU as a reviewing court requires decision-makers, including the legislator, to identify, consider and balance costs against benefits.[27] Where this is not sufficiently established, the CJEU can void the act or decision. However, it is not appropriate for the Court to venture upon the fact finding and weighing itself.

The crux of the matter, explaining the reticence of the CJEU when assessing subsidiarity, is thus the problem of judicially manageable standards. Confronted with a lack of these standards, the Court has allowed the legislator in the past a large margin of discretion, and in essence conducted a formal and procedural review, invariably (thus far) upholding the legislator's justifications.

The older case law offers little clues, and indeed, reveals a certain uneasiness on the part of the Court.[28] De Burca convincingly argues that the review for compliance with Article 5(3) in these cases boils down to a mere justification requirement without any scrutiny on the part of the Court.[29]

More recent cases, *Vodafone*[30] and *Luxembourg v Parliament and Council*,[31] show a substantial improvement qua legal reasoning on the subsidiarity review. The essence of the Court's reasoning goes to the justification offered by the Legislator in order to demonstrate the added value of EU action and the insufficiency of action at Member State level.[32] This justification requirement is an aspect of the judicial standard of evidence-based lawmaking, thus furthering the notion of procedural rationality.[33]

[24] J Bast and A von Bogdandy, 'Art 5 EUV' in E Grabitz, M Hilf, M Nettesheim (eds), *Das Recht der Europaïschen Union: Kommentar* (Munich, Beck, 2010) 20; G Bermann, 'Taking Subsidiarity Seriously' (1994) 94 *Columbia Law Review* 391.

[25] D Valentine, *The Court of Justice of the European Communities* (London, Stevens & Sons, 1961) 388.

[26] CJEU, Opinion 01/60 of 4 March 1960 on the Procedure for the amendment of the Treaty pursuant to the third and fourth paras of Art 95 of the ECSC Treaty, ECR (spec ed) 69.

[27] D Partan, 'The Justiciability of Subsidiarity' in C Rhodes and S Mazey (eds), *The State of the Union* vol 3 (London, Longman, 1995) 70.

[28] See CJEU Cases 415/93 *Bosman* [1995] ECR I-5040; Case 84/94 *UK v Council* [1996] ECR I-5793; Case 233/94 *Germany v Parliament and Council* [1997] ECR I-2441; Case 377/98 *Netherlands v Parliament and Council* [2001] ECR I-7149.

[29] G De Burca, 'The Principle of Subsidiarity and the Court of Justice as Institutional Actor' (1998) *Journal of Common Market Studies* 223–26.

[30] CJEU Case 58/08 *Vodafone* [ECLI:EU:C:2010:321].

[31] CJEU Case 176/09 *Luxembourg v Parliament and Council* [ECLI:EU:C:2011:290].

[32] Elsewhere, I have written at length about both cases, see for instance W Vandenbruwaene, 'The Ambivalent Methods of Subsidiarity Review' in M Cartabia, N Lupo and A Simoncini (eds), *Democracy and Subsidiarity in the EU* (Bologna, il Mulino, 2013) 371–98.

[33] See for this term P Popelier and C Van de Heyning, 'Procedural Rationality: Giving Teeth to the Proportionality Analysis' (2013) 9 *European Constitutional Law Review* 230–62.

In a recent case, on the prohibition of menthol tobacco, the CJEU for the first time indicated directly that the Impact Assessment (IA) contains valuable information with respect to the determinants comprised by article 5(3).[34] Indeed, in the *Vodafone* case, the reference to the IA was only indirect,[35] because the Court invoked in its reasoning recital 14 of the Regulation, which in turn referred to the IA. The Opinions of the AG in both *Vodafone* and *Luxembourg v Council* did substantially discuss the IA, and now the Court has taken up this call.[36]

With regards to marginal scrutiny of legislative discretion, it is interesting to note that in the recent case *Estonia v Parliament and Council*, the Commission reiterated its longtime view that the Court could only marginally scrutinise the legislative assessment,[37] and the Court did not limit its review to a manifest error of assessment: 'the legislature has concluded on the basis of detailed evidence and without committing *any* error of assessment that the general interests of the EU could be better served by action at that level.'[38]

In the case of *Menthol Tobacco*, the Court clearly indicated its double task with respect to subsidiarity:

> An initial review of compliance with the principle of subsidiarity is undertaken, at a political level, by national parliaments in accordance with the procedures laid down for that purpose by Protocol (No 2).
>
> Subsequently, responsibility for that review lies with the EU judicature, which must verify both compliance with the substantive conditions set out in Article 5(3) TEU and compliance with the procedural safeguards provided for by that protocol.[39]

AG Kokot opined that mere 'boilerplate language' asserting compliance with subsidiarity could potentially infringe upon the duty to state reasons under Article 296 TFEU.[40] How both roles could become intertwined and reinforce one another will be dealt with in section III.

III. National Parliaments and the Early Warning System

Although numerous scholarly analyses of the Early Warning System have been conducted, this enforcement mechanism nevertheless draws our attention as it is relevant for our present inquiry to see whether the contributions of the national Parliaments[41] can in effect heighten the scrutiny of subsidiarity, specifically in light of the ex post judicial phase.

[34] Case 547/14 *Philip Morris*, above n 5, para 226: 'In the present case, it is undisputed that the Commission's proposal for a directive and its impact assessment include sufficient information showing clearly and unequivocally the advantages of taking action at EU level rather than at Member State level.'

[35] D Keyaerts, 'Ex Ante Evaluation of EU Legislation Intertwined with Judicial Review? Comment on Case C-58/08 Vodafone' (2010) 35 *European Law Review* 869–84.

[36] See also the suggestions by Craig, above n 1; Vandenbruwaene, above n 17.

[37] Case 508/13, *Estonia v Parliament and Council* [ECLI:EU:C:2015:403] para 43.

[38] ibid para 54, emphasis added.

[39] CJEU, Case 547/14, *Philip Morris* [2016] ECLI:EU:C:2016:325, paras 216–17.

[40] Case 547/14, Opinion AG Kokott, 290–91.

[41] See the contribution by N Lupo, Ch 9 in this volume.

The question that arises is whether the Reasoned Opinions can add an additional dimension to the subsidiarity scrutiny process before the Court.

Although both the Italian Chamber and the Senate enjoy equal legislative powers[42]—the so-called perfect bicameral system—both chambers have adopted rather different procedures with respect to the Early Warning System. In the Senate, as a rule, all draft legislative acts emanating from the EU are sent both to the standing sectoral committee and the Committee on EU Policies.[43] In the House on the other hand, only the Committee on EU policies selects which draft legislative acts are susceptible to the Early Warning procedure for analysis. Lupo has labelled this model 'decentralised' for the Senate, and 'mixed' for the House. The attempt on the part of the House to endow a specific committee with the scrutiny of subsidiarity seems to reflect a desire for a more uniform approach to the question of compliance with subsidiarity. This Committee is also supported by a specific administrative staff devoted to EU issues. Practice reveals though, that Italian Parliament opts for 'a wide and dynamic conception of subsidiarity',[44] thus rejecting a narrow legalistic view.

The European Parliament has called for 'guidelines [that] could be prepared, outlining criteria for reasoned opinions on subsidiarity issues'.[45] Since parliamentary practice in Italy does not find itself hampered by the need to conduct a stringent and legally oriented subsidiarity analysis, Reasoned Opinions and their content seem indeed rather broad in their scope. Guidelines bringing together the case law of the CJEU and the Impact Assessment Guidelines could meaningfully strengthen the operability of EU subsidiarity as aimed at in the EWS, specifically with a view to using reasoned opinions in a subsequent annulment procedure under Article 263 TFEU (see section III). The CJEU itself has noted that its review for compliance with subsidiarity is twofold, ie '[to] verify both compliance with the substantive conditions set out in Article 5(3) TEU and compliance with the procedural safeguards provided for by that Protocol [No 2].'[46] The Reasoned Opinions could serve as a more elaborate argumentation on a possible defective reasoning with subsidiarity, much like inversely the EU legislator relies on preparatory documents to argue its case. What is needed in that hypothesis, though, is more substantive alignment between the RO and the legal conception of subsidiarity.

In order to render the standing rights for national Parliaments operational, prevailing law dictates that the executive branch is empowered to bring a procedure before the Court of Justice, under article 8 of Protocol No 2. Article 42(4) of the Law No 234/2012 holds that the government should lodge a complaint, both for violations of subsidiarity and proportionality, and that the acting Chamber may stand in the trail.[47]

[42] For the perspective of the regional assemblies in the EWS, see C Fasone, 'Italian Regional Councils and the Positive Externalities of the Early Warning Mechanism for National Constitutional Law' in A Jonsson Cornell and M Goldoni (eds), *National and Regional Parliaments in the EU-Legislative Procedure Post-Lisbon* (Oxford, Hart, 2016) 155–79.

[43] N Lupo, 'The Scrutiny of the Principle of Subsidiarity in the Procedures and Reasoned Opinions of the Italian Chamber and Senate' in Jonsson Cornell and Goldoni, ibid 225–52; see also S Cavatorto, 'Italy' in C Hefftler et al, *The Palgrave Handbook of National Parliaments* (London, Palgrave Macmillan, 2015) 214–15 (the composition and functioning of the Committees in EU Policy).

[44] Lupo, ibid 250.

[45] European Parliament Resolution of 4 February 2014 on EU Regulatory Fitness and Subsidiarity and Proportionality, (2013/2077(INI)), para 31.

[46] CJEU, Case 547/14, *Philip Morris*, para 216.

[47] Art 42(4) Law No 235/2012.

From a procedural point of view, two questions arise: firstly, can a national Parliament successfully argue that the principle of proportionality has been infringed even though the Protocol only mentions subsidiarity as grounds for annulment in this procedure? Second, if the Court of Justice only recognises Member States as privileged applicants under article 263 TFEU, how will it deal with institutions of that Member State in the annulment proceeding?

First, many national Parliaments opt to discuss subsidiarity and proportionality together. From a political and policy-oriented point of view, this makes sense. Legally though, the annulment proceeding for a breach of proportionality is not covered by the standing rights under Article 8 Protocol No 2. This means that the Italian Parliament, should it opt to trigger this procedure, is best advised to limit its argumentation to subsidiarity if it wants to stand in the trial itself. Here, Article 8 functions as a special category of the broader annulment proceedings of Article 263 TFEU, where proportionality obviously can feature as a ground for objection.

As for the second question—there is no legal problem. Procedural law allows representation to be organised according to national law, but the process has to be initiated, the appeal lodged, by the Member State.[48] Analogous reasoning to representation of regions before the CJEU[49] offers the answer that nothing precludes national law from arranging the Member State agent and/or the legal representation to work under instructions of a particular institution, in this case one or both Houses of Parliament.

IV. Maximising Scrutiny: Alignment of the Different Mechanisms

The primary function of the justification requirement is to enable the Court to conduct judicial review.[50] Indeed, 'subsidiarity cannot be easily validated by operational criteria.'[51] This does not imply, however, that the CJEU should refrain altogether from reviewing because it lacks a certain epistemic ability to deal with findings of fact. The judicial scrutiny of subsidiarity demonstrates the need for an intensity and scope of interpretation by the Court that reconciles judicial restraint with the operational demands of legitimacy. The hypothesis of judicial review of compliance with subsidiarity requires courts to address two questions: (a) Can the legislator demonstrate that the interests of other levels are taken into account,[52] and (b) can the legislator demonstrate with empirical evidence the adequacy (or added value) of his action? These two questions relate to the functioning of subsidiarity at a procedural and a substantial dimension respectively. However, classical legal methodology

[48] See Art 19 of the Statute of the Court of Justice and Art 119 of the Rules of Procedure of the Court of Justice.

[49] W Vandenbruwaene, P Popelier and C Janssens, 'Article 260 TFEU Sanctions in Multi-Tiered Member States' (2015) 7(2) *Perspectives on Federalism* 146–47 (discussing regional representation before the CJEU in Austria, Belgium, Germany, Italy, Spain and the United Kingdom).

[50] ie a functional interpretation of Art 296 TFEU: see eg Joined Cases 154/04 and 155/04, *Alliance for Natural Health and Others* [2005] ECR I-6451 paras 133–34.

[51] European Commission, *18th Report on Better Lawmaking*, COM (2011) 344, 2.

[52] Which is an inverse translation of Member State insufficiency.

leaves the court ill-equipped to deal with these questions. What standards should be upheld? How can sufficient latitude or discretion be ascertained for the legislator because of his democratic legitimacy?

The main argument in the context of judicial review of subsidiarity is functional in the sense that a court is ill-equipped to assess the underlying socio-economic determinants, especially when they have a forward-looking or speculative character. Nonetheless, there is a difference between the open character or indeterminate of the legal norm and a pure political question, constitutionally required to be assessed by the legislature.[53]

The Impact Assessment Guidelines[54] posit five questions that reiterate the determinants on subsidiarity issued by the Edinburgh Council, and address subsidiarity in particular the transnational aspects of the issue at hand and possible negative consequences of regulation by the Member States alone. Substantial benefit could be gained from the application of impact assessment, as an instrument of ex ante evaluation, in the initial compliance with subsidiarity of the legislative act, but also with respect to other enforcement mechanisms.[55] Indeed, 'the very fact that there is a framework within which these issues are considered is, however, a positive step, which facilitates scrutiny as to the nature of the justificatory arguments and their adequacy.'[56]

The question then becomes: how to integrate impact assessments in a judicial proceeding, and how can courts review these arguments? The main argument in the context of judicial review of subsidiarity is functional in the sense that a court is ill-equipped to assess the underlying socio-economic determinants, especially when they have a forward-looking or speculative character.[57] IA has the potential to mitigate the concerns under the functional political question doctrine by offering interpretation guidance to the judiciary. However, 'the standard of review derives from the Treaty and is therefore autonomous of the declarations.'[58] Standards of evidence-based lawmaking thus serve to frame and limit legislative discretion.

In her study on impact assessments in EU lawmaking, Meuwese concluded that IA may serve as a catalyst for legal principles, amongst which subsidiarity. 'IA reports tend to contain the kind of information that is needed for a more rational consideration of the opportunity of Community action.'[59] Insofar that the instrument of IA encourages deliberative dialogue, and functions as a template along which lines the argument proceeds, it shows benefits in the parliamentary ex ante dialogue[60] on compliance with subsidiarity. Furthermore, consistency warrants the application of subsidiarity by the judiciary to the

[53] N Achterberg, *Theorie und Dogmatik des Öffentlichen Rechts* (Berlin, Duncker & Humblot, 1981) 229.

[54] See above s I.A.

[55] A Meuwese, *Impact Assessment In EU Lawmaking* (The Hague, Kluwer, 2008) 257; A Alemanno, 'The Better Regulation Initiative at the Judicial Gate: a Trojan Horse Within the Commission's Walls or the Way Forward?' (2009) 15 *European Law Journal* 382–401.

[56] Craig, above n 1, 78.

[57] K Meßerschmidt, *Gesetzgebungsermessen* (Baden Baden, Nomos, 2000) 964–69.

[58] M Doherty, 'Judicial Review in the European Community: the Environment, Subsidiarity, and the Question of Intensity' (2000) 22 *Liverpool Law Review* 113.

[59] Meuwese, above n 55, 257.

[60] See on the general conception of national parliaments as guardians, rather than co-legislators: P Kiiver, 'The Early-warning System for the Principle of Subsidiarity: the National Parliaments as a Conseil d'Etat for Europe' (2011) 36 *European Law Review* 106–07; I Cooper, 'The Watchdogs of Subsidiarity: National Parliaments and the Logic of Arguing in the EU' (2006) 44 *Journal of Common Market Studies* 291.

same extent as the legislator is constrained by the principle in the ex ante phase.[61] Von Bogdandy and Bast refer to the possible 'mutual reinforcement' of the ex ante Protocol mechanism and the judicial review of subsidiarity, but warn for political framing.[62] IA can provide the rational framework to alleviate this risk. But are judges equipped to deal in a substantive manner with these instruments? Alemanno encourages the recognition of instruments of Better Regulation as essential procedural requirements, reviewable by the Court, but recognises the difficulty of reviewing substantive aspects.[63] In that same vein, Keyaerts argues that the Court could approach in a formal and procedural manner the assessment by the legislator of complex underlying socio-economic indicators, by using the preparatory studies by the Commission, the impact assessments.[64] In *Afton Chemical*,[65] the CJEU investigated the manifest error of assessment proposed by the litigant on the basis of the Commission's impact assessment. The starting point for the Court is the broad discretion on functional grounds. The legislature is better equipped than the Court to assess 'highly complex scientific and technical facts'. This explains the reduction of judicial review to a marginal control, ie to bar manifest errors of assessment. Afton Chemical submitted that the IA did not support the Commission's conclusions. The Court developed its view on IA: it noted its non-binding character[66] toward other institutions, it observed moreover the 'scientific basis' that the Commission is to take into account, the obligation to take new evidence or date into account, and reiterated its view on the judicial review of legislative discretion, ie that the legislature can demonstrate that it has taken 'into consideration of all the relevant factors and circumstances of the situation the act was intended to regulate.'[67] In *Spain* v *Council*[68] the Court strengthened the intensity of review of discretion.[69] The CJEU confirmed this approach to legislative discretion in *Bressol* where a Member State sought to derogate from the freedom to reside *juncto* the prohibition of discrimination in a matter of higher education, by requiring 'specific evidence … an objective, detailed analysis, supported by figures, must be capable of demonstrating, with solid and consistent data, that there are genuine risks …'.[70] This coincides with the approach to the European Commissions' IA procedure which is aimed at securing 'a balance between political discretion and enhancing objectivity in law-making'.[71]

[61] E Swaine, 'Subsidiarity and Self-Interest: Federalism at the European Court of Justice' (2000) 41 *Harvard International Law Journal* 64, arguing that it would be 'an anomaly for the Community institutions to be constrained by subsidiarity in framing legislation, only for the Court to freely construe legislation … without further regard for the principle.'

[62] A Von Bogdandy and J Bast, 'The Federal Order of Competences' in A Von Bogdandy and J Bast (eds), *Principles of European Constitutional Law* (Oxford, Hart, 2009) 304.

[63] Alemanno, above n 55,395.

[64] D Keyaerts, *Better Regulation en de EU-rechter: een overbrugbare kloof* (Mechelen, die Keure, 2012) 149–72; Alemanno, above n 55, 400.

[65] CJEU, Case 343/09 *Afton Chemical* [2010] ECR I-7027.

[66] Para 30: 'In that regard, it should first be observed that the impact assessment carried out by the Commission, … was not binding on either the Council or the Parliament, who, under the co-decision legislative procedure laid down by Article 251 EC, were entitled to make amendments to that proposal'.

[67] Case 343/09 *Afton Chemical*, above n 65, paras 31–33.

[68] CJEU, C-310/04, *Spain v Council* [2007] ECR I-7318, paras 122–23.

[69] Alemanno, above n 55, 398.

[70] CJEU, C-73/08, *Bressol v Gouvernment de la Communauté française* [2010] ECR I-2735, para 71.

[71] Meuwese, above n 55, 91.

Thus, impact assessments are the main instrument through which the EU legislator can demonstrate the compliance with EU subsidiarity.[72] The Court may rely on two interpretative modi: one substantial and one procedural. In a substantial sense, in order to strengthen the Court's handling of the material indicators construing subsidiarity, the CJEU may turn to the impact assessment, as it did in the *Menthol Tobacco* case. At the procedural plane, one needs to discern between the standard of proof required from the legislator, and a judicial decision whether this standard has been met by the primary decision-maker.[73] This second-order review, albeit of a marginal intensity, may not be overlooked. In other words, even if the Court defers to the legislative findings to constitute a subsidiarity assessment, it should not—and does not—relinquish its secondary function. This begs the question: what modus of review would be optimal for subsidiarity scrutiny?

A. Inverse Semi-procedural Review

The principle of subsidiarity functions in analogous manner to the principle of proportionality, offering an argumentative scheme. Judicial review of the principle of subsidiarity reflects this function. The justification requirement that rests upon the legislator can be structured along the determinants offered in Article 5(3). There are two essential questions: a) how to interpret these determinants and b) how to set out the argumentation. These questions direct towards a substantial and a procedural modus of review.

Bar-Siman-Tov has coined the notion semiprocedural review aimed to prescribe a modus of review for human rights violations. In his words:

> Semiprocedural review is a model of judicial review which merges the examination of the statute's enactment process with the substantive judicial determination of the statute's constitutionality. [Semiprocedural review] is divided into two stages. At the first stage, courts engage in substantive judicial review: they examine the content of a certain statute and determine whether it infringes upon constitutionally protected rights or other constitutional values. At the second stage, courts turn to an examination of the legislative process in order to determine the permissibility of the infringement.[74]

His idea is thus to structure the review of human rights violations in two steps: first, the most patent violations, and in a second step, the less obvious cases. In the second step, procedural safeguards justify the legislative act. This idea relates to what Popelier and Van de Heyning have labeled 'procedural rationality'[75] in the context of a proportionality review.

[72] In this sense, IA are the focal point of the justification requirement in art 5 of Protocol No 2. A specific—and stronger—justification requirement would enable the Court to conduct ist review better, see N Colneric, 'Der Gerichtshof der Europäischen Gemeinschaften als Kompetenzgericht' (2002) *Europäische Zeitschrift für Wirtschaftsrecht* 714.

[73] P Craig, *EU Administrative Law* (Oxford, Oxford University Press, 2012) 432–33.

[74] I Bar Siman Tov, 'Semiprocedural Review' (2012) 6 *Legisprudence* 271. See also the critique of A Alemanno, 'The Emergence of the Evidence-Based Judicial Reflex: A Response to Bar-Siman-Tov's Semiprocedural Review' (2013) 1 *Theory and Practice of Legislation* who argues that is is not a real model of review but rather an example of a more rational and evidence based approach to lawmaking that shows itself in judicial review.

[75] '[T]he requirement of procedural safeguards in the decision-making process, denominated here as "procedural rationality", is a way to deal with constitutional adjudication in cases of wide discretion.' Popelier and Van De Heyning, above n 33, 232.

From the comparative overview above, it appears that courts turn towards procedural mechanisms to place a justification requirement of the legislator in order to structure his discretion.[76] Combining certain traits, I suggest that subsidiarity review is best conducted through an inverse semi-procedural model. In the first stage, certain 'flags' are checked to buttress the rationality of the legislative findings and the interlevel legitimacy subsidiarity entails.

The following questions serve that purpose:

1. A justification requirement
   a. Is the data adequate and conform methodological standards?
   b. are the determinants that construe subsidiarity (ie added value of the higher level intervention and the insufficiency of lower level action) adequately construed?
2. Has a consultation requirement been adhered to?
3. What information results from other enforcement mechanisms such as the EWS?

However, a mere procedural look does not suffice because it relies very much on the legislator's own assessment. Therefore, an additional substantive phase of review is warranted, which can take a more severe form if one of the questions in the procedural frame does not convince. The hypothesis may rise that after a yellow card, the Commission maintains its proposal with a summary justification.

B. Interaction with other Enforcement Mechanisms

An obvious point in this discussion concerns the interaction between the different enforcement mechanisms laid out. More precisely, how can the Impact Assessment, a Reasoned Opinion, and judicial scrutiny be connected? Writing on the constitutional responsibility resting on Congress to uphold and shape the federal balance, Justice Kennedy put forward that 'the absence of structural mechanisms to require those officials to undertake this principled task, and the momentary political convenience often attendant upon their failure to do so, argue against a complete renunciation of the judicial role.'[77] This conveys nicely the idea that the enforcement mechanisms should be complementary, and may conversely potentially reinforce each other.

i. Judicial Review and IA

Basing subsidiarity review on the IA merely relocates the problem of substantive assessment. Can the Court second-guess the IA? Is the Court obliged to accept whatever the IA concludes? Three points are in order to gain an understanding of this aspect of the problem: first, legislative discretion is not eradicated by a procedural requirement to demonstrate the basis of evidence and rationality of the decision-making. Second, the use of the IA has to be viewed in conjunction with other enforcement mechanisms on subsidiarity, such as the

[76] K Lenaerts, 'The European Court of Justice and Process-Oriented Review' (2012) 31 *Yearbook of European Law* 4: 'judicial deference in relation to "substantive outcomes" has been counterbalanced by a strict "process review"'.

[77] *US v Lopez*, 514 US (1995) at 577 (Kennedy J, concurring).

Early Warning System. And, third, the qualitative guarantees surrounding the IA have to be taken into account such as the control by the Impact Assessment Board, and the methodological standards in the IA Guidelines.

First, the procedural requirements stemming from the Better Regulation programme, including subsidiarity, do not restrict the substantive scope of the legislator to the point of substitution. Instead, they aim at providing a rational basis for making policy-choices. The balancing act of different values and trade-offs is enlightened by the articulation of the evidence at hand, not threatened. The deployment of IA in judicial reasoning should reflect this propriety. Nonetheless, the IA can aid the Court to construe the degree of discretion, as shown in the *Menthol Tobacco* case.[78]

Second, methodological standards for the use of IA should to a certain extent be taken into account by the Court. Minimum standards extracted from the IA Guidelines may be brought into the legal realm through the self-binding effect of these 'codes of conduct' and based on the principle of careful preparation.[79] Barbier de La Serre and Sibony propose standards for the use of partisan expert evidence in judicial procedures to ensure reliability and procedural fairness.[80] Analogous standards should be taken into account with respect to the methodology of subsidiarity IA: peer review (eg screening by the Impact Assessment Board), publication and contestability. For example, in case of controversy on the methodological rigour of an impact assessment, the CJEU may appoint assistant rapporteurs or external experts to review the drafting of the IA.[81]

ii. *Judicial Review and the EWS*

This point concerns the dialogue of the EU legislator with the national Parliaments. Insofar that the instrument of IA encourages deliberative dialogue, and functions as a template or *topos* along which lines the argument on subsidiarity proceeds, it carries benefits into the parliamentary ex ante dialogue on compliance with subsidiarity. There exists a possibility for 'mutual reinforcement' of the ex ante Protocol mechanism and the judicial review of subsidiarity. The CJEU could—hypothetically—in future cases rely on the process of the Early Warning System to rule on the compliance with subsidiarity. For example, if after a yellow card (ie reasoned opinions from at least 19 national Parliaments) the Commission decides to maintain its proposal, the CJEU could rely on both the IA, and the reasoned opinions to see if there has been an error in assessment. The degree of discretion should be commensurate with the degree of substantive reply, and adjustment to interlevel concerns. This proposition is evidently to be confined in relationship to the substantive coherence of the reasoned opinions of the national Parliaments. This point reinforces the need for coordination between the national Parliaments, also with regards to the procedure to adopt a Reasoned Opinion, specifically its legal content.

78 Case 547/14, *Philip Morris*, above n 5.

79 Alemanno, above n 55, 392–93.

80 E Barbier de la Serre and AL Sibony, 'Expert Evidence before the EC Courts' (2008) 45 *Common Market Law Review* 973–77.

81 See the analogous suggestion by Barbier de la Serre and Sibony, ibid 981 and Art 24 of the Statute of the Court of Justice, and arts 63 to 79 of the Rules of Procedure on measures of inquiry.

V. Conclusion

The EU law version of the principle of subsidiarity is, contrary to the mainstream opinion, justiciable in its nature. Problems in interpretation and scrutiny do arise however, given the underlying determinants of socio-economic complexity such as added value and Member State insufficiency. Case law reveals a progressive trend of heightened scrutiny, which however, still falls short given the legitimising function of article 5(3) and the nexus with the EU's democratic legitimacy as laid bare by the involvement of the national Parliaments through the EWS procedure.

This chapter has suggested three remedies to intensify the judicial scrutiny of compliance with article 5(3) TEU. First, I have argued that the Impact Assessment can offer inspiration and evidence to assess the legislator's discretion. Second, a semi-procedural model of review can adequately unify respect for this margin of discretion and simultaneously ensure a rational procedural obligation to adhere to standards of evidence-based lawmaking. Third, the different mechanisms to ensure compliance with subsidiarity should interact more, and take each other existence into account. Specifically, the Reasoned Opinions of the national Parliaments should be drafted more strategically to anticipate later judicial proceedings, and their juxtaposition to the Impact Assessment's part on subsidiarity. This later recommendation pertains both to the content of the Reasoned Opinions and the respective parliamentary proceedings.

A stronger judicial scrutiny of subsidiarity is no quantitative call for annulment of legislation. The hallmark of constitutionalism resides with compliance. If annulment is a necessary step, so be it, but stronger justification of compliance, and indeed compliance with the principle itself, is the ultimate end.

13

Procedures vis-à-vis the Institutions of the New Economic Governance

MASSIMO NARDINI

I. The Evolution of the Role of the Italian Parliament under EU Constraints, from the European Monetary System to the 'Fiscal Compact'

In 2012, for the first time in its history, the Italian Fiscal Constitution was modified by introducing the balanced budget principle. Four articles were amended, among them Article 81 about budgetary policy. Just as the way Article 81 was written in the Constituent Assembly established after the Second World War[1] took into account the relationship between the executive and the legislative branches on the public budget, its reform will have important effects on Italian institutions, notably on the role of the Houses in the Euro-national

[1] About the debate in the Constituent Assembly, see N Lupo, 'Art 81' in R Bifulco, A Celotto and M Olivetti (eds), *Commentario alla Costituzione* Vol II (Torino, Utet giuridica 2006) 1579 ff and G Rivosecchi, 'Parlamento e sistema delle autonomie all'ombra del governo nelle trasformazioni della decisione di bilancio' (2012) 1 *Rivista AIC*, available at www.rivistaaic.it/parlamento-e-sistema-delle-autonomie-all-ombra-del-governo-nelle-trasformazioni-della-decisione-di-bilancio.html.

budgetary process, that is, the annual process which consists of the so-called 'EU semester' and the national semester.

The basis of the original Article 81 was the idea that the fulfilment of the financial objectives and the pursuit of the other public interests must be differentiated. Consequently, any legislative initiative from MPs should indicate the means of financing new or major expenditures in compliance with Article 81(4), and the government could freely amend the financial guidelines in the annual budget without changing the 'substantive' legislation, in line with the formal budget theory expressed in Article 81(3).[2] Moreover, the financial constraints provided by Article 81(4) were intended to ensure a 'substantial' balance between revenues and expenditures in the long term, rather than a 'pure' balanced budget at any given time.[3]

Even with these constitutional rules, Italian Constitutional Court decision no 1/1966 allowed for the creation of public debt. Italian public accounts deteriorated in the second part of the twentieth century, with Italian debt becoming out of control in the 1980s. The substantial causes of the debt dated back to financial decisions made at the end of the 1960s. It was not a matter of structural inadequacy of Article 81 that led to that issue, but rather the effect of the Italian parliamentary system's failure to implement it.[4]

The fiscal Constitution, instead of being 'a rigorous and effective bulwark' for the financial responsibility of policy-makers (as Einaudi, a famous Italian economist and politician who served as the second President of the Republic between 1948 and 1955, said in a meeting during the Constituent Assembly works on 24 October 1946), became a 'fortress under siege' by pressures for more spending by political parties. The institutional system was unable to make concessions among different public needs by following priority criteria in consideration of the financial resources effectively available.

In the 1980s the budgetary policy was changed; the internal legal framework was modified with the aim of pursuing a financial renewal of the national public accounts. This objective was partially reached in 1991 with a primary surplus (0.1 percent to GDP).[5] The main reason for the progressive change in the Italian budgetary policy can be identified as the European Monetary System, which capped the 'monetisation of debt' which had previously been filled by the Italian Central Bank's constant 'accommodations' of the Treasury's financial needs.[6]

[2] About the effects of the original Art 81 on the fiscal power of the government and the parliament, see F Forte, 'The Italian Post war Constitution: Reasons of a Failure' (1999) 7(2) *European Journal of Law and Economics* 103–16. See also V Onida, 'The Historical and Constitutional Foundations of the Budgetary System in Italy' in D Coombes (ed), *The Power of the Purse. The Role of European Parliaments in Budgetary Decisions* (London, Allen & Unwin, 1976).

[3] For a critical point of view on this decision, see P De Ioanna and A Monorchio, 'Le nuove procedure di contabilità e il bilancio dello Stato' (1978) 3 *Democrazia e Diritto* 491–92. See also G Di Gaspare, 'Innescare un sistema di equilibrio: ritornando all'articolo 81 della Costituzione' in *Le procedure finanziarie in un sistema istituzionale multilivello* (Milan, Giuffré Editore, 2005).

[4] See P De Ioanna, 'Forma di governo e controllo della finanza pubblica' (1991) 4 *Democrazia e Diritto* 143 ff, R Perna, 'Le procedure di bilancio, fra Governo e Parlamento, in una democrazia maggioritaria' in *Costituzione e pareggio di bilancio* (Napoli, Jovene Editore, 2012) 26.

[5] See A Monorchio and N Quirino, *Economia della finanza pubblica* (Bari, Cacucci Editore, 2005) 51–55.

[6] See A Simoncini, 'Back To "Flexible" Constitutions? The Impact of Financial Crisis and the Decline of the European Constitutionalism' (2013) 2 *Italian Journal of Public Law* 169. For a deep analysis of the functioning of the EMS, see P De Grauwe, *The Economics of Monetary Integration* (Oxford, Oxford University Press, 2014).

When the Maastricht Treaty was signed in 1992, the main problem for Italian policymakers was reducing the enormous amount of debt accumulated in previous years. The size of this debt had systematically turned the primary surplus into a chronic deficit because of the amount of interest on it.

Since 1992, it became clear that the financial adjustment programme required budgetary planning with an adequate legal framework and a clear division of power between the Executive and the Parliament.[7] To do so, in 1997, the Houses approved the reform of the Public Accounts Law (Law No 97 of 1997). According to this law, the contents of the budget were simplified to allow the Houses to vote on macro-budgetary items, connected to specific administrative units, and provide better oversight for government expenses. This budgetary reform was in line with the legislative changes made at both local and central levels (introduced with Law No 421 of 1990 and Law No 59 of 1997), which were aimed at reinforcing responsibility and transparency in public choices,[8] as well as the reform of the Assemblies' internal rules.

In the context of EU economic governance, the rules of which were tightened by the Euro-Plus Pact, the 'six pack', the 'two pack' and the 'Fiscal Compact', not only did the Member States have to fulfil a medium term objective (MTO) of a balanced budget in structural terms, but they were also forced to introduce the balanced budget rule as an express clause into their national legal frameworks, preferably at the constitutional level.

These 'external' rules put increased attention on procedures rather than just the quantitative financial targets and also made some innovations on the longstanding operation of national parliaments, whose loss of autonomy during the crisis seemed to be less pronounced than that which had affected national governments. These innovations were transposed into the Italian legal framework by Constitutional Law No 1 of 2012, aimed at introducing the balanced budget principle, and elaborated in Law No 243 of 2012.[9] In particular, this reform amended Article 81 of the Constitution[10] by introducing the principle according to which public revenues and expenditures must be in balance.

[7] See L Verzichelli, *La politica di bilancio* (Bologna, Il Mulino, 1999); F Russo and L Verzichelli, *Budget Punctuations and Budgetary Regimes in Italy*, Paper of the Fifth Annual Conference of the Comparative Agenda Project (Science Po Reims, June 2012).

[8] See MV Lupò Avagliano, *Temi di contabilità pubblica. La riforma del bilancio dello Stato* (Padova, CEDAM 2010); M Nardini, 'Politica di bilancio e programmazione della spesa. Dalla legge n 62/1964 alla legge n 196/2009 di riforma della contabilità dello Stato', 7 October 2011, available at: www.amministrazioneincammino.luiss.it/2011/05/07/politica-di-bilancio-e-programmazione-della-spesa-dalla-legge-n-621964-alla-legge-n-1962009-di-riforma-della-contabilita-dello-stato.

[9] See E Griglio and N Lupo, 'Parliamentary Democracy and the Eurozone Crisis' (2012) 1 *Law and Economics Yearly Review* 342.

[10] The new Art 81(1) and (2) provide that 'The State shall balance revenue and expenditure in its budget, taking account of the adverse and favourable phases of the economic cycle. No recourse shall be made to borrowing except for the purpose of taking account of the effects of the economic cycle'. About the Italian constitutional reform, see A Brancasi, 'L'introduzione del principio del cd. pareggio di bilancio: un esempio di revisione affrettata della Costituzione' (2012) 1 *Quaderni costituzionali* 108 ff, N Lupo, 'La revisione costituzionale della disciplina di bilancio e il sistema delle fonti' in *Costituzione e pareggio di bilancio* (Napoli, Jovene Editore, 2012) 89 ff, T Groppi, I Spigno, N Vizioli, 'The Constitutional Consequences of the Financial Crisis in Italy' in Xenophon Contiades (ed), *Constitutions in the Global Financial Crisis. A Comparative Analysis* (Farnham, Ashgate Publishing Limited, 2013) 89–113. See also I Ciolli, 'The Balanced Budget Rule in the Italian Constitution: It ain't necessarily so … useful?' (2014) 4 *Rivista AIC*, available at www.rivistaaic.it/the-balanced-budget-rule-in-the-italian-constitution-it-ain-t-necessarily-so-useful.html.

Article 3(5) of Law No 243 of 2012 specifies that public accounts are in balance when the structural balance is equal to the medium term objective or shows a deviation lower than that considered significant by the Stability and Growth Pact and international agreements like the 'Fiscal Compact'; in the alternative, the adjustment path towards the MTO must be ensured respect in the case of exceptional events (Article 6) and programmatic differences which give place to correction mechanisms (Article 8).

Therefore, the balanced budget is indicated in the medium term objective agreed upon year by year with the EU institutions. According to Article 126 of the Treaty on the Functioning of the European Union (TFEU) and its annexed Protocol No 12, any Member State's deficit-to-GDP ratio up to the three per cent threshold expressed in annexed Protocol 12 should be formally accepted.

Consequently, the conceptual distinction between the MTO and the balanced budget principle at the basis of Law No 243 of 2012 appears to be in line with Article 126 of the Treaty, according to which 'excessive' government deficit (not deficit itself) must be avoided. By referring to the balanced budget principle and the financial margins allowed by the Treaties (even if the Stability and Growth Pact and the 'Fiscal Compact' offer a tighter interpretation of them), procedural budgetary rules have gained ground as the way to set the medium term objective time after time. The national Parliaments can now play a role in setting the budget, instead of following a pure balanced budget clause to fulfil in any case.

Furthermore, according to the constitutional reform in 2012, the recourse to borrowing is permitted for negative economic cycles or exceptional circumstances; in the first case the balanced budget is intended as structural (involving only a technical approach) while in the second case a parliamentary authorisation with a qualified majority is required.

Indeed, according to Article 81(2) of the Italian Constitution and Article 6(3) of Law No 243 of 2012, the Houses have an important say in deciding the recourse of public debt, and there is no limit on the maximum amount fixed into law. This power was used for the first time on 17 April 2014 (during the first year that these provisions were applied) when the Chamber of the Deputies and the Senate of the Republic, following the Economic and Financial Document (EFD) of 2014, approved a deliberation proposed by the Government through which, given the deepening of the financial recession, the balanced budget target was delayed to 2016.

Another deliberation postponing the balanced budget target to 2018 was approved by the Parliament on 8 October 2015, paralleling the resolution on the Update of the Economic and Financial Document of 2015, as well as on the 12 October 2016 on the occasion of the parliamentary approval of the Update of the Economic and Financial Document of 2016.[11]

It is important to note that according to article 6(3) of Law No 243 of 2012, an absolute majority was needed to approve a temporary deviation in the achievement of planning objectives aimed to guarantee the structural balance.[12] Hence, the 2014 EFD and the Update of the 2015 EFD needed to be approved with a stronger majority than a simple one.

[11] In particular, according to Law No 196 of 2009 as modified by Law No 169 of 2016, in case of exceptional events just before the EFD and the Update of the EFD, the Government's relation on the recourse to borrowing can be annexed to these documents.

[12] See A Ferreri, '"No more Waiting?" The "European Semester" as a Time for bringing Europe back to Parliamentary Debating: an Analysis of the Italian Sase (2011–2014)', in Centro Einaudi, Working Paper-LPF, no 9, 2014.

II. The Italian Budgetary Policy as a Process: The European Semester and the National Semester

The first step towards this new view of budgetary policy was the introduction of the European semester. It is legally based on Article 121 TFEU and detailed in Article 2 of EU Regulation No 1466/1997, as modified by EU Regulation No 1175/2011 (one of those included in the 'six pack'). This innovation is aimed at strengthening the EU's economic governance by harmonising the timing of policy formulation between the Member States and keeping their national budgetary procedures aligned with European requirements.[13]

This evolution can be better understood by considering that the European economic governance now focuses more attention on the budgetary process. This is confirmed not only by the attention now paid to some macroeconomic factors (starting with growth estimations, which represent the basis for the revenue side of the budget), but also by the programming approach that has been extended to a multi-annual timeframe that focuses on the individual actions of the budgetary session throughout each year.

In this context, the new supranational rules have had a structural impact on national budgetary procedures because European institutions are now directly involved in them. At the same time, each national Parliament can have a say in the European semester to influence the 'bargaining' between the government and the EU institutions, the final result of which is expressed in the medium term objective.[14]

In the case of Italy, the financial crisis could have provided a chance for an effective restructuring of the balance between the executive and the legislative powers: indeed, the loss of decision-making powers in the budgetary process caused by the strengthening of fiscal measures has been compensated for by new procedures and tools for parliamentary scrutiny and oversight. These were introduced at both the national and supranational levels.

This evolution can be observed when analysing Italian budgetary law, which changed entirely in 2009 with Law No 196 of 2009, which was subsequently amended two years later with Law No 39 in 2011 in order to comply with the new timeline established at the European level and provided specific provisions regarding the role of the parliament in the budgetary process.

In particular, there is a specific section in Article 4 of Law number 196 of 2009 on parliamentary scrutiny: Article 4(1) allows the Parliament to give directions to the Executive on the application of the law's provisions, notably concerning the preparation of the budgetary documents and procedures, while Article 4(2) promotes forms of bicameral cooperation on the scrutiny of public accounts which involve the Presidents of the two Houses.

[13] About the innovations introduced by the European Semester, see M Hallerberg, B Marzinotto, GB Wolff, 'How Effective and Legitimate is the European Semester? Increasing the Role of the European Parliament' Bruegle Working Papers, no 9, 2011, S Verhelst, 'The Reform of European Economic Governance: Towards a Sustainable Monetary Union', (June 2011) 47 *Egmont Papers* 50. See also O Clerc and P Kauffmann, 'Vers une Nuovelle Gouvernance Macro-économique dans la Zone Euro' (2011) 552 *Revue de l'Union Européenne* 589–96 and B Marzinotto, GB Wolff, M Hallerberg, *An Assessment of the European Semester*, in www.europarl.europa.eu/studies, 1 October 2012, p. 68 ff.

[14] See again G Rivosecchi, 'Il governo europeo dei conti pubblici tra crisi economico-finanziaria e riflessi sul sistema delle fonti' (2011) 1 www.osservatoriosullefonti.it 13.

Another section (Article 6) allows the Parliament to access public administrations' databases in order to improve their oversight power on public finance and fill in the previous information gap. Also, according to Articles 7, 10 and 10 bis of Law No 196 of 2009, the Parliament gives directions to the government in the preparation of the budget for the next year by debating and adopting the Economic and Financial Document (EFD) by resolution. This sets the multi-annual financial framework and the projection of the macroeconomic indicators made by the government itself. Meanwhile the Houses are informed and consulted during a process that monitors the deviations from programmatic objectives and adopts correction mechanisms.

The EFD contains Italy's Stability Program and the National Reform Program which are examined by the Parliament before their transmission to the European Commission. It can be updated by the Executive in September of that year to take into account the evolution of macroeconomic and financial variables, as well as the content of the Council's recommendation on the first version of the EFD. This new Document also must be approved by the Houses.

Unlike the previous document provided by the old Italian legislation (the Economic and Financial Planning Document, EFPD), which was merely confined to the relationship between the national institutions involved (the executive and the legislative branches), the EFD now provides the 'key point' of European economic governance, with a sort of interaction between the EU level and the national one.

In this context, the EFD provides a real chance for the Italian Parliament to play an active role in the budgetary process from the very beginning, when the main financial guidelines are fixed at the national level before being examined by the European Commission and the Council.[15] This document is based on and parallels the Annual Growth Survey published by the European Commission in the November of the previous year, as well as on the economic priorities adopted by the European Council in the month of March, when the EFD is prepared.

The EFD is the central moment when the Government and the Houses can establish a common position on budgetary targets. These are intended to be achieved in subsequent budgetary policy and transposed into the medium term objective agreed upon with the EU institutions during the next European semester.[16]

Following these conclusions, these reforms before the constitutionalisation of the balanced budget rule had partially aligned the national semester with the European one. Initially, the effects of these procedural innovations were blocked, however, because, according to the 'quantitative' EU rules, national budgetary policy was aimed at pursuing a balanced budget at any cost. In Constitutional Law No 1 of 2012, the budgetary rule was

[15] See G Rizzoni, 'Il "semestre europeo" fra sovranità di bilancio e autovincoli costituzionali: Germania, Francia e Italia a confronto' (2011) 4 in *Rivista AIC*, available at www.rivistaaic.it/il-semestre-europeo-fra-sovranit-di-bilancio-e-autovincoli-costituzionali-germania-francia-e-italia-a-confronto.html, 9 ff and J Wehner, *Legislatures and the Budget Process. The Myth of Fiscal Control* (London, Palgrave MacMillan, 2010) 3 ff.

[16] According to Arts 10 and 10-bis of the Law No 196 of 2009, as modified by the Law No 169 of 2016, the contents, respectively, of the EFD and the Update of the EFD have to be related to the medium term objective. About the relationship between national states and the European integration process, see N Lupo, 'Il ruolo delle burocrazie parlamentari alla luce dell'assetto istituzionale, nazionale e sovranazionale' (2012) 1 *Rassegna Parlamentare* 84–85.

intended to create a balance between revenue and public expenditure which Italy now achieves when the medium-term objective, to which the EU authorities during the yearly budgetary process agree, has been effectively accomplished.

At the national level, the new budgetary principle represents a clear parameter for the Houses' evaluation of the public policies, given that each expenditure decision must be financed by taxes and/or by a reduction of public expenditure in other sectors. At the same time, the very idea of balance contains a certain degree of flexibility, notably because public debt is allowed in order to address 'exceptional circumstances' (after an express authorisation by the Houses) or to take into account the effects of the businness cycle on the budget.[17]

Moreover, the Law No 243 of 2012 explains the relevance of the decisions taken at the European level about which medium term objective Italy must achieve. In other words, the balance is achieved not only when deviations from the MTO are authorised by the Parliament for the aforementioned reasons, but also when the national authorities and the European institutions 'agree' to a certain amount of deficit.

III. The Italian Way to Solve the Asymmetrical Information Problem between the Executive and the Legislative Branches

As analysed above, budgetary policy is not simply an issue of what to do but must also be considered to be the outcome of a process in which various actors are involved. For this reason, it is important to look at the role the national Parliament will be able to play in it. A more thorough analysis about the relationship between the Italian Houses and the institutions of the European economic governance is needed in order to do so.

It can be said that, unlike in Germany where the Constitutional Court has guaranteed the prerogatives of the Bundestag in the budgetary domain at the domestic level, in Italy the Parliament has had to defend its role as an actor in the long procedure of the multi-level economic governance since its very beginning. Furthermore, the Houses in participating in this policy-making process require more information so that they can control the government's action during the entire budgetary process, from the European semester to the national one.

The national legal framework has provided many tools to reinforce the Houses' right to information, notably with Constitutional Law No 1 of 2012 and with Law No 234 of 2012. Article 6(1) of Constitutional Law No 1 of 2012, as detailed by Articles 16–19 of Law No 243 of 2012, provides the establishment of a 'fiscal council' (the Parliamentary Budget Office, or PBO). The PBO is an independent body responsible for analysing and assessing the Government's macroeconomic and fiscal forecasts and verifying compliance with national and European fiscal rules. In particular, it is required to be an objective provider of

[17] About the deviation from the medium term objective in 2014, see C Fasone, 'Taking Budgetary Powers away from National Parliaments? On Parliamentary Prerogatives in the Eurozone Crisis', in EUI Working Papers, no 37, 2015, 23.

economic and financial analysis to Parliament during the entire decision-making process, from the European semester to the national semester.[18]

The Italian PBO publishes its report twice a year, the first (called the Budgetary Planning Report, which analyses the Economic and Financial Document) in March/April when the Stability Program is presented, and the second (called the Budgetary Policy Report, which analyses the update to the EFD, the Stability Bill and the Draft Budgetary Plan) in September/October before the start of the 'budgetary session'. In each of these reports there is a chapter which refers to supranational fiscal rules: 'Compliance with the Fiscal Rules' in the Budgetary Planning Report and 'Fiscal Policy Targets in Light of European Fiscal Rules' in the Budgetary Policy Report.

Should there be different estimations between the Government and the PBO, the executive, upon request of at least one third of Members of the Parliamentary Budget Commissions, shall explain to the Parliament the reasons why it intends to confirm its own assessments per the 'comply or explain' procedure. This setup means that the PBO tends to reinforce the position of the Houses in the debate on the Economic and Financial Document by giving credible and independent support to the Houses' estimates.

Parliamentary hearings are also very important, especially those made during the budgetary sesssion. On 3 November 2015, the Chariman of the PBO, Giuseppe Pisauro, for instance, testified before the Joint Budget Committees of the Senate and the Chamber of Deputies as part of the consideration of the budget for 2016–2018. On that occasion, Pisauro showed that the macroeconomic scenario presented in the Draft Budgetary Plan (DBP) differed slightly from the policy scenario set out in the Update to the Economic and Financial Document. In particular, while the growth forecasts for 2015–2016 were acceptable, those for 2017 and 2018 were imprudent and excessively optimistic, in a context where the macroeconomic outlook could be affected by the slowdown in emerging economies and the deflationary impact of weak oil prices.

On that matter, it is important to address the position assumed by the Chairman of the PBO in a parliamentary hearing on 3 October 2016 that the validation process for the 2017 policy scenario would have produced an unfavourable finding, as the growth estimations indicated in the Update of the Economic and Financial Document could have been too optimistic. Only after the presentation of the 2017 Draft Budgetary Plan by the Government, where the growth estimations were justified by the fiscal stimulus detailed in that document, did the Parliamentary Budget Office validate these growth forecasts.

During the national semester, should there be recommendations by the European Commission about the contents of the budgetary draft, the fiscal council could give empirical support to the Government's different estimations or macroeconomic projections. It must be considered that the Italian government must present the Update of the EFD by the end of September each year, which comes after the recommendation of the European Council made during the month of July of the same year. Even if the initial estimates to which the EU institutions agree cannot be reversed completely, in this part of the Italian semester there is

[18] The principles at the basis of the fiscal council's activity have been explained by OECD in the Draft principles for independent fiscal institutions. About the Parliamentary Budget Office, see D Cabras, 'Un Fiscal Council in Parlamento' in www.federalismi.it, 17 October 2012, available at www.federalismi.it/nv14/articolo-documento.cfm?artid=21019; M Chiti, 'L'Ufficio parlamentare di bilancio e la nuova governance della finanza pubblica' (2014) 1 www.astrid-online.it.

a potential path for changes that the Government could justify without invoking a negative economic cycle, but by referring to data provided by an independent institution.

According to Article 5 of Law No 234 of 2012 concerning the Italian participation in the formation and adoption of EU law and policies, the Government promptly shall inform the Houses about any initiative aiming to conclude agreements between EU Member States that introduce or strengthen financial or monetary rules. The same obligation is applied to agreements that have relevant consequences on public finance.

Subsequently, if the position taken by the Government during the negotiation of these agreements is not in line with the resolutions adopted by the Parliament, the Prime Minister or a delegated Minister shall promptly provide the Houses with an explanation.[19]

Finally, these provisions also are applied to international agreements which are not part of the European legal framework. This is in order to prevent the representative Assemblies from being excluded from the negotiations of such agreements, as had happened with the European Stability Mechanism and the 'Fiscal Compact'.

Other important powers aimed at reducing the problem of asymmetrical information between the Parliament and the Government and reinforcing parliamentary control over the executive have been introduced by Law No 234/2012. This law governs the participation of the Italian institutions to the formation and execution of EU legislation.

Article 4(4) of Law No 234 of 2012 states that the Government shall periodically inform and consult the Houses, according to the procedures indicated in Constitutional Law No 1 of 2012 and Law No 243 of 2012, for supranational documents, acts or agreements that involve coordinating budgetary and economic policies or provide for the functioning of the mechanisms of financial stabilisation.

Articles 6 and Article 7 of Law No 234 of 2012 contain specific rules about the participation of the Italian Parliament in the creation of EU legislation, notably addressing when the Parliament agrees with the Government about the guidelines to be followed in the EU context.

By invoking the aforementioned articles, as well as Article No 10 of the Treaty of the European Union, on 26 January 2016 some deputies from an opposition party (the 5 Star Movement) asked the Government during a parliamentary question why the Parliament was not consulted on the Executive's proposal for a different European Monetary Union (EMU). This proposal was prepared on the basis of the so-called 'Five Presidents' Report' on 'Completing Europe's Economic and Monetary Union' examined during the informal meeting of the EU Council on 12 February 2015.

It is interesting to note that in its reply to this questioning, the Government explained that the content of the proposal was based on the 2015 Programming Resolution (on which various parliamentary resolutions were proposed, including Resolution No 6-00155, proposed by the leader of the Democratic Party's parliamentary group at the Chamber of Deputies), as well as on the results of fact-finding investigations in the specialised Committees, in order to emphasise the 'parliamentary coverage' this initiative had already received. Ironically, the purpose of this proposal was intended by the Government as a way to empower the democratic control of the Houses.

[19] For an analysis of the reform in 2012 in connection with the Law No 234/2012, see G Piccirilli, 'Il Parlamento italiano: le procedure europee nella legge n. 234 del 2012' in A Manzella and N Lupo (eds), *Il sistema parlamentare euro-nazionale* (Torino, Giappichelli, 2014) 211–13.

IV. The Italian Parliament and the European Central Bank in the Context of Monetary Policy and the Banking Union

Since the budgetary policy in the Euro-zone has progressively focused on the balanced budget principle, the management of the financial crisis has been handled primarily by the European Central Bank, which has provided emergency funding packages coupled with economic adjustment programs, notably after Mario Draghi's famous announcement at the Global Investment Conference in London on 26 July 2012 ('within our mandate, the ECB is ready to do whatever it takes to preserve the Euro').[20]

For Italy, the actions recently adopted by the European Central Bank (ECB) to contain the financial crisis have had the positive effect of depressing yields for national bonds and helping it return to the financial markets. They also have caused an important reduction on the interest Italy owed on the high level of public debt that it had accumulated in the past.

However, some scholars have argued about specific initiatives taken by the Governor of the European Central Bank during the financial crisis which affected Italy in 2011. One of these disputed intiatives happened when a letter was sent to the Italian Prime Minister by the President of the ECB Jean Claude Trichet and his designated successor Mario Draghi on 5 August 2011, where the Italian government was required to take the necessary emergency measures in order to restore the country's credibility in the financial markets. This letter was kept secret from the Parliament until it was published in a major national newspaper (the *Corriere della Sera*) on 29 September. Most of all, it indicated not only the measures to be adopted but also the legal instrument to use to do so, specifically the decree-law that the Houses needed to make into law by the end of September 2011.

Apart from the specific content of the reforms required by the European Central Bank, the letter limited the role of the national Parliament in two ways. First, the decree-law itself is a Government instrument of a temporary nature, having the force of law in extraordinary cases of necessity and urgency, alternative to the 'classic' formal law enacted by Parliament. Second, the traditional timing for the parliamentary conversion into law seems to have been negatively affected from the very beginning, given that the letter referred to 'the end of September' regardless of when the decree was effectively adopted, while according to Article 77 of the Italian Constitution, the Parliament has 60 days from the Executive's adoption of a decree-law to convert it into a formal law. At the same time, it must be considered that the decree-law was adopted on 13 August, which is during the traditional summer recess, in order to inhibit the parliamentary discussion on it even further.[21]

Furthermore, the inclusion of Italy in the ECB's Securities Market Program was disclosed by the national Government only in late-2011 and, in any case, it has never been debated by

[20] About the role of the ECB in the European Monetary Union, see W Buiter, 'Alice in Euroland' (1999) 37(2) *Journal of Common Market Studies* 181–209; O Issing, 'The Eurosystem is Transparent and Accountable, or Willem in Wonderland' (1999) 37(3) *Journal of Common Market Studies* 503–19.

[21] The Decree-law 13 August 2011, no 138 was ratified with modifications by the Italian Parliament with the Law on 14 September 2011, no 148. See M Luciani, 'L'equilibrio di bilancio e i principi fondamentali: la prospettiva del controllo di costituzionalità'; in *Corte Costituzionale, Atti del seminario sul principio dell'equilibrio di bilancio secondo la riforma costituzionale del 2012* (*Milano, Giuffré Editore*, 2014), 11–12. About the structural problems of the Italian legislative decisions, see generally L Duilio, *Politica della legislazione, oltre la crisi* (Bologna, Il Mulino, 2013).

the two Houses of Parliament.[22] Therefore, the relationship between the Italian Parliament and the European Central Bank seems controversial.

In light of this, it should be noted that the European Central Bank is now paying more attention to the role of national assemblies than it had in the past, as shown by various hearings with the President Mario Draghi before the competent Committees of the Houses in the most important EU Member States. In particular, he visited the Bundestag on 24 October 2012 and explained the effects of the OMT Decision of the ECB Governing Council on 6 October 2012 to the Committees on Budget, Finance and European Affairs in a joint session. On 26 June 2013 he had a hearing in front of the Finance Commission of the French National Assembly; thereafter, on 26 March 2015 he also made a speech to the Committees on Budget, Finance and European Affairs of the Italian Parliament. Following this, there has been a major involvement of national Parliaments in monetary policy as part of the ongoing project to build up a European Banking Union.

It is important to focus on the way that the European Central Bank's decisions have an impact on the economy. In other words, it is necessary to pay attention to the monetary policy's transmission mechanisms, in which the banking system plays an important role in giving effect to the decisions taken by the monetary institutions.

In the EU, the Banking Union appears to reinforce the position of the European Central Bank even more than it had in the past. Therefore, the ECB can be considered to be the most independent central bank, with even less accountability than other central banks such as the German Bundesbank or the American Federal Reserve.[23]

According to various scholars, the ECB actually plays an 'executive' role; while at the same time the very fact that it is considered as a component of the EU's 'fragmented executive' implies that not only the European Parliament but also national Parliaments should be informed about and engaged in a dialogue with it. This approach has its root in both article 21 of Regulation No 1024/2013 and article 46 of Regulation No 806/2014, which contain specific articles dedicated to national Parliaments and aimed at reinforcing their oversight powers. The involvement of national Parliaments in a domain strictly devoted to the 'technical' institutions is an important innovation for Italy.

It should be remembered that in 1981 a mere exchange of letters between the Treasury Minister and the Governor of the Italian Central Bank was sufficient to create the famous 'divorce' between these two institutions. It also broke down the practice of the 'monetisation' of the public deficit without any change to the national legislative framework and consequently without any involvement of the Italian Parliament in this decision. During that period, the need for major parliamentary control over the Central Bank's activities became an important issue of political debate, even if it did not produce any notable result.[24]

Today, the Italian Parliament's new information rights and oversight powers in the banking sector are specifically recognised in the EU legal framework, which was not the case before in the national legislation. It is equally important to pay attention to the fact that these competences expressed in the form of EU regulations become automatically part of the Italian legal system without the need of a separate national legislative procedure to enter them into national law.

[22] See again Fasone, above n 17, 18.

[23] See P De Grauwe, *Economics of Monetary Union* (Oxford, Oxford University Press, 2014) 157.

[24] See S Ortino, *Banca d'Italia e Costituzione* (Pisa, Pacini Editore, 1979) 411–12; A Predieri, 'Sistema bancario e istituzioni: un nuovo compito per il Parlamento?' (1976) 2 *Città e Regione*, 12 ff.

In particular, the Italian Houses, as the other national Parliaments, receive the annual reports from the European Central Bank and the Single Resolution Board, from which they can make reasoned observations. They also can request that these institutions reply in writing to any observation or question submitted to them.[25]

In this context, it has to be emphasised that on 3 March 2015 the first Chairman of the European Banking Authority, Andrea Enria, intervened in the Finance and Treasury Committee of the Senate during a fact-finding investigation about the Italian banking system regarding the prospect of European supervision, soon followed on 23 June 2015 by the Italian representative of the Supervisory Board, Ignazio Angeloni.

Moreover, it is interesting to highlight that the Italian Senate, whose role in the national institutional system would have radically changed if the constitutional reform had been approved in the referendum held on 4 December 2016, is the only Upper Chamber of the countries joining the Banking Union which seems to have exploited the aforementioned oversight powers.[26]

V. Interparliamentary Cooperation as a Basis for a Euro-national Budgetary Process

Based on the preceding analysis about the ongoing Euro-national budgetary process, it appears an interparliamentary coordination is needed: the European Parliament is unable to play an effective role during the European semester and, at the same time, national Parliaments are far more directly involved in bugetary decisions than in the past.

Generally speaking, according to Article 10 of the Lisbon Treaty, the EU's representative democracy is based on both the European Parliament and the national Parliaments, which are required to cooperate in order to face the 'fragmented' but even more powerful executive power in the EU system, as it has emerged in recent years.

In other words, given that the European Council has been considered a part of the EU institutional system following the Lisbon Treaty and since the start of the financial crisis has acquired an important role in managing it, the national Houses are now asked to be part of the budgetary decisions taken at the EU level, as a necessary counterpart of this kind of 'Euro-national executive field'.[27]

Specifically for Italy, this means that specific tools must be provided in order to rebalance the position of the Houses with respect to the national government, the latter being strengthened by the EU in parallel with the tightening fiscal measures adopted in the last years.[28]

[25] See N Lupo and R Ibrido, 'Which Democratic Oversight on the Banking Union? The Role of the Euro-national Parliamentary System' (2015) 4 *Law and Economics Yearly Review* 301.

[26] About the role played by the Italian Senate in exploiting oversight powers of the Banking Union, see Lupo and Ibrido, ibid 317.

[27] See N Lupo, 'Parlamento europeo e parlamenti nazionali nella costituzione "composita" nell'UE: le diverse letture possibili' (2014) 3 *Rivista AIC*, available at www.rivistaaic.it/parlamento-europeo-e-parlamenti-nazionali-nella-costituzione-composita-nell-ue-le-diverse-letture-possibili.html, 5–6.

[28] Actually this process dates back to the aftermath of the joining of Italy to the European Monetary Union, that is well before the financial crisis in 2008; see S Fabbrini and A Donà, 'Europeanisation as Strengthening of Domestic Executive Power? The Italian Experience and the Case of the Legge Comunitaria' (2003) 25 *Journal of European integration* 31 ff.

The empirical evidence shows that the core competences of the legislative branch cannot be exercised only on the basis of the national legal framework, especially given the influence exercised by the supranational level on the relationship between the Houses and the executive power.

Today, the necessary coordination between the European Parliament and the national Parliament can take the form of the interparliamentary cooperation provided in Article 13 of the 'Fiscal Compact', in line with Title II of Protocol (No 1), annexed to the European Union Treaties, on the role of national Parliaments in the European Union.[29]

Given that the European Parliament alone is unable to oversee the economic policy decided in the Euro-zone, the national Parliaments are forced to be conscious of their crucial role in this sector by orienting and controlling the activity of their respective governments, notably in the European Council and in the Euro-summit. However in order to do it effectively, parliamentary control must be homogeneous at the level where the decision is taken.[30]

In compliance with Article 13 of the Treaty, the European Parliament and the national Parliaments of the contracting parties must determine together the organisation and promotion of this conference, formed by the representatives of their relevant committees, in order to discuss budgetary policies and other issues covered by the 'Fiscal Compact' itself.[31]

The sharing of different points of view and experiences can help to counter-balance the major role assumed by the executive in the budgetary process in favour of the representative assemblies, by allowing the latter to use the powers attributed by the European legal framework.[32] Indeed, because of this Conference, parliamentarians from all EU countries can meet, interact and exchange information and knowledge, as was already happening in the previous interparliamentary institutions.[33]

The Conference's very existence is important in causing a balance effect by reinforcing the role of the representative institutions both in the European Union and in the national context.[34] This means that the Conference can strengthen accountability and give some directions to the European Council and the Euro-summit.[35] Furthermore, it is interesting

[29] See V Krelinger, 'La nouvelle conférence interparlementaire pour la gouvernance économique et financiére' (2013) Notre Europe Institut Jacques Delors, Policy paper, no 100; A Manzella, 'Verso un governo parlamentare euro-nazionale?' in Manzella and Lupo (eds), above n 19, 13 ff, V Krelinger, 'The Making of a New Treaty: Six Rounds of Political Bargaining' (2012) 32 *Policy Brief—Notre Europe*.

[30] See N Lupo, 'La Conferenza interparlamentare sulla governance economica e finanziaria:la deludente attuazione dell'art 13 del Fiscal Compact' (2014) 1 *Quaderni costituzionali* 113–14.

[31] See C Fasone, 'European Economic Governance and Parliamentary Representation. What Place for the European Parliament?' (2014) 20(2) *European Law Journal* 168.

[32] As remarked by E Griglio and N Lupo, 'Parliamentary Democracy and the Eurozone Crisis' (2012) 1 *Law and Economics Yearly Review* 336 'in the new EMU scenario, in fact, Executives dispose of less margins for playing as free riders, while national Parliaments can count on the traditional and new instruments of inter-parliamentary cooperation'.

[33] About the importance of information in shaping the relations between the Government and the Parliament, see JO'Brennan and T Raunio, 'Deparliamentarization and European Integration' in J O'Brennan and T Raunio (eds), *National Parliaments within the Enlarged European Union. From 'Victims' of Integration to Competitive Actors?* (London and New York, Routledge, 2007) 8. See also B Crum and J E Fossum (eds). *Practices of Inter-Parliamentary Coordination in International Politics—The European Union and Beyond* (Essex, ECPR Press, 2013).

[34] See A Manzella, 'Parlamento europeo e parlamenti nazionali come sistema' (2015) 1 *Rivista AIC*, available at www.rivistaaic.it/parlamento-europeo-e-parlamenti-nazionali-come-sistema.html, 12

[35] See again Lupo, above n 27, 18.

to observe that the discussions at the Conference have involved the President of the EU Council as organiser or co-organiser, in consideration of the potential influence that this connection could potentially have on the activity of each Presidency in the specific sector of budgetary policy.

At the same time, the Conference organised in January 2014 during the European Parliamentary Week, which was introduced for the first time in January 2013 as a response to the European semester,[36] shows that this possible link between the activity of the Conference and the Euro-national budgetary process has existed from its start.

The presence of the European Parliament in the Conference allows the Italian Parliament to have a direct link to the EU institutional system without the interposition of its own government. Adding to the classical relationship between legislative and executive, now the Houses (in particular, the Budget and the Finance Committees in both of them)[37] can have an important chance to influence the EU decision-making process regarding budgetary policy, in line with Article 12 of the Lisbon Treaty which affirms that

> national parliaments contribute actively to the good functioning of the Union … by taking part in the inter-parliamentary cooperation between national parliaments and with the European Parliament, in accordance with the Protocol on the role of national parliaments in the European Union.

In this context the introduction of the European semester can be considered as an intermediate step forward the interparliamentary cooperation of Article 13 of the 'Fiscal Compact', given that the budgetary planning presented to the European Commission takes into account their 'parliamentary sustainability'.[38]

VI. Conclusions

The relationship between the Italian Parliament and the institutions of the European Economic Governance is strictly connected to the evolution of the Euro-national budgetary process. After a long period when the supranational financial constraints were considered as mere quantitative targets, aimed at forcing each state to balance its budget, now the rules introduced by the 'six pack', the 'two pack' and the 'Fiscal Compact' have brought more attention to the idea of the budgetary decision as a process, in which all the institutions involved both at the national and the EU level are asked to participate.

In this context, thanks to the balanced budget principle introduced by Constitutional Law No 1 of 2012 and Law No 243 of 2012, now the Italian budgetary MTO is not a mere numerical financial target fixed ex ante (as it would be if it was a pure balanced budget rule), but rather depends on complex interactions that occur between the national Parliament and the executive as well as between those Italian policy-makers and the EU institutions.

[36] See C Hefftler and K Gattermann, 'Interparliamentary Cooperation in the European Union: Patterns, Problems and Potential' in C Hefftler, C Neuhold, O Rozenberg and J Smith (eds), *The Palgrave Handbook of National Parliaments and the European Union* (Hampshire, Palgrave Macmillan, 2015) 99–100.

[37] See the chapter by Griglio in this volume.

[38] See A Manzella, 'La cooperazione interparlamentare nel "trattato internazionale" europeo' (2012) 4 www.astrid-online.it 4.

In the new legal framework, there can be an earlier involvement of the Parliament in the budget formulation process during the European semester than in the past, since there are discussions and deliberations of the Economic and Financial Document which represents the basis on which the following 'bargaining' between the national government and the European institutions involved in the process takes place.

The reforms approved in Italy since 2012 reflect the major role recognised for the national Parliaments at the EU level. The oversight function of the Houses has been positively affected by the possibility for them to authorise temporary public borrowing in exceptional circumstances, as well as by the institution of a Fiscal Council which, combined with specific informational rights, can strenghten the scrutiny of the Executive's budgetary policy.

Also, in the monetary and banking domain, the Italian Parliament can now have a say that it could not before when these competences where attributed to the national Central Bank. Finally, budgetary policy is a matter of politics, which in turn involves institutional aspects. As demonstrated by Italian history, only rules which directly affect the budgetary process (and the players) can promote fiscal responsibility in the policy-makers' behaviour. Awaiting a new design for the EU institutional architecture, each state joining the EMU must adapt its national form of government to the European economic governance in the budgetary domain, from where historically representative democracy has grown.

14

Procedures vis-à-vis the 'Masters of the Treaties': The Parliamentary Role in the Revision of the Treaties

BARBARA GUASTAFERRO

I. Introduction

The process of democratisation of the European Union through its progressive 'parliamentarisation'[1] has recently affected also the revision of the Treaties. The strong intergovernmental connotation characterising EU Treaty amendments so far—through the Intergovernmental Conferences—was familiar to international law and to a tradition which, in the sensitive field of foreign policy, mainly empowers representatives of the Governments of the Member State. By way of contrast, the experience of the Convention on the future of Europe, drafting the 2004 Treaty establishing a Constitution for Europe, paved

[1] On parliamentary democracy in Europe see M Cartabia, N Lupo and A Simoncini (eds), *Democracy and Subsidiarity in the EU* (Bologna, Il Mulino, 2013) and A Manzella, *Sui principi democratici dell'Unione europea* (Napoli, Editoriale Scientifica, 2013).

the way for the involvement of both national and European Parliaments in the revision process. Indeed, thanks to the so-called 'Convention method', already used for the drafting of the Charter of Fundamental Rights, the possible revision of the treaties was discussed at an assembly composed of representatives of national Parliaments, governments of the Member States, the European Parliament and the Commission.

Democratising the European Union and bringing it closer to the citizens was the main challenge launched by the Laeken European Council in December 2001 and by the 'Declaration on the future of the Union' which paved the way for the constitutionalisation of the European integration process. One of the most effective strategies to respond the this challenge was the involvement of national Parliaments into future projects of reform of the Treaties. Indeed, neither the governments of individual Member States (although accountable to their Parliaments through indirect democratic legitimacy) nor the European Parliament (although directly elected by citizens) were perceived as sufficiently qualified to give light, alone, to a 'Constitution for Europe'.[2] On the one hand, the European Parliament was not considered to hold the legitimacy deriving from popular sovereignty, not representing a European *demos*.[3] On the other hand, the referendum against the European Constitution in France and Holland in 2005 emphasised a possible mismatch between the national executives and their respective national Parliaments and public opinions.

It is in the light of the insufficiency of the indirect democratic legitimacy (which wants national Parliaments to have a say only in monitoring their respective Governments in the European arena) that the European Constitution, first, and the Lisbon Treaty, after,[4] started to recognise a 'direct role of national parliaments (independent from their respective governments)'[5] within the EU legal framework. Most importantly, the Lisbon Treaty 'constitutionalised' the 'Convention method', requiring as a general rule a more representative Treaty amendment procedure.

This chapter will explore the 'parliamentarisation' of the Treaty amendment process, as provided by the novel formulation of Article 48 Treaty on European Union (TEU)[6] introduced by the Lisbon Treaty, and will assess how it worked in practice. The chapter will then devote specific focus to the Italian Parliament, showing not only that during the European Convention the delegates of the Italian Parliament gave a significant contribution to the drafting of the Constitution for Europe, but also that the Italian Parliament made a specific effort to safeguard national parliamentary prerogatives in the post-Lisbon revision of EU Treaties.

[2] A Duff, *The Struggle for Europe's Constitution* (London, Federal Trust for Education and Research, 2005).

[3] G Ress, *Parlamentarismo e democrazia in Europa* (Napoli, Guida, 1999). An 'ironic parallel' exists between the increasing competences and functions of the European Parliament, on the one hand, and the decreasing affection of citizens showed by the low turnout in European elections (JHH Weiler, 'European Parliament Elections 2014: Europe's Fateful Choices' (2014) 24(3) *European Journal of International Law* 247).

[4] On the powers of national Parliaments after Lisbon see, among others, N Lupo, 'I parlamenti nazionali e le istituzioni europee' in G Amato and R Gualtieri (eds), *Prove di Europa unita. Le istituzioni europee dinanzi alla crisi* (Firenze, Passigli, 2013).

[5] Manzella, above n 1, 17.

[6] In line with the suggestions by the Constitution for Europe: see B De Witte, 'Entry into Force and Revision' in B de Witte (ed), *Ten Reflections on the Constitutional Treaty for Europe* (Firenze, EUI, 2003); L Gianniti, 'La revisione del futuro trattato costituzionale ed il diritto di recesso: sull'ambiguo processo di costituzionalizzazione dell'Unione, in www.associazionedeicostituzionalisti.it; M Cartabia, 'La ratifica del Trattato costituzionale europeo e la volontà costituente degli Stati membri' in *Forum quaderni costituzionali*, www.forumcostituzionale.it/ (2.10.2004).

II. The Power of Revision of the Treaties between International Law and Constitutional Law

Before entry into force of the Lisbon Treaty of 2009, the amendment procedure was divided into three phases:[7] the 'Community' phase, in which both the Commission and the governments of the Member States could make proposals for amendments to the Council, which, after seeking a (non-binding) opinion to the European Parliament (and possibly the Commission), could decide to convene an intergovernmental conference, through its Chairman; an 'international-diplomatic' phase, characterised by the political negotiation between the representatives of the Governments of the Member States within the Intergovernmental Conference; a 'national phase', related to the ratification of the treaty in accordance with Member States' constitutional traditions.[8]

Scholarly literature is divided about the nature itself of the power to revise the Union Treaties: is this power entrenched within an international law framework, which deems the Member States as the 'Masters of the Treaty' (Herren der Verträge),[9] or within a constitutional law framework, which circumscribes the Member States' power in the amendment procedure? The question could also be framed in the following way: is the procedure provided by the Treaties optional ('Sollvorschrift', ie non mandatory) or compulsory for Member States[10]—thus restricting, in some ways, their *jus contrahendi*? While some commentators have argued that a mutual agreement between the parties, in conformity with the Vienna Convention on the Law of Treaties,[11] may at any time revoke or modify the provisions of the Treaty,[12] other commentators have noted that the constitutional character of the Community Treaties would prevent the classic rules of international law from being applicable to the revision process.[13]

Indeed, the Court of Justice excluded the possibility for a mere practice, or a simple agreement between states, albeit in accordance with the rules of international law, to change

[7] See the former Art 48 of the Treaty on European Union, governing the amendment of the Treaties and replacing Arts 96 of the ECSC, 204 of the EURATOM and 236 EEC Treaty.

[8] *Political analysis of the internal reporting and decision-making of the EP delegation to the European Convention*, Study Directorate General for Internal Policies Policy Department C: Citizens' Rights and Constitutional Affairs Constitutional Affairs PE 419.592 (2010), 9.

[9] According to the formulation of the German Constitutional Court provided in both the *Maastricht* and the *Lisbon Urteil.*

[10] J Da Cruz Vilaca and N Ficarra, 'Y a-t-il des limites matérielles à la révision des traités instituant les Communautés européennes?' (1993) 1–2 *Chaiers de droit européenne* 15: 'le débat doctrinal portant sur l'article 236 (est) centré … sur la question de savoir si ses disposition sont facultatives ("Sollvorschrift") ou au contraire obligatoires pour les Etats membres et si, en fin de compte, ceux-ci peuvent réviser ou non légalement le traité sur la base des principes juridiques internationaux de l'*actus contrarius* et de la liberté quant à la forme, tout en ignorant les limites formelle set processuelles prévues dans lecit article 236'. The authors thus wonder whether it would be legal or unlawful to revise the Treaties by circumventing the formal limits envisaged by the EU Treaties.

[11] See arts 39, 54 and 57 of the Vienna Convention on the Law of Treaties.

[12] M Deliege-Sequaris, 'Révision des Traités européenne en de hors des procédures prévues' [1980] *Cahiers de Droit Européen* 539 and cp, JV Louis, 'Quelques considérations sur la révision des traités instituant les Communautés européennes' [1980] *Cahiers de Droit Européen* 553.

[13] JP Jacqué, *Cours général de droit communautaire*, RCADE 1990, vol I-1, quoted in K Boskovitz, *Le juge communautaire et l'articulation des compétences normatives entre la Communauté européenne et ses Etats Membres* (Athenes-Bruxelles, AntN Sakoulas/Bruylant, 1999) 27.

the founding Treaties.[14] In *Defrenne*, the Court held that any modification of the Treaty can only take place within the limits of the procedure contemplated by the Treaty in Article 236 Treaty Establishing the European Economic Community (TEEC). In its opinion 1/92, the Court ruled that the powers of the Court can only be changed within the framework of that article. Therefore, some scholars suggested to qualify the provisions of the Treaty related to the amendment procedure as a *lex specialis* in relation to the rules of international law, and that failure to comply with the procedure could be scrutinised by the Court of Justice through an action for failure to act.[15]

While I will not focus on the question on the possible existence of material and *substantive* limits to the revision of the Treaties,[16] it is clear that there exist some *procedural* limits to it. The Masters of the Treaty are not 'unconstrained' while amending the Treaty, because of the involvement, mandatory and not discretionary, of the Community institutions. The limits imposed by the formal revision procedure, and their defence by the Court of Justice,[17] are important in the light of the significant and new role allocated to elective assemblies in the course of the same procedure. This role cannot be circumvented by the Member States, at least when they act within the Union's institutional framework.

III. The New Revision Procedure Introduced by the Lisbon Treaty

During the European Convention drafting the 'Treaty establishing a Constitution for Europe', not surprisingly, the question of the revision process was one of those pivotal issues which measured the 'constitutional ambitions' of the European integration process.[18] While the supporters of such constitutional ambitions proposed the introduction of qualified majority rule for revising at least some parts of the Treaties, the requirement of a necessary unanimous agreement among Member States is still present in the revision

[14] Case C-327/91 *France v Commission*, para 36; Case C-149/85 *Wybot/Faure*, para 23; Case C-84/94 *United Kingdom v Council*, para 19; Case C-68/86, *United Kingdom v Council*, para 38; Case C-59/75, *Pubblico Ministero v Manghera*; Case C-43/75, *Defrenne v Sabena*.

[15] Boskovitz, above n 13, 28.

[16] According to some scholars there are no substantive limits to the revision of the Treaties, which, as long as the procedural rules are respected, could also affect the fundamental articles related to the institutional balance, or to the values and objectives of the Union (enshrined respectively in Arts 2 and 3 TEU): 'Le traités ne fixent aucune limite expresse aux révisions constitutionnelles; c'est ainsi, par exemple, qu'ils ne disent rien sur l'intangibilité des règles fondamentales énoncé aux articles 2 et 3 CEE, non plus que sur l'interdiction de modifications profondes des dispositions institutionnelles … En tout état de cause, dès lors que le procédures prescrits sont respectés, toutes les révisions sont possibles'. See R Bernhardt, 'Les sources du droit communautaire; la "Constitution" de la Communauté' in *Trente ans de droit communautaire* (Luxembourg, OPOCE, 1982) 79. cp R Passchier and M Stremier, *Unconstitutional Constitutional Amendments in European Union Law: Considering the Existence of Substantive Constraints on Treaty Revision*, in www.ssrn.com (19 February 2015).

[17] It is interesting to note that the Court of Justice might use the same restrictive approach towards the respect of procedural constraints if called to judge upon Art 50 TEU, when the UK's withdrawal from the EU triggered by the Brexit referendum will start.

[18] L Gianniti, 'Brevi note sui profili interni del procedimento di revisione dei trattati europei' in *Studi in onore di Franco Modugno* (Napoli, ES, 2011) and C Pinelli, 'Formazione e revisione del Trattato costituzionale europeo, in S Panunzio (ed.), *I diritti fondamentali e le Corti in Europa* (Napoli, Jovene, 2005).

procedure currently provided for in Article 48 TEU. Nevertheless, probably in the light of a compromise between a *constitutional* reading and an *international* reading of the founding Treaties, the revision process attaches a fundamental role to the EU institutions and a completely new power to the national Parliaments.[19]

The Lisbon Treaty introduces both an 'ordinary' and a 'simplified' revision procedure of the Treaty. It is only the first procedure, nevertheless, which guarantees the participation of representative assemblies to the amendment process and can be used to increase the powers of the Union. The opportunity to create a less cumbersome revision procedure arose during the late 1990s as one of the institutional implications of the enlargement process, which increased the number of Member States and consequently decreased the likelihood of a unanimous agreement. The group of wise men led by former Belgian Prime Minister Dehaene, which studied the prospects for institutional reform following the Treaty of Amsterdam in 1997, suggested to differentiate the revision procedures, reserving a more flexible procedure for the 'less essential' parts of the treaties.[20]

A. The Participation of National Parliaments and the European Parliament to the Ordinary Revision Procedure

Article 84 of the so-called Spinelli project, drafted by the Commission of Institutional Affairs of the European Parliament in 1984, already provided that representatives of the Council, one third of the members of Parliament, or the Commission could submit to legislative authorities a proposal to amend one or more provisions of the Treaty,[21] but it took more than 20 years to include the European Parliament in the process. In light of the new ordinary revision procedure envisaged by the Lisbon Treaty,[22] the European Parliament, the Government of any Member State and the Commission may submit to the Council proposals for the amendment of the Treaties. The Council must transmit the above projects to the European Council and notify them to national Parliaments. Before the President of the Council may decide to convene an intergovernmental conference, there is a long preliminary stage. Indeed, the European Council (which was not originally included in the procedure) may decide—as long as there is a simple majority in favour of the examination of the amendment—to convene a Convention composed of representatives of national Parliaments, of Heads of State or Government of the Member States, of the European Parliament and of the Commission. In fact, the European Council may also decide by a simple majority, with the approval of the European Parliament, not to convene a Convention in case of less significant amendments. It will eventually be for the Convention to examine the proposals for amendments and to adopt by consensus a recommendation to an intergovernmental conference.

[19] On the same issue see C Pinelli, 'The Convention Method' in N Lupo and C Fasone (eds), *Interparliamentary Cooperation in the European Composite Constitution* (Oxford, Hart Publishing, 2016).

[20] R Von Weizsacker, J Dehane and D Simon, *The Institutional Implications of the Enlargement*, Report to the European Commission, 18 October 1999, 12–13.

[21] F Capotorti, M Hilf, FG Jacobs and JP Jacqué, *The European Union Treaty. Commentary on the Draft adopted by the European Parliament on 14 February 1984* (Oxford, Clarendon Press, 1986).

[22] See from Art 48(2) TEU to Art 48(5) TEU.

It is clear that the most important innovation of the Lisbon Treaty concerns the institutionalisation of the 'Convention method'[23]—inaugurated for the drafting of the Charter of Fundamental Rights of the European Union. Such an institutionalisation entails that, before reaching the merely intergovernmental stage of the Treaty amendment process, the 'Community' phase of such a process is expanded and consolidated, and, most importantly, it involves representative assemblies.

As for the European Parliament, the powers of this institution are significantly increased. First, the European Parliament may submit proposals for amendments to the Treaties, whereas such a prerogative used to be reserved to the Commission or to the government of one of the Member States. Second, the European Parliament shall participate with their representatives to the Convention examining the proposals for amendments. Several studies on the internal functioning of the European Convention[24] attributed to the delegation of the European Parliament the substantive amendments—of a purely constitutional nature—introduced by the 'Treaty establishing a Constitution for Europe'.[25] Third, the same consultation powers of the Parliament—already existing—are strengthened by the Lisbon Treaty.

Prior to the latter, the European Parliament needed to be consulted by the President of the Council in the choice of convening an Intergovernmental Conference (IGC). Nowadays, the European Council must consult the European Parliament before taking a decision in favour of examining the proposed amendments through a Convention, but, if the European Council decides not to convene a Convention, the prior approval of the European Parliament—and not the mere consultation—is required. Therefore, the participation of the European Parliament in the amendment process becomes a generalised priority: either the Parliament is involved through its representatives in the Convention, or it agrees not to convene a Convention, and thus it voluntarily gives up the possibility to have a say in the amendment of the Treaty and gives a waiver to proceed at the merely intergovernmental level. The explicit approval of the Parliament in this case to a certain extent compensates for the lack of parliamentary representation in the Convention.

It should be noted that the European Parliament already used this possibility, following the European Council's proposal not to convene a Convention to change the composition of the European Parliament, adding 18 new members.[26] The amendment to a protocol

[23] C Closa, 'The Convention Method and the Transformation of EU Constitutional Politics' in EO Erikssen, JE Fossum and A Menéndez (eds), *Developing a European Constitution* (London, Routledge, 2004) 183–206. See also C Closa, *Ratifying European Union Treaties. Processes and Actors* (London, Routledge, 2013).

[24] GG Floridia and L Sciannella, *Il cantiere della nuova Europa. Tecnica e politica nei lavori della Convenzione europea* (Bologna, Il Mulino, 2003).

[25] D Beach, 'The European Parliament in the 2000 IGC and the Constitutional Treaty Negotiations: from Loser to Winner' (2007) 14 (8) *Journal of European Public Policy* 1271–92 and 'A New Pragmatism. The Role and Impact of the EP in the European Constitution Negotiations' in F Laursen (ed), *The Rise and Fall of the EU's Constitutional Treaty* (Leiden, Martinus Neijoff Publishers, 2008) 323–42. On the particular expertise of the EP delegation itself in the field of institutional affairs see O Costa, 'La contribution de la composante "Parlement européen" aux négociations de la Convention' (2004) 13 *Politique européenne* 21–41, in particular 24–29.

[26] The question arose to adapt the composition of Parliament emerged from the last elections in spring 2009 to the new composition provided by the Treaty of Lisbon, which entered into force after the elections. See B De Witte, 'The European Treaty Amendment for the Creation of a Financial Stability Mechanism' (2011) 6 *European Policy Analysis*, www.sieps.se, 4–5.

annexed to the Treaties was finalised through a short intergovernmental conference convened by the European Council Decision of 17 June 2010 which explicitly refers to consent by the European Parliament not to convene a Convention.[27] More recently, Parliament gave its approval to the European Council's proposal not to convene a Convention in order to add a protocol to the Treaty of Lisbon on the concerns of the Irish people on the right to life, family and education, taxation and security and defence.[28] Moreover, the European Parliament did not consider it necessary to convene a Convention to examine the proposal to extend to the Czech Republic Protocol 30 on the application of the Charter of Fundamental Rights of the European Union to Poland and the UK, as the possible effects of the proposal would be limited.[29]

Moving on to analyse the role of national Parliaments within the ordinary revision procedure of the Treaties, it must be stressed that for the very first time they can participate in the modification of the European Treaties through their representatives in the Convention. Nevertheless, national Parliaments do not have the power of initiative conferred by the Treaty of Lisbon to the European Parliament, nor the right to be consulted in the event there is the proposal to revise the Treaties without convening a Convention. It should however be noted that, unlike previous Treaties, the proposals for revising the Treaties submitted to the Council, must be 'notified to the national parliaments', consistently with the more general obligation to inform the national Parliaments under the Treaty of Lisbon.[30] Last but not least, the national Parliaments essentially take over the process of ratification. Under Article 48(4) TEU, the changes to the founding Treaties 'enter into force after being ratified by all the Member States in accordance with their respective constitutional requirements'.

The fragility of the involvement of national Parliaments, especially in cases where it is decided not to convene a convention, was emphasised. In these cases, the role of national Parliaments in amending the Treaty, which essentially consists of the participation in the Convention, can be overcome by a convergent will of the Council and the European Parliament. By way of contrast, such a convergent will could never affect the primary role of national Parliaments in ratifying the Treaties, thus providing an 'external legitimacy' to the revision process, while approving, at least in Italy, the law authorising the ratification of the Treaty.[31]

[27] This consent was expressed by the European Parliament decision of 6 May 2010 on the European Council's proposal not to convene a Convention for the revision of the Treaties with regard to transitional measures concerning the composition of the European Parliament (17196/2009—C7-0002/2010—2009/0814(NLE)).

[28] European Parliament decision of 18 April 2012 on the European Council's proposal not to convene a Convention for the addition of a Protocol on the concerns of the Irish people relate to the Lisbon Treaty, the Treaty on European Union and to the Treaty on the Functioning of 'European Union (00092/2011—C7-0388/2011—2011/0816(NLE)).

[29] European Parliament decision of 22 May 2013 on the European Council's proposal not to convene a convention to add to the Treaty on European Union and the Treaty on the Functioning of the European Union a protocol on the application of the Charter of Fundamental Rights of the European Union to Czech Republic (00091/2011—C7-0386/2011—2011/0818(NLE)).

[30] Protocol No 1 attached to the Treaty of Lisbon specifies the information duties upon the European institutions.

[31] Gianniti, above n 18, 4.

B. The Participation of National Parliaments and the European Parliament under the Simplified Revision Procedures

The 'simplified' revision procedure, which can never increase Union competences and can only be used to modify the third part of the TFEU concerning internal policies of the EU, is provided for by Article 48, paragraph 6 and 48, paragraph 7, of the TEU.

As per Article 48(6) TEU, the Government of any Member State, the European Parliament or the Commission shall submit to the European Council proposals to amend Part Three of the TFEU. The European Council may adopt a decision amending the Treaty, acting unanimously after consulting the European Parliament, the Commission and in some cases the European Central Bank. This Decision shall enter into force only if approved by Member States in accordance with their respective constitutional requirements.

In this simplified revision procedure, the participation of Parliaments is visibly reduced if compared to the ordinary revision procedure. At a general level, the non-establishment of a Convention does not allow the European Parliament and national Parliaments' representatives to discuss the proposals for amending the Treaties. As to the specific powers of the European Parliament, it retains the possibility of submitting proposals for amendments to the European Council, but it is simply consulted before the Council takes the final decision to amend the Treaties.

National Parliaments also see their role reduced. First of all, there is no express reference to a European obligation to notify the national Parliaments of draft amendments adopted through the simplified procedure. Furthermore, in order to enter into force, draft amendments require the simple 'approval', rather than 'ratification' by the Member State, which is required by the ordinary procedure. The difference in terminology covered by the Treaty could, in fact, solicit some national laws to avoid the ratification procedure which generally allows the appropriate involvement of national Parliaments. The German Constitutional Court, in fact, criticised the simplified revision procedure introduced by the Lisbon Treaty for blurring the role of national Parliaments, allowing a substantial change in the Treaty without the procedural guarantees that the ordinary revision procedure attaches to the involvement of national Parliaments.[32]

For this reason, the German Constitutional Court made the ratification of the Lisbon Treaty subject to the previous amendment of the law extending the powers of the two branches of the German Parliament in European affairs.[33] Indeed, the Court invited the Parliament, as the highest expression of popular sovereignty, to exercise the so-called 'responsibility for integration' (*Integrationsverantwortung*), that it holds in accordance with Article 23 of the German Constitution. The law on the participation of the Bundestag and the Bundersat to the integration process, in order to respect the guidelines of the Constitutional Court, required the involvement of the German Parliament comparable to that provided in the ordinary revision procedure of the Treaties, also in all the other cases that would have allowed—in the words of the Court—'a dynamic development of the Treaties'.[34]

[32] BVerfG, 2 BvE 2/08, 2 BvE 5/08, 2 BvR 1010/08, 2 BvR 1022/08, 2 BvR 1259/08, 2 BvR 182/09, 30 June 2009 (*Lisbon Urteil*).

[33] The law (*Gesetz über die Ausweitung und Stärkung der Rechte des Bundestages und des Bundesrates in Angelegenheiten der Europäischen Union*) has been modified in 2009 so to authorise the ratification of the Lisbon Treaty.

[34] BVerfG, 2 BvE 2/08, 2 BvE 5/08, 2 BvR 1010/08, 2 BvR 1022/08, 2 BvR 1259/08, 2 BvR 182/09, 30 June 2009 (*Lisbon Urteil*), para 411.

Those cases included exactly the simplified revision procedures provided for in Articles 48(6) and 48(7) TEU, as well as the 'flexibility clause' in article 352 TFEU.[35]

Finally, the Lisbon Treaty provides for another form of simplified procedure laid down in Article 48(7) TEU: when the TFEU or Title V of the TEU (on foreign policy) requires the Council to act unanimously in a sector or in a particular case, the European Council may allow the Council to act by a qualified majority in that same area.[36] Moreover, when the TFEU requires the Council to adopt legislative acts under a special legislative procedure, the European Council may allow the adoption of such acts in accordance with the ordinary legislative procedure. The European Council's decision must be unanimous, it needs the approval of the European Parliament, and it is transmitted to the national Parliaments. If even one single national Parliament contests such a decision within six months from the date of its transmission, the decision is not adopted.

In this case, therefore, the national Parliaments do not participate in the 'ratification' of the proposed amendment, as in the ordinary revision procedure, nor do they participate to its 'approval', as in the simplified revision procedure as per Article 48(6) TEU: national Parliaments hold a sort of 'oppositional power', being able to block the decision by exercising their veto.[37] Also the procedure contemplated by Article 48(7) TEU was contested by the German Constitutional Court: although its activation requires a unanimous vote in the European Council, the possibility of veto enjoyed by the executive does not necessarily reflect the will of the German Parliament, as if the position of the Government implicitly entails the consent of its Parliament.[38] For this reason, the activation of the procedure in article 48(7) TEU also requires an Act of Parliament's authorisation under Article 23.1 of the Basic Law. In other words, the possibility for each Parliament to veto the application of the 'bridging clause' is not a sufficient device to safeguard parliamentary democracy.[39] As showed by the following paragraphs the Italian Parliament also found a way to safeguard national parliamentary prerogatives even in the simplified revision procedure.

IV. The Italian Parliament and the First EU Treaties Revision after the Entry into Force of the Lisbon Treaty

A. The Amendment of Article 136 TFEU via the Simplified Revision Procedure

The European Council of 16–17 December 2010 took the first decision to launch a simplified revision procedure of the Lisbon Treaty in order to introduce some permanent

[35] The position of the German Constitutional Court on these provisions is analysed in B Guastaferro, 'Il Trattato di Lisbona tra il "custode" della sovranità popolare e il "custode" della Costituzione: la triplice "riserva" apposta al Trattato dalla Corte costituzionale tedesca' (2011) 1 *Rassegna di diritto pubblico europeo*.

[36] The procedure is not applicable to decisions that have military implications or which fall within the field of defence.

[37] On such a distinction see M Olivetti, 'Parlamenti nazionali nell'Unione europea' in *Digesto delle discipline pubblicistiche* (Torino, Utet, 2012).

[38] German Constitutional Court, *Lisbon Urteil*, para 413.

[39] ibid, para 414.

mechanisms to ensure the financial stability of the euro-zone and replace the transitional measures launched in May 2010 to deal with the Greek economic crisis.[40] In fact, the European Council of 25 March 2011[41] added a new paragraph to Article 136 TFEU[42] in order to create a permanent stability mechanism to help Member States whose currency is euro who are experiencing a financial and economic crisis. Such supporting financial assistance is subordinated to strict conditionality.

It is interesting to note that, although Article 48.6 TEU requires the European Parliament to be consulted before taking the decision to amend the Treaty, the decision of the Council did not in any way take into account the position of the European Parliament (expressed in a resolution of 23 March 2011).[43] The latter required EU institutions to fully participate to the new European Stability Mechanism, believing that the intention to establish the mechanism outside the institutional framework of the European Union could be a threat to the integrity of the system based on the Treaties.[44] The European Parliament also called for respect of the basic principles of democratic decision-making, such as transparency and parliamentary control,[45] inviting the European Council to adopt the Regulation on conditionality in accordance with the ordinary legislative procedure of the Union (which sees the involvement of the European Parliament on an equal footing alongside the Council). It also stressed that each national Parliament should be fully involved at all stages, in accordance with its budgetary and monetary powers, in order to increase transparency, ownership and accountability of the decisions taken.[46]

The European Council Decision of 25 March 2011, adopted just two days after the resolution of the Parliament, did not modify the 2010 draft decision in light of the considerations and suggestions of the European Parliament. It was observed that, while the amendment to Article 136 TFEU created a new legal basis to establish a stability mechanism through an intergovernmental agreement outside of the Treaties, the European Parliament's call for involving EU institutions would have required the granting of new powers to the Union. This would have precluded the possibility of amending the Treaty by using the simplified revision procedure, particularly appropriate in the emergency context which characterised the economic and financial crisis of the Union.[47]

Whatever the reasons for the simplified procedure, it is clear that the contribution of the representative assemblies to amend the Treaties in these cases is marginal. It is telling

[40] On the reasons behind the choice to revise the Treaty, rather than using the procedures already envisaged by the Treaty, such as Art 122, para 2, TFEU see De Witte, above n 26. For a criticism on such a choice see L Gianniti, *Il meccanismo di stabilità e la revisione semplificata del Trattato di Lisbona: un'ipoteca tedesca sul processo di integrazione?* Documenti IAI, febbraio 2011.

[41] European Council Decision of 25 March 2011 amending Art 136 of the Treaty on the Functioning of the European Union with regard to a stability mechanism for Member States whose currency is the euro (2011/199/UE).

[42] The new paragraph states: 'The Member States whose currency is the euro may establish a stability mechanism to be activated if indispensable to safeguard the stability of the euro area as a whole. The granting of any required financial assistance under the mechanism will be made subject to strict conditionality'.

[43] *Amendment of the Treaty on the Functioning of the European Union with regard to a stability mechanism for Member States whose currency is the euro*, European Parliament resolution of 23 March 2011 on the draft European Council decision amending Article 136 of the Treaty on the functioning of the European Union with regard to a stability mechanism for Member States whose currency is the euro (00033/2010—C7-0014/2011—2010/0821(NLE)).

[44] ibid, point 7 of the Resolution.

[45] ibid, point 8 of the Resolution.

[46] ibid, point 17 of the Resolution.

[47] De Witte, above n 26, 6.

that in the same resolution the European Parliament submitted that 'the use of Article 48, paragraph 6, TEU is an extraordinary procedure' and recalled that 'in accordance with Article 48, paragraph 3, TEU, Parliament has the right to request the convening of a convention to reshape the institutions, procedures and policies defining the Union's economic governance'.[48]

B. The Italian Parliamentary Experience

Italy implemented the amendment of Article 136 TFEU through a law authorising the ratification,[49] opting, therefore, for the procedure which most protects parliamentary prerogatives. According to Italian constitutional provisions, indeed, the intervention of the national legislature is not required for all Treaties. Indeed, as a general rule, Article 87(8) of the Italian Constitution empowers the President of the Republic to ratify international treaties and Article 80 provides for the necessity of legislation enabling the ratification only with reference to some particular Treaties. When this is the case, as an additional safeguard to parliamentary prerogatives, the same Parliament should intervene through the regular legislative procedure (since article 72, last paragraph, Constitution dictates that 'The regular procedure for consideration and direct approval by the House is always followed in the case of bills on constitutional and electoral matters, enabling legislation, the ratification of international treaties and the approval of budgets and accounts').

It might be argued that the choice of the Italian Government to opt for the procedure which most guaranteed parliamentary prerogatives, even in the case of a Treaty amendment process through the 'simplified' procedure, might have benefited from the fact that the Italian Parliament has jointly examined the decision to amend Article 136 TFEU, the decision to ratify the so called 'Fiscal Compact',[50] and the decision to ratify the European Stability Mechanism.[51] The Parliament, indeed, approved three different laws authorising the Treaties' ratification during the same day, in light of a parliamentary debate addressing the implications of all the above-mentioned proposals.[52] In this respect, since the Parliament's authorisation by law of the ratification of international Treaties is required by Article 80 of the Constitution when those Treaties are 'of a political nature' or 'entail changes to the national territory or financial burdens or changes to legislation', the undoubtedly 'political nature' of the Fiscal Compact, as well as the 'financial burdens' entailed by it and by the European Stability Mechanism, triggered the two Houses of the Parliament to authorise their ratification through the regular legislative procedure.

The serious involvement of a representative institution such as the Parliament, at least in the ratification process, is very important if we consider that there is no popular

[48] Point 20 of the Resolution quoted in footnote 43.

[49] Law No 115 of 23 July 2012.

[50] Law No 114 of 23 July 2012.

[51] Law No 116 of 23 July 2012.

[52] L Pierdominici, *Constitutional Change through Euro Crisis Law. Report on Italy* (2014) available at http://eurocrisislaw.eui.eu/italy/: 'in both the Houses, and for both the initial part in front of the competent Parliamentary Committees and the discussion in the House of Deputies, the procedure of authorisation by law of the Fiscal Compact was joined with the other procedures related to the Treaty amendment article 136(3) TFEU and the European Stability Mechanism (ESM)'.

participation in the Treaty amendment process, in that the ratification of EU Treaties does not require a referendum.[53] The only EU-related referendum in Italy was held in 1989, but it was 'consultative', as it asked whether the Italian population was in favour of the transformation of the European Communities into a European Union with a Government accountable to the European Parliament, and with a European Parliament entitled to draft a Constitution for Europe. The outcome was highly positive, with 88.03 per cent of the voters in favour and only 11.97 per cent of the voters against.[54] So, no referendum was held at the major steps of the European integration process, and no referendum was held on the Fiscal Compact.[55] Indeed, article 75(2) Constitution excludes this possibility for the ratification of international Treaties as 'Referenda are not admissible in the case of tax, budget, amnesty and pardon laws, or laws authorizing the ratification of international treaties'.

Even if the parliamentary debate on the domestic impact of European economic governance arising from the financial crisis was not particularly significant, at least some criticisms were raised,[56] since Italy was already experiencing clear problems in its budgetary situation. Especially as far as the most austerity oriented measure was concerned, namely the Fiscal compact, some MPs raised clear concerns about its insufficient democratic nature, criticizing 'European bureaucrats'' decisions, about the unwillingness of the citizens to participate in the hard process of reduction of the debt.[57] This is in contrast with the history of the Italian Parliament, which always showed its almost bi-partisan support to the European integration process. Notoriously, Italy proved its adaptability to the EU legal order in ratifying very quickly and with large majorities almost all EU Treaties.[58] Sometimes the Italian Parliament even showed its enthusiasm in furthering and deepening the European integration process. Just to give an example, it was the first Parliament to ratify the Treaty establishing a Constitution for Europe (never entered into force because of the failure of the referenda in France and the Netherlands).[59] Moreover, it approved the Lisbon Treaty in 2008 with a unanimous vote within both the Chamber of Deputies and the Senate.[60]

It is telling that within the joint parliamentary debates on Article 136 TFEU, on the ratification of the European Stability Mechanism (ESM), and of the Fiscal Compact, the same

[53] Moreover, the Italian legal order does not contemplate the possibility that the Constitutional Court might ex ante review the law authorising the ratification of the Treaties.

[54] Nevertheless, the referendum was conceived to have symbolic value rather than any legal implication, also since in the Italian legal order referendums are only allowed either to abrogate parliamentary laws (as per Art 75 of the Constitution) or to confirm a parliamentary constitutional law aimed at revising the Constitution (as per Art 138 of the Constitution). In this respect, a specific constitutional law was adopted (Law No 2 of 3 April 1989) in order to have such a 'consultative referendum' on the future of the EU.

[55] Nevertheless, it is interesting to note that some scholars, economists, and politicians proposed a referendum on the Law No 243 of 2012 (namely the law implementing the balanced budget principle introduced by amending Italian Constitution in light of EU guidelines).

[56] The Fiscal Compact obtained 368 votes in favour and 68 votes against it in the Chamber of Deputies, coming from two political parties (Italia dei valori and Lega Nord).

[57] See in particular the intervention of some MPs during the exam of the III Commission on Foreign Affairs of the Camera dei Deputati, 18 July 2012, reported by Pierdominici, above n 52.

[58] See the chapter in this volume by G Vosa, 'The Role of the Italian Parliament in the Stipulation of International Treaties: Rise and Decline of the "Authorisation Model"', who nevertheless emphasises that, at the very beginning, the left wing political parties were against the process of European integration.

[59] The Chamber of Deputies approved the draft Constitutional Treaty on 25 January 2005, with only 28 contrary votes, and the Senate voted on 6 April 2005 with only 16 votes against.

[60] See M Cartabia and B Guastaferro, 'Italy' in S Griller (eds), *Member States' Constitution and European Integration*, (Oxford, Hart, forthcoming 2017).

rapporteurs emphasised the difference with the old times in which the ratification of the EU-related bills were seen as only 'technical' debate. The political echo and the sensitiveness of the issues involved, not only triggered some resistance, but sometimes turned the discussion on the long-standing problems of the so called democratic deficit in the European Union, with strong arguments, from both the centre right and the centre left, for the need of a more 'political' Union.[61]

V. The Choice of the Italian Legislator to Safeguard the National Parliament in the Treaty Amendment Process: Articles 11 and 5 of Law No 234 of 2012

The previous paragraph showed that Italy tried to ensure an appropriate involvement of the national Parliament to the first Treaty amendment process after the entry into force of the Treaty of Lisbon. As a matter of fact, the simplified nature of the revision of Article 136 TFEU did not affect the choice of the Italian Parliament, which decided to approve a statutory law authorising the ratification of the Treaty as if it was dealing with an ordinary revision procedure. Moreover, following the above-mentioned Treaty revision process, with the Law of 24 December 2012, no 234,[62] which regulates methods and procedures concerning the Italian participation to the EU, Italy to a certain extent generalised this sort of 'safeguard' to protect national Parliaments also in case of simplified revision procedure of the Treaties.

Indeed, Article 11 of the Law No 234 of 2012 is expressly dedicated to the simplified revision of the EU Treaties. It is possible to say, in this respect, that the Italian Parliament was concerned about ensuring its adequate participation in the EU amendment process, also when it takes the simplified forms enshrined in Article 48(6) and 48(7) TEU. It followed the path of the German Parliament, which was, nevertheless, only pushed by its Constitutional Court in the Lisbon *Urteil* to take more seriously its involvement in the Treaty amendment process.

The first paragraph of Article 11 requires the Government to promptly inform both the Houses of the Parliament on any initiative carried out within the framework of the simplified revision procedure as per Article 48(6) and 48(7) TEU as well as in the framework of the common Union defence policy as per Article 42(2) TEU. This is extremely important because, at the EU level, the requirement to notify to national Parliaments of any proposals to amend the Treaty is enshrined only in case of ordinary revision procedure.

The third paragraph of Article 11 provides that, in cases where the entry into force of a decision of the European Council or the Council of the European Union is subject to

[61] See for instance MP Tempestini (PD), 17 July 2012, Exam in the III Commission for Foreign Affairs, http://leg16.camera.it/824?tipo=C&anno=2012&mese=07&giorno=17&view=&commissione=03&pagina=data.20120717.com03.bollettino.sede00010.tit00020#data.20120717.com03.bollettino.sede00010.tit00020, 42, as quoted in Pierdominici, above n 52.

[62] A Esposito, 'La legge 24 dicembre 2012, n 234, sulla partecipazione dell'Italia alla formazione e all'attuazione della normativa e delle politiche dell'Unione europea. Parte I—Prime riflessioni sul ruolo delle Camere', in www.federalismi.it, 23 January 2013.

the prior approval of the Member States in accordance with their respective constitutional requirements, 'the decision shall be considered adopted in case of a positive resolution of both Houses.'[63] Most importantly, when a simplified Treaty revision procedure is at stake, the legislature makes it clear that the approval must follow the rules of the legislative process,[64] even if such a procedure is not properly the same of the procedure on the ratification of the Treaties envisaged by Article 80 of the Italian Constitution.[65] Indeed, as specified by the fourth paragraph of Article 11, the Government submits to the Parliament, within 30 days after such adoption, a draft law on the approval of any decision taken by the European Council pursuant to Article 48(6) TEU.

It might be argued that the rationale behind this choice of the Italian legislator is the following: the 'simplification', in fact, would lie primarily in the development of the decision at the European level (which simply requires a unanimous decision of the European Council without the necessity to convene a Convention), and not at the domestic level. Against this backdrop, during the ratification process, it would be necessary to follow a procedure at least 'inspired' by article 80 of the Constitution,[66] in order to ensure the involvement of the Parliament through the legislation authorising the ratification. To conclude, Article 11 of Law No 234 of 2012 also requires the Government to inform both the Houses of the Parliament on the process of approval of the concerned decisions by other Member States of the Union (see paragraph 7).

It is also important to underline that the Italian legislator, through Law No 234 of 2012, wants to guarantee an appropriate participation of the national Parliament also in case of future Treaties signed outside the institutional framework of the EU. Article 5 of the Law No 234 of 2012, indeed, requires the Government to promptly inform the Parliament of any initiative concerning the conclusion of agreements between Member States of the European Union aimed at introducing or strengthening the rules on financial or monetary or otherwise producing significant consequences on the public finances (paragraph 1). Moreover, the Government ensures that the position represented by Italy in the negotiation of the agreements takes into account the guidelines *(atti di indirizzo)* adopted by the Houses. In the event that the Government does not comply with those guidelines, the Prime Minister or a Minister appointed by him needs to report to the Houses, providing the appropriate justification of the position taken (paragraph 2). Most importantly, Article 5, paragraph 3, requires these provisions to apply also in the case of agreements concluded outside the EU Treaties framework as well as in case of change of previous agreements. In this respect, Italy ensures an appropriate involvement of the Parliament, which could be otherwise excluded by the European economic governance when it is carried out with instruments of international law outside the procedural guarantees of EU law towards elective assemblies.

[63] Art 11, para 3 of the Law 24 December 2012, no 234. See on this provision G Piccirilli, 'Il Parlamento italiano: le procedure europee nella legge n 234 del 2012', in A Manzella and N Lupo, *Il sistema parlamentare euro-nazionale* (Torino, Giappichelli, 2014) 215–17.

[64] More specifically, the German law provides for the approval of the simplified revision procedure by constitutional law, under Art 23, para 1, of the Basic Law (which requires two-thirds majority of the members of the Bundestag and two-thirds of the votes of the Bundesrat).

[65] Esposito, above n 62, 52.

[66] G Piccirilli, 'Il ricorso alla legge per l'esercizio dei poteri "europei" da parte del Parlamento italiano. Spunti per una lettura costituzionalmente orientata' (2013) 2 *Osservatoriosullefonti.it*.

VI. The Delegates of the Italian Parliament within the European Convention

While the previous paragraphs accounted for the choice of the Italian Parliament in managing the simplified Treaty revision process, there is no empirical evidence of the role of the Italian Parliament in the ordinary revision process, which never occurred after the entry into force of the Lisbon Treaty. Nevertheless, as we have seen, the new Treaty of Lisbon's ordinary revision procedure is the same procedure used for the drafting of the Treaty adopting a Constitution for Europe, in that it requires a Convention where also parliamentary delegates and not simply executive delegates are represented. The 2001 Laeken European Council defined the composition of the Convention: in addition to its Chairman and Vice-Chairmen, the Convention was composed of 15 representatives of the Heads of State or Government of the Member States (one per Member State), 30 members of the national Parliaments (two per Member State), 16 members of the European Parliament and two representatives of the Commission.[67]

Representatives of the Italian Parliament to the Convention were the deputy Marco Follini and Senator Lamberto Dini; their substitutes, respectively, the deputy Valdo Spini and Senator Filadelfio Guido Basile. The Representative of the Italian Government was the Deputy President of the Council of Ministers Gianfranco Fini, and some Italian MEPs (Cristiana Muscardini, Antonio Tajani and, as a substitute, Elena Paciotti) were part of the European Parliament delegation to the Convention. Last but not least, one of the two Vice-Presidents of the President of the European Convention Giscard d'Estaing, namely Giuliano Amato, was Italian, and he was the former President of the Italian Council of Ministers.

Within the biggest delegation of the Convention, namely that of national Parliaments, Italian delegates played a pivotal role. In particular, the figure of the Senator Lamberto Dini was decisive in expressing the concerns and requests of the national parliamentarians vis-à-vis the Presidium and in linking with the Liberals' leader Andrew Duff, member of the European Parliament, in order to create a sort of 'integrationist side' within the parliamentary delegation within the Convention.[68] Indeed, within the national parliamentarians' delegation, there was an 'integrationist bandwagon organized by van der Linden, Dini and Meyer'.[69] More generally, Lamberto Dini was deemed to be one of 'the most influential member's of the Convention, becoming 'a decisive figure in the frantic politicking of the Convention's final months'.[70] This was also because he had the chance to chair the national parliamentarians' group in the final (and decisive) moments of the Convention by dint of Italy having the EU's rotating presidency.

Together with Andrew Duff and the French parliamentarian Perre Lequiller, the delegates of the Italian Parliament suggested the Union should aim for a single President,

[67] The accession countries will participate fully in the work of the Convention (with one government representative and two national Parliament members) and will participate in the proceedings without, however, being able to prevent any consensus which may emerge among the Member States.

[68] P Norman, *The Accidental Constitution. The Making of Europe's Constitutional Treaty* (EuroComment, 2003) 45.

[69] ibid 249.

[70] ibid 33.

who would unify the positions of President of the European Council and Commission.[71] Moreover, they opposed the UK position in the sensitive issue of enhanced cooperation, which triggered continued discord among the Members of the Convention especially in the field of foreign policy and defence. In particular, Senator Dini, as a former foreign minister, stressed in the discussion that 'enhanced cooperation was necessary if the UK insisted on continuing restrictions to more QMV in the Union'.[72] He also proposed an alternative to unanimity and to qualified majority voting (QMV) which could have taken the form of a super-qualified majority.[73]

In the final months of the Convention, Duff, Dini and Brok produced a 'key-point' paper which showed the strengths of the cooperation between the integrationist side of both national parliamentarians and MEPs and listed few demands 'of pivotal importance', to be transmitted to the Intergovernmental Conference, including: a) QMV in foreign policy when the foreign minister's initiatives were supported by the Commission; b) the external Action Service as a single administration within the Commission; c) greater scope for the Court of Justice in the field of common foreign and security policy; d) QMV for legislation harmonising indirect tax measures relating to administrative cooperation, tax fraud and tax evasion; e) the express requirement that the European Parliament must consent should a future European Council decide *not* to call a convention to revise the Constitution. This last requirement, in particular, was of pivotal importance to safeguard parliamentary prerogatives within the Treaty amendment procedure, and was eventually included into the final text of the Constitution for Europe, and later on into the Lisbon Treaty.

The Italian parliamentary position was also crucial in the discussion on the role of Parliaments in the subsidiarity scrutiny, and led to the abandonment of the idea of the 'red card' proposed by the UK representative Gisela Stuart (namely the possibility for two-thirds of parliamentary votes to force the Commission to withdraw a legislative proposal). As it was reported, 'Lamberto Dini poured scorn on Stuart's idea … (and) demanded the red card idea be dropped because "it means giving national parliaments the power of veto over the initiative of the Commission and that we should not do"'.[74]

VII. Concluding Remarks

The involvement of Parliaments in the process of revision of the Treaties is an important step towards the legitimacy of the European Union. It introduces elements of democratic representation in a long-standing tradition of merely international-diplomatic negotiations between the executives of the Member States. The road to effective involvement of representative assemblies in this area has been rather difficult.

As to the European Parliament, it is only with the Treaty of Lisbon that the assembly directly elected by the citizens can make proposals for amendment of the Treaties, despite the proposals of the 1984 Spinelli project. As to national Parliaments, their path towards

[71] ibid 113.
[72] ibid 208.
[73] ibid 239–44.
[74] ibid 170.

the participation in the Treaty amendment process has been even more difficult. The European Parliament did not consider them in the various initiatives presented throughout the European institutional history to include representative assemblies in the revision procedures of the Treaties, escaping their 'genuinely' executive nature.[75] Moreover, the coexistence of representatives of elected assemblies in the European Convention was sometimes characterised by competitive dynamics. The alliance of the European Parliament with national Parliaments was jeopardised sometimes by 'an inferiority complex of the European Parliament' in respect of national Parliaments, sometimes by a certain 'mistrust'.[76] For a long time, the European Parliament conceived of itself as the only legitimate body to 'draft a European Constitution bearing in mind the *European* perspective', considering national parliamentary delegations as expression of 'necessarily divergent *national* claims' exactly like their national governments.[77]

The idea that national Parliaments—as *national* institutions—were not necessarily oppositional stakeholders, able to jeopardise the growth of supranational institutions, was difficult to establish.[78] However, the invitation to consider the European Parliament and national Parliaments as complementary, and both necessary to the EU's democratic growth, was finally welcomed by the Lisbon Treaty. Indeed, the 'parliamentarisation' of the Union needs to lie on two pillars, the European Parliament, on the one hand, and national Parliaments, on the other. The Lisbon Treaty, indeed, institutionalised the so-called 'Convention method', which involves both the representative assemblies in the delicate phase of revision of the Treaties.

Besides this major 'formal' achievement, the praxis developed in the aftermath of the Lisbon Treaty is not promising. First, this praxis created a sort of imbalance between the European Parliament and national Parliaments. While the ordinary revision procedure establishing a Convention (where the European Parliament and national Parliaments are equally represented), has never been used so far, several minor amendments to the Treaties, thanks to the consent of the European Parliament, occurred not convening a Convention. As we saw, this precluded national Parliaments from having their voice heard.[79] Indeed, an excessive use of the ordinary revision procedure not requiring the Convention could deprive national Parliaments of the 'constituent power' they enjoy in light of the Lisbon Treaty. Rather than directly participating in the proposal and drafting of the amendments, national Parliaments could only exercise their 'counter-constitutional power', and possibly block decisions taken by Governments' representatives.[80]

[75] See the Study quoted above n 8, 13.

[76] ibid 54.

[77] See the speech by Altiero Spinelli during the plenary session of 14 February 1984 at the European Parliament (italics added by the author).

[78] On the importance of the cooperation between national Parliaments and European Parliament see C Decaro and N Lupo, 'Introduzione' in C Decaro and N Lupo (eds), *Il 'dialogo' tra parlamenti: obiettivi e risultati* (Roma, LUISS University Press, 2009).

[79] See s III.A of this chapter.

[80] On the concept of 'contre-pouvoir constituant' see E Maulin, 'Le pouvoir constituant dans l'Union européenne' (2007) 45 *Droits: Revue francaise de théorie, de philosophie et de culture juridique* 33: 'le pouvoir constituant qu'ils exercent resemble alors plutot à une faculté d'empecher, à une contre-pouvoir constituant suscepltible de faire obstacle … à la constitution éuropéenne'. According to the author, national Parliaments' constituent power resembles more to a power to oppose to the European integration process, which is why it could be qualified as a 'counter-power'.

Second, in order to revise Article 136 TFEU, the simplified revision procedure was used. If, more generally, the simplified procedure does not contemplate adequate representation of national Parliaments as it does not convene a Convention, in this specific case also the European Parliament's formal power to be consulted was dismissed. None of the EP's preferences were channelled in the final unanimous decision of the European Council, although it concerned a very sensitive issue related to economy and finance.

Third, international law instruments used to deal with the economic and financial crisis favoured intergovernmental negotiations outside the Union's institutional framework, thus circumventing the procedural safeguards introduced by the Treaty of Lisbon in favour of representative assemblies.[81] The Treaty establishing the European Stability Mechanism and the Treaty on Stability, Coordination and Governance in the Economic and Monetary Union (the so-called Fiscal Compact) are just examples of the agreements adopted during the sovereign debt crisis of 2010–2012 between the governments of Member States. According to some scholars, this wave of cooperation agreements is not symptomatic of a kind of 'intergovernmental conspiracy'[82] designed to undermine the role of supranational institutions. Moreover, the actions taken in the intergovernmental sphere share the same 'teleological context' of Union actions aimed at stabilising the economic and financial situation, and would still pursue the 'objectives of the Union.'[83]

Nevertheless, it is submitted that the use of public international law allows the circumvention of the rules governing the amendment of the Treaties. This runs counter to the efforts of the Court to affirm the binding nature of the procedural limits to the revision of the Treaties, requiring the involvement of the EU institutions and representative assemblies, able to 'circumscribe' the constituent power of the Member States' 'Masters of the Treaties'.[84] Against this backdrop, it is important to emphasise that the choice of the Italian legislator to protect the involvement of national Parliaments, not only in case of simplified revision procedure but also in case of future Treaties signed outside the institutional framework of the EU and concerning financial and monetary issues, represent a major contribution to the parliamentarisation of the Treaty amendment process.

[81] For an analysis on the fragile parliamentary representation in the European economic governance (with particular reference to the role of the European Parliament), which could result in a violation of the democratic principle 'no taxation without parliamentary representation' see C Fasone, 'European Economic Governance and Parliamentary Representation: What Place for the European Parliament?' (2014) 20 *European Law Journal* 164–85.

[82] B De Witte, *Using International Law in the Euro Crisis: Causes and Consequences*, ARENA working paper no 4/2013.

[83] Manzella, above n 1, 36. On the institutional aspects related to the European framework on budgetary issues see GL Tosato, *La riforma costituzionale del 2012 alla luce della normativa dell'Unione: l'interazione fra i livelli europei ed interno*, Paper presented at the Conference 'Il principio dell'equilibrio di bilancio secondo la riforma costituzionale del 2012', Roma, Palazzo della Consulta, 22 November 2013.

[84] Suffice here to recall that while the Parliament's request to be consulted in the negotiations for the Treaty on the European Stability Mechanism was dismissed, the presence of four representatives of the EP in the negotiations for the fiscal Compact was crucial to try to make as much as possible in line with the new Treaty the legal framework of the Union (Fasone, above n 81, 9–10).

Part IV

The Italian Future in a European Perspective

15

Understanding the Impact of the Autonomy of National Legislatures on the EU Policy Process

AMIE KREPPEL

I. Introduction

Democratic legislatures fall into two broad categories by virtue of the constitutional character of their relationship with the executive branch. Parliament type legislatures are those with hierarchical executive–legislative relationships based on fused powers and mutual dependency, while congress type legislatures have a largely transactional relationship with the executive branch due to their formal independence and separated character.[1] There exists a great deal of variation within each of these categories, both between legislatures and within individual legislatures across time. Though it is rare for the core character of the executive–legislative relationship to change (from fused to separation of powers or vice versa), the legislative autonomy of a legislature can (and does) shift for a variety of reasons impacting its relative power and influence in terms of both policy-making and executive oversight. Most analyses of changing legislative powers and shifting legislative–executive relations have focused on the domestic political sphere. Less attention has been

[1] A Kreppel, 'Typologies and Classifications' in S Martin, T Saalfeld and KW Strøm (eds), *The Oxford Handbook of Legislative Studies* (Oxford, Oxford University Press, 2014); M Shugart, 'Comparative Executive-Legislative Relations' in RAW Rhodes, S Binder, B Rockman (eds), *The Oxford Handbook of Political Institutions* (Oxford, Oxford University Press, 2006).

given to links between legislative autonomy and policymaking in context of the European Union (EU).[2]

Historically the Italian Parliament has been one of the more autonomous and influential within Europe in terms of shaping domestic policy outcomes for a variety of institutional and partisan reasons.[3] Reforms since the mid-1990s have served to reduce that autonomy to some extent, though perhaps not to the degree some had envisioned. The impact of the Chamber of Deputies' changing levels of legislative autonomy on Italian engagement with EU level governance remains largely unexplored. Though the subject of national parliamentary participation in (or exclusion from) the EU-level political process in general has been studied comparatively[4] and through case studies[5] the impact of the *character* of national legislatures, including their relative institutional and partisan autonomy, remain largely unexplored. An analysis of the Italian case may provide useful insights in this regard.

On its surface, the Italian Parliament would seem to be well placed to influence the implementation, and even the formation of EU-level legislation due to its powerful role within the Italian policy-making landscape. The historic weakness of the Italian executive combined with the policy-making powers of the legislature could be interpreted as providing the opportunity for parliamentary influence during both the ascending (policy formation) and descending (implementation) phases of the EU legislative process.[6] However, the structure of EU decision-making, including the constraints created by tight time lines and often extensive legal guidelines, together with changing domestic political contexts have served to weaken significantly the policy influence of the Italian Parliament over time. Recent treaties have exacerbated this trend as the policy domain of the EU has grown, the need for expertise to analyse EU policy initiatives expanded, and the time constraints on domestic legislatures tightened. Thus, despite the new early warning system to provide additional input from domestic legislatures, greater emphasis on subsidiarity at the EU level and a long history of parliamentary strength vis-à-vis the executive, Italy appears to be following recent trends across the EU of empowering the executive within an expanding EU policy framework. Indeed, in the Italian case a past legacy of legislative power may have inspired the Parliament to actively participate in the reduction of its own influence relative to the executive in the name of increased efficiency in both domestic and EU policy arenas.

To examine why this is the case, this chapter provides a brief overview of a framework for comparing legislatures across political systems. This is then applied to the Italian Chamber of Deputies, before and after the significant restructuring of the party system and

[2] For consistency and clarity, I use the current title of European Union throughout. The reader will recall that between its creation in 1957 and the Single European Act (SEA) in 1987 the official title was the European Economic Community. This was briefly changed to European Community between the SEA and the adoption of the Maastricht Treaty in 1992, which formally changed the name to the European Union upon implementation in 1993.

[3] Throughout this chapter I am focusing explicitly on the Chamber of Deputies, however much of the analysis holds true for the Senate as well given the highly symmetrical character of Italian bicameralism.

[4] K Goetz and JH Meyer-Sahling, 'The Europeanization of National Political Systems: Parliaments and Executives' (2008) 3 *Living Reviews in European Governance.*

[5] A Maurerand and W Wessels (eds), *National Parliaments on their Ways to Europe: Losers or Latecomers?* (Baden Baden, Nomos Verlagsgesellschaft, 2001); K Featherstone and C Radaelli, *The Politics of Europeanization* (Oxford, Oxford University Press, 2003); S Brouard et al (eds), *The Europeanization of Domestic Legislatures. The Empirical Implications of the Delors' Myth in Nine Countries*, (New York, Springer-Verlag, 2012).

[6] See the chapter by R Ibrido, in this book.

internal parliamentary reforms of the 1990s. A summary review of the evolution of the structures and procedures for managing EU policy at the domestic level and the interaction between these trajectories follows. This analysis highlights two general trends. The first is the rise and decline of the legislative power and obstructionism of the Chamber of Deputies because of changes in both structural and partisan autonomy. The second is the increasing formalisation of the process for managing Italy's participation in policy-making at the EU level focused on the role of the executive, with a corresponding marginalisation of the legislature. The possible links between these two trends are discussed in the concluding section of the chapter.

II. Comparing Legislative Influence

Legislatures within democratic political systems play several critical roles. They serve as an important *link* between voters and government and they are the central *representative* political institution at the national level.[7] They also are the primary mechanism for executive *oversight*, to insure against government over-reach and mismanagement.[8] Of course, as indicated by the term 'legislature,' they also engage in the legislative process or *policy-making*. All legislatures in democratic systems engage in all four of these core tasks (linkage, representation, oversight and policy-making) to some degree. However, while the significance and character of the first two core tasks of linkage and representation are largely consistent across democratic political systems, there is a high degree of variation in both the character and centrality of the oversight and policy-making functions of legislatures. This variation is determined largely by the nature of the broader political system, and in particular the institutional structure of the relationship between the legislature and the executive branches.

There are two basic models of executive–legislative relations: fused powers and separation of powers, also referred to as parliamentary and presidential systems respectively. The fundamental difference between the two is the level of institutional autonomy between the executive and legislative branches. In separation of powers (SoP) systems, the executive is elected, directly or indirectly, by citizens for a fixed term and is completely separate from the legislative chamber. The executive is neither selected nor maintained in office by the legislature, and in turn has no ability to shorten the legislative term. The constitutionally designed institutional structure is one of independence and autonomy between the two branches of government.

The situation is quite different in fused powers systems in which voters directly elect only the members of the legislature, who are, in turn, tasked with confirming and/or maintaining the executive in office through a vote of investiture (or at least abstaining from a vote of censure). In most cases, the executive also has the ability to call for early legislative elections, though there may be some restrictions on this power. Thus, the relationship is one of mutual dependence between the executive and legislative branches, with no fixed terms for either institution, and more or less extensive powers of 'mutually assured destruction'

[7] M Mezey, *Comparative Legislatures* (Durham, Duke University Press, 1979).
[8] G Loewenberg, 'Paradoxes of Legislatures' (2007) 3 *Daedalus* 56.

between the two branches. Figure 1 presents these two very different models of executive–legislative relations.

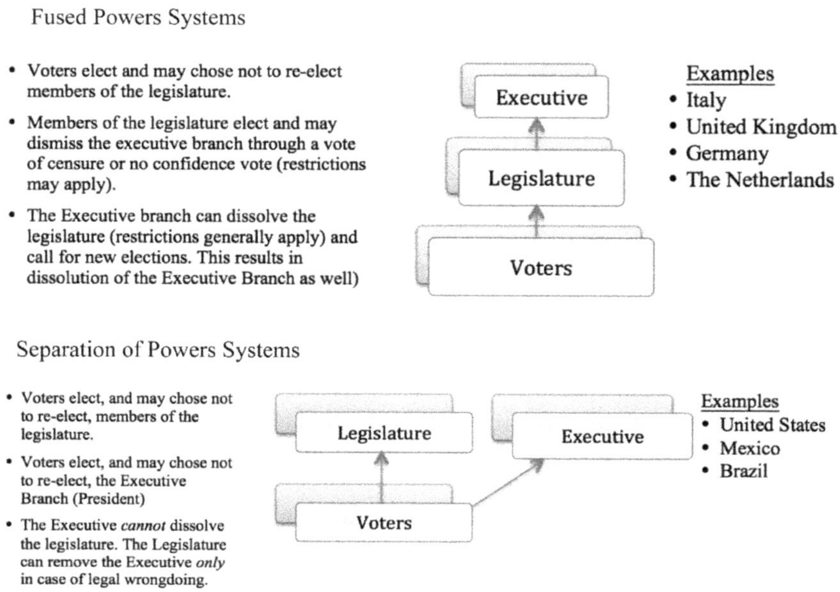

Figure 1: Executive-Legislative Relations in Separation and Fused Powers Systems

These broad structural differences in the relationship between the executive and legislative branches have a profound impact on their relative policy-making influence. In general, despite what the names might suggest, parliamentary systems empower the executive and presidential systems result in more influential legislatures.[9] These are simplifications, however, and while the basic inter-institutional relationships are generalisable, there are a great many *institutional* and *partisan* variables that can affect the autonomy, and subsequent policy influence of legislatures within these two broad types of political systems.

Institutional variables are usually constitutional or statute based and tend to effect the legislature as a whole and all legislators within it equally, while partisan variables are a function of both electoral rules (systemic), as well as internal party rules and norms (party specific) and can therefore have mixed effects. Examples of the former that can tilt the balance of legislative powers in favour of the executive include the character of executive veto power (super majority to override and/or line item) and decree powers (emergency or legislative; immediate effect and/or possibility to reiterate repeatedly).[10] These powers can be present in either separation of powers or fused powers systems and either balance the policy powers of the legislature (SoP) or tilt the scale more heavily in favour of the executive branch (fused).

[9] G Tsebelis, *Veto Players: How Political Institutions Work* (Princeton, Princeton University Press, 2002).

[10] This is by no means intended to be an exhaustive list of possible executive powers, though these are the most common with direct policy-making influence. For additional discussion and details, see Kreppel, above n 1.

Partisan variables are both broader and more difficult to measure. In both SoP and fused powers systems, regardless of the formal rules governing the policy process, political parties play a significant role. Even when legislatures are equipped formally and structurally to be highly influential in the policy process, policy-making may actually occur externally, with the leader(s) of the majority party/parties effectively determining legislative outcomes. If members of the legislature are not autonomous actors, then the institution will have weak partisan autonomy and be less able to influence policy outcomes independently. Member autonomy is a function of the dependence of individual legislators on their parties for their continuation in office. A number of variables determine this, but among the most important systemic causes are the characteristics of the electoral system. Electoral systems determine the ease with which new parties can be formed and win seats (proportional versus plurality) and the reliance of candidates on their party leadership for re-election (candidate based versus list-based elections, the existence of preference votes, etc) and for resources (public funding, registration requirements for new parties, ballot access rules etc).

In general, institutional aspects of legislative autonomy tend to remain consistent, while the partisan autonomy of the legislature can vary from election to election depending on the character of the party/parties in power. Institutional shifts in the relative autonomy of legislatures do occur, more often because of changes to laws or legal decisions than actual constitutional reform, though of course the latter is also possible. Other statutory changes that can influence relative legislative autonomy include changes to the electoral system that impact party strength and partisan autonomy. The legislature itself can initiate some changes through reforms to internal structures or rules of procedure that shape inter-institutional relations or the role of parties within the legislative organisational structure.

Italy has witnessed nearly all of these varieties of reforms, in some cases in multiple iterations. As a result, the relative institutional and partisan autonomy of the Italian legislature has varied substantially over time. These changes occurred concurrently with the evolution of the European Union. Like all EU Member States, Italy has had to adapt to the changing character of the EU and the sometimes rapid expansion of EU policy jurisdiction and production. The discussion below examines the extent to which the high level of autonomy enjoyed by the Italian Parliament has had an impact on the character of the institutional adaptations made to adjust to changes at the EU level and whether or not the demands of EU membership have affected the relative autonomy of the Italian Parliament. I first present a review of changing character of the Italian Parliament through the lens of institutional and partisan autonomy and then discuss the changing character of the tools that structure its engagement with the EU legislative process. This is followed in the conclusions by an assessment of the interactions between these two aspects of policy-making in Italy.

III. Origin and Changes in Institutional and Partisan Autonomy in Italy

The origins of contemporary parliamentary power in Italy are embedded in the Constitution and the legacies of the Fascist era. The focus of the Constituent Assembly, elected in 1946 to draft a new Constitution, was on the Parliament and, unsurprisingly, on limiting executive power.[11] Indeed the Parliament 'was the most celebrated body in the new institutional framework'.[12] Of particular importance was the institutional autonomy afforded to the Parliament through control of its internal organisational structures and rules, including, but not limited, to legislative agenda setting. Though not fully evident during the early decades of the new Republic, these elements of institutional self-determination, in conjunction with the evolving character of the party system, would provide the Italian Parliament with a level of institutional autonomy and potential policy influence largely unmatched in Europe.

The electoral laws adopted in the immediate post-war period also provided a high level of partisan autonomy to members of the Italian legislature. The electoral law that reigned between 1946 and 1993 was one of the most purely proportional in Europe, facilitating the growth of small parties and increasing the viability of splinter groups. In addition, until 1991, voters had up to four preferential votes (for elections for the Chamber of Deputies) that they could use to re-arrange party determined candidate lists, providing incentives for members of Parliament to seek a personal vote.[13] The extreme proportionality of the electoral system, potential for personal vote and relatively easy ballot access, combined to provide individual members with a high level of partisan autonomy. Added to this was the frequent recourse to secret voting within the Chamber of Deputies, which was initially a requirement for all final votes until the 1971, and allowed at the request of 20 or more deputies in most other cases until 1988. Generalised use of the secret ballot reduced the ability of party leadership to police their members and led to frequent defection by members of the governing coalition significantly reducing its legislative efficacy.[14]

Despite these opportunities for institutional and partisan autonomy, the full potential of the Parliament's ability to influence policy-making in Italy was not immediately apparent. It was only following a period of executive–legislative cooperation during the 1950s and 1960s that the Parliament's institutional autonomy became apparent.[15] Indeed, the 'role of the parliament remained very limited for the first decade or two' of the new Republic.[16] The shift in the character of executive–legislative relations was in large part a function of the changing dynamics of political party competition. From the post-war period through the political crises that ended the so-called 'First Republic' in the 1990s an increasingly polarised form of party competition dominated the Italian party landscape and shaped executive–legislative relations.[17]

[11] G Pridham, *Political Parties and Coalitional Behaviour in Italy* (New York, Routledge, 1988).

[12] M Cotta and L Verzichelli, *Political Institutions in Italy* (Oxford, Oxford University Press, 2007) 141.

[13] This was decreased to a single preference vote by referendum in 1991 and ultimately removed altogether with the more comprehensive electoral reform of 1993. Although intended to give voters more say in elections and weaken the control of the party elite, many viewed the existence of preferences as a tool of the parties and an opportunity for corruption.

[14] D Giannetti, 'Secret Voting in the Italian Parliament' (unpublished manuscript, 2010) presented at the Rationalité et science sociale Colloque 'Scutin secret et vote public, huis clos et débat ouvert' Elester Collége de France, Paris; S Koff and S Koff, *Italy: From the First to the Second Republic* (New York, Routledge Press, 2000).

[15] F Bindi, *Italy and the European Union* (Washington DC, Brookings Institution Press, 2011).

[16] G Pridham, *Political Parties and Coalitional Behaviour in Italy* (New York, Routledge, 1988) 64.

[17] G Sartori, 'Proporzionalismo, Frazionismo e Crisi dei Partiti' in G Sartori (ed), *Correnti, Frazioni e Fazioni nei Partiti Politici Italiani* (Bologna, Il Mulino, 1973); G Galli, *I Partiti Politici Italiani (1943–2004)* (Milano, BUR Rizzoli, 2010).

This transformation began with the rising popularity of the Italian Communist Party (PCI). Because of its exclusion from government (due to its perceived anti-systemic nature) the steady increase in support for the PCI eventually led to structural changes that ended the previous period of inter-institutional consensus, and ushered in a new era of parliamentary obstructionism. During the 1970s and 1980s, the Chamber of Deputies emerged as a highly autonomous legislature founded upon a thorough reform of its internal Rules of Procedures (RoP), a permissive electoral system and an increasingly narrow set of possible governing coalition options.

In 1968, the PCI won nearly 27 per cent of the popular vote and 28 per cent of the seats in the Chamber of Deputies. By 1976 its support had grown to 34.4 per cent of the vote and 228 seats, just 4.3 per cent and 35 seats behind the ruling Christian Democratic Party (DC), which had governed Italy since 1948.[18] The increasing popularity of the PCI led to a reconsideration of the internal organisational structure of the Parliament, resulting in a fundamental revision of the Rules of Procedure in 1971. The changes adopted during the 1971 reforms were intended to normalise and depolarise the Italian Party system through increased power sharing and opportunities for the opposition to participate in the policy process.[19]

The critical element of the reforms was the decentralisation of the internal mechanisms of control previously concentrated almost exclusively in the hands of the President of the Assembly (which had been under the exclusive control of the Government) through the establishment of the Conference of Party Group Leaders. This new body was given control over the majority of internal decision-making functions, including the critical task of setting the institution's agenda. Most importantly, the Conference adopted its decisions by *unanimous* consent. This meant that the parties of the opposition (and in particular the PCI) were granted the ability to block the legislative process if they did not approve of the agenda. Additional internal changes followed introducing new informal norms of power sharing such as, since 1976, the selection of a member of the opposition to serve as President of the Chamber of Deputies, which, despite the 1971 reforms, was still an influential position.[20] Combined with the changes made in the 1971 reforms, this gave an unprecedented level of internal institutional control to the opposition and significantly hindered the ability of the Government to control the destiny of its initiatives within the Parliament.

Thus, the 1970s was a transformative period for the Italian political system, and executive legislative relations in particular. The confluence of a significant increase in the electoral popularity of the main party of the opposition with dramatic internal reforms of the Chamber of Deputies combined to significantly weaken the executive in absolute and relative terms. As the popularity of the PCI increased the number of feasible majority coalition opportunities available to DC decreased, eventually leading to the introduction of

[18] D Nohlen and S Philip, *Elections in Europe: A Data Handbook* (Baden Baden, Nomos, 2010).

[19] A Manzella (ed), *I Regolamenti Parlamentari a Quarant' Anni dal 1971* (Bologna, Il Mulino, 2012); R Leonardi, R Nanetti and G Pasquino, 'Institutionalization of Parliament and Parliamentarization of Parties in Italy' (1978) 3(1) *Legislative Studies Quarterly* 161.

[20] A Kreppel, 'Executive-Legislative Relations and Legislative Agenda Setting in Italy: From Leggine to Decreti and Deleghe' (2009) 1 *Bulletin of Italian Politics* 125, 151. Presidential powers included setting the agenda when the Conference of Party Groups Leaders could not come to an agreement, determining the order of the day, allocating speaking time and determining the order and acceptability of amendments on the floor (RoP, Arts 8 and 12).

the '*pentapartito*' coalition formula, which endured until the end of the First Republic.[21] The combination of a weak, ideologically broad coalition, a norm of secret voting and a powerful opposition that could demand nearly 30 per cent of the legislative calendar and obstruct the policy process at will, all combined to ensure a high level of institutional and partisan autonomy for the Chamber of Deputies. As a result, the Italian executive was severely hampered in its attempts to pursue a cohesive legislative agenda. By the end of the 1970s the standard hierarchical style relationship between the executive and legislative branches in Italy had been thoroughly undermined.

The result, not surprisingly, was to severely limit the policymaking efficacy of the executive, resulting in a decline in legislative production and an increasing tendency by the government to rely on alternative legislative strategies. Most notable among these was increasing reliance on decree-laws.[22,23] Although the ability to issue decrees is embedded in the 1948 Constitution, it had been used only occasionally until the 1980s, when it became increasingly the default mechanism for government legislation. The decree-law procedure provided much needed access to the legislative calendar and took immediate effect. Moreover, if the Parliament failed to convert decrees to ordinary laws within the required 60 days, the government quickly learned it could simply reintroduce (sometimes with modifications) the previous decree repeatedly, giving it force of law and effectively legislating 'over the heads of the parliament.'[24] This led to an increase from an average of less than one decree per month in the 1950s and 1960s and about two per month in the 1970s to nearly seven per month in the 1980s and more than 20 per month in the final years of the First Republic.[25]

By the end of the 1980s it was clear that the combination of very high levels of institutional autonomy (both constitutional and statutory) and increasing partisan autonomy (as a result of weak discipline with coalition parties and high fragmentation) had created a nearly dysfunctional political system. Several initiatives to ameliorate the situation began in the late 1980s and early 1990s. In 1988 the Chamber of Deputies reformed its internal rules to reduce recourse to the secret ballot and strengthen party discipline, to only partial effect. Both the fragility and the ineffectiveness of the governing *pentapartito* formula led to widespread calls for electoral reform and the introduction of a majoritarian system that

[21] The '*pentapartito*', or five-party, formula was an ideologically broad, and often internally unstable, coalition that included the Socialist, Social Democratic, Republican, Liberal and Christian Democratic parties. During this period there were times when one or more of these parties left the coalition, but the basic format remained consistent.

[22] A Kreppel, 'The Impact of Parties in Government on Legislative Output in Italy' (1997) 31 *European Journal of Political Research* 327; S Vassallo, 'Le leggi del Governo: come gli esecutivi della transizione hanno superato i veti incrociati' in G Capano and M Giuliani (eds), *Parlamento e processo legislativo in Italia: continuità e mutamento* (Bologna, Il Mulino, 2001) 85.

[23] Art 77 of the Italian Constitution allows for government initiated decree laws in cases of 'extraordinary urgency', but these must be presented to the legislature the same day they are issued for conversion to regular laws. Furthermore, although such urgent decree laws immediately take effect, they are valid for only 60 days and lose all validity (retroactively to the date of their issuance) if not converted by the legislature within that time frame.

[24] The Constitution prohibits the government from issuing measures with the same force of ordinary laws without an explicit delegation from the legislature (Art 77), but is silent on reiterating decrees repeatedly. This practice was determined to be unconstitutional by the Constitutional Court in a 1996 ruling that also required the government to provide justification of the use of the decree-law procedure (No 360).

[25] Kreppel, above n 20.

would lead to Westminster style majorities and alternation in government.[26,27] In 1991, voters supported a referendum to reduce the number of voter preferences to just one and in 1993, another referendum abrogating the existing highly proportional electoral law leading to the adoption of a mixed system passed.

The early elections of 1994 witnessed the implosion of the previous party system. The People's Party (previously the Christian Democrats) that had dominated Italian politics for the entire post war era declined from 209 to just 29 seats in the Chamber of Deputies. The combination of a new more majoritarian electoral system, corruption scandals surrounding the governing parties and generalised frustration with government ineffectiveness, resulted in significant losses for all parties that had participated in the government. Instead the newly created Forza Italia party of Silvio Berlusconi and the Democratic Party of the Left (a rebranded Communist party, minus the splinter '*Rifondazione Communista*' party), together with their respective electoral coalitions, emerged as the dominant political actors.

The emergence of a new party system and an electoral system that resulted in a comparatively clear majoritarian victory for the centre-right signalled the beginning of yet another phase in the legislative autonomy of the Chamber of Deputies.[28] The most notable change was the emergence of a much clearer demarcation between government and opposition, which now divided the parties ideologically between left and right, establishing a form of bipolarism in contrast to governments of the moderate centre opposed by the ideological extremes, as had been the norm throughout the 1980s. Politically, the norms of bipolarism and alternation have increased the potential costs of party and coalition disloyalty. The impact of this reality can be seen in the increasing stability of governments and coalitions in the 'Second Republic'. While the average duration of a government in the First Republic was less than a year, in the two decades between 1996 and 2015 governments have lasted an average of almost two and half years, still well below most bipolar systems, but a notable improvement.[29] Further increasing the potential for party discipline are electoral rules that prioritise party over personality, particularly since the 2005 return to a more proportional electoral system with closed lists.

Despite the upheaval of the 1990s there were no substantive changes to the constitutionally protected institutional autonomy of the Chamber of Deputies. However, following the perceived shift towards bipolar competition the Chamber took it upon itself to revisit its Rules of Procedure and internal organisational structures. The result was a comprehensive

[26] A Pappalardo, 'La Nuova Legge elettorale in Parlamento: chi, come e perche' and R D'Alimonte and A Chiarmonte, 'Il nuovo sistema elettorale Italiano: le opportunità e le scelte' in S Bartolini and R D'Alimonte (eds), *Maggioritario ma non troppo* (Bologna, Il Mulino, 1995).

[27] During this same period Italy experienced one of the most encompassing corruption scandals in the history of modern democracies. The 'Bribe City' (*Tangentopoli*) scandal and broad 'clean hands' (*mani pulite*) judicial investigation that uncovered it consumed the Italian political sphere throughout much of the 1990s and served as an impetus for public and political support of the institutional reforms introduced during this period.

[28] The mixed system adopted in 1996 was used again in 2001; however, in late 2005 a new electoral system was adopted. The 2005 law was a return to proportional representation, but with closed lists and a majority bonus grants the largest electoral coalition a minimum of 340 seats. This provides a strong incentive for electoral coalitions, even between parties that might have significant different policy goals.

[29] This does not include the technical governments of Dini (1995–96) or Monti (2011–13).

revision of the Rules of Procedure, including several reforms designed to reduce the institutional autonomy of the legislature vis-à-vis the executive in the name of legislative efficacy.[30] Among the most significant were changes to the rules governing the establishment of the legislative calendar (Section VI, Articles 23, 24 and 25). The rules established in 1971 required the unanimous agreement of all party group leaders in the Conference of Presidents. Lacking this, it was left to the President of the Chamber to determine the legislative calendar (Articles 23 and 26, RoP 1971).[31] The 1997 reforms reduced the required majority to party leaders representing 75 per cent of the Chamber (Article 23.6, RoP 1997). The new rules also provided an opportunity for the government to prioritise among its proposals (Article 23.3, RoP 1997). In the absence of an agreement, the authority still reverts to the President of the Chamber (Article 26), however, since the emergence of the Second Republic (1994), the position of President of the Chamber is once again strictly under the control of the governing majority. With these changes the executive branch made substantial inroads in terms of managing the policy-making process. Though still far short of what occurs in most other (bipolar) parliamentary systems, these changes represent a marked improvement for Italian executives, and a reduction in the legislative influence of the Parliament.

These changes have occurred within a generalised pattern of decline in legislative production. The total of all laws adopted has declined from an average of nearly 17 (15.3 excluding ratifications) per month during the last full legislative term of the First Republic (the X legislative term) to just 6.2 (3.85 excluding ratifications) per month during the XVI legislative term.[32] The increasingly prominent role of the executive in the legislative process is evident by the growth in the percentage of all successful initiatives introduced by the executive. This increased from just over 65 per cent during the X legislative term to nearly 80 per cent during the XVI legislative term, and reached nearly 90 per cent during the XV legislative term.[33] At the same time, there has been a substantial growth in the use of delegated legislation during the Second Republic. Legislative decrees (not to be confused with decree laws) are the result of the legislature actively devolving decision-making on a specific topic to the executive (a '*deleghe*' or delegation).[34] Once the legislature has passed a delegating act the executive is empowered to adopt legislative decrees, which unlike decree laws, do not require conversion and cannot be modified by the legislature.

The possibility of legislative delegation has existed since the entry into force of the Constitution,[35] but it was not until 1988 that rules governing the procedure were effectively

[30] Camera dei Deputati, *Modificazioni al regolamento della Camera dei Deputati* (Rome, 1998).

[31] Although these rules were amended in 1981 and again in 1990 to provide some additional details and rationalise the process somewhat, the central reliance on unanimity remained severely limiting the government's access to the legislative calendar.

[32] Camera dei Deputati (1998) *Rapporto 1998 sullo Stato della Legislazione*, consulted online December 2014 at http://leg16.camera.it/397?documenti=54.

[33] ibid, Camera dei Deputati (2012) *Rapporto 2012 sulla legislazione tra Stato, Regioni e Unione europea*, consulted online December 2014 at http://leg16.camera.it/cartellecomuni/Leg16/documenti/Tomo_II.pdf.

[34] One delegating law may contain many *deleghe* and thus result in many legislative decrees.

[35] Art 76 of the Constitution allows the Parliament to delegate the exercise of the law making function to the executive but only when the 'principles and guiding criteria have been established by the Houses, and then only for a limited time and for specified ends'.

implemented (Article 14 of Law No 400, 1988). The real growth in the use of delegating legislation for non-EU related legislation occurred during the Second Republic.[36,37] During the X legislative term there were just three delegating laws adopted and 129 legislative decrees issued, by the XIII those numbers has increased to 55 and 378 respectively.[38] More recently, the number of delegating laws has decreased, but the number of delegations included in each one has increased. During the first four years of the XVI legislative term, 22 delegating laws were approved, but these included 377 delegations.[39] The shift away from decree laws, which require conversion and provide opportunities for parliamentary modification, towards legislative decrees that require neither is another indication of the decreasing autonomous policy role of the legislature. Moreover, like the reforms of 1997 that granted the executive greater access to the legislative calendar, the decision to delegate legislative powers to the executive is voluntary and represents an intentional self-inflicted reduction in legislative autonomy by the Chamber of Deputies. While the Italian executive still cannot claim to have the policy dominance exerted by the executive in other, more strongly hierarchical, parliamentary systems, these changes demonstrate a clearly less obstructionist legislature.

The Chamber of Deputies has experienced dramatic shifts in its role in policy-making in the absence of any constitutional revisions directly affecting its autonomy. Its history began in the early decades of the new Republic, when its full potential legislative influence went largely unrealised. This was followed by a period of increasing autonomy and obstructionism enabled by internal reforms. Together with an extraordinarily proportional party system, and inherently weak coalition governments, these reforms led to a period of executive policy impotence. The result was an attempt to govern by executive decree to bypass parliamentary obstructionism. By the early 1990s, the system imploded, weakened by incapacity, corruption and popular frustration. Changes to the party system, only partially inspired by electoral reforms, allowed for the emergence of a kind of weak bipolarism. In response, the legislature once again revised its internal rules, organisational norms and legislative behaviour, but this time in an effort to provide a reliable system of legislative support for the policy initiatives of the executive. Though still significantly more influential in policy-making than most parliaments, the Chamber of Deputies of the Second Republic is a very different institution from its predecessor.

At the same time as these changes in the character of the Chamber of Deputies were occurring, the European Union was developing and the resulting policy opportunities and legislative burdens imposed on national political systems increasing. The next section briefly examines the ways in which national legislatures in the Member States can engage in the EU policy-making and the evolution of the legal and structural mechanisms developed over time to manage this process in the Italian case.

[36] G Tarli Barbieri, 'La Grande Espansione della Delegazione Legislativa nel più Recente Periodo' in P Caretti and A Ruggeri (eds), *Le deleghe legislative: riflessioni sulla recente esperienza normativa e giurisprudenziale* (Milano, Giuffrè, 2003).

[37] For additional information on the growing use of delegated legislation by the legislature, see E Malfatti, *Rapporti tra deleghe legislative e delegificazioni* (Torino, G Giappichelli Editore, 1999) and the various contributions to Caretti and Ruggeri, ibid.

[38] Kreppel, above n 20.

[39] Camera dei Deputati, above n 33.

IV. The Influence of the Chamber of Deputies on EU Policy-making

National legislatures have the possibility to engage with EU policy-making in two very distinct ways at the beginning and the end of the process. In the pre-legislative or 'ascending' phase, domestic legislatures can potentially influence the positions taken by their national leaders at the EU level through their powers of executive oversight and control.[40] During this phase, the goal is to help to shape the national position and place constraints on members of the executive negotiating at the EU level. Legislatures are engaged once again during the 'descending' phase[41] of the legislative process when they are tasked with implementing EU laws. This occurs through the adoption of new legislation or the adaptation of existing statutes.[42]

The legislature has the ability to exercise any direct influence on the substance of policy formation only during the ascending phase, but this is a relatively limited opportunity. Until very recently the Italian Parliament simply lacked both the information and the institutional capacity to engage with the EU policy process early enough in its development to have an impact. Despite recent reforms (discussed below) the actual impact of the Chamber of Deputies on EU policy through its engagement during the ascending phase remains minimal.[43] Partially, this is simply a function of the reality that legislating at the EU level is a complex process conducted between 28 Member States. As a result, no one state can determine outcomes in most cases. However, even influencing the position of the Italian executive at the negotiating table is difficult. Gathering and processing information on EU legislative initiatives (including Commission green and white papers as well as early draft bills) is burdensome, even with recent attempts to automatise and streamline the process (discussed below). Making specific tangible policy recommendations to the executive is a challenge the Chamber of Deputies has had a difficult time overcoming.[44]

Since the eventual outcome of a European Union law is fixed, the ability to affect policy-making substantially during the descending phase is limited, but not inconsequential.[45] The role of the legislature during this phase is also generally less challenging objectively. The policy goals of the legislation have already been determined, as has the timeline for implementation in most cases. The role of the legislature is therefore simply to determine

[40] The Lisbon Treaty added to the potential of national legislatures to engage early in the legislative process through the Subsidiarity Control Mechanism, also known as the early warning system (Lisbon Treaty, Protocol No 2). This process is limited to areas of shared EU-Member State competence. At best, however, this process merely demands that the Commission reconsider its proposal in light of the subsidiarity concerns of national legislatures.

[41] See chapter by R Ibrido, in this book.

[42] EU laws have supremacy (*Costa v Enel*, case 6/64) over national laws, regardless of which came first. The Commission can bring an infringement case against a Member State to the European Court of Justice for non-compliance if domestic laws are believed to conflict with EU laws.

[43] E Borghetto, M Giuliani and F Zucchini, 'Leading Governments and Unwilling Legislators: The European Union and the Italian Law Making (1987–2006)' in Brouard et al, above n 5; S Fabbrini and A Donà, 'Europeanisation as Strengthening of Domestic Executive Power? The Italian Experience and the Case of "Legge Comunitaria"' (2003) 25 *Journal of European Integration* 31.

[44] Bindi, above n 15.

[45] How a law is implemented can have significant political and distributive impacts that can lead to conflicts over the selection of implementation strategies.

the most appropriate method of implementation given the domestic circumstances and resources. However, successfully completing these tasks requires a legislature with the capacity to adopt legislation efficiently, and this has been a challenge for the Italian Parliament historically (as discussed above). The result has been a series of institutional reforms and legal mechanisms adopted with the goal of streamlining the process and improving the institutional capacity of the Chamber of Deputies. These were late additions in Italy, however, largely inspired by changes at the EU level (Single European Act and the Lisbon Treaty most notably), and in the character of legislative autonomy and executive–parliamentary relations.

Although Italy was one of the founding members of the European Economic Community in 1957, it was not until the 1971 revision of the of Chamber of Deputies' Rules of Procedure that the European Community was directly mentioned, and it took until 1990 for the creation of even an ad hoc committee on EU affairs.[46] The absence of clear institutional provisions for dealing with EU legislation within the legislature reflected the general absence of clear mechanisms for managing the transposition of EU laws at the national level. A comprehensive structure for dealing with EU legislation was not introduced in Italy until 1987, when the legislative implications of the Single Market initiative within the Single European Act (SEA) made it unavoidable. By this time, the impossibility of utilising the standard legislative process to pass the implementing legislation required by EU directives had resulted in regular use of legislative delegation to the executive. However, this process was unregulated, disorganised and not without opposition, leading to significant delays. As a result, in 1987 the Parliament passed the 'Fabbri Law' (183/1987) followed quickly by the 'La Pergola Law' (86/1989), which further regulated the process in an attempt to move away from the inefficient use of ad hoc delegating laws.

These laws established the general mechanisms for integrating the Parliament formally into the EU legislative process and restructured the management of EU legislation within the executive branch. The new regimen 'made it the government's duty to transmit EC draft legislation to parliament; and they formalized the parliament's right to adopt resolutions on EU matters.'[47] Perhaps most critically, the La Pergola law created a new consolidated mechanism for dealing with EU legislation through the introduction of an annual 'Community Law' (*Legge Communitaria*). This new format required, among other things, that the government submit to the legislature a clear accounting of EU related legislation anticipated for the coming year in a single package by the end of January each year.[48] Moreover, for the first time the executive was also tasked with keeping the legislature informed regarding the activities of the government in developing new initiatives at the EU level through biannual reports.

The Chamber of Deputies responded to the new Fabbri and La Pergola laws by reforming their Rules of Procedure (rules 125–127) in 1990 to make the most of the newly formalised

[46] The Senate actually introduced a *Guinta per gli affari delle communità europee* in 1968, but it was limited to fact-finding and consultative functions and had relatively little impact, Bindi, above n 15.

[47] ibid, 85.

[48] It is important to note that the Community Law did not actually adopt or transpose any EU initiatives directly; rather it set the rules for how these would be adopted in the future including administrative acts, secondary legislation or legislative decrees, with the latter accounting for more than 50 per cent; Borghetto, Giuliani and Zucchini, above n 43.

opportunities to participate in EU law-making. However, the combination of new laws and internal rules reforms still failed to resolve fully the shortcomings of EU policy management. Difficulties in adopting the annual Community Law led to long delays in implementing EU directives, including both the passage of new initiatives and the adaptation of existing laws to meet EU commitments. This resulted in increasingly numerous infringement proceedings being initiated against Italy.[49]

The continued weaknesses of the process together with the further development of the EU itself led to the introduction of a new law for managing EU law.[50] Adopted in 2005, the 'Buttiglione Law' (11/05) officially replaced the previous law while maintaining many of its provisions, such as the centrality of the annual Community Law. It did add some new aspects to the process, however, including the creation of an inter-ministerial committee within the government for the coordination of European Community affairs (*Comitato interministeriale per gli affari comunitari europei*) or CIACE.[51] The Buttiglione Law also further regulated the formation of the Italian position during the preparation of Community acts of the European Union and aimed to better fulfil the obligations arising from Italy's membership in the European Union based on the principles of subsidiarity, proportionality, efficiency, transparency and democracy.

Despite the commitments within the Buttiglione Law to increase the involvement of the Parliament in both the ascending and descending aspects of the EU legislative process, the influence of the legislature remained under-developed.[52] The annual Community Law forced EU policy to centre stage, but only for a relatively short period. The capacity and interest of the dedicated EU committee in the Chamber of Deputies to fully engage with the establishment of the government's policy positions at the EU level remained minimal, while at the same time the breadth of the EU policy domain continued to expand.[53]

The newest incarnation of the rules regulating the management of EU law within Italy was adopted in 2012 (234/2012). Once again, the reforms were inspired by a combination of failures at the national level and changes at the EU level, most significantly, the implementation of the Lisbon Treaty in late 2009. The new law changed the mechanism for transposing EU directives, implementing regulations and responding to infringement proceedings by dividing the previous Community Law into two distinct initiatives. The new European Delegation Law and the European law replaced the previous annual Community Law.[54]

[49] Just between 1997 and 2005, Italy had 211 infringement cases opened against it, the highest number of any Member State: P Nicolaides and AM Suren, 'The Rule of Law in the EU: What the Numbers Say' (2007) *EIPASCOPE* 35.

[50] The modifications included in the new law were also inspired by the revisions adopted in 2001 to Ch V of the Constitution empowering the regions and decentralising the law-making process in some arenas.

[51] The previous La Pergola law had shifted responsibility for Community legislation form the Ministry of Foreign Affairs to the office of the President of the Council (Prime Minister).

[52] Fabbrini and Donà, above n 43; Bindi, above n 15; F Zucchini, 'Government Alternation and Legislative Agenda Setting' (2011) 50 *European Journal of Political Research*; Borghetto, Giuliani and Zucchini, above n 43.

[53] Bindi, above n 15; Borghetto, Giuliani and Zucchini, above n 43; M Drigani, 'La legge 24 dicembre 2012, n 234: analogie e differenze con la legge Buttiglione' (2013) 5–6 *Le Regioni* 905.

[54] For more details on the new law, how it differs from its predecessors and its impact see the contribution by Renato Ibrido in this volume.

The European Delegation Law includes only legislative delegations and authorisations to allow the government to implement EU related initiatives via executive regulation. The President of the Council of Ministers (Prime Minister) or the Minister for European Affairs, in consultation with the Minister of Foreign Affairs and the other ministers concerned, must submit this bill to the Houses by 28 February each year. In contrast, the newly designed European Law can include any legislation necessary to repeal or amend existing state regulations that are in violation of the obligations deriving from Italy's membership in the European Union or the subject of infringement proceedings by the Court of Justice.[55] Unlike the annual delegating law, the European Law does not have a specific timeline for submission, and can be presented to the legislative chambers separately or together with the annual European Delegation Law.

The comprehensive character of the previous annual Community Law, because of its diverse content, resulted in long periods of delay during the parliamentary approval process. The result was a continued inability of Italy to comply promptly with the provisions of the European Union and continued high rates of infringement proceedings. The hope is that the division of EU related initiatives into two bills; with the European Delegation Law comprising exclusively powers to be delegated to the government will facilitate quick passage through Parliament. This, in turn, should allow the executive to implement quickly the acts of the European Union over which it has been granted sole jurisdiction. The relatively recent implementation of the new law makes it difficult to assess its success accurately, though it does clearly continue the trend of reducing the role of the legislature during the descending phase of EU policy-making in the name of increased efficacy.[56]

The newest law regulating the process of managing the transposition of EU directives and adaptation of Italian law to meet EU requirements marks the fourth such initiative since the passage of the SEA. Each successive incarnation has attempted to streamline the process to overcome, or at least decrease, the seemingly unavoidable delay imposed by the Italian legislative process. In the more recent iterations, there have also been attempts to improve the Parliament's timely access to information on EU initiatives, its expertise in EU policy-making and thus, its involvement in the development of Italy's policy positions at the EU level (ascending phase). These initiatives have been even less successful than the attempts to increase the efficiency of the Parliament during the descending phase.[57] As in other EU Member States, the burdens of shaping, implementing and complying with EU level policies have served to increase the policy-making power of the executive branch in Italy.[58] In Italy, however, this has occurred alongside a process of systemic political reform and shifting power dynamics between the executive and legislative branches. The extent to which these two different sources of institutional change have influenced, or even inspired each other, is unclear and difficult to untangle given the often intertwined chronology.

[55] The European Law may additionally include any provisions necessary to comply or to ensure the application of acts of the European Union and the international treaties concluded by the European Union.

[56] As of December 2015, there have been no additional modifications of the Chamber of Deputies' Rules of Procedure as a result of the procedural changes introduced by law 234/2012.

[57] Borghetto, Giuliani and Zucchini, above n 43.

[58] Goetz and Meyer-Sahling, above n 4; Brouard et al, above n 5.

V. Correlation or Causation?

The power dynamics between the executive and legislative branches in Italy have tilted back and forth from over the decades. Beginning with an initially dominant executive and passive legislature in the 1950s and 1960s, shifting to an increasingly assertive and obstructive legislature during the 1970s and 1980s, through the crises of the 1990s, and culminating in the emergence of the Second Republic and a newly (re)empowered executive facing a legislature actively working to diminish its own powers. As discussed above, some of these shifts have resulted from changes in the party system (with and without electoral reforms), while others have resulted from well-intentioned, but often problematic internal reforms within the legislature.

The character of the relationship, if any, between these shifts in the legislative autonomy/ policy influence of the Italian legislature and the development of the EU, is difficult to assess. The pattern of increased executive dominance in the legislative realm since the 1990s is repeated across the Member States of the EU, and thus is not a specific characteristic of the Italian state.[59] However, in Italy this shift has occurred despite the presence of a legislature with very real institutional powers and a party system that still restricts executive dominance by forcing coalitions among parties with significant ideological and policy differences. To what extent then have the demands of EU membership affected the development of legislative autonomy in Italy, and how has the relative power and high degree of policy influence wielded by the Chamber of Deputies in the 1970, 1980s and 1990s shaped Italy's engagement with EU policy-making?

Looking at the second question, first, it seems clear that the obstructive power of the Italian Parliament derived from its legislative autonomy significantly influenced Italy's ability to meet the legislative demands of EU membership. Italy has consistently been among the worst performers in terms of the transposition and implementation of EU directives, regulations, decisions and European Court of Justice infringement rulings.[60] The inability to deal with the transposition of EU directives and respond to infringement proceedings in a timely manner has been a driving force behind the repeated revisions of the laws governing the management of EU policy at the domestic level up to and including the most recent law 234/2012.[61]

The expansion of EU related policy demands occurred independently of the changes occurring within the Italian political system, but they served to underscore their significance and the policy consequences. Reduction in executive dominance of the policy process began in the 1970s, when the demands of implementing EU-level directives were still relatively limited. However, there was a steady increase in the number of EU directives requiring transposition at the national level with precipitous growth following the implementation of the Single European Act (1987) and Maastricht Treaty (1993), both of which ushered in

[59] Goetz and Meyer-Sahling, above n 4.

[60] T Borzel, T Hofman, D Panke and C Sprungk, 'Obstinate and Inefficient: Why Member States Do Not Comply with European Law' (2010) 43 *Comparative Political Studies* 1363; Borghetto, Giuliani and Zucchini, above n 43.

[61] A Esposito, 'Le Legge 24 Dicembre 2012, N 234, sulla Partecipazione dell'Italia alla Formazione e all'Attuazione della Normativa e delle Politiche dell'Unione Europea' (2013) 2 *Federalisimi.it*; Drigani, above n 53.

significant expansions in the EU policy domain.[62] Prior to the Single European Act, there was no established specific mechanism for dealing with EU directives, which were dealt with in an often ad hoc, and extremely inefficient manner. However, the growing stalemate between the Parliament and the government in the 1980s combined with the impending burdens of the single market programme made it clear that alternative tools were required to meet growing demands leading to the adoption of the Fabbri and La Pergola laws. However, neither of these was sufficient to overcome the entrenched institutional and partisan autonomy and subsequent legislative obstructionism of the Chamber of Deputies.

The inability of Italy to meet its EU commitments fully or in a timely fashion was just one of the many significant failures of the First Republic, and clearly not the driving force behind the reforms that led to the Second Republic. Moreover, as evidenced by the need to introduce the Buttiglione Law and the most recent 234/2012 Law, the changes in executive–legislative relations that have developed over the past two decades have not been sufficient to fully overcome the legislative challenges posed by Italy's EU membership. Despite recent improvements in the overall efficiency of the process, Italy remains a 'laggard' in EU compliance.[63] That said, the evolution of the tools used to meet EU commitments have contributed to the broader trend of executive empowerment in the policy process.

From the beginning, EU policy transposition has been devolved largely to the executive by delegating laws that allow the executive to act unilaterally through legislative decrees and regulations. While the manner in which this process occurs has become more formalised, first through annual Community Laws and now through the European Delegating Law and European Laws, the underlying character of the process remains one of empowering the executive and marginalising the legislature. If anything this pattern has been intensified by the Parliament's more general willingness to abdicate its legislative autonomy through internal rules revisions and a general willingness to use increasingly expansive delegating laws.

Thus, as far as the descending phase of EU policy-making is concerned the general trend has been one of increasingly formalised delegation to the executive, even when transposition might offer the legislature some control over the means, if not the ends, of the policy process. The trend may be moving in the other direction as regards the ascending phase of EU policy-making. Structurally the committee dedicated to the European Union within the Chamber of Deputies is still relatively new. However, its powers have been enhanced consistently over time, as it moved from its initial ad hoc incarnation with an open structure to a permanent committee with dedicated members and staff and a leading position for the consideration of all legislation related to the EU (Rules 125–127 as revised in 1990, 1996 and 1999).

Moreover, both domestically and at the EU level there has been increasing attention to the principle of subsidiarity, which has resulted in new initiatives to keep national Parliaments informed about EU policy initiatives in a timely manner. Even before the Lisbon Treaty, the Buttiglione Law (2005) required the executive to provide preparatory information and all draft EU legislation to the Parliament. The Lisbon Treaty now requires the

[62] For details on the growth of EU legislation, including information on distribution across policy areas see the API for European Union legislation by Buhl & Rasmussen 2011 (http://api.epdb.eu).

[63] Borzel, Hofman, Panke and Sprungk, above n 60.

Commission to directly provide all relevant documentation to national legislatures and at the domestic level, the 234/2012 Law places increased constraints on the executive to engage the Parliament during the formation phase of the national position.[64] Despite these developments, the impact of the Chamber of Deputies, like most other national Parliaments, remains marginal during the ascending phase of EU the policy process. Even a comparatively powerful and autonomous legislature with historically strong committees and a high degree of institutional and partisan autonomy (despite recent efforts to reduce it) is easily overwhelmed by the quantity and character of EU policy. The frequently technocratic character of EU policies and tight timelines, combined with the need to coordinate decision-making across 28 countries, frequently results in the marginalisation of even a highly autonomous legislature.

Overall, this analysis suggests that the character of the national legislature can affect the EU only as far as it can obstruct (intentionally or accidentally) the implementation of EU-level policies. Changes in the nature of the domestic legislature may increase or decrease that delay, and certainly systems with dominant executives and weak legislatures are likely to be more efficient in the transposition process. Indeed, as the autonomy of the Chamber of Deputies has decreased during the Second Republic, new mechanisms for managing EU policy at the national level have been adopted that delegate increasing authority to the executive resulting in some increases in efficiency. Thus far, however, the challenges of meaningful participation during the ascending phase of the legislative process have largely proven to be too much for Chamber of Deputies to overcome. Continued development of the Committee for European Union Policy and initiatives to improve the participation of national legislatures taken at the EU level may improve the situation. Ultimately, however, real change would require a concerted effort by the government. This seems an unlikely strategy for the Italian executive having only recently, and incompletely, improved its hierarchical relationship with the Chamber of Deputies.

[64] Esposito, above n 61.

16

The Italian Symmetrical Bicameral System in EU Affairs

MARIA ROMANIELLO

I. Introduction

The negative outcome of the referendum of 4 December 2016 reconfirmed the status quo of the Italian bicameral system, characterised by the perfect symmetry of functions between the two Houses of Parliament which not only implies that the two Houses hold the same powers but also assures their constitutional autonomy. According to Article 64.1 Constitution 'Each House adopts its own rules by an absolute majority of its members'. This internal autonomy is the essential prerequisite of a symmetrical bicameral system, which guarantees the complete independence of the two branches of the Parliament from any mutual interference and from any other constitutional body. However, this autonomy determines counterproductive consequences which mitigate the perfect symmetry between the two Houses and fosters practical differences in terms of organisation and procedures. Those differences create important distortions in the rationale and in the functioning of the symmetrical bicameral Parliament and, consequently, in the functioning of the whole institutional system.

This, already evident in the national practices, appears far more emphasised in EU affairs, where the two Houses differ not only in terms of structural organisation, but also in terms of procedures developed for monitoring EU legislation.

Moreover, since the introduction of the Lisbon Treaty and the Early Warning System (EWS), each House has further acquired—according to article 6 Protocol No 2—autonomous powers to participate directly in the EU decision-making process. The system recognises the power to review EU draft legislative acts and to express concerns on subsidiarity—within eight weeks from the date of transmission—and made directly to the European institutions through a written objection, called reasoned opinions, which are finally counted in terms of vote. Namely, the provision allocates to each national Parliament—regardless of its unicameral, bicameral or multi-cameral composition—two votes, which in bicameral systems cannot be freely assigned in line with the national division of competences, but rather each House must have one vote each.

The provision thus establishes a unicameral logic, and each House now holds an independent power to issue a subsidiarity concern directly to the EU institutions. Therefore, at first glance, upper chambers seem to have acquired the power to participate in the EU decision-making on equal footing with the lower ones. However, this is not the case, and most Member States with bicameral systems started introducing legal provisions limiting the participation of their upper chambers coherently with the national division of competences.

Theoretically, for a symmetrical bicameral parliamentary system like Italy, the implementation of the mechanism should have not been as problematic, since both Houses hold the same powers. However, the system is characterised by strong structural and organisational differences, which accentuate the anomalies of the symmetrical bicameral system. Moreover, as already unanimously accepted, the European Union has influenced the core of the national forms of government of its Member States and the mechanism has an important impact on the Member States' executive–legislative relationships and, further, their effective participation in EU decision-making.[1] Namely, any diverging position of the two Houses with respect to the assessment of the subsidiarity principle risks undermining the political majority at the national level and fragmenting its position at the EU one. In other words, in a symmetrical bicameral system, where both Houses stand with equal power, the two Houses can adopt different political approaches with respect to their participation in the EU. This represents a threat for the same principle of parliamentary democracy, since it can lead the national Parliament, or one of the two Houses, to be in opposition with its own government.[2]

This is the case for the Italian Parliament: the two Houses not only diverge indeed in the practical implementation of the EWS but also have two different approaches with respect to procedure.

The aim of this chapter is to first give an overview of the Italian bicameral system. Second, it analyses the implications of the EWS on bicameral parliamentary systems. Third, it

[1] On the impact of EU integration on the national forms of government see: M Cartabia, *Principi inviolabili e integrazione europea* (Milano, Giuffré, 1995); S Fabbrini and A Donà, 'Europeanisation as Strenghtening of Domestic Executive Power? The Italian Experience and the Case of the Legge Comunitaria' (2003) 25 *Journal of European Integration* 32; V Schmidt, *Democracy in Europe. The EU and National Politics* (Oxford, Oxford University Press, 2006); KM Johansson and J Tallberg, 'Explaining Chief Executive Empowernment: EU Summitry and Domestic Institutional Change' (2010) 2 *West European Politics* 208; N Lupo and G Rivosecchi, 'I limiti di un approccio esclusivamente nazionale ai problemi della forma di governo' in R Cerreto (ed), *La democrazia italiana: forme, limiti, garanzie* (Roma, Italianieuropei, 2010).

[2] T Raunio, 'National Legislatures in the EU Constitutional Treaty' in J O'Brennan and T Raunio (eds), *National Parliaments Within the Enlarged European Union* (Abingdon, Routledge, 2007) 86.

investigates how the two Houses of the Italian Parliament diverge in terms of participation and involvement in the EU decision-making process. Fourth, it examines the impact of those differences on the rationale of a symmetrical bicameral system. Methodologically, the chapter not only scrutinises the internal structure and the procedural regulations of both Houses but also looks at the practical development and their effective participation in the EU, namely in the EWS.

II. The Constitutional Setting of the Italian Symmetrical Bicameral System

Fearing the risk of authoritarian degenerations, the Italian political parties almost unanimously supported the establishment of the parliamentary form of government, while strongly diverging in terms of parliamentary organisation.[3] Despite those divergences, the need to assure stability and protection for the newly established democratic principles was the priority and the symmetrical bicameral system was the best compromise. Hence, based on the argument that it would have 'not [been] suitable to centralise in one sole chamber such a power as the legislative one, which for its nature is inclined to be omnipotent',[4] the Italian Senate was designed as a *chambre de réflection* and was vested with the role of 'guarantor' of the legislative process.[5] The Italian Senate is, thus, rooted in the idea of separation as a method for limiting, and when appropriate blocking,[6] potential impetuous decisions.[7] In this way, the Italian Senate was designed for playing the role of guarantor of 'institutional "equilibrium" between political conservation and innovation and a "sustainability" of constitutional development',[8] having responsibility for guarding the Constitution[9] and for preserving liberties and individual rights.

According to the constitutional provisions, 'the Parliament consists of the Chamber of Deputies and the Senate of the Republic' (Article 55(1) Constitution), and the two chambers are symmetrical in terms of functions and in relation with the executive. Specifically, 'the legislative function is exercised collectively by both Houses [of Parliament]' (Article 70

[3] G Ferrara, 'Commento all'art 55' in G Branca (ed), A.A.VV, *Commentario della Costituzione* (Bologna-Roma, Zanichelli e Soc ed del Foro Italino, 1984).

[4] Santi Romano, *Principi di Diritto costituzionale generale* (Milan, Giuffré, 1945) 307.

[5] A Barbera, 'Parlamento' (1996) 6 *Enciclopedia delle scienze sociali* (Roma, Istituto della enciclopedia italiana) 472; E Cheli, 'Bicameralismo' (1987) 2 *Digesto delle discipline pubblicistiche*, (Torino, Utet) 318; A Manzella, *Il Parlamento* 3rd edn (Bologna, Il Mulino, 2003); S Mattarella, 'Il bicameralismo' (1983) 3 *Rivista Trimestrale di diritto pubblico* 1161; L Paladin, 'Tipologia e fondamenti giustificativi del bicameralismo. Il caso italiano' (1984) 4 *Quaderni Costituzionali* 219.

[6] L Carlassarre, 'Un bicameralismo discutibile', in L Violante (ed), *Il Parlamento*. Storia d'Italia. Annali 17 (Torino, Einaudi, 2001).

[7] C Lodici, 'Parliamentary Autonomy: The Italian Senato' in SC Patterson and A Mughan (eds), *Senates. Bicameralism in the Contemporary World* (Columbus, Ohio State University Press, 1999).

[8] J Luther, 'The Search for a Constitutional Geography and Historiography of Second Chambers' in J Luther, P Passaglia and R Tarchi (eds), *A World of Second Chambers. Handbook for Constitutional Studies on Bicameralism*, (Milano, Giuffré Editore, 2006).

[9] L Campion, 'Second Chamber in Theory and Practice' (1953) 7 *Parliamentary Affairs* 17.

Constitution), which implies that all legislation must be approved, with the same text, by both.[10] As for the executive, the Government must receive the confidence of both Houses (Article 94(1) Constitution). Within the symmetrical bicameral system provided for by the Constitution, the two Houses are autonomous and independent from each other and from the other constitutional organs, which impedes any interference in their respective internal organisation and working procedures. Hence, the two Chambers enjoy normative, financial and internal jurisdictional autonomy. The first, normative autonomy, which is provided for by Article 64(1) Constitution, states that 'Each House adopts its own Rules by an absolute majority of its members'. Accordingly, each Chamber drafts its own Rules of Procedure (RoP), which represent the most important source governing the internal parliamentary organisation and procedures. The second, financial autonomy, refers to the power recognised for each Chamber to draw up and approve its own budget, which is not subject to review by the Court of accounts. Finally, the third regards judicial autonomy, which implies that everything concerning internal disputes is subject to the sole jurisdiction of the Chambers, so called *autodichia.*[11]

This internal autonomy is the essential prerequisite of a symmetrical bicameral system, which assures the complete independence of the two branches of the Parliament from any mutual interference and, also, from any other constitutional body. However, this general autonomy, and mainly the normative one, mitigates the perfect symmetry between the two Chambers and fosters practical differences in terms of organisation and procedures. In other words, while autonomy was conceived as the expression of the symmetrical bicameral system, it nonetheless causes the emergence of divergences between the two chambers, which create important distortions in the rationale and functioning of the perfect bicameral system.

Moreover, according to the Constitution, the two Houses formally diverge in terms of composition and electoral criteria. Starting with the electoral criteria, 'the Senate is elected on a regional basis, with the exception of the seats assigned to the overseas constituency' (Article 57(1) Constitution). The reference to 'regional basis' is not intended in terms of regional representation, but rather it specifies only the Senate electoral districts, which are drawn on regional boundaries. Moreover, the constitutional provisions provide for differences between the two Chambers regarding both the active and the passive electorate: senators are elected by voters who have reached 25 years of age (18 for the Chamber of Deputies), and voters are eligible only if they have reached the minimum age of 40 years old (25 for the Chamber of Deputies). This difference, today strongly criticised for its diachronic nature,[12] was based on the Constituents' idea that the Senate should have acted as the chamber of reflection, aimed at 'cooling off' the potential impulsive decisions of the Chamber of Deputies. As for the composition, the Chamber of Deputies is composed of 630

[10] N Lupo, 'L'art 70 della Costituzione: una disposizione poco valorizzata' in M Ruotolo (ed), *La funzione legislativa, oggi, Atti del Convegno tenutosi presso l'Università di Camerino* (Napoli, Editoriale Scientifica, 2007).

[11] see ECHR *Savino and Others v Italy*, 28 April 2009. In this case the ECHR issued a decision concerning the balance between the principle of autonomy of the Parliament and the right of judicial protection. The Court, while recognising and to some extent reinforcing the principle of 'autodichia', nonetheless claimed the lack of objective impartiality of the appellate body of the Chamber of Deputies.

[12] N Lupo, 'Una misura a favore dei giovani: far votare per il Senato anche chi ha tra 18 e 25 anni' (2011) *nelmerito.com.*

elected members (Article 56(2) Constitution), while the Senate is made up of 315 elected Senators (Article 57(2) Constitution) in addition to the 'Senators for life by right' and the 'Senators for life'. The former are the former Presidents of the Republic (Article 59(1) Constitution), who at the end of their mandate become 'Senators by right and for life unless they renounce the office. The latter are five in total and are appointed by the President of the Republic from those citizens 'who have honoured the Nation through their outstanding achievements in the social, scientific, artistic and literary fields' (Article 59(2) Constitution).[13] Finally, among the elements of asymmetry of the Italian bicameralism were the different terms of the two Houses as designed by the constituents. According to the original Article 60 Constitution, the Chamber of Deputies lasted five years, while the term of the Senate was fixed at six years. Practically, this provision was never applied and the Senate twice was dissolved prior to the completion of its term. Finally, in 1963, with Constitutional Law No 2, the constitutional provision was revised and the same term—five years—was established for both Chambers.

III. The Lisbon Treaty and Implications for Bicameral Parliamentary Systems

Announced as a step ahead in the strengthening of the representative democracy in the EU, the entry into force of the Lisbon Treaty increased the general expectation about enhancing the legitimacy of EU institutions. The real novelty is the formal recognition of an active role to the national Parliaments (NPs), which are finally called to actively contribute to the good functioning of the Union.

Under the new heading 'Provisions on democratic Principles', the Lisbon Treaty remarks that the 'functioning of the Union shall be founded on representative democracy' (Article 10.1 Treaty on European Union (TEU)). The principle establishes the basis for EU legitimacy and becomes one of the founding principles of the EU,[14] which is based on a dual system of direct and indirect legitimacy.[15] It follows that the citizens 'are directly represented at Union level in the European Parliament' and indirectly represented through

[13] Since 1984, the interpretation of the constitutional provisions has been that five should be the maximum number of senators for life in the Senate. In 1984, with the consent of the President of the Senate Cossiga and the Senate Committee on the Elections, the President of the Republic Pertini decided to follow a different interpretation to which each President of the Republic could nominate up to five senators, regardless the number of the Senators for life already serving. This interpretation was further followed by President Cossiga, however with President Scalfaro, it was restored to the previous interpretation, and today the senators for life, nominated by the President, are only five.

[14] A Von Bogdandy, 'A Disputed Idea becomes Law: Remarks on European Democracy as a Legal Principle' in B Kohler-Koch and B Rittberger (eds), *Debating the Democratic Legitimacy of the European Union* (Lahman, Rowman and Littlefield, 2007); A Von Bogdandy, 'Founding Principles' in A von Bogdandy and J Bast (eds), *Principles of European Constitutional Law* (New York and Munich, Hart/CH Beck, 2009).

[15] P Casalena, N Lupo and C Fasone, 'Commentary on Protocol No 1 annexed to the Treaty of Lisbon (On the role of National Parliaments)', in H-J Blanke and S Mangiameli (eds), *The Treaty on European Union* (Berlin-Heidelberg, Springer, 2013); N Lupo, 'National and Regional Parliaments in the EU Decision-making Process, after the Treaty of Lisbon and the Euro-crisis' (2013) 5 *Perspective on Federalism*; L Verhey, 'Fostering Executive Accountability in the EU: a Key Issue' in J Wouters, L Verhey and P Kiiver (eds), *European Constitutionalism Beyond Lisbon*, (Antwerp/Oxford/Portland, Intersentia, 2009).

their Heads of State or Government in the European Council and through the governments in the Council, with both being 'democratically accountable either to their National Parliaments, or to their citizens' (Article 10.2 TEU). All those provisions build up a 'Euro-national parliamentary system'[16] rooted on a double and complex[17] process of legitimacy: at the European level, through the European Parliament and, at the national level, through the NPs.

The Lisbon Treaty has thus introduced important novelties aimed to improve the participation of NPs in the EU decision-making. NPs are finally called to actively contribute to 'the good functioning of the Union' (Article 12 TEU), and the same Article 12 TEU identifies the ways this should be assured. However, the Article does not contain an exhaustive list of all the new powers conferred to by the Treaty to the NPs, and it should be read jointly with the content of the two Protocols,[18] namely, on the role of national Parliaments in the EU (No 1) and on the control of the application of the principles of subsidiarity and proportionality (No 2), which have the same legal force as the Treaties.[19] Specifically, Protocol No 2 on the application of the principles of subsidiarity and proportionality introduces the EWS (Article 6 Protocol No 2) which formally recognises an involvement of NPs in the European legislative procedure and, precisely, in the early phase of the EU decision-making process. Hence, NPs have acquired an individual power with respect to the scrutiny of compliance of EU draft legislative acts with the principle of subsidiarity.

This mechanism is thus an ex ante subsidiarity control to EU draft legislative acts, which recognises an individual power to each parliamentary House to express concerns on subsidiarity. However, the mechanism can be triggered only collectively and two different procedures are established: the so-called 'Yellow and Orange cards'.

In the scholarship, there have been many attempts to classify the new powers conferred to the NPs[20] with all focusing on specific patterns and configurations.[21] Beyond those theoretical classifications, scholars have already pointed out the negative consequences determined by the blind and 'equal' distribution of powers among all NPs. Namely, the Treaty does not ponder the heterogeneity of the national constitutional realities and their parliamentary

[16] A Manzella and N Lupo (eds), *Il Sistema parlamentare euro-nazionale* (Torino, Giappichelli, 2014).

[17] Scholars developed different theories describing the EU system: 'multilevel' I Pernice, 'Multilevel Constitutionalism in the European Union' (2002) 27 *European Law Review* 511; 'compound' S Fabbrini, *Compound Democracies: Why the US and Europe are becoming similar?* (Oxford, Oxford University Press, 2010); 'pluralistic' M Kumm, 'The Jurisprudence of Constitutional Conflict: Constitutional Supremacy in Europe Before and After the Constitutional Treaty' (2005) 11 *European Law Journal* 262; M Maduro, 'Conceptual Law: Europe's Constitutional Pluralism in Action' in N Walker (ed), *Sovereignty in Transition* (Oxford, Hart Publishing, 2003); N Walker, 'The Idea of Constitutional Pluralism' (2002) 65 *Modern Law Review* 317; 'intertwined' J Ziller, 'Conclusions' in A Albi and J Ziller (eds), *The European Constitution and National Constitutions. Ratification and Beyond* (The Netherlands, Kluwer Law, 2007).

[18] P Craig, 'The Treaty of Lisbon: Process, Architecture and Substance' (2008) 33 *European Law Review* 137.

[19] Those provisions are further completed by other provisions of the Treaty, specifically: (i) Art 71 TFEU; (ii) Art 48(7) TEU and Art 6 Protocol No 1; (iii) Art 352 TFEU; (iv) Art 81(3) TFEU.

[20] N Lupo, 'National Parliaments in the European Integration Process: Re-aligning Politics and Policies' in M Cartabia, N Lupo and A Simoncini (eds), *Democracy and Subsdiarity in the EU. National Parliaments, Regions and Civil Society in the Decision-Making Process*, Series 'Percorsi- Nova Universitas' (Bologna, il Mulino, 2013).

[21] P Kiiver, *The Early Warning System for the Principle of Subsidiarity. Constitutional Theory and Empirical Reality* (London and New York, Routledge, 2012); Lupo, ibid; M Olivetti, 'Parlamenti nazionali nell'Unione europea' in R Bifulco et al (eds), *Digesto delle discipline Pubblicistiche, Aggiornamento* (Torino, UTET, 2012); M Olivetti, 'Article 12 (The Role of National Parliaments)' in Blanke and Mangiameli, above n 15.

structure.[22] The sole difference explicitly acknowledged by Article 8 of Protocol No 1 and Article 7(1) of Protocol No 2 is between unicameral and bicameral parliaments. Article 7(2) Protocol No 2 TEU/Treaty on the Functioning of the European Union (TFEU) states, 'Each National Parliament shall have two votes, shared out on the basis of the national Parliamentary system. In the case of a bicameral Parliamentary system, each of the two chambers shall have one vote'. In bicameral systems, the two votes are assigned regardless of their internal distribution of competences and regardless of the formal role played by each Chamber in the national decision-making process. According to the Treaty provision, the votes cannot be liberally assigned in line with national division of competences but rather, in a bicameral system, the Houses must have one vote each.

Contrary to this approach, the institutional landscape of NPs is profoundly heterogeneous.[23] In bicameral systems, diversity has been the rule over time and among countries. In this sense, the institutional arrangements and the powers recognised to upper Houses vary a lot and any generalisation risks losing the peculiarity of each constitutional setting.

With 28 Member States and 41 parliamentary chambers in total, in the EU 13 countries have a bicameral system. These are Austria, Belgium, the Czech Republic, France, Germany, Italy, Ireland, the Netherlands, Poland, Romania, Slovenia, Spain and the United Kingdom. Among them, only three countries hold the classical territorial model, which identifies bicameralism as the characteristic feature of federal systems.[24] While in the other Member States, the presence of the upper House is justified on other important reasons but mainly focused on the need to assure a balance of power in the system, with the upper House playing the role of chamber of reflection against the lower one and providing 'second thoughts'[25] to the legislative process, as well as assuring stability in policy and government.

Therefore, the complexity and the high heterogeneity of bicameral systems strongly clash with the European approach and the establishment of the EWS based 'on unqualified equality of Member States'.[26] Because, in bicameral systems, the two votes are assigned regardless of their internal distribution of competences and regardless of the formal role played by each chamber in the national decision-making process, it appears that upper Houses have seen their positions reinforced at the European level. Usually, in asymmetrical bicameral systems, upper Houses have fewer formal powers than lower ones: ie the confidence relationship is the prerogative of the lower chamber—and they also play a marginal role in the legislative process. Contrary to the national settlement, today, upper chambers have autonomous power to participate in the EU decision-making on equal footing with the lower ones.

[22] The use of the term 'national parliaments' proved to be extremely inadequate for the complex Belgian constitutional settlement. In this way, Belgium enlarged the understanding of the term and added the Declaration n 51 to the Lisbon Treaty. M Romaniello, 'Upper Chambers in EU Affairs. Scrutinising German and Belgian federalism' (2015) 16 *federalismi.it Rivista di diritto pubblico italiano, comparato, europeo.*

[23] Kiiver, above n 21; PM Kaczyński, 'Paper Tigers or Sleeping Beauties? National Parliaments in the Post-Lisbon European Political System' (2011) CESP Special Reports; Olivetti, 'Article 12 (The Role of National Parliaments)', above n 20; Lupo, above n 20; N Lupo, 'I Parlamenti nazionali e le istituzioni europee' in G Amato and R Gualtieri (eds), *Prove di Europa Unita. Le Istituzioni europee di fronte alla crisi* (Firenze, Passigli Editore, 2013).

[24] S Levmore, 'Bicameralism: When are two Decisions better than One?' (1992) 12 *International Review of Law and Economics* 145.

[25] Campion, above n 9, 20.

[26] Kiiver, above n 21.

This provision not only impacts at the EU level but also creates considerable repercussions in the national constitutional framework, mainly concerning the executive–legislative relationship. In other words, 'If we reason that subsidiarity enforcement is about keeping the exercise of legislative competences domestic where possible, under the EWS senates enjoy a voice that is completely out of proportion with the voice that they have when legislative competences actually are domestic'.[27] However, against this 'enforcement thesis', since the adoption of the Lisbon Treaty, the EU Member States—with bicameral parliaments—tried to accommodate the EWS coherently with the national division of competences and powers between the two parliamentary Houses; therefore, legal provisions limiting upper Houses' participation in the EU have been introduced.[28]

Based on this, the implementation of the EWS in a symmetrical bicameral system, such as Italy, may appear unproblematic. However, as I will underline in the following sections, the system clashes with the persistence of procedural and structural asymmetries, which together with the different approaches that two Houses have adopted with respect to the EWS accentuate the anomalies of the Italian symmetrical bicameral system.

In the following sections, I investigate in more detail the impact of the mechanism on the Italian symmetrical bicameral system.

IV. The Italian Slow Process of Adaptation to the EU

In Italy, the process of adaptation has been slow and tardy,[29] not only in terms of the structural adaptation of the Parliament, but also, in more general terms, with respect to the national legislative framework. For more than 50 years, Article 11 Constitution was deemed sufficient to legitimise the Italian membership to the EU. Legally, the Italian participation in the EU was thus accomplished through ordinary laws, and the first provision, which mentioned the involvement of the Italian Parliament in the decision-making process, was Law No 871 on 12 July 1965.[30] This law introduced the obligation for the Executive to provide to Parliament an annual report on the European Economic Community (ECC) and the European Atomic Energy Community (Euratom). However, excluding this unique provision, for more than 20 years the issue was completely unregulated, and it was up to each House to establish, through its RoP, the mode of scrutiny of EU proposals and to take the executive into account in the EU decision-making process.[31]

[27] ibid.

[28] Highly interesting is the case of the Slovenia National Council. See M Romaniello, 'Assessing Upper Chambers' role in the EU Decision-making Process' (2015) 27 SOG Working Paper Series.

[29] F Bindi Calussi and B Grassi, 'The Parliament of Italy. From Benevolent Observer to Active Player' in A Maurer and W Wessels (eds), *National Parliaments on their Ways to Europe: Losers or Late comers?* (Baden-Baden, Nomos, 2001).

[30] See more in detail the chapter by Vosa in this volume.

[31] See G Gaja, 'Per un controllo parlamentare dell'attività normativa delle Comunità europee' (1973) *Politica del diritto* 11; AM Calamia and C Mordivucci, 'Istituzione di un Ministero per gli affari comunitari?' (1977) *Rivista diritto Internazionale* 822 and C Mordivucci, 'La politica comunitaria e il ruolo svolto dalle Commissioni Affari Esteri e dalla Giunta per gli Affari delle Comunità europee' in A Cassese (ed), *Parlamento e politica estera* (Padova, CEDAM 1982).

In 1971, the two Houses reformed their respective RoP and introduced special provisions, which could assure, on the one side, a direct relationship with the European institutions and, on the other side, the development of domestic scrutiny procedures for EU draft legislation. However, the special procedures were not effectively exploited, and both Houses showed some reluctance in scrutinising EU matters. This was mainly caused by the restrictive internal provisions, which forbade the adoption of any parliamentary resolution on EU draft proposals.[32]

At the end of the 1980s, the Italian Parliament adopted two laws, which defined the framework for parliamentary involvement in the EU decision-making process: Law No 183 of 1987 and Law No 86 of 1989. The new set of rules, followed by new provisions established in the parliamentary RoP, recognised important rights for the Parliament. First, it formalised the Parliament's right to adopt resolutions on EU matters. Second, the government was required to transmit EU draft legislation to both chambers of the Parliament. Finally, in order to solve the high number of Italian infringements in the transposition of the European legislation, Law No 86 of 1989 introduced the Annual Community Law, as the legal instrument for the prompt implementation of the European directives. The ratification of the Maastricht Treaty did not lead to relevant changes in the already established legal framework; only with the Amsterdam Treaty did we witness a new wave of reforms, which were aimed to assure a proactive national participation in the EU decision-making and reinforce the involvement of the Parliament and its information rights. The amendments were nonetheless fragmented and embodied in different legal provisions. After the ratification of the Nice Treaty and the overture of the constitutional convention on the future of the European Union, in 2001 the Italian Constitution was amended, and today the revised article 117 Constitution proclaims that national legislation shall be in compliance with the constraints deriving from EU legislation. In 2005, the Parliament adopted Law No 11,[33] which clarified the fragmented legal framework for the Italian participation in the EU decision-making process. After the entry into force of the Lisbon Treaty[34] and the constitutional amendments of Articles 81, 97 and 119 Constitution[35]—brought about by the ratification of the Treaty on Stability, Coordination and Governance in the Economic and Monetary Union (known as Fiscal Compact TSCG)—in 2012 Law No 11 of 2005 was abrogated[36] and replaced by the new legal provisions established in Law No 234.[37]

Thus, after four years of legislative inertia,[38] the new law no 234/2012 finally implemented the provisions established in the Lisbon Treaty and it completely—although still

[32] G Gaja, 'Proposta di riforma della Giunta per gli affari europei del Senato' (1977) *Rivista di diritto internazionale* 398; V Lippolis, 'Il parlamento nazional-comunitario' (1991) XI(2) *Quaderni costituzionali* 319; G Girotto, 'Parlamenti e diritto comunitario: gli atti parlamentari di indirizzo politico in Italia e in Francia' (2002) 23 *Quaderni Costituzionali* 577.

[33] M Cartabia and L Violini, 'Le norme generali sulla partecipazione dell'Italia al processo normativo dell'Unione europea e sulle procedure di esecuzione degli obblighi comunitari. Commento alla legge 4 febbraio 2005, n. 11' (2005) 4 *Le Regioni* 474; P Gambale, 'Le "garanzie Parlamentari" nella fase del diritto comunitario: cenni di diritto comparato e novità dell'ordinamento italiano' (2006) 48 *Rassegna Parlamentare* 834.

[34] The Italian ratification on 2 August 2008.

[35] Constitutional Law 1/2012 adopted in April 2012.

[36] Art 61(1), b) of the Law 243/2012.

[37] Law 24 December 2012, no 234 General provision on the Italian participation to the formulation and implementation of the European Union policies.

[38] C Fasone, 'Qual è la fonte più idonea a recepire le novità del trattato di Lisbona sui parlamenti nazionali?' (2010) 3 *Osservatorio delle fonti*.

not satisfactorily—revises the scheme and the procedures which regulate Italian participation in the EU decision-making process.[39]

A. The Evolution of the Structural Organisation of Scrutiny in the Italian Parliament

In 1968, the Senate had already established an ad hoc body focused on EU Affairs, then called *Giunta per gli Affari delle Comunità europee*. The 'Giunta' lacked the same legal prerogatives of the other parliamentary standing Committees and also lacked the same legal status. Initially, it mainly had 'fact-finding and consultative functions'.[40] In 1971 with the reform of the RoP, the Senate reinforced its prerogatives in scrutinising EU affairs. However, as already highlighted, its role was still very limited; and until 1988 the plenary and the standing Committees could not adopt resolutions on EU draft proposals. This limitation was justified by the need to not excessively restrain the negotiation capacity of the executive. Only after the Fabbri Law—Law No 183 of 1987—in 1988, did the Senate revise again its RoP and empower its standing Committees to adopt resolutions on EU draft legislative acts. Up until 2003, the Italian Giunta on European Affairs lacked the status of a full Senate Committee, and it did not enjoy the legislative and drafting capacity recognised for the other standing Committees of the Senate. The Giunta was composed of 24 members, all of whom simultaneously held membership in one of the standing Committees of the Senate. The members were selected on political bases, reflecting the balance of representation of the political forces in the plenary. Only in 2003 was the former advisory Committee completely reformed; at that time, it acquired the status of full standing Committee, maintaining its 'overall responsibility on domestic legislation emanating from activities and measures of the European Union and the EU institutions, and the implementation of Community agreements' (article 23(1) RoP). Moreover, under the new RoP, membership continued to be based on the logic of the double mandate. This provision represents an exception to the general rule, that 'each Senator can be member of only one Standing Committee' (article 21(5) RoP). The Chamber decided to maintain this ratio for two main reasons. First, it would have assured the transversality of knowledge[41] between European issues and the specific subject matters on which each standing Committee was expert. Second, it would have guaranteed an increased awareness among the Senate's standing Committees on European Union Policies.[42]

During the XV legislative term, the standing Committee set up two subcommittees, respectively called the sub-Committee for the 'ascending phase' and the sub-Committee for

[39] G Piccirilli, 'Il Parlamento italiano: le procedure europee nella legge n 234 del 2012' in Manzella and Lupo, above n 16.

[40] F Bindi, *Italy and the European Union* (Rome and Washington DC, Scuola Superiore della Pubblica Amministrazione and Brookings Institution Press, 2011) 88; see also E Vinci, 'La giunta consultiva del Senato per gli affari comunitari' (1968) *Studi parlamentari e di politica costituzionale* 135.

[41] Manzella, above n 5, 342; A Vuolo, 'Il Parlamento nella fase ascendente della formazione del diritto comunitario' in R Dickman and S Staiano (eds), *Funzioni Parlamentari non legislative e forma di governo: esperienza dell'Italia* (Milano, Giuffrè, 2008) 537.

[42] MV Agostini, 'I rapporti fra i Parlamenti dell'Unione europea' in E Rossi (ed), *Studi pisani sul Parlamento II* (Pisa, Plus-Pisa University Press, 2008).

the 'descending phase'.[43] 'The first [is] competent in scrutinising when a decision is taken at [European] level and the second [is] when European legislation is implemented at national level'.[44] The two subcommittees mainly have a consultative role and the choice of members reflects the political representation of the parliamentary groups existent in the main standing Committee. The subcommittee responsible for the 'ascending phase' supports the main Committee in scrutinising all the draft legislative and non-legislative acts of the European Union and preliminarily verifies their compliance with the principle of subsidiarity and proportionality, as well as the merits and the legal basis of the proposals.[45] The subcommittee responsible for the 'descending phase' is focused on the national legislation and mainly on scrutinising bills implementing treaties and EU measures, as well as verifying the compliance of national legislation and the implementation of EU measures.

Differently from the Senate, the Chamber of Deputies only established its Special Committee on European Affairs in 1990. Its structure and procedural organisation was very similar to the Senate's Giunta. It was an ad hoc Committee, with no legislative and drafting capacity. However, unlike the Senate, the Chamber of Deputies already transformed its ad hoc Committee into a standing Committee by 1996, namely the XIV European Union Policies Committee. The main structural difference between the two Committees is based on membership. In the Senate, the 14th Committee is characterised by the ratio of double membership. Conversely, in the Chamber of Deputies, members of the standing Committee on European Union Policies, who are approximately 40, are not allowed to be full members of any other standing Committee at the same time.[46]

B. The Evolution of the Procedural Organisation of Scrutiny in the Italian Parliament

The progressive rationalisation of the legislative framework and the extension of the parliamentary prerogatives to participate in the EU decision-making process was not accompanied by a practical parliamentary involvement in EU issues. It was only in 2005, with the adoption of Law No 11, that a shift of attitude emerged; and, finally, in 2012 a new law was adopted for filling the domestic structural gaps. This law represented an important recognition of the new powers introduced by the Lisbon Treaty. However, this has not yet been followed by a contextual revision of the parliamentary RoP, but rather 'experimental' procedures were introduced in both Houses of the Parliament.

According to article 6 of the new law no 234 of 2012, the executive shall forward to the Parliament all EU draft legislative acts and any related preparatory work, as well as any successive modifications. In the Senate, the EU proposals are then forwarded to the relevant standing Committees and the Committee on European Union Policies. The latter

[43] For a more in-depth analysis on the use of this dichotomy see chapter by Ibrido in this volume.

[44] Guizzi, 'Italy: A Consideration of the Position of the National Parliaments in the European Union' in F Laursen and SA Pappas (eds), *The Changing Role of Parliaments in the European Union* (Maastricht, European Institute of Public Administration, 1995) 152.

[45] C Tucciarelli, 'Parlamento italiano, forma di governo ed Unione europea al termine della XV legislatura' (2008) 18 *Quaderni Costituzionali* 630.

[46] This was not the case with the previous ad hoc Commission, but it also enjoyed 'a sort of traversality', ie it was made up of members of other committees.

since 2007 has introduced a preliminary scrutiny of EU documents through the so-called Subcommittee for the 'Ascending Phase', which selects the most relevant proposals to be further examined in the main Committee. Moreover, to assure effective parliamentary scrutiny of EU affairs, since 2003 article 29(2–bis) of the Senate's RoP[47] has established that 'the program and calendar of business of each committee shall also be drafted to ensure that preparatory documents for European Union legislation published in the Official Journal or notified by the government may be scrutinised in a timely manner'. These provisions aim at assuring the prompt and greatest involvement of the parliamentary standing Committees in scrutinising EU draft legislative acts. Hence, according to article 144(1) RoP, each EU draft legislative act shall be forwarded to the specific standing Committee responsible by subject matter, which in order to deliver its opinion shall scrutinise all the 'government's progress reports on EU procedures for adopting the draft instruments, and the government's progress report on the transposition of EU legislation into Italian law'. Moreover, the responsible standing Committee shall include in its reports the opinion expressed by the 3rd (Foreign Affairs, Immigration) and 14th (European Union Policies) standing Committees. However, if the standing Committee responsible by subject matter does not issue an opinion within 15 days after referral, the standing Committee on European Union Policies 'may request that its opinion, comments and proposals be forwarded to the Government, through the President of the Senate' (article 144(5) RoP). Thus, in case of inertia of the competent standing Committee, the Senate's RoP give the Committee on European Union Policies a right of intervention. This intervention has been the rule so far, which proves the failure of the efforts to increase the involvement of the other standing Committees in EU affairs.[48]

According to article 23(1) RoP of the Senate:

> The Committee on European Union Policies shall have overall responsibility on domestic legislation emanating from activities and measures of the European Union and the EU institutions, and the implementation of Community agreements. The Committee shall also have responsibility in respect of compliance with obligations following EU law. The Committee, in so far as it lies within its powers, shall also be responsible for relations with the European Parliament and with the Conference of Community and European Affairs Committees of parliaments of the European Union.

Thus, if the EU draft legislative acts refer to institutions or broad EU policies, the Committee on EU Policies is the competent committee in scrutinising those acts. In this case, the 1st and 3rd standing Committees 'may submit their comments and proposals to the 14th Committee', which shall be annexed to the opinion of the 14th Committee (article 144(4) RoP). If, within 15 days from referral, the 14th standing Committee does not issue an opinion, the 1st and the 3rd standing Committee may request that their opinions, comments and proposals be forwarded to the Government, through the President of the Senate (article 144(5) RoP).

Procedurally, The Committee of the Chamber of Deputies holds similar competences to the Senate's. According to the Chamber's RoP—as last amended in 2001—article 126(1) 'The European Union Policy Committee shall have overall responsibility for the general

[47] Similar provision was established in the Chamber of Deputies Art 25(4) RoP.

[48] C Fasone, 'Gli effetti del Trattato di Lisbona sulla funzione di controllo parlamentare' (2011) 2 *Rivista italiana di diritto comunitario* 361.

legal aspects of the activity and measures of the European Communities and for the implementation of Community agreements'. Moreover, like in the Senate, all Committees have competence according to subject matter to scrutinise EU legislation. Namely, article 127(1) Chamber's RoP ordains that any EU legislative acts and EU draft legislative acts 'shall be referred for consideration to the appropriate Committee according to subject matter, with the opinion of the European Union Policy Committee'. However, differently from the Senate, in case of *inertia*, the XIV Committee does not have a power to substitute for the competent standing Committee. Then, the competent standing Committee, according to Article 127(2) RoP:

> [I]n not more than thirty days ... shall consider the legislative text in question and may express in a final document their own opinion on the appropriateness of any possible initiatives. The document shall be printed and distributed and shall be transmitted by the President of the Chamber to the President of the Senate and the President of the Council of Ministers.

C. The Experimental Procedure for Subsidiarity Assessment

After the Lisbon Treaty, neither the Italian Senate nor the Chamber of Deputies introduced a specific procedure for assessing the compliance of EU draft legislative acts with the principle of subsidiarity. However, awaiting a complete reform, on 1 December 2009, the President of the Senate addressed a letter to all Presidents of the standing Committees, specifying which provisional procedure should be implemented. The President of the Senate stated that the assessment of the compliance with the principle of subsidiarity should follow the regular scrutiny procedure, as established in article 144 of the Senate's RoP.[49] Moreover, the President made clear that any 'acts of political orientation' adopted by the standing Committees competent by subject matter and the opinion delivered by the 14th Committee shall contain an assessment on both the merits of the proposals and the respect of the principle of subsidiarity. As well, established in article 144(5) RoP, in the case of inertia of the competent standing Committee, the Committee on European Union Policies 'may request that its opinion, comments and proposals be forwarded to the Government' and to the European Institutions 'through the President of the Senate'. Also in this case, the 14th Committee acts as a replacement of the standing Committees competent by subject matters.[50]

With the Lisbon Treaty, as happened for the Senate, the Chamber of Deputies did not reform its RoP. Thus, in order to implement the novelties of the Treaty and wait for a formal reform, the Rules Committee of the Chamber of Deputies issued an opinion on 6 October 2009. The Rules Committee gave indications about the 'experimental' procedure to be adopted in the House for controlling compliance with the principle of subsidiarity. It extensively interpreted the provision established in article 127 RoP as the legal ground for forwarding opinions to the European Institutions. Different from the Senate, the Chamber does not give all standing Committees the power to control the respect of the principle of subsidiarity; rather, this is an exclusive competence of the standing Committee on

[49] The same happened with the Barroso Procedure, which was implemented in the regulatory scrutiny procedure. This was clarified by the letter of the President of the Senate, October 2006.

[50] DA Capuano, 'Il Senato e l'attuazione del trattato di Lisbona, tra controllo di sussidiarietà e dialogo politico con la Commissione europea' (2011) in www.amministrazioneincammino.luiss.it.

European Union Policies. In other words, that Committee is responsible for verifying the compliance of EU draft legislative acts, mentioned in article 6 of Protocol No 2, with the principle of subsidiarity, while the competence on the merits of the proposal continues to be conferred to the standing Committees according to subject matters.[51] The Rules Committee of the Chamber of Deputies further indicated that the scrutiny of EU draft legislative acts, namely the pre-legislative scrutiny phase in the standing Committee, shall follow the ordinary procedure established for national pre-legislative scrutiny (articles 72–81 RoP) and, thus, conduct all necessary actions for gathering information on the proposal.

On 14 July 2010, the Rules Committee of the Chamber issued another opinion, which integrated the existing procedure and clarified the legal ground for referring the vote on a reasoned opinion to the plenary—as provided by Article 72(3) Constitution—specifically stating that

> the reasoned opinion of the XIV Committee containing a decision on subsidiarity matters may be put to the Assembly upon request by the Government, by a fifth of members of the Committee itself (or representatives of the Groups in the Committee representing equal numbers), or a tenth of the members of the Assembly (or presidents of the Groups of equal numbers).[52]

When the opinion is adopted, the President of the Chamber of Deputies forwards the decision to the European institutions and sends the same documents also to the President of the Senate and to the Government.

The 'experimental' procedure set up in the Chamber of Deputies has already been criticised by Scholars.[53] Practically, the procedure is burdensome and complex, and it creates problems in terms of coordination among all the standing Committees of the Chamber. In this respect, the Senate's choice appears more appropriate, since all Committees competent by subject matter can express their own opinions both on the merits of the proposal and on the compliance with the principle of subsidiarity, with the possibility that the 14th Committee can act, in cases of inertia, in substitution of the other Committees. However, in practice, the Senate also had some problems with coordination, and in some cases the standing Committees adopted different opinions in assessing the compliance of the EU draft legislative act with the principle of subsidiarity.[54]

V. Participation in the EU Decision-making Process and the Assessment of the Principle of Subsidiarity

Since the inception of the Barroso procedure, and mainly with the Lisbon Treaty and the setup of the EWS, the Italian Senate has proven to be among the most active chambers in the EU.

[51] A Esposito, 'Il Trattato di Lisbona e il nuovo ruolo Costituzionale dei Parlamenti nazionali: prospettive per il Parlamento Italiano' (2009) 51 *Rassegna Parlamentare* 1119.

[52] HJ Blanke et al, 'Protocol (No 2)' in Blanke and Mangiameli, above n 15, 1685.

[53] N Lupo, 'I Parlamenti nazionali nell'Unione europea e il principio di sussidiarietà: qualche suggestione per la Camera dei deputati' (2014) *Amministrazioneincammino.luiss.it.*

[54] See the Senate's reasoned opinions on COM/2012/0576 and on COM/2012/0788.

In the so-called political dialogue, the number of opinions sent by the Italian Senate were significantly more numerous than the Chamber of Deputies. This difference is based on two main reasons. The first is mainly procedural. As was already highlighted, according to article 144(5) RoP, in the event that the Committee responsible by subject matter does not issue an opinion within 15 days of referral, the 14th Committee of the Senate can act in substitution and 'may request that its opinions, comments and proposals be forwarded' to the EU institutions and 'to the Government, through the President of the Senate'. In practice, in the XVI legislative term (2008–2013), the 14th Committee used this provision extensively: a total of 95 times. Moreover, different from the Chamber of Deputies, the Senate established that after the elapse of the eight-week deadline, the opinions approved would have been forwarded to the European institutions. This applies not only in cases where the Senate finds a breach of the principle of subsidiarity, but also when the Senate just approves an opinion containing some reflections on or a positive assessment of European proposals.

The second reason is strictly related to the executive–legislative relationship and to the different approaches adopted in this respect by both Chambers. It is important to stress that these different approaches, more than being based on strict political reasons, are determined by the different views that the officials have with respect to their participation in the EU. The Chamber of Deputies is much more concerned about the possible negative implications that the 'independent' parliamentary participation in the EU decision-making process may have on the national form of government[55] and on the path of the European integration process. Meanwhile, the Senate considers this direct dialogue with the Commission a positive feature, since it enables the Houses to act—up to a certain extent—independently from the Government.[56]

On this, the different approach between the two Houses with respect to the executive was evident in both the EU draft legislative acts on matrimonial property regimes[57] and property consequences of registered partnerships.[58] In both cases, the Senate issued a reasoned opinion regardless of the Government's position. Conversely, the Chamber of Deputies, although expressing some concerns about the issues, stated that any definitive position could only be taken in accordance and coordination with the Government. Since the two acts were subject to unanimity in the Council, a negative opinion of the Chamber not only would have limited the Government's powers of negotiation, but rather would have completely blocked any discussions at the EU level. Moreover, the Chamber did not raise a reasoned opinion because it argued that any assessments of compliance with the principle of subsidiarity should have been based on an evaluation of the merits of the proposal and its respect of the principle of proportionality, which should have been issued by the respective standing Committees competent by subject matter.[59]

[55] A Esposito, 'La legge 24 Dicembre 2012, 234, sulla partecipazione dell'Italia alla formazione e all'attuazione della normativa e delle politiche dell'Unione Europea. Parte I—Prime riflessioni sul ruolo delle Camere' (2013) 2 *federalismi.it.*, 9.

[56] Capuano, above n 50, 5.

[57] Document COM(2011) 0126 Proposal for a Council Regulation on jurisdiction, applicable law and the recognition and enforcement of decisions in matters of matrimonial property regimes

[58] Document COM(2011) 0127 Proposal for a Council Regulation on jurisdiction, applicable law and the recognition and enforcement of decisions regarding the property consequences of registered partnerships.

[59] See www.camera.it/_dati/leg16/lavori/bollet/201105/0526/html/14/comunic.htm#4n2.

Obviously, this different approach risks fragmenting the Italian position in the EU affairs, with divergences not only between the two Houses but also with respect to the Government. In the first reasoned opinion issued by the Senate on Greenland's fishery products,[60] while the Senate's Committee claimed a breach of the principles of subsidiarity and proportionality, the Italian Government supported the proposal in the Council. In this case, the different positions that emerged proved not only the lack of coordination between the Government and the Senate acting independently in EU affairs, but also the fact that the Government was eluding its obligations, as established in Law 11 of 2005. It follows that the reasoned opinion adopted by the Senate was more a national warning toward the Government to respect its obligations,[61] rather than a real European concern.

In an examination of the overall reasoned opinions sent by the two Houses to the European institutions, through the EWS, the first item of note is that the two Houses only have adopted a reasoned opinion on the same issue once. Considering the perfect symmetry of the Italian Parliament, we would have expected more joint positions and more coordination between the two Houses. However, the practice contradicts these expectations and shows that the two Chambers act as individual players in the EU decision-making process.

This lack of coordination is far more evident in the only case where the two Houses adopted a reasoned opinion on the same issue, namely on 'approximation of laws, regulations and administrative provisions on the manufacture, presentation and sale of tobacco and related products'.[62] The reasons developed by the two Houses were slightly different, although converging on the same argument. In this respect, the Chamber of Deputies[63] disputed the legal basis of the proposal (Article 114 TFEU), which it deemed to be not in line with the CJEU's decision[64] on the issue. According to the Court 'the use of Article 114 is not justified if the main and immediate purpose of the proposed act is the protection of health, and if the harmonizing of market conditions within the Community is merely a secondary consequence'. Following this reasoning, the Chamber argued that the EU draft legislative act appeared to not satisfy 'in full the conditions laid down by the CJEU for using art 114 as the legal basis'. Moreover, the Chamber further argued that the proposal would have had a negative impact on the same objective was aiming to achieve, since 'by encouraging Member states to act independently in certain areas [it would] bring about a situation of significant divergences among Member States with the consequent effect of restricting the free movement of goods'.[65] Different from the Chamber of Deputies, the Senate[66] did not only dispute the legal basis of the EU draft legislative acts,[67] but rather

[60] Doc XVIII n 41 Resolution of the 9° standing Committee, adopted the 8th June 2010 on the Proposal for a Council Decision laying down rules for imports into the European Union from Greenland of fishery products, live bivalve molluscs, echinoderms, tunicates, marine gastropods and by-products COM(2010) 0176.

[61] C Fasone, 'Il Senato approva il primo parere contrario sul rispetto del principio di sussidiarietà' (2010) *forumcostituzionale.it.*

[62] COM/2012/0788.

[63] Reasoned opinion issued on 19 February 2013.

[64] See in particular the judgments of 10 December 2002, *British American Tobacco (Investments) and Imperial Tobacco*, Case C 491/01, ECR page I-11453, para 60; and of 12 July 2005, *Nutritional Supplements*, Joined Cases C-154/04 and C-155/04, para 28.

[65] Reasoned opinion of the Chamber of Deputies issued on 19 February 2013.

[66] Reasoned Opinion of the Senate adopted on 30 January 2013.

[67] It is interesting to note that the Senate made reference to the same CJEU decision but with the opposite purpose to support the legal basis of the EU draft legislative Act, namely the C-491/01.

it raised further arguments against the proposal. The reasoned opinion argued that the legislative proposal had improperly used the power of delegation as regulated by Article 290 TFEU. Thus, according to the Treaty provision which limits the use of delegated acts only for 'non-essential elements of the legislative acts', the Senate found a breach of subsidiarity 'for an excessive and unjustified conferment of power on the Commission' for essential elements of the act, which may not be the object of delegation. According to the Senate, this delegation was deemed 'unjustified and prejudicial to the competence of Member States', since they were considered outside the criteria of the necessity and added value tests. Moreover, the arguments of the Senate seemed to go beyond the assessment of the compliance with the principle of subsidiarity and also be based on proportionality. This can be seen in its argument that 'a delegation of powers on such essential elements produces an excess of federal over national regulatory authority'.[68]

Despite all of the above, in general, both Houses do not restrict their reasoned opinions to a strict legal assessment of compliance with the subsidiarity principle, but rather they both adopt a wide approach; all reasoned opinions contain a general scrutiny on the choice of the legal basis, on the merits of the proposal, and on its respect of the principle of proportionality. On this, it is interesting to note the reasoned opinion issued by the Chamber of Deputies on COM(2011) 615 final,[69] which did not argue that there had been a breach of the subsidiarity principle; but rather, the Chamber clearly stated that the 'proposal fully compli[ed] with the principle of subsidiarity'.[70] The Chamber of Deputies disputed only one article of the Proposal, specifically article 21 which 'provided for conditionalities linked to the coordination of the economic policies of the Member States'.[71] Hence, it developed its reasoning claiming that the article could not be justified under the legal basis established by the proposal and that the Commission did not provide convincing arguments which could justify the introduction of those conditionalities. Thus, a reasoned opinion was issued although the Chamber did not dispute the compliance with the principle of subsidiarity.

In general, it is evident that coordination procedures between the two Houses of the symmetrical Parliament, on the one side, and between the Parliament and the Government, on the other side, shall be established. The need of those coordination mechanisms is further confirmed in light of the new provisions introduced by Law No 234 of the 2012. Although this law finally implemented the provisions established in the Lisbon Treaty, it introduces new interpretative concerns, for example regarding the different degrees of parliamentary participation in EU special procedures. According to article 11 paragraphs 1 and 2 of the law, the procedures which refer to (i) the framing of common Union defence policy (article 42(2) TEU); (ii) the simplified revision procedure of the European Treaties (article 48(6) TEU); and (iii) implementation measures for the Union's own resource system (article 311(3) TFEU), shall be adopted by law.

[68] Reasoned Opinion of the Senate adopted on 30 January 2013.

[69] COM/2011/0615 Proposal for a Regulation of the European Parliament and of the Council laying down common provisions on the European Regional Development Fund, the European Social Fund, the Cohesion Fund, the European Agricultural Fund for Rural Development and the European Maritime and Fisheries Fund covered by the Common Strategic Framework and laying down general provisions on the European Regional Development Fund, the European Social Fund and the Cohesion Fund and repealing Regulation (EC) No 1083/2006.

[70] Opinion adopted by the Chamber of Deputies on 14 December 2011.

[71] ibid.

Unlike the above, article 11 paragraph 3 of the law, regarding all the cases where the entry into force of a decision of the European Council and of the Council of the EU is subordinated to a prior national approval 'by the Member States in accordance with their respective constitutional requirements' and article 11 paragraph 5, referring to NPs' power of opposition to initiatives of the European Council,[72] require two further and different parliamentary acts. It requires in the first case a 'positive deliberation' of the two Houses, in the second case, a simple 'deliberation of the two Houses'. These new provisions raise new ambiguities regarding both the legal form of the act to be adopted and the procedure to be followed. In both cases, the law requires two general deliberations and appears to recognise an autonomous and independent power for each House, at the detriment of a unitary approach of the Italian Parliament at the EU level.[73]

Moreover, under article 12, the law regulates the so-called 'brake clauses' that shall apply in all cases where the TFEU establishes the possibility that 'a member of the Council [could] suspend the procedure and refer the matter to the European Council'. In those cases, the two Houses shall express their position to the Government through a political resolution. The same applies if the Parliament declares that 'for vital and stated reasons of national policy' the proposal should be opposed in the Council (article 31(2) TEU). Also, in this case, the Government is obliged to follow the position adopted by the two Chambers (article 12(2) law no 234 of 2012).

From the analysis of Law No 234 of 2012 and its procedural implications for the Parliament, it appears clear that the lack of constitutional provisions with respect to parliamentary participation in EU decision-making fostered an extensive interpretation of the parliamentary mechanisms to take the Government into account. However, those powers are individual powers that each chamber can independently adopt, without any previous coordination with the other chamber. It follows that in a symmetrical bicameral Parliament if the position of the two chambers diverge, the risk is the fragmentation of the country's political position at the EU level, which would cause a complete decisional blockage.

VI. Conclusions

The Italian Parliament is based on a symmetrical functional structure, where both Houses not only hold the same powers, but also enjoy constitutional autonomy. This autonomy is an essential feature of the symmetrical bicameral system, which guarantees the independence of the two branches of the Parliament. Paradoxically, this autonomy undermines the perfect symmetry between the two Houses and fosters practical differences in terms of organisation and procedures.

This chapter investigated those differences at the EU level and, by looking at both the structural and procedural organisation of the two Houses, pointed out how they diverged in terms of both adaptation to and participation in the European decision-making process. In structural terms, the main difference between the two Committees on European

[72] Art 48 para 7 TEU the passerelle clause and art 81 para 3 TFEU opposition in the matter of family law.

[73] See more in detail Piccirilli, above n 39, 205.

Affairs is based on membership. In the Senate, the 14th Committee is characterised by double membership, while in the Chamber of Deputies, members of the XIV Committee are not allowed to be full members of any other standing Committee at the same time. As for the scrutiny procedure, the two standing Committees hold similar competences; however, the important difference between the two Houses is the power given to the 14th Committee of the Senate to intervene and, in cases of inertia, to replace the competent standing Committee.

Moreover, since the introduction of the political dialogue and the EWS with the Lisbon Treaty, the two Houses adopted two different approaches. In the political dialogue, the Senate is much more active than the Chamber of Deputies. This difference can be explained by the procedural organisation set up in the Italian Senate, which is much more effective than the one established in the Lower House. However, besides the procedural dissimilarities, the two Houses also have different approaches determined by the different views that their respective officials have with respect their participation in the EU. The Chamber of Deputies is much more concerned about the possible negative implications that its participation in the EU decision-making process may create on the national form of government.[74] Conversely, the Senate considers this direct dialogue with the Commission a positive feature, since it enables the Houses to act independently from the Government and to participate directly in the EU decision-making process.

This divergence is also evident in the practice of the EWS. In fact, the two Houses have always adopted reasoned opinions on different subject matters, except in one case. Moreover, even in that case there was no evidence of coordination between the two Houses.

In summation, with the Lisbon Treaty and the establishment of the 'unicameral logic', the Italian symmetrical bicameral system came to be further imbalanced by the emergence of important structural and procedural differences. Those divergences imply that both Houses, possessing equal powers, differ in terms of practical implementation. The two Houses adopted two different approaches and, today, the Italian Senate remains among the most active chambers at the European level, while the Chamber continues to have a more watchful approach.

[74] Esposito, above n 55, 9

17

The 2016 Attempted Reform of the Italian Senate in a European Perspective

LUIGI GIANNITI

I. The Italian Constitutional Revision Bill: Still a Symmetrical Bicameralism in the Management of EU Affairs?

On 4 December 2016, a constitutional revision bill that was meant to reform Part II of the Italian Constitution was rejected by a large majority of voters through a referendum. The constitutional revision bill, approved by both Houses, was meant to reform one of the most symmetrical existing bicameralisms, differentiating the composition and the functions of the two branches of Parliament.

While the Chamber of Deputies would have been confirmed in its current political composition, the Senate was going to be transformed into an assembly representative of territorial autonomies (both the regions and the municipalities), indirectly elected by regional councils. Additionally, concerning functionality, the two Houses would have been entitled with different functions and powers. The legislative function, in particular, would have been vested primarily in the Chamber of Deputies as, in the ordinary procedure, the Senate could deliberate to participate in the legislative procedure and formulate amending proposals which were not binding for the Lower House, as the latter would have always adopted the final decision on the bill.

Few bills (constitutional revision bills and, as will be discussed in the present chapter, also bills authorising the ratification of European treaties and those concerning the shape and the terms of the Italian participation to and execution of EU laws and policies) would have been subject to the approval of both Houses through the traditional bicameral procedure.

As for non-legislative functions, the so-called *indirizzo politico* (translatable as the general political direction, which is to say the function which allows participation in the definition of political goals and the means to attain them) would have been attributed exclusively to the Chamber of Deputies; that Chamber, moreover, would have exercised the oversight of governmental activity and performance. The Senate would have been responsible for the evaluation of public policies and the activity of public administrations. This function had been extended during the *navette* to also cover the impact assessment of EU policies on territories (see below Section V).

The constitutional revision bill, although designing an intense differentiation of Houses in Italian bicameralism,[1] seemed like it would not have substantially would have altered the symmetrical position of the two Houses in the management of EU affairs.[2]

The present chapter is meant to analyse the position that would have been assigned to the two Houses in this field, focusing on the role of the reformed Senate. In particular, Section II, on the basis of a general recognition of the constitutional provisions affecting the Italian participation in the European Union, focuses on the symmetrical procedures provided by the constitutional revision bill for the approval of laws authorising the ratification of European Treaties. An insight into the potential exercised by the constitutional reform on the law regulating Italy's participation at the EU is provided in Section III which, starting from an analysis of Law No 234/2014, highlights the role of the revised Senate in the management of EU affairs. The role of the reformed Upper House in the procedures for the transposition of EU law is analysed in Section IV.

II. The Symmetrical Bicameralism for the Approval of Laws Authorising the Ratification of European Treaties

A. Constitutional Provisions Affecting the Italian Participation at the European Union: A General Overview

In Italy, unlike the majority of other EU countries, for a long time participation in the European Union has not been regulated at the constitutional level. However, the Constitutional Court in its jurisprudence has been ensuring the primacy of EU law through

[1] For a general overview of the features introduced by the constitutional revision bill affecting the Italian bicameral system, see, *ex multis*, C Pinelli, 'Le funzioni del Senato in ordine all'adesione della Repubblica all'UE' (2016) *Rivista AIC*; L Violini, 'Il bicameralismo italiano: quale futuro?' (2013) 3 *Rivista AIC*; A Manzella, 'La riforma del bicameralismo' (2013) 4 *Rivista AIC*; M Luciani, 'La riforma del bicameralismo, oggi' (2014) 2 *Rivista AIC* and, in the same issue, B Pezzini, 'La riforma del bicameralismo'; M Olivetti, 'Alcune osservazioni sulla riforma del Senato e del Titolo V nel disegno di legge costituzionale n. 1429, approvato dal Senato l'8 agosto 2014' (2014) *Amministrazioneincammino.it*; E Gianfrancesco, 'I numeri del Senato' (2014) www.gruppodipisa.it.

[2] On the prospects of the constitutional reform of the Senate, in the light of the full implementation of the features introduced by the Treaty of Lisbon, see the proceedings of the seminar on the topic 'La riforma del Senato nella prospettiva europea dopo Lisbona', held in Rome at AREL on 26 June 2014.

the interpretation of Article 11 of the Constitution.[3] In 2001, this principle was enshrined, with regard to legislation, in a constitutional norm, according to which 'legislative powers shall be vested in the State and the Regions in compliance with the Constitution and with the constraints deriving from the EC legal order and from international obligations' (article 117(1)).[4]

Manifold discussions were held about the possibility of bringing in a new constitutional norm regulating the participation of Italy in the EU.[5] A model for reference might have been detected in the German Constitution, as amended starting from the Single Act. Before 1990, in fact, the predominance of EU law had been ensured in Germany by the interpretation of a broader norm,[6] similar to article 11 of the Italian Constitution. Other proposals of reform were meant to authorise the ratification of European treaties through constitutional laws.

Yet, unlike other European countries, Italy chose to keep on ratifying treaties through ordinary laws. This was also the case with the most exhaustive European treaties: the so-called Constitutional Treaty (which never entered into force after the French and Dutch referendums)[7] and, more recently, the Treaty of Lisbon. In the current constitutional framework, the procedure followed for the ratification of European treaties does not differ in fact from the one applied to the ratification of international treaties.[8] On this point, a rather significant feature would have been introduced by the constitutional revision bill which, as will be highlighted (see below, Section I.B), provided two distinct parliamentary procedures for authorising the ratification of European and international treaties respectively.[9]

[3] Art 11 of the Italian Constitution reads: 'Italy rejects war as an instrument of aggression against the freedom of other peoples and as a means for the settlement of international disputes. Italy agrees, on conditions of equality with other States, to the limitations of sovereignty that may be necessary to a world order ensuring peace and justice among the Nations. Italy promotes and encourages international organizations furthering such ends'. See M Cartabia and L Chieffi, 'Art 11' in R Bifulco, A Celotto and M Olivetti (eds), *Commentario alla Costituzione* (Torino, UTET, 2006) 263 ff. See also V Barsotti, PG Carozza, M Cartabia and A Simoncini, *Italian Constitutional Justice in Global Context* (New York, Oxford University Press, 2016) 207 ff. See also N Lupo and G Piccirilli in the 'Conclusion' to this book.

[4] A Pajno, 'Il rispetto dei vincoli derivanti dall'ordinamento comunitario come limite alla potestà legislativa nel nuovo Titolo V della Costituzione' (2003) 5 *Le istituzioni del federalismo* 813–42. Pinelli, above n 1.

[5] The introduction of a 'European clause' in the Italian Constitution has represented a long debated issue; see for instance the debate carried out by the Joint Committee for Constitutional Revision settled in 1997: S Faro, 'Il tema della partecipazione dell'Italia all'Unione europea nei lavori della Commissione parlamentare per le riforme costituzionali' (1997) 6 *Rivista italiana di diritto pubblico comunitario* 1323 ff; F Sorrentino, 'La partecipazione dell'Italia all'Unione europea' in MP Chiti and L Sturlese (eds), *La riforma costituzionale: atti del convegno di studi in ricordo di Silvano Tosi, Firenze, 27–28 marzo 1998* (Milano, Giuffrè, 1999) 117 ff. On more recent constitutional revision bills directed at modifying art 11 of the Italian Constitution, see P Benvenuti, 'L'art 11 della Costituzione e il progetto di legge costituzionale n 218' (2003) 2 *La comunità internazionale* 201 ff.

[6] Art 24 of the Basic Law.

[7] Some scholars maintained that the Constitutional Treaty was to be ratified in Italy through a constitutional law; among them, M Cartabia, 'La ratifica del trattato costituzionale e la volontà costituente degli Stati membri' (2004) *Forumcostituzionale.it*, and L Gianniti and C Pinelli, 'Una scelta due questioni' (2004) *La Stampa*, 10.10.2004.

[8] For further details, see the chapter by G Vosa, in this volume.

[9] As for the execution of European obligations, the constitutional law no 1/2012 which, in coherence with the Treaty on Stability, Coordination and Governance in the Economic and Monetary Union (so called 'Fiscal Compact'), introduced in the Italian Constitution the budget balance formally recognised (art 97) the responsibility of public administrations, in line with the EU legal order, in granting balanced budgets and the sustainability of public debt. On the impact of the 2012 constitutional revision on the relationship between the Italian and the European legal orders, see G Tosato, 'La riforma costituzionale del 2012 alla luce della normativa dell'Unione: l'interazione

B. The Bicameral Procedure for the Approval of Laws Authorising the Ratification of European Treaties in the Constitutional Revision Bill

With the approval of the constitutional revision bill, laws authorising the ratification of European treaties would have been among the few laws still needing approval by both Houses under the procedure laid down by article 70.

According to the new wording of proposed article 80 of the Constitution, only the Chamber of Deputies would have been needed in order to approve the law authorising the ratification of international treaties. An explicit exception was set for those 'laws authorizing the ratification of international treaties concerning Italy's participation in the European Union'. Those needed to be approved by both the Chamber of Deputies and the new Senate, as it happens today in the context of a bicameral system where the two Houses enjoy the same powers.

Significantly, in the constitutional revision bill, the procedure for constitutional revisions and for amending other constitutional bills (article 138 Constitution) remained unchanged. Both Houses were entitled to approve the constitutional amendments on an equal basis, with a qualified majority and through two subsequent votes.

As a result of their being bicameral, laws authorising the ratification of European treaties would have held a peculiar place in the system of norms.[10] They would have always needed to be approved by both the Senate and the Chamber of Deputies, whereas ordinary laws would only possibly have been subject to a non-binding examination by the Senate. It should be remembered that the Senate was not supposed to participate in the confidence relation with the Government: a majority supporting the Government might therefore not have been guaranteed at all times in the Upper House.

The reason to propose a bicameral approval of laws ratifying European treaties lied in the fact that the norms of the treaties prevail over ordinary laws[11] and eventually also over constitutional ones.[12] It would have been peculiar if the national instrument for their

fra i livelli europeo e interno', Conference 'Il principio dell'equilibrio di bilancio secondo la riforma costituzionale del 2012', Italian Constitutional Court, 22 November 2013, available at www.cortecostituzionale.it. On the implications of the new constitutional reference to the EU legal order, see M Luciani, 'L'equilibrio di bilancio e i principi fondamentali: la prospettiva del controllo di costituzionalità', Conference 'Il principio dell'equilibrio di bilancio secondo la riforma costituzionale del 2012', Italian Constitutional Court, 22 November 2013, available at www.cortecostituzionale.it. On the issue, see also M Nardini, 'La legge n 243/2012 e l'adeguamento dell'ordinamento nazionale alle regole europee di bilancio' (2013) 1 *Osservatoriosullefonti.it*.

[10] Likewise, in Germany the law authorising the ratification of EU treaties is, according to the Constitution (art 23 of the Basic Law), a perfect bicameral law. Unlike the Italian procedure, however, such law requires an approval by a two-thirds majority, similar to the one provided for constitutional revisions. Recently on this point, strengthening the role of art 23 as a specification related to the participation to the EU of the eternity clause enshrined in art 79.3 of the Basic Law, see the *Einleitung* to the volume by C Calliess and T Beichelt, *Die europapolitische Rolle von Bundestag und Bundesrat. Die Europäisierung des Parlaments* (Gütersloh, Verlag Bertelsmann Stiftung, 2015) 21 ff.

[11] The primacy of EU law over national law has been recognised by the Italian Constitutional Court, although in different jurisprudential stages. S Cassese, *Ordine giuridico europeo e ordine nazionale*, Introduction to the meeting with the German Constitutional Tribunal, Karlsruhe, 20 November 2009, available: www.cortecostituzionale.it/documenti/convegni_seminari/19-21_11_09_Cassese.pdf has, in particular, detected four stages.

[12] Among the latest jurisprudential developments on this point see the *Melloni c Ministerio Fiscal* case, decided by the Court of Justice on 26 February 2003 (C-399/11, l) and referred to the application of art 53 of the Charter of Nice, which clearly confirmed the need to preserve the primacy of EU law even when a national constitutional provision may prevent or obstacle its application. For details, see A Ruggeri, 'La Corte di giustizia, il primato

ratification would have been submitted to a single House. In that case, the authorisation to ratification of European treaties through constitutional norms would have soon been called for. The issue might have been raised by the new Senate itself free from the confidence relationship.

As a consequence, the solution envisaged in the constitutional revision bill, by differentiating laws authorising the ratification of European treaties through a bicameral approval, qualified the same laws as special sources of law, characterised by a strengthened approval process.

C. Fallouts of the Constitutional Revision Bill on the Procedures for the Ratification of European Treaties

The very wording used by the constitutional revision bill ('laws authorizing the ratification of treaties regarding Italy's participation in the EU') surely applies to international treaties like the Treaty of Lisbon, which modifies and adopts the Treaty on the European Union (TEU) and the Treaty on the Functioning of the European Union (TFEU). Yet, it might not have included in its scope treaties which affect the EU legal system but are not formally part of the EU legal framework. This would have been the case for the so-called 'Fiscal Compact' (the aforementioned Treaty on Stability, Coordination and Governance in the Economic and Monetary Union).[13]

A strict interpretation of article 80 of the constitutional revision bill would have included the law authorising the ratification of the Fiscal Compact amid the ordinary laws, approved in only one House, as a treaty of a political nature. After all, in the constitutional revision bill (article 55(4)), only the Chamber of Deputies would have wield the *indirizzo politico*.

Nevertheless, a more careful reading of the impact of such a treaty on the Italian legal system might have led to a more open interpretation of the last paragraph of proposed article 80. In other EU countries, in fact, no doubts were expressed as to the opportunity to resort, for the Fiscal Compact, to the procedure prescribed for amending European treaties which, in Germany, is similar to those applied to constitutional revisions.[14]

incondizionato del diritto dell'Unione e il suo mancato bilanciamento col valore della salvaguardia dei principi di struttura degli ordinamenti nazionali nel loro fare "sistema"' (2013) www.diritticomparati.it and M Iacometti, 'Il caso Melloni e interpretazione dell'art 53 della Carta dei diritti fondamentali dell'Unione europea tra Corte di giustizia e Tribunale costituzionale spagnolo' (2013) www.associazionedeicostituzionalisti.it.

[13] Art 16 of the Treaty on Stability, Coordination and Governance in the Economic and Monetary Union confirms that the Fiscal Compact is not part of EU legal system, but it is functionally connected to EU law: 'Within five years, at most, of the date of entry into force of this Treaty, on the basis of an assessment of the experience with its implementation, the necessary steps shall be taken, in accordance with the Treaty on the European Union and the Treaty on the Functioning of the European Union, with the aim of incorporating the substance of this Treaty into the legal framework of the European Union'. Despite this provision, the Treaty does not enjoy the supremacy and direct effect of EU law; see, among others, P Craig, 'The Stability, Coordination and Governance Treaty: Principle, Politics and Pragmatism' (2012) *European Law Review* 231 ff; Loïc Azoulai et al, 'Another Legal Monster? An EUI Debate on the Fiscal Compact Treaty' (2012) 9 EUI Department of Law, Working Paper available at http://cadmus.eui.eu/bitstream/handle/1814/21496/LAW_2012_09_Kocharov_ed.pdf?sequence=1; GL Tosato, 'Il Fiscal compact' in G Amato and R Gualtieri (eds), *Astrid. Le istituzioni europee alla prova della crisi* (Firenze, Passigli, 2013) 1 ff.

[14] Gesetz zu dem Vertrag vom 2. Februar 2012 zur Einrichtung des Europäischen Stabilitätsmechanismus (Bundestagsdrucksachen 17/9045, 17/10126); Gesetz zu dem Vertrag vom 2. März 2012 über Stabilität,

It might be objected that in Germany, France and other EU Member States—unlike Italy—the Constitution lays down specific rules for the participation in European integration.[15] Article 117(1), of the Italian Constitution, by contrast, refers to the Community legal order (an obsolete concept after the Lisbon Treaty) and to the engagements assigned to Italy, which are generically mentioned aside other international engagements. Under this point of view, the Italian constitutional revision bill would not have changed the legal regulation of the European integration process, thus allowing manifold interpretations of the procedure to be followed for authorising the ratification of European treaties.

To solve such interpretative doubts, the procedure aimed at solving controversies between the two Houses, described by the constitutional revision bill (article 70, paragraph 6), might have been used. It, however, would have been more likely to cause problems than to offer real solutions. The Presidents of the Senate and the Chamber of Deputies, in fact, should have solved, through an agreement, those controversies concerning the competence of the two Houses, raised in accordance with their respective rules of procedure. The decision as to whether adopt a single-chamber or a bicameral procedure might therefore have been left, as a last resort, to an agreement between the two Speakers. It may be wondered whether such a mechanism would have revealed itself effective, especially when dealing with delicate matters such as the procedure to be followed for the ratification of treaties like the Fiscal Compact or the establishment of the European Stability Mechanism, given the fact that the two Speakers might well have found no agreement, or else made no choice at all.

III. The Bicameral Law on the Italian Participation in the EU

A. Law No 234/2012, Approved after the Treaty of Lisbon and Designed for a Symmetrical Bicameral System

The constitutional revision bill would have included among the (very few) categories of bicameral laws the ones 'establishing general norms, the shape and the terms of Italian participation to and execution of EU laws'.

As, prior to 2001, there was no reference, in the written Constitution, to the European Union, a particular importance was given, in the Italian experience, to the general law on the Italian participation to the EU: Law No 86/1989 and, later, Law No 11/2005, approved alongside the Constitutional Treaty, which was ratified by Italy, even though the latter never entered into force.

Koordinierung und Steuerung in der Wirschafts—und Währungsunion (Bundestagsdrucksachen 17/9046, 17/10125); both approved by the Bundestag and the Bundesrat on 29 June 2012 (*Zustimmungsgesetze*, majority of two-thirds). See Calliess and Beichelt, above n 10, 287 ff.

[15] According to the German Basic law (art 23 GG), the participation of the Federal Republic in the development of the European Union is a tool for the fulfilment of a 'United Europe'. By interpreting and applying such a provision, the German Constitutional Tribunal has evaluated the compliance to Constitution of the Fiscal Compact and of the Treaty establishing the European Stability Mechanism.

Law No 234/2012, approved after the entry into force of the Treaty of Lisbon,[16] deals thoroughly with the instruments and procedures of the Italian participation in the adoption of EU law, the decision-making procedure of common institutions in general (Headings I–V) and the transposition of EU norms into national law. It also sets norms about parliamentary information and participatory tools relating to 'agreements'—such as the Fiscal Compact—'between EU Member States which foresee the introduction or strengthening of rules in the financial or monetary sector or else have a relevant impact on public finance'. This structure provides an argument in support of an interpretation that includes such agreements among those to be ratified and executed through a bicameral law.

Beyond this unique aspect, which is a sign of the most recent evolution of EU law, the first aim and content of Law No 234/2012 is to regulate the powers enjoyed by the Italian Parliament under the Treaty of Lisbon. These powers are positive (of approval) and negative (of opposition); some are allocated to each Chamber and some to the Parliament *tout court*.[17]

The law, designed for a bicameral system, stipulates for instance that the Government state its intentions to both Houses before each Council meeting and that the Houses have the chance to adopt resolutions or other relevant documents. In the constitutional reform, however, only the Chamber of Deputies would have exerted general policy functions. It would therefore have not made sense for the President of the Council of Ministers to brief Senators personally about the European Council meetings.[18]

If the constitutional revision bill had entered into force, only the Chamber of Deputies would have been entitled to adopt political guidelines, which as a result might have been even more binding for the Government.[19] Nevertheless, the role of the Parliament in European affairs still would have needed to be governed by a bicameral law, which might have allowed the Senate to shape a role for itself, as will be highlighted in the following paragraphs.

B. The Placement of the Revised Senate with Regard to Information and Participatory Rights in EU Affairs

Law No 234/2012 sets a wide range of rights for the Houses to receive information from the Government. In this regard, the position of the Houses should stay perfectly balanced. In the European experience, upper Houses, albeit excluded from the confidence relationship,

[16] In Germany, the issue is regulated by a plurality of statutory laws: in particular, the EUZBBG (last revised in 2013) affects the cooperation between the Federal Government and the Bundestag, whereby a distinct law (the EUZBLG, which has been completed by an agreement among the Federation and the *Länder* of 10 June 2010) regulates the cooperation between the Federal Government and the Bundestag.

[17] For a general overview, see D Fromage, *Les parlements dans l'Union européenne après le Traité de Lisbonne* (Paris, L'Harmattan, 2015).

[18] On the prospects of the Law No 234/2012 in the light of the constitutional revision bill, see E Albanesi, 'Il nuovo Senato e i raccordi con l'Unione europea' in P Costanzo, A Giovannelli and L Trucco (eds), *Forum sul d.d.l. costituzionale 'Renzi-Boschi'* (Turin, Giappichelli, 2016) 73 ff at 86.

[19] In Germany, the EUZBBG punctually defines the information to be addressed only to the Bundestag on the meetings of the European Council, the Council and also other institutions—such as the EuroGroup and the directing bodies of the European Stability Mechanism—which are not provided by the EU Treaties, but share a special relationship with the EU legal order and contribute to complete it. See Fromage, above n 7, 209 ff.

generally enjoy a full set of rights to information about European affairs. European treaties themselves directly grant to each House of the national Parliaments rights to information and rights of participation in the formation of EU decisions. It might be questioned, however, how upper Houses which do not participate in the confidence circuit make use of the influx of information which European institutions provide them.[20] It should be noted that Law No 234/2012 also sets upon the Government some specific obligations to provide information concerning foreign and security policy (article 4, paragraph 2), about which the reformed Senate would have had no competence.

The constitutional revision bill, if approved, would have led to a wide range of interpretative issues. This is one of the main reasons why it was radically criticised both in the debate that led to its parliamentary approval and in the period preceding the referendum.[21]

C. The Relationship between the Lower and the Upper Houses on EU Affairs in the Proposed Asymmetrical Bicameralism

Law No 234/2012, setting norms on aspects of parliamentary life falling under the scope of the Houses' rules of procedure, permits each of them to adopt resolutions on EU draft documents, as well as on any other EU-related issue brought to its attention by the Government.[22]

A reduction of the influence of the Senate would have been predictable as a result of its exclusion from the confidence relation.[23] On the other hand, however, a certain degree of authority still would have been ensured by the norm of the proposed article 55(5), of the Constitution, according to which the Senate would have 'participate[d] … in the function as liaison between the State, the other constitutive entities of the Republic and the EU'.[24] Law No 234 also sets norms directed at promoting the two Houses' early participation in

[20] In the case of Italy, the flow of information coming from European institutions is, to some extent, the mirror of the one coming from the Government. Yet, under Law No 234/2012, the Government must accompany most relevant documents with a report on the effects on the national legal system and the Government's political opinions.

[21] See the relevant perplexities set by G Tremonti in his piece for *Corriere della Sera*, 'Il progetto di potere della nuova Costituzione', where he notes that 'The competence of the new Senate has not been limited to 'territories' and to regional or municipal issues, as it would have been logical, but has been extended to European matters. Therefore, given the range of matters the EU legislates on, the Senate will be endowed with an almost universal competence. Starting from the EU treaties, that will be decisive for our future, everything will bicamerally depend from a Chamber dramatically and grotesquely inadequate …' (our translation)

[22] See D Capuano, 'Il Senato e l'attuazione del trattato di Lisbona, tra controllo di sussidiarietà e dialogo politico con la Commissione europea' (2011) *Amministrazioneincammino.it*; P Caretti, 'La legge n 234/2012 che disciplina la partecipazione dell'Italia alla formazione e all'attuazione della normativa e delle politiche dell'Unione europea: un traguardo o ancora una tappa intermedia?' (2012) 5–6 *Le Regioni* 837 ff; G Rivosecchi, 'La partecipazione dell'Italia alla formazione e attuazione della normativa europea: il ruolo del Parlamento' (2013) 5 *Giornale di diritto amministrativo* 463 ff; A Esposito, 'La legge 24 dicembre 2012, n 234, sulla partecipazione dell'Italia alla formazione e all'attuazione della normativa e delle politiche dell'UE. Parte I—Prime riflessioni sul ruolo delle Camere' (2013) 2 *Federalismi.it.*

[23] The French Senate, for instance, may adopt '*des résolutions europennes*' (Constitution, art 88–4) that do not qualify as actual recommendations but as mere guidelines. *cf* H Haenel, 'Rapport d'information fait au nom de la commission des affaires européennes sur le développement du role européen du Sénat' (Paris, 2009) 17.

[24] Specifically on the function of 'liaison' (or 'linkage' function) between the state, the other constituting entities of the Republic and the EU, in the light of the evolutions in the debate on the constitutional revision bill, see LS Rossi, 'La 'funzione di raccordo' con l'Unione europea nella riforma dell'art 55 Cost' (2015) www.forumcostituzionale.it.

the conclusion of agreements among EU Member States that are outside the Union institutional framework (article 5).

The reason why the distinction between the 'political' Chamber and the Senate reveals itself to be less striking in EU-related matters should be understood in light of the role that the reformed Senate would have played in a multilevel constitutional system. The majority of EU legislative acts, in fact, are approved by the European Parliament (EP) and the Council of the European Union with procedures based on the majority principle. Only in limited cases (those where a unanimous vote is required) can a single Member State veto EU procedures.[25]

In those fields where unanimity is the rule, only the Chamber of Deputies might have been entitled to approve binding resolutions.[26] That would have been the only case in which a 'parliamentary reserve'[27] could turn into a veto. Otherwise, the political Chamber's guidelines could not have gone beyond a mere influence on the behaviour of the Executive within the Council. This is the reason why even a House devoid of a political general direction power may nevertheless make a contribution to the national stance on the adoption of European laws and policies.

Other European Upper Houses have the same experience, directly participating in the political dialogue with the European Commission. Hence, a constitutional definition of the way in which the Senate could contribute to the adoption of European Union laws and policies (the so-called 'participation') would have revealed itself to be highly appropriate.[28] Also, in this case, the interpretative problems and the operative difficulties inherent in the way that the constitutional revision bill was formulated emerge very clearly.

D. Other Cases of Equal Involvement of the Revised Senate in the Management of EU Affairs

As has been highlighted, the role of the new Senate would have remained perfectly equal to the Chamber of Deputies in amending treaties and defining the 'organic' law on the participation of Italy in the adoption of EU laws and policies. A bicameral law would have been required for the authorisation to ratify changes to the Treaties. Likewise, the

[25] In such cases, whereby each Member State has a veto power (under provisions of the EU treaties and others such as the one establishing the European Stability Mechanism), the role of the political House completely differs from that of the upper House. This is the experience featuring, for instance, the German Bundestag.

[26] After the entry into force of the Treaty of Lisbon, the Council is required to adopt unanimity only in a few areas which are, however, among the most important (taxation, finances, social security and protection, common foreign and security policy, common security and defence policy etc). See, among others, art 19, para 1; art 21, para 3; art 22, paras 1–2; art 25 of the TFEU. On this point, see G Tsebelis, 'Bridging Qualified Majority and Unanimity Decision-making in the EU' (2013) 20 (8) *Journal of European Public Policy* 1083 ff. On the new tendencies towards intergovernmentalism affecting the Council, see M Kloka and SK Schmidt, 'Legislative and Judicial Politics in the Post-Masstricht Era: the Intergovernmentalist Paradox in the Council of Ministers' in CJ Bickerton, D Hodson and U Puetter (eds), *The New Intergovernmentalism. States and Supranational Actors in the Post-Maastricht Era* (Oxford, Oxford University Press, 2015) 227 ff.

[27] See art 10 of the Law No 234/2012, governing the parliamentary scrutiny reserve. For a comparative overview on the issue, see K Auel, O Rozenberg and A Thomas, 'Lost in Transaction? Parliamentary Reserves in EU bargains' (2012) 10 *OPAL Online Paper Series*.

[28] On the experience of the French, English and German Upper Houses, see finally Fromage, above n 17.

norm that also requires a bicameral law for a simplified revision of the treaties (article 48, paragraph 6, TEU) should have remained unchanged. Additionally, Law No 234/2012 requires approval by law for the starting of a common defence (article 42(2), TFEU) and for setting the EU's own resources (article 311(3), TFEU). The former procedure is similar to a simplified revision, even if it would have fallen among those areas of competence which acknowledged the primacy of the Chamber of Deputies. The latter procedure, which at the EU level requires a unanimous vote, rather could have been considered as part of the general political direction power; as a consequence, with regard to the overall legal framework, it was not likely that the national law would have been approved through a bicameral procedure after the entry into force of the constitutional revision.

It was an open question, though, whether the revised Senate would have followed such an interpretation. The following example contributes to demonstrate how wide the spaces left open to interpretation by the constitutional revision bill were: Law No 234/2012 sets a general clause to be applied every time EU treaties establish that the entry into force of a European Council or a Council decision is subject to Member States' approval in accordance with their constitutional norms. This is the case, for instance, of the EU accession to the European Convention on Human Rights (ECHR)[29] or the single procedure for the election of the European Parliament.[30] In such cases, article 11(3) of Law No 234/2014 provides that the decisions by the European Council or Council 'are considered as approved in case of a positive deliberation of both Houses'; this deliberation is not a bicameral law, but a political guideline adopted by each House and having the same content.

Whether single decisions might be comparable to real treaty revisions should be subject to a case-to-case evaluation. The Parliament will need to make a decision upon the approval of a 'perfect' bicameral law. Generally speaking, decisions concerning the election of the EP and the accession to the ECHR undoubtedly have a constitutional nature.

The so-called 'emergency brake'[31] is another case in point: article 12 of Law No 234/2012 enables both Houses to adopt guidelines in order to define the Government's stance at the European level. Likewise, should vital national policy problems arise against the adoption of a decision at the European level (article 31(2)), the Government is today required to abide by the policy advice provided by the Houses.

If a political interpretation of the nature of these instruments had prevailed, the power to 'hit the brakes' only would have been recognised for the Chamber of Deputies.[32] As a matter of fact, keeping a decision-making role for the Senate after the entry into force of the constitutional revision bill would have reinforced the Government's independence and weakened the power of the Chamber of Deputies. The same reasoning would have been applied whenever the treaties explicitly involve national Parliaments in stopping

[29] Art 218(8) TFEU.

[30] Art 223(2) TFEU. Other cases are provided by art 25(1) (concerning the adoption by the Council of provisions to strengthen or to add to the rights recognised to the citizens of the Union) and art 262(1), TFEU (on the provisions adopted by the Council to confer jurisdiction on the Court of Justice of the European Union in disputes relating to European intellectual property rights).

[31] Art 48(2); art 82(3); art 83(3), TFEU allow a Member State to bring to a halt the negotiations at the Council level in order to refer the discussion to the European Council.

[32] In other Member States (Germany, for instance), the recourse to such *passerelle* clauses is subordinated to a preliminary agreement with the Parliament, namely only of the Bundestag if the *passerelle* clause concerns a subject listed within the exclusive competences of the Federation or otherwise also of the Bundesrat.

the ongoing decision-making procedure (article 11(5) Law No 234/2012 concerning the so-called general 'bridging clause' of article 48(7) TFEU and the opposition in family law under article 81(3) TFEU).

These examples show that, also in this case, the constitutional revision bill would have opened the way for a series of interpretative questions and difficulties, as well as for a potential conflict between the two Houses that could have involved the Constitutional Court.

IV. The Potential Role of the Revised Senate in the Transposition of EU Law into Italian Law

Proposed article 55 of the Constitution would have stated that the Senate should participate in the 'implementation of legislative acts and policies of the European Union'. A bicameral law would therefore have set norms for the role of the Senate.

Law No 234/2012 also provides for the transposition of EU law into Italian law. In Italy, the majority of EU norms are transposed through primary sources which, after the approval of the constitutional revision bill, would have generally fallen under the competence of the Chamber of Deputies. In this procedure (ie, the ordinary legislative procedure under the constitutional revision bill), the intervention of the Senate would have been possible only at the request of a quorum of Senators and within strict time limits, and the Chamber of Deputies could anyway overtake that intervention.

Though Law No 234/2012 foresees the annual 'European Law' ('legge europea') and 'European Delegation Law' ('legge di delegazione europea')[33] (both to be approved as bicameral norms in the current symmetrical bicameral system)[34] as the main tools for EU law transposition, the more general and constitutional provisions entrusting only the Chamber of Deputies with the political direction power apparently confirmed that the implementation laws should be part of the category of ordinary laws to be approved with a predominant role of the Chamber of Deputies. The Senate would have been entitled only to 'participate' in the forms granted by the constitutional revision bill.

The 2016 Stability Law (Law No 208/2015) includes, for example, some modifications of Law No 234/12, concerning the relationship between central and regional governments in the execution of the Court of Justice's judgments, according to article 260 of TFEU (article 1, paragraphs 813 and 814). While these modifications do not create any problems in a perfectly bicameral system, one should wonder if such an intervention would have been the object of a bicameral legislative procedure or (as it inevitably would have happened if included again in the Stability Law) of the new ordinary one, in which the Chamber of Deputies had the final say.

[33] On the introduction of two distinct types of legislative acts for the transposition of EU law and the fulfilment of EU obligations provided by Law No 234/2012, see Esposito, above n 22, and D Paris, 'Le leggi europea e di delegazione europea 2013: osservazioni sulla prima attuazione dello 'sdoppiamento' della legge comunitaria' (2014) 1 *Osservatorio sulle fonti*.

[34] For further details on the Italian legislative mechanisms of transposition of EU law into the national legal order, see the chapter by R Ibrido, in this volume.

Conclusion: 'Silent' Constitutional Transformations: The Italian Way of Adapting to the European Union

NICOLA LUPO AND GIOVANNI PICCIRILLI

I. The Composite Nature of the European Constitution

This volume analysed the evolution and the current features of the Italian Parliament through the lens of the European integration process. Since the 1950s, when the two Houses supported the Government in its being a founding member of European Communities, the Chamber of Deputies and the Senate of the Republic have undergone deep transformation processes, although there has been substantial stability of the constitutional provisions devoted to them (with the only exception of the constitutional amendment of 1963, regarding the equalisation of the two Houses' terms and the stabilisation of their number of members).[1]

Especially in its first decades, the European integration process—to which some specific provisions of the rules of procedure have been devoted since 1968 at the Senate and since 1971 at the Chamber—apparently played a very marginal role in this transformation. Only recently has the Italian Parliament fully acknowledged the political and institutional relevance of the European dimension. Similar to what happened in many other Member States, and in particular in the other founding ones, the first institutional actors to adapt to the European dimension were (some of) the judges. In parallel, the Government and its administration also started a transformation process aimed at adapting and profiting from

[1] See Constitutional Law No 3/1963. In the original text of the Constitution, the Senate legislative terms lasted six years, instead of five, and the members of both Houses were determined according to the most recent census, in proportional terms. However, this difference never had practical applications: in all legislative terms up to 1963, the Senate was dissolved one year prior to its 'natural' deadline, in order to have a single election day for both Houses.

the needs and opportunities deriving from it. Conversely, the Parliament was among the last national institutions to start its Europeanisation process.

As already has been remarked, it is especially the constitutional dimension of this transformation that has been brought to the fore by the contributions included in this volume. The Italian Parliament, like every other national Parliament in the European Union, is called upon to play a significant constitutional role, taking full advantage of its position among the institutions of the Euro-national parliamentary system and contributing to the composite European Constitution. That is why this concluding chapter is also focussed on re-examining the main features of the Italian Parliament and its evolution, as analysed in the volume, wondering whether and how it influenced the European Constitution. This means that in this conclusion the constitutional approach will be more explicit and that, most of all, a reverse viewpoint will also be adopted: instead of looking exclusively at how the European integration process transformed the Italian Parliament, the analysis will try to shed some light also on how the European Union has been influenced, for better or for worse, by the Italian Parliament, and more generally by some institutional features of the Italian Constitution.

Of course, the editors of the volume are fully aware of the vivid and still ongoing debate about the existence and the characteristics of the European Constitution, which would not make sense to summarise here.[2] Among the different and alternative ways of defining and qualifying the European Constitution, all of them share the theory according to which in the European Union a Constitution in a modern sense exists,[3] although it is not codified and has a composite nature. This means that it is not embedded in a unique legal document and that it cannot to be derived exclusively by EU law (treaties and other sources of EU law), as it is composed of elements of both EU law and national constitutional law.[4]

That is why an analysis of the Italian Parliament would be, in our opinion, significant also to understand better how the European Constitution actually works and why it has acquired some features and not others. More specifically, it aims to investigate one of the elements of this Constitution clearly attributable to the 'political constitutionalism' dimension of this Constitution.[5] Especially in the absence of a popular constituent act, it is precisely on the will of national Parliaments that the EU legal order was founded and on them,

[2] For an updated picture see R Schuetze in his 'Introduction' to the second edition of *European Constitutional Law* (Cambridge, Cambridge University Press, 2016) Lxiii ff. For the origins of the debate, JHH Weiler, *The Constitution of Europe: 'Do the New Clothes Have An Emperor?' And Other Essays on European Integration* (Cambridge, Cambridge University Press, 1999) and I Pernice, 'Multilevel Constitutionalism in the European Union' (2002) 27 *European Law Review* 511–29.

[3] On the notion of 'Constitution' in a modern sense, deriving from the two Revolutions at the end of the 18th Century and defined by Art 16 of the French Declaration of the Rights of Man and of the Citizen in 1789, according to which 'Toute Société dans laquelle la garantie des Droits n'est pas assurée, ni la séparation des Pouvoirs déterminée, n'a point de Constitution', see V Onida, *La Costituzione. La legge fondamentale della Repubblica* (Bologna, Il Mulino, 2007).

[4] See L Besselink, *A Composite European Constitution* (Groningen, Europa Law Publishing, 2007) and L Besselink and JH Reestman, 'The Fiscal Compact and the European Constitutions: "Europe speaking German" (2012) 8 *European Constitutional Law Review* 1–8. Somewhat convergent seems the approach proposed by A Manzella, who even anticipated the idea of a 'union of constitutions' ('Dopo Amsterdam. L'identità costituzionale dell'Unione europea' (1997) 5 *Il mulino* 906–25) and then, in the light of the evolution of the European treaties, concluded with the 'constitutional unity' of the European legal order ('L'unitarietà costituzionale dell'ordinamento europeo' (2012) 3 *Quaderni costituzionali* 659–64).

[5] The reference here is naturally to the contribution by R Bellamy, *Political Constitutionalism. A Republican Defence of the Constitutionality of Democracy* (Cambridge, Cambridge University Press, 2007).

together with the European Parliament that, according to Article 10 Treaty on European Union (TEU), it derives its own democratic legitimacy.[6]

The 'political constitutionalism' dimension of this story, indeed, has been often overlooked or neglected, especially by EU law scholars, also because it has played, at least until very recently, a very limited role in the setting up of European institutions and in the EU decision-making.[7] As it is generally recognised, in fact, the most relevant role in fostering the European integration process and in designing the features of the European Constitution was played by the judiciary: that is, consistently with the composite nature of this Constitution, by the Court of Justice of the EU as well as by the national judges, especially (some) Constitutional Courts.[8] As has been remarked, in the EU judges operate in a 'space of *constitutional interdependence*', as they are 'embedded in a constitutional fabric made of national constitutions, European Union (EU) law, European treaties, and conventions'.[9]

Further, this judicial and legal prevalence in the setting up of the European Constitution helps to explain some of the issues currently at stake within the European project. Namely, it definitely confirmed its elitist origins[10] and confined the place of national Parliaments—and national public opinions—to a marginal one: essentially, Parliaments have been called upon to intervene in the ratification phase of every new treaty, often without much debate on the merits of the main choices and steps of the integration process, already defined at the inter-governmental level.[11] As for the rest, oversimplifying a bit, it is probably not utterly improper to state that the overall mood in Brussels, among EU institutions and their bureaucracies, was that the less national Parliaments and national politics had to do with European affairs, the better.

[6] See L Besselink, 'The Place of National Parliaments within the European Constitutional Order' in N Lupo and C Fasone (eds), *Interparliamentary Cooperation in the Composite European Constitution* (Oxford, Hart, 2016) 34 ff.

[7] Among others, N Scicluna, *European Union Constitutionalism in Crisis* (Basingstoke, Routledge, 2014) 3 ff. and C Fasone and N Lupo, 'Constitutional Review and the Powers of National Parliaments in EU Affairs Erosion or Protection?' in D Jancic (ed), *National Parliaments after the Lisbon Treaty and the Euro Crisis: Resilience or Resignation?* (Oxford, Oxford University Press, 2017) 59–75.

[8] See, respectively, the classic studies by A Stone Sweet, *The Judicial Construction of Europe* (New York, Oxford University Press, 2004) 1 and M Claes, *The National Courts' Mandate in the European Constitution* (Oxford, Hart, 2006). More recently, among others: M Dawson, 'The Political Face of Judicial Activism: Europe's Law–Politics Imbalance' in M Dawson et al (eds), *Judicial Activism at the European Court of Justice* (Cheltenham, Edward Elgar Publishing, 2013) 11–31; J Komárek, 'The Place of Constitutional Courts in the EU' (2013) 9 *European Constitutional Law Review* 420–50.

[9] M Cartabia, 'Europe as a Space of Constitutional Interdependence: New Questions about the Preliminary Ruling' (2015) 16 *German Law Journal* (conclusion of the Special Issue on Preliminary References to the CJEU), 1791–96 (with specific reference to the Constitutional Courts, but both the concept and the terminology seem to work for any European judge).

[10] In general, on the role (real or aspired) of the elites in the European integration, see JHH Weiler, 'Europe in Crisis. On "Political Messianism", "Legitimacy" and the "Rule of Law"' (2012) *Singapore Journal of Legal Studies* 248–68. The influence of elites in the Italian public discourse on Europe is deepened by di M Cotta et al (eds), *L' Europa in Italia. Élite, opinione pubblica e decisioni* (Bologna, Il mulino, 2005). More specifically, on the legal elites (the 'community of lawyers') who drove the integration process, see A Vauchez, 'Introduction. Euro-Lawyering, Transnational Social Fields and European Polity Building' in A Vauchez and B De Witte (eds), *Lawyering Europe: European Law as a Transnational Social Field* (Oxford, Hart, 2013) 1–20.

[11] See the chapter by G Vosa, in this Book.

II. The Wide Scope and the Stability of the 'European Clause' Embedded in Article 11 of the Italian Constitution

In the composite European Constitution a crucial role is exercised by the so-called 'European clauses': namely, specific clauses embedded in almost all the Member States' Constitutions that implicitly or explicitly aim at opening the internal constitutional order to norms and principles adopted at European level.[12] Together with some provisions of the EU treaties—like, for instance, Article 4(2) TEU, with its reference to 'national constitutional identities',[13] and Article 6(3) TEU, with its reference to 'constitutional traditions common to the Member States', just to quote the two clauses with general contents[14]—such 'European clauses' entailed in national Constitutions enable the 'communication' between the EU and the domestic legal orders and support once more the idea of the existence of a composite Constitution. They operate with mutual reference to each other and ensure the openness of both the EU and national legal orders, acting like 'valves': that is, like mechanical switches that can raise or lower the amount of (normative) fluid flowing through them, making the two legal orders communicate and interact as components of a unique whole.[15]

The existence of clauses of 'openness' towards the international legal order is an original feature of the Italian and German Constitutions. Both contained clauses allowing—respectively—'limitations' (Article 11, in 1947) or 'transfers' (Article 24, in 1949) of sovereignty since the beginning, and they have been immediately used as ways for European Communities law's accession into internal legal orders. The same model was then followed by other Member States, like the Netherlands (Article 62 in 1953, now Article 92), Luxembourg (Article 49 bis, in 1956), and Denmark (Section 20, in 1953), with the introduction of general constitutional clauses used as mechanisms for acceding to the European integration process.[16]

Especially with the Treaty of Maastricht, when the constitutional nature and effects of the European Union were about to become more evident—after having been dissimulated for a long time[17]—a new series of clauses referring to the European Union was inserted in

[12] M Claes, 'Constitutionalizing Europe at its Source: The "European Clauses" in the National Constitutions: Evolution and Typology' (2012) 1 *Yearbook of European Law* 81–125; M Claes, 'Le "clausole europee" nelle costituzioni nazionali' (2005) 2 *Quaderni costituzionali* 283–320. See also, mainly from a EU law perspective, J Wouters, 'National Constitutions and the European Union' (2000) 1 *Legal Issues of Economic Integration* 25–92.

[13] It is known that the wording of Art 4(2) TEU is broader and more complex, including not only the 'constitutional identity', but more precisely 'national identities, inherent in their fundamental structures, political and constitutional, inclusive of regional and local self-government'. On the recurring simplification of this formula see E Cloots, *National Identity in EU Law* (Oxford, Oxford University Press, 2015).

[14] It is necessary to add also all the times that TEU and TFEU state that some decisions are taken by each Member State 'in accordance with its own constitutional requirements' (for instance arts 42(2) TEU; 25; 218(8); 223(1); 262; 311 TFEU). More elaboration on this point is made in the chapter by G Piccirilli, in this book.

[15] M Avbelj, 'Supremacy or Primacy of EU Law-(Why) Does it Matter?' (2011) 17 *European Law Journal* 744–63 reconstructs the mutual relationship between national and European law as 'heterarchical' and thus to be reciprocally coordinated rather than considered one subordinated to the other.

[16] Claes, above n 12.

[17] This dissimulation was fully consistent with the approach followed among others by Jean Monnet, according to which the best way to conduct the integration process was to avoid dramatic (and so too-evident) spurts, and to proceed with the 'politique des petits pas'.

many Member States' constitutions. Their main aim was to make possible the adaptation of internal legal orders to some of the provisions included in the Treaty of Maastricht, but often it was also to put a series of conditions and requirements to further developments of the European integration process.[18]

When a rather strict European clause was in force, national Constitutions needed to be amended consistently with every Treaty revision taking place at EU level. This is the case of the French Constitution, which has been amended several times in order to: ratify the Treaty of Maastricht[19] and the Treaty of Amsterdam;[20] proceed to the ratification of the Constitutional Treaty, which, as is known, was then-nullified by the popular referendum;[21] and finally to ratify the Treaty of Lisbon.[22] These constitutional adaptations were required also as an effect of a procedural mechanism (Article 54 French Constitution) that allows the pre-emptive involvement of the Conseil constitutionnel before the ratification of a new international treaty (and therefore any new European treaty), asking this body whether the Treaty complies with the Constitution or whether, on the contrary, a constitutional amendment is required.[23]

It can be worth considering more deeply, through some comparative elements, the relationship between constitutional amendments and ratification of European treaties in order to underline the Italian particularity of 'silent' adaptation. Many European clauses, in fact, different from the Italian one, refer explicitly or implicitly to constitutional amendment procedures to ratify new European Treaties.

As a matter of common knowledge, this is the option embraced by the (new) Article 23 of the German Basic Law, inserted in 1992, in view of the ratification of the Treaty of Maastricht and prior to its approval by the German institutions. According to it, every modification to the European treaties that substantially amends or supplements the Basic Law must be subject to the constitutional amendment procedure entailed in Article 79(2) and within the limits of Article 79(3) of the Basic Law.[24] The rationale of this clause is to ensure the rigidity of the Basic Law vis-à-vis the evolution of the European integration both procedurally (by requiring the same procedures and majorities of constitutional amendments) and substantially (by setting the same limit of the 'eternity clause' of Article 79(3) of the Basic Law to both 'domestic' constitutional amendments and 'EU-driven' ones).[25]

[18] Along the same line of reasoning, see the analytic examination of the individual clauses (updated after the Lisbon Treaty) that is presented in the Annex III of the study commissioned by the European Parliament (PE 493.046) and conducted by L Besselink et al, *National Constitutional Avenues for Further EU Integration* (Brussels, European Parliament, 2014) 263 ff.

[19] Loi constitutionnelle no 92-554 of 25th June 1992, adding to the Constitution the title: 'The European Communities and the European Union'.

[20] Loi constitutionnelle no 99-49 of 25 January 1999, amending ss 88-2 and 88-4 of the Constitution.

[21] Loi constitutionnelle no 2005-204 of 1 March 2005 amending Title XV of the Constitution.

[22] Loi constitutionnelle no 2008-103 of 2 February 2008 substituting again the Title XV of the Constitution, at the moment of the entry into force of the Treaty of Lisbon.

[23] See P Gaïa, 'Le Conseil constitutionnel français et le contrôle de conformité à la Constitution des engagements internationaux et européens de la France' in N Zanon (ed), *Il controllo preventivo dei trattati dell'Unione europea* (Milan, Giuffré, 2015) 2–79.

[24] Art 79(2) requires the approval by two-thirds of the Members of each House of the Federal Parliament. Art 79(3) prohibits constitutional amendments affecting the division of the Federation into Länder, affecting their participation on principle in the legislative process, or affecting the principles of human dignity (set in Art 1) and those of the democratic and welfare state (Art 20).

[25] However, this link between (further) European integration and constitutional rigidity is not to be seen as an element of closure of the German constitutional order to external interactions: see A Di Martino, 'The "Open

Not too dissimilar from the German solution tends to be, at least in practice, the Irish approach. Starting with the decision of the Supreme Court in the case *Raymond Crotty v An Taoiseach and Others* in 1987,[26] any significant modification to the European Treaties requires a correspondent amendment to the Irish Constitution. The procedure tends to be even more complex and difficult, however, as constitutional amendments in Ireland necessarily imply the approval by popular referendum.[27] In order to ratify the Treaty of Lisbon, after the negative result of a first referendum held in Ireland on 12 June 2008, a new referendum was celebrated on 2 October 2009 in the light of the negotiations that led to some concessions for the Republic of Ireland.[28] The positive result of the second referendum allowed the entry into force of the 28th Amendment of the Constitution of Ireland, which affirmed the 'commitment' of Ireland to the European Union, enabled the ratification of the Treaty of Lisbon and made specific reference to some of the innovations introduced with it (such as the *passerelle* clauses, the adhesion to forms of enhanced cooperation, the establishment of a common defence, etc).[29]

Slightly different is the French example, in which, as already recalled, it is the interaction between political will (the decision of the President of the Republic, or the Prime Minister, or the President of one of the two Houses or, since 1992, 60 deputies or 60 senators, to involve the Conseil Constitutionnel) and legal elements (a negative outcome of the preliminary *saisine*, by the same Conseil Constitutionnel, provided by Article 54 Constitution) that may lead to a constitutional amendment, in order to ratify a European treaty. In the case of the Treaty of Lisbon, for instance, the political element is quite evident, with the neo-President of the Republic, Nicolas Sarkozy, invoking the intervention of the Conseil Constitutionnel on the same day that he himself signed it (13 December 2007). Then the legal element followed shortly after, with the Conseil Constitutionnel deciding on the matter in just one week,[30] asking for a constitutional amendment (… that arrived within a couple of months).[31]

At the opposite extreme, the main and original European clause embedded in the Italian Constitution has an extremely wide scope and did play a crucial role in the last 60 years, granting a smooth adaptation of the Italian legal order to the different stages of the European integration process.

Constitutional State": Germany's responses to International and European Pluralism' in L Mezzetti (ed), *International Constitutional Law* (Turin, Giappichelli, 2014) 109–40, who reconnects the way in which Germany participates in the European integration to the ideas of the 'open constitutional state' (K Vogel, *Die Verfassungsentscheidung des Grundgesetzes für eine internationale Zusammenarbeit* (Tubingen, Mohr, 1964)) and of the 'cooperative state' (P Häberle, *Der kooperative Verfassungsstaat aus Kultur und als Kultur* (Berlin, Duncker und Humblot, 2013)), fostering the adhesion to the concept of a constitutional integration in terms of 'Verfassungsverbund' that ends to be not dissimilar from that of the composite European constitution (see at 131 ff).

[26] Decision [1987] IESC 4, released on 9 April 1987 and specifically related to the ratification of the Single European Act.

[27] Art 46(2) of the Irish Constitution.

[28] The agreement between Ireland and other Member States are attached to the conclusions of the Presidency of the European Council, held in Brussels on 18/19 June 2009: Annex 1 (Decision of the Heads of State or Government of the 27 Member States of the EU, meeting within the European Council, on the concerns of the Irish people on the Treaty of Lisbon); Annex 2 (Solemn declaration on workers' rights, social policy and other issues) and Annex 3 (National declaration by Ireland).

[29] See, in particular, the new Arts 29.4.4–29.4.9 of the Irish Constitution.

[30] Judgement No 2007-560 DC, on 20 December 2007.

[31] See the already quoted loi constitutionnelle no 2008-103, 4 February 2008. On this, see X Magnon, 'Le traité de Lisbonne devant le Conseil constitutionnel: non bis in idem?' (2008) 74 *Revue française de droit constitutionnel* 310–33.

According to Article 11 of the 1947 Italian Constitution, placed since the beginning among its fundamental principles (Articles 1–12), 'Italy agrees, on conditions of equality with other States, to the limitations of sovereignty that may be necessary to a world order ensuring peace and justice among the Nations' and 'promotes and encourages international organisations furthering such ends'.

The provision was originally conceived mainly for the membership to the United Nations, but was drafted in a way that allowed its extension to the multiple projects of European integration that were taking place after the Second World War.[32] In it, there are also some traces of the openness to the international order requested in the Constitutions of the three main defeated military powers, Germany,[33] Japan,[34] and, precisely, Italy.[35]

Thanks to the constitutional reference to sovereignty and its limitations, Italy has been capable to ensure the ratification of all the European Treaties by means of ordinary legislation and the legal effectiveness of EU law to the domestic legal order, allowing also the Italian Constitutional Court to progressively adapt its case law to the early affirmation of the primacy and direct effect by the European Court of Justice as early as the 1960s.[36]

More recently, in addition to Article 11, a limited number of specific references to the European Union and some of its institutions appeared in the text of the Italian Constitution.

A first step was made in 1999, when Article 122 Constitution was amended in a comprehensive reorganisation of the regional form of government. Among other changes, the new discipline of incompatibility that excluded the possibility of being a member, at the same time, of elected assemblies at different levels of government, made the first explicit reference to one of the EU institutions, namely the European Parliament.

A second (and more telling) step was taken in 2001. Here, in the framework of a general re-thinking of the distribution of legislative competences between state and regions, a reference to the 'constraints deriving from Community Law' was set in Article 117(1), together with the Constitution itself and 'international obligations', as limits common to both state and regional legislation. It was probably intended as a mere reaffirmation of limits already recognised by the case law of the Constitutional Court to state as well as regional legislation, but it raised a certain debate especially where it referred also to 'international obligations'.

[32] A Cassese, 'Commento all'articolo 11' in G Branca (ed), *Commentario della Costituzione, articoli 1–12, Principi generali* (Bologna-Rome, Zanichelli, 1975) 569 ff. See also M Cartabia-L Chieffi, 'Art 11' in R Bifulco, A Celotto and M Olivetti (eds), *Commentario alla Costituzione* (Turin, Utet, 2006) 264–305.

[33] See, in particular, Art 24 of the 1949 German Basic Law, which states, inter alia, that 'The Federation may by a law transfer sovereign powers to international organisations' and that 'With a view to maintaining peace, the Federation may enter into a system of mutual collective security; in doing so it shall consent to such limitations upon its sovereign powers as will bring about and secure a lasting peace in Europe and among the nations of the world'.

[34] See Art 9 of the 1946 Japanese Constitution, according to which 'Aspiring sincerely to an international peace based on justice and order, the Japanese people forever renounce war as a sovereign right of the nation and the threat or use of force as means of settling international disputes. In order to accomplish [this aim], land, sea, and air forces, as well as other war potential, will never be maintained. The right of belligerency of the state will not be recognized'.

[35] M Cartabia, 'The Legacy of Sovereignty in Italian Constitutional Debate' in N Walker (ed), *Sovereignty in Transition* (London, Hart Publishing, 2003) 305–26 (analysing the uses of 'sovereignty' in the Italian legal scholarship and case law).

[36] The now-classic reference to this path is P Barile, 'Il cammino comunitario della Corte' (1973) *Giurisprudenza costituzionale* 2406. More extensively see M Cartabia and JHH Weiler, *L'Italia in Europa. Profili istituzionali e costituzionali* (Bologna, Il Mulino, 2000) and GL Tosato, 'L'articolo 11 della Costituzione e il diritto dell'Unione europea' in N Ronzitti (ed), *L'articolo 11 della Costituzione. Baluardo della vocazione internazionale dell'Italia* (Neaples, Editoriale scientifica, 2013) 69–85.

The applicability of this limit also to state legislation, indeed, brought the Constitutional Court to overcome the traditional principle according to which international treaties had, in the internal legal order, the same legal status of the law executing them (that is, ordinary law) and could therefore be repealed by more recent piece of legislation according to the *lex posterior* criterion. According to its decisions nos 348/2007 and 349/2007, the Constitutional Court in particular can use the European Convention on Human Rights as a standard for judicial review of state legislation[37] (insofar its provisions, as interpreted by the European Court of Human Rights, conform with the Constitution): so, it acquired an intermediate position between ordinary law and the Constitution.[38]

Finally, with the constitutional revision that in 2012 introduced the balanced budget principle in Article 81 Constitution, also Article 97, containing the basic principles for public administration, was amended. A new paragraph was added, at its beginning, addressed to all 'general government entities' (ie the public administration in a subjective sense), now asked to ensure balanced budgets and sustainability of public debt 'in accordance with European Union law'.[39]

However, contrary to what happened in Germany with the aforementioned replacement of Article 23 Constitution,[40] the modifications to the Italian Constitution did not touch the essence or the letter of the original European clause, which is still contained in Article 11.[41] At the most, some scholars as well as several decisions of the Italian Constitutional Court combine Article 117(1) with Article 11, using both as constitutional bases for justifying the constitutional need to adapt the internal legal order to EU law. Yet, it would be incorrect to rely on Article 117 alone, as it solely implies a constraint for the internal legislators (the state as well as the regions), whereas Article 11 refers to wider limitations of sovereignty that thus include the constitutional level of the sources of law and also the other branches of the Republic. Indeed, when the Constitutional Court wished to recap the main elements of the composite European Constitution, obviously as seen from an Italian perspective, it did not need to recall also Article 117, as the referral to Article 11 is sufficient to recognise the '*primautè*' of EU law on national law (with the only exception of the so-called 'controlimiti').[42]

[37] See G Repetto (ed), *The Constitutional Relevance of the ECHR in Domestic and European Law. An Italian Perspective* (Cambridge, Intersentia, 2013).

[38] See V Barsotti, PG Carozza, M Cartabia, A Simoncini, *Italian Constitutional Justice in Global Context* (Oxford, Oxford University Press, 2016) 226–30.

[39] On the importance of this addition see GL Tosato, 'La riforma costituzionale del 2012 alla luce della normativa dell'Unione: l'interazione fra i livelli europeo e interno', available at www.cortecostituzionale.it/documenti/convegni_seminari/Seminario2013_Tosato.pdf. More broadly, see the special issue of *Il Filangieri. Quaderno 2011, Costituzione e pareggio di bilancio* (Naples, Jovene, 2012).

[40] However, see also the opening words of the Preamble of the Basic Law, as originally drafted in 1949: '[the German people] inspired by the determination to promote world peace as an equal partner in a united Europe'.

[41] See C Pinelli, 'I limiti generali alla potestà legislativa statale e regionale e i rapporti con l'ordinamento internazionale e con l'ordinamento comunitario' (2001) 5 *Foro italiano* 194.

[42] See the recent order no 24/2017 of the Constitutional Court, which issued a preliminary reference to the Court of Justice in reaction of the latter's judgment on the 'Taricco case', para 2 ('The recognition of the primacy of EU law is an established fact within the case law of this Court pursuant to Article 11 of the Constitution; moreover, according to such settled case law, compliance with the supreme principles of the Italian constitutional order and inalienable human rights is a prerequisite for the applicability of EU law in Italy. In the highly unlikely event that specific legislation were not so compliant, it would be necessary to rule unconstitutional the national law authorising the ratification and implementation of the Treaties, solely insofar as it permits such a legislative scenario to arise (see Judgments No 232 of 1989, No 170 of 1984 and No 183 of 1973)'). More on the 'controlimiti' doctrine also below, at n 61.

The choice to make use of Article 11 of the Italian Constitution as a European clause and, consequently, not to amend the 1947 Constitution to include a reference to the European communities was originally due to political reasons. During the 1950s, the majority required for passing any constitutional amendment was at least two-thirds of the members of each House.[43] Because of the opposition of the communist and socialist parties it was practically impossible to reach that threshold for the ratification of European Communities' founding treaties.[44]

In a different political context, after the crisis of the party system in the early 1990s, in the framework of an attempt to comprehensively reform the Constitution, there also has been the idea of inserting a new European clause.[45] It would have included a list of (rather vague) limits to the participation in the European Union[46] and a specific procedure to allow further limitation of national sovereignty (apparently applicable also to the ratification of new European treaties) that would have requested even a popular referendum.[47] However, after the failure of that constitutional reform, no further (significant) proposals have been examined to amend or integrate Article 11 Constitution.[48]

Thus, under the wide umbrella of Article 11 Constitution, the Italian participation in the European Union has been relying essentially on just legislative means, starting from the choice made when authorising the ratification of the first European treaties,[49] soon confirmed and refined by the Italian Constitutional Court. Even though it took some time

[43] According to Art 138 of the Italian Constitution, any approval with a mere absolute majority would have allowed the possibility for requiring a popular referendum. However, as the ordinary legislation implementing the referendum itself was passed only on 1970, before that date all the constitutional amendments needed to be approved with a two-thirds majority by both Houses.

[44] A Barbera, 'Costituzione della Repubblica italiana', in *Enciclopedia del diritto. Annali*, VII (Milan, Giuffré, 2015) 263–358, at 352; A Varsori, *La Cenerentola d'Europa? L'Italia e l'integrazione europea dal 1947 ad oggi* (Soveria Mannelli, Rubbettino, 2010) 34 ff. More specifically, with regard to the evolution of the communist party on the European integration, that brought it to have, as elected in its own lists, Altiero Spinelli as member of the Italian Chamber in 1976 and of the European Parliament in 1979, see interviews and documents in M Maggiorani and P Ferrari (eds), *L'Europa da Togliatti a Berlinguer. Testimonianze e Documenti (1945–1984)* (Bologna, Il mulino, 2005).

[45] See Art 114 of the draft constitutional amendment elaborated by the Bicameral Committee for constitutional reforms in 1998, on which C Curti Galdino, 'Il progetto di revisione costituzionale sui temi attinenti all'Unione europea nei lavori della Bicamerale' in Società Italiana Diritto Internazionale, *Riforme costituzionali, Prospettiva europea e prospettiva internazionale* (Neaples, Editoriale scientifica, 2000) 27.

[46] Limits were identified with the 'supreme principles of the legal order and the respect of the human being'.

[47] The Law to allow further limitations to national sovereignty would have been approved by absolute majority in both Houses and submitted to popular referendum upon the request of one-third of the members of each House, 80,000 voters or five regional assemblies.

[48] For the sake of completeness, some proposals for constitutional amendments to Art 11 have been submitted, in particular by MPs members of the Northern League, in order to tighten the constraints to the participation of the EU. See, in the XVI legislative term (2008–2013), the two identical constitutional bills nos AS 769 by Sen Bricolo and AC 1329, by Hon Cota, submitted in 2008 (and later copied and pasted in 2016, during the subsequent legislative term, by AS 2396, by Sen Consiglio). These proposals aimed at introducing the necessity for the approval of further limitations to national sovereignty both by the Parliament (by absolute majority) and by the people with a referendum. However, no discussion of any of these constitutional bills has ever been started in parliamentary committees. More recently, also Sen Tremonti, a former finance minister in the Berlusconi governments, submitted a proposal aimed to add to Art 11 Const a new sentence, self-declared inspired by the German Constitution (that EU law is applicable only 'if compatible with principles of sovereignty, democracy, subsidiarity and with the other principles of the Italian Constitution') as well as to restore the original version of Art 117(1) Const (AS 2693, submitted on 10 February 2017).

[49] Law 14 October 1957, no 1203.

to combine the dualist approach of the Italian legal order with the early affirmation of the primacy and direct effect made by the European Court of Justice,[50] the Italian Constitutional Court never called for the need of a constitutional reform in order to participate in the integration process, affirming the possibility to cope with it by the means of interpreting the Constitution in force.[51]

The same model was then followed for authorising the ratification of all treaty revisions. A bill was submitted by the Government and approved, as quickly and plainly as possible, by a large parliamentary majority—which enlarged even more as the parties of the left became gradually more in favour of European integration—and no referendum or prior judicial check of compatibility with the Italian Constitution was required.[52] This model was applied also to the Treaty of Lisbon, even more because the Italian Parliament had been among the first to ratify the constitutional treaty three years earlier. This helps to explain why neither in the Senate (on 23 July 2008) nor in the Chamber of Deputies (31 July 2008) a single negative or abstention vote was cast on the bill authorising its ratification.[53] If for ratifying the constitutional treaty there was no need for any constitutional amendment, this was evidently true for a treaty as that of Lisbon which, at least formally, intended to downgrade the constitutional impact (as well as some constitutional rhetoric) of its immediate precedent.

The approach chosen by the Italian constitutional order doubtless offers some advantages, both from the point of view of the domestic level as well as from that of the European one.

Starting from the former, such an approach keeps the constitutional norms (ie the most rigid and fundamental rules at the basis of the legal order) as open as possible to supranational interaction, ready to adapt to the evolving reality of European integration via interpretative evolutions, without the need for formal revisions of the constitutional text. This openness allowed the incorporation of the most innovative steps of the process of European integration via a mere ordinary law authorising the ratification of the individual treaty at stake. No constitutional amendments have been approved (or required) in order to originally take part in the European Coal and Steel Community (ECSC), European Atomic Energy Community (EAEC) or European Economic Community (EEC); to adhere to the European Union after the Treaty of Maastricht; to join the single currency; or to complete the domestic procedure for the (later-failed) Constitutional Treaty. In other words, the absence of rigid constitutional barriers in the communication between the two legal orders has facilitated the 'incorporation' at the constitutional level of interpretative conventions, filling the void of what the Constitution does not say.[54]

[50] Barile, above n 36. See also F Sorrentino, 'La Costituzione italiana di fronte al processo di integrazione europea' (1993) *Quaderni costituzionali* 71–112 and M Cartabia, 'The Italian Constitutional Court and the Relationship Between the Italian Legal System and the European Union' in AM Slaughter et al (eds), *The European Court and National Courts: Doctrine and Jurisprudence: Legal Change in Its Social Context* (London, Hart Publishing, 1998) 133–46.

[51] Barsotti et al, above n 38, 205 ff.

[52] See chapters by P Falletta and G Vosa.

[53] In the final vote on the bill authorising the ratification of the Treaty of Lisbon the Senate registered 286 votes in favour out of 286 members participating in the vote (consisting of the plenum of 321 members, as at that time there were seven life senators, plus the President). At the Chambers of Deputies there were 551 votes in favour out of 551 voting members (plenum 629, plus the President).

[54] This may represent a case of 'informal constitutional change by incorporation', according the classification proposed by R Albert, 'How Unwritten Constitutional Norms Change Written Constitutions' (2015) 2 *Dublin*

There is also a specific advantage for the Italian Parliament, which had been the protagonist, together with its Government, of the founding of the European Communities and remains. No place was left for actors like the Constitutional Court (at least in the ratification phase) or the Italian people. Regarding the latter, the only exception was the 1989 referendum, provided by an 'ad hoc' constitutional law (so approved by the Parliament itself), and devoid of any binding value. Through the advisory referendum in 1989 Italian citizens were asked—on the same day in which they were called to elect, for the third time, the members of the European Parliament—whether they wanted to transform the European Communities into a Union, with a Government responsible before the European Parliament, and to confer to the European Parliament a mandate to draft a project of a European Constitution. The result confirmed the wide pro-European orientation of the Italian public opinion at that time, as 88.1 per cent of the voters gave a positive reply (and the turnout was rather high, at 81 per cent also because it was held on the same day of the EP elections).[55]

Also, the European level can benefit from such an interpretative way of approaching the constitutional coping with continental integration. It allows a (founder) Member State to promptly follow the evolution and the different phases (and fashions) at the European level, keeping the 'constitutional avenues for further integration'[56] as accessible and large as possible. It seems also fully consistent with the idea of a constant evolution of the European Union, as stated in the motto 'an ever closer Union'.[57]

Beyond the just mentioned advantages, there can be some risky drawbacks. Generally speaking, progressive affirmation of non-written norms integrating and lying beside the Constitution risks affecting and weakening the Constitution's effectiveness,[58] as it loses its communicative potential to be perceived as a point of reference of the common values of the society.[59]

University Law Journal 387–417, namely 'the evolution in the tacit understanding of law and politics held by governors and accepted by governed'.

[55] P Costanzo, 'La Costituzione italiana di fronte al processo costituzionale europeo' in F Modugno (ed), *Attuazione e integrazione della costituzione* (Naples, Jovene, 2009) 85–100 and B Caravita, 'Il referendum sui poteri del Parlamento europeo: riflessioni critiche' (1989) 2 *Politica del diritto* 319–27.

[56] For the use of this expression see Besselink et al, above n 18.

[57] Similarly, the evolving idea entailed in the motto was deemed consistent with the absence of a rigid hierarchy of norms among sources of EU secondary law: R Bieber and I Salome, 'Hierarchy of Norms in European Law' (1996) *Common Market Law Review* 907–30, at 911.

[58] T Ginsburg, 'Constitutional Specificity, Unwritten Understandings and Constitutional Agreement' in A Sajó-R Uitz (eds), *Constitutional Topography: Values and Constitutions* (The Hague, Eleven International Publishing, 2010) 69 ff.

[59] The risk of affecting the continuity in popular consent by informal constitutional changes has been described by W Dellinger, 'The Legitimacy of Constitutional Change: Rethinking the Amendment Process' (1983) 97 *Harvard Law Review* 383 ff. More specifically R Albert, 'Counterconstitutionalism' (2008) 31 *Dalhousie Law Journal* 1 ff, elaborates on the relationship between constitutionalism and constitutional culture, underlining that when the constitutional text loses contact with the reality of the law in action, the consequence is the people's loss of faith in the constitution. A recent example of this 'distance' can be exemplified by the rather surreal debate on the occasion of the constitutional referendum on 4 December 2016, stimulated by warnings related the replacement of 'community constraints' with 'EU constraints' in the wording of Art 117(1) of the Constitution. This elementary drafting update had been presented to the public opinion as a way to limit national sovereignty with an uncontrolled expansion of EU powers (so claimed the leader of the Northern League Matteo Salvini during the TV debate on the constitutional referendum with the Minister for Constitutional reforms Maria Elena Boschi held on 7 October 2016).

Specifically with regard to the 'openness' of the Italian Constitution towards European integration, the elasticity of constitutional requirements has often meant that the Italian interest can be underestimated during the negotiation that leads to the signature on a treaty reform, as it is not protected by a specific constitutional provision. If you add in the relative weakness of parliamentary mechanisms for directing and engaging in oversight of the behaviour of the Italian Government in the European negotiations, it is rather easy to understand why, in fact, Italy has hardly asked for 'special' treatment or specific clauses in the treaty revisions in order to convince its citizens in a referendum, or its opposition parties, or even its Constitutional Court. As has been already remarked, Italian electors were never called to vote on any treaty revision, while the consent of the opposition parties was generally taken for granted, at least until the ratification of the Treaty of Lisbon, which still was authorised with an extremely wide consensus. Even the Constitutional Court, although invoking, as a kind of last resort, the possibility of using its supreme principles as counter-limitations to the limitations of sovereignty allowed by Article 11 Constitution (the so-called 'controlimiti' doctrine), did not identify, at least until very recently, any effective constitutional element that EU law could not alter.[60]

Under a certain point of view, this rather smooth and almost uncritical acceptance of European integration, without any affirmation of elements of the Italian constitutional identity—as the German Constitutional Tribunal did with reference to the democratic principle, as derived from the right to vote—and without any request for opt-outs, derogations, legal guarantees or forms of differentiated integration,[61] may be interpreted as a weak ex ante protection of the Italian constitutional identity,[62] or even as the confirmation of a weak (sense of) identity.

[60] The expression 'controlimiti', although widely diffused in the scholarly debate (introduced as 'contro-limitazioni' by Barile, above n 36, commenting on the decision no 183/1973), has been used by the Italian Constitutional Court just once, in the decision no 238/2014. Even in the order no 24/2017 (above n 42) when the Court was asked to apply them, it preferred to recur to the wording of Art 4(2) TEU, also in order to leave some margin of dialogue with the CJEU. Diffusely on the 'controlimiti' doctrine M Cartabia, *Principi inviolabili e integrazione europea* (Milan, Giuffrè, 1995), P Faraguna, *Ai confini della Costituzione. Principi supremi e identità costituzionale* (Milan, FrancoAngeli, 2015) and G Piccirilli, 'L'unica possibilità per evitare il ricorso immediato ai controlimiti: un rinvio pregiudiziale che assomiglia a una diffida', in A Bernardi, C Cupelli (a cura di), *Il caso Taricco e il dialogo tra le Corti. L'ordinanza 24/2017 della Corte costituzionale* (Naples, Jovene, 2017) 327–44.

[61] The main exception was probably the allocations of seats at the European Parliament on the occasion of the Treaty of Lisbon, in order to equalise the number of those attributed to Italy and France (then incorporated in the Declaration No 4, and supported by the further Declaration No 57 for subsequent terms). See C Fasone, 'Quando i seggi … non tornano. A proposito dei membri del Parlamento europeo spettanti all'Italia e del trattato di riforma' (2007) *Amministrazione in cammino* 1-32, and F Fabbrini, 'La composizione del Parlamento Europeo dopo il Trattato di Lisbona' (2011) 61 *Rivista trimestrale di diritto pubblico* 787–802.

[62] P Faraguna, 'Taking Constitutional Identity away from the Courts' (2016) 41 *Brooklyn Journal of International Law* 491–578, at 525 ff, considers these forms of differentiation in participating in the European Union exactly as forms of (ex ante) protection of the national constitutional identity, that—diversely from Italy—have been pursued by other Member States such as the United Kingdom, Ireland (see also at n 28 above), but also Denmark (which opted out from the EMU and later from the single currency, and in various forms from the AFSJ: see in detail L Miles and A Wivel (eds), *Denmark and the European Union* (London-New York, Routledge, 2014) and specifically the chapters by M Marcussen, 'Denmark and the Euro opt-out' 47–64; R Adler Nissen, 'Justice and Home Affair: Denmark as an Active Differential European' 65–79; and the conclusion of the editors 'A Smart State Handling a Differentiated Integration Dilemma? Concluding on Denmark in the European Union' 228–38). Finally consider the distinguishing in the application of the Charter of Fundamental Rights of the EU made by the United Kingdom, Poland and the Czech Republic in Protocol No 30: S Peers, 'The "Opt-out" that Fell to Earth: The British and Polish Protocol Concerning the EU Charter of Fundamental Rights' (2012) 12 *Human Rights Law Review* 375 ff.

At the same time, from another perspective, this constitutional approach might be seen as a demonstration of the closeness and even of the high degree of overlap between Italian and European constitutional identities. In other terms, in Italy the consensus for the European integration process has been very wide and the 'European choice' seemed rather natural, 'given the three bases of Italian foreign policy. These are Europeanism, Atlanticism and a Mediterranean orientation'.[63] It comes as no surprise, thus, that Italy did not feel the need to affirm values and principles other than those that it found in the European integration process, and even its constituent fathers could have seen this process as a continuation of its constitutional foundations, aimed at securing peace and justice among nations and recognising the principle of equality and fundamental rights and freedoms. Whether, 70 years later, this means that the EU could be qualified as a 'fulfilment' of the Italian Constitution—as recently maintained[64]—seems, indeed, an open and more debatable issue.

III. The Italian Parliament in the 'Silent' Evolution of the Composite Constitution

The same openness and adaptability to the evolution of the political context that has been found in the constitutional principles related to the Italian participation in the EU can be traced in the constitutional provisions related to the role of the Parliament in the Italian form of government.

In the name of its institutional autonomy, only a few constraints are defined in the Constitution's text, leaving a wide margin of interpretation for the institutional practice and political dynamics. As shown in the book,[65] this approach, originally conceived to leave the hands of political parties rather free to pursue their own choices and alliances,[66] allowed the Italian Parliament to redefine several times its role in the constitutional system (especially vis-à-vis the Government) according to the evolution of electoral legislation and the reshuffling of the political parties that took place in 1993. Moreover, it allowed the Parliament itself to silently evolve its own functioning by modifications of the rules of procedure or, even, more recently, by innovative interpretations of the parliamentary rules and precedents.

The phenomenon of implied constitutional amendments has already been the subject of an influential book in the late 1950s by Silvano Tosi,[67] who, following an interpretation

[63] So, synthetically, SZ Koff and SP Koff, *Italy. From the First to the Second Republic* (London and New York, Routledge, 2000) 197–210.

[64] See (also relying on some speeches by Italian Presidents of the Republic rhetorically highlighting the common origins and values of integrated Europe and the Italian Republic) F Fabbrini and O Pollicino, 'Constitutional Identity in Italy: European Integration as the Fulfilment of the Constitution', EUI Working Paper LAW 2017/06.

[65] See the chapter by P Falletta.

[66] See G Amato, 'Constitution' in E Jones and G Pasquino (eds), *The Oxford Handbook on Italian Politics* (Oxford, Oxford University Press, 2015) 71 ff, at 78 (also highlighting that the Constituent Assembly did not know which parties would have prevailed in the subsequent elections of 1948).

[67] S Tosi, *Modificazioni tacite della Costituzione attraverso il diritto parlamentare* (Milan, Giuffrè, 1959).

of the Italian constitutional history proposed by Giuseppe Maranini,[68] elaborated on the discrepancies between the form of government enshrined in the Constitution and its actual functioning after 15 years of practice. He found in the two Houses' rules of procedure, similar to what happened pending the Albertine Statute the key factor in the significant detachment from the written constitutional provisions, pinpointing in their flexibility the cause of 'silent' (ie 'unsaid', not formalised via an actual constitutional amendment) modifications of the constitutional order.

More recently, the same process seems to have been brought to its extremes. Not only is the constitutional text stable, notwithstanding the political and electoral change that happened in 1993, but even the two Houses' parliamentary rules of procedure have not been significantly amended, at least in the last 20 years. The shift to a quasi-majoritarian form of government, fostered by the different reforms of the electoral law, did not bring any major formal adaptation of the rules internal to the Houses.[69] What facilitated this most recent evolution has been the capacity of the Presidents of the two Houses to find increasingly innovative interpretations of the existing rules, progressively detaching them from their original intent and even their wording. The result—as it has been remarked[70]—is a paradoxical inversion of the hierarchy of the sources of law in the parliamentary context that puts 'precedents' at the top of the pyramid, so weakening the effectiveness of parliamentary rules of procedure. This evolution also created the necessity of allowing the accessibility and verifiability of the collection of precedents, as happens in many Parliaments, in order to ensure forms of control by individual MPs, parliamentary minorities and also the general public.[71]

The relevance of parliamentary rules of procedure and even of the inner practices of the Houses confirms, once more, the idea that parliamentary law is an essential element of constitutional law. Consequently, their evolution—although 'silent'—deserves to be considered and deeply investigated. After all, the history of parliamentary bodies is, to some extent, a history of silent evolutions, progressive adaptation and increasing exploitation of the (often meagre) constitutional provisions on the role of elected assemblies and their relationship with the Government. Parliamentary rules at every level tend to prefer continuity and adaptation to ruptures and revolutions.[72]

This is surely true for the Italian Parliament in the nineteenth century, which progressively achieved the right to vote on the initial confidence to Government, that was not

[68] The most complete exposition of Maranini's interpretation is in G Maranini, *Storia del potere in Italia (1848–1967)* (Firenze, Vallecchi, 1967), but was anticipated also in previous writings. For an accurate reconstruction of the relationship between Maranini and his pupil Tosi, see F Lanchester, 'Politica e diritto in Silvano Tosi' (2009) 1 *Federalismi.it* 1–18.

[69] The need for such reforms stimulated two collections of essays: E Gianfrancesco and N Lupo (eds), *Le regole del diritto parlamentare nella dialettica tra maggioranza e opposizione* (Rome, Luiss University Press, 2007) and E Gianfrancesco and N Lupo (eds), *La riforma dei regolamenti parlamentari al banco di prova della XVI legislatura* (Rome, Luiss University Press, 2009).

[70] C Bergonzini, 'La piramide rovesciata: la gerarchia tra le fonti del diritto parlamentare' (2008) 4 *Quaderni costituzionali* 741–62.

[71] A specific attention on the elaboration, selection and application of parliamentary precedents is paid by the essays collected in N Lupo (ed), *Il precedente parlamentare tra diritto e politica* (Bologna, Il Mulino, 2013).

[72] See P Ungari, 'I precedenti storici del diritto parlamentare vigente in Italia', in V Longi et al (eds), *Il regolamento della Camera dei deputati. Storia, istituti, procedure* (Rome, Camera dei deputati, 1969) 39–95 at 95, and L Gianniti and N Lupo, *Corso di diritto parlamentare*[2] (Bologna, Il mulino, 2013) 21 ff.

foreseen by the Albertine Statute.[73] Then, it is also the case of the Italian Parliament in the Republican period, with its subsequent adaptations to societal evolutions by modifying the rules of procedure (completely rewritten in 1971)[74] or interpreting them in evolutionary manners. The same can be probably said also for the European Parliament, which notoriously expanded its powers in the decision-making process vis-à-vis the Council, anticipating in its rules of procedure the treaty revisions that formally increased its role.[75]

Finally, a similar conclusion can be reached with regard to the evolution of the European role of the Italian Parliament. Coherently with the silent integration of the Italian legal order within the European Communities (and later Union) and in line with the continuous modification of the parliamentary function in the domestic form of government, the Euro-national procedures of the Italian Parliament also have been evolving progressively and mainly informally. As is already known, until recently the 'European' role of national Parliaments was left entirely to each Member State's Constitution.[76] Thus, in Italy some 'European' procedures emerged long before the formal acknowledgement of the powers listed by the Treaty of Lisbon and have been expanding in new directions in the last few years.[77] Also in this context the road was opened not by a formal amendment to the rules of procedure, but by simpler innovations to the parliamentary practice.

Already before the approval of the Law No 234/2012, some important (and informal) innovations were reached through the application by analogy of existing procedures aiming to ensure mechanisms of parliamentary oversight of the Government's activity in European affairs.

For example, with an autonomous decision of the (then-just-appointed) President of the Council of Ministers Mario Monti, the Government started to report to the Houses regularly before each meeting of the European Council. This parliamentary practice inaugurated by the Monti Government seems particularly telling, as it needs to be set in the framework of a general attitude of governments—and especially of the so-called

[73] Again Maranini, above n 68 and also S Labriola, *Storia della costituzione italiana* (Rome, ESI, 1995); F Rossi, *Saggio sul sistema politico dell'Italia liberale: procedure fiduciarie e sistema dei partiti fra Otto e Novecento* (Soveria Mannelli, Rubbettino, 2001). R Ferrari Zumbini, 'La Torino del 1848-49 come laboratorio costituzionale: la nascita spontanea della fiducia parlamentare' (2016) 2 *Le Carte e la Storia* 75–85.

[74] In 1971 the adoption of new rules of procedure helped the Italian Parliament to open itself to the society that was undergoing deep transformations. For a re-reading on the role of the new rules of procedure see A Manzella (ed), *I regolamenti parlamentari a quarant'anni dal 1971* (Bologna, il Mulino, 2012) and F Lanchester (ed), *Regolamenti parlamentari e forma di governo: gli ultimi quaranta anni* (Milan, Giuffrè, 2013). The reversion of the secret/open ballot rule with two parallel modifications of the rules of procedure of both Houses was a way to register the end of the so called 'consociational democracy' in the late 1980s: see A Lijphart, *Patterns of Democracy: Government Forms and Performace in Thirty-Six Countries* (New Haven, Yale University Press, 1999), A Pizzorno, 'Le difficoltà del consociativismo' in A Pizzorno, *Le radici della politica assoluta* (Milan, Feltrinelli, 1993) 285–313, S Vassallo, 'Parliament' in Jones and Pasquino (eds), above n 66, 107–18.

[75] G Tsebelis, 'The Power of the European Parliament as a Conditional Agenda Setter' (1994) 88 *American Political Science Review* 128–42; B Rittberger, *Building Europe's Parliament: Democratic Representation Beyond the Nation State* (Oxford, Oxford University Press, 2005).

[76] This specific point has been developed in the Introduction to this book.

[77] See the extensive research, committed by the European Parliament (PE 474.392) and edited by W Wessels and O Rozenberg, *Democratic Control in the Member States of the European Council and the Euro Zone Summits* (Brussels, European Parliament, 2013).

'technocratic governments'[78]—to act (and feel) quite independent from their respective Parliaments at the European level.[79]

This practice was later formalised in Article 4 Law No 234/2012 and regularly followed by subsequent Governments led by Enrico Letta and Matteo Renzi, as well as the first months of the one led by Paolo Gentiloni.[80] Significantly, the President of the Council of Ministers has been directed to assume the duty to stand before the plenary to present the Government's position. Even more interestingly, the Parliament has reacted as it usually does on the occasion of communications by the Government, namely by approving resolutions in order to give political directions in light of the European Council meetings.[81] Far less frequent have been the reports in the plenary on the outcome of the same meetings, also because in these cases a hearing of the minister or undersecretary of state on EU policies in front of the two Houses' joint committees is usually preferred.[82]

Moreover, it is also possible to find interesting innovations in the organisation of parliamentary bodies that has occurred without formal amendments to the parliamentary rules of procedure. For instance, the Committee on EU Policies at the Senate established a subcommittee for the relationship with the regions in matters of EU affairs[83] (its second subcommittee, in addition to that in charge of draft opinions on EU legislative proposals on behalf of the whole body). The potential impact of a dedicated body in charge of overseeing the cooperation with regions (which in Italy hold legislative powers) might be very incisive in composing the Italian position on EU policies, also considering the representatives of the regions' permanent lack of participation in parliamentary bodies.[84]

This is, more or less, the state of the art regarding the Italian Parliament, and its European powers, which this book has sought to analyse. It is difficult to imagine what the future could be, in a time in which political and constitutional changes happen so fast. From a certain point of view, the described 'silent' evolution and the progressive adaptation of both the Italian Constitution and the Italian Parliament were possible in and consistent

[78] On the experience of the so-called 'technocratic governments' see D McDonnell and M Valbruzzi, 'Defining and Classifying Technocrat-led and Technocratic Governments' (2014) 53 *European Journal Political Reserarch* 654–71 and N Lupo, 'I "governi tecnici". Gli esecutivi Ciampi, Dini e Monti nel difficile equilibrio tra tecnica e politica' (2015) *Rassegna parlamentare* 57–120.

[79] See, significantly, the statement by the same Monti few months later during an interview with *Der Spiegel* ('A Front Line Between North and South', 6 August 2012, available at www.spiegel.de/international/europe/interview-on-the-euro-crisis-with-italian-prime-minister-mario-monti-a-848511.html) when he stated that 'If governments let themselves be fully bound by the decisions of their parliaments without protecting their own freedom to act, a breakup of Europe would be a more probable outcome than deeper integration'. Critically on this point S Puntscher Riekmann and D Wydra, 'Representation in the European State of Emergency: Parliaments against Governments?' (2013) 5 *Journal of European Integration* 565–82.

[80] In 2013–2016, with regard to such purpose, the Government went before the Chamber of Deputies 16 times (and just as many before the Senate).

[81] More details in the chapter by A Esposito.

[82] In the same time span, the President of the Council went only once before the plenary of the Chamber of Deputies (and never in the Senate) after the meeting of the European Council (Mario Monti on 25 March 2013). In the XVII parliamentary term (started in 2013), joint meetings of the committees on EU policies (sometimes together with the committees on foreign affairs and less frequently also with the committees on budget) have been convened for reporting the outcome of the European Council meetings on 22 May 2013, 17 July 2013, 15 January 2014, 9 July 2014, 12 November 2014, 20 May 2015, 1° July 2015, 2 March 2016.

[83] More information in the chapter by C Fasone, in this book.

[84] However, at least in its first paths, the subcommittee seems to be not extremely active. It convened only four times in 2014 and never again in 2015–16.

with a context of a general 'permissive consensus' on the European integration process.[85] Currently, as is well-known, the economic crisis and the difficulties of the EU in facing it caused a standstill of the European integration process, which also brought within the Italian Parliament a division between pro-European and anti-European political parties, formerly unknown to Italian politics. At the same time, the rejections by the referendum of 4 December 2016 of the constitutional reform proposed by the Renzi government seems to question the validity of the majoritarian transformation begun in 1993.

It will be interesting to see whether the main features of the Italian Parliament will continue as they are and allow it to play a significant role in the Euro-national parliamentary system, or whether its being inserted into the Euro-national parliamentary system and the new political and electoral reality will oblige it to increase the formalisation and even the rigidity of its channels of communication with the EU legal order, once the evolution of the political system may it become less valid as a common list of widely shared principles and core values.

[85] S Kröger and R Bellamy, 'Beyond a Constraining Dissensus: The Role of National Parliaments in Domesticating and Normalising the Politicization of European Integration' (2016) 14 *Comparative politics* 131–53. The concept of 'permissive consensus' is taken from L Hooghe and G Marks, 'A Postfunctionalist Theory of European Integration: From Permissive Consensus to Constraining Dissensus' (2009) 39 *British Journal of Political Science* 1–23.

Afterword: European Democracy and National Parliaments (Through the Prism of Matteo Renzi)[1]

PETER L LINDSETH

I. The Power–Legitimacy Disconnect and the Limits of EU 'Democratisation'

European integration is characterised by a fundamental disconnect. On the one hand, there is the vast amount of regulatory *power* that has been transferred to the supranational level, which has grown considerably as a consequence of the various crises facing the EU over the last decade (notably in the Eurozone). On the other hand, there is the failure of EU bodies to attain an autonomous democratic and constitutional *legitimacy* commensurate with that transfer of power, despite the fervent hopes of integration's most enthusiastic advocates. For better or worse, even with the diffusion of regulatory and disciplinary power to the supranational level, democratic and constitutional legitimacy in the most robust sense has remained wedded to national bodies—parliaments, executives, and judiciaries.[2] One obvious way that European public law has attempted to overcome

[1] This contribution builds on a lecture originally delivered at the Summer School on 'Parliamentary Democracy in Europe' at the LUISS Guido Carli School of Government in Rome on 18 July 2014. It has been expanded to account for the result of the referendum in Italy on 4 December 2016.

[2] See generally PL Lindseth, *Power and Legitimacy: Reconciling Europe and the Nation-State* (New York, Oxford University Press. 2010); for more on the disconnect at the heart of integration, see PL Lindseth, 'Delegation Is Dead, Long Live Delegation: Managing the Democratic Disconnect in the European Market-Polity' in Christian Joerges and Renaud Dehousse (eds), *Good Governance in Europe's Integrated Market* (Oxford, Oxford University Press, 2002).

this power–legitimacy disconnect has been through an effort to 'democratise' and 'constitutionalise' supranational institutions themselves, whether through the elected European Parliament (EP) or through the Court of Justice of the European Union (CJEU) as the constitutional arbiter of the European system. Although this strategy has certainly not been a complete failure (far from it), it has nevertheless been a very uphill struggle, much more so than the most idealistic advocates of European unity care to admit. The EU possesses many kinds of legitimacy—legal, technocratic, even electoral in some sense, at least with regard to the EP. But what events have repeatedly affirmed is how much the EU lacks autonomous democratic and constitutional legitimacy in its own right—that is, as a 'government of the people', or the institutional expression of an historical identity between a population and a set of governing institutions that is the ultimate basis of democracy and constitutionalism.[3]

As Neil MacCormick has shown, this identity need not be grounded in exclusionary ethnic, religious or linguistic affinities, nor does it preclude cooperation with other polities on the basis of reciprocity and interdependence. This consciousness can instead be 'civic'—based on shared ideals rather than ethnic, linguistic or religious connections—but it still must be grounded in a 'historical' and indeed 'cultural' experience for that particular community.[4] The sort of legitimacy that flows from this experience lays the foundation for a political–cultural perception that institutions of government are genuinely the people's 'own', which they have historically constituted for the purpose of self-government over time, rather than being mere functional expressions of regulatory authority, whether national or supranational, technocratic or juristocratic.

Lacking this robust form of democratic and constitutional legitimacy, European integration has ultimately relied on national institutions and the historic identity that they share with their national or sub-national political communities. It is for this reason that the EU remains almost entirely dependent on the Member States for the *sine qua non* of genuine democratic and constitutional power: the legitimate capacity to extract in a compulsory fashion and then redirect—ie 'mobilise'—either fiscal resources (taxing and spending) or human resources (policing and defence) for the benefit of the polity as a whole.[5] The manner in which the Member States may choose to use these resources (including any borrowing to make up for fiscal shortfalls) is of course increasingly subject to supranational surveillance and discipline—something to which each Member State has pre-committed by way of the EU treaties. Nonetheless, what the multiple crises of the last decade have made repeatedly clear is that the EU lacks the legitimacy to take over this mobilisation function itself in any macro-economically or geopolitically significant sense. This may change in the future, but as of this writing (December 2016) this anchoring of legitimate compulsory

[3] PL Lindseth, 'Of the People: Democracy, the Eurozone, and Lincoln's Threshold Criterion' (2012) 22 *Berlin Journal* 4.

[4] N MacCormick, *Questioning Sovereignty : Law, State, and Nation in the European Commonwealth* (Oxford, Oxford University Press, 1999) 169–74.

[5] PL Lindseth, 'Between the "Real" and the "Right": Explorations Along the Institutional-Constitutional Frontier' in M Adams, EH Ballin and A Meuwese (eds), *Constitutionalism and the Rule of Law: Bridging Idealism and Realism* (Cambridge, Cambridge University Press, 2017).

extraction at the national level suggests a crucial fault line between the EU's primarily regulatory as opposed to potential future democratic and constitutional character in its own right.

From a scholarly standpoint, therefore, a focus on the attempted 'democratisation' and 'constitutionalisation' of European institutions—no matter how prominently this effort has figured in the traditional narrative of European public law—can be misleading. What the legal-scholarly fascination with the EU's purportedly autonomous democratic and constitutional character obscures are the less celebrated but arguably more persistent dimensions of European public law and institutional change, ones that ultimately draw on the more robust sense of legitimacy on the national level. Over the last six decades, a central goal of European public law has been to reconcile the functional demands of integration with the continued political–cultural attachment to ideals of representative government and constitutional democracy on the national level. These ideals were a crucial inheritance of nineteenth-century liberal nationalism, most importantly (but not exclusively) expressed in the national parliament, readjusted to the demands of mass democracy, public welfare and international cooperation after the catastrophe of 1914–1945. Since its inception, the public law of European integration has quietly and in some sense unconsciously sought to effectuate this reconciliation by establishing, over time, a range of *national* mechanisms to oversee and legitimise (if not necessarily directly control) supranational regulatory power.

The aim of these mechanisms has been to borrow legitimacy from the national level even as regulatory power has shifted, sometimes massively, beyond the confines of the nation-state. These national legitimating mechanisms include, of course, the well-known collective oversight of supranational policy-making exercised by national executives via the Council of Ministers and the European Council (this mechanism is indicative of the decisive role played by national executives under the post-war constitutional settlement). But national oversight also includes judicial review by national high courts with respect to certain core democratic and constitutional commitments—the so-called *Kompetenz-Kompetenz* jurisprudence in Germany, for example, or the *contro-limiti* jurisprudence in Italy. Finally, and most recently, these national mechanisms include increasing recourse to national parliamentary scrutiny of supranational action. This has been particularly pronounced over the last two decades, whether involving national parliaments scrutinising national executives individually or supranational bodies more generally, the latter primarily through the new subsidiarity 'early warning mechanism' of the Treaty of Lisbon.

These national mechanisms exist, I would argue, to strike a balance. On the one hand, they seek to accommodate the evident functional and political demands for supranational regulatory solutions—a fact whose significance cannot be denied. On the other, they build on the continued political–cultural attachment to the nation-state as the primary locus of democratic and constitutional legitimacy in Europe, *despite* the shift in regulatory power beyond the confines of the nation-state. Put another way, these national legitimating mechanisms establish a framework within which the otherwise undoubted complexity of Europe's policymaking processes, distributed across multiple levels of governance, can operate *without evident democratic and constitutional legitimacy of their own*, at least as classically understood.

II. Democratic Legitimacy and the Elusive Search for 'Large-scale Solidarity' in Europe

To explore this dynamic of reconciliation further, particularly in the context of the Eurozone crisis, I will take a little bit of an analytical detour. What I propose to do is to deconstruct, if you will, a speech given by Matteo Renzi, the then-Italian Prime Minister, before the European Parliament on 2 July 2014.[6] The purpose of the speech was ostensibly to present the objectives and priorities of the forthcoming six-month Italian presidency of the Council. Instead, Renzi used the speech as an opportunity to make some broader observations about the state of the integration process, and more particularly about its socio-political/socio-cultural underpinnings.

The speech was resolutely pro-European in its rhetoric and tone but was also surprisingly frank in its assessment of integration and the challenges before it. As noted in contemporaneous press accounts, Renzi's presentation was full of historical allusions, both classical and contemporary. I am less interested in Renzi's many allusions to antiquity—in which, for example, he called on today's generation of Europeans to show themselves, like Telemachus in *The Odyssey*, to be worthy heirs of the founding generation of the integration project. Rather, I am more interested in Renzi's allusions to contemporary history—that is, to the nineteenth, twentieth and twenty-first centuries—as well as what these allusions suggest about the current state and potential future of integration, not to mention the reconciliation of Europe and national parliaments that is my topic here.

Renzi began by offering congratulations to the members of the EP for their recent election in May 2014. He spoke of the 'great responsibility' of the EP to bring 'trust and hope' (*fiducia e speranza*) to European institutions.[7] But note what he did not say: he did not say that EP brought democratic legitimacy to European policy-making. He did say that it was 'only right and politically just' for the European Council to respect 'the results of the recent electoral campaign' and hence the EP's 'prerogatives' in the choice of the new Commission president. But he avoided using the language of EU 'democracy' to describe this step.

Of course, I have no special access to the workings of Renzi's mind. Nevertheless, I think it fair to say that he deliberately avoided the language of democratic legitimation with regard to the EP. The prior week, in a speech before the Italian Chamber of Deputies, Renzi stated: 'Those who imagine that the democratic "gap" in Europe will be overcome simply by the appointment of Juncker as President of the European Commission are living on Mars'.[8] In this earlier speech he went on to describe not only the low turnout in the European elections but also the significant percentage of the vote that went to parties hostile to the European project. From there he segued to a theme that would be central to his speech

[6] M Renzi, 'Programme of Activities of the Italian Presidency', European Parliament (2 July 2014) www.europarl.europa.eu/sides/getDoc.do?pubRef=-//EP//TEXT+CRE+20140702+ITEMS+DOC+XML+V0//EN&language=EN#creitem13.

[7] The translations of Renzi's statement here and elsewhere in this contribution are my own. I take full responsibility for any errors.

[8] M Renzi, 'Intervento del Presidente del Consiglio', Camera dei Deputati, Parlemento Italiano (24 June 2014) www.camera.it/leg17/410?idSeduta=0251&tipo=stenografico#sed0251.stenografico.tit00040.

in Strasbourg the following week: 'It is not enough to have a currency in common, or a President in common, or a source of funding in common'. Rather, what is needed is for Europe to 'accept the idea that we have a common destiny and common values'. In his speech the following week before the EP, Renzi elaborated: 'The real challenge confronting our continent is to find the *soul of Europe*, to find the profound *meaning of our being together*' (emphasis added).

Now I know as scholars we are not supposed to pay much attention to these sorts of rhetorical flourishes by politicians or their speechwriters. Nevertheless, I found this entire line of discussion fascinating. Perhaps Renzi did not intend it but his reference to finding Europe's 'soul' and 'the meaning of our being together' brought to mind a similar line of thinking in Ernest Renan's famous 1882 lecture, '*Qu'est-ce qu'une nation?*' ('What is a Nation?'). According to Renan: 'A nation is a soul, a spiritual principle … [It is] the possession in common of a rich legacy of memories [but also] present-day consent, the desire to live together …'.[9] In speaking of the current ills afflicting the EU, it is interesting to ponder whether Renzi intentionally meant to evoke this paean to liberal nationalism of the nineteenth century. After all, isn't European integration supposed to be a post-national project, something designed to transcend the legacy and evils of nationalism?

Perhaps Renzi was not intending to evoke Renan specifically, but there is much in the speech to suggest that Renzi would like nothing more than for integration to emulate at least some aspects of liberal nationalism as Renan articulated in his famous 1882 lecture. Most importantly, for Renan, nationalism entailed a 'large-scale solidarity'—something that Renzi would love to see replicated on a European scale, particularly in response to the Eurozone crisis, with its asymmetric shocks and needs for intra-European transfers.

The clearest indication of this attitude was Renzi's invocation—and rejection—of the famously dismissive observation of Metternich in 1847 describing pre- *Risorgimento* Italy as nothing more than 'a geographical expression'.[10] For Renzi, today's Europeans must demonstrate that Europe too is something more than a 'geographical expression'. According to Renzi:

> There will be no space for Europe if we remain only a dot on Google Maps We are a community, a people, we are not a geographical expression—to use the phrase applied to Italy by a great Austrian statesman of the nineteenth century.

The idea that EU citizens constitute 'a people' (rather than 'peoples') is of course a bold claim—that is, if you take it as a description of the current state of European political culture. I take it, however, as aspirational. It is a statement of what Renzi felt Europe must become ('a community, a people, not a geographical expression'); otherwise, as Renzi pointed out, integration amounts to little more than an exercise in 'unit[ing] our bureaucracies'—a process of integration ultimately of an administrative character. And as he continued, 'I can assure you that we Italians have enough of our own bureaucracy. Either we recover a strong, deep identity together or we lose the challenge we face'.

[9] E Renan, 'What Is a Nation?' in G Eley and R Grigor Suny (eds), *Becoming National: A Reader* (New York, Oxford University Press, 1996).

[10] CWL (Fürst von) Metternich, *Mémoires, documents et écrits divers laissés par le prince de Metternich, chancelier de cour et d'Etat: 2. ptie.: L'ère de paix (1816–1848)* (A Klinkowström ed, E Plon, Nourrit et cie, 1883) 415.

Renzi did not engage in all this high-minded rhetoric for its own sake. Rather, he had a specific policy agenda in mind: to escape the austerity that has been the cornerstone of the response to the Eurozone crisis so far; to add flexibility to the interpretation of the Stability and Growth Pact; and perhaps, even more ambitiously, to augment the fiscal capacity of the supranational level—perhaps through Eurobonds—in order to help counteract the asymmetric economic and financial effects of monetary union. As Renzi's rhetorical flourishes all suggested, however, the lack of a robust, shared identity at the supranational level in Europe was and is a barrier to institutional change that might permit policies with real macro-economic significance in the Eurozone—not the mere one per cent of European GDP that is the current EU budget.

The problem is that fiscal capacity of such macro-economic importance still remains fundamentally national, in the hands of national parliaments, despite the supranational discipline to which national parliaments have subjected themselves. Without autonomous supranational fiscal capacities—and more importantly without the autonomous democratic and constitutional identity to support them—the central instrument used to pay for the Eurozone crisis has necessarily been national austerity, combined with national pre-commitments to fiscal discipline enforced by supranational institutions. Conveniently, this combination of national austerity and supranational surveillance/discipline has to date made little or no redistributive demands on 'Europe' as a collectivity. All essential costs—political and economic—have been and continue to be borne internally, by the individual states. This may well change if the crisis once again intensifies (for example through a Greek default or an Italian banking crisis). Regardless, what is important to recognise is that the dominant approach to resolving the crisis has ultimately relied on, and in fact validates, the democratic and constitutional legitimacy of national institutions as a central foundation of the European project. At this stage in Europe's development it is there, and apparently only there, that one can mobilise the necessary fiscal resources and democratic legitimacy to address the crisis in an effective manner, even if decisions on all these questions happen under the watchful eye of European partners and supranational institutions.

It is this reality that Renzi apparently wanted to transcend in his July 2014 speech, by exhorting Europe to find its 'soul', 'the meaning of [its] being together', and a 'strong, deep identity' based on a 'common destiny and common values'. What Renzi seemed to be seeking was a transformation of nineteenth-century liberal nationalism's emergent 'large-scale solidarity'—something that would obviously be so crucial to the welfare state in the twentieth century—into a supranational reality for the twenty-first century. And without that sense of intra-European solidarity, genuine fiscal capacity at the EU level (whether in the form of Eurobonds or otherwise) would of course be impossible. Renzi was speaking, in other words, of the necessary 'phase-transition' whereby a bureaucratic process of integration might become a genuine expression of democratic constitutionalism in its own right, one with both the necessary *power*, but more importantly, the *legitimacy* to address the challenges that Europe faces.[11]

[11] Lindseth, above n 5.

III. European Technocracy and 'Building Europe Without Europeans'

At this point, I cannot help but think of the famous statement attributed to Massimo d'Azeglio in the aftermath of the *Risorgimento*, that 'we have made Italy; now we must make Italians'.[12] As Renzi's speech before the EP suggested, creating a European polity beyond the nation-state is not simply a matter of institutional engineering—that is, of creating an institutional apparatus called 'Europe' with all its seemingly autonomous democratic and constitutional features, whether via the EP, the CJEU, or otherwise. Rather, Renzi seemed to be saying that 'we have made Europe; now we must make Europeans' in order to achieve the necessary 'large-scale solidarity' that Europe now demands.

If that is the case, then I cannot help but also think of Paul Reuter, the French law professor instrumental in writing the Schuman Plan that kicked off the integration process in 1950. It was Reuter who came up with the proposal to Monnet to create the High Authority, the forerunner of today's European Commission.[13] And Reuter's reasons for placing a technocratic body at the heart of the integration project are telling. The creation of the High Authority (the future Commission) was, according to Reuter, 'in some sense a desperate solution' because, as he put it, there was 'neither a European parliament, nor government, nor people' on which to build an integrated polity or market.[14] In something of the inverse of d'Azeglio's aspiration for Italy, Reuter said that the purpose of supranational technocracy was 'to build Europe without Europeans' by 'address[ing] ourselves to independent personalities'.[15] The decisions of these independent personalities would then be binding on national governments and parliaments—a formula that has since been expanded to include not merely the Commission but also the Court of Justice and the European Central Bank (ECB).

Of course, much has changed since the 1950s but perhaps less than is often supposed. As Joschka Fischer famously pointed out in his speech on Europe's constitutional future at Humboldt University in 2000, European governance has long been afflicted by the broadly held sense that integration is a largely 'bureaucratic affair run by a faceless, soulless Eurocracy in Brussels'.[16] Many citizens in the Eurozone periphery today might modify this statement slightly, in order to add (at least) 'Frankfurt' to 'Brussels' as an additional locus of this 'faceless, soulless Eurocracy'. But you get the point: whether we are referring to the Commission in Brussels or the ECB in Frankfurt, the sad truth is that many Europeans still experience the exercise of authority by supranational institutions in Europe as technocratic and distant.

[12] For a sense of the debate surrounding this attribution, see, eg, C Gigante, '"Fatta l'Italia, Facciamo gli Italiani". Appunti su una massima da restituire a d'Azeglio' (2011) 26 *Incontri. Rivista europea di studi italiani* 5.

[13] For background, see Lindseth, *Power and Legitimacy*, above n 2, 96.

[14] P Reuter, *La Communauté européenne du charbon et de l'acier* (Paris, Librairie générale de droit et de jurisprudence, 1953) 51.

[15] ibid 51–52.

[16] J Fischer, 'From Confederacy to Federation: Thoughts on the Finality of European Integration', Speech at Humboldt University Berlin (12 May 2000) www.futurum.gov.pl/futurum.nsf/0/1289AFAAE84E5075C1256DA2003D1306; also www.jeanmonnetprogram.org/papers/00/joschka_fischer_en.rtf.

The official response to this broad political perception toward the EU—beginning with the SEA in 1986, continuing with every subsequent treaty up to Lisbon in 2009, and intensifying in the Eurozone crisis—has been to increase the role of the European Parliament in the supranational policy process. Today, the EP now plays the decisive role in choosing the Commission president while also enjoying the right of co-decision in nearly every regulatory domain within the competence of the EU. However, the problem with this formal 'parliamentary democratization strategy' (as I called it in an article published in 1999)[17] is its failure to stem the perception of the EU as fundamentally technocratic and distant. This failure is reflected not just in low turnouts in EP elections or in the votes given to parties hostile to integration, as Matteo Renzi stressed in his speeches in the summer of 2014.[18] Rather, it is also reflected in the stubborn refusal to confer on the EP autonomous taxing, spending and borrowing authority (again, beyond the one per cent of EU GDP that the current budget comprises). The power of legitimate compulsory mobilisation of fiscal resources remains almost entirely national, even if the exercise of those powers is subject to supranational surveillance.

To put it in the terms I have used elsewhere,[19] the problem at the EU level is not 'input legitimacy' (government 'by' the people) or even, surprisingly, 'output legitimacy' (government 'for' the people). Rather, as mentioned above, the problem is Lincoln's threshold criterion: government 'of' the people. This refers to the historical identity between a population and a set of governing institutions, no matter how flawed or criticised (Italians know well how to criticise the flaws of their national institutions). It refers to the political–cultural perception that the institutions of government are genuinely the people's 'own', which they have historically constituted for the purpose of self-rule over time. It refers to assemblies and institutions, in the sense of nineteenth-century liberal nationalism, which might serve as instruments of 'large-scale solidarity'.

Antecedent to this perception, of course, is the perception of the existence of a 'people' itself, ie a historically constructed sense of communal solidarity within a political grouping. It is out of this historically constructed sense that the capacity of the majority to rule over the minority becomes legitimate in a political–cultural sense without that rule being regarded as 'foreign' domination (subject, of course, to the protection of human rights). Within such a demos-legitimate polity, it is 'we' who are governing 'ourselves' rather than being governed by 'others'. And it is this sense that creates the 'large-scale solidarity' described by Renan, most importantly including common fiscal capacity—taxing, spending and borrowing—that has been at the heart of the 'remarkably resilient'[20] function of national parliaments since the nineteenth century.

[17] PL Lindseth, 'Democratic Legitimacy and the Administrative Character of Supranationalism: The Example of the European Community' (1999) 99 *Columbia Law Review* 628.

[18] See, eg, Renzi, above n 8.

[19] See, eg, Lindseth, above n 3.

[20] *cf* G Eley, 'The Social Construction of Democracy in Germany, 1871–1933' in G Reid Andrews and H Chapman (eds), *The Social Construction of Democracy, 1870–1990* (New York, New York University Press, 1995) 110 (referring to 'the constitutional frameworks fashioned [throughout Europe] in the 1860s' as 'remarkably resilient').

IV. National Parliaments as Repositories of Demos-legitimacy

In his quest for Europe's 'soul', for a sense of Europe's 'being together', etc, I would suggest that Renzi was aware of this fundamental socio-political / socio-cultural obstacle to European legitimacy—even as supranational institutions now exercise a great deal of normative power across a whole range of regulatory and disciplinary domains. In fact, I would argue that this sense of demos-legitimacy (government 'of' a people) is not merely essential to democracy but also to constitutionalism in the most robust sense of the term. It is on the basis of this demos-legitimacy that merely functional institutions of rule—like those in the EU—are transformed into genuinely 'constitutional' bodies for a political community, because these bodies have come to be understood as the institutional expressions of the right of the demos to rule itself.[21] It is in this sense that democracy and constitutionalism crucially overlap in the modern world, making it difficult to fully have one without the other.

To put it in the terms of Massimo d'Azeglio's famous expression, the process of 'making Italy' and 'making Italians'—or 'making Europe' and 'making Europeans' for that matter—are in fact deeply intertwined, something that Renzi in 2014 appeared to understand. Where one finds this robust sense of demos-legitimacy, one finds the true locus of 'self-government' in a normative-legal as well as fiscal-mobilisation sense, even as functional demands of modern governance often compel the diffusion and fragmentation of regulatory power to other bodies, whether subnational, national or supranational. Regardless of any legal, technocratic, input, output, or even 'messianic'[22] legitimacy that the integration process might otherwise possess, what integration lacks, for the present, is the necessary sense of Europe as a 'large-scale solidarity' (Renan), something ultimately beyond a 'geographical expression' (Metternich). As Renzi stressed before the Italian Chamber of Deputies in the summer of 2014, Europe is too often still regarded as 'another place … [W]e go to Europe not just when we go to Brussels or Strasbourg or Ypres', the location of the European Council meeting from which Renzi had recently come. Rather, he stressed that '[w]e go to Europe when we leave the house in the morning, when we walk the streets of our cities, when we look in the mirror. This is Europe; it is not different from us'.[23] And yet, there remained the nagging sense—whether in Italy or other Member States—that 'Europe' was distant, technocratic, indeed 'soulless', despite all that has occurred in the integration project over the last 70 years. The more robust sense of demos-legitimacy, the sense of 'large-scale solidarity' sufficient to mobilise resources in common, continues to depend on the EU's Member States.

It is for this reason that I am generally cautious about using the terminology 'Europeanisation' to describe the current changes in national parliamentary responsibilities and

[21] Lindseth, above n 5.
[22] JHH Weiler, 'The Political and Legal Culture of European Integration: An Exploratory Essay' (2011) 9 *International Journal of Constitutional Law* 678.
[23] Renzi, above n 8.

procedures as a consequence of integration. The label is undoubtedly accurate in important respects—national parliaments are undoubtedly evolving in response to the shift in normative and regulatory power to the supranational level, as the many contributions to this volume demonstrate with regard to Italy. The problem with the label is that it risks suggesting a questionable teleology, in which, as former EU Council President Herman Van Rompuy once put it, 'national parliaments have become, in a way, European institutions' themselves.[24] The term also implies that national parliaments have little or no agency in the process of integration and are merely 'acted upon' rather than 'actors' in their own right (a viewpoint also defied by the many contributions to this volume). What national parliaments possess, above all, is the great store of 'legitimacy resources' that come with being the constitutional expression of self-government in a demos-legitimate polity rather than mere functional cogs in the European system (as might be suggested by one reading of Article 12 of the Treaty on the Functioning of the European Union (TFEU)).

It is hardly surprising, therefore, that over time the integration process has needed to involve national parliaments more directly, to draw on their 'legitimacy resources'—resources that European institutions, and notably the EP, otherwise lack. This is particularly the case as integration has, by way of the Eurozone crisis, cut increasingly close to national parliaments' core historical prerogatives: taxing, spending and borrowing. This increased involvement of national parliaments in European affairs should not be regarded as some retrogression or sign of crisis in the system, as if this is merely part and parcel of the 'renationalisation' of European politics. Rather, the demand for national-parliamentary involvement is evidence of an ongoing process of 'reconciliation', as I argue extensively in my book *Power and Legitimacy*.[25] This process is born of the essential reality of European governance, in which significant normative *power* has shifted to the supranational level in response to functional demands, but democratic and constitutional *legitimacy* has remained fundamentally wedded to the nation-state and its core institution, the national parliament. Despite the very significant changes in the place and role of national parliaments over the last six decades, they remain the preeminent expression of the desire of the various national 'demoi' in Europe to rule themselves.[26] The deeper grammar of European public law takes cognisance of this fact, despite the increasing role of the EP across a range of domains.

V. A National '*Riserva di Legge*' in European Integration?

There is another implication of this crucial role of national parliaments in the integration process that one might explore. The question is whether the *power-legitimacy disconnect* in the European system, as well as the continued dependence of integration on national institutions for democratic and constitutional legitimacy in the most robust sense, implies any

[24] Herman van Rompuy, 'The Discovery of Co-Responsibility: Europe in the Debt Crisis', Speech at Humboldt University, Walter Hallstein Institute for European Constitutional Law (6 February 2012) http://europa.eu/rapid/press-release_PRES-12-35_en.htm?locale=en.

[25] Lindseth, *Power and Legitimacy*, above n 2.

[26] PL Lindseth, 'Equilibrium, Demoi-cracy, and Delegation in the Crisis of European Integration' (2014) 15 *German Law Journal* 529.

limits on the nature and scope of authority transferrable to the supranational level. In other words, does European public law need to develop an integration analogue to the Italian *riserva di legge* or the German *Vorbehalt des Gesetzes* on the national level, ie, a constitutionally enforceable limitation on the scope of authority delegable to supranational bodies, consistent with the need to preserve the role of the national parliament in a democratically recognisable sense?

In my view, unless Europeans are prepared to change fundamentally their understanding of what democratic self-government means, or where it is located, then the answer to this question is 'yes'—outer constraints on supranational delegation are necessary in order to fully reconcile Europe and national parliaments.

Whenever we talk about the legitimacy of European integration, we must always ask the question 'legitimate for what?' I am speaking here of the linkage between the nature of the legitimacy enjoyed by a legal or political order (legal, technocratic, functional, or robustly democratic and constitutional) and the scope of power that the legal order can then successfully exercise. We can call this *the power-legitimacy nexus*. The EU is clearly legitimate when it acts as a vehicle to harmonise regulatory standards in various domains. Indeed, it may well also be legitimate, in certain circumstances, as a vehicle to enforce national 'pre-commitments' to fiscal discipline—but this is only true if the foundation of such pre-commitments come from informed sovereign decisions made on the national level. But what is also clearly the case, as the Eurozone crisis has repeatedly demonstrated, is that the EU is not (yet) sufficiently legitimate in its own right to exercise taxing, spending or borrowing power of any real macro-economic significance, precisely because the EU does not (yet) possess the demos-legitimacy to support the exercise of such power. 'Large-scale solidarity', such as it is in Europe, remains wedded to the nation-state.

This perspective helps to explain some of the notorious—particularly German—judicial decisions emerging out of the crisis, especially in how they have articulated the so-called *Demokratieprinzip*.[27] In my reading of the German decisions (admittedly as an outsider, always subject to correction), the *Demokratieprinzip* has both a substantive and procedural dimension. The substantive dimension defines the outer bounds of constitutionally permissible delegation in terms of maintaining the national parliament's budgetary autonomy. The procedural dimension, by contrast, focuses on the nature of national—particularly parliamentary—oversight that is constitutionally mandated in order to legitimise otherwise delegable powers to the supranational level. This German jurisprudence, in my view, in fact expresses general principles regarding the relationship between national parliaments and European governance that should be available to any national high court in Europe, not just in the 'core' but also in the 'periphery'. Jurisprudentially, what is good for the German 'goose' should also be good for the Greek, Irish, Portuguese, Italian, or Spanish 'gander'.

[27] *Greek Bailout Decision*, 2 BvR 987/10, 2 BvR 1485/10, 2 BvR 1099/10, 7 September 2011, www.bundesverfassungsgericht.de/pressemitteilungen/bvg11-055en.html; *Bundestag Right of Participation/EFSF*, 2 BvE 8/11, 28 February 2012, www.bundesverfassungsgericht.de/pressemitteilungen/bvg12-014en.html; *Bundestag Right of Information ESM/Euro Plus Pact*, 2 BvE 4/11, 19 June 2012, www.bundesverfassungsgericht.de/en/press/bvg12-042en.html; *Rejection of Temporary Injunctions ESM/Fiscal Compact*, 2 BvR 1390/12, 2 BvR 1421/12, 2 BvR 1438/12, 2 BvR 1439/12, 2 BvR 1440/12, 2 BvE 6/12, 12 September 2012, www.bundesverfassungsgericht.de/en/press/bvg12-067en.html.

Lurking in the background here is, of course, the increasingly important role of supranational technocracy in the Eurozone crisis: the ECB along with its fellow members of the erstwhile 'troika', the European Commission and the International Monetary Fund (IMF). The increasing disconnect between the supranational technocracy and national political life creates the danger of a kind of Weberian nightmare involving supranational technocratic domination without the possibility of any kind of legitimation via representative government in a historically recognisable sense. Throughout his 1000 days in office, Matteo Renzi seemed very much alive to this concern. In remarks made in July 2014, Renzi noted that Europe was at risk of becoming home simply for 'bureaucracies and banks'. 'It serves no purposes to share a currency', he insisted, 'if you do not share a destiny. We must defend Europe from the assault of technocracy'.[28]

VI. Leadership, Technocracy and … Tradition

Again, I know as scholars we are not supposed to pay much attention to political speeches. However, as I bring this contribution to a close, I am struck that this sort of rhetoric would likely have also caught the attention of no less a scholar than Max Weber. For Weber, the very purpose of the national parliament was as a forum for developing charismatic political leaders capable of projecting national power and resisting the claims of technocracy.[29] If Max Weber were alive today, I think he would have been following Renzi's efforts along these dimensions quite closely. Renzi's rhetoric and political trajectory could be understood as a test case for whether such political leadership can successfully emerge from today's national parliaments, in order to counteract new forms of technocratic domination in the very challenging context of the ongoing crisis of European integration.

The ultimate irony, however, is that Renzi was felled two years later not by the growing European technocracy (even if, as with Berlusconi before him, it might well have had its chance soon enough, in the emerging Italian banking crisis). What felled Renzi, rather, was the overwhelming victory of the 'No' in the constitutional reform referendum of 4 December 2016. Renzi, for all his seeming charismatic potential at the outset of his 1000 days, was in the end unable to overcome a peculiar kind of traditional legitimacy—that belonging to the long-criticised but nonetheless deeply-entrenched 'perfectly symmetric bicameralism' that had been a feature of the modern Italian Parliament since it first came into being under the post-war republican constitution in 1948. The fact that Renzi's defeat was at the hands of an eclectic (and, arguably for any other purpose, incoherent) majority of Italians was of little moment—a classically 'negative' majority was all it took to preserve this tradition.

One might fault Renzi, as many in Italy did in the referendum's aftermath, for attempting to turn the vote into a direct plebiscite over his leadership and policies. But Renzi's tact

[28] M Renzi, 'Difendiamo l'Europa dall'assalto della Tecnocrazia', *Partito Democratico* (5 July 2014) www.partitodemocratico.it/doc/269735/renzi-difendiamo-leuropa-dallassalto-della-tecnocrazia.htm.

[29] PL Lindseth, 'The Paradox of Parliamentary Supremacy: Delegation, Democracy, and Dictatorship in Germany and France, 1920s–1950s' (2004) 113 *Yale Law Journal* 1341, 1409–10, citing Max Weber, 'Parliament and Government in a Reconstructed Germany (A Contribution to the Political Critique of Officialdom and Party Politics)' in *Economy and Society : an Outline of Interpretive Sociology* vol 2 (Guenther Roth and Claus Wittich eds, Berkeley, University of California Press, 1978).

was entirely understandable given national constitutional histories in Europe over the last 70 years. The proposed reform—however flawed it might have been in particulars—was in keeping with similar efforts in leading European countries in the post-war decades to find a balance between parliamentarism (government by assembly) and the increasingly apparent need for some form of what Weber called 'plebiscitarian leadership democracy'.[30] In effect, Renzi was simply unable to achieve a long-delayed Italian version of the same constitutional form—one that, say, Adenauer or de Gaulle were able to achieve in their respective countries in the 1940s and 1950s. This failure perhaps suggests that Italy's efforts to assert itself within Europe will continue to fall short: Italian prime ministers, lacking the same executive prerogatives of a German chancellor or French president, will have difficulty in pressing their case in intergovernmental fora like the European Council, or in resisting the technocratic demands of the Commission or the ECB elsewhere.

Perhaps that is how the Italians want it, more trusting ultimately of EU discipline than the mischief that domestic politicians might effect if given too free a rein. Even if a particular institutional design may seem functionally more apt for certain purposes (like European integration), there is no guarantee that it can overcome the diverse political interests that might oppose it. This is particularly true where, in a country such as Italy, political interests are able to mobilise powerful discourses of legitimacy and 'right'—sometimes cynically but more often sincerely—that tend to favour government by assembly over executive leadership, 'plebiscitarian' or otherwise. Renzi's failure in constitutional reform was simply a testament to the difficulty of institutional change, which ultimately requires a special confluence of functional demand, political interest, and cultural conceptions of right (legitimacy) to break through the constraints of path-dependence and tradition.[31]

This was not to be the moment for Renzi or his proposed reform in December 2016. But in choosing to resign after the referendum defeat, Renzi also sought to exemplify an ethic of political transformation and responsibility that his proposed reform sought to institutionalise. In a graceful concession speech, Renzi lamented that '[a]fter every election everything stays the same … I believe that to change this political system in which leaders are always the same, shifting their assignments but not changing the country', it was no longer possible to pretend that all politicians 'are as stuck to their traditions as they are to their own seats'.[32] Hence his decision to step down.

But whether Renzi's departure from active politics is enduring remains to be seen. The tradition of Italian parliamentarism may have prevailed for the moment, but its functional flaws remained. Italy, and indeed the EU, may not have seen the last of Matteo Renzi. And if he finds a way to return, it will be an interesting experiment in whether he has the credibility, skill and, yes, charismatic legitimacy to transform the same national Italian parliamentary system *indirectly* that he was unable to do *directly*. And if he is able to do so, then he might also be able to challenge the dominant technocratic character of European integration and perhaps achieve the sort of 'large-scale solidarity' on the EU level that it undoubtedly needs. As of this writing (December 2016) I would not hold out too much hope, but then again, anything is possible.

[30] For an overview, see Lindseth, ibid, 1407–11.

[31] Lindseth, above n 5.

[32] 'Il testo integrale del discorso di Matteo Renzi dopo la sconfitta al referendum costituzionale' (*LaStampa.it*) www.lastampa.it/2016/12/05/italia/speciali/referendum-2016/il-testo-integrale-del-discorso-di-matteo-renzi-dopo-la-sconfitta-al-referendum-costituzionale-OVHGkFwXHabc2u1HRMIeBJ/pagina.html.

INDEX

NB–Page numbers in **bold** denote information in tables and those in *italics* denote information in figures

www.ingramcontent.com/pod-product-compliance
Ingram Content Group UK Ltd.
Pitfield, Milton Keynes, MK11 3LW, UK
UKHW051449290926
15471UKWH00008B/1103

9 781509 936670